International Handbook of Selection and Assessment

International Handbook
of Selection
and Assessment

Edited by

Neil Anderson

Goldsmiths College, University of London

and

Peter Herriot

Institute for Employment Studies, Brighton

JOHN WILEY & SONS

Chichester · New York · Weinheim · Brisbane · Singapore · Toronto

National   01243 779777
International (+44) 1243 779777
e-mail (for orders and customer service enquiries): cs-books@wiley.co.uk
Visit our Home Page on http://www.wiley.co.uk
or http://www.wiley.com

Other Wiley Editorial Offices

John Wiley & Sons, Inc., 605 Third Avenue,
New York, NY 10158-0012, USA

VCH Verlagsgesellschaft mbH, Pappelallee 3
D-69469 Weinheim, Germany

Jacaranda Wiley Ltd, 33 Park Road, Milton,
Queensland 4064, Australia

John Wiley & Sons (Canada) Ltd, 22 Worcester Road,
Rexdale, Ontario M9W 1LI, Canada

John Wiley & Sons (Asia) Pte Ltd, 2 Clementi Loop #02-01,
Jin Xing Distripark, Singapore 129809

Library of Congress Cataloging-in-Publication Data

International handbook of selection and assessment / edited by
    Neil Anderson and Peter Herriot.
        p.   cm.
    Includes bibliographical references and index.
    ISBN 0-471-96638-X
    1. Employee selection—Cross-cultural studies.   2. Employment
tests—Cross-cultural studies.   3. Employees—Recruiting—Cross-
cultural studies.   I. Anderson, Neil (Neil D.)   II. Herriot,
Peter.
    HF5549.5.S38I56   1997
    658.3'11—dc21   96–40878
                                                                    CIP

British Library Cataloguing in Publication Data

A catalogue record for this book is available from the British Library

ISBN 0-471-96638-X

Typeset in 10/12pt Palatino by Dorwyn Ltd, Rowlands Castle, Hants
Printed and bound in Great Britain by Bookcraft (Bath) Ltd, Midsomer Norton, Somerset
This book is printed on acid-free paper responsibly manufactured from sustainable forestation, for
which at least two trees are planted for each one used for paper production.

Contents

List of Contributors   ix
Preface   xiii
Acknowledgements   xv
About the Editors   xvii
About the Contributors   xix

1   Selecting for Change: How will Personnel and Selection Psychology
    Survive?   1
    Peter Herriot and Neil Anderson

    Section 1: Technological, National, and Professional Cultures

2   Human Resources are Local: Society and Social Contracts in a
    Global Economy   39
    Denise Rousseau and Catherine Tinsley
3   Integrated Personnel Selection, Appraisal and Decisions: A Chinese
    Approach   63
    Zhong-Ming Wang
4   International Assessment and Selection   81
    Viv Shackleton and Sue Newell
5   Network and its Implications for Assessment   97
    José M. Prieto and Cristina Simón
6   Assessment in a Technological World   125
    Paul Jansen
7   Selection and Training of Expatriate Employees   147
    Samuel Aryee
8   Selection of Military Staff   161
    N.M. Hardinge
9   Selection for a Profession: A Case Study   183
    Robert Wood, Graham Hamer, Charles Johnson and Tim Payne
10 Tacit Knowledge and Job Success   201
    Robert J. Sternberg

Section 2: Business Change and Psychological Responses

11 Personnel Selection and Corporate Strategy 219
    Allan P.O. Williams and Paul Dobson
12 Selection and Assessment During Organizational Turnaround 247
    Marise Ph. Born and Paul G.W. Jansen
13 Criterion Measures and the Criterion Dilemma 267
    Robert Guion
14 Criterion Development: The Unknown Power of Criteria as
    Communication Tools 287
    Wieby M.M. Altink, Coert F. Visser and Michiel Castelijns
15 Utility Analysis: What Are the Black Boxes, and Do They Affect
    Decisions? 303
    John W. Boudreau, Michael C. Sturman and Timothy A. Judge
16 Meta-analysis and Validity Generalization 323
    Kevin R. Murphy
17 Organizational Competencies: Creating a Strategic Behavioural
    Framework for Selection and Assessment 343
    Paul R. Sparrow
18 Assessing Honesty, Integrity, and Deception 369
    Kevin R. Murphy and Nathan Luther

Section 3: Personnel Selection and Assessment

19 What Is This Thing Called Fit? 393
    Benjamin Schneider, Amy L. Kristof-Brown, Harold W. Goldstein and
    D. Brent Smith
20 Selection as Socialization 413
    Neil Anderson and Cheri Ostroff
21 From Job Analysis to Work Profiling – Do Traditional Procedures
    Still Apply? 441
    Coert F. Visser, Wieby M.M. Altink and Jen A. Algera
22 Structured Selection Interviews: Why Do They work? Why Are They
    Underutilized? 455
    Robert L. Dipboye
23 The Big Five as a Framework for Personality Assessment 475
    Gerald Matthews
24 Selecting for Teamwork 493
    Michael A. West and Natalie J. Allen
25 Selection for Potential: The Case of Graduate Recruitment 507
    Tony Keenan

Section 4: Individual Assessment for a Changing Context

26 Interrelationships between the Foundations for Selection and
    Training Systems 529
    Irwin L. Goldstein

27　The Impact of Personnel Selection Procedures on Candidates 543
　　Paul A. Iles and Ivan T. Robertson
28　Performance Appraisal in Context: Organizational Changes and
　　their Impact on Practice 567
　　Clive Fletcher
29　Assessing Developmental Needs 581
　　Jeroen J.J.L. Seegers
30　Assessment for Self-Managed Career Development 599
　　Jennifer M. Kidd
31　Downsizing and Deselection 619
　　Paul R. Jackson

Index 637

List of Contributors

JEN ALGERA — *ARBONED hoogovens, P.O. Box 10.000, CA Ijmuiden, The Netherlands*

NATALIE J. ALLEN — *Center for Administration and Information Studies, University of Western Ontario, Ontario, Canada*

WIEBY M.M. ALTINK — *Adviesbureau Psychotechniek Utrecht B.V., Arthur van Schendelstraat 612, P.O. Box 1047, 3500 BA Utrecht, The Netherlands*

NEIL ANDERSON — *Department of Psychology, Goldsmiths College, University of London, New Cross, London, UK*

SAMUEL ARYEE — *Department of Management, School of Business, Hong Kong Baptist University, 224 Waterloo Road, Kowloon, Hong Kong*

MARISE BORN — *Faculty of Psychology & Pedagogics, Vrije Universiteit, Amsterdam, The Netherlands*

JOHN W. BOUDREAU — *Center for Advanced Human Resource Studies, New York State School of Industrial and Labor Relations, Cornell University, Ithaca, NY 14853-3901, USA*

MICHIEL T. CASTELIJNS — *Adviesbureau Psychotechniek Utrecht B.V., Utrecht, The Netherlands*

ROBERT L. DIPBOYE — *Department of Psychology, Rice University, Houston, Texas, USA*

PAUL DOBSON — *Personnel Research & Enterprise Development, City University Business School, London, UK*

CLIVE FLETCHER — *Department of Psychology, Goldsmiths College, University of London, New Cross, London SE14 6NW, UK*

HAROLD W. GOLDSTEIN — *Department of Psychology, New York University, New York, NY, USA*

IRWIN L. GOLDSTEIN   *College of Behavioral and Social Sciences, University of Maryland, 2141 Tydings Hall, College Park, MD 20742-7225, USA*

ROBERT M. GUION   *Bowling Green State University, Bowling Green, Ohio, USA*

GRAHAM HAMER   *Inns of Court School of Law, London, UK*

NEIL HARDINGE   *Defence Evaluation and Research Agency, Centre for Human Sciences, Farnborough, Hampshire GU14 6TD, UK*

PETER HERRIOT   *Institute for Employment Studies, Mantell Building, University of Sussex, Falmer, Brighton, UK*

PAUL ILES   *Liverpool Business School, Liverpool John Moores University, 98 Mount Pleasant, Liverpool L3 5UZ, UK*

PAUL R. JACKSON   *Institute of Work Psychology, University of Sheffield, Sheffield, UK*

PAUL JANSEN   *Department of Business Administration, Vrije Universiteit, Amsterdam, The Netherlands*

CHARLES JOHNSON   *Psychometric Research & Development Ltd, St Albans, Herts, UK*

TIM JUDGE   *Center for Advanced Human Resource Studies, New York State School of Industrial and Labor Relations, Cornell University, Ithaca, NY 14853-3901, USA*

TONY KEENAN   *Department of Business Organization, Heriot-Watt University, Chambers Street, Edinburgh, UK*

JENNIFER M. KIDD   *Department of Organizational Psychology, Birkbeck College, University of London, Malet Street, London WC1E 7HX, UK*

AMY KRISTOF-BROWN   *College of Business Administration, University of Iowa, Iowa City, IA, USA*

NATHAN LUTHER   *Department of Psychology, Colorado State University, Fort Collins, CO 80523, USA*

GERRY MATTHEWS   *Department of Psychology, University of Dundee, Dundee, UK*

KEVIN MURPHY   *Department of Psychology, Colorado State University, Fort Collins, CO 80523, USA*

SUE NEWELL   *Warwick Business School, University of Warwick, Coventry, UK*

CHERI OSTROFF — *School of Management, Arizona State University West, Phoenix, Arizona, USA*

TIM PAYNE — *Pearn Kandola, Oxford, UK*

JOSÉ M. PRIETO — *Faculty of Psychology, Complutense University, Somosaguas, Madrid, Spain*

IVAN ROBERTSON — *Manchester School of Management, UMIST, PO Box 88, Manchester M60 1QD, UK*

DENISE ROUSSEAU — *Heinz School of Public Policy & Management, Carnegie-Mellon University, Pittsburg, PA 15213, USA*

BENJAMIN SCHNEIDER — *Department of Psychology, University of Maryland, College Park, Maryland, USA*

JEROEN J.J.L. SEEGERS — *Assessment and Development Consult, Zypendaalseweg 47, 6814 CC Arnhem, The Netherlands*

VIV SHACKLETON — *Aston Business School, Aston University, Birmingham, UK*

CRISTINA SIMÓN — *Educational Technology Office, Technical University of Madrid, Madrid, Spain*

D. BRENT SMITH — *Department of Psychology, University of Maryland, College Park, Maryland, USA*

PAUL SPARROW — *Management School, Sheffield University, Sheffield, UK*

ROBERT J. STERNBERG — *Department of Psychology, Yale University, New Haven, USA*

MICHAEL C. STURMAN — *Center for Advanced Human Resource Studies, New York State School of Industrial and Labor Relations, Cornell University, Ithaca, NY 14853-3901, USA*

CATHERINE TINSLEY — *Department of Management, Hong Kong University of Science & Technology, Clearwater Bay, Kowloon, Hong Kong* and *School of Business, Georgetown University, Washington, DC 20057, USA*

COERT F. VISSER — *Adviesbureau PsychoTechniek Utrecht B.V., Arthur van Schendelstraat 612, P.O. Box 1047, 3500 BA Utrecht, The Netherlands*

ZHONG-MING WANG — *Department of Psychology, Hangzhou University, Hangzhou, People's Republic of China*

MICHAEL A. WEST — *Institute of Work Psychology, University of Sheffield, Sheffield, UK*

ALLAN WILLIAMS — *Personnel Research & Enterprise Development, City University Business School, London, UK*

ROBERT WOOD — *Pearn Kandola, Oxford, UK*

Preface

This *International Handbook of Selection and Assessment* is the successor to the volume *Assessment and Selection in Organizations*, originally published by John Wiley & Sons in 1989. The process of developing toward this Handbook was intentionally undertaken in stages. Over the eight-year period which has elapsed between these editions there have been a multitude of changes in the theory and practice of employee selection. Our interpretation was that the field was developing at such a pace that periodic updates were necessary and desirable as 'milestones' along the way toward the second edition proper.

The publication of the First Update in 1994 was followed by the Second Update in 1995. The contents (11 Chapters) of these two updates are incorporated into this volume which is, in many respects, the follow-up to the first edition. The change of title was decided upon as this project progressed. This volume is indeed now pre-eminently an *International Handbook* with contributors from several countries across three continents—Europe, North America and Asia.

A total of 31 chapters comprise this Handbook, authored by some 48 contributors across seven countries. Contributors originate from Britain, Canada, the People's Republic of China, Hong Kong, The Netherlands, Spain, and the United States of America. Such diversity and multi-national heterogeneity was intentional on our part as Editors: global business demands a global but diverse science of personnel and selection psychology. This volume, we hope, represents just one early step toward integrating perspectives from different countries and in bringing together a set of eminent contributors from such diverse national backgrounds.

NEIL ANDERSON
PETER HERRIOT
August 1996

Acknowledgements

Many people have contributed to the publication of this International Handbook. First and foremost we must acknowledge the professionalism, commitment and efforts of all the authors who have contributed chapters to this volume. Without exception, they responded willingly and constructively to our editorial feedback, which we feel must at times have felt rather demanding and opinionated in our attempts to address particular emerging themes in employee selection. Such a publication is also dependent upon the diligence and support of able secretarial and administrative staff. In this respect we would particularly thank Sue Weston, Elaine Webb, Jane Halfpenny and Sue Jeffrey.

Equally, the on-going support of our publishers, John Wiley & Sons, has been invaluable over the period that it has taken to move from the First and Second Updates to this Handbook. Amongst the staff at Wiley, we would especially wish to extend our gratitude to Michael Coombs, Steve Hardman, Diane Taylor and Claire Plimmer for all their efforts. They have been a pleasure to work with. Finally, our families. For their tolerance of the long hours we have spent holed-up in our offices working on this Handbook and their ever-present personal support, we are hugely indebted.

NEIL ANDERSON, *Goldsmiths College, University of London*
PETER HERRIOT, *Institute for Employment Studies, Brighton*

About the Editors

Neil Anderson is Senior Lecturer in Occupational Psychology and Course Director of the MSc in Occupational Psychology at Goldsmiths College, University of London. He is Founding Editor of the *International Journal of Selection and Assessment* and formerly an Associate Editor of the *Journal of Occupational and Organizational Psychology*. His research interests span recruitment and selection, organizational and work group socialization, innovation at work, and organizational climate. He has co-authored or edited five books and his work has appeared in several scholarly journals including the *Journal of Applied Psychology*, the *Journal of Organizational Behavior*, the *Journal of Occupational and Organizational Psychology* and the *International Journal of Selection and Assessment*.

Neil has on-going research projects, collaboratively or alone, into the socialization of recruits into the British Army, work group socialization of graduates, the structure and psychometric properties of popular 'Big Five' measures of personality, telephone-based interview decision-making, and cognitive aspects of organization socialization. He is committed to cross-cultural personnel psychology, having been Visiting Professor to the Universities of Minnesota (USA) and Hangzhou (China).

Peter Herriot is Associate Director of the Institute for Employment Studies, Brighton, a not-for-profit multi-disciplinary research and consultancy organization. He is also Visiting Professor at the City University Business School and at the University of Surrey. He is currently Editor of the *European Journal of Work and Organizational Psychology*, which seeks to appeal to both practitioners and academics by avoiding the twin traps characteristic of each: untheorized practice and irrelevant theory.

Peter has consistently championed the approach to selection as a social and organizational process rather than as assessment of the individual. More recently, he has broadened his area of interest to incorporate the management of careers, defining the organizational career as the repeated renegotiation of the psychological contract. He is a confirmed Europhile and a strong believer in the unique character and value of national, regional, occupational and organizational cultures.

About the Contributors

Jen Algera is Professor of Personnel Management at Eindhoven University of Technology, the Netherlands. The main focus of his work is on the design of performance management systems. He is also active in the fields of personnel selection, job design and organization design.

Natalie J. Allen is an Associate Professor in the Department of Psychology at the University of Western Ontario (London, Canada). Much of her research focuses on the development and consequences of employee commitment to the organization and other work-related domains. Other areas of research interest include cross-cultural issues within organizational behaviour and the composition of, and processes within, work teams. Her work appears in the *Journal of Applied Psychology, Journal of Occupational and Organizational Psychology*, and the *Academy of Management Journal*.

Wieby M.M. Altink studied work and organizational psychology and started her career as a lecturer and researcher in selection and psychometrics (PhD on selection activities in developing countries). After that she worked as Associate Professor in the field of human resource management at the University of Amsterdam; her main areas of research were selection, appraisal and personnel development. Currently she is working at the human resource consultancy firm Psycho Techniek as a senior consultant. Her main consultancy areas are human resource management, management development and organizational change processes.

Samuel Aryee is an Associate Professor of human resource management and organizational behaviour in the Department of Management at Hong Kong Baptist University. He obtained his PhD from McMaster University in Hamilton, Canada. His areas of research interest include careers, expatriate management, human resource management in high-technology firms, women and employment and work–family interface.

Marise Born is Assistant Professor at the Department of Work and Organizational Psychology, Vrÿe Universiteit, Amsterdam, The Netherlands. Her interests are in the area of assessment of individual differences, personnel selection, meta-analysis and gender issues. She has published some 30 articles in Dutch and English books or journals.

John W. Boudreau is Associate Professor of Human Resource Studies, and Director of the Center for Advanced Human Resource Studies at Cornell University. His research includes human resource (HR) management decision-making; HR information systems; applications of economics, accounting and financial theories to HR decisions; computer applications to HR management decisions; organizational staffing; and HR strategic planning in the United States, Asia, Australia and Europe. He founded and co-ordinates HRNET, a leading internet HR discussion group. He also founded and directed the Central Europe Human Resource Education Initiative in the United States and the Czech and Slovak Republics. He has served on the editorial boards of *Human Resource Costing and Accounting, Human Resource Management, Personnel Journal, Personnel Psychology,* and *Journal of Applied Psychology.* His published research has won the 'New Concept Award' and 'Scholarly Contribution Award' from the Academy of Management.

Michiel T. Castelijns studied neuropsychology and work and organization psychology in Tilburg, The Netherlands. He is Senior Consultant at Psycho Techniek. He is responsible for the individual assessment consultancy and assessment centres. He has published on organizational culture, assessment centres, psychological testing and the selection of pilots.

Robert L. Dipboye is a Professor of Psychology and Administrative Sciences at Rice University, Houston, Texas, where he is director of the Industrial and Organizational Psychology program and chair of the Psychology Department. He is an associate editor of the *Journal of Applied Psychology,* and is on the editorial boards of the *Journal of Organizational Behavior* and the *Academy of Management Review.* He has published numerous journal articles on the interview and is the author of *Selection Interviews: Process Perspectives* and *Understanding Industrial and Organizational Psychology: An Integrated Approach.*

Paul Dobson is a chartered psychologist and lectures in organizational behaviour on the MBA programme at City University Business School. He read psychology at the University of East London and undertook research in occupational psychology at Birkbeck College. He obtained his PhD at the City University. Prior to his present appointment he was a Research Fellow in the Centre for Personnel Research and Enterprise Development, where he carried out research in the areas of selection and assessment and organizational development. He has published widely in the former area and is co-author of the book *Changing Culture.*

Clive Fletcher is Professor and Head of the Department of Psychology at Goldsmiths College, University of London. After completing his PhD studies he worked for some years as a consultant psychologist in the UK Civil Service before taking up his first academic post. A Fellow of the British Psychological Society and a former Chair of its Occupational Psychology Section, Professor Fletcher has been involved in teaching and research in the field of managerial assessment and appraisal for over 20 years, and has published many books and articles in this area. He is a member of a number of journal editorial boards, and editor of the *Essential Business Psychology* book series.

Harold W. Goldstein is a visiting Assistant Professor of Psychology at New York University. He received his BA degree (1987) from the University of Michigan and his MA (1991) and PhD (1993) degrees from the University of Maryland at College Park, all in psychology. His primary research interests include leadership and crisis management, organizational climate and culture, personnel selection and equal employment opportunity issues.

Irwin L. Goldstein is Professor of Psychology and Dean, College of Behavioral and Social Sciences at the University of Maryland. His research interests focus on needs assessment, evaluation models and personnel systems, including selection and training systems. He is the author of *Training in Organizations*. He has served as President of the Society of Industrial and Organizational Psychology and in 1992 he was awarded their Distinguished Service Award. In 1995 he was honoured with the American Society for Training and Development Swanson award for research excellence. He has served as associate editor for the *Journal of Applied Psychology* and *Human Factors*.

Robert M. Guion received his PhD from Purdue University in 1952. From there he went to Bowling Green State University in Ohio where, except for leaves to the Universities of California and New Mexico, to the state personnel division of Hawaii, and the Educational Testing Service, he remained until retirement as Distinguished University Professor Emeritus. He is the author of *Personnel Testing*, the forthcoming *Assessment, Measurement, and Prediction for Personnel Decisions* and several articles and chapters.

Graham Hamer is Registrar of the Inns of Court School of Law. After a first university post at Goldsmiths College, University of London, he moved to the Medical College of St Bartholomew's Hospital in 1981, becoming Academic Registrar in 1987. He is a member of the steering group of the Higher Education Equal Opportunities Network, and is on the editorial advisory board of the journal *Perspectives: Policy and Practice in Higher Education*.

Neil Hardinge is a Senior Principal Psychologist in the Defence Evaluation and Research Agency's Centre for Human Sciences at Farnborough, where he is a Resource Manager for the Training Needs and Effectiveness group. Neil joined the Civil Service in 1967. He has extensive experience of human factors research in the public sector having worked in the Ministry of Defence for the Royal Navy, Royal Air Force and Army for the home Civil Service on a wide variety of human factors topics. His main interests include selection and training.

Paul Iles is the Littlewood's Professor of Human Resource Development and Head of the Liverpool Centre for Human Resource Development at the Liverpool Business School, Liverpool John Moores University. A chartered psychologist and Fellow of the Institute for Personnel and Development, he was formerly a senior lecturer in human resource strategies at the Open University School of Management and Director of its Diploma in Management programme. His research interests are in managerial assessment and development, career and organization development, international human resource management/development, equal opportunities/managing diversity and organizational learning.

Paul R. Jackson completed a PhD on interview search styles at the University of Sheffield, and has worked at the MRC/ESRC Social and Applied Psychology Unit and the Institute of Work Psychology. His current post is as Senior Lecturer in the Department of Psychology in Sheffield. His research interests include primary work design interventions to reduce work-related stress, the psychological impact of unemployment, and research design and methodology.

Paul Jansen is Professor of Industrial Psychology at the Department of Business Administration, Faculty of Economics and Econometrics, Vrÿe Universiteit, Amsterdam, the Netherlands. In addition, he is Director of the Limperg Institute, the Universities Institute for Research in Accountancy. He has published, in Dutch, a book on assessment centres, and has co-edited a number of books on management (development), assessment and selection. Paul has published over 80 articles in Dutch, English and German books or journals.

Charles Johnson is currently Managing Director of Psychometric Research & Development Ltd, which he joined in 1986, and a director of Crisis Management Associates, where his work involves him in a wide range of human resource programmes and developments, market research and the development of computer-based crisis simulations. He is also the author/co-author of a large number of tests used widely in the United Kingdom for occupational purposes. His first job was as an assistant lecturer in psychology at University College, London, after completing a PhD in psycholinguistics. He spent three years doing research of various sorts in psychiatric hospitals, plus a short period doing free-lance work for magazines, before joining the British Civil Service as the senior psychologist in its test construction unit, and later working as a principal psychologist in the Cabinet Office (MPO) Recruitment Research Unit.

Tim Judge is Associate Professor of Management and Organizations in the College of Business at the University of Iowa. Prior to receiving his PhD at the University of Illinois, Tim was employed as a manager at Kohl's Department Stores. He also served on the faculty at Cornell University. His primary research and teaching interests are in the areas of staffing career systems, personality assessment, and organizational behaviour. He has published articles on these topics in the *Academy of Management Journal*, *Journal of Applied Psychology*, *Organizational Behavior and Human Decision Processes*, and *Personnel Psychology*. Tim serves on the editorial boards of *Journal of Applied Psychology, Journal of Management,* and *Personnel Psychology.* In 1995 he received the Ernest J. McCormick Award for distinguished early career contributions from the Society for Industrial and Organizational Psychology. Tim is a member of the Academy of Management, American Psychological Association, and Society for Industrial and Organizational Psychology. He serves on the Executive Committee of the Human Resource Division of the Academy of Management and on the Steering Committee of the Careers Division of the Academy of Management. Tim is also serving as Programme Chair for the Society for Industrial and Organizational Psychology's 1998 Annual Meeting.

Tony Keenan is Professor of Organizational Behaviour in the Department of Business Organization at Heriot-Watt University in Edinburgh. He has held a variety of positions in the university, including Head of Department, Dean of Faculty, and Head of the Business School. His main research interests and publications have been in the areas of graduate recruitment, stress, and careers of professional engineers. He is currently Editor-in-Chief of *The Journal of Occupational and Organizational Psychology.*

Jennifer M. Kidd is a Senior Lecturer in the Department of Organizational Psychology, Birkbeck College, University of London, and a Chartered Occupational Psychologist. Previously she worked as a career counsellor in further education and as a Research Fellow at the National Institute for Careers Education and Counselling. Her main areas of research and publication are career guidance and career development and her books include the co-authored text *Rethinking Careers Education and Guidance* (1996).

Amy Kristof-Brown is a PhD student in Organizational Behavior at the University of Maryland's College of Business and Management. She has published articles in *Journal of Applied Psychology* and *Personnel Psychology* and is an author on several book chapters. Her primary research interests include person–environment fit and impression management in the context of organizational selection decisions and work teams.

Nathan Luther is a doctoral student in Industrial/Organizational Psychology at Colorado State University. His research interests include personality, organizational dishonesty, corruption, and counter-productive work behaviours.

Gerry Matthews received his BA (1980) and PhD (1984) in experimental psychology from the University of Cambridge. He is currently Reader in Psychology at the University of Dundee, where he has worked since 1989. Previously, he held posts at the University of Wales Institute of Science and Technology, and Aston University. His research interests include the relationship between personality and performance, individual differences in stress vulnerability, and driving behaviour. He has co-authored a book on *Attention and Emotion: A Clinical Perspective* (Lawrence Erlbaum, 1994).

Kevin Murphy is a Professor of Psychology at Colorado State University. He serves as Incoming Editor of *Journal of Applied Psychology*, and as a member of the editorial boards of *Personnel Psychology, Human Performance*, and *International Journal of Selection and Assessment*. He is the author of over 60 articles and book chapters, and author or editor of six books. His research interests include performance appraisal, psychological testing, individual differences, personnel selection and assessment, and honesty in the workplace.

Sue Newell is a lecturer at the Warwick Business School, University of Warwick. She is a chartered occupational psychologist, lecturing in the area of Organizational Behaviour. Her main research interest involves studying the inter-organizational networks that influence the diffusion of new ideas. Other research interests include evaluating management development programmes, especially those that involve using the outdoors as a medium, examining equal opportunity initiatives implemented by business organizations and looking at international differences in selection and assessment.

Cheri Ostroff is an Associate Professor of Management at Arizona State University West. She served on the Industrial Relations Faculty at the University of Minnesota for eight years. Her areas of expertise include: human resource management systems and firm performance; levels of analysis; person–organization fit; training; and socialization. In 1994 she received both the Ernest J. McCormick Award for Early Career Contributions from the Society of Industrial Organizational Psychology, and the American Psychological Association's Distinguished Scientific Award for Early Career Contribution in Applied Research. Dr Ostroff is Associate Editor of the *International Journal of Selection and Assessment*, and serves on the Editorial Board of *Journal of Applied Psychology*. Dr Ostroff has provided human resource consulting to a variety of firms in the United States.

Tim Payne is a chartered occupational psychologist with Pearn Kandola where he specializes in the fair assessment of people at work. His main involvement is with assessment and development centres, and he has published articles in this area. He is Editor of the Professional Forum Section of the *International Journal of Selection and Assessment*.

José M. Prieto is a tenured Professor of Work and Organizational Psychology at the Complutense University of Madrid. From 1972 to 1996 he has combined consulting experience and a scientific approach with the psychological framework of research and practice. He is a member of several executive committees and editorial boards of national and international associations and journals in the field of personnel assessment. In 1994 he chaired the 23rd International Congress of Applied Psychology where about 40% of the program was circulated in digital form throughout Internet. The book of abstracts was made available in HTML within the World Wide Web several weeks in advance of the printed version.

Ivan Robertson is a chartered psychologist and Fellow of the British Psychological Society. He is co-editor of the *International Review of Industrial and Organizational Psychology* and past Chair of the North of England Branch of the British Psychological Society. His work experience includes several years in industrial/national government as an occupational psychologist. Since taking up an academic post in 1979 he has produced 20 books and over 100 scientific articles/conference papers. He is now Professor of Occupational Psychology and Head of Manchester School of Management, UMIST.

Denise Rousseau is a Professor of Organization Behavior at Carnegie-Mellon University, jointly in the Heinz School of Public Policy and Management and in the Graduate School of Industrial Administration. She has been a faculty member at Northwestern University, the University of Michigan, and the Naval Postgraduate School (Monterey). Her research addresses the impact of work group processes on performance and the changing psychological contract at work. Her recent books include: *Psychological Contracts in Organizations: Written and Unwritten Agreements* (Sage), and *The Boundaryless Career* (Oxford) with Michael Arthur.

Benjamin Schneider is Professor of Psychology at the University of Maryland at College Park. He has taught at Yale University, Michigan State University, Bar-Ilan University (Israel), Peking University (People's Republic of China), and at the University of Work and Economics Aix-Marseilles (France). He serves on a number of journal editorial boards, he edits a new series of books for Sage on *Organizational Behavior*, and was the editor from 1984 to 1994 (with Arthur P. Brief) of Lexington Books' *Issues in Organization and Management* series. He has published six books, the latest, *Winning the Service Game* with David E. Bowen, is published by the Harvard Business School Press, and more than 80 journal articles and book chapters.

Jeroen J.J.L. Seegers is founding partner and director of ADC: Assessment & Development Consult. Before this he worked as senior occupational and industrial psychologist for a large Dutch consultancy firm. He was managing director of GITP Focus Benelux and European United Consultants. He has been working with the assessment centre method since 1977 and was trained in the United Kingdom and United States. He published several articles on assessment centres and wrote the first Dutch book on the assessment centre, published in 1982. Seegers has implemented the assessment centre method in numerous organizations in the Netherlands and Europe and worked for organizations like Heineken, NCR, ABN-AMRO, MARS, Siemens and Merck Shape & Dohm.

Viv Shackleton is currently Senior Lecturer and Convenor of the Organization Studies Group at Aston Business School, Aston University, Birmingham, UK. His teaching and research interests are in employee recruitment and selection, especially in a European context, managerial assessment, and career counselling. His most recent book publications are *Successful Selection Interviewing* (with Neil

Anderson) and *Business Leadership*. He has held university appointments and conducted consulting assignments in continental Europe and the United States, as well as in Britain.

Cristina Simón holds a graduate degree in cognitive psychology from the Universidad Autonoma de Madrid. In 1995 she obtained her PhD in training technology from the Faculty of Technology of the Open University, UK. She started her professional experience at the Foundation for the Development of the Social Function of Communications (Fundesco). In 1991 she joined the Educational Technology Office of Madrid Technical University as project manager of the Educational Telematics area. She is currently Senior Consultant in the Division of Human Resources and Training of Ernst & Young in Madrid.

D. Brent Smith is a PhD student in Industrial and Organizational Psychology at the University of Maryland at College Park. He has published on the topic of personality in the workplace and his research interests concern level of analysis and methodological issues in understanding the role of personality at work.

Paul Sparrow is a Reader in International Human Resource Management at Sheffield University Management School. He worked as a freelance consultant, Research Fellow at Aston University then Senior Research Fellow at Warwick Business School. In 1988 he joined PA Consulting Group working as a consultant and finally a principal consultant. In 1991 he returned to academia, lecturing at Manchester Business School. He has written a number of books including *European Human Resource Management in Transition* and *Designing and Achieving Competency*, and published articles concerning the future of work, human resource strategy, management competencies, the psychology of strategic management and international human resource management. He is an Associate Editor of the *Journal of Occupational and Organizational Psychology*.

Robert J. Sternberg is IBM Professor of Psychology and Education in the Department of Psychology at Yale University. A Stanford PhD, he is a Fellow of the American Academy of Arts and Sciences, American Association for the Advancement of Science, American Psychological Association, and American Psychological Society. He is the author of over 500 publications, including, recently, *Successful Intelligence* (Simon & Schuster, 1996).

Michael C. Sturman is a PhD candidate studying personnel and human resources at Cornell University's School of Industrial and Labor Relations. His research interests include predicting job performance and understanding judgement and decision-making for human resource problems.

Catherine Tinsley is an Assistant Professor at Georgetown University, currently visiting at the Hong Kong University of Science and Technology. She examines how management theories and models differ across various contexts, focusing on issues of work place relationships, conflict, and conflict management. She has published in *Research in Organizational Behaviour* and *Organizational Behavior and Human Decision Processes*.

Coert F. Visser studied work and organizational psychology and clinical psychology in Groningen (the Netherlands). He works at Psycho Techniek as a consultant and member of the management team. His main activities are in the areas of assessment and development of people, work and organizations. He has written on several topics including self-assessment, assessment centers, self-managing teams and management development.

Zhong-Ming Wang is Professor of Management and Industrial/Organizational Psychology at the School of Management, Hanhzhou University, China. He received an MA in Organizational Psychology from Hangzhou University (1982), an MA in applied psychology from the Gothenburg University, Sweden (1985) and a PhD (1987) in Industrial/Organizational Psychology from Hangzhou University. He is currently Dean of School of Management and Vice-President of Hangzhou University. He is also Vice-President of the Chinese National Committee of Personnel Assessment. Wang is the associate editor of both the *Chinese Journal of Applied Psychology* and *Chinese Ergonomics*, and is on the editorial boards of *International Journal of Human Resource Management, International Journal of Selection and Assessment, Applied Psychology, Journal of Cross-Cultural Psychology, Journal of Management Development*, and *Journal of Managerial Psychology*. He has published several books, including *Work and Personnel Psychology* and *Research Methods in Psychology*, and more than 100 articles in China and abroad. His main research areas include personnel selection/assessment, organizational decision-making, leadership, organization development, cross-cultural organizational behaviour and human resources management.

Michael A. West is Professor of Work and Organizational Psychology at the Institute of Work Psychology, the University of Sheffield, and co-director of the Corporate Performance Programme of the Centre for Economic Performance at the London School of Economics. He has authored, edited or co-edited eight books including *Managerial Job Change* (1988), *Women at Work* (1990), *Innovation and Creativity at Work* (1990), *Effective Teamwork* (1994) and the *Handbook of Workgroup Psychology* (1996). He has also written more than 100 articles for scientific and practitioner publications, and chapters in scholarly books. His research interests are in innovation and creativity at work; team and organizational effectiveness; and mental health at work.

Allan Williams is Professor of Organizational and Occupational Psychology at the City University Business School. He heads the Business Studies Department and is Director of the Centre for Personnel Research and Enterprise Development. He read psychology at Manchester University, and received his MA and PhD in Occupational Psychology at Birkbeck College, University of London. After a spell in commerce he entered the management education field in 1963. He has researched and consulted in many well-known organizations, and published in the human resource management and organizational development literature. Recent co-authored books include: *Changing Culture* (IPD, 2nd edition, 1993), and *The Competitive Consultant* (Macmillan, 1994).

Robert Wood is a chartered occupational psychologist, and a partner with Pearn Kandola. The first 20 years of his career were spent in education, including a PhD from the University of Chicago and a University Chair. He was made a Fellow of the British Psychological Society in 1986. His book *Assessment and Testing* is published by Cambridge University Press, and a book on recruitment and selection (with Tim Payne) is due to be published by Wiley in 1997 as part of the *Best Practice in HRM* series.

Chapter 1

Selecting for Change: How will Personnel and Selection Psychology Survive?

PETER HERRIOT

Institute for Employment Studies, Mantell Building, University of Sussex, Brighton BN1 9RF, UK

NEIL ANDERSON

Goldsmiths College, University of London, New Cross, London SE14 6NW, UK

INTRODUCTION

Traditional personnel and selection psychology is in danger of terminal decline. What an opening assertion in an editorial for the *International Handbook of Selection and Assessment*! Overwhelming changes in the international business environment have fundamentally shifted the nature of work, and therefore the aetiology of organization structures and work design in most industrialized countries over recent years. Personnel and selection psychologists have operated within a period of disjuncture and threat virtually unparalleled in our history. As many practitioners would willingly testify, the demand characteristics on their role in the recruitment process have been transformed from fitting individuals into discrete and stable jobs into selecting for newly created jobs, flexible and transient work roles, innovation potential, organizational fit, teamworking skills, and de-selection, amongst many other newly emergent pressures. This shift is the result of global changes in the business environment, changes that strike at the heart of the dominant criterion-related validity paradigm in personnel and selection psychology and which are rendering it increasingly outmoded and impotent in the world of work.

But surely the evidence fails to support our prophecy of gloom and doom? Membership numbers of both the American Psychological Association Division

International Handbook of Selection and Assessment, Edited by N. Anderson and P. Herriot.
© 1997 John Wiley & Sons Ltd.

14 (SIOP) and the British Psychological Society Occupational Division continue to rise, as do the figures for organizational psychology professional bodies in many other countries. Attendances at organizational psychology conferences are growing in both Europe and the United States; new journals have been launched in several countries; and there has been an increasing number of university programmes in organizational psychology, particularly outside the United States. All of these 'health of the profession' indicators are surely positive? But all are input and demand indicators, driven by an international recognition of the potential role that personnel and selection psychology could play in the modern, post-bureaucratic business environment. None points up the growing concerns, voiced in several quarters over recent years, that elements of traditional selection theory and practice are becoming noticeably obsolete and archaic.

The tenets of traditional selection theory and practice remain rooted in an era of bureaucratic work organization, where stable, specialized jobs in large numbers were prevalent and which largely supported assumptions key to the paradigm. Post-bureaucratic forms of work organization have shifted the ground under the feet of personnel psychologists, resulting in the dominant paradigm becoming increasingly maladaptive. Cascio (1995) aptly quotes Albert Einstein's comment following the first atomic reaction in 1942: 'Everything has changed, except our way of thinking' (*Workplace of the Future*, 1993, p. 2). We hope that this editorial chapter will serve as a paradigmatic 'wake-up call' for personnel and selection psychology, since continuing to ignore the sweeping changes in the environment upon which we theorize and in which we practice will undoubtedly lead to marginalization and eventually to terminal decline. No institution or organization survives unless its culture adapts to the changing demands of its environment (Schein, 1985). We will demonstrate in this chapter that the culture of personnel psychology is changing painfully slowly in response to the immense global challenges of today. And the task is indeed immense. As Howard (1995, p. 548) observes: '. . . the practice of I/O psychology in the twenty-first century will need to be more like the work environment—fluid, varied, and complex, but customer oriented and just in time'.

We put forward four main arguments. First, that there exist a number of hugely powerful 'environmental drivers' in modern day international business. Secondly, that these drivers have resulted in deep rooted changes in the nature of work within organizations. Thirdly, that the dominant predictivist paradigm is curtailing selection psychologists' responses to these changes, and is becoming increasingly maladaptive to its environment. Fourthly, and by inescapable implication, that these changes in the context of personnel psychology give rise to several far-reaching challenges for selection research and practice, among them the following four:

(i)   selecting for change,
(ii) multiple and interactive levels of analysis,
(iii) cross-cultural applicability of meta-analytical findings, and
(iv) generating wider theoretical frameworks.

Figure 1.1 illustrates these themes and therefore overviews the structure of this chapter.

THE DRIVERS OF CHANGE

The changes currently assailing us all are each huge in their own right. In sum they are formidable; in interaction, feeding off each other as they do, they represent a revolutionary shock, a discontinuity in the development of human society (Davis, 1995). Perhaps the most fundamental of them all is 'globalism'. The barriers of space and time are overturned, and finance capital can be transferred at a moment's notice. Tiny changes in interest or exchange rates can have global consequences. Organizations can transfer their functions to wherever offers the most cost-competitive business environment. Some are so at home anywhere in the world that they are no longer identified with a particular country; they are truly transnational (Bartlett and Ghoshal, 1989). Huge corporations can form alliances with each other to open up new markets on the other side of the globe. We are all interdependent now—in terms of our environment, finance, health, safety, mobility and careers.

The main engine for change is information technology (IT). The instantaneous transfer of capital, for example, depends upon the communicative power of IT. Research and development (R&D) teams on the opposite sides of the world can interactively formulate and reformulate scientific models (Sproull and Kiesler, 1986). IT also offers the possibility of adding to our knowledge by enabling us to perceive patterns in data—of 'informating' (Zuboff, 1988). It helps us to learn by providing instant symbolic feedback from our actions. And it can control processes or aid decisions.

The growth of knowledge is exponential, and according to Prahalad and Hamel (1990), knowledge in the form of the core competence of the corporation is now the major source of competitive advantage. Such knowledge is hard to imitate and adds unique value to the customer. Knowledge is three sided—*knowing that, knowing how, and knowing beyond* (Herriot and Pemberton, 1994). Gaining information, using it in practice, and learning from that use to envisage a different future are now the key processes in knowledge-based organizations.

With the erosion of many trade barriers and the deregulation of various industry sectors, new markets are constantly opening up, and competition for them is ever keener. Organizations both annexe and create new niche markets for themselves, and prospector companies (Sonnenfeld and Peiperl, 1988) move into and out of markets with speed and effect. The need to satisfy the short-term requirements of the shareholders for dividends, especially in the United States and the United Kingdom (Hutton, 1994), adds to the attractiveness of such a strategy.

The diversity of the new markets results in strongly differentiated demand and the need to customize goods and services to suit different markets and even individual customers or clients. 'Think global but act local' is the new motto. And speed to market of goods and services is a source of competitive advantage, with compressed design cycles being critical in the time spent in development,

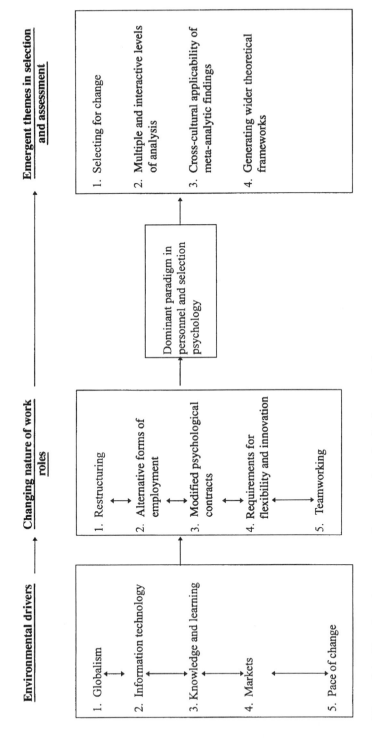

Figure 1.1   The changing nature of personnel and selection psychology

production and transportation. Moreover, obsolescence of these same goods and services is even faster, so the product cycle is under constant pressure from both ends.

The pace of change is thus increasing exponentially, with its speed and unpredictability making long-term planning next to impossible (Hosking and Anderson, 1992). Furthermore, the adaptations required of organizations and individuals are now so frequent that the pressure of new learning and new relationships, and feelings of never returning to a steady, routinized state, are highly prevalent amongst individuals at work. As we mentioned above, the impact of each of these environmental drivers is multiplicative and is a function of their interaction with one another. For example, globalism continuously opens up new markets, which further differentiate demand. Information technology adds to knowledge, which increases the rate of change.

THE CHANGING NATURE OF WORK ROLES

Organizational responses

Faced with an environment that is transforming itself, how are organizations to survive? The evolutionary analogy has proved irresistible to commentators. To quote Howard again (1995, p. 522):

> An organism's survival doesn't depend on overall 'fitness', which is impossible to define, but on the niche it is filling, what other organisms are around, what resources it can gather, and to some extent its past history. Organizations likewise must engage in this dance of co-evolution with their wafting webs of economic and political dependencies. They must keep open as many options as possible and strive for what is not necessarily optimal, but advantageous and workable.

But this is a prescriptive rather than a descriptive account. There are three strategic responses which organizations have favoured over the last decade: cost-cutting, customer-facing and innovation (Williams and Dobson, Chapter 11 in this volume). Of these, cost-cutting has been favoured in the Anglo-Saxon countries (e.g. North American and Northwest European countries), and has consequently received most attention. Moreover, when we consider the drivers of change to which cost-cutting is a strategic response, it is clear that it is only the increase in competition that this strategy is fundamentally designed to address.

Cost-cutting has been addressed in two basic ways. First, by various forms of restructuring, and secondly by attempts to increase productivity so that the same amount of work can be done by fewer and fewer employees. Restructuring has had the fundamental purpose of reducing headcount and hence employment costs. The reduction of cost is immediate, and is instantly recognizable to shareholders and financial analysts as a response to the impact of competition. Downsizing, often by means of compulsory redundancies, is the favoured option. Delayering (the elimination of levels in the hierarchy) and devolution of the corporation to profit centres are also frequent, and these latter restructurings also have the purpose of empowering those who deal with customers to meet their needs faster and more flexibly.

Mergers, acquisitions and bankruptcies are ever more frequent; the first two have the purposes of adding to the organization's core capability and at the same time ridding it of a competitor. They often have the additional longer-term consequence of reducing overall headcount. Finally, much of what is not core to the organization's purpose is now being contracted out to external suppliers, on the grounds that this decreases costs by removing the expense of permanent employment. A wide variety of temporary and part-time employment contracts are also now in vogue (Feldman, 1995). Such contracts enable organizations both to reduce costs and also to have employees available for periods of peak demand. There are even so-called zero hour contracts, whereby 'employees' are guaranteed no work at all, but required to work whenever they are needed. It is important to note that while operatives and others at the lower levels of the organizational hierarchy have historically been liable to suffer from these uncertainties, they are now universal throughout organizations (Heckscher, 1995). There are, of course, unavoidable and far-reaching implications from these contractual developments for the theory and practice of personnel selection.

The second major element of the strategy to survive by means of cost competitiveness has been the attempt to increase productivity. This has taken many forms, and has been dominated by a series of management fads (Huczynski, 1993). These have been marketed as packaged solutions by management consultants, and include individual performance-related pay as a means of performance management, and business process re-engineering to reduce and simplify the work-flow. While many organizations have quietly filleted these fads for those elements that are appropriate to their own needs and culture, others have believed that they are the solution to their problems. In general, such fads have been sold to top management, who then passed down the responsibility for implementation to middle managers already doing the work of two. Fads have a shelf life of about two years, and few become deeply embedded in organizations. The consequence is a sequence of fads to which employees have to pretend to adapt.

The results of evaluations of corporate restructuring and management fads are now beginning to come through. It seems that financial performance assessed in a variety of ways has not reliably improved as a consequence of downsizing (DeMeuse, Vanderheiden and Bergmann, 1994). Moreover, a variety of other often deleterious consequences has ensued (Cascio, 1995). These include a variety of hidden costs, such as the need to manage external contractors, and loss of reputation as a good employer. The same applies to the fads, where the psychological consequences of the various interventions were unforeseen, in particular the concerns for equity. Indeed, it is important to explore the impact of restructuring and management fads on individuals and groups in the workplace in more detail, since it is the arena in which we would have expected personnel psychologists to have had an influence. Again, these changes are not without impact upon the field of selection psychology, whether one sits on the practitioner or the academic side of the fence.

Moreover, what we know of the process of innovation in organizations suggests that the psychological consequences of restructuring are actively hostile towards innovation. Yet innovation and creativity at work have become the norm in employers' expectations of the day-to-day behaviour of their staff, not merely a desirable supplementary quality displayed periodically by just a few. Innovation requires: a degree of security so that risks may be taken; autonomy from over-zealous control; a sense of agency such that individuals believe that they can have an impact upon outcomes: and working in teams so as to benefit from diverse perspectives (West and Altink, 1996). Yet restructuring has resulted in job and personal insecurity; tighter control through budget targets; helplessness engendered by a series of organizational and environmental events over which one has had no control; and the reward of individual performance rather than teamwork. It will consequently be extremely difficult to move from a strategy of cost cutting to one of innovation, since the consequences of the former are actively hostile to the latter. Conversely, it is arguable that in the longer term this is the only alternative for post-industrial societies; cost competitiveness will be a necessary but not a sufficient condition for survival. And certainly, many organizations are already selecting for innovation potential amongst prospective employees (King and Anderson, 1995).

The decline of jobs and the emergence of work roles

One way to understand the consequences of restructuring on jobs and individuals is to use the concept of the psychological contract, i.e. the perception of what each party to the employment relationship owes the other (Rousseau, 1995; Herriot and Pemberton, 1996). Downsizing and delayering may be construed by employees as reneging on an existing contract by the organization in which individuals had historically traded their loyalty, expertise and conformity for security and regular promotion and pay increases. As a consequence, both those made redundant and those who survive are likely to experience a range of emotional responses. Insecurity, inequity, powerlessness and loss of organizational commitment are amongst them (Stroh, Brett and Reilly, 1994), especially if the manner of the redundancy pays no attention to the relational nature of the psychological contract (Brockner, Tyler and Cooper-Schneider, 1992; Jackson, Chapter 31 in this volume). Long-serving employees are likely to have gone the extra mile for the organization and been good organizational citizens over and above their job descriptions. Is this the way they are to be repaid from now on, think the survivors? Rousseau (1990) distinguishes such relational from strictly explicit and transactional contracts, and believes (Rousseau, 1995) that the trend will be towards the latter. The employment relationship is becoming shorter; it is moving from insiders to outsiders; and it is changing from being implicit to being explicit in its terms and conditions. And the ideology of human resource management, which construes employees as human capital to be used to achieve business objectives, has taken fast hold upon Anglo-Saxon business culture.

The consequences of such pressures toward business restructuring are already being acutely felt in most sectors of business, whether public service or private sector. The traditional Taylorian-derived, specialized job consisting of discrete tasks and activities is dying, and is being replaced by ever-more flexible forms of work organization (Bridges, 1994; Cascio, 1995; Howard, 1995). Larger organizations which for years had been structured around classical principles of bureaucratic control, authority structures and job specialization (e.g. the armed forces, public sector utilities, monopolistic and oligopolistic companies) are being decentralized, privatized and downsized, and many of their job tasks out-sourced to sub-contractors. And these organizations, we need to acknowledge, are inextricably tied into the historical roots of personnel and selection psychology, particularly in Anglo-Saxon countries. In these organizations stable jobs in large numbers permitted the application of various assumptions, validation techniques, methods and practices. But this context is disappearing, with an increasing emergence of small to medium sized companies, the downsizing of military personnel numbers, sub-contracted labour, homeworking and teleworking, and the inexorable trend toward more flexible, changeable work roles as the latter-day replacements for stable, specialized jobs (see also Sackett and Arvey, 1993; Schmidt, 1993; and Howard, 1995). Of course, we acknowledge that probably there will always be job roles in organizations structured around the design principles of classical bureaucracy, but these are rapidly declining in numbers as internal markets, outsourcing and sub-contracting all take their toll.

Six specific responses

These pressures have resulted in six main responses:

- flexible work roles
- newly created jobs (NCJs)
- teamworking
- concerns over organizational fit
- moves towards a segmented labour market
- proactive career management by the individual

Work roles

Work roles less and less consist of predictable and regular tasks, but of high involvement in solving problems and adding value in new ways (Lawler, 1992). Role-senders are many and varied—colleagues, bosses, customers, clients, suppliers and allies. To meet their changing expectations requires flexibility and adaptability. Employees need a whole range of skills and knowledge over and above their functional or technical competence (which, of course, is itself subject to ever faster obsolescence). Yet the dominant paradigm presupposes a set of tasks that can be defined and which will remain the same for the predictable future (Lawler, 1994).

Newly created jobs

An increasing proportion of job roles being recruited for have not previously existed. Organizational restructuring, downsizing programmes, entry into new markets and the impact of new technology are all drivers toward newly created jobs (NCJs). In a survey of British managers conducted by Nicholson and West in the 1980s (Nicholson and West, 1988), between one-third and one-half of respondents reported that their last move was into an NCJ. It is impossible to use traditional methods of job analysis for jobs that do not yet exist, and so the classical opening gambit of selection psychologists—job analysis—is not relevant.

Teamworking

Innovation and speed to market require teamworking of a high order (Mohrman and Cohen, 1995). Individuals are increasingly interdependent, and work is coming to be seen more and more as the completion of projects. Hence analysis by the organization at the level of individual performance is becoming increasingly questionable and obsolete. The team itself can manage its own members' contributions. Moreover, if selection is for team role rather than for job, then it will have to be for the short term and just-in-time. So will the selection of those on temporary contracts. People will be selected on the basis of reputation, recent performance and team fit. Yet the dominant paradigm implies that selection is always of individuals for long-term jobs, and its artefacts are designed to that end.

Organization fit

For the organizational core, however, selection will be for the longer term. But it is more for organization fit than for job fit that they will be assessed (Schneider, 1987, and Schneider *et al.*, Chapter 19 in this volume). This does not necessarily imply homogeneity, however. To meet its needs for innovation, the organization may require a variety of perspectives (Amabile, 1983; West and Farr, 1990). To understand and deal with its customers better, it may need a comparable demographic mix of employees. In both cases the criterion is fit to the organization rather than to a job. Again, the dominant psychological culture makes the wrong assumption that it is person-job fit which is the sole concern in selection decision-making.

Segmented labour market

As organizations become more knowledge based, the labour market will become more segmented and differentiated; for many of their core experts and managers, the labour market will become a seller's rather than a buyer's one (Mirvis, 1993). Where labour market power is more evenly divided than recently has been the case, the selection procedure becomes more of a negotiation. Each party is trying to decide whether it wishes to select the other as employee or employer, and on what terms. The procedure is a subjective dynamic social process rather than a one-way objective assessment (Herriot, 1989). This is perhaps one of the reasons why the interview is so popular, together with the belief that organization fit is best assessed face-to-face (Anderson, 1992). As Murphy (1986) pointed out, utility estimates are of little use when your first choice turns you down. Of course, these changes in labour market power will not be true of all sectors of the labour market. For unskilled and semi-skilled or workers whose activities can be out-sourced or sub-contracted to developing countries to reduce labour costs, the picture looks increasingly bleak. Without reskilling, the labour market (for these workers) looks set to reduce or even disappear. We are therefore facing an in-creasingly segmented and divided labour market; not by sex or race, as has been the concern for affirmative action over recent decades, but by skills and knowl-edge. Moreover, selection practices will need to cope with new contractual and geographically distant forms of employment—fixed-term contracts, zero hours contracts, international secondments and placements, and homeworking and tele-working, to name but a few. Once again, we need to critically review the capabil-ity of the dominant paradigm to embrace such a diversity of selection scenarios.

Career management

The rapidity of change and the need for everyone in the organization to adapt implies a requirement for career-resilient employees who can take charge of their own development and manage their own careers (Waterman, Waterman and Collard, 1994). Yet at the same time organizations will seek to ensure that their supply of top management talent is developed by job moves designed to remove the gaps in their experience (Hall and Associates, 1986). Self-management implies ownership of assessment information by the individual, and the use of instru-ments that have other purposes than to predict job performance (see Kidd, Chap-ter 30 in this volume). And developmental job postings imply selecting people who may not be the best performers. The implication is that selection will change from being a one-off barrier to entry into the organization, so long a taken-for-granted assumption in the predictivist paradigm. It will become a continuous and repeated internal process where appraisal increasingly begins to take on facets of re-assessment and attempted behaviour modification. We return to this final im-plication later in this chapter.

The compound effect of these six major drivers is to raise pertinent questions over the paradigm–environment fit of personnel psychology, and whether such a fit as presently exists is less than compelling and becoming ever less so. More seriously, we may argue that the dominant paradigm fails to address the present and future needs of organizations. If customer-facing and innovation strategies are going to become more necessary in an era of demanding markets, sharp competition and increasing knowledge, then various changes in personnel strat-egies and practice become inevitable.

THE DOMINANT PARADIGM

Cultural assumptions

If these environmental drivers and the organizational responses to them are the environment in which personnel and selection psychology itself has to survive, how well adapted is its culture? The dominant paradigm in personnel psychology derives from North America, and may be described in terms of a set of fundamental assumptions, general beliefs, specific values and artefacts. While the following account is doubtless sufficient of an over-simplification as to invite the charge of caricature, it is a useful starting-point.

The culture of the dominant paradigm may be described briefly as follows (Herriot, 1992). Its *fundamental assumptions* are:

- Work is done by individuals
- Work consists of tasks
- Groups of tasks form jobs
- Jobs do not change very much
- Individuals' job performance can be measured and attributed to the individual
- Job tasks require specific attributes
- Individuals' attributes predict job performance
- Individual differences in attributes are the biggest source of performance variability
- Attributes can each be measured independently of each other
- Attributes change relatively little over time
- Selection is by the organization of the applicant, not the reverse
- The main purpose of selection is to predict job performance
- The best job performers are the most suitable employees
- The better the selection, the better the job, team and organizational performance.

In addition to these assumptions about work, people and selection, there are certain more *general beliefs* about the nature of personnel psychology itself, as follows:

- Personnel psychology is a branch of academic psychology
- Psychology is a science
- The theories and findings of science are universal
- Personnel psychology is therefore universal.

Among the *specific values* of the dominant culture in the academic wing of the discipline are the following:

- Approval of one's academic peers and seniors
- Publication in prestigious scientific journals
- Analysis rather than intervention
- Methodological rigour
- Quantitative and statistical sophistication
- Continued membership of invitation-only researcher discussion groups and workshops
- Conferment of honorary awards and titles by academic peers.

The *artefacts* of the dominant culture include:

- Selection procedures designed in terms of the classic criterion-related validity paradigm
- Meta-analysis, validity generalization and utility analysis
- Job analysis and job descriptions
- Theories of individual differences
- Performance ratings of individuals

The consequence of these latter assumptions is a stance towards the environment whereby personnel and selection psychologists perceive themselves as detached scientists and expert practitioners, standing outside both the environmental drivers and the efforts of organizations to adapt to those drivers. They have formulated a body of esoteric knowledge of which, if they are wise, organizations will take account in their personnel policies and practices. This is the classic self-definition of scientists as objective external investigators of the phenomena that they seek to explain and control. Unfortunately, the ground has moved under the feet of academic personnel psychologists: selection research is now *following slowly* after changing events in the workplace in a reactive manner, *not* generating novel perspectives to drive innovative practice.

Problems with the culture

Let us begin by debunking some of these rather grandiose assumptions. Foremost amongst them is the myth that personnel psychology could ever attain the status of a 'pure science'. We would strongly endorse the recent stance of Landy, Shankster-Cawley and Moran (1995, pp. 253–254):

> Adopting a systems perspective requires that we discard the traditional view of selection and placement activities as neutral technologies to be inserted into a system in a rational manner. Personnel activities are part of a system, and as they change or are developed, they influence and are influenced by social, economic, and organizational contexts.

Likewise, the role of the personnel psychologist can never be that of a completely detached expert-scientist, and it is folly to believe that surrounding ourselves with the 'trappings of scientism' will ever raise the status of the discipline. It will not; it will merely marginalize the profession and reduce its influence upon its environment.

The dominant paradigm in personnel psychology values quantified empirical studies, formulaic reconfigurations of established methods and the production of generalized knowledge, the jewels in the crown of the profession over the last two decades being meta-analysis and validity generalization. But the maturation of personnel psychology as a scientific discipline, whilst reaping the benefits of increasingly robust and sophisticated empirical research, has led to a predominant cultural code of mass epistemological conformity. No other sub-discipline in the organizational sciences has exhibited such a paucity of theoretical perspectives, such a lack of debate over guiding paradigmatic assumptions and such unquestioned conformity to naive, managerialist positivism. And if the discipline fails to stimulate a diversity of theoretical perspectives and epistemological approaches, then it runs the risk of becoming an overheated enginehouse of remote, blind empiricism.

Already, the opportunities for an academic personnel psychologist to hole-up in her or his office have become seductive. One can quite feasibly nowadays handle most communications by electronic media, request offprints by remote electronic means, send graduate students out to do all necessary fieldwork, run analyses of secondary data sets, and thus never have to leave the office. Indeed, for academic personnel psychologists there are strong pressures toward isolationism: analysis and writing-up work is less interrupted, a degree of detachment from the day-to-day hubbub of the commercial world helps independent reflection; and one can avoid those troublesome queries from people who should know better (organizational clients, human resource practitioners, students, colleagues, etc.). And if one specializes in meta-analytic procedures, then one need only ever collect-in reports of other people's data sets, thereby avoiding entirely the tiresome need for fieldwork which, after all, is the demeaning workaday world of 'second division' academics.

This leads on to the second concern we have over prevalent beliefs, values and assumptions, namely that the dominant predictivist paradigm can only *ever* furnish an incomplete understanding of the myriad of phenomena and issues that go to make up the dynamic, social psychological milieu of current selection processes. Again, the list that follows is not exhaustive but illustrative of phenomena in the selection process that the dominant paradigm either cannot account for, or would dismiss as inappropriate or inconsequential research questions:

- The processes of selection as opposed to the validity of individual methods
- Psychological and developmental processes that occur in applicants between the times a predictor measure and the criterion measure are taken
- The impact of selection procedures upon applicants
- Applicant rights
- Recruiter abuse of applicants and power-based mistreatment of candidates
- Irrational beliefs and practices amongst recruiters and applicants
- Processual variance between recruiters in their idiosyncratic styles of conducting even highly structured methods
- Erosion of standardization over time (e.g. following the organization-wide introduction of structured interviewing)
- Candidate decision-making—whether to apply, to remain in the selection process, or to accept a job offer
- Impression management by recruiters and candidates
- How the psychological contract is formed and developed by both parties throughout the selection process
- The 'socialization impact' of selection methods as a moderator of predictive validity

- Changes in the job role that alter the criterion domain
- Selecting for organizational and team-level fit
- Cultural, national, historical and societal impacts upon recruitment and selection processes
- The reasons *why* discrimination occurs in practice.

Scientific paradigm or psychic prison?

The above list is clearly a lengthy one, and no amount of organization-specific validity studies or large-scale meta-analyses will begin to address these phenomena. All these practical issues are, in our view, worthy of research attention, and ironically, many will directly impact upon predictive validity but have received little or no attention within the dominant paradigm. Nonetheless, the dominant paradigm is extremely coherent; the values and artefacts that underpin its culture follow logically from its assumptions. We venture that these assumptions have now taken on the characteristics of an ideology, in the sense of an explicit set of beliefs that are embraced as a whole; to question a part is tantamount to rejecting the whole (see also Dachler, 1994). It is likely to be extremely difficult to adapt the culture to its environment if its assumptions are not capable of being evaluated in terms of their appropriateness to the current and future environment. So potent and pervasive is this culture that it almost feels sacrilegious to dare to raise questions over its value.

A comparison with other sub-disciplines in the organization sciences reveals, in stark contrast, just how restrictive the predominant paradigm in personnel psychology has become. In management science and organizational behaviour, for instance, a vociferous dialectic has raged for years between managerial-positivists, post-bureaucratic organization theorists and advocates of labour process theory (Legge, 1995). So vigorous has this debate been that, in comparison, the field of personnel psychology appears bland beyond belief, at least in terms of published outputs and the near absence of theoretical debate. In personnel psychology we have allowed a creeping asphyxiation of published disagreement to occur in which a conservative and conventional epistemological stance has become ingrained into the deepest layers of our culture. It may be that differences of opinion are now only expressed under the cover of the anonymous review process, but certainly the situation has not been helped by our main journals publishing almost exclusively quantitative, empirical studies. Why does selection psychology have no equivalent journal to the *Academy of Management Review* which specializes in theory-building articles? Of course, the *Journal of Applied Psychology* includes theoretical papers in its terms of reference, but how many have appeared over the years? And this is not, we believe, a function of over-restrictive editorial policy so much as a manifestation of the cultural artefacts we listed earlier in this chapter.

The paucity of theoretical frameworks has serious implications, for it limits the range of topic areas that are considered appropriate subjects for study. Yet the environment is forcing governments, organizations and individuals to address other and quite different issues. If the dominant paradigm prevents these issues being addressed, then other professions will annex our territory (Abbott, 1988). It is no accident that, certainly in the Anglo-Saxon countries, HR practitioners and academics have gained prominence in recent years. It is a salutary lesson for personnel psychologists that this increase in the influence of human resource management (HRM) has occurred despite its prescriptive nature and the relative paucity of the evidence it quotes. Whilst personnel practitioners have moved with the times to embrace many of the issues in selecting for change, academic personnel psychologists appear to have fortified themselves into a paradigm that has begun to take on the appearance of a psychic prison. Researchers at times have appeared to obstinately cling to taken-for-granted assumptions that have been by-passed in the real world of post-bureaucratic work organizations. The psychic prison may indeed be built upon the impressive foundations of pure science, its facade monolithic and imposing to the uninitiated, and its interior culture safe and predictable to the privileged longer-term guests, but it is a prison nevertheless. And its institutionalizing effects undoubtedly need to be challenged periodically.

Academic conformity

We raised the spectre earlier that the structure of rewards in the academic wing of our discipline has become dysfunctional. Excessive conformity pressures have starved the discipline of paradigmatic innovation, radical theoretical perspectives, alternative model-building, and attempts toward and the acceptance of novel methodological approaches to applied studies. Many readers will have heard similar arguments in the past, but usually confined to hushed conversations between small cliques of trusted friends in darkened corners of conference anterooms. What exactly are the conformity pressures, how are they enacted, and what effects are they ultimately having upon the well-being of our discipline?

The competition for tenure-track posts amongst early-career faculty is intense, and is followed up by a three-, five- or seven-year period (dependent upon the country in question) of what is effectively probation and socialization. Allying oneself with a powerful senior professor as mentor, together with ingratiating oneself to senior colleagues in the department and in the wider scientific community, are further determinants of survival. Altruistic contributions to the professional society and upholding journal standards by furnishing timely reviews of manuscripts both help. But above all, avoiding controversy, radicalness or ostracism by one's peers is crucial in the repertoire of impression management tactics learned by early-career faculty. The advancement of scientific understanding in personnel psychology would be immensely better served if younger researchers perceived themselves as radical academicians rather than as fledgling apparatchiks of their respective professional societies; and if this was reflected by the reward structure. Regrettably, many countries with developed selection research communities have allowed the opposite to become the case.

But such pressures are not confined solely to pre-tenured academics. Far from it. The pressures to 'play the game' by sticking to safe empirical studies, to locate oneself within the confines of the predominant managerialist–positivist paradigm, and not to alienate oneself from an academic elite who wield considerable power have become excessive. Taken in combination, these pressures have resulted in theoretical stagnation, methodological homogeneity, piecemeal deductivism, and the hegemony of 'dust-bowl' empiricism. The evidence of constructive controversy and challenge to the predominant paradigm is sparse, let alone any signs of radical theoretical advance. What controversy there is appears to be almost entirely within-paradigm: disagreements over the calculation of SDy estimates, banding procedures for test cut-off scores, parameters for including studies in meta-analyses, the number of generic personality dimensions, and so forth. Academic endeavour in personnel psychology seems to have been reduced to a cosy quasi-bureaucratic industry, where multiple empirical factories compete with one another, playing out a game for which the rules are well known, the norms for output type and frequency well established, and an accommodation reached between academics that managerialist-positivist paradigmatic assumptions are better left unchallenged.

How maladaptive is the dominant culture?

What are the indicators that an applied scientific discipline is becoming isolated from its environment? They include:

- An increasing gulf between the interests of academics, consultants and practitioners
- Segregation of practitioners from academics and early-career exclusive specialization into either branch
- Growth of academic numbers sufficient to permit the evaluation of colleagues on all occasions by fellow academics
- Increasing competition for funding from government grants reviewed by academic peers and a decline in direct industrial funding of research
- Acceptance of the need to publish a quantity of outputs above the desire to contribute to an understanding of, or impact upon, phenomena in the field
- Concerns expressed by practitioners that tenure is no longer needed to protect academics engaged in radical or politically sensitive research
- Concerns expressed by academics that practitioners are more at the cutting edge of developing innovative responses in the field
- Practitioners regarding the premier journals in the field as 'irrelevant'
- Academics regarding the premier journals in the field as 'boring'.

Of course, the presence of just one or two of these indicators in isolation does not imply maladaption or marginalization. It is their combined effects over time that is likely to lead to this. There are two lines of argument which suggest that the dominant culture in personnel and selection psychology is on the verge of becoming maladaptive. The first consists of evidence that those who should be acting upon the understandings and recommendations of its exponents are failing to do so. The second delineates the inappropriateness of its assumptions, values and artefacts to either its present and likely future environment or to developing scientific understanding of phenomena in the selection process.

Organizations are part of the environment to which personnel psychology has to adapt, although whether organizations rather than other academics are the more powerful role-senders in the research environment is open to debate. What is clear from the evidence is that although the use of psychometric instruments is widespread, actual practice in organizations does not follow the recommendations that are implied by the dominant culture. If it did, then those instruments most used would be those that had high validity; and selection decisions would be made on an actuarial rather than a clinical judgemental basis.

Smith and Abrahamsen (1992) brought together survey results from six countries: France, Germany, Israel, the Netherlands, Norway, and the United Kingdom. Interviews and application forms were the most frequently used selection techniques in all of them, with cognitive, personality and trainability tests used for between 10% and 20% of vacancies, and assessment centres and biodata used very rarely. The correlation between the frequency of usage of instruments and their validity was negative: $r = -0.25$. The same infrequency of usage of the most valid instruments is also true in the United States (Muchinsky, 1994), where it is rare for information derived from psychometric instruments to be used actuarially (Ryan and Sackett, 1987). Whatever the reasons for these findings, it is clear that the findings from validation studies and meta-analyses as key artefacts of the dominant academic culture have had only a limited impact upon their supposed constituency.

Other evidence suggests that researchers have committed substantial effort toward questions which are regarded by practitioners as being banal, esoteric and self-indulgent. In no other area has this been more blatantly obvious than in utility analysis. Countless minor modifications in the calculation of SDy estimates, excruciatingly slight twists in the configuration of formulae, and tweaks to include hitherto overlooked variables, have spawned literally hundreds of published papers. Many are impressively sophisticated and intricately detail-conscious in their endeavour, but all are grounded upon the fundamental premiss that financial payback is a critical factor in practitioner choice between selection methods. In other words, that the rational-quantitative assumptions and cultural artefacts prevalent amongst the personnel psychology research community will naturally be applicable to practising HR specialists and line managers. They simply are not. In a paper provocatively titled '*The futility of utility analysis*', Latham and Whyte (1994) found that experienced managers were indeed influenced by the provision of utility analysis findings in addition to general validity information and expectancy tables—but in a negative direction! Managers were *less* likely to implement more valid selection methods when given the financial payback results of utility analysis. Yet, the power to persuade practitioners to adopt more valid methods supposedly conferred upon personnel psychologists by utility analysis has been the justification offered for the monumental research effort in this area.

The thorny question of whether researchers have wasted their time, undoubted talents and technical expertise is subservient in our view to the concern we have of why it has taken so long for a paper challenging the guiding premise that financial payback is paramount to be published. Our point then is not to criticize utility analysis *per se*. Indeed, Boudreau, Sturman and Judge (Chapter 15 in this volume) present a cogently argued case for on-going and important work in this area. Rather, this is just one of several possible exemplars of taken-for-granted assumptions in personnel psychology being unchallenged and left uncriticized. In such a climate there is always a danger that false consensus may lead to the myopia of technical–statistical sophistication over-stepping its rational and epistemological bounds. It may remain unchecked by a telling lack of constructive controversy over underlying assumptions within the research community, or by any concern about whether practitioners find it in the least useful. We argue that researchers need to critically examine more often the veracity of taken-for-granted assumptions in personnel psychology; in short, to ask of ourselves the ultimatums *why* and *for what purpose* much more frequently than seems to be the case at the moment.

A multi-cultural framework

Questions of reason and purpose are critical. We argue that the fundamental beliefs of the dominant paradigm about the nature of personnel psychology itself are now outmoded. If we are to adapt successfully, then we will have to engage in double-loop learning (Argyris and Schon, 1978), which forces us to reflect upon our beliefs and activities. We need to question why particular research questions are being pursued, who is likely to benefit from such knowledge, and make self-regulatory judgements over the appropriate level of resourcing and time dedicated to each, competing research question. Personnel psychology, particularly in North America, has developed notable strengths in single-loop learning—questioning and improving how we do what we do (Argyris and Schon, 1978). Indeed, it can be argued that this is one factor that accounts for the methodological sophistication and quantitative–empirical excellence so evident in North American journals. Our point is that, in a period of environmental disjuncture and upheaval such as we are presently witnessing, single-loop learning alone is not enough. We need to critically appraise our underlying beliefs and values.

To recapitulate, these beliefs suggest that personnel and selection psychology is an objective body of knowledge that has universal application; it is an applied science. Such assumptions reflect a narrow, largely Anglo-Saxon view of the way in which psychological knowledge is acquired and applied. We would argue that national cultures are pivotal. It is true that they are being affected by the environmental drivers, but cultural differences are deep and will ever remain so. Such differences will profoundly influence the ways in which organizations and individuals in those nations or regions respond to the environmental drivers. They will also influence the culture of personnel psychology within them in two ways. First, the assumptions, values and artefacts of the national culture will affect those of its psychologists, just as they influence the organizations based in that country. Secondly, different stakeholders in personnel psychology have different degrees of influence in different countries; such differences in role-senders affect the culture's response to them. Hence the impact of personnel psychology upon organizations is mediated through national cultures. It follows that to ignore such

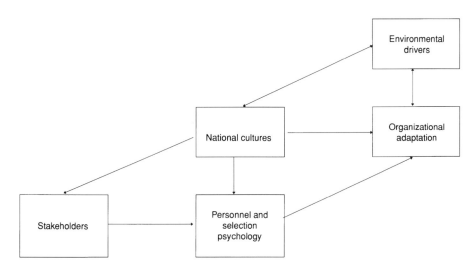

Figure 1.2   The role of personnel and selection psychology: a cross-cultural perspective

differences and to attempt to apply globally the assumptions, values and artefacts of the dominant Anglo-Saxon personnel culture is doomed to failure (see Figure 1.2).

Recently, the effects of national cultural differences upon business and organization have been suggested (Hofstede, 1980; Trompenaars, 1993). Underlying dimensions of the different assumptions embodied in various national cultures are now clear. They are (with some differences in terminology and emphasis): *universalism* versus *particularity; individualism* versus *collectivism; affectively neutral* versus *affectivity; specific* versus *diffuse; achievement* versus *ascription;* and *internal* versus *external locus of control.* The Anglo-Saxon cultures tend towards the first-mentioned polarity of each of these dimensions.

So, universalist Anglo-Saxons are more likely to believe the abstract generalizations and moral laws apply everywhere, whereas other cultures (e.g. Japan) are more likely to think differently about particular situations or relationships. Individualist Anglo-Saxons focus on their own individuality and their personal objectives rather than on their group or community membership and common objectives. The French, Italians, Irish and Japanese are more collective. Objectivity, detachment and instrumentality are recommended in American and Northwest European business activity, allowing people to remain affectively neutral, or at least to separate the emotional from the reasoning processes. Others such as the Italians mix them together. Specific Anglo-Saxons split up relationships at work into areas, e.g. collaboration on a task, whereas others generalize across from the particular to the diffuse, or require general personal relations to be established before specific business can be done (China, Japan and South America). Accomplishments and recent performance are what counts in an achievement-oriented country such as the United States, where you are only as good as your last success. In Germany and Japan, individual status is ascribed as a result of your position and in France of your education. Particularly in Germany and Japan, however, there is a strong emphasis on corporate rather than individual achievement. A strong tendency towards an internal locus of control enables Americans to attribute outcomes to individual effort and ability almost regardless of context; hence individual performance-related pay is a natural artefact. Reference outwards to the situation or to other people as determinants of outcomes (Japan and Singapore) may actually lead to better adaptation to customers and better response to feedback. As Trompenaars (1993) observes, feedback can be used to help us change our objectives in response to external realities, or it can simply inform as to how well we are achieving our internally set targets.

National cultures and personnel and selection psychology

Clearly, the above account of differences in national cultures is grossly oversimplified. However, it can be argued that national cultures affect the personnel psychology culture in two ways: directly, inasmuch as psychologists themselves embody their national culture and operate within it, and indirectly, different stakeholders have more influence in some cultures than in others. We characterized the American and British cultures as typical Anglo-Saxon cultures operating towards one end of each of the six cultural dimensions above. It is only too clear how closely these national assumptions and values are related to the dominant personnel psychology culture. It, too, is individualist, concentrating on the individual level of analysis; it is universalist, assuming its scientific theories can be applied everywhere; it is specific, concerning itself with analysis down into job tasks and personal attributes; it is achievement oriented, concentrating as it does on performance; it largely ignores emotions, assuming rationality and measuring aptitudes; and it assumes that individuals are responsible for outcomes, an internal locus of control. The dominant personnel psychology culture admirably reflects the culture of its nation of origin. This is why it has been so successful in its idiosyncratic context.

Other countries, however, have different psychology cultures which accord with their national culture and situation. In Spain, for example, academics and practitioners are closely aligned in the development of theory and practice (Prieto and Avila, 1994). In China, group structure and processes have long been major areas of applied research (Xu and Wang, 1991). In Latin America, the major emphasis of applied psychology is on community psychology (Wiesenfeld and Sanchez, 1991), and personnel psychology needs to treat organizations as impacting upon local communities.

Moreover, different stakeholders dominate in different countries. In the United States, for example, academics are well supported by their universities (although some might not think so!) which provide them with research facilities and support staff. Their academic peers are consequently their main reference group and stakeholders since they are not forced to go externally for their resources, and the origin of issues and problems is mainly the academic literature. It is reviewers and editors of the academic journals who determine what are the issues worth addressing, since the most valued product is the refereed journal article. In Britain and the Netherlands, the same stakeholders are gaining power, but indirectly: their national governments award resources partly on the basis of research performance, which is assessed by publications in prestigious European and American journals. In Western Europe, large organizations have close connections with university-based consultancies, and individual tenure is partially determined by the value of external funding won by faculty members. In Eastern Europe, national government is often the most prominent stakeholder, demanding help from psychologists in addressing pressing economic and social issues. Clearly, stakeholders have a profound effect on which issues are addressed and how, and on what behaviour is valued—methodological purity or practical intervention, for instance.

There are therefore many cultural influences upon the role of personnel psychologists in different countries. What are the implications of this realization? The most important is surely the need to stand outside one's own cultural perspective and view it in comparison with the perspectives of others. Attempts to transpose the dominant North American culture and paradigm in personnel psychology to other countries and cultures are thus again doomed to failure. The second is the ability to work through the consequences of each of these different perspectives for organizations and work in different countries. And the third is the willingness and ability to engage in these latter two activities in collaboration with people from other countries, since without such collaboration the enterprise is doomed to failure. These activities are obviously necessary for those engaged in work in an international context. They are also increasingly vital for people working in their own national culture, since it may well be crucial to the successful local adaptation of personnel psychology to incorporate a few assumptions, values and artefacts from elsewhere. Those who happen to work in one of the countries where personnel psychology is more developed would benefit from expanding their field of vision and experience beyond the source of the next refereed article to collaborating with international colleagues. Assumptions of scientific superiority need to be kept carefully in check since personnel psychologists in different countries can learn much from each other, and the profession stands to gain immeasurably from an internationalization of its perspectives and *modus operandi*.

EMERGENT THEMES IN PERSONNEL SELECTION AND ASSESSMENT

The preceding sections of this chapter offer little comfort to personnel psychologists who would prefer a universally applicable system in a steady state where routinized responses are the order of the day. We have suggested that overwhelming forces in globalized business markets have, and will continue, to transform work organizations. If this is not enough, then we have argued, perhaps more controversially, that the dominant paradigm in personnel psychology is outmoded and retrogressive; maladaptive to its changing environment; and incapable of sustaining an eclectic culture of research able to generate a wider understanding of recruitment selection processes across the world. We expect that some will disagree with our broad-brush analysis and applied cross-cultural stance—fine. Whatever the reader's impressions so far, the conclusion that issues and challenges in personnel selection running into the next millennium will dictate core rather than superficial, artefactual revisions to the scientific paradigm and organizational practice is inescapable. We now identify four main issues that will have to be addressed, each subsuming a number of specific themes. In this way we seek to make more specific some of the ways in which the dominant paradigm will have to change. These issues and themes are as follows:

1. Selecting for change
   - bimodal prediction
   - compressed validation cycles
   - selecting for emergent knowledge, skills, abilities and other factors (KSAOs)
   - the need for on-going, internal re-assessment.

2. Multiple and interactive levels of analysis
   - Person–team (P–T) fit
   - Person–organization (P–O) fit
   - Complementary, neutral and contradictory interactive terms.

3. Cross-cultural applicability of meta-analytic findings
   - International generalizability
   - Generalizability to expatriate selection.

4. Generating wider theoretical frameworks
   - Examples of innovative perspectives
   - Facilitating theoretical eclecticism.

Selecting for change

Our first theme—selecting for change—subsumes four interdependent issues: *bimodal prediction, compressed validation cycles, selecting for emergent knowledge, skills, abilities and other factors (KSAOs)* and *the need for on-going internal re-assessment.*

Bimodal prediction

The traditional paradigm in selection has, as we have already argued, assumed the existence of on-going, stable, analysable jobs comprised of discrete sets of tasks. Person–job fit was therefore the primary concern, with the job being conceptualized as a given 'target' to be hit through the application of valid and reliable methods of candidate assessment. The responsibility of the personnel psychologist was one of *unimodal prediction*—predicting the degree of fit to a given job. Increasingly we will be responsible for what can best be termed *bimodal prediction*—predicting the likely composition of the work role *as well as* person–work role fit. And we use the term 'work role' intentionally: as we have seen, clusters of activities and tasks performed by employees are likely to be much more fluid and transient in the future (Howard, 1995).

Predicting person–job fit alone was difficult enough, but bimodal prediction constitutes a daunting challenge, and one which demands a reconceptualization of the predictivist paradigm. In the past, as long as a job analysis had been performed, personnel psychologists could safely concentrate their efforts on the development of methods to evaluate applicant qualities. In the future, we will need to have available valid and reliable methods to predict the short- and medium-term composition of work roles (see also Visser *et al.*, Chapter 21 in this volume). This challenge, we believe, is one of crucial import to the survival of the discipline. There is thus a demonstrable need for personnel psychologists to turn their attention to the development of projective methods and techniques to predict future work roles. There is also the need for a major paradigmatic shift to incorporate this expansion of the prediction equation, and to refocus theory and practice around the strictures of bimodal prediction.

Some evidence of activity in bimodal prediction is already apparent by both American and British personnel psychologists. In the United States, Arvey, Salas and Gialluca (1992) used a task–ability intercorrelation matrix for present jobs to forecast the requirements for future possible job scenarios. In Britain, Henderson, Anderson and Rick (1995) report the development of a future-oriented competency framework for use as assessment centre dimensions. Structured interviews and repertory grids were conducted with groups of organizational staff to elicit expected competency dimensions for the job–family (graduate entrant jobs) for three to five years in the future. The assessment centre was subsequently reorganized around these future-oriented competencies. Sparrow (Chapter 17 in this volume) describes competency-based approaches to selection which depend upon the organization identifying and recruiting for a 'stock' of behavioural competencies. He argues persuasively that some clusters of competencies will be maturing (declining in importance), some emerging (increasing in importance) and some core (of on-going importance). The organization thus selects to develop or re-stock the behavioural repertoire present in its labour pool.

Compressed validation cycles

Production engineers talk of 'compressed design cycles' to indicate that the time needed to move from a product prototype to the finished and saleable item is now considerably shorter than in the past. In personnel psychology, the shorter-term stability of work roles presents a series of challenges to the classical paradigm, which historically has rightly emphasized the value of predictive validity studies. Why bother to validate a selection method or procedure against a criterion which is already out of date by the time the study has been completed? Validation cycles, which in the past could quite conceivably have held true over a period of several years, are becoming of increasingly dubious value. This, we believe, will lead to the need for *compressed validation cycles*. By this we mean that validation studies will need to be conceived of and completed in a period of weeks/months rather than months/years. The 'shelf-life' of validation study findings will be determined by how quickly the work role changes; the quicker the change, the shorter the shelf-life.

Of course, the wider availability of personal computers loaded with powerful database management and statistical analysis programs should help. But the challenge to our way of thinking is that in future the criterion problem, as we have already implied, will be of a magnitude and transience hitherto not conceived of. Personnel psychologists will need to adapt their approach from being that of a 'one-off' definitive validation study, maybe spanning years, toward an ethos of continuous improvement through a series of shorter-cycle validation studies followed by selection system re-adjustment (see also Roe, 1989). Moreover, as Fletcher (1996) argues, it is likely that concurrent validation studies will become more prevalent than predictive designs, since they are quick to complete because they do not rely on longitudinal data collection. Whatever the strengths of the traditional purist stance that predictive validity studies will always be needed, the imperative is for personnel psychologists to develop methodological approaches which are rapid enough to function within compressed validation cycles. Shorter delays after selection and before taking initial performance measures; using ratings of potential given in appraisal as predictors of performance over subsequent months; and regularly updating the criterion space for alpha, beta and gamma changes in dimension composition are just some of the possible ways of responding to the challenge of compressed validation cycles.

Selecting for emergent KSAOs

The changes in work organization described earlier in this chapter have given rise to several applicant KSAOs becoming more attractive to employers. Sparrow (Chapter 17 in this volume) would describe these as 'emergent competencies'. Amongst other factors, it is clear that organizations are placing greater emphasis on employee *flexibility*, *personality*, and *potential to innovate*.

First, *flexibility* and adaptability, in technical and social competencies, attitudes to work, and task- and non-task-related behaviour will be called for. As work roles will themselves be transient, assessment criteria for selection will widen from being the evaluation of specific technical competencies, to the assessment of flexibility as a psychological–behavioural construct. To our knowledge, little research exists into how to evaluate flexibility or its psychological antecedents. Indeed, personnel researchers will need initially to establish whether it makes sense to talk of 'flexibility' as a single construct—it may conceivably break down into several antecedent attitudinal dimensions (e.g. openness to change, rule independence, openness to experience, etc.) and observable, behavioural dimensions (e.g. ease of transition between task domains, ability to learn new skills, adaptability to work role changes, etc.). Each set of dimensions might be best assessed by different methods (e.g. attitudinal domains by personality instruments, behavioural domains by assessment centre exercises), so it is clear that much further research and applied technical development is called for.

Secondly, as several recent reviews have concluded, *personality* assessment is currently enjoying something of a renaissance in interest (Robertson, 1993; Robertson and Kinder, 1993; Landy, Shankster-Cawley and Moran, 1995; Ostroff and Rothausen, 1996; Hogan, Hogan and Roberts, 1996; Borman, Hanson and Hedge, in press). Landy, Shankster-Cawley and Moran quote Goldberg (1993): *'Once upon a time, we had no personalities. Fortunately, times change.'* Times do indeed change, but it still seems rather peculiar for *psychologists* to admit to a resurgence of interest in personality. Indeed, this appears largely specific to the context of the United States where the popularity of personality testing was adversely affected by earlier sceptical reviews and the strict legislative framework (e.g. Guion, 1991; Landy, Shankster-Cawley and Moran, 1995; Hough and Schneider, 1996). In many European countries, particularly Britain and the Netherlands, personality testing has long been popular (Shackleton and Newell, 1994; and Chapter 4 in this volume). In Britain, for instance, personality inventories are used by up to 80% of all organizations in recruitment for graduate and managerial vacancies (Keenan, 1995). Debate continues over the 'Big Five' structure of personality (e.g. Barrick and Mount, 1991; Schneider and Hough, 1995), as does discussion over the bandwidth-fidelity dilemma (e.g. Barrett *et al.*, 1996; Hough and Schneider, 1996; Ones and Viswesvaran, 1996). However, from the perspective of this chapter the critical point is that the need to assess personality is inextricably linked to the emergence of flexible job roles which permit greater behavioural freedom and expression at work.

Thirdly, selecting for *innovation potential* is becoming more prevalent amongst organizations. We have confined our comments so far in this chapter to situations where changes in the work-role are imposed from above as a result of environmental, technological or business pressures. Somewhat different implications arise for selection where organizations are actively recruiting for individuals with the motivation, skills and knowledge to change their work-role from within—that is, to innovate. Two challenges arise in relation to selection decision making. First, there is a dearth of methods specifically designed and validated to measure applicants' propensity to innovate (King and Anderson, 1995). Several personality instruments contain innovation or creativity-type dimensions, but little dimension-specific evidence exists to support their construct or criterion-related validity (King and Anderson, 1995). This leads on to the second major challenge in selecting for innovation potential. By definition, innovation implies changing the work role for the better in some *unforeseen* way, and therefore shifting the criterion domain in a manner which is unknown at the time of prediction. Of course, this is not such a new phenomenon; innovation research has long shown that jobholders in even non-discretionary and extensively regulated roles attempt to modify their position through innovation (Amabile, 1983; Van de Ven, Angle and Poole, 1989; West and Altink, 1996). The challenge for selection psychologists is thus to adapt to new recruits' *wilful disruption*, as it were, of the criterion domain.

The need for on-going, internal re-assessment

The fourth and final issue subsumed within our 'selecting for change' theme is the need for assessment to be viewed as an on-going activity rather than as a one-off barrier to entry into an organization. Why is this so, especially as some would hold that it is sufficient to measure general intellect (g) and possibly conscientiousness (c) as stable 'panacea predictors' of any foreseeable criterion? The reasons stem from our assertion that work-role change is endemic, exponential in its effects, and the only likely stable characteristic of future work organization.

Again, selection psychologists need literally to 'select for change', whether the causes of such instability are environmental pressures, the changing of roles from below by innovative employees or, most likely, a mixture of the two.

Here the implication is that we will need to extend our traditional restricted focus on organizational entry up until the first or second performance appraisal (although, of course, longer-term validity and validity decrement studies have been conducted). Selection needs to shift from being a one-off barrier to entry to being an on-going, periodic re-appraisal of the fit between individual competencies and organizational, team and work-role demands. The timing and duration of this cycle will be determined by how quickly the work-role changes, how fundamental the changes are, and how 'fine-tuned' an organization wishes to maintain the degree of fit between employee competencies and work-role demands. Of course, in these circumstances, the staff appraisal procedure of an organization is likely to take on this function of the periodic re-assessment of individual competency. This raises the question: Are many organizational appraisal processes up to the task? The valid and reliable measurement of cognitive and behavioural dimensions has always been treated as critical in selection procedures, but less so in appraisal where the fidelity of measurement has taken second place behind concerns over facilitating performance feedback. Appraisal schemes may therefore need considerable upgrading if they are to meet this challenge.

Multiple and interactive levels of analysis

Organizations of the future will need to select not only for person–work role fit but also for person–team (P–T) fit and for person–organization (P–O) fit. This trend has certainly been acknowledged elsewhere (e.g. Chatman, 1991; Guion, 1991; Ostroff and Rothausen, 1996; Borman, Hanson and Hedge, in press) where excellent reviews of studies into P–T fit and P–O fit are presented. Again, we confine our comments to the implications for the dominant scientific paradigm and for practice implied by the need to select for P–T fit and P–O fit. The critical challenge is to expand our conceptual horizon beyond the level of person–job fit and to incorporate multiple and interactive levels of analysis into selection decision-making. Fortunately, progress has already been made in theorizing issues for multiple levels of analysis in I/O psychology (e.g. Ostroff, 1993; George and James, 1994). At the team level of analysis, the work of Campion and Stevens shows considerable promise in elucidating the range of individual KSAOs needed to be an effective team member (Campion, 1994; Stevens and Campion, 1994a; see also West and Allen, Chapter 24 in this volume). These authors have also developed a useful psychometric test (Stevens and Campion, 1994b) which shows promise as a diagnostic tool to evaluate P–T fit. In a similar vein, Cannon-Bowers *et al.* (1995) propose an alternative typology of individual-level KSAOs for team-working. Other recent research by Borman and Motowildo (1993) into *contextual performance*—performance on non-task-related elements of a job—also shows real promise in advancing our understanding of, and methods to predict, P–T fit.

However, all these approaches are again grounded firmly in the dominant paradigm since they focus exclusively at an individual level of analysis. Assessing

P–T fit and P–O fit comprehensively demands that personnel psychologists extend their foci of analysis beyond solely the individual level. The selection of entire *ad hoc* project teams, selecting a cohort of newcomers into an organization, and selecting for longer-term fit into the organization culture are all instances where P–T and P–O fit are crucial and cannot be accounted for by individual-level measurement alone. We therefore coin the term *multiple and interactive levels of analysis* to highlight this challenge.

In terms of *multiple* levels of analysis, we refer to P–T fit and P–O fit in addition to the traditional concern for person–job fit. Of course, these three levels of analysis are interdependent and, to some extent, overlapping. Contextual performance, as operationalized by Borman and Motowildo (1993), clearly encroaches upon many micro-analytical issues of team level fit, for example. So the dividing lines between the three levels of analysis will inevitably be somewhat arbitrary.

Furthermore, we propose that there is an *interaction* between the levels of analysis. Interaction terms will be either *complementary, neutral*, or *contradictory*. A *complementary* interaction occurs where a high scale score at one level of analysis is desirable in combination with a high scale score at another level of analysis. For example, in a work-role involving substantial interpersonal contact the criterion of a high scale score on sociability is likely at the individual level of analysis, and if this work-role also requires team-working skills, then this criterion is appropriate also at the team level of analysis. *Neutral* interactions, if not a contradiction in terms, occur where a high scale score desired at one level combines with a middling scale score or where this dimension is simply not applicable at another level of analysis. More problematic, naturally, are *contradictory* interactions. Here an organization simultaneously desires a high scale score at one level of analysis, but a low scale score at another. For instance, high sociability at the individual level, but a low scale score on this dimension in order for the person to fit into an organization culture which values modesty, introspection and self-effacing behaviour by its employees. Given three levels of analysis (individual, team and organization) in combination with three interaction terms (complementary, neutral and contradictory) being applied to multiple measurement dimensions, the opportunities for research and improving current practice are immense.

Cross-cultural applicability of meta-analytic findings

Meta-analysis and validity generalization techniques have contributed much to the development of knowledge in selection psychology. The combination of multiple validity studies involving up to several thousand subjects in procedures that allow the analyst to partial-out measurement errors omnipresent in individual studies have permitted definitive conclusions over the mean validity of selection methods (e.g. Schmidt *et al.*, 1995; Schmitt *et al.*, 1984). Of course, the vast majority of meta-analyses have been conducted in the United States, inputting the findings of validity studies almost all of which were also conducted there. This is understandable since it has been eminent American I/O psychologists who have championed developments in meta-analysis and their computation procedures. However, the findings from meta-analyses have been unreservedly cited by

personnel psychologists in other countries and appear to have been unques-
tioningly accepted as being generalizable to different national contexts. Social,
cultural, legislative, and recruitment and appraisal differences have been overlooked, and certainly in many European countries the results of meta-analyses
conducted in the United States have been cited as applying without caveat. These
findings may indeed be transferable to other countries, but then again they may
not be, given the pervasive cultural differences we outlined earlier in this chapter.

Schmidt (1993) quotes the intriguing statistic that the United States has around
5% of the world's population but 70% of the world's lawyers. This inequality of
distribution is probably quite comparable to the numbers of personnel psychologists, and even more so in terms of the citation impact of published papers,
especially in the area of meta-analysis. At a rough guess, possibly up to seven-
tenths of the world's personnel psychologists reside in the United States, whereas
at least nine-tenths of the citation impact of published articles is probably attributable to American academic personnel psychologists. The distribution is changing
rapidly, however, with considerable growth in the numbers of personnel psychologists in other countries. Although some meta-analysts have not been shy or
reticent in their claims over the generality of their findings (see Guion, 1991; and
Murphy, Chapter 16 in this volume), claims of *international generalizability* are
notably absent. In fact, proponents of meta-analysis have often supported their
efforts by citing the possible utility payback to the American economy of using
more valid methods of staff selection (e.g. Schmidt, 1993; Schmidt, Ones and
Hunter, 1992). It is therefore down to personnel psychologists in other countries
who have been remiss in not establishing the international generalizability of
meta-analytic findings.

We would argue that international generalizability will inevitably be influenced
by the selection method in question. For example, interviews will be subject to
national, social and cultural differences in their format and conduct. Thus, the
findings from US meta-analyses may be generalizable to those Northwest European countries which share an Anglo-Saxon culture, but not to countries in Southern Europe, Asia or Africa. For other methods, for instance ability and personality
tests, the tests comprising the original meta-analytic samples need to be
established. Popular tests in America (e.g. the Wonderlic, DAT, GATB, HPI, and
MMPI) and others upon which several meta-analyses have been based, are virtually unused for selection in other countries. Consequently, the generalizability
of meta-analytic findings may be questionable, especially as some countries (e.g.
Britain) have moved toward the use of tests of specific cognitive ability and tests
of work-related or occupational personality.

Two issues warrant further comment. First, the generalizability of findings to
expatriate selection, and secondly, the situation-specific reactions of personnel
practitioners regardless of the country in question. In relation to the former,
Schmidt, Ones and Hunter (1992) claim:

> We would add that ability and some personality-based predictors used in *expatriate
> selection* (selection of overseas assignees) may prove to be valid and generalizable
> across cultures as well (p. 661).

The authors clearly stop short of claiming the international generalizability of American meta-analytic findings *per se*, but suggest they may be so for recruitment decisions for foreign assignments. This is not an uncontroversial claim. Are we really to believe that validity findings will generalize to expatriate assignments in *all* other countries in the world from Afghanistan to Zambia? This is a claim of incredible scope which cries out for empirical research given the trends toward globalization outlined earlier in this chapter. It is, perhaps, based upon the assumption that 'scientific' findings must in principle be universally applicable.

Finally, we must acknowledge the reality of the position of personnel practitioners in any country. Being employed by a single organization and perceiving this employer as the focus of their loyalties inevitably moderates their reactions to meta-analytic and validity generalization findings. Why should HR practitioners pay any attention to average validity findings, especially if these findings emanate from another country? Certainly, the variations in every organization-specific validity study so clinically (and quite correctly) dispatched to measurement error by meta-analysts are more likely to be perceived by that organization's personnel practitioners as verification of its uniqueness, individuality and their own *raison d'être*. However irrational it may appear to academic selection psychologists, practitioners are likely to value above all the situational specificity of their employing organization and, paradoxically, to dismiss the claim that validity findings will be generalizable to their own context as being equally irrational.

Generating wider theoretical frameworks

As noted earlier in this chapter, the dominant concern in much selection research has been the prediction of person–job fit. As a consequence, the organizational perspective has tended to be emphasized above all other considerations. This, in itself, is of course an entirely legitimate concern. It is the circumscription of this focus within the predominant predictivist–quantitative paradigm that has falsely restricted the range of issues and phenomena addressed by personnel researchers. One cannot deny the methodological and statistical sophistication with which researchers are nowadays examining relationships between predictors and criterion, and undoubtedly Anglo-Saxon cultures lead the world in the statistical–analytical complexity of their research in selection psychology. Whether such a degree of statistical complexity is warranted given the unreliability of measures of many variables in applied-organizational settings is a moot point. Nevertheless, in our attempts to mimic the physical sciences personnel psychology has been successful in constructing a body of research that exhibits all the hallmarks of 'proper' scientific enquiry: hypotheses specified a priori, state-of-the-art statistical analyses, empirical incrementalism, quantitative studies grounded upon existing theory and previous findings, acknowledged limitations of the study design, sanitized study reports which obscure the messy realities of conducting organizational research and, above all, responsibly conducted and written-up deductivism.

Having stated that the dominant vantage point has been that of the organization, there have been several themes of research which have expounded quite different views. These include:

- Applicant rights in the selection process (e.g. de Wolff and Van den Bosch, 1984)
- The psychological impact of selection procedures upon candidates (e.g. Iles and Robertson, Chapter 27 in this volume; Fletcher, 1991; Rynes, 1993).
- Procedural and distributive justice in the selection process (e.g. Gilliland, 1993).
- Selection as a social negotiation of the psychological contract (e.g. Herriot, 1989).
- Selection as a developmental model of mutual accommodation (e.g. Hesketh and Robertson, 1993).
- Selection as mutual attraction and bi-directional decision-making (e.g. Schneider *et al.*, Chapter 19 in this volume; Wanous *et al.*, 1992).
- Selection as the co-construction of mutual realities (e.g. Dachler, 1994).
- Selection as the domination of one group over another (e.g. Hollway, 1991).
- Radical feminist perspectives of the selection process (e.g. Hollway, 1991).

The themes of concern underlying all of these innovative perspectives are worlds away from those that preoccupy those at the heart of the predictivist paradigm. But these are the few exceptions to the overwhelming volume of work which sits neatly within the dominant and convergent paradigm. Our call, then, is for greater divergence and diversity of theoretical perspectives, but also for such radical approaches to embrace an appropriate level of methodological rigour. Only through this combination of theoretical innovation coupled with methodological rigour will the discipline flourish in response to environmental changes.

CONCLUSION

We are presently witnessing a watershed in personnel and selection psychology. To attempt to stand above this in aloof splendour, relying upon the regalia and the trappings of scientism built up over the years, is a temptation especially for the academic wing of our discipline. Personnel psychologists, we argue, need to put down their calculators and pick up their thought processes. The time has come for a moratorium on any further meta-analyses of popular selection methods in the United States, slight modifications to the configuration of utility formulae, and replication studies in areas that have been intensively researched. The opportunity costs are simply too great. Instead, it is time to take stock of the theoretical health and dynamism of the discipline; to rejuvenate its early roots as an applied science, but one which is becoming increasingly influenced by the globalization of business and therefore needs to become a truly global applied science that reflects important national and cultural differences.

We return to our opening aim that this chapter should be a 'paradigmatic wake-up call' and our original statement that *traditional* personnel and selection psychology is in danger of terminal decline. Unless we can stimulate a quantum leap in our paradigmatic assumptions, beliefs, values and artefacts, the prospect of marginalization will loom ever larger. We need to break free of the restrictive and narrow paradigm that has dominated our thinking and practice hitherto. For only by engaging in critical, self-imposed constructive controversy, healthy epistemological debate and dialectic, are we likely to be able to stimulate the double-loop learning in personnel psychology needed to cope with an environment that is changing at an exponential rate. Only then will we begin adequately to understand and address the issues facing our key clients: individuals, work groups, organizations and governments. Applied personnel psychology is not primarily an academic discipline with academic peers as clients; it is psychology applied to the world of work.

REFERENCES

Abbott, A. (1988). *The System of Professions.* Chicago: University of Chicago Press.

Amabile, T.M. (1983). *The Social Psychology of Creativity.* New York: Springer-Verlag.

Anderson, N.R. (1992). Eight decades of employment interview research: A retrospective meta-review and prospective commentary. *European Work and Organizational Psychologist,* **2**, 1.32.

Argyris, C. and Schon, D.A. (1978). *Organisational Learning.* Reading, MA: Addison-Wesley.

Arvey, R.D., Salas, E. and Gialluca, K.A. (1992). Using task inventories to forecast skills and abilities. *Human Performance,* **5**, (3), 171–190.

Barrett, P., Kline, P., Paltiel, L. and Eysenck, H.J. (1996). An evaluation of the psychometric properties of the concept 5.2 Occupational Personality Questionnaire, *Journal of Occupational and Organizational Psychology,* **69**, 1–20.

Barrick, M.R. and Mount, M.K. (1991). The big five personality dimensions and job performance: A meta-analysis. *Personnel Psychology,* **44**, 1–26.

Bartlett, C.A. and Ghoshal, S. (1989). *Managing Across Borders.* London: Hutchinson.

Borman, W.C. and Motowildo, J.J. (1993). Expanding the criterion domain to include elements of contextual performance. In N. Schmitt, W.C. Borman & Associates, *Personnel Selection in Organizations.* San Francisco: Jossey-Bass.

Borman, W., Hanson, M. and Hedge, J. (in press). Personnel selection, *Annual Review of Psychology.*

Bridges, W. (1994). *Jobshift.* Reading, MA: Addison-Wesley.

Brockner, J., Tyler, T.R. and Cooper-Schneider, R. (1992). The effects of prior commitment to an institution on reactions to perceived unfairness: The higher they are, the harder they fall. *Administrative Science Quarterly,* **37**, 241–261.

Campion, M.A. (1994). Job analysis for the future. In M.G. Runsey, C.B. Walker and J.H. Harris (eds.) *Personnel Selection and Classification.* Hillsdale: NJL Erlbaum.

Cannon-Bowers, J.A., Tannenbaum, S.I., Salas, E. and Volpe, C.E. (1995). Defining competencies and establishing team training requirements. In R.A. Guzzo and E. Salas (eds.), *Team Effectiveness and Decision Making in Organizations.* San Francisco: Jossey-Bass.

Cascio, W.F. (1994). Downsizing: What do we know? What have we learned? *Academy of Management Executive,* **7** (1), 95–104.

Cascio, W.F. (1995). Whither industrial and organizational psychology in a changing world of work? *American Psychologist,* **50** (11), 928–939.

Chatman, J.A. (1991). Matching people and organisations: Selection and socialisation in public accounting firms. *Administrative Science Quarterly,* **36**, 459–484.

Dachler, M.P. (1994). A social-relational perspective of selection. Paper presented at the 23rd International Congress of Applied Psychology, Madrid, Spain, July 1994.

Davis, D.D. (1995). Form, function and strategy in boundaryless organisations. In A. Howard (ed.), *The Changing Nature of Work.* San Francisco: Jossey-Bass.

DeMeuse, K.P., Vanderheiden, P.A. and Bergmann, T.J. (1994). Announced lay-offs: Their effect on corporate financial performance. *Human Resource Management,* **33** (4), 509–530.

Feldman, D.C. (1995). Managing part-time and temporary employment. In M. London (ed.), *Employees, Careers, and Job Creation*. San Francisco: Jossey-Bass.

Fletcher, C. (1991). Candidates' reactions to assessment centres and their outcomes: A longitudinal study. *Journal of Occupational and Organizational Psychology*, **64**, 117–127.

Fletcher, C. (1996). Challenge and change for psychometrics: The need for a new approach. Paper presented at the Conference on Ethics and Good Practice in Assessment and Psychological Testing, Cheltenham, UK, July 1996.

George, J.M. and James, L.R. (1994). Levels issues in theory development. *Academy of Management Review*, **19**, 636–640.

Gilliland, S.W. (1993). The perceived fairness of selection systems: An organizational justice perspective. *Academy of Management Review*, **18**, 694–734.

Goldberg, L.R. (1993). The structure of phenotypic personality traits. *American Psychologist*, **48**, 26–34.

Guion, R.M. (1991). Personnel assessment, selection, and placement. In M.D. Dunnette and L.M. Hough (eds.), *Handbook of Industrial and Organizational Psychology*, Vol. 2, Palo Alto, CA: Consulting Psychologists Press, Inc.

Hall, D.T. and Associates (1986). *Career Development in Organisations*. San Francisco: Jossey-Bass.

Heckscher, C. (1995). *White Collar Blues*. New York: Basic Books.

Henderson, F., Anderson, N.R. and Rick, S. (1995). Future competency profiling. *Personnel Review*, **24**, 19–31.

Herriot, P. (1989). Selection as a social process. In M. Smith and I.T. Robertson (eds.), *Advances in Staff Selection*. Chichester: John Wiley.

Herriot, P. (1992). Selection: The two subcultures. *European Work and Organizational Psychologist*, **2**, 129–140.

Herriot, P. and Pemberton, C. (1994). *Competitive Advantage through Diversity*. London: Sage.

Herriot, P. and Pemberton, C. (1996). Contracting careers. *Human Relations*, **49**, 757–790.

Hesketh, B. and Robertson, I.T. (1993). Validating personnel selection: A process model for research and practice. *International Journal of Selection and Assessment*, **1**, 3–17.

Hofstede, G. (1980). *Culture's Consequences*. London: Sage.

Hogan, R., Hogan, J. and Roberts, B.W. (1996). Personality measure and employment decisions. *American Psychologist*, May, 469–477.

Hollway, W. (1991). *Work Psychology and Organizational Behaviour*. London: Sage.

Hosking, D.M. and Anderson, N.R. (eds.) (1992). *Organizational Change and Innovation: Psychological Perspectives and Practices in Europe*. London: Routledge.

Hough, L.M. and Schneider, R.J. (1996). Personality traits, taxonomies, and applications in organizations. In K.R. Murphy (ed.), *Individual Differences and Behaviour in Organizations*. San Francisco: Jossey-Bass.

Howard, A. (1995). Rethinking the psychology of work. In A. Howard (ed.), *The Changing Nature of Work*. San Francisco: Jossey-Bass.

Huczynski, A.A. (1993). Explaining the succession of management fads. *International Journal of Human Resource Management*, **4** (2), 443–464.

Hutton, W. (1994). *The State We're In*. London: Heinemann.

Keenan, A. (1995). Graduate recruitment in Britain: A survey of selection methods used by organizations. *Journal of Organizational Behavior*, **16**, 303–317.

King, N. and Anderson, N.R. (1995). *Innovation and Change in Organizations*. London: Routledge.

Landy, F.J., Shankster-Cawley, L. and Moran, S.K. (1995). Advancing personnel selection and placement methods. In A. Howard (ed.), *The Changing Nature of Work*. San Francisco: Jossey-Bass.

Latham, G.P. and Whyte, G. (1994). The futility of utility analysis. *Personnel Psychology*, **47**, 31–46.

Lawler, E.E. (1992). *The Ultimate Advantage: Creating the High-involvement Organisation*. San Francisco: Jossey-Bass.

Lawler, E.E. (1994). From job-based to competency-based organizations. *Journal of Organizational Behavior*, **15**, 3–15.

Legge, K. (1995). *Human Resource Management: Rhetorics and Realities*. London: Macmillan.

Mirvis, P.H. (ed.) (1993). *Building a Competitive Workforce*. New York: John Wiley.

Mohrman, S.A. and Cohen, S.G. (1995). When people get out of the box: New relationships, new systems. In A. Howard (ed.), *The Changing Nature of Work*. San Francisco: Jossey-Bass.

Muchinsky, P.M. (1994). A review of individual assessment methods used for personnel selection in North America. *International Journal of Selection and Assessment*, **2**, 118–124.

Murphy, K.R. (1986). When your top choice turns you down: Effects of rejected offers on the utility of selection tests. *Psychological Bulletin*, **99**, 133–138.

Nicholson, N. and West, M.A. (1988). *Managerial Job Change: Men and Women in Transition*. Cambridge: Cambridge University Press.

Ones, D.S. and Viswesvaran, C. (1996). Bandwidth-fidelity dilemma in personality measurement for personnel selection. *Journal of Organizational Behavior*, **17**, 609–626.

Ostroff, C. (1993). Comparing correlations based on individual-level and aggregated data. *Journal of Applied Psychology*, **78**, 569–582.

Ostroff, C. and Rothausen, T.J. (1996). Selection and job matching. In D. Lewin, D.J.B. Mitchell and M.A. Zaidi (eds.), *Human Resource Management Handbook*. Greenwich, CT: JAI Press.

Prahalad, C.K. and Hamel, G. (1990). The core competence of the corporation. *Harvard Business Review*, **90** (3), 79–91.

Prieto, J.M. and Avila, A. (1994). Linking certified knowledge to labour markets. *Applied Psychology*, **43** (2), 113–130.

Robertson, I.T. (1993). Personality assessment and personnel selection. *European Review of Applied Psychology*, **43**, 187–194.

Robertson, I.T. and Kinder, A. (1993). Personality and job competencies: The criterion-related validity of some personality variables. *Journal of Occupational and Organizational Psychology*, **66**, 225–244.

Roe, R.A. (1989). Designing selection procedures. In P. Herriot (ed.), *Assessment and Selection in Organizations*. Chichester: John Wiley.

Rousseau, D.M. (1990). New hire perceptions of their own and their employer's obligations: A study of psychological contracts. *Journal of Organizational Behavior*, **11**, 389–400.

Rousseau, D.M. (1995). *Psychological Contracts in Organisations*. California: Sage.

Ryan, A.M. and Sackett, P.R. (1987). A survey of individual assessment practices by I/O psychologists. *Personnel Psychology*, **40**, 455–488.

Rynes, S.L. (1993). Who's selecting whom? Effects of selection practices on applicant attitudes and behavior. In N. Schmitt, W.C. Borman and Associates, *Personnel Selection in Organizations*. San Francisco: Jossey-Bass.

Sackett, P.R. and Arvey, R.D. (1993). Selection in small N settings. In N. Schmitt, W.C. Borman and Associates, *Personnel Selection in Organizations*. San Francisco: Jossey-Bass.

Schein, E. (1985). *Organizational Culture and Leadership*. San Francisco: Jossey-Bass.

Schmidt, F.L. (1993). Personnel psychology at the cutting edge. In N. Schmitt, W.C. Borman and Associates, *Personnel Selection in Organizations*. San Francisco: Jossey-Bass.

Schmidt, F.L., Ones, D.S. and Hunter, J.E. (1992). Personnel selection. *Annual Review of Psychology*, **43**, 627–670.

Schmidt, F.L., Pearlman, K., Hunter, J.E. and Hirsch, H.R. (1985). Forty questions about validity generalization and meta-analysis. *Personnel Psychology*, **38**, 697–798.

Schmitt, N., Gooding, R.Z., Noe, R.A. and Kirsch, M. (1984). Meta-analyses of validity studies published between 1964 and 1982 and the investigation of study characteristics. *Personnel Psychology*, **37**, 407–422.

Schneider, B.W. (1987). The people make the place. *Personnel Psychology*, **40**, 437–453.

Schneider, R.J. and Hough, L.M. (1995). Personality and industrial-organisational psychology. In C. Cooper and I.T. Robertson (eds.), *International Review of Industrial and Organisational Psychology*. Chichester: John Wiley.

Shackleton, V.J. and Newell, S. (1994). European management selection methods: A comparison of five countries. *International Journal of Selection and Assessment*, **2**, 91–102.

Smith, M. and Abrahamsen, M. (1992). Patterns of selection in six countries. *The Psychologist*, **5**, 205–207.

Sonnenfeld, J.A. and Peiperl, M.A. (1988). Staffing policy as a strategic response: A typology of career systems. *Academy of Management Review*, **13**, 588–600.

Sproull, L. and Kiesler, S. (1986). Reducing social context cues: Electronic mail in organisational communication. *Management Science*, **32** (11), 1492–1512.

Stevens, M.J. and Campion, M.A. (1994a). The knowledge, skill and ability requirements for teamwork: Implications for human resource management. *Journal of Management*, **20**, 503–530.

Stevens, M.J. and Campion, M.A. (1994b). Staffing work teams: Development and validation of a selection test for teamwork settings. Unpublished manuscript.

Stroh, L.K., Brett, J.M. and Reilly, A.H. (1994). A decade of change: Managers' attachment to their organisations and their jobs. *Human Resource Management*, **33** (4), 531–548.

Trompenaars, F. (1993). *Riding the Waves of Culture.* London: Nicholas Brealey.

Van de Ven, A., Angle, H.L. and Poole, M.S. (eds.) (1989): *Research on the Management of Innovation: The Minnesota Studies.* New York: Harper & Row.

Wanous, J.P., Poland, T.D., Premack, S.L. and Davis, K.S. (1992). The effects of met expectations on newcomer attitudes and behaviours: A review and meta-analysis. *Journal of Applied Psychology*, **77**, 168–176.

Waterman, R.H., Waterman, J.A. and Collard, B.A. (1994). Toward a career-resilient workforce. *Harvard Business Review*, **12** (4), 87–95.

West, M.A. and Altink, W. (1996). Innovation at work: Individual, group, organizational and socio-historical perspectives. *European Journal of Work and Organizational Psychology*, **5**, 3–11.

West, M.A. and Farr, J.L. (eds.) (1990) *Innovation and Creativity at Work.* Chichester: John Wiley.

Wiesenfeld, E. and Sanchez, E. (1991). Introduction: The why, what, and how of community social psychology in Latin America. *Applied Psychology*, **40** (2), 113–118.

de Wolff, C.J. and van den Bosch, G. (1984). Personnel selection. In P.J. Drenth, H. Thierry, P.J. Willems and C.J. de Wolff (eds.), *Handbook of Work and Organizational Psychology*, Vol. 1. Chichester: John Wiley.

Workplace of the Future: A report of the Conference on the Future of the American Workplace (1993). New York: US Departments of Commerce and Labor.

Xu, L-C. and Wang, Z.-M. (1991). New developments in organisational psychology in China. *Applied Psychology*, **40** (1), 3–14.

Zuboff, S. (1988). *In the Age of the Smart Machine.* Oxford: Heinemann.

Section 1

Technological, National, and Professional Cultures

We have divided the Handbook into four sections, which reflect the argument we put forward in our editorial chapter. Section 1 considers the overall global context of national *cultural diversity* and the spread of *information technology* (IT). The implications of these two overarching features of change for assessment for specific occupational groups, and indeed for occupational know-how in general, are explored. Section 2 focuses more upon the *business changes* that have occurred recently, and upon the attempts by psychologists to address some of the tactical and strategic issues with which business people are daily confronted. Section 3 reviews the efforts of selection psychologists to deal with the *changing recruitment requirements* of organizations, and contrasts the elegant academic models with the needs at the sharp end. The question of what people are actually being selected for is the crucial one here. Finally, in Section 4 we carry through this analysis to the *individual applicant*, and to the effects of assessment upon him or her. In all four sections we move from early chapters which set the context to later ones which describe and evaluate psychologists' response to that context.

First, then, to Section 1. Standing outside our own national culture and being faced in detail with the professional practices of another very different culture is a difficult, painful but ultimately rewarding experience. In the case of different cultures, we have to take an overarching perspective and move beyond our own cultural framework; in the case of the development of IT, we have to admit that our present perspective is bound to be far narrower than the ultimate extent of its application. Our efforts to assess others for their ability to take a wider perspective have hitherto been limited in the extreme, although they are certainly more advanced when it comes to assessment within occupational and professional cultures.

In an intellectual tour-de-force in Chapter 2, Denise Rousseau and Catherine Tinsley succeed brilliantly in standing outside their own culture. They argue that despite the globalization of business and the pervasive spread of information technology, there are at least three reasons why such human resource (HR) processes as recruitment and selection will differ across the world. These are, first, local constraints on the relevant labour market; secondly, varying legal regulatory constraints upon practice; and finally, broader institutional forces such as educational practices and local cultures. Differences between local cultures lead to different unspoken social and psychological contracts at the workplace, and imply that multi-national organizations need to accommodate their assessment processes to local conditions. Rousseau and Tinsley conclude by turning Ben Schneider's well-known dictum on its head; as well as recognizing that 'the people make the place', we should also remember that the place makes the people.

There are few places of which we Westerners are more ignorant than China. Yet that great nation is currently an emerging market of the utmost importance, to which Western organizations are keenly attracted. In Chapter 3 Zhong-Ming Wang gives us a first-hand and authoritative account of the long historical development of Chinese assessment methods to the present day. His chapter clearly supports Rousseau and Tinsley's argument that these will be adapted appropriately to local culture. As one might have expected, Chinese assessment is much more holistic than is Anglo-Saxon assessment. Moreover, given the strong emphasis on group and social ties in China, we should not be surprised that both social assessment criteria and also social methods of selection predominate. We wonder whether these fundamental elements of local culture will be recognized by incoming Western organizations, or whether they will make the universalist assumptions typical of the Anglo-Saxon culture and seek to impose 'scientific' methods.

There has been much recent research upon the differing usage of selection methods in different countries, which Viv Shackleton and Sue Newell ably review in Chapter 4. They start from the common situation of the selection of expatriate workers, and show how the traditional method of selection by the organization is inappropriate to a situation where the individual also has to choose the organization, or at least, the posting. The considerable diversity of selection methods, even within Europe, is described. The authors explain this diversity in terms of national culture and, more specifically, of the ways in which psychologists and HR professionals are trained. They conclude that national preferences rather than homogenization will continue to exert a strong influence.

Information technology and its applications force us to reconstruct the nature of work, and hence the nature of assessment and selection for that work. José-Maria Prieto and Cristina Simón encourage us to face the future in Chapter 5. The removal of the barriers of place and time means that work is mobile, so that teleworking and teletrading are becoming daily more common. Information technology is giving workers remote access to organizational information; enhancing communication with colleagues; and providing the opportunity of monitoring and evaluating work processes and the enlargement of individual work profiles. How, ask Prieto and Simon, is selection going to be carried out for the new jobs? Criteria such as effectiveness, commitment and autonomy will predominate, they argue. Clearly, oral and written communication skills will be at a premium, as will deep knowledge of product/service and a mature and self-motivating attitude to work.

In Chapter 6, Paul Jansen goes on to explore in more detail the implications of the information technology revolution for selection and assessment. He enumerates seven trends in the nature of organizational work which are matched by seven corresponding trends in the nature of assessment. In line with our analysis in Chapter 1, Jansen emphasizes the unpredictability of future work functions and their increasing velocity. Hence, more general, holistic and just-in-time assessment will be required. Criteria will be dynamic in nature, and given a context of constant change, learning potential will be the most important criterion. This chapter is essential reading for a strategically oriented practitioner.

We now move on to some specific areas that appear by their culture to require their own appropriate methods of assessment. First, though, in Chapter 7 we investigate with the help of Sam Aryee the issue introduced by Shackleton and Newell—expatriate selection and training. As Aryee remarks, the consensus in the literature is that expatriate retention failure stems from the practice of using domestic staffing policies in staffing overseas subsidiaries. He too argues that so pervasive is the effect of an overseas posting upon the life of the employee that negotiation rather than traditional one-way selection is more appropriate. Criteria of success, also, are much broader than the traditional performance measures. Ability to relate to others from the host country and to adapt successfully to its culture are among them. However, as Aryee notes, the danger is that firms will adopt the compensatory strategy of selecting according to one prominent criterion, namely technical competence, on the grounds that other criteria are less important and harder to assess. Clearly, we still have a long way to go in this important cross-cultural area.

National cultures are of course only one source of cultural differences. Professions and occupations also have their own cultures, and therefore selection for them and assessment within them need to be designed with such differences in mind. The armed services have long proved a fertile research field for applied psychologists, and their bureaucratic culture and structure has strongly influenced the historically dominant selection paradigm. However, in military organizations too, organizational and work changes are profound, as Neil Hardinge explains in Chapter 8. Fewer employees have to perform a greater variety of work tasks, and so competency-based assessments are becoming more favoured. Moreover, there are strong pressures for service employees to become more representative demographically of the civil society, so equal opportunity issues are at a premium. However, there remains as a unique and fundamental element of the armed services the total immersion in the military culture and, ultimately, the willingness to kill an enemy if necessary.

Equally unique is the law. In Chapter 9 Robert Wood, Graham Hamer, Charles Johnson, and Tim Payne give a vivid blow-by-blow account of the problems encountered in introducing a selection system for entry into the profession. In such a high status profession, acceptability of the system is absolutely fundamental, over and above considerations of technical adequacy. Credibility was finally achieved by the involvement of legal professionals in the design and execution of a selection process which sought to achieve both technical acceptability and face validity. This chapter is essential reading for all who appreciate that applied psychology is psychology applied, not an academic discipline!

Finally, Section 1 concludes with Chapter 10 by Robert Sternberg, entitled 'Tacit Knowledge and Job Success'. Tacit knowledge is defined as 'the knowledge that you need to succeed in an endeavour, that is not formally taught, and that often is not even verbalized'. It is practical knowledge, not just about what goes on but also about what to do in particular situations. It includes how to organize your own activity, how to get along with others, and how to get a job done. Clearly, tacit knowledge is best assessed through practical exercises, though Sternberg proposes the use of scenarios where the assessee is required to say what they would do. This latter method implies that the assessee can make the tacit explicit. Judgements on the part of the assessor as to what constitutes an appropriate response are dependent upon the values of the assessor and those of their employing organization. As Sternberg rightly argues, this is a strength rather than a weakness of the method, since it allows for selection for organizational fit. The appropriate way to approach a boss, for example, differs across organizations. Tests of tacit knowledge clearly have a big future at a time when national, organizational and occupational cultural differences are at last being recognized.

PETER HERRIOT
August 1996

Chapter 2

Human Resources are Local: Society and Social Contracts in a Global Economy

DENISE M. ROUSSEAU

Heinz School of Public Policy and Management, and Graduate School of Industrial Administration, Carnegie-Mellon University, Pittsburgh, PA 15213, USA

CATHERINE TINSLEY

Department of Management, Hong Kong University of Science and Technology, Clearwater Bay, Kowloon, Hong Kong
and
School of Business, Georgetown University, Washington, DC 20057, USA

We pretend to work and they pretend to pay us—Soviet worker.

The iron rice bowl means a job for life—Communist China.

Japan is sociology's revenge on economics—Anonymous.

An astute politician once said, 'All politics is local.'[1] Human resource management (HRM) activities are often local too—despite the globalization of economies and the internationalization of corporations. Effective recruitment and performance management practices in Canada are not the same as in Mexico, Britain, or Germany, even if the skills sought *are* (e.g. for production work at Ford plants). Nonetheless, in the 1980s about 25% of all American Industrial/Organizational Psychology journal articles dealt with performance appraisal and selection, virtually all of them in the United States (Erez, 1993). British journals (e.g. *Journal of Occupational and Organizational Psychology*), offer similar approaches to performance review and selection (Arvey, Bhagat and Salas, 1991), limited in this case to Great Britain. Little explicit attention is given to location (i.e. region or country) and how it might impact the ways organizations obtain and manage people.[2] This chapter addresses the role of location, particularly the societal and cultural context, in shaping recruitment and performance management.

International Handbook of Selection and Assessment, Edited by N. Anderson and P. Herriot.
© 1997 John Wiley & Sons Ltd.

Increased travel, capital flows, trade and globalization of taste have encouraged businesses to penetrate foreign markets and to set up shop in many countries. The isolationist policies of many governments have been overcome with their efforts to raise foreign equity investment in both developed and developing countries. Ironically enough, this globalization of business affairs has yielded little research on the influence of location on HR practices. Rather, local concerns have been pushed aside by an assumption of a global 'universal' culture, at least for managers. HR mavens encourage multinationals to build broad global HR practices and international managerial career paths (Pucik, Tichy and Barnett, 1992), activities presuming universality.

Organizational research seems to have globalized, too. Gomez-Mejia (1986) details a 'universal set of scales' that can be used to assess different work aspects across cultural groups in many languages (including Swedish, Korean, Hebrew, and English among others) and argues for its 'pan-cultural validity'.[3] MOW International Research Team (1987) and Hofstede (1980) provide widely cited comparative research on work motives and broader cultural differences. Globalization has created awareness of the differences between doing business in Europe, Asia and elsewhere. But for the most part, the problems created by local differences are being solved by emphasizing ways to integrate business strategies and HR practices (Pucik, Tichy and Barnett, 1992). We know much less about the durable differences in HR practices that local institutions create.

This chapter maintains that HR practices will to an extent continue to be local even when they form part of a global HR strategy (Figure 2.1). To date there is little systematic research on the impact of local differences on HR practices. What does exist are descriptions of differences in education, laws and culture provided by writers more interested in social institutions than in organizations *per se* (e.g. Klitgaard, 1986). This chapter will use these descriptions and current organizational research into cross-national HR practices to illustrate local conditions that HR researchers and practitioners must take into account. We acknowledge that our efforts in this chapter constitute a risky venture, with little cross-national research on HR practices, epistemological difficulties in putting experiences from different societies into one framework, and with frank acknowledgement of our own inevitable cultural blinders and unannounced assumptions. Nonetheless, our goal is to highlight local factors that can affect recruiting and performance management and in doing so help pave the way for more globally informed HR research and practice.

There are three basic reasons for the local nature of HR practices:

- constraints on the relevant labor pool,
- legal requirements, and
- broader institutional forces such as educational practices and local culture.

Labor markets remain local in many respects simply because Parisians or Pittsburghers may not want to leave home. The relevant labor pool, defined as those people with appropriate skills available for employment, is not fluid but can be tied to specific towns, regions or countries. Economic development in Mexico, for

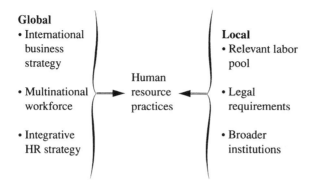

Figure 2.1 Environmental forces on human resources

instance, has been constrained by a general reluctance in the population to move away from extended families. Constrained mobility makes location an important HR issue. Differing legal systems also constrain local HR practices. Governmental regulations covering health and safety, fair employment practices, and limitations on personnel actions (e.g. job property rights) mandate variation in HR practices across states and countries. Constraints on firing poor performers in France or Venezuela alter the way in which performance measures can be used. While performance appraisal may produce a paper-trail to document substandard performance in America, its use in countries with greater employment protections may be limited to employee development if used at all. Lastly, a broad spectrum of institutional forces intertwined with nation-wide social structures (education, industrial policy and culture) require accommodations from any organization that would form a part of a society (Drucker, 1994; Perrow, 1996).

These three localizing forces account for much of the tremendous variety in HR practices even among multinationals, which can range from 'ethnocentric' (where staffing is largely made up of people from the country of the parent firm), 'polycentric' (decentralizing staffing and practices within local units), to 'geocentric' (placing the 'best' people where needed regardless of nationality) as described by Heenan and Perlmutter (1979) and DeCieri and Dowling (1995). Both science and practice are beginning to assess the usefulness of existing HR practices in a global economy. To better understand local factors in global HR, in this chapter, we address:

1. The limits of current research into HR practices, particularly the relevance and legitimacy constraints on this research for recruitment and performance management in different societies.
2. Societal institutions that create the need for variations in HR practices, particularly the social contracts of employment that create 'taken for granted' personnel practices.
3. A research agenda that takes into account both local and global HR concerns.

LIMITS OF OUR CURRENT HR THINKING: RELEVANCE AND LEGITIMACY

Scientifically researched and validated HR practices, especially technologies for selection (e.g. tests, assessment centers) and performance appraisal (e.g. ratings scales, management by objectives, and 360 degree appraisals), are largely Anglo-American in derivation and use. Few validation studies are conducted on tests in France, Greece or China and little research appears in the literature on performance appraisal in these or other non-English-speaking countries.[4] Organizational scholars increasingly have recognized national variation in HR practices (e.g. Herriot, 1992). Entire issues of journals have been devoted to variations in HR practices and work values across nations (e.g. in the case of the European Community, *Employee Relations*, volume 14, 1992; *The European Work and Organizational Psychologist*, volume 1 (2–3), 1991). However, the tools that research-based HR focuses on, such as physical and cognitive abilities tests, worker-oriented job analyses, biodata and behaviorally anchored ratings scales, which are a mainstay in organizational psychology (e.g. *Journal of Applied Psychology, Personnel Psychology*), are themselves culturally limited. In I/O psychology, state-of-the-art research is today characterized by certain culturally tied features:

- *Individual* as the typical subject (far less often the work group or larger unit)
- *Managerial* skills and development (less emphasis on workers)
- *Short-term*, readily quantifiable criteria (rather than long-term or complex results)
- *Internal* to the organization (de-emphasizing customers, clients, or community).

Despite the local (i.e. Western) nature of scientifically developed HR tools, these practices are still potential exports. 'Scientific' HR tools are often packaged along with one of the most robust of all locally grown Western products—higher education. US business schools, for instance, can have upward of 25%–30% foreign nations enrolled in their MBA programs,[5] and a comparable if not greater percentage in executive programs, where organizational research and HR practices are a large portion of the curriculum.

HR practices are forms of technology, ways of doing work, which, in this case, means recruiting people and measuring performance. Which HR technologies are chosen depends on their relevance and legitimacy in a particular context. For instance, abilities testing may be seen as inappropriate if society maintains that access to jobs should be based on status or ascription rather than personal achievement. Testing here might be illegitimate even when it is relevant to local problems (e.g. poor performance). Extrapolating from the literature on technology transfer (e.g. the seminal work of Rogers and Shoemaker, 1971), we propose four possible outcomes from exposing foreign students to local (e.g. American) HR technology:

- *Rejection* of science-based HR technologies as culturally irrelevant (e.g. Japanese MBA students react with disbelief to a performance feedback exercise where they are asked to directly confront a recalcitrant subordinate).

- *Adoption* of science-based HR technologies practices (e.g. Mexican executives initiating job analyses to identify current skills and training needs in a water purification business).
- *Adaptation* of HR technologies to suit a local environment (e.g. in hierarchically oriented France, a bank manager returned from participating in an American executive development program and began creating a more customer-oriented bank by empowering employees to solve customer problems. Anticipating employee sensitivity to passing off 'managerial' duties onto them, the manager made it clear that he now had to perform new and greater responsibilities *and* that these changes were being mandated by *his own boss*. Thus, the traditional hierarchy remained while greater teamwork and customer orientation were introduced).
- *Creation* of distinct locally derived responses to a need recognized through management education (e.g. in Mexico, a manager begins advertising jobs with good pay and work conditions aimed at the *parents* of teen-age prospective employees, who exert a good deal of influence on the occupational choices of their children, especially daughters).

This taxonomy of alternative outcomes in the diffusion of HR technologies suggests that awareness of locational factors is needed to advance their use, adaptation and development. To broaden the relevance and legitimacy of scientific HR across national boundaries, and in regional or local settings, we must understand the link between HR technologies and society.

SOCIETAL FACTORS AND THE SOCIAL CONTRACT

Key features of the environment shape the structure of organizations and the behavior of their members (DiMaggio and Powell, 1983). The broader societal setting comprises bundles of resources, culture, media, educational systems, laws, courts and governmental requirements. Created by these societal institutions, social contracts comprise the pervasive beliefs regarding obligations within a society, including beliefs about employment relations.

Elements of a social contract include widespread social judgments regarding fair and appropriate conduct, entitlements (including job property rights or owner authority over employees), and basic concepts of employment (e.g. permanent versus temporary). These beliefs can be conscious and easily identified (e.g. whether terms such as 'full-time' are interpreted to mean 'permanent' or 'works a 40 hour week') or unconscious and tough to access (e.g. entitlements such as whether the employee or employer is responsible for staff development and education). Social contracts are the context for understanding the individual psychological contracts that employment creates (Rousseau, 1995). Practices that are the product of ongoing repetitive interactions, such as children following their parents into factories or remaining in their hometown with an extended family, gradually take on a rule-like quality that makes them a social fact. Social contracts are not entered into by choice. Rather, they are 'taken-for-granted' realities,

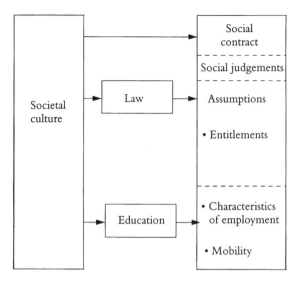

Figure 2.2   Social contract framework. Adapted from Rousseau (1995)

assumptions people may not know they have until they are violated. Elements of the social contract stem directly from the broader societal culture as well as indirectly through a culture's impact on education, law, industry and related institutions (Figure 2.2).[6]

The three quotes that open this chapter manifest well-established cultural beliefs. In the former Soviet Union, 'we pretend to work and they pretend to pay us' reflected the widespread lack of production incentives, particularly for individual effort in a communist country where the emphasis was on bureaucratic consistency and informal norms of working no harder than one's peers. The 'iron rice bowl' in China's centralized economy is a guaranteed standard of living unrelated to effort or performance, a very valuable feature in a country where starvation and famine are in living memory. Viewing Japan as 'sociology's revenge on economics' reflects contradictions between how work is organized in Japan and the assumptions of traditional economics where atomized workers pursue self-interested aims and shirk if not closely monitored or paid so highly that they do not dare lose their current job. The communal system that sociologists document in Japanese organizations (e.g. Dore, 1983; Lincoln and Kalleberg, 1985) challenges the individualistic assumptions of both traditional economics *and* traditional Western I/O psychology. In all three cases we have society-wide social contracts regarding employment relations.

The subconscious nature of social contracts in the workforce means that HR practices imported from one setting may send unintended messages to workers in the new context. For instance, broad-banding of job classifications or reliance on teamwork can mean flexibility and interpersonal support in Japan or in Canada but convey that top management is no longer 'doing its job' (i.e. controlling and making decisions) in France. Social contract features include (but are not limited to): societal-based work and family role, patterns for distributing risk from occupational injuries between employee and employer, entitlements and forms of social security, culturally supported mobility patterns, and 'guaranteed' school-to-work transitions (e.g. guaranteeing important jobs for university graduates). Taken-for-granted social contracts affect selection and performance management by constraining conditions of entry, participation, and exit (Figure 2.3). Entry refers to how people are recruited into the organization and includes pipelines between institutions such as universities and employers and criteria used to select recruits. Participation refers to the contributions members make to organizations, including the quality and kind of job performance they manifest. Exit refers to the conditions under which members are retained or terminated. Contract features affecting entry, participation and exit emerge from the confluence of societal culture, educational system and law.

Societal culture

Culture has been defined as the integrated set of interrelated beliefs and behavioral patterns shared by a group of people (Kroeber and Kluckhohn, 1952). Numerous researchers have generated dimensions that might characterize a culture (Hofstede, 1980; Kluckhohn and Strodtbeck, 1961; Parson and Shils, 1951;

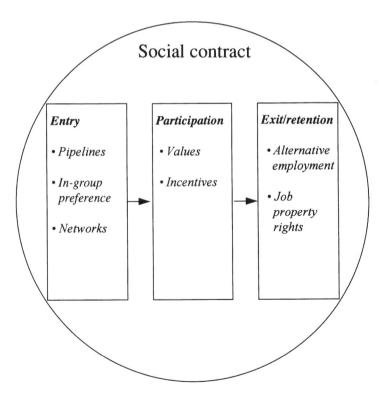

Figure 2.3   Social contract effects on workforce

Ronen and Shenkar, 1985; Triandis, 1982). And while culture is inherently complex, any one culture might be compared with another relative to a particular dimension, for example how individualistic, how egalitarian, and how risk-seeking it is. Furthermore, there will clearly be wide variations within a culture (Los Angeles to Iowa, London to Exeter, Paris to Nice) and between immigrant groups and communities within a single country.

Acknowledging the proliferation of cultural dimensions offered by anthropologists and organizational researchers, certain dimensions have particular relevance to practices of recruitment and performance management, including individualism/collectivism, independent/interdependence views of self and beliefs about in-groups and out-groups. Individualism/collectivism reflects values and assumptions of self, self–other relations, and beliefs regarding people who are not closely related, i.e. 'out-group members' (Hofstede, 1980; Triandis, 1989). Individualistic values manifest as concerns for individual interests, self-promotion and self-reliance. Collectivist values evince concerns for the integrity, harmony and solidarity of one's in-group. It tends also to create a sense of disparity or difference between beliefs regarding one's in-group and outsiders ('out-groups'). Social contracts regarding employment are affected by this cultural dimension through the assignments of responsibility (for education, welfare and support) to one's self or others and to the social obligations to which people are bound (to family and friends in collectivist societies and to self-reliance in individualistic ones).

The incompatibility of many features of Western employment in less industrialized parts of the world (e.g. Bhagat *et al.*, 1990) is linked, at least in part, to more collectivist emphases in less developed countries. In Mexico, for instance, the value placed on family is so strong that surveys indicate consistently that the major motivators in the Mexican workforce are to support one's family and to provide for the education of one's children (Abitia, 1986, 1991). In contrast, surveys typically indicate job challenge, autonomy and advancement as the primary motivators of the American workforce (Hofstede, 1993; Kovach, 1987). Development of the Mexican economy is tied to business growth, expansion of the middle class, and development of Mexican managers. But, as already noted, a barrier to this development has been widespread reluctance of the population to move away from extended family ties. If career mobility and development require willingness to leave traditional roots, then it may be slowed by the collectivistic ties of Mexican culture where family concerns often dominate individual careers.

Conditions of entry are tied to cultural assumptions regarding the self. An individualist views the self as an atomized, discrete entity (Triandis, 1989). The boundary of 'self' is one's own skin, and distinctly separates one's self from others. A collectivist assumption of self would extend the notion of self to other group members (Triandis, 1989). Culture-based views of self can lead recruiters to evaluate selection information quite differently. Where *inter*dependent views of self predominate, recruiting tends to be more person-centered, focusing on the 'fit' of the new recruit with the rest of the company. Who that new recruit is as a person, and how s/he might interact with other company employees becomes a critical concern in a more collectivistic environment (Herriot, 1992).[7] Efforts to understand the 'whole person' are associated with use of non-scientific techniques such as handwriting analyses (far more common in Europe than in North America. Similarly, managers in collectivistic Peru are screened by narrative descriptions of their global traits (Salas, 1984) while emphasis on interpersonal relations predominate in employee selection in Arab countries (Ali, 1988). On the other hand, the independent view of self characterizing individualist cultures such as the United States promotes a more task-oriented selection procedure. Here emphasis is placed on identifying recruitees with appropriate skills for discrete jobs.[8] US firms also tend to have supervisors do the hiring and to give more weight to their input even when potential co-worker input is requested. In Japan, on the other hand, future co-workers' evaluations have a significant influence on the hiring decisions: 'a job candidate cannot count on his or her excellent qualifications when competing for a job opening. Without gaining favorable opinions from future co-workers, winning the job offer would be very difficult' (Huo and Von Glinow, 1995). A significant contrast has been observed between domestic Japanese recruiting and that in Japanese transplants to the United States. While few tests are employed domestically, Japanese transplants screen American workers through extensive use of test batteries.[9] Linked both to lack of confidence in the American educational system and to views regarding out-group members, this practice suggests that both cultural and workforce characteristics can shape use of HR practices. In general, we observe the trend toward recruitment in individualistic cultures relying more on 'objective' or 'validated' standard measures and collectivistic cultures relying on socially constructed methods (meetings, unstructured interviews, dinners, etc.) and word-of-mouth recruitment.

Attitudes toward out-group members (e.g. foreign nationals, people who graduated from a different university) influence the emphasis on personal qualifications versus social acceptability in recruiting and performance reviews as well as tolerance of co-workers from different backgrounds. The economies of the past have shaped today's societal cultures. Societies that have traded actively with other nations tend to manifest greater flexibility in dealing with 'out-group members' (i.e. foreign nationals; Glenn, 1981; Triandis, McCusker and Hui, 1990). The Dutch are a case in point:

> Dutch people are, and will remain, well-prepared to take up international careers—not because of their capacity to force locals to adapt (as in the case of the ubiquitous American manager) but because of their own capacity to adapt to local circumstances . . . instilled by a socialization process requiring individuals to be open toward actual or potential clients—a traditional Dutch virtue which follows the trader posture (Sorge, 1992, p. 75).

Similarly, countries that have historically been isolated from other cultures by geography or governmental decree tend to make strong distinctions between in-groups and out-groups, placing much greater emphasis on obedience, duty, sacrifices for the welfare of the group, social support, loyalty to in-groups, and interdependence. Such orientations are widely discussed with respect to Pacific

Rim nations such as Japan and Korea, and may apply to developing nations too, where one might expect a general reluctance to hire individuals who are out-group members (e.g. ethnic minorities, foreign nationals), at least not without extensive screening in some form (Triandis, 1989).

Because cultural patterns are correlated with economic activity, they are vulnerable to change. If the definition of what is an economically beneficial activity changes over time, then cultural patterns may also change. There appears to be a shift from collectivism to individualism in many parts of the world, largely attributed to increasing affluence (Hofstede, 1980), compounded by urbanism, migration and exposure to the mass media. Consistent with this observation, as affluence increases in Mexican society, Abitia (1986, 1990) reports some decline in the importance of family relative to personal goals.[10]

Implications

Culture affects HR practices in numerous ways, for example:

- emphasis on individual skills versus organizational or work-group fit in selection
- appropriateness of individual versus group measures of performance
- recruitment and career patterns owing to (a lack of) employee mobility
- openness to out-group members in recruiting or in evaluating performance.

Finally, one major impact of culture on HR practices is a link we hypothesize between individualism/collectivism and selection criteria. Individualism is associated with objectivist practices such as skill assessment and other forms of standardized testing. Collectivism is expected to be associated with nepotism and other relationship-based recruiting processes.

Education

Primary and secondary schooling is typically the pipeline on which careers are founded. Several qualities of this schooling can have a powerful impact on workforce entry, participation, and exit.

1. Availability of education—the ability of the present and future workforce to access education.
2. Job-relatedness—the extent to which educational content mirrors skills and knowledge relevant to occupations.
3. Institutional linkages between education and organizations—how tightly connected educational institutions are with employers, particularly in terms of established pipelines between schools and jobs.
4. Cultural socialization through education—the extent to which education reinforces local cultural differences in values and beliefs or reinforces social stratification.

The *ability of the workforce to access education* is a function of societal wealth and social stratification. Poorer societies offer less access to education. Access to quality primary and secondary schooling is typically socially stratified in developing countries (Klitgaard, 1986). This means that the most educated are often from the elites and have attained that education based on ascription rather than merit. In fact, recruitment in countries where education is not widely available is often based on social relations. Entry can be more of a political and social activity than a skill assessment, in part also, because education can be a surrogate for skill or ability in societies where few people are educated. Mexico provides a case in point where being part of a social network is a powerful predictor of ability to access jobs. Relationships among these elite members are often formed in universities and remain powerful forces in individual careers. In contrast, developed countries where education is more widely available tend to emphasize individual competence to a greater extent in recruitment—though social networks from Yale to Oxford can create access to employment opportunities in developed countries as well. When developed countries are socially stratified, as in the case of Great Britain, the ability to behave as a member of an elite group (e.g. table manners and conversational skills, Derr, 1987) may be a condition of employment or advancement. Education, particularly private education, often reinforces these social norms and the interpersonal skills that come with them. Quality education is widespread in those developed countries with low social stratification (e.g. Sweden and Norway) and leads to greater emphasis at entry upon personal capabilities.

The *work-relatedness* of public education varies greatly even in highly developed countries. Educational content reflects cultural values regarding the relative standing of intellectual activities and economic success, and can impact access to prestigious careers as well as worker ability to exit for jobs elsewhere. The general content of French education, which emphasizes philosophy and Cartesian rationality (Brunstein, 1992), bears little relationship to actual job duties. In contrast, German education emphasizes employment opportunities beginning at the secondary level with clearly defined vocational training tracks for mechanical, technical, scientific and other occupations. The Dutch system, despite local variation, is a sort of middle ground emphasizing practical but generalist skills.

Brunstein (1992) comments:

> The (French) education system has an even more pronounced impact on individuals than generated by their general cultural background . . . Manual work is given little value and so has a tendency to absorb young people with narrower perspectives. This is one of the reasons for the high level of unemployment among young people, which stands at 19 per cent in France, compared to a rate of only 4.5 percent in Germany (1991–2) . . . A clear distinction prevails between school education and professional training; companies do not consider themselves responsible for education . . . the elite among higher education students are selected for entry into exclusive fee-paying *grand ecoles* (specialist graduate schools), and are provided with a semi-guarantee of a prestigious professional career; the remaining masses have free access to the universities, which are of a markedly lower standard of prestige, resourcing and career preparation (p. 55).

In contrast, Sorge (1992) offers the Dutch as an example of the inherent connection between education and work but with very distinct terms to the social contract:

> . . . education in The Netherlands is radically different from that in France. Breeding intellectual high-flyers or technocratic elites, and setting yourself apart from less talented people, are culturally and institutionally resented, like a kind of original sin against Dutch social responsibility, modesty, and sobriety . . . For any employer, the Dutch university engineer or business administrator, like the Dutch technician . . . no matter what institution has trained him or her, is a reliable and competent educational 'product' (Sorge, 1992, p. 75).

Both the Dutch and French demonstrate the tight connection between education, culture and a social contract of work (albeit with distinctly different terms). Their nexus gives rise to opportunities for Dutch workers to bridge between different vocational tracks and creates for them employment stability. In France, it reinforces one's *cadre* or social standing but can reduce employability due to limits on inter-firm mobility and limited use of organization-based training.

Institutional linkages refer to ways in which schooling is directly tied to organizations and organizations to schooling. Certain organizational forms may only be achievable when an educational system provides particular forms of support. This is most likely to be the case in a society where knowledge provides a competitive edge. According to Drucker (1994):

> knowledge workers gain access to jobs and social position through formal education . . . the education that is required . . . can be acquired only through formal schooling. It cannot be acquired through apprenticeship (pp. 65–66).

In-depth scientific or mathematical knowledge requires a decade or more before sufficient understanding is gained for an individual to contribute productively. Since organizations typically cannot afford to bear these costs, they benefit from a closer link to schools in obtaining appropriately skilled workers, and institutional linkages can be expected to impact employment considerably at entry and in the nature of member participation.

Japan provides an illustration of the substantive link between education, industry and social contracts of employment. The pervasive emphasis in Japanese employment is that a good employee is a generalist, capable of playing whatever role is required without being differentiated from fellow group members (Huddleston, 1990) at least for those in large firms. Specialization is not valued since it emphasizes difference as opposed to similarity. The emphasis on generalists is rooted in the high performance standards of the educational system. High competition weeds out those people not able to master broad academic disciplines, depriving them of the university admission critical to attaining professional roles in industry and government. The social contract in Japan inextricably ties lifetime career to successful performance in rigorous pre-university schooling. It is no surprise, therefore, that formal assessment methods play only a small role in Japanese hiring, being reserved for developmental purposes.

Instead, promising candidates are repeatedly asked to interview and to particip-ate in social events, lunches and dinners (Arvey, Bhagat and Salas, 1991). However, it could be argued that if the educational system does foster stratifica-tion based on ability and skills, educational background might tell would-be employers more about prospective new hires than any test could. Any move-ment to alter work roles, careers and skills in Japanese firms has powerful implications 'upstream' for the educational institutions that provide the corpor-ate labor force, since students work long and hard in school in pursuit of the promised career pay-off.

In China, access to both schooling and jobs is controlled by the central govern-ment. Educational institutions cooperate with industrial and agricultural minis-tries in placing graduates. Some graduates are placed through 'side door' arrangements with family and friends in high places. Strong education-to-organization links can be expected to reduce employment screening, particularly reliance on conventional testing.

Education shapes HR practices in organizations and organizations themselves can shape the educational system. Increasing concerns over the quality of the American workforce have led organizations to develop stronger ties to education. In Battle Creek, Michigan, Nippondenso was a leading force in the restructuring of community college programs and the creation of advanced industrial services to support its supplier base. Motorola has invested in transforming the entire educational program of five school districts serving its major production facilities (Florida, 1994). Such links provide firms with additional information about poten-tial employees than is normally available during recruiting and provide alterna-tives to conventional selection testing.

Education-to-organization links have a solid historical foundation. These links are institutionalized in many countries, and have become durable and taken-for-granted. The organization-to-education links, on the other hand, are newer, re-flecting firms' more recent efforts to access scarce appropriately trained workers. This connection between education and worker skills and performance is likely to be strengthened in the emerging knowledge organizations, and can be expected to vary by country and region. According to Drucker (1992):

> The knowledge society will inevitably become far more competitive than any society we have yet known—for the simple reason that with knowledge being universally accessible, there will be no excuses for nonperformance. There will be no 'poor' countries. There will be only ignorant countries (p. 68).

Lastly, education affects HR practices through the extent to which a society's educational system *socializes* people to hold common values and beliefs that enhance their ability to work effectively in organizations. The movement toward team-based education in the United States, where classroom teachers coordinate with each other to give an integrated education and where students work cooper-atively on group projects, is an effort to promote both better learning in school but also team-based skills required in the new workforce. In contrast, the competitive educational system in France focuses on individuals as independent contributors

(Brunstein, 1992). Values espoused in public education can have long-term and enduring effects on workforce behavior. Socialization particularly affects the nature of worker participation, including characteristic terms of performance (e.g. group or team versus individual), which in turn shapes the process of performance appraisal.

Implications

Education is tied to the social contract largely through its effects on how people in a society commonly access and join organizations. The effects of education on entry include the following:

- Widespread quality education directly increases the quality of the workforce, its versatility, and ability to respond to technological and market changes.
- Identifying appropriately skilled workers is easier in societies where education is highly job-related, where certifications and credentials reflect meaningful skills, and where there is often a greater emphasis on individual assessment. Selection will be more social and political in societies where education is largely unrelated to job requirements. Job-related education increases the opportunities workers have to change employers.
- Institutional links between organizations and educational settings reduce the use of conventional tests as selection devices.

Education also can create and or reinforce distinct values and behavioral norms characterizing organizational members.

- Socialization through education will increase the similarity of values and behaviors among the workforce and influence performance appraisal, practices and content.

Law

Like education, a country's legal structure is formed by social and cultural forces, and influences the employment relationship. HR practices as we know them are made possible and perhaps even necessary because of the governance structures to which organizations are subject. The Nobel Prize winner Douglas North has argued:

> Political institutions are as important as economic institutions . . . What happened in Central and Eastern Europe radically changed views about economic theory . . . (typical organizational practices) won't work unless there is body of law—patent law, contract law, property rights—that gives people the right incentives to engage in economic activity (quoted in the *New York Times*, 13 October 1993).

Law shapes HR practices by influencing conditions under which workers enter, work in, or exit the organization, though enforcement can vary widely across nations. Entry effects are evident in societies where equal employment opportunity and/or merit are in some ways mandated. The development of HR technologies such as test fairness techniques, sophisticated job analyses, and other innovations can be directly linked to the implementation of the Civil Rights of 1964 in the United States, particularly Title VII. Conditioning differential impact of hiring decisions on evidence of *job relatedness* spawned an industry wherein Title VII was somewhat aptly termed 'a guaranteed income for psychologists' experienced in job analyses and test validation. Similarly, governments often support other values in hiring such as preferential treatment for legal citizens or veterans of the armed forces.

Legal effects on performance practices are closely tied to the existence of governmental restrictions on terminations. Employee job property rights and entitlement to due process in termination are the norm in many nations (cf. France (Brunstein, 1992); Germany (Wachter and Stengelhofen, 1992)). Job property rights are misnamed. Where laws exist protecting workers' rights to employment, it means that recruitment is for membership not just a particular job. The United States has been the exception until recently. Although at-will employment practices have in the past made terminations easier in the United States than in most of the industrialized world, a few entitlements are now expanding, particularly with regard to due process. Performance appraisal increasingly forms part of the 'paper trail' required to terminate employees for 'cause'.

Despite these developments in the rights of American workers, worker rights are much greater and more widespread in certain other countries. Although both the United States and Canada developed labor laws protecting workers following World War II, Canadian worker rights have proven stronger and more durable (Europaisches Gewerkschaftsinstitut, 1992). In Sweden, worker directors have acted for decades as representatives on boards of directors, a legally required component of worker participation in larger companies. In Germany, there are legally fixed rules and regulations for many job-related features including hiring and firing, wages and other incentives (Trimpop, 1995). Constraints on firing in a country creates limited use of performance appraisal, even for developmental purposes. Nonetheless, in nations where the government owns a considerable proportion of the enterprises (e.g. Nigeria), government-owned or regulated organizations (e.g. public utilities or railroads) tend to observe bureaucratic-based practices in both recruitment and performance measurement reflecting institutional demands for consistency. Here, performance measurement may be conducted to reinforce conformity and role behavior (but not necessarily results). Note, however, that these effects are due to governmental forces shaping the type or organizations that exist, not due to laws *per se*.

One final local difference linked to law, governance structures and local culture are *within*-country ethnic difference (e.g. racial in the United States, caste in India, immigrant workers in the United States and Europe). Legal stipulation regarding affirmative action (the United States), reserved positions (India), and immigrant rights (Germany) are tied to broader societal beliefs and structures.

Implications

Laws and governance structures impact the entry, performance and exit dimensions of the social contract in employment, for example:

- Law impacts selection by specifying hiring criteria (e.g. job relatedness in the United States in the case of potential adverse impact on protected minority groups and women) or by creating non-market-based forces allocating labor to jobs (e.g. Communist China's centralized assignment of workers to employment).
- Where organizations maintain greater control over whom they employ, job property rights and other restrictions on terminations also create incentives for organizations to carefully recruit potential employees since the risks associated with selecting an incompetent or poorly motivated employee are greater when termination is difficult.
- Strong job property rights and other governmental limitations on termination reduce incentives for firms to develop sophisticated performance monitoring.
- Within-country ethnic differences are linked to local variations in policy and intra-nation variation in HR practices.

IMPLICATIONS: ORGANIZATIONAL THEORY AND A GLOBAL HR RESEARCH AGENDA

We really know very little about how local factors affect HR practices. This chapter has knitted together a loose collection of qualitative and quantitative findings in a range of literatures from educational sociology to economics to provide evidence of how societal culture, education and law affect the entry, performance and exit conditions of social contracts in employment. This line of reasoning suggests that different societal contracts will grow out of local cultural, educational and legal systems; hence, human resources are local.

Yet, postulating that human resources are local is like opening Pandora's box. It unlocks a myriad of questions concerning what localization means and how organizations might deal with it. A more comprehensive research agenda is needed to respond to a rapidly globalizing workforce. A research agenda focusing on the effects of society and social contracts on the workforce would address questions regarding when, where and how HR practices should be localized, which HR practices might generalize and to where. Organizations must balance strategic concerns with local social contracts when shaping their HR practices. Conformity to cultural and institutional pressures clearly eases implementation of HR practices. However, within the constraints of these pressures there still can be some HR practices that are more suited to the organization's specific recruiting and performance management needs than are others. How should organizations and researchers approach this heightened awareness of the local nature of HR?

Organizational theorists offer two explanations which can guide our thinking regarding the impact of local environments on work life: resource dependence and institutional legitimacy. Resource dependence, i.e. doing things to satisfy exchange partners such as employees, suppliers, clients, and other stakeholders affects how organizations achieve strategic goals (e.g. hiring computer-literate employees to support a technological change). Resource-based effects are evident in selection where the quality of the educational system shapes the quality of workers available. A German manufacturer recruiting workers from a trade school bases hiring decisions on a referral and a certificate, while for comparable jobs a British firm administers a test to screen applicants on manual dexterity and literacy regardless of education.[11] Because the quality of training can differ greatly between two countries, applicant screening will differ too.[12] Institutional legitimacy, in contrast, means doing things because it would be 'unthinkable to do otherwise', engaging in practices predominating in the larger society (e.g. giving employees days off in accordance with local holidays—Canada Day, Boxing Day in Great Britain, or Casimir Pulaski's Birthday in the State of Illinois, USA). Organizations compete not just for resources but also for political clout and institutional legitimacy, 'for social as well as economic fitness' (DiMaggio and Powell, 1983, p. 150). Although resource-based pressures are economic in nature, organizational responses to institutional pressure, specifically social contract conditions, are guided by external norms and established societal practices. Just as Ebenezer Scrooge risked doom for not giving his employee Bob Cratchit Christmas Day off in Charles Dickens's *A Christmas Carol*, defiance of institutional pressure challenges the organization's propriety and legitimacy.

Earlier we discussed the options for rejecting, adopting, adapting or creating specific HR practices. Despite a good deal of related research on diffusion of new technologies within and between societies (e.g. Rogers and Shoemaker, 1971), we know very little about the conditions under which these options will be exercised regarding HR practices. A critical element of a global HR research agenda is understanding the interplay between institutional and resource pressures as well as the choices that can be made within institutional constraints.

In their study of the benefits HR practices bring to organizations, Ingram and Simons (1995) suggest that those firms adopting HR innovations *when they first appear* do so to gain economic benefits. Those who adopt later (after the innovation has gained wide industry acceptance) do so to avoid being out of step with the rest. With respect to a recent HR innovation, working at home, Ingram and Simon point out that in the 1990s those organizations where employees are permitted to work at home have done so in response to needs to respond to a diverse workforce (e.g. working mothers). Firms lacking the demographic diversity to motivate such a change may not do so unless or until it becomes *de rigueur* or politically correct to do so. In contrast, flexible work schedules, an innovation that caught on in the 1970s, are increasingly the norm in organizations, regardless of the workforce's demographic composition. Twenty years after its introduction, flexible scheduling is part of the institutional fabric of many organizations, a way to be a 'supportive employer'. Its adoption reflects less a strategic concern and more a desire to gain institutional respect. In sum, resource-based practices will reflect strategic choices while institution-based practices will represent 'taken-for-granted' and widely shared societal routines.

But the reasons why some employers successfully innovate in ways at odds with prevailing institutions are not well understood. What factors affect a firm's capacity to adopt HR practices at odds with prevailing institutions? Since resource-based reasons reflect the organization's strategic choices, and in particular its degree of dependence on a given labor pool, we might expect that firms which target a labor pool different from conventions in their industry might be subject to fewer or different institutional pressures than others in that industry. Thus, firms with more diverse nationalities, more women, or some other mix of people, might be less constrained by pressures from dominant institutions. Reasons for adopting such distinct HR practices are driven by concern for economic outcomes such as cost and productivity and innovative firms might place greater emphasis on those outcomes than others in their industry.

What factors affect a firm's need for compliance with social contracts and other institution-based pressures? Institution-based reasons reflect the organization's geopolitical setting. Such reasons for adopting HR practices are driven by concern for social acceptability and may be more characteristic of certain kinds of organizations, e.g. large firms or those with governmental ties. In contrast, smaller firms or those with independent ownership may be less subject to such pressures. Institution-based HR practices can impede or enhance productivity. Under what conditions does adopting a practice for social acceptability reduce conflict, smooth social interaction and promote better coordination of efforts? When is social acceptability less relevant? We know little as yet about the conditions under which responses to institutional forces help or impede organizational success.

Many challenges remain for future research:

- How might researchers move beyond the historical focus on individuals, managers, short-term outcomes, and internally focused criteria that characterize most research in I/O psychology? (Shifting research to work group dynamics, including inter-group and extra-organizational relations, can broaden its cross-cultural relevance.)
- Under what circumstances should a multinational's HR practices be uniform throughout the entire organization, and to what extent should HR practices differ by locality? (We may need to move beyond studying only managers, professionals and other organizational elites to investigate the HR practices applied to the broader global workforce.)
- How can we effectively implement changes in HR practices derived in one society in another? For example, whether, when and/or how should merit-based selection systems be introduced into traditionally politicized or in-group oriented work environments (e.g. Eastern Europe)?
- How should local in-group/out-group relations be addressed? In lower-level work situations where cosmopolitan education is less likely? Throughout organizational and managerial ranks? When is 'who you know' critical to business success and how should organizations take into account the political ties of recruits and members in personnel-related decisions?
- As an organization's workforce moves from being mono-national to multi-national, how does this affect employee perceptions of an organization's

practices? How does cultural context affect the way HR practices are understood by organization members? How can multinational organizations avoid sending mixed signals or the wrong message to employees of different backgrounds?

• How should organizations choose the proper unit of analysis in creating and implementing an HR strategy? Traditional HR focuses on individual background and skill variables. (In some circumstances the appropriate focus might be the team or other work group.)

Because of local constraints on the labor force's mobility, questions arise regarding HR practices for accessing and effectively developing the labor pool:

• How can organizations effectively adjust their recruiting and performance management practices to accommodate the available labor pool? (The utility of various HR technologies across employee skill and education levels needs further study.)
• What kinds of relationships should organizations develop with secondary schools and universities to access appropriately skilled workers? (Forms of school-to-work transitions reflect an alternative to conventional selection methodologies and can supplement other forms of recruiting and socialization.)

Lastly, but of course very important, are questions pertaining to enhanced understanding of the role of social contracts of employment:

• How can organizations come to understand and work within the social contracts, taken-for-granted entitlements and guarantees their local members are party to? Under what conditions can and should these contracts be challenged? Under what conditions can these contracts be effectively sustained?

Social contracts in employment are part of the taken-for-granted realities of a place. They embody what employees collectively expect from their relationship with an organization and weave together the forces of culture, education and law into the fabric of everyday work life. Resource dependence and institutional legitimacy offer two reasons why organizations should be concerned with the local nature of HR. Doing business in several places at once means that organizations may need to accommodate their HR practices to garner resources and win institutional respect.

Scientific HR itself is a cultural phenomenon, operating on the assumption that practices for acquiring a workforce and supporting its performance are, with inevitable qualification, generalizable across settings. And it is the Western and particularly Anglo-American cultures that hold beliefs in the existence of universal principles and general categories (a belief system Glenn (1981) refers to as 'abstractive'). Schneider (1985) persuasively argued that 'the people make the place'. Now, science-based human resource practice must give more serious attention to the effect of place on people.

ACKNOWLEDGEMENTS

We thank both editors and our colleagues Steve Appold and Caroline Gomez for helpful comments on this chapter. We also appreciate all the help and support Carole McCoy provided us in preparing this chapter.

ENDNOTES

1. Tip O'Neill, Speaker of the House of Representatives, United States Congress, was fond of making this statement, based on his experience of having represented for over 30 years the Boston neighborhood where he grew up. For those who wonder about the grammatical nature of the saying, 'All politics is local' is correct since there is an implied 'of' as in 'All *of* politics is local'. Our thanks to Erik Devereux for pointing this out.

2. Although systematic research on cross-national HR issues may be relatively new, there is a longer tradition of practical experience with cross-national HR in continental Europe driven by the need to deal with a workforce composed of foreign guest workers as well as local people.

3. Bass and Berger (1979) argue that validity generalization is the exception, with little evidence of validity across countries. Arvey, Bhagat and Salas (1991) concur that test publishers have diversified into international markets without too much attention to validity.

4. Israel is an exception with a large number of American-educated scholars holding doctorates in business or psychology.

5. These percentages are based on data from admission rates in our previous and present universities and their schools of business and management over the past five years.

6. Note that this figure is adopted from Rousseau (1995) and addresses the determinants of social contract most relevant to *cross*-cultural or *cross*-societal differences.

7. It is perhaps significant, however, that in the United States the open-ended, unstructured interview persists as a common selection device despite a corpus of selection research that argues that such interviews do not successfully predict success at discrete jobs. If we examine what organizations actually do, as opposed to what psychologists say they ought to do, it may be that even American organizations select for person–organization fit rather than person–job fit, and have done so for years. Thus, it may be that the research of psychologists is individualistic, but the behavior of organization members less so.

8. Culture can mean that people not only consider different criteria but seek out different sources of information. Greeks asked to make selection decision gave greater weight to information given by relatives and friends for candidates than the American sample. Interestingly, however, the rank ordering of the applicants in terms of acceptability between Greeks and Americans was fairly high (0.75), suggesting agreement in terms of their hireability.

9. Similarly, Shackleton and Newell (1991) found that the only British organizations using graphology were subsidiaries of French-owned corporations.

10. Despite cultural trends toward individualism worldwide, organizations, particularly in the United States and the United Kingdom, are moving toward teamwork and team-based work structures.

11. Although the European economic community is moving toward the 'free movement' of labor between member countries, each member state still has to recognize the qualifications of another country. The need for credible signals of worker qualification is a major problem in the creation of boundaryless careers and a global work force (Arthur and Rousseau, 1996).

12. Many resource-based differences in HR practices derive from the quality and availability of the relevant labor pool. The relevant labor can be the community (for the local

McDonalds), the state or province (for a large public utility), or the larger region, country to international depending on the employer's size and attractiveness in a competitive market. HR practices adopted for rational, resource-based reasons reflect strategic differences between organizations, and organizational differences within a country can be as great as the variation between countries. Organizations with different strategies use different HR practices (Miles and Snow, 1984; Jackson, Schuler and Rivero, 1989; Rousseau and Wade-Benzoni, 1994). To date the focus of this resource-based research has been North American and Japanese firms, raising the possibility that resource-based reasons for adopting HR practices may take as yet un-investigated new forms in other settings.

REFERENCES

Abitia, E.A. (1986, 1991). *Los valores de los Mexicanos*, Vols. 1 and 2. Mexico City: Banamex.

Ali, A. (1988). A cross-national perspective of managerial work value systems. In R.N. Farmer and E.G. McGowen (eds.), *Advances in International Comparative Management*. Greenwich, CT: JAI Press.

Arthur, M.B. and Rousseau, D.M. (eds.) (1996). *The Boundaryless Career: Work, Mobility, and Learning in the New Organizational Era*. New York: Oxford University Press.

Arvey, R.D., Bhagat, R.S. and Salas, E. (1991). Cross-cultural and cross-national issues in personnel and human resources management: Where do we go from here? *Research in Personnel and Human Resources Management*, **9**, 367–407.

Bass, B.M. and Berger, P.C. (1979). *Assessment of Managers: An International Comparison*. New York: Free Press.

Berridge, J. and Brunstein, I. (eds.) (1992). Human resource management in the European Community. *Employee Relations*, **14**.

Bhaghat, R.S., Kedia, B.L., Crawford, S.E. and Kaplan, M.R. (1990). Cross-cultural issues in organizational psychology: Emergent trends and directions for research in the 1990s. In C.L. Cooper and I.T. Robertson (eds.), *International Review of Industrial/Organizational Psychology*, Vol. 5, Chapter 3.

Boas, F. (1940). *Race, Language and Culture*. New York: Macmillan Co.

Brunstein, I. (1992). Human resource management in France. *Employee Relations*, **14** (4), 53–70.

DeCieri, H. and Dowling, P. (1995). Cross-cultural issues in organizational behavior. In C.L. Cooper and D.M. Rousseau (eds.), *Trends in Organizational Behavior*, Vol. 2, pp. 127–143. London: John Wiley.

Derr, C.B. (1987). Managing high potentials in Europe: Some cross-cultural findings. *European Management Journal*, **5**, 72–80.

Deutsch, M. (1973). *The Resolution of Conflict: Constructive and Destructive Processes*. New Haven: Yale University Press.

DiMaggio, P.J. and Powell, W.W. (1983). The iron cage revisited: Institutional isomorphism and collective rationality in organizational fields. *American Sociological Review*, **48**, 147–160.

Dore, R. (1983). Goodwill and the spirit of market capitalism. *British Journal of Contemporary Business*, **8** (2), 27–35.

Drucker, P.F. (1994). The age of social transformation. *The Atlantic Monthly*, **274**, November, 53–80.

Erez, M. (1993). Towards a model of cross-cultural I/O psychology. In M.D. Dunnette and L. Hough (eds.), *Handbook of Industrial and Organizational Psychology*, 2nd edn, Vol. 4. Palo Alto, CA: Consulting Psychologists Press.

Erez, M. and Earley, P.C. (1993). *Culture, Self-identity and Work*. New York: Oxford University Press.

Europaisches Gewerkschaftsinstitut (1992) *Gewerken und Arbeitsbeziehungen in den USA und Kanada—Eine vergleichende Studie der gegenwartigen Situation*. Brussels: Europaisches Gewerkschaftsinstitut.

Florida, R. (1994). *Economic Transformation, Regions, and Development Policy.* Pittsburgh: Center for Economic Development, Heinz School of Public Policy and Management, Carnegie-Mellon University.

Glenn, E. (1981). *Man and Mankind: Conflicts and Communications Between Cultures.* Norwood, NJ: Ablex.

Goodenough, W. (1964). *Explorations in Cultural Anthropology: Essays in Honor of George Peter Murdock.* New York: McGraw-Hill.

Gomez-Mejia, L.R. (1986). The cross-cultural structure of task-related and contextual constructs. *The Journal of Psychology,* **120** (1), 5–19.

Hampton, W.J. (1988). How does Japan, Inc. pick its American workers? *Business Week,* October 3, 84, 88.

Hennan, D.A. and Perlmutter, H. (1979). Multinational organization development. Reading, MA: Addison-Wesley.

Herriot, P. (1992). Selection: The two subcultures. *European Work and Organizational Psychologist,* **2**, 129–140.

Hofstede, G. (1980). *Culture's Consequences: International Differences in Work-related Values.* Beverly Hills, CA: Sage.

Hofstede, G. (1993). Cultural constraints in management theories. *Academy of Management Executives,* **7**, 81–94.

Huddlestone, J.N. (1990). *Gaigin Kaisha: Running a Foreign Business in Japan.* Armour, NY: Sharpe.

Huo, Y.P. and Von Glinow, M.A. (1995). Managing human resources across the Pacific Ocean: A tri-national comparison of staffing practices.

Ingram, P. and Simons, T. (1995). Disentangling resource dependence and institutional explanations of organizational practice: The case of organization's adoption of flextime and work at home. *Academy of Management Journal,* **38**, 1466–1482.

Jackson, S.E., Schuler, R.S. and Rivero, J.C. (1989). Organizational characteristics as predictors of personnel practices. *Personnel Psychology,* **42**, 727–786.

Janssens, M. and Brett, J.M. (1994). Coordinating global companies: The effects of electronic communication, organizational commitment, and multi-cultural managerial workforce. In C.C. Cooper and D.M. Rousseau (eds.) *Trends in Organizational Behavior, Vol 1.* Chichester: John Wiley.

Klitgaard, R. (1986). *Elitism and Meritocracy in Developing Countries: Selection Policies for Higher Education.* Baltimore: Johns Hopkins University Press.

Kluckhohn, F. and Strodtbeck, F.L. (1961). *Variations in Value Orientations.* Evanston, IL: Row, Peterson.

Koenig, R. (1987). Toyota takes pains, and time, filling jobs at its Kentucky plant. *Wall Street Journal,* December 1.

Kovach, K.A. (1987). What motivates employees? Workers and supervisors give different answers. *Business Horizons,* September–October, 61.

Kras, E.S. (1988). *Management in Two Cultures: Bridging the Gap Between U.S. and Mexican Managers.* US: International Press.

Kroeber, A.L. and Kluckhohn, F. (1952). Culture: A critical review of concepts and definitions. *Peabody Museum Papers* **47**, 1. Cambridge, MA: Harvard University.

Lincoln, J.R. and Kalleberg, A.L. (1985). Work organization and workforce commitment: A study of plants and employees in the U.S. and Japan. *American Sociological Review,* **50**, 738–760.

Lytle, A.L., Brett, J.M., Barnsness, Z.B., Tinsley, C.H. and Janssens, M. (1995). A paradigm for confirmatory cross-cultural research in organization behavior. *Research in Organizational Behavior,* **17**, 167–214.

Malinowski, B. (1944). *A Scientific Theory of Culture and Other Essays.* Chapel Hill, NC: The University of North Carolina Press.

MOW International Research Team (1987). *The Meaning of Work.* London/New York: Academic Press.

Miles, R.E. and Snow, C.C. (1984). Designing strategic human resource systems. *Organizational Dynamics,* 36–52.

Parson, T. and Shils, E. (1951). *Towards a General Theory of Action.* Cambridge, MA: Harvard University Press.

Perrow, C. (1996). The bounded career and the demise of civil society. In M.B. Arthur and D.M. Rousseau (eds), *The Boundaryless Career: Work, Mobility and Learning in the New Organizational Era.* New York: Oxford University Press.

Pucik, V., Tichy, N.M. and Barnett, C.K. (eds.) (1992). *Globalizing Management: Creating and Leading the Competitive Organization.* New York: Wiley.

Robertson, I.T. and Makin, P.J. (1986). Management selection in Britain. A survey and critique. *Journal of Occupational Psychology,* **59**, 45–57.

Rogers, E.M. and Shoemaker, F.F. (1971). *Communication of Innovations.* New York: Free Press.

Ronen, S. and Shenkar, O. (1985). Clustering countries on attitudinal dimensions: A review and synthesis. *Academy of Management Review,* **10**, 435–454.

Rousseau, D.M. (1995). *Psychological Contracts in Organizations: Understanding Written and Unwritten Agreements.* Newbury Park, CA: Sage.

Rousseau, D.M. and Wade-Benzoni, K.A. (1994). Linking strategy and human resource practices: How employee and customer contracts are created. *Human Resource Management,* **33**, 463–489.

Ruiz Quintanilla, S.A. (ed.) (1991). Work centrality and related work meanings. *European Work and Organizational Psychologist,* **1** (2–3).

Salas, E. (1984). Factors that facilitate or hinder the implementation of managerial technology: A sociotechnical systems process. Unpublished dissertation. Old Dominion University.

Schneider, B. (1987). The people make the place. *Personnel Psychology,* **40**, 437–453.

Shackleton, V. and Newell, S. (1991). Management selection: A comparative study of methods under top British and French companies. *Journal of Occupational and Organizational Psychology,* **64**, 23–26.

Scott, W.R. (1987). Introduction: From technology to environment. In J.W. Meyer and W.R. Scott (eds.), *Organizational Environments: Ritual and Rationality,* pp. 13–17. Beverly Hills, CA: Sage.

Sorge, A. (1992). Human resource management in The Netherlands. *Employee Relations,* **14** (4), 71–84.

Smith, D.F. and Florida, R. (1994). Agglomeration and industrial location: An econometric analysis of Japanese-affiliated manufacturing establishments in automotive-related industries. *Journal of Urban Economics,* **36**, 23–41.

Tannen, D. (1979). What's in a frame? Surface evidence for underlying expectation. In K. Kressel, D.G. Pruitt and Associates (eds.), *Mediation Research,* pp. 166–189. San Francisco: Jossey-Bass.

Tinsley, C.H. and Lytle, A.L. (1994). Is mediation best? An examination of dispute resolution in Mexico. Paper presented at the International Association of Conflict Management meetings, Eugene, Oregon, June.

Triandis, H. (1982). Dimensions of cultural variations as parameters of organizational theories. *International Studies of Management and Organization,* **12** (4), 139–169.

Triandis, H. (1989). Cross-cultural studies of individualism–collectivism. In J.J. Berman (ed.), *Nebraska Symposium on Motivation: Cross-Cultural Perspectives,* Vol. 37, 41–133. Lincoln: University of Nebraska Press.

Triandis, H.C., McCusker, C. and Hui, C.H. (1990). Multimethod probes of individualism and collectivism. *Journal of Personality and Social Psychology,* **59**, 1006–20.

Trimpop, R.M. (1995). Union commitment: Conceptual changes in the German context. *Journal of Organizational Behavior,* **16**, 597–608.

Two Americans Win Nobel Economics Prize, *New York Times,* 13 October 1993.

Wachter, H. and Stengelhofen, T. (1992). Human resource management in a Unified Germany. *Employee Relations,* **14** (4), 21–37.

Chapter 3

Integrated Personnel Selection, Appraisal and Decisions: A Chinese Approach

ZHONG-MING WANG

Department of Psychology, School of Management, Hangzhou University, People's Republic of China

INTRODUCTION

China has a long tradition of ancient ideas and practices on selection and appraisal. The national and cultural context of selection and appraisal is characterized by its large labour population, dynamic changes in personnel reform and institutional approach labour management. Under the recent economic reform, systematic research and applications of personnel selection, appraisal and decisions on the basis of measured qualities have been encouraged and implemented. Since the 1980s, various kinds of selection and appraisal techniques have been developed and more widely accepted and used in personnel management in China. In the meantime, a series of studies on selection and appraisal has been carried out. On the basis of the recent practice and research, three important characteristics of an integrated selection and appraisal are highlighted as a Chinese approach to staffing decisions.

CHINESE TRADITIONS IN SELECTION AND ASSESSMENT

Chinese ancient views on personnel characteristics

China has a long tradition of job categorization, personnel assessment and selection. As early as the twelfth and eleventh centuries BC, *The Rites of the Chou Dynasty*, China's classical ancient literature, systematically defined the selection

International Handbook of Selection and Assessment, Edited by N. Anderson and P. Herriot.
© 1997 John Wiley & Sons Ltd.

requirements of managerial positions for the first Chinese bureaucratic system with six categories of official ranks. In ancient Chinese culture (about 313–238 BC), human traits were widely discussed in terms of three dimensions of predispositions:

- Basic characteristics: economic, cooperative and specialty predispositions, which determine people's behavioural orientations and styles.
- Capability characteristics: the ability to study and understand (cognitive ability); the ability to direct and manage (administrative ability); and the ability to evaluate and hire (personnel ability).
- Moral characteristics: teamwork potential with the collectivist value as its core element (Wang, 1993).

Apparently, basic characteristics represented general abilities, capability characteristics indicated more dynamic and problem-solving skills, whereas moral characteristics formulated social and team abilities. These ancient conceptions of human characteristics formed a holistic view of personnel characteristics and have some close links with modern Chinese thinking on the integration of multiple personnel characteristics in selection and appraisal.

Personnel selection and appraisal systems

During the ancient period, personnel appraisal and examinations were popular practices in China. The most common aspects of personnel assessment included various kinds of examinations in music, archery, horsemanship, writing, mathematics and public affairs. Around the year AD 587, China started the world's first comprehensive national system of personnel examination and selection for civil service, *the Imperial Examination Systems* (Wang, 1993). During the Ming and Qing dynasties (1368–1900), the system became more complicated and included more comprehensive aspects of examination and appraisal. This personnel system lasted over 1300 years, perhaps the longest in history, with an emphasis on both basic knowledge and problem-solving abilities (Li, Song and Li, 1989).

In general, this ancient personnel selection system had three significant features. The first feature was its nature of public competition. The selection procedures, examination rules and results were widely publicized. Anybody could apply for the positions, undertake examinations, and compete with each other in selection. The second feature was its multiple-assessment approach. The selection was mainly based on the performance of examinations and later dependent upon four types of appraisal: (i) ability, (ii) morality, (iii) performance, and (iv) seniority. Using essays, oral exams and performance tests, a typical examination package consisted of three parts: general composition (written expression and verbal ability), policy judgement (problem-solving) and commentary (discussion and proposals). The third feature was its multi-level screening and decision-making procedure which involved county, provincial and state levels of examinations and selection. The final examination was usually held in front of the Emperors themselves. To a large extent, many of those features and practices are still reflected in current Chinese personnel selection, appraisal and decision-making.

Testing and assessment

In ancient China, testing and assessment were popular in education and management. Confucius first classified people into three categories on the basis of three levels of 'wisdom' (great, average and little wisdom), representing his early ideas emphasizing individual differences in assessment. Mencius (327–289 BC), another well-known Chinese philosopher, advocated the importance of quantitative measurement of human mind through scaling (Zhang, 1988). In addition, a variety of psychological measurement methods were widely developed such as the Chinese puzzles and situational interviews to measure behavioural traits (Lin, 1983). From the Jin Dynasty (265–420) through to the Tang Dynasty (618–907), a series of appraisal systems was developed. For example, a 'periodic appraisal system' was used to determine promotion and demotion. A 'merit record system' was developed for rewarding and promoting officials, while a nine-rank 'performance assessment system' was adopted to appraise the performance of official work. In the Tang Dynasty, sentence completion tests became popular. These appraisal systems emphasized multiple measures and time-series assessment. The current testing approach and practice of selection and appraisal in China are largely rooted in this tradition.

THE CONTEXT AND PRACTICE OF SELECTION AND APPRAISAL IN MODERN CHINA

Labour market development and needs for selection and appraisal

The development of the modern Chinese labour market has gone through two stages, i.e. from an early stage of a central planning system to the current stage of a market-economy-oriented system. During the early period of the founding of the People's Republic of China in the 1950s, a central planning system of labour employment, i.e. the National Committee for Labour Employment, was established which was responsible for introducing jobs to reduce unemployment. Generally speaking, this early system had three components: the national labour administration and enterprise labour system, the national planned job assignment system, and the life employment system. Under the national labour administration and enterprise labour system, the governmental bureaux of various industries administered labour planning, selection, recruitment, placement and transfers within industrial sectors, while the governmental labour departments organized labour introduction to companies and its recruitment. This central planning system was also extended to the national planned job assignment system for the selection and recruitment of graduates from schools and universities. The number of jobs to be assigned was planned when the admission plan was formulated, i.e. before the students entered universities. After graduation, students could not choose a different job. The administration of the schools and universities was responsible for the one-way job assignment. Once recruited or assigned to jobs, employees put themselves into the 'iron bowl employment', i.e. a life employment system. It was not only very difficult for employees to move or quit jobs, but also almost impossible for organizations to fire or dismiss employees. This made the selection and recruitment so crucial in determining the life careers among Chinese employees on the basis of the evaluation of political background (family background and political memberships) and schooling. No systematic job analysis was conducted. Therefore the person–job fit was low priority.

This central planning system was somewhat workable under the early development of the central planning economy with a relatively low rate of unemployment and an emphasis on ideology. However, by the beginning of the Chinese economic reform in 1979, after the ten-year cultural revolution, there was an urban labour population of 15 million looking for jobs. Labour management reform was then carried out nationwide with programmes of labour departmental job introduction, self-organized employment, and autonomous employment. This reform has been effective in dealing with unemployment and promoting flexible selection and recruitment practice. In the following 14 years, while the urban-employed labour population increased by 64%, from 95 million in 1978 to 156 million in 1992, the rate of urban labour population looking for jobs decreased from 5.4% in 1979 to 2.3% in 1992 (Chen *et al.*, 1993). By 1994, the population of employees in State-owned enterprises, collective-owned companies, private firms, township companies and international joint ventures were 111 million, 31 million, 13 million, 120 million and 7 million, respectively (Ma and Sun, 1995; Chen, 1995). In the meantime, a dual-track labour management system was trialled including the labour planning administration and the labour market adjustment mechanism. Many thousands of labour markets have been established. Various kinds of assessment techniques have been adopted for selection and recruitment. The one-way job assignment and placement system has been changed into a two-way job choice and selection system. There have been great demands and potentials for more effective selection and appraisal. In addition, with the rapid development of management reform and technological innovations in State- and collective-owned enterprises, more and more employees became redundant and needed to be either re-trained or re-employed. In 1994, a nationwide re-employment programme was launched among 25 large- and medium-sized cities and 1.06 million were re-employed and got new jobs (Chen, 1995). An important feature of this programme was its re-training and re-selection based on comprehensive assessment and appraisal.

The structure of personnel systems

To fully understand the modern approaches and practice of selection and appraisal in China, it is necessary to consider the structure of the Chinese personnel management system. Generally speaking, this system has two major branches: the labour management system and the cadre management system. On the one hand, the labour system is mainly designed to manage ordinary workers and staff, including pre-job vocational training, selection, recruitment, appraisal, placement, on-the-job training, work quota design, performance evaluation, rewarding and punishment. On the other hand, the cadre system involves the management of two categories of personnel: (i) general administrative cadres such as management staff, technicians and engineers; and (ii) leading cadres such as executives, middle managers, party officials and trade union leaders. The main tasks of the cadre system include the selection, placement, transfer, promotion, appraisal, training, rewarding and punishment of cadres.

During the early 1980s the focus of Chinese personnel management reform was shifted from labour evaluation and reward design to the selection and appraisal for more competent and qualified managers and cadres. Especially in recent years the cadre system has implemented the principles of selecting more politically competent, younger, more knowledgeable and more professionally specialized cadres, while the labour system has emphasized the principles of public recruitment, voluntary application, comprehensive evaluation and selection by merit. More and more younger and competent managers have been selected for leading positions. In the process of the current personnel management reform towards a market economy, the labour system has made more efforts to train more qualified and skilful workers and to help them adapt to the rapid development in technological innovations, whereas the cadre system has focused more on leadership appraisal and selection (Wang, 1989; Wang, 1991).

Institutional single-pattern approach in selection

For many years most of the Chinese State- and collective-owned enterprises followed the same regulations and practice in personnel selection. In a series of in-depth case studies on personnel decision procedures among Chinese organizations, Wang and Wang (1989) found that most Chinese enterprises and organizations adopted a relatively identical single pattern of institutional approach in personnel selection, evaluation, recruitment and placement, and a similar centralized procedure with relatively strict sequences of decisions through different levels of authorities. However, many enterprises, especially collective-owned companies and joint ventures, had some local autonomy in decisions concerning selection and placement within the range of State policies for personnel management. Moreover, it was shown that educational qualifications were still a major requirement for personnel selection while psychological characteristics such as abilities, personality, interests and attitudes were increasingly being taken into account in personnel decisions. The study called for designing more adaptive decision procedures, developing decision information systems and using multiple predictors and utility analysis to improve personnel decisions in Chinese enterprises.

Comprehensive leadership appraisal

Throughout recent decades a comprehensive approach to leadership appraisal has been emphasized in China. The practice of Chinese leadership appraisal in the 1950s and 1960s was more centralized and had three significant characteristics.

- To emphasize political competence and commitment, particularly ideological background;
- To observe and examine personnel in practical situations and through real tasks.
- To encourage mass evaluation and co-worker assessment.

During this long period, little attention was paid to the quantitative assessment of personnel characteristics. The person–job fit issue was often neglected. In the late 1960s and through the 1970s when the so-called Cultural Revolution took place in China, personnel management was disrupted and in chaos. However, since the mid-1980s, with the rapid developments of economic reform in all industrial sectors, a series of leadership appraisal research and applications have been actively conducted. Most of this research first started from industry and then expanded into governmental organizations. The objectives of this leadership appraisal research were two-fold:

1. To change the traditional practice of evaluating enterprise leaders by personal impressions or simply political affiliations, and
2. To build up comprehensive and standardized appraisal systems for cadre selection and promotion. Among others, leadership appraisal research included studies of performance–maintenance leadership behaviour, cadre leadership assessment and selection, situational simulation and assessment centres, and job and task analysis.

PERSONNEL ASSESSMENT AND APPRAISAL

The CPM leadership study

One of the main tasks in leadership appraisal research was to develop effective assessment models and reliable instruments suitable for specific cultural contexts. A large-scale research project was therefore carried out with the appraisal of leadership behaviour involving 16 260 respondents from 53 factories in a number of industries in northern China (Xu, 1987). At the first stage of this project, a Japanese two-dimensional instrument for leadership appraisal was adapted to the Chinese management situation, measuring task performance and relationship maintenance (the so-called performance–maintenance (PM) scale) (Misumi, 1985). Eight situational criteria were used in the Chinese performance–maintenance (PM) study: work motivation, satisfaction with income, work environment, mental health, teamwork, efficiency of meetings, communications, and performance. However, the Chinese research data soon revealed that despite some cultural similarities between China and Japan, a third dimension of leadership appraisal, namely moral character, was significant, in addition to the original two dimensions of performance and maintenance (Lin, Chen and Wang, 1987). It was recognized that as an important cultural characteristic of Chinese tradition, moral character was highly valued throughout Chinese history. It generally includes personal characteristics such as honesty, integrity, positive attitudes toward employees and leadership, beliefs in team cooperation, and organizational commitment. It was believed that any leadership perspective that did not emphasize the moral character of leaders was incomplete (Peterson, 1988). Therefore, the PM scale was modified and the moral character factor was added so that a three-dimensional scale of character, performance and maintenance (CPM) was formulated. The CPM scale was then implemented in a number of Chinese governmental organizations and industrial enterprises and proved to be a reliable and valid appraisal instrument of leadership behaviour. The CPM study indicated that in assessing leadership behaviour in Chinese organizations, an integrated approach of moral, relationship and performance was more suitable for Chinese cultural and managerial situations (Xu et al, 1985; Wang, 1991).

Cadre leadership assessment and selection

There have been many other studies on psychological assessment and appraisal of personnel and leadership behaviour in Chinese industries. The early work of personnel assessment and appraisal was carried out among middle managers and supervisors in the machine industry in Shanghai in the early 1980s. Self-designed tests of abilities were also used in establishing a psychological archive databank for 4,448 ordinary factory workers as well as 37 different kinds of work groups. During the mid-1980s, cadre assessment and selection became an important task in personnel management. Several kinds of more comprehensive assessment systems were developed in Beijing, Shanghai and Hangzhou which included three components of assessment: political predisposition (political competence, responsibility, modelling behaviour, open-mindedness, progressive spirit, etc.), abilities (ability to make decisions, to be creative, to solve problems, to communicate verbally, and to be good at social coordination and interpersonal relationships), and performance (both productivity and social efficiency). In Beijing, for example, more than 2000 employees took part in the appraisal study which provided data for selection, placement and training (Zhang, 1986). In Hangzhou, an assessment instrument was developed and used for leadership appraisal which included 30 items of four aspects: political predisposition, knowledge structure, ability level and work performance. On the basis of the Chinese tradition of mass consultation in personnel management, a role-set method of multi-level assessment was adopted in many industries and governmental departments (e.g. Zhang, 1986). Each role-set involves the candidate, and his/her supervisors, subordinates and peers. The abilities and performance of candidates or incumbents were assessed for leading management positions. Therefore, more accurate and comprehensive data for personnel decisions were obtained.

Situational simulation and assessment centre

In a series of selection and assessment activities, Lu (1986) used the assessment centre method in appraising and selecting factory managers. A simulated management situation test was designed including four work samples for the candidates:

- Document review—15 common documents about middle management.
- Group discussion—a management meeting for personnel placement.
- Supervisor–subordinate conversation—a role-playing task.
- Work-planning speech—a plan for new production.

The whole session of situational simulation emphasized policy-making and usually took two or three days. The results from the assessment and selection study in a sewing machine company in Shanghai and a gas engine company in Beijing showed that 89% of candidates selected after assessment proved to be effective managers at work. In another study of an assessment centre involving 38 cadres in a research institute in Shanghai, the validity coefficient between the situational assessment score and work performance was 0.48. It was therefore shown that, by evaluating verbal ability, written expression ability, interpersonal ability, delegating ability, organizing ability, analytic ability, management creativity and policy implementation ability, the simulation test was more effective and valid in selecting and assessing Chinese cadres than traditional paper-and-pencil tests.

A more sophisticated assessment centre was designed and validated in Beijing for evaluating managerial potential (Liang *et al.*, 1991). Altogether, about 150 executives and middle managers participated in this assessment centre study. Fourteen cases of in-basket documents were used with tasks such as bonus allocation, new product development, marketing for PCs, user needs analysis, accident insurance, market research, safety regulations, annual reporting, recruiting secretaries, coordinating conflicts, complaint resolution, cost and profit analysis, and product structure analysis. The results showed that evaluations were consistent with what was found from the mass evaluation and that a four-factor construct structure of the nine ability measures by the in-basket tasks was obtained:

1. Analytical and judgemental decision-making, operating and managing abilities.
2. Motivational and delegational abilities.
3. Organizing and coordinating, interpersonal relationships.
4. Written ability, management beliefs.

The use of situational appraisal methods and an assessment centre approach has indicated a significant development and change in personnel management practice in the Chinese industrial enterprises and governmental organizations. In a large field survey of the attitudes on the situational assessment among personnel managers, 53% of respondents reported that they thought the method was suitable, whereas 32% expressed their reluctance in adopting the methods (Lu, 1991).

Job analysis and task analysis

The personnel selection was also conducted in relation to job analysis. Using methods of case analysis, work diary records, a questionnaire survey and cadre assessment, a study of job analysis was made in 60 Chinese factories (Wu, 1986). It was shown that there were seven main categories of management functions in

Chinese enterprises: general administration, ideological work, production management, technical work, marketing, welfare, and personnel management. The results of this job analysis were used in designing assessment scales for managers and supervisors. In a recent research project to develop selection tests for pilots, Wang (1995) conducted a comprehensive task analysis and identified six task factors including team information exchange, multi-information discrimination, uncertain information processing, abstract information recognition, regular information recognition, and operation and recording. This project has adopted an integrated approach to include basic cognitive abilities, decision skills under dynamic tasks as well as team compatibility in pilot selection.

PERSONNEL SELECTION AND DECISION-MAKING

Three aspects of personnel decisions

To a large extent, the effectiveness of selection and appraisal lies in the improvement of personnel decision-making procedures in various organizations, especially relating to the decentralization of decision-making power and the enhancement of decision-making quality. By 1986, developing more standardized and democratic procedures for personnel decision-making had become a major task of personnel management in China. It was then a very active area in the research and application of selection and appraisal. Research has been carried out along three lines of personnel decision-making:

1. Cognitive process and information utilization in personnel decision-making.
2. Participation in personnel decision-making in organizations.
3. Decision support for personnel selection.

The process of personnel decision-making has been an important research topic in China. The information-processing perspective is adopted in examining task structures, decision procedures, information utilization and judgement strategies in personnel decisions. It is suggested that the decision process and personnel information utilization are more crucial than personnel information itself (e.g. personnel appraisal data).

Public bidding in the selection of management teams

Another research area in Chinese personnel decisions is the selection of top-level managers for the director–management contract systems, i.e. deciding on who should be the director responsible for enterprise management through a bidding process of public selection and competitive recruitment, a nationwide practice in management reform since 1987. Wang and Fan (1990) conducted a large-scale field survey in 27 Chinese enterprises (15 State-owned and 12 collective-owned enterprises) to reveal the psychological characteristics and effective strategies for facilitating and improving the selection decisions by management teams for director–management responsibility contract systems. Both managers and worker representatives from those companies, together with supervisors from the industrial bureaux (level above the plant), were interviewed. Applications, proposals and records of the recruitment meetings were carefully examined in order to understand the general procedures and task structures of personnel decision-making. It was found that the decisions by public election and competitive recruitment of top-level managers in Chinese enterprises had five important features:

1. Selection decisions were heavily based on economic and personal information while overlooking information about management tasks and human resources in enterprises.
2. Information-gathering relied more on official examinations, but there was a lack of quantitative appraisal and mass evaluation.
3. Personnel decisions were made among fewer candidates or proposals with more short-term benefits and therefore needed coordinating long-term objectives of State, collective and individual interests.
4. There was a lack of participation by worker representatives in the appraisal and selection committee at various stages of decision-making.
5. Public assessment had the advantage of facilitating information gathering and utilization.

The results of this study provided systematic evidence and decision support strategies for improving the selection and recruitment procedure of director–management responsibility contract systems in Chinese organizations.

Information utilization in personnel selection

More recently, research efforts have been made to investigate the patterns of utilization of personnel information in personnel selection in Chinese companies. For example, Wang and Wang (1991) completed a field research project among over 200 personnel managers representing 132 Chinese companies with nine indicators of personnel selection information:

1. Job requirements with working conditions and interpersonal job requirements.
2. Ability requirements with educational qualifications and job-related ability information.
3. Personnel management context including labour supply, personnel management policies and regulations, and selection experience among personnel managers.
4. Personnel archives with candidates' background records, interview results and previous performance.
5. Appraisal results such as mathematics and Chinese language, technical skill tests and physical examinations.
6. Psychological characteristics including personality, job interests and general abilities.

7. Selection criteria including selection ratio and weighting structure of different aspects of the job requirements for various positions.
8. Person–job fit with candidates' job adaptability, suitability and performance of the personnel selected using similar procedures.
9. Non-procedural information including personal relationships and top-down interventions.

In addition, multiple indicators were used to measure the effectiveness of personnel selection including absenteeism, accident rate, productivity, technical skill ratings, training ratings, performance ratings by supervisors and peers, number of awards, work attitudes, job preference, intention of leaving the company, relationships with direct supervisors and subordinates at work, use of ability potentials, and adaptations at work.

Table 3.1 and Table 3.2 present the general results of this study. It is shown that personal archive information and ability requirements were among the most utilized personnel information, whereas non-procedural information, performance appraisal results and psychological ability information were among the least utilized ones. The multiple regression analysis of personnel information with the person–job fit indicator showed that non-procedural personnel information had a negative effect on the degree of person–job fit while the utilization of other personnel information had different influences on the quality of person–job fit in Chinese companies.

Table 3.1 Personnel information utilization

Selection information	Mean	SD
Job characteristics	3.45	0.63
Ability requirements	3.74	0.66
Organizational environment	3.60	0.74
Personal archives	3.99	0.54
Appraisal results	2.90	1.12
Psychological characteristics	3.01	0.69
Selection criteria	3.52	0.72
Non-procedural information	2.02	0.74
Person-job fit	3.48	0.85

Scale = 1–5; 1 = very low level, 5 = very high level.

Table 3.2 The effectiveness of personnel selection

Effectiveness indicators	Mean	SD
Quantitative performance	4.13	0.59
Quantitative appraisal	3.94	0.49
Qualitative appraisal	3.05	0.57
Motivational appraisal	3.72	0.55
Interpersonal appraisal	3.64	0.64
Adaptability appraisal	3.29	0.81

Scale = 1–5; 1 = very low level, 5 = very high level.

The results of this study present a general picture of information utilization patterns in personnel selection in Chinese industrial organizations. Among other indicators, the two key predictors in the Chinese personnel selection appeared to be (i) person–job fit, and (ii) non-procedural information. The results revealed that the person–job fit indicator had positive effects on effectiveness of personnel selection, while non-procedural information showed more negative effects on personnel performance. Adopting non-procedural information would largely reduce the effectiveness of personnel selection and appraisal.

The main suggestion from these results was that instead of ignoring the non-procedural information which was actually often affecting the selection process, identifying and structuring the degree and effects of non-procedural information would certainly enhance the quality of selection and decision-making.

SELECTION AND APPRAISAL IN STATE-OWNED COMPANIES AND JOINT VENTURES

In recent years much attention has been paid to the selection and appraisal practice in different kinds of Chinese industrial organizations, especially State-owned enterprises and international joint-venture companies. Wang, Drenth and Koopman (1994) reported the results of an international collaborative project on human resource management in China, comparing State-owned companies and joint ventures. In a large-scale field study, 40 companies were investigated (20 State-owned vs. 20 joint ventures). Altogether, ten aspects of human resource management were measured: personnel selection and placement, personnel training, performance appraisal, career development and promotion, pay and rewards, participation and trade unions, quality control, management by objectives, corporate culture compatibility, and risk management. Table 3.3 presents the HRM formalization scores from those companies. The results show significant differences between the two kinds of enterprises in most of HRM practice. In general, Chinese State-owned enterprises had more formalized procedures in performance appraisal, whereas joint ventures were better at personnel selection, placement, promotion, career development and risk management.

SOME METHODOLOGICAL CONCERNS

In using quantitative measurement in personnel selection and appraisal in China, some methodological concerns about the quality of assessment instruments were raised. From recent Chinese experience of selection and appraisal, several methodological issues need to be mentioned:

- independent criteria
- social desirability effect
- psychometric training
- rating bias.

Table 3.3   HRM formalization scores in State-owned companies and international joint ventures

HRM aspects	Chinese State-owned (N = 20)	Joint ventures (N = 20)
Selection and placement	5.90	7.40*
Personnel training	2.20	3.10
Performance appraisal	7.80	6.40*
Career development and promotion	2.30	6.30*
Pay and rewards	6.10	7.20*
Participation and trade unions	3.40	2.10
Quality control	4.30	4.20
Management by objectives	6.40	6.10
Corporate culture compatibility	na	5.80
Risk management	3.50	4.80*

Scale: 1 = very low, 8 = very high; na: not available.
* Significant difference.

Adopting independent criteria in personnel selection

Although some recent studies in personnel selection used tests and assessment data as predictors, there were few well-designed validation studies in which predictors were tested by independent criteria or real performance data. Often, self-rating of performance and satisfaction was obtained from the same questionnaire and assessment scales, which by itself had close relationships with the ratings of the predictor measures from the same instruments and by the same respondents. This would result in fake and inflated correlations between predictors and criteria. It is therefore crucial that independent measures are adopted in selection and appraisal studies by different raters or sources so that more adequate validity evidence could be obtained.

The control or elimination of social desirability effects

For a long time, social and ideological influences were quite significant on personnel evaluation, personal archives and selection in China. Personnel assessment, especially for cadres, was traditionally considered to be an organizational control. Therefore, the social desirability effect should be seriously addressed and controlled in personnel selection, appraisal and decisions. Since many items in leadership appraisal instruments were direct expressions of socially desirable concepts, such as political predispositions or public relations, special attention needs to be paid to possible bias in question design and ratings. In addition, in using the role-set methods of assessment, the ratings might be under-estimated or over-estimated if interpersonal relationships among the role-set were over-emphasized and turned into strong social desirability.

The training of psychometric knowledge and rating skills

The Chinese personnel evaluation and selection for the 1950s and 1960s, before the economic reform, were mostly qualitative, mainly based on political criteria and conducted by personnel departments. For the new practice in leadership and personnel appraisal there has been a great need in training of personnel psychological theories and appraisal techniques for people at various levels of organizations in order to eliminate rating errors and judgement bias. Since the mid-1980s, to meet the new needs of personnel management systems, many special training programmes in personnel management have been developed and offered to personnel managers by various companies, of which the learning of psychometric principles and appraisal methods is an important part. Many industries, particularly international joint ventures, require that their managers and supervisors join those training programmes to learn appraisal techniques and performance appraisal so as to better carry out their management responsibilities. Moreover, a number of universities and research institutes have offered training programmes in selection and appraisal for managers, party secretaries and supervisors from various industries and governmental organizations. Trainees are usually required to take part in field projects at local enterprises. This has not only popularized the theoretical knowledge and methods of selection and appraisal, but also established close working relationships between psychologists and practitioners, managers and governmental officials.

Adaptation issues and rating bias

In recent years many selection and appraisal instruments have been translated from the West and have needed to be adapted to the Chinese work situations. Chen (1983) called for special attention to methodological issues in adapting Western tests and developing models of Chinese psychological testing in industrial psychological research and applications. Chen (1987) reported the results of a recent study on rating biases of commonly used leadership appraisal scales in Chinese enterprises. Several factors were found to be biased, severely affecting the accuracy of ratings:

- leniency or severity of ratings;
- conservative bias, such as regression towards the mean and restriction of rating range; and
- halo effects.

It was also shown that there were five main defects in the current personnel appraisal activities in Chinese organizations:

1. Ambiguity in the meanings of appraisal items, e.g. some items were too general and global.
2. Lack of training of rating skills, especially in dealing with negative statements.
3. Lack of familiarity and supplementary information about the ratees.
4. Raters' attitudes or favouritism toward certain ratees.
5. Rater irresponsibility.

This study and other relevant work suggested that the systematic training of personnel psychology and assessment be organized for factory managers and supervisors in personnel and labour management. More reliable and valid instruments of personnel appraisal need to be developed to improve personnel appraisal in the reform of personnel systems in China.

TOWARDS AN INTEGRATED APPROACH TO SELECTION, APPRAISAL AND DECISIONS

Several characteristics of an integrated approach to selection, appraisal and decisions are revealed from recent developments in personnel selection and appraisal in China:

- multi-faceted models of assessment and appraisal;
- mass assessment and organizational appraisal;
- procedural and non-procedural control; and
- multi-stage selection and decisions.

Multi-faceted model of personnel assessment

One significant feature of the Chinese approach to assessment and appraisal is the use of a multi-facet comprehensive model with cognitive, social and moral characteristics. From the ancient Chinese view of a three-dimensional predisposition (basics, capability and moral) and the Imperial Examination Systems with four types of appraisal (ability, morality, performance and seniority), to the three-dimensional scale (performance, maintenance, and character) of leadership assessment in the 1980s, a holistic appraisal has been emphasized and implemented.

Mass assessment and organizational appraisal

Another important feature of the Chinese approach is the emphasis on mass evaluation and organizational appraisal with a core component of team assessment. To a large extent, evaluation and assessment in China has had a collective nature, in comparison with the individual style of evaluation in Western countries. Usually, in selecting cadres from the ordinary faculty, interview evaluation and group discussions will be conducted among supervisors, co-workers and colleagues from the same working units in order to formulate a general picture of the candidate. Most recent selection practices involve wide mass assessment and multi-level organizational appraisal.

Procedural and non-procedural control

In most selection and appraisal activities there is a feature for procedural orientation, i.e. a relatively similar formal procedure is followed under the State personnel policy and labour regulations. More effort has also been put into the identification and control of non-procedural factors (especially personal relationships, top-down administrative interventions, etc.) which often distort the normal process of selection and appraisal in organizations. Restructuring those non-procedural factors may reduce bias and unfairness in selection, recruitment and decision-making.

Multi-stage selection and decisions

In recent research into the practice of selection, appraisal and decision-making in China, an integrated approach has been revealed. As a long-term plan for personnel management, a new approach is needed in order to integrate comprehensive evaluations in the multi-stage selection decisions. This is particularly true when senior managers or officials are under selection. The multi-stage personnel decision includes the following four stages.

1. Base-line screening stage: screening based on performance in written examinations or background information assessment to shorten the list.
2. Organizational profiling stage: assessment of candidates above the cutoff score through organizational interviews among supervisors, colleagues and key people in the organization by an independent outside selection work team.
3. Team interview interaction stage: face-to-face oral information checking and questioning by a group of experts, supervisors and personnel officials.
4. Person–job–team matching and decision-making stage: personnel information integration and person–job–team matching for final selection and nomination.

In this multi-stage process of decision-making, an integrated approach of selection, appraisal and decisions is adopted, emphasizing multi-level screening, team assessment, comprehensive appraisal and organizational control.

ACKNOWLEDGEMENT

Research was supported by a grant from the Chinese National Science Foundation.

REFERENCES

Chen, J.H. (1995). *A Report of China's National Economy and Social Development*. Beijing: China Planning Press (in Chinese).
Chen, L. (1983). *Essentials of Industrial Psychology*. Hangzhou: Zheijang People's Press (in Chinese).
Chen, L. (1987). Recent research on organizational psychology in China. Paper presented at the Sixth Annual Conference of Chinese Psychology Society, September, Hangzhou.
Chen, N.X. *et al.* (1993). *The Organization and Management of the Chinese Labour Market*. Beijing: Economics and Management Press (in Chinese).
Li, C.G., Song, X.H. and Li, J. (1989). *An Introduction to Chinese Ancient Civil Service Systems*. Beijing: Labour and Personnel Press (in Chinese).

Liang, K.G., Deng, T., Xu, Y.L. and Fu, Y.H. (1991). An application of assessment centre in managerial potential evaluation and its construct validity. *Chinese Journal of Applied Psychology*, **7** (4), 50–57 (in Chinese).

Lin, C.D. (1983). Methodology of Chinese ancient psychological testing. In S. Pan and J.F. Gao (eds.), *Studies on Chinese Ancient Psychological Thinking*, pp. 304–312. NanChang: Jiangxi People's Press (in Chinese).

Lin, W.Q., Chen, L. (Long) and Wang, D. (1987). The construction of the CPM Scale for leadership behavior appraisal. *Acta Psychologica Sinica*, **19** (2), 199–207 (in Chinese).

Lu, H.J. (1986). An application of situational simulation appraisal in selecting of managerial personnel. *Information on Psychological Sciences*, **2** (in Chinese).

Lu, H.J. (1991). *Cross-Cultural Theories for Human Resource Development*. Shanghai: BaiJia Press (in Chinese).

Ma, H. and Sun, S.Q. (1995). *Economic Situation and Prospect of China*. Beijing: China Development Press (in Chinese).

Misumi, J. (1985). *The Behavioral Science of Leadership*. Ann Arbor: University of Michigan Press.

Peterson, M. (1988). PM theory in Japan and China: What's in it for the United States? *Organizational Dynamics*, pp.22b.

Wang, Z.M. (1989). Human resource management in China: Recent trends. In R. Pieper (ed.), *Human Resources Management: An International Comparison*, pp. 195–210. Berlin: Walter de Gruyter.

Wang, Z.M. (1991). Recent developments in industrial and organizational psychology in People's Republic of China. In C. Cooper and R.T. Robertson (eds.), *International Review of Industrial and Organizational Psychology*. London: John Wiley.

Wang, Z.M. (1993). Culture, economic reform and the role of industrial/organizational psychology in China. In M.D. Dunnette and L.M. Hough (eds.), *Handbook of Industrial and Organizational Psychology*, 2nd edition, pp. 689–726. Palo Alto, CA: Consulting Psychologists Press.

Wang, Z.M. (1995). An integrated task analysis for Chinese pilot assessment selection. *Chinese Ergonomics* (in press) (in Chinese).

Wang, Z.M., Drenth, P.J.D. and Koopman, P.L. (1994). Human resource management practices in China, Paper presented at *23rd International Congress of Applied Psychology*, 17–22 July, Madrid, Spain.

Wang, Z.M. and Fan, B.N. (1990). The task structure and information processing requirement of decision making on director responsibility systems in enterprises. *Chinese Journal of Applied Psychology*, **5** (1), 1–8 (in Chinese).

Wang, Z.M. and Wang, Y.B. (1989). Some characteristics and strategies of personnel decisions in Chinese enterprises. *Chinese Journal of Applied Psychology*, **4** (3), 8–14 (in Chinese).

Wang, Z.M. and Wang, Y.B. (1991). The network structure of information and decision support strategies in personnel decision making. Chinese Journal of Applied Psychology, **6** (3), 18–25 (in Chinese).

Wu, L.L. (1986). A job analysis of management cadres in enterprises. *Chinese Journal of Applied Psychology*, **1** (3), 12–16 (in Chinese).

Xu, L.C. (1987). Recent development in organizational psychology in China. In B. Bass (ed.), *Advances in Organizational Psychology: An International Review*, pp. 42–251. London: Sage Publications.

Xu, L.C., Chen, L. (Long), Wang, D. and Xue, A.Y. (1985). The role of psychology in enterprise management. *Acta Psychologica Sinica*, **17** (4), 339–345 (in Chinese).

Zhang, H.C. (1988). Psychological measurement in China. *International Journal of Psychology*, **23**, 101–117.

Zhang, P.Q. (1986). *Personnel Assessment in Industrial and Governmental Organizations*. Beijing: Beijing Science and Technology Press (in Chinese).

Chapter 4

International Assessment and Selection

Viv Shackleton

Aston Business School, Aston University, Birmingham, UK

Sue Newell

Warwick Business School, University of Warwick, Coventry, UK

INTRODUCTION

Most human resource management textbooks and many company vision statements make reference to the fact that 'people are our greatest asset'. Attracting, developing and retaining high quality personnel is seen as a key to success (Pfeffer, 1994). Yet increasingly, as firms make their plans to employ and develop core employees, they need to consider the labour market in international, rather than domestic, terms. This is because successful companies are increasingly operating at a global, rather than a national, level and this trend appears set to continue and intensify. Within Europe, the opening up of the Single European Market in 1992 has been a further spur to companies to move beyond national borders.

Bartlett and Ghoshal (1989) identify different strategies that companies are using to expand into this global market. In some cases companies operate as *international* organizations, transferring services and products developed in the home country to markets overseas, so that the world is treated as a portfolio of market places. Other companies operate as *transnationals*, seeing the world as a reservoir of resources and capabilities which can be captured and utilized to provide a powerful source of innovation in products and services. It is the latter strategy that Bartlett and Ghoshal assume to be the more successful long-term strategy for ensuring competitive advantage. From a recruitment and selection perspective this has enormous implications, as will be seen below.

International Handbook of Selection and Assessment, Edited by N. Anderson and P. Herriot.
© 1997 John Wiley & Sons Ltd.

However, whichever strategy is adopted, there is likely to be a much greater emphasis on internationally mobile employees (Bruce, 1989). It is true, of course, that even in large multinationals the great majority of employees will not be internationally mobile, and local conditions of employment will remain the norm for the majority (Hendry, 1994). However, a small core of international employees will be a key to successful globalization. So the focus will be on the international mobility of particular groups of employees. Atkinson (1989) identifies four such groups, namely senior managers, leading scientific and technical staff, young managers during their development programmes, and graduate recruits.

Senior managers are the group which is seen to be most crucial for developing the business overseas, but suitably experienced international senior managers are in short supply. For example, Scullion (1992) found that two-thirds of the 45 British and Irish firms that he looked at had experienced such a shortage, and an even larger proportion envisaged such shortages in the future. Atkinson (1989) found very similar proportions, even though, as he noted, the numbers of such employees are very small in virtually all firms. He described them as 'numerically insignificant but qualitatively vital'. Atkinson also found that most firms relied on recruiting such personnel externally, rather than developing this international experience from within the organization. This is one of the major reasons for the shortage itself. However, Atkinson also noted that, in response to this shortage, companies were putting more emphasis on designing development programmes for young managers and graduates which could eventually feed into these senior positions. European initiatives, such as the ERASMUS programme, which aims to develop comparability in qualifications across countries, to promote language development, and to encourage student mobility, are also facilitating such company developments, even though the number of students involved is small. For example, ERASMUS originally aimed to involve 10% of the student population in such exchanges by 1992/93, but the actual numbers are much smaller (The Higher, 1991).

SELECTING MANAGERS FOR AN INTERNATIONAL COMPANY: THE ROLE OF EXPATRIATES

Adopting an international strategy for global expansion is likely to lead to the extensive use of expatriate managers. These are managers from the home country who are recruited to work overseas. Such expatriates will typically fill the key positions in the overseas operation (Adler, 1984). Selection of such expatriates is, therefore, crucial as they will determine the success or failure of the overseas operation. As early as 1966 (Byrnes, 1966) it was noted that selection and training for international assignments were inadequate. This situation appears to have changed little, with few companies systematically attempting to develop selection methods which accurately predict overseas assignment success (Adler and Kiggundu, 1983).

Research in this area of selection is limited, although it is clear that the successful use of expatriate managers depends on a number of variables, including technical competence on the job, personality traits or relational abilities, environmental variables and the family situation of the individual (Tung, 1982). Moreover, research suggests that a majority of firms base their selection decisions mainly on technical abilities and do not assess the individual's personality, adaptation skills or family issues (Mendenhall and Oddou, 1985; Marx, 1994). Perhaps not surprisingly, therefore, the failure rate for expatriate assignments is high. In the United Kingdom, it is estimated that one in seven such assignments ends in failure. In the United States, Mendenhall and Oddou (1985) estimated that between 1965 and 1985 the premature return rate for expatriates had fluctuated between 25% and 40%, while Hogan and Goodson (1990) give a figure of 40% for failure in overseas assignments.

The cost of such a high level of failure is enormous (Mendenhall and Oddou, 1985; Adler and Kiggundu, 1983). These include start-up costs, costs of increased salaries as a result of working abroad, opportunity costs, psychological costs for the expatriate brought on by the recognition of failure, damage to the credibility of the parent organization in the eyes of host country nationals, and the costs of projects that have been left unfinished (Worst, 1992). Given this failure rate it would seem important to develop more stringent selection methods which included the evaluation of an individual's ability to adapt to the new culture. Utility analysis demonstrates very clearly how even small improvements in selection validities can improve job performance markedly (Schmidt *et al.*, 1979). Thus, much work remains to be done in this area of predicting expatriate success on overseas assignments.

SELECTING MANAGERS FOR TRANSNATIONAL COMPANIES: THE ROLE OF FOREIGN EMPLOYEES

Recruitment for the transnational company, however, depends on the selection of individuals from the countries in which it is developing the business, in order to fully utilize the resources and capabilities present in these countries. In this strategy, rather than attempting to export national ways of operating, cultural diversity is encouraged and extolled. However, this strategy will only be successful if those recruited from the importing country have the skills, expertise and attitudes that are needed to develop the business in this overseas location. While the selection of personnel for overseas assignments (expatriates) is not without its difficulties, as already noted, the selection of personnel from different countries is likely to be an even greater challenge.

Any company wishing to recruit someone from outside its own country will have problems because there are a number of challenges to be overcome. Hendry (1994) lists some of these (p. 152):

- Lack of knowledge of local labour markets.
- Lack of presence in the other country which makes it harder to attract good candidates.
- Ignorance of the local education system and the status of qualifications.

- Variability in the experience and qualifications of graduates, given the different structures of national systems (e.g. German students graduate in their late twenties).
- Trying to transfer native recruitment methods to other countries where different systems may apply.
- Language and cultural problems at interviews.
- Pay differences and expectations about pay.
- Lack of pension portability (less an issue when recruiting graduates).
- Constraints on, and attitudes to, mobility.

Selection is thus only one of the challenges to such international recruitment, but it is nevertheless an important issue which companies need to consider. This is because approaches to selection and recruitment vary significantly across cultures. In this chapter we look at some of these differences and address the implications of these for successful recruitment by transnational companies.

The traditional psychometric view of selection and recruitment can be compared with an obstacle race, where the recruiting organization puts up the hurdles over which potential recruits have to jump. The recruit who manages to get over the most hurdles, while knocking the fewest over, will be taken on by the company. In this perspective, recruitment and selection are seen as a managerial decision-making task, in which managers have to erect 'cunning hurdles' to outwit all but the most able candidates. These 'hurdles' might be in the form of interviews, references, psychological tests, group discussions and so on. One of the main problems with this approach is that it ignores the fact that the candidates themselves are making decisions throughout the process. They have to decide whether to follow up a particular job advertisement, complete an application form, attend the selection process and take up any job offer.

THE EXCHANGE PERSPECTIVE

In the light of these limitations, Herriot (1984) developed an alternative exchange perspective. This views selection as a process of negotiation between two parties— the employing company and the potential recruit. Throughout the selection process both parties are exchanging information which allows each to address the 'fit' between their own expectations and the expectations of the other. Where there is an evident lack of fit, as perceived by either party, the exchange will either be terminated, or some form of negotiation will take place which accommodates the differences. The key to the success of selection from this perspective is that both parties are open and honest about their expectations so that the other 'side' can accurately make a decision as to the fit. The selection methods that are used during this process of exchange should thus allow both parties to learn more about the expectations of the other. A candidate learns more about the organization, its culture and its work environment and his/her own potential role within this, both long-term and short-term. The organization learns more about the individual candidate, his or her personality, abilities, skills, attitudes and expectations.

One can imagine that this exchange might well be more problematic when the two parties are from different national backgrounds. This is exacerbated by the differences in selection methods used in different countries, as will be discussed below. Thus, an overseas candidate, faced with selection methods which are unfamiliar and/or perceived as invalid, may be more likely to perceive that s/he will not 'fit in'. And the recruiting company may likewise feel that the overseas candidate will not 'fit in' because s/he does not do well on the various tests and assessments—even though this is because of a lack of familiarity with the 'rules of the game' rather than incompetence.

In terms of the implications of this for international recruitment, there are a number of fundamental differences between the United Kingdom and other countries, for example in graduate recruitment (Keenan, 1991). Other countries do not operate any equivalent to the British 'milk-round', where companies come to university campuses on particular dates arranged with the university career service, and undertake first-round interviews with all those graduates who are interested in them. In Europe the system of direct applications is encouraged, stimulated by company links with academics and with students on work placement. This means that UK firms that do not have a strong presence in other countries through personal links will find it much more difficult to attract graduates from these countries.

Research has found that British firms have been slow to consider attracting overseas graduates, rather than 'home-grown' ones. Keenan (1991), in a survey of 127 large UK firms and 62 similar French firms, found 45% of the French firms were actively recruiting non-French graduates, while only 20% of the UK firms were seriously looking to recruit non-UK graduates. Furthermore, of those not involved in this type of recruitment, only 25% of the UK firms indicated that they were planning to do this, compared with 60% of the French firms. French firms thus appear to be embracing the concept of international recruitment, at least at the European level, much more seriously than British firms.

At the same time, there are a number of reasons why British firms may need to be more, rather than less, active than their continental equivalents. Most obvious is the fact that English is the language of international business, so that British graduates are attractive recruits. Given the predicted shortage of UK multi-lingual graduates, British firms need to look elsewhere to make up the shortfall. Bruce (1989) also found that many British graduates, especially those who achieve high qualifications, are quite willing to move abroad in the early stages of their career. This might be because managerial salaries in the United Kingdom remain lower than in other European countries (Scullion, 1992).

Keenan (1991) goes on to suggest what UK firms need to do in order to be able to attract from the wider European pool, if not the international pool. First, it is necessary to identify additional qualities or skills, such as foreign languages, that people will need to exhibit if they are to operate effectively in an international context. Secondly, it will be necessary to develop an understanding of the different educational systems that operate in other countries, so that they know where graduates that they want to attract are located. For example, in France the universities tend to attract less able students than the Grandes Écoles. Lastly, they need to identify institutions that have developed truly international courses. Those institutions that offer European degrees, in terms of both the syllabus and the students attending the courses are likely to provide the richest source of future international employees. It is these institutions that need to be targeted.

Turning to look at international differences in selection methods, a good example of the impact of cultural diversity is evident from recent research which has compared the methods used across different countries within Europe. This illustrates that even in countries that are geographically quite close, there is tremendous diversity.

DIFFERENCES IN SELECTION METHODS

There is only a small amount of empirical evidence on the relative use of the various methods of selection by different countries. Thus, as Sparrow and Hiltrop (1994) point out, we must be careful in making sweeping generalizations, because without a large-scale comparative study, the data that are available need to be treated as a 'series of snapshots and insights into national practice' (p. 340). Nevertheless, this does provide an indication of the diversity.

Shackleton and Newell (1991) compared the methods used to recruit managers in France and the United Kingdom. The samples for this survey were drawn from directories listing the top 1000 companies in each country. Two hundred and fifty companies from each of these two directories were randomly selected and a questionnaire was mailed to the personnel manager of each. These questionnaires asked a range of questions relating to the frequency with which a variety of selection methods was used. The results from this survey found that while larger companies in both countries tended to use selection methods that psychologists advocate as having higher reliability and validity (e.g. assessment centres and psychological tests), French companies, in general, continued to use methods that have lower reliabilities and validities, especially graphology. Companies in the United Kingdom also made extensive use of references that are known to have a low validity in the typical open format. Moreover, on virtually every method that was included in the survey (interviews, references, psychological tests, hand-writing analysis, biodata and assessment centres) there was a significant difference between its use in France and the United Kingdom. For example, even though interviews were the dominant selection method in both countries, the format of these interviews differed. Over 90% of the respondents from the French companies used more than one interview for each candidate, compared with only about 60% of the respondents from British firms.

In an attempt to look more broadly at the diversity in selection across Europe, Shackleton and Newell (1994) expanded this comparison to include Belgium, Germany and Italy. The same questionnaire and sampling method were used so that direct comparison across five European countries was possible. The overall results from this comparison can be seen in Table 4.1. Also included in Table 4.1 are indications of the extent of usage of the various methods in Australia and North America. The data from Australia are directly comparable, because Di

Table 4.1 Percentage use of different selection methods to recruit managers all of the time and some of the time

	Interview		Application form		References		Personality tests		Cognitive tests		Handwriting		Biodata		Assessment centre	
	All	Some	All	Some	All	Some	All	Some	All	Some	All	Some	All	Some	All	Some
UK	91	100	70	93	74	96	10	64	12	70	0	3	4	19	4	59
France	94	100	89	98	11	78	17	62	8	49	17	77	0	4	0	19
Germany	60	100	83	100	76	100	2	19	2	21	0	9	2	11	3	60
Italy	96	100	46	68	32	88	8	20	8	20	0	12	0	0	0	8
Belgium/Flemish	92	100	75	96	15	85	35	83	30	77	2	21	12	34	2	42
Belgium/French	100	100	92	96	13	67	25	62	32	73	12	44	4	8	0	24
Australia	91	99	60	86	77	98	12	61	11	56	0	3	10	18	3	22
North America (estimates*)	99	99	Unknown		91	97	16	33	16	50	Very rare		6	11	16	44

* The data for North America are based on various sources and provide only an indication of the overall extent of usage.

Milia, Smith and Brown (1994) used the same questions as Shackleton and Newell (1994). The data on North America are not based on the same set of questions but on a number of published studies of selection method usage (Rowe, Williams and Day, 1994; Gowing and Slivinski, 1994; Muchinsky, 1994). For this reason the North American data present a range of reported usage, rather than specific percentages.

The conclusion drawn from the analysis of these data was that the methods used to select managers vary significantly across countries in Europe. From the perspective of international recruitment these differences are likely to be important. For example, an Italian candidate, on the basis of common practice in his or her own country, is likely to expect to be faced with some interviews and to have a reference taken up about his or her suitability. However, if an Italian candidate applies for a job with a Belgian company, and that company uses selection methods typical in Belgium, then he or she will be asked to sit various cognitive and personality tests, may be asked to supply some handwriting for analysis if the company is based in the French-speaking part of Belgium, and may have to go to an assessment centre, as well as go through the more familiar interviews and supply references. Given this dramatic difference, expectations of both parties (company and candidate) are unlikely to be met.

SUMMARY OF SOME OF THE DIFFERENCES IN SELECTION METHODS

Since Shackleton and Newell (1991), there have been a number of studies of international differences in selection methods. There are some difficulties in drawing comparison between studies and countries, since different samples and methods have been used. In addition, there are methodological limitations in many of the existing surveys. However, it is possible tentatively to highlight some differences by amalgamating the various studies. The published work includes Shimmin (1989), Income Data Service (1990), Smith and Abrahamsen (1992), Bournois (1993), Brewster et al. (1993), Gunnigle (1993), Vincente (1993), reports from the Price Waterhouse/Cranfield project (various years), a special edition of the *International Journal of Selection and Assessment* (1994), and Shackleton and Newell (1994).

Application forms, biodata and curriculum vitae

In some countries the application form is the dominant way in which individuals apply for jobs (e.g. the United Kingdom, the United States, Ireland), while in other countries the c.v. is much more prevalent (e.g. Denmark). In the United Kingdom, application forms are increasingly being tailored to the needs of the specific company and the specific job within that company, with the questions designed to assess competencies which will be related to success on the job. However, in Germany there is much more use of standard application documents. This is linked to the involvement of works councils and formalized vocational training systems in Germany which place more emphasis on ensuring uniformity of information.

Biodata, as a systematic way of using information about past performance and life style, are less commonly used in all countries for which data are available, despite the good predictive validities that can be achieved with this method (Drakeley, 1989).

References

While the reference can be described in a number of ways (e.g. testimonial), it refers to the assessment of the individual by some third party. In Ireland, the reference is the most popular source of selection. It is also common in the United Kingdom, Australia and North America, although it tends to be used as a final check on a selection decision, rather than as a predictor on its own. In Belgium, references are often taken up over the phone. However, in other countries, including France, Sweden, the Netherlands and Portugal, references are much less common.

Interviews

Interviews are the most common selection method used, irrespective of country. However, there are major differences in the format and structure of the interview, as seen above in the comparison of France and the United Kingdom. The interview remains dominant in selection globally, despite the fact that research has repeatedly found it to have relatively low validity in the commonly employed unstructured form.

In certain countries, notably the United Kingdom and the United States, competency-based interviews are becoming increasingly popular, especially with large companies that recruit a considerable number of graduates. There are a number of forms of competency-based interviews which are variously described as behavioural, situational or criterion-based. They share the common feature of comprising questions that systematic research has shown tap job-related competencies and differentiate good performers from poor ones. Such attempts to re-model the usual unstructured interviews are aimed at making the interview more valid and fair, and look likely to increase in popularity.

Graphology

Graphology is concerned with deducing personality descriptions or behaviour predictions from a sample of an individual's handwriting. It is most common in French-speaking cultures (especially France and francophone Belgium). While in most countries this technique is typically portrayed as having no validity, France shows considerable enthusiasm for the method. Undergraduate students of business in France may well have lectures from graphologists advocating the benefits of such a technique (Bulois, 1995). Bournois (1993) suggests that its popularity is due to the fact that it is 'quick and cheap'. However, this does not account for the cultural specificity of its use. Interestingly, in studies of methods of selection in

North America, graphology is not even reported as a *potential* method of selection, suggesting that it is not used as a technique by companies in the United States and Canada, even French-speaking Canada.

Psychological tests

In some countries, notably Britain and Belgium, the use of psychological tests is fairly widespread and growing, especially in large companies. In some countries personality tests are more often used than cognitive tests (e.g. Australia), while in other countries cognitive tests are more often used than personality tests (e.g. the United States). However, the results in Table 4.1 shows that there is a high relationship between the use of these two types of psychological tests. Thus, both types of tests are rarely used in some countries (e.g. Germany and Italy), while both types are much more common in other countries (e.g. Belgium, the United Kingdom and Australia). However, in other countries their use is limited because of social, economic, political and religious influences (Sparrow and Hiltrop, 1994). For example, the Catholic Church tends to disapprove of psychological tests, so that in predominantly catholic countries (e.g. Italy) their use may be limited. In apparent contradiction to this, though, there is evidence that test use is growing in Portugal. At the same time, unions tend to favour tests in so far as they can counter patronage and nepotism. In other countries, such as Sweden, there is increasing concern over the use of tests because they are seen as an invasion of privacy.

Assessment centres

Again, there are large national differences in the frequency of use of assessment centres. For example, they are fairly common in large organizations in the United Kingdom, the United States, Belgium, Denmark and Germany, but relatively uncommon in Australia, France, Switzerland, Spain and Italy. However, to date, the published comparative analyses do not allow many comments to be made about the content of assessment centres. Anecdotal evidence suggests that an assessment centre in the United Kingdom is likely to be very different from one in, say, Germany or France. A typical assessment centre in these latter countries is unlikely to include psychometric tests, while in the United Kingdom and the United States, testing as part of the process is common practice. More qualitative analysis is needed to really understand these differences.

Other methods of selection

In studies of North America, evidence is emerging that new methods are being used as part of the selection process. Muchinsky (1994), for example, looks at the use and effectiveness of integrity (honesty) testing, drug testing and even genetic testing to assess, respectively, moral character, drug usage and genetic compatibility. However, their usage is not yet widespread even in North America and these techniques have not really been diffused to Europe or Australia, at least as reported in surveys of selection method usage. (See also Murphy, Chapter 16 in this volume.)

EXPLANATIONS FOR INTERNATIONAL DIFFERENCES IN SELECTION METHODS

In trying to understand the observed differences in selection methods used in different countries, national culture appears to be the most obvious starting point. Hoecklin (1993) suggests that in Anglo-Saxon cultures, selection methods are devised to test how far an individual is likely to be able to contribute to the tasks of the organization. Assessment centres, intelligence tests and measurements of competence, each of which can be designed to measure such attributes, will thus be the norm in such cultures. In Germanic cultures, selection will focus on the quality and specialization of the education standard reached. Finally, in Latin cultures (as well as Far Eastern cultures), selection methods will focus on establishing how well the candidate is likely to get on with those in his/her prospective working group. There are two aspects that are seen as important in such cultures. First, the elitism of the higher educational establishments attended, for example attending a prestigious Grand École in France, is taken as 'evidence' of managerial quality. Secondly, the interpersonal style of the individual and his or her ability to develop networks. Such abilities will typically be assessed during interviews, but if tests are used they are likely to be tests that assess personality, communication and social skills, rather than the more Anglo-Saxon tests that measure intelligence or cognitive ability.

Hoecklin suggests that these differences in the focus of assessment, and thus the selection methods used, can be understood in terms of the relative position of countries on the cultural dimensions of universalism–particularism, achievement–ascription and the differences in how people from different cultures perceive the organization (see also Rousseau and Tinsley, Chapter 2 in this volume). Thus, countries that are more universalist and achievement-oriented (e.g. the United Kingdom, North America and Australia) tend to use more objective criteria, which are measurable, such as intellectual abilities or technical skills, and so assess the ability to satisfy technical task demands. More particularist, ascription-oriented countries (e.g. France and Italy) are more concerned with assessing whether the personality of the individual is likely to match the work group. Thus, for example, in France and Italy there is a tendency to use a number of interviews and inter-viewers. This is sensible if one believes that organizational success depends on the ability to function in a 'web of relationships and hierarchies' (p. 78). In this context, it is more plausible to assess interpersonal skills than more objective technical skills. (See also Schneider *et al.*, Chapter 19 in this volume.)

THE ROLE OF PSYCHOLOGY AND PERSONNEL SPECIALISTS

There are two other factors that may account for some of the national differences, namely the role played by applied psychology and by personnel and human resource management (HRM) specialists.

Different countries have embraced the scientific method in the social sciences, especially psychology, to varying extents. In the United States, Australia, the

United Kingdom, the Netherlands and Flanders (Belgium), for example, psychology is well established in universities and business schools. Moreover, the psychology embraced is a scientific, applied variety. The enormous research base of industrial and organizational psychology in the United States is known and taught. American and British textbooks are used in further and higher education. It may be no coincidence that it is in these countries that we find the use of more valid and reliable selection techniques.

Similarly, the 'professionalization' of psychology and HRM is different in different countries. Some countries, including Belgium, Denmark, Finland, Italy and the United States have laws regulating psychologists. Britain has legal protection for the term 'Chartered Psychologist' and the British Psychological Society (BPS) is currently moving towards proposing and supporting an Act of Parliament to protect the more general term 'Psychologist'. This is not the case in some other countries. Moreover, the role of the BPS in Britain is a relatively strong one for encouraging professional practices among its constituents. The same cannot always be said for the psychological societies in some other countries. This 'professionalization' of psychology may go some way to explaining the take-up of testing, assessment centres, etc. and to the absence of less scientifically respectable methods such as graphology, or indeed the absence of any method other than interviews.

In similar vein, the professionalization of HRM can be seen to help or hinder the diffusion of different methods. In France, for example, the Association Nationale des Directeurs et Cadres de la Fonction Personnel (ANDCP), a professional society for HRM practitioners, does not play a strong role in the education, training and research of HRM. In contrast, the Institute of Personnel and Development (IPD) in Britain plays more of a role in accrediting HRM courses; educating its membership with publications, conferences and its own training courses; sponsoring research; and laying down guidelines for professional practice, including recruitment and selection.

So, the diffusion and adoption of selection methods that are valid, reliable, fair and acceptable to all parties may well be more likely in countries where the relevant professional societies are strong and themselves influenced by a social scientific tradition. Yet this explanation is only part of a wider factor, i.e. the country's culture, referred to above. Some cultures are more likely to provide fertile ground for the professionalization of a group, or for the acceptance of applied social science, than are others. One cannot underestimate 'cultures' consequences'.

SUCCESSFUL INTERNATIONAL RECRUITMENT

From the point of view of international recruitment, this wide diversity, whatever its origins, may cause confusion and frustrated expectations in those seeking employment in countries other than their own. Yet, as we have seen, recruitment of 'other-nationals' is a major factor in the long-term global success of companies. It might be that simply understanding the differences in methods and approaches that exist between countries, and communicating these to potential candidates, is enough. Then they can modify their expectations concerning the methods they are likely to face if they apply for a job in a foreign country. However, given the importance of expectations and 'mindsets', and their resistance to change, communication alone is unlikely to be enough.

To overcome this problem the most common strategy appears to be simply to devolve selection to allow for local differences in testing and language differences (Hoecklin, 1993). In this strategy the host country is supplied with a set of personal qualities or characteristics they consider to be most important and decisions about the methods used to assess these qualities are left to the managers in the foreign subsidiary. However, this has proved somewhat problematic because of the way these qualities are culturally defined, and the fact that they are often culture-specific. Ikea, the Swedish-based international furniture company, for example, selects individuals whose personal values match those of the organization. So they look for frugality, humbleness, lack of concern for status, attention to costs and a preference for a casual lifestyle. Difficulties have been reported in communicating these values across countries. In one or two languages there is even no easy translation of the adjective 'humble'! Similarly, Body Shop, the British-based retailer of fragrances and toiletries, gives subordinates and peers responsibility for a large part of the interviewing process. The strong cultural bias towards green issues is very prevalent in the recruitment process. But such concerns and values are not always appreciated in countries outside the developed Western world.

A less common, but potentially more successful, strategy was reported by Bulois (1995). Shell recruits graduates for its international division centrally, but arranges assessment centres by country. That is, graduates from the United Kingdom attend a different assessment centre to graduates from Scandinavia, who attend a different assessment centre to graduates from Latin countries. Moreover, the methods used at each of these nationally or regionally focused assessment centres are modified to match more closely the kinds of methods that would be used in the particular countries of those being assessed. They also use assessors from the same cultural or national background.

While there are no published objective data as to the relative success of these approaches, the companies themselves are happy with them. They would appear to overcome the potential problems of requiring candidates to face unfamiliar selection methods. Clearly, comparative case studies are needed in this area.

SUMMARY AND CONCLUSIONS

The world of work is changing fast, as everyone is aware; nowhere more so than in the area of internationalizing. Mergers, acquisitions, take-overs, joint ventures and collaboration across borders are taking place like never before. The truly global product, be it cars, furniture, jeans or audio equipment, is getting ever closer. The people managing this process in the transnational and international companies are themselves more and more international in outlook. Yet recruitment and selection methods seem, for the most part, to have maintained a strange imperviousness to these internationalizing trends. The British or North American undergraduate is no stranger to assessment centres or psychometric tests. The French manager or professional is quite familiar with graphology. Yet each is likely to be unfamiliar with, and even hostile towards, the other country's methods. The Italian undergraduate is unlikely to meet any of these three methods, even if he or she joins an Italian multinational. An appreciation of such diversity is long overdue. Current trends and anecdotal evidence from companies suggest that the future is unlikely to witness an international homogenizing of methods. Rather, it is likely that national preferences will continue to exert a strong influence on selection methods. Making systematic and valid comparisons of other countries' nationals for selection purposes will remain a difficult art.

REFERENCES

Adler, N.J. (1984). Women in international management: Where are they? *California Management Review,* **26,** 78–89.

Adler, N.J. and Kiggundu, M.N. (1983). Awareness at the crossroad: Designing translator-based training programs. In D. Landis and R.W. Brislin (eds.), *Handbook of Intercultural Training,* vol. II, pp. 125–132. New York: Pergamon.

Atkinson, J. (1989). *Corporate Employment Policies for the Single European Market.* IMS report No. 179. University of Sussex: Institute of Manpower Studies.

Bartlett, C.A. and Ghoshal, S. (1989). *Managing Across Borders: The Transnational Solution.* Boston, MA: Harvard Business School Press.

Bournois, F. (1993). France. In C. Brewster, A. Hegewisch, J.T. Lockhart and L. Holden (eds.), *The European Human Resource Management Guide.* London: Academic Press.

Brewster, C., Hegewisch, A., Lockhart, J.T. and Holden, L. (eds.) (1993). *The European Human Resource Management Guide.* London: Academic Press.

Bruce, L. (1989). Wanted: More mongrels in the corporate kennel. *International Management,* January, 35–7.

Bulois, N. (1995). Recruitment in Europe: A study in cultural contrasts. Unpublished MSc dissertation, Aston Business School.

Byrnes, F.C. (1966). Role Shock: An occupational hazard of American technical assistants abroad. *The Annals of the American Academy of Political Social Science,* 95–108.

Di Milia, L., Smith, P. and Brown, D. (1994). Management selection in Australia: A comparison with British and French findings. *International Journal of Assessment and Selection,* **2** (2), 80–90.

Drakeley, R. (1989). Biographical data. In P. Herriot (ed.), *Assessment and Selection in Organisations: Methods and Practice for Recruitment and Appraisal.* Chichester: John Wiley.

Gowing, M. and Slivinski, L. (1994). A review of North American selection procedures: Canada and the USA. *International Journal of Assessment and Selection,* **2** (2), 103–114.

Gunnigle, P. (1993). Ireland. In C. Brewster, A. Hegewisch, J.T. Lockhart, and L. Holden (eds.) *The European Human Resource Management Guide.* London: Academic Press.

Hendry, C. (1994). *Human Resource Strategies for International Growth.* London and New York: Routledge.

Herriot, P. (1984). *Down From the Ivory Tower.* Chichester: John Wiley.

Hoecklin, L.A. (1993). *Managing Cultural Differences for Competitive Advantage.* The Economist Intelligence Unit, Special Report No. P656.

Hogan, G.W. and Goodson, J.R. (1990). The key to expatriate success. *Training and Development Journal,* **44** (1), 50–53.

Income Data Service (1990). *European Management Guide to Recruitment*. Wimbledon: Institute of Personnel Management.

Keenan, T. (1991). Graduate recruitment à la Française. *Personnel Management*, December, 34–37.

Marx, E. (1994). Selecting strategies. *Interviewer*, 8–22 December, 13.

Mendenhall, M.E. and Oddou, G. (1985). The dimensions of expatriate acculturation: A review. *Academy of Management Review*, **10** (1), 39–47.

Muchinsky, P. (1994). A review of individual assessment methods used for personnel selection in North America. *International Journal of Assessment and Selection*, **2** (2), 118–124.

Pfeffer, J. (1994). *Competitive Advantage Through People. Unleashing the Power of the Work Force*. Boston, MA: Harvard Business School Press.

Rowe, P., Williams, M. and Day, A. (1994). Selection procedures in North America. *International Journal of Assessment and Selection*, **2** (2), 74–79.

Schmidt, F.L., Hunter, J.E., McKenzie, R.C. and Muldrow, T.W. (1979). Impact of valid selection procedures on workforce productivity. *Journal of Applied Psychology*, **64**, 604–626.

Scullion, H. (1992). Attracting management globetrotters. *Personnel Management*, January, 28–32.

Shackleton, V.J. and Newell, S. (1991). Management selection. A comparative survey of methods used in top British and French companies. *Journal of Occupational Psychology*, **64** (1), 23–36.

Shackleton, V.J. and Newell, S. (1994). European management selection methods: A comparison of 5 countries. *International Journal of Selection and Assessment*, **2** (2), 91–102.

Shimmin, S. (1989). Selection in a European context. In P. Herriot (ed.), *Assessment and selection in organisations: Methods and practice for recruitment and appraisal*. Chichester: John Wiley.

Smith, A. and Abrahamsen, M. (1992). Patterns of selection in six countries. *The Psychologist*, 205–207.

Sparrow, P. and Hiltrop, J.M. (1994). *European Human Resource Management in Transition*. Hemel Hempstead: Prentice-Hall.

Tung, R.L. (1982). Selection and training procedures of U.S., European and Japanese Multinationals. *California Management Review*, **25** (1), 57–71.

Vincente, C.S. (1993). Human resource management in Spain: Strategic issues, the economic and social framework. In S. Tyson, P. Lawrence, P. Pirson, L. Manzolini and C.S. Vincente (eds.), *Human Resource Management in Europe: Strategic Issues and Cases*. London: Kogan Page.

Worst, J. (1992). Selecting employees for international assignments: What little we do know. Paper presented at the International Congress of Psychology, Brussels, Belgium.

Chapter 5

Network and its Implications for Assessment

JOSÉ M. PRIETO

Department of Individual Differences and Work Psychology, Faculty of Psychology,
Complutense University of Madrid, Campus of Somosaguas, 28223 Madrid, Spain
jmprieto@psi.ucm.es

CRISTINA SIMÓN

Educational Technology Office, Technical University of Madrid, Madrid, Spain

THE ASSUMPTION OF GOING TO WORK

For centuries, a large majority of people used to work at home or in the nearby surroundings, for instance the farm or the workshop. One of the consequences of the Industrial Revolution was that machines allowed workers to earn a living, but kept them hostages within offices and factories. Homeworking had been discouraged during the nineteenth and twentieth centuries by trade unions. However, from 1990 to 1995, shrinking and downsizing companies have forced us to go back to old ways or to begin a new style of out-of-office employment. Under certain circumstances and for certain jobs, going to work starts to be considered a waste of time and money (Coates, 1994). Nowadays it is possible to work at a distance and rely on telematic systems to facilitate communication with the supervisor, co-workers and customers.

For centuries, successful merchants used to make a fortune buying products somewhere and selling products somewhere else. It became clear in the business world that there was a lot of money to be made trading and shipping over long distances. The ability to cross regional or national boundaries, within the framework of import and export activities by appointment to their majesties, was a standard trick of wealthy traders. One of the consequences of the Industrial

International Handbook of Selection and Assessment, Edited by N. Anderson and P. Herriot.
© 1997 John Wiley & Sons Ltd.

Revolution was that a large majority of entrepreneurs and employers almost always wanted to introduce further protectionist legislation in each country against foreign merchants and traders. They were, however, open to free migratory movements of potential workers in so far as it contributed to a reduction in wage claims. By contrast, trade unions favoured protectionist legislation against a foreign workforce but not against foreign employers and merchants.

Technologies backing a networked economy enhance the idea that it is no longer necessary to do the work in the office or to do the trade in a protectionist market. Tiny laptop computers allow workers to make any place their workplace at any time or to connect to potential customers across wired boundaries. For many workers the job is wherever they go, wake up or stay. The main office becomes a support centre. The number of people who work from home at least one business day a week is growing rapidly. In a similar vein, for a new set of customer products, information and services must be made available by vendors and malls that never close. They consider themselves on-line shoppers. With the touch of a finger they can browse product descriptions, flip back and forth, view full colour images and order right on the spot. Conservative estimates indicate that one in eight Europeans working are part-time, white-collar employees at the office and part-time, blue-jeaned employees at home (Moorcroft and Bennett, 1995). Thousands of companies and stores, from large corporations to one-man firms, support their products and services on-line within the wide limits of telecommuterland. Table 5.1 lists some of the dial-up networks and services that already exist. The list is incomplete because, inside telecommuterland, there is not a general register of networked *landers*. Changes are rapid in so far as a merger between two networks takes place without a public notice. Customers ask questions and company representatives respond to user posts in the area devoted to on-line services. Issue-driven libraries serve as official posting areas for demo versions, program patches, screen shots, new jobs and vacancies, training packs, beta testers, press releases, classifieds and frequently asked questions.

By the year 2000 teleworking and electronic trading will be a common activity and not an out-of-the-ordinary setting as it was in 1990 (IBM Europe, 1994). It already raises specific demands in the domain of personnel selection and appraisal and in the realm of customer behaviour. These demands affect both employees and managers, full-time and part-time, skilled or unskilled workers involved in establishing and developing teleworking schemes and occupational categories (Blanch, 1990).

The under 35s is the first genuine computer generation in many European countries. They are the *chip's cohort*, not *generation* X. Telework schemes have already started to influence their careers because they feel at ease in this domain and are aware of its potential. In some countries, like Spain, the under 35s is also the first generation whose second language is English. Both factors interact together to favour the adoption of teleworking and teletrading practices in a very open global market.

Teleworking and teletrading provide a different framework to deal with difficult circumstances such as complaining employees or customers, with care responsibilities of children or the elderly, with minor sick leave or injuries, with a

Table 5.1 Some dial-up networks and services present inside telecommuterland

On-line networks	American Online	Internet
	AT&T Interchange	Minitel
	Bitnet	MCI/DELPHI
	BIX	Microsoft Network
	BT Tymnet	MindVox
	CompuServe	Netcom
	Exec-PC	Prodigy
	GEnie	Sierra Online
	IGC Networks	USENET
	Infovia	The Well
	Interchange	The World BBS
On-line services	Banking and Finance	Investments
	Business Network	Kids
	Computer Support	Leisure
	Connections to external	Magazines
	resources	Membership Service
	Chat and Talk	Newspapers
	Discussion Forums	Professional
	E-mail	Product Support
	Education	Reference
	Entertainment	Search-ability
	Fun	Shopping
	Games	Sports
	Home and Family	Travel
	Health	Weather

physical or a temporary disability, with a long commute from home to the workplace, with persistent interruptions in the job, with projects requiring great dedication from a single person, with peaks and troughs in the workload (Davies, 1995). It is also quite convenient in big cities such as Madrid where overheads are high or the contingent rent of space for expansion or relocation is very expensive.

The introduction of information technologies has been one of the most important phenomena that companies and institutions have faced in the twentieth century. The unavoidable and rapidly growing use of computers and telecommunication networks has had relevant organizational implications for work group collaboration at many levels: economic, social, managerial, psychological and, of course, technological (Olson, 1989). Now it is quite difficult to distinguish when information technologies take full advantage of people in their jobs, and when people take full advantage of information technologies in their jobs. In a similar vein, information technologies have been classified as variegated and highly sophisticated forms of organization, and organizations have been classified as rather conventional and ornate varieties of information technology (Beniger, 1990).

The statement that the introduction of technology brings about important organizational changes emerged in the context of an argument about technological determinism (Peiró, 1984). Key variables affecting success in organizations were systematically analysed, and scientists and practitioners started to recognize their leading role (Peiró, 1990). The Contingency Theory approach (Burns, 1992) considered technology as one of the three main variables determining the structure of organizations, together with environment and size. Classical studies such as those of Woodward (1958) and Perrow (1970), empirically supported this statement, and proposed specific aspects (e.g. the degree of predictability of technology mediated activity) as key issues to be analysed for an effective organizational design. From the very beginning technology was understood not just as a set of more or less complex machinery, but also covering the new forms of organizational activity, procedures and roles associated with it (Prieto *et al.*, 1990).

The great explosion of information technologies during the last 50 years has caused a pervasive introduction of applications to support potentially every activity, from factory work to the highest management decision-making procedures, and mainly addressing clerical tasks (Peiro and Prieto, 1994). It was recently announced by one of the largest software providers, Lotus Development Corporation, that one trillion dollars had been invested by organizations in information technologies in the 1980s. The expected increases in productivity, however, are being questioned by recent research results comparing investment and benefits achieved by companies (Auerbach Report, 1993).

Even if the long assumed improvements in productivity as a result of investment and installation of technology may not turn out to be so great, what is in any case clear is that 'technology is here to stay', and that new forms of working are starting to emerge (Prieto and Martin, 1990). One of the most dramatic changes that information technology allows is precisely the opportunity for workers to perform their activities at a distance, either in groups at scattered centres or simply as individuals from their homes.

The present chapter tries to throw some light on the main issues raised by technology-supported telework and telecommuting, and the consequent implications for selection and appraisal in organizations. The focus of interest is bluejeaned employees at home or well-to-do, self-employed people doing their jobs at a telework or teleshopping centre. These settings shape their alternative office, factories, mall. They say they go to work and in fact they stay at home (Dawnson and Turner, 1989). It seems that the assumption of going to work is a rapidly decreasing necessity. The issue-driven question here is how all this works out as far as recruitment and personnel policies are concerned.

OFF-SITE WORK AND TRADE

In the 1970s, J. M. Nilles coined a rather broad term, *telecommuting*, that comprised 'the partial or total substitution of telecommunication technologies, possibly with the aid of computers, for the commute to work'. It meant any way of networking in which the computer terminal allowed the individual to commute and communicate, by sharing the working time while staying out of the office. This expression goes back to an old idea in Industrial and Organizational Psychology: 'moving the work to the workers instead of moving the workers to the work' (Nilles, 1994, p. xix). The International Labour Organization definition highlighted 'the combination of information technologies with the concept of a flexible workplace. Work is carried out in a location which is remote from central offices or production facilities where employees have no personal contact with co-workers' (Di Martino and Wirth, 1990).

In 1988, Nilles introduced another term, *telework*, and proposed a definition that included 'ANY form of substitution of information technologies (such as telecommunications and computers) for work-related travel' (Nilles, 1994, p. xix). In more operational terms, Chapman *et al.* (1995) meant by telework 'the performance of work activities at a distant location from employing/contracting organizations that is enabled by information and telecommunications technologies' (p. 230).

Another related term is *electronic trade* or *teletrade* because the same technology is used to promote a wide range of marketing strategies across borders to make available not only information about goods or services but also ordering and payment systems through the information highways across boundaries (Mitchell, 1995).

These terms forecast the idea that

- some conventions in labour conditions approach their sell-by-date because flexible workplaces and flexible working hours take the lead in a digital world of production and service, and
- the days of most customers spending most of their time in the shopping centre or in the local market premises are beginning to fade away.

Telecommuting

Teleworkers use terminals to establish dial-up connections or to maintain continuous on-line network connections. Mitchell (1994) has coined a new expression, *open electronic networking*, to describe the technology that enables the existence and maintenance of productive networks of individuals overcoming the barriers of space and time. The purpose is to make contacts, to reach, distribute or share information with colleagues, employers or clients, to team up with other teleworkers and set up a business developing a common project or support service. They gain access to a network of computers that provide several services.

A very simple classification of telecommuting services relies on the concept of *modes of remote activity* (Simón, 1995). It can be assumed that any scenario in which a teleworker or a telecustomer has to perform a task remotely is built around two main dimensions: the *interlocutor* providing the service and the *time frame* for the completion of a task.

The *interlocutor* may be *a database* as a source of information for the teleworker or the telecustomer, or *a person* who communicates and interacts with the telecustomer or other teleworkers. All that generates the existence of an *information service* or of a *communication service*.

The *time frame* arranges events to occur *simultaneously* or *sequentially*. Simultaneous tasks adjust to each other at the same time and speed *on real time*, whereas a time-lag is expected in sequential tasks, performed *at a deferred time* and probably *at a different rhythm*.

Table 5.2   Scenarios for open electronic networking inside telecommuterland

		Time frame	
Interlocutor	Service	Deferred time	Real time
Persons	Communication	E-mail Discussion lists Newsgroups	Talk Videoconference Screen sharing
Database	Information	Libraries Bulletin boards Search Engines	Remote log on WWW Home Pages CD-ROM

The interaction of these two dimensions, i.e. the *interlocutor* and the *time frame*, results in a table of telecommunication services (Table 5.2). Some examples for each case are included.

Communication between persons with a time-lag

The basic element is electronic mail. Initially e-mail systems were designed to exchange messages about a given subject among several users at a very low cost, at any time, at any distance without being too much concerned about the interval of time between the date of dispatch and the date of reception or about the sender and the receiver's computer compatibility. Teleworkers use e-mail to keep in touch with supervisors or colleagues and to react to customers' questions, doubts, complaints. The e-mail provides an opening for follow-ups, feedback and reinforcement systems just-in-time.

A new variant is the voice e-mail, which combines the richness and impact of digital audio with the speed and reach of electronic mail. Voice e-mail programs as well as MIME protocols allow the sending of messages containing speech, music and images.

A discussion list is a meeting point somewhere in cyberspace for people who share common interests and points of concern. They use e-mail as the basic tool to circulate and accumulate messages around the same subject. People post a message on-line and read the reactions to it that build up over time. Teleworkers ask their customers to submit their questions concerning failures or improvements. In this way other users obtain the benefit of having access to comments and suggestions made in the past to similar inquiries. Frequently asked questions (FAQs) are accumulated to make these files publicly available as a part of the after-sales system. Teleworkers involved in maintenance services join related discussion lists, forums and conferences as a refresher course. Other related networks are *forums* in CompuServe, *special interest groups* in DELPHI, *rounded tables* in GEnie, and *news groups* in USENET.

Via CompuServe, forums related to the main subject of this chapter are open to the exchange of comments and reactions:

- Entrepreneurs' small business forum (GO SMALLBIZ)
- Telework Europa forum (GO TWEUROPA)
- UK professionals forum (GO UKPROF)
- Working from home forum (GO WORK)

The following addresses are the right place to find out an updated database of discussion lists devoted to telework, telecommuting, teletrading and entrepreneurship issues.

Through the WWW: http://www.neosoft.com/internet/paml/
Through USENET: news.lists and news.answers

The following list of news groups related to common areas of interest for people involved in telework and electronic trade has been identified in USENET:

- alt.business.misc   General business and commerce topics
- alt.business.multi-level   Multi-level marketing businesses
- altr.business.seminars   Business seminars
- clari.nb.business   Real stories in business and industry news
- clari.biz.misc   Business news
- misc.job.labor   Contract labour
- misc.jobs.misc   Employment, workplaces, careers
- misc.jobs.offered   Announcements of positions available
- misc.jobs.offered.entry   Job listings, entry-level positions only
- misc.jobs.resumés   Postings of résumés and jobs wanted

Communication between persons on real time

Real time conversations also may take place in the network. The conventional approach is written conversations. There are handy programs currently called *talk* or *chat* that let teleworkers, customers or supervisors maintain a dialogue. Each person sits at the terminal and one of them sends a *talk* message to the e-mail address of the person to be contacted. A message is displayed on the screen of the receiver asking if she or he is ready for a talk. If the person agrees to initiate a two-way dialogue, the program splits the screen to work with the other person at the same time. Each person writes a sentence that appears on the screen of the other person when she or he presses the **return** key. It is also possible to transmit a voice message, but the system is still in an experimental phase. It requires the use of special broadband connections, algorithms and sound cards.

The simultaneous videoconference basically consists of the dynamic exchange of files that include sound and image as attachments to messages. It is still in a trial-and-error period. It requires high-speed transmissions (a minimum of 128 kb/s) at both ends to recreate the idea of animation and to integrate both image and sound in a natural manner. Sophisticated equipment for moving audio and visual information over the net must be present at both ends of the transmission system. The consequence is that the videoconference is rarely used between tele-workers and teletraders; they prefer to connect both computers at a certain moment sharing the screen text and images. They interact remotely in real time with the same document in their word processor or graphics application. It seems most appropriate to the domain of telehealth and emergency situations when the expert cannot travel to the location where an incident has occurred.

Information from a database with a time-lag

Thousands of electronic libraries exist in each network and in each service mentioned in Table 5.1. Each library is organized into folders offering programs and text files contributed by authors, administrators and participants. Each file can be reached by following strategic searches. Moving files between computers is one of the handiest features of telecommuting. It allows teleworkers to easily track down the program or the document they need to cope with an occurrence or an emergency. These libraries and sites are considered very specialized catalogues. Often teleworkers download files from the source computer to directories in their desktop computers. In this way they gather the sort of valuable information they need to put in order tailored databases. Afterwards these databases find their way into the support system provided by each teleworker to peers and clients.

Bulletin boards are dial-up systems (BBS) designed for individual users interested in very specific subjects. In universities, campus wide information systems (CWIS) have been created to share information among community members. Both BBS and CWIS serve internal news, messages, articles, announcements, directories, library connections, very specific databases for their staff and for some regular customers. For this purpose sysops and system administrators open a port in the internal network or create gateways to handle the movement of data from the firm's network to the desktop or portable computer.

Information from a database on real time

Teleworkers regularly log onto the remote computer of the organization where they are employed and work with it on an interactive basis. Menu-driven systems make interactive sessions intuitive. Sometimes they can also log onto their customers' computers to look for information they need to deal with crucial questions submitted and discussed by both interlocutors.

The Home Pages in the World Wide Web are written in hypertext and are just the buoys marking the route in a point-and-shoot environment. A click of the mouse is enough to track the information and to pursue key elements in a nonsequential manner through the text or through the images. In this way each individual reader determines which links to follow when reading a document in a host computer or when moving through several networked computers, because the document is one of several interconnected documents. It is the reader, not the author, who fixes the beginning and the end of a meaningful search, of a given document, of a series of associated paragraphs. Teleworkers and telecustomers currently tailor the catalogue of the hot lists they need to visit regularly.

The Home Pages in the World Wide Web devoted to telework and electronic trade are located in two addresses:

- http://www.fed.org/   Foundation for Enterprise Development
- http://www.eotw.com/   Entrepreneurs on the Web

CompuServe, for instance, distributes a CD-ROM that includes summaries of a huge amount of files available in the databases and a selection of images of some products available in the shopping centre. Teleworkers or telecustomers off-the-line find and mark each file or product they are looking for. Immediately they click for a connection and the computer automatically downloads the file or sends an order to the store in the electronic mall that includes a payment against a credit card. When the computer is disconnected users have the targeted files in the computer at minimum cost, or the product starts the handling and shipping process to reach the customer a few days afterwards via express services.

Teleworking

A standard classification of telework modalities is based on the alternative place where the individual carries out the activities (Qvortrup, 1993), and includes five categories:

- Home-based telework
- Satellite work centres
- Shared facility centre
- Private teleworking companies
- Mobile work

Home-based telework, or electronic homework

As its name indicates, the individual spends some or all his/her working time at home. This modality is frequent among freelance professionals, but it may also be the case of a company providing the facilities for working from home (e.g. in cases of maternity leave). Currently, most electronic homework is asked for by the worker, rather than proposed by the employer. Recent studies do not foresee a large extension of full-time home-based telework (COBRA Project, 1994), but instead advocate a combination of home and office, or home and TeleCentres, which are the second way of technology-supported distance working that will be defined.

Satellite work centres or TeleCentres

TeleCentres usually are premises equipped with computers and telecommunications facilities to support workers in their distant activities. TeleCentres can be created following the initiative of a company or a consortium of firms, generally to carry out activities that can easily be split from the traditional offices, such as telemarketing, programming and certain types of clerical work.

Shared-facility centre or community teleservice centre

Such centres are mainly funded by regional governments aiming to stimulate the local economy. In such cases, by contrast with the former modality, the centre serves the needs of small businesses and workers who cannot afford to install their own telecommunications services. Examples of shared-facility centres are the ones set up in Scotland in 1991 (TelePrompt Project, 1994); along these lines, the United Kingdom has a Telecottage Association covering a wide range of centres. The Nordic countries have long experience with this innovation, reporting in 1993 on more than 100 centres (Qvortrup, 1993).

Private teleworking companies

In the early 1990s, initiatives by new companies offering services via telework have emerged in the market. One of the most successful cases is the French firm Telergos, which was created in 1990 with the aim of commercializing clerical and secretarial work, and has met with a significant degree of success.

Mobile work

In its simplest meaning, mobile work is possibly the most extended modality of telework. It covers all professionals having to spend most of their working time travelling, visiting or in other kinds of external arrangements. The growing use of mobile telephones and faxes has allowed people to have a permanent communication link with their companies, either for consultation or just simply for permanent messaging and contact. More sophisticated applications of mobile work, for example, involve the use of multi-media devices for fault repairing of complex equipment. Another interesting working environment is telemedicine, especially in facilitating joint diagnosis.

In the above five modalities, individuals are regarded as 'tele-employees', who play their professional role for a traditional firm at a distance with the aid of technologies. However, a more advanced concept from an organizational outlook is also starting to be implemented, in which workers maintain very different links with their employers.

The list of occupations where the idea of telework has been launched is quite narrow yet but has been growing regularly during the last 10 years: accountants, accounting clerks, architects, bank officials, bookkeepers, clerical support, computer analysts, computer operators, computer programmers, counsellors, data entry clerks, engineers, insurance agents, lawyers, managers, marketing managers, purchasing agents, real estate agents, salespersons, secretaries, securities brokers, translators, travel agents, tutors, word processor operators and writers.

Teletrading

A direct consequence of the concurrence of telework and telecommuting has been the emergence of two new business concepts:

- virtual firms and
- electronic trading.

Virtual firms

A virtual firm is a network of creative experts telecommuted to band together to introduce a commercial innovation or to produce a tailored product or service.

The virtual firm pivots on one leading figure (the entrepreneur), who coordinates the contribution of a team of associates (third-party developers). The virtual firm also requires high-quality or innovative products developed by a team of associates. Each associate is an expert in a very specific domain.

The entrepreneur organizes the strategy of the virtual firm, obtains funds, provides management and marketing support to products and services built up by independent associates teleworking in the same project. There is not a binding contract between the entrepreneur and each associate. The entrepreneur is not an employer. Each associate is not an employee, but a partner. The entrepreneur keeps the register of partners, their activity ratios and their real contributions to the final product. Making a profit and distributing incomes is the responsibility of the entrepreneur. Each product is introduced into the market by the entrepreneur. Often virtual firms take advantage of mailing lists and the Home Pages at the World Wide Web.

A large majority of people enrolled in virtual firms are well trained and educated experts in the following fields: advertising, catering, clerical and secretarial staff, computer consulting, design and implementation of on-line training courses, financial counselling and planning, marketing, outplacement, sales, secretarial, temporary employment agencies, software designers, and technical writers for manuals and handbooks in CD-ROM. Initially they do not know each other but they have expert knowledge and experience. One of them knows how to generate and develop new ideas or technical projects; another knows how to commercialize products; a third knows how to get subsidies and sponsorships to support novel projects in the initial phase. Thus, the virtual firm allows them to band together by teleworking and telecommuting.

In so far as each associate is an owner who contributes to the success or failure of the virtual firm, selection procedures to be used must take into account virtual jobs and virtual partners (but not real jobs or past and future incumbents). The classical paradigm of the person–job fit must undoubtedly be reviewed in this context. The new paradigm person–team fit (Prieto, 1993; see also West and Allen, Chapter 24 in this volume) must be also reviewed because there are only virtual teams. Some ideas will be explored and outlined below.

Electronic trading

Brand-name commercial sites are available in information networks such as those mentioned in the upper half of Table 5.1. Almost all computer software and hardware vendors have created on-line support areas. However, museums and art galleries, for instance, also exhibit their catalogues in the net. Universities and research centres announce their syllabuses as well as their enrolment procedures. Scientific journals and popular magazines introduce past editions in the net that any user may download. Electronic malls remain open 24 hours a day, 365 days a year displaying a wide array of products, information and services. Orders and payments are accepted on-line if the name, address and credit card information of the user is already stored in the database.

The US Government has decided that all governmental purchases will resort to electronic trade methods by 1997. In a similar vein, EU Commissions will start to accept submissions for projects and proposals in electronic forms also by 1997.

The consequence of these approaches in marketing is a new term, the *electronic customer* or *telecustomer*. This is a new kind of customer who knows how to telecommute and reaches the kind of product or service he or she is looking for from a teleworker or from a database.

FITTING THE JOB: THE INCUMBENT AND THE CLIENT

It has already been remarked that it was only after the evolution of information technologies that new forms of working such as telework and teletrade started to emerge. In fact, nowadays organizations are more and more designed around the extensive use of telecommunications and computers. Now it is quite difficult to imagine what any clerical job would be without a telephone or fax, or how daily affairs would be managed without the credit card! The pervasiveness of telecommunications in social and organizational contexts is now being realized in the popularity of the information highways and the long list of corporate on-line networks open to external users mentioned in Table 5.1.

Obviously, teleworkers strongly depend on technological aids to become productive and motivated in their daily activities. The teleworker should be able to recreate the office environment in a distant place, both in terms of facilities and communication flow.

Many classifications of telecommunication and information technologies have started to emerge, mainly because of the growing number of applications and their rapid expansion in many human and social areas; the interested reader can refer to works such as Grover and Goslar (1993) and Zorkoczy (1991). For the purposes of this chapter, however, it is more relevant to observe technologies from the role they may (in many cases, eventually) play in the organization, rather than attending to technical aspects.

This functional approach to technology is shared by research groups currently working on Business Process Re-Engineering and Telework in Europe (COBRA Project, 1993). They state that '. . . in general, real quantum leaps in productivity improvement can only take place if people, processes and technology are considered together, within a holistic framework' (Deliverable 1, p. 74). Systems of this kind have been conceptualized in previous work, particularly in the field of organizational training (Zorkoczy, 1989; Simón and Zorkoczy, 1991; Simón, 1995).

There are four main categories among the specific functionalities that technology currently supports:

- Remote access to organizational information
- Communication with colleagues
- Enlargement of individual work profiles
- Monitoring and management of work processes

We look briefly at each of them, and illustrate how each category operates.

Remote access to organizational information

The centralization of information has been one of the first achievements of introducing technologies in working environments, and was made possible through the implementation of local area networks (LANs). From their desktop, workers can navigate through different types of information, from personnel data to bibliographic references, databases, etc. In the case of large, multinational companies, several LANs are linked together with a common interface which is transparent for the user, thus putting in common information available from different countries. It receives a new name: INTRANET.

The centralization of information in such a way is called an *information system*. This term was introduced early in the 1960s when the first computer equipment was implemented in organizations with a view to centralizing the relevant information and providing comfortable ways of retrieving it. It was originally defined as 'the mechanism which provides the means of storing, generating and distributing information for the purposes of supporting the operations and management functions of an organization' (Layzell and Loucopoulos, 1989). Information systems can be considered as the first 'global' introduction of technologies to try out and enhance different areas of human performance. Because of its long tradition, there is a large (and very useful) history of implementations in which critical issues and 'lessons learned' have arisen (e.g., Nickerson, 1981; Avgerou and Cornford, 1993; Damodaran, 1991).

Information systems originally involved a minicomputer or data-processing centres, with multiple dumb terminals connected from which users were allowed to manipulate data. This panorama has greatly changed in the last few years, and therefore, although the concept of an information system is still widely used, it has started to coexist with many others.

The information system has been opened to teleworkers and telecustomers: they are able to access databases or reach each other by dialling up with a modem connected to their computers. An example of a corporate but open information system that is accessible throughout the world is the CompuServe on-line service. A monthly subscription rate and a dial-up local connection via a modem currently allows more than four million people to share information via this distributed system. This is approximately the population of Laos, Norway or Nicaragua. In Europe alone there were more than 500 000 members by December 1995, around the average population of many middle-sized European cities. The information is stored in electronic libraries, covering a wide area of subjects outlined in the lower half of Table 5.1.

Communication with colleagues

Even if teleworkers and telecustomers are able to access organizational information, they may feel isolated in their home or remote telecentre. Consequently, they require some sort of communication device to develop social interaction. They also should be able to cover the need for informal communication with peers.

The effects and the strategic potential of technological aids introduced in the processes of human communication stress the importance of collaboration and joint actions among teleworkers coping with similar problems and dilemmas. It has become a highly interdisciplinary mode of research, in which computer scientists, engineers, sociologists and psychologists are contributing to the debate on how to improve the multiple-interactivity aspect of human performance in different situations.

Many products have been developed, and extensively used. Such tools have been mentioned in Table 5.2 and discussed in the section Off-site Work and Trade earlier this chapter. One of them requires further attention as a consequence of its relevance for teleworkers and teleconsumers.

The accumulation of individual e-mail messages around a very specific product or service in a common reservoir generates very popular files known as FAQs (frequently asked questions already mentioned earlier). They are public archives of basic information on a given topic stated in question-and-answer formats. FAQ files are considered a technical vade-mecum for ready reference and regular use. Teleworkers from all around the world share their concerns and strategies through FAQ files served in secluded but specialized libraries.

Enlargement vs. enrichment of job profiles

The augmenting capabilities and user friendliness of computer interfaces mean that users are actually able to perform very easily activities that some years ago required specialized skills, such as controlling costs or just simply editing documents. Technology has frequently been regarded as 'enabling', and in this sense the use of software packages such as word processors, spreadsheets, project management and navigators allow users to expand the range of tasks they perform in an organization. Therefore, the profile is enriched. It can therefore be claimed that technology also calls for job enlargement and for increases in productivity caused by the use of technology. It also allows users to cope with a larger workload.

Monitoring and management of work processes

Computer and telecommunication devices such as automatic logs of activity, analysis of work performed within the network, random calls for checking of tasks, etc. are increasingly being used to monitor and manage certain types of work in organizations.

An example will allow us to clarify this functionality by considering the case of a computer firm that started a 7-day, 24-hour telephone hotline providing support to users. The firm made a decision to implement the service using a telework and teletrade scheme, instead of purchasing premises and central infrastructure for employees.

Teleworkers perform their activities from their homes. The firm installs for them a computer with a modem and an ISDN (Integrated Services Digital Network) line for this use, which is charged directly to the firm. The workers also receive a timetable, so that shifts are established. Within their planning, some breaks are also agreed, so that continuity of attention to calls is guaranteed.

During their specified working time teleworkers receive calls and interact with users. The teleworkers have to abstract and understand the users' explanations of the problem, and discover and transmit the solution to them whenever possible, following the guidelines provided by the firm. If the problem requires a deeper level of consultancy, a commitment to call back as soon as possible is made to the client, and a note is sent to the group coordinator, who redirects it to the specialist in the firm. FAQ files are used by teleworkers and distributed to telecustomers as a first-aid instrument.

Daily tasks also include reporting on every call by filling out standard templates which are sent via a modem to the centralized server of the network. Teleworkers are also connected via a modem to a computer conferencing system where they can share problems and issues with their managers and colleagues.

A monitoring and control system has been set up by the firm, including the following procedures:

- Automatic storing of statistical data for every call received, including duration, start and ending times. Such information also helps in controlling the peaks throughout the day and the corresponding suitability of the timetable.
- A random record of calls, for examining the competence of the teleworkers in dealing with clients and providing solutions.
- Monitoring of reports elaborated by the teleworkers.

BARRIERS TO TELEWORK

A good number of constraints affecting adoption and acceptance of telework have been identified:

1. Organizational barriers.
2. Psychological barriers (ATTICA Project, 1994; Simón, 1995).

We discuss each in turn.

Organizational barriers

- Factors affecting the security and confidentiality of information transmitted, which is an important focus of reluctance in organizations.

- The need to place the emphasis on job outputs (results) rather than inputs (e.g. hours at the work place) implies a dramatic change in the organizational culture.
- Telecommunications-supported work requires from the manager a different role regarding the aspects of control, turning from monitoring the process toward assessing the result at a distance.
- An effective use of the technology requires that the organization implements actions (information and training, evaluation) which represent additional resources accumulated to the investments made in the technology itself.

Psychological barriers

- The sense of isolation associated with an activity performed on a distance basis is one of the most important barriers at this level, and has been extensively studied in more specific fields such as distance education (Kaye, 1992). In the situation of telework, the position of the individual in the organization should not be forgotten; in this sense, the concept of an interface should be extended to include not just human–computer interaction, but also human–organization interaction, for example through the use of graphical metaphors (Warburton, 1993).
- The fear of losing promotion opportunities by comparison with non-teleworking peers raises negative attitudes.
- The personal implications of getting much closer to the family context are not necessarily positive (e.g. if the worker does not have a proper place to work at home).
- Telework undoubtedly places a greater level of accountability for the job on employees, who have to assume a larger range of activities (text processing, formatting documents, managing appointments, etc.). Therefore, the individual has to acquire a greater level of discipline, as well as a broader set of skills, demanding extra time and effort compared with traditional workplace-based modalities (Prieto, 1989a, b).

IMPLICATIONS FOR SELECTION AND APPRAISAL

Telecommuting, teleworking and virtual firms are different forms of de-centralized employment, jobs, and work settings. In this context, conventional approaches to personnel selection and appraisal turn into a nightmare of lab-yrinthine bureaucratic procedures to gather congruous information about performance criteria and about appropriate predictors.

Performance criteria in terms of conventional concepts such as office hours, working hours, overtime, spare time, close down, set hours and workplaces lose relevance. Person-centred managers find it quite difficult to supervise the time spent on tasks by each individual teleworker: they cannot influence them because there is no face-to-face contact. Quite often, only output measures of performance are immediately available. This is not the case with regard to task-centred managers: they are used to monitoring results by objectives, providing feedback and influencing standard work performance (Heilmann, 1988). They know about the product or service that is brought out.

Increased levels of productivity have been detected as a direct consequence of high levels of flexibility in the organization of working days (Gordon, 1988). During the Olympic Games in Los Angeles (1984), Pacific Bell launched a program favouring telework to contribute to a reduction in traffic congestion. A case study suggests that managers detected an improvement of 10%–20% in productivity among their subordinates appointed as teleworkers during a month (Bailey and Foley, 1990).

Compensation systems based on piecework, payment by results, job-and-finish, copyrights, royalties, share-out payments, production bonuses and so on are based on whether such products or services meet technical standards and whether they actually work. Quite often, however, teleworkers' productivity is tied to the development of an idea, a project or a course of action. Under such circumstances the measurement of effectiveness makes sense if prime objectives are achieved. It requires a completely different reward structure associated to the political feasibility and the social acceptance of such an idea, project or course of action. Actual evaluation procedures must be based on the same criteria for all kinds of employees of the same firm, teleworkers and on-site workers. Effectiveness, a sense of commitment and autonomy are the targets.

Moreover, teleworkers are free to leave the work or to change their functions once they have completed the set task. Under certain circumstances supervisors are convinced of teleworkers' loyalty to the firm because they behave in a very professional manner (Pratt, 1984) whereas teleworkers feel they are loyal to their professionalism because they are proud of what they have done (Kinsman, 1987).

Filling the bill

The selection of teleworkers in a real or in a virtual firm is essentially a problem of discovering the personal characteristics, job characteristics and workplace circumstances needed to achieve the level of effectiveness expected in the set task. The fundamental aim of each individual teleworker, or of each team of teleworkers, is to find ways in which a particular task, project or contribution can best be accomplished with a minimum of errors and a maximum of acceptance by potential and loyal customers. The manager's function in a real firm and the entrepreneur's function in a virtual firm do not differ from that of the so-called efficiency expert, who places primary emphasis on increased productivity and effectiveness. The psychologist's aim seems to be directed toward the identification of factors that determine the quality of the contribution of individual teleworkers or of teams of teleworkers involved in a task or in a project and the strategies needed to ensure effectiveness as well as cooperation.

Teleworkers interact among themselves, with the supervisor, with the entrepreneur or with the customer in a dynamic, interdependent and an adaptive manner. Each teleworker has been assigned specific functions or roles to perform, whereas they remain connected with the task or the project.

However, there remain a few conundrums surrounding the efficient supervision of teleworkers which are not in clear focus. How to deal with non-performers who cannot produce as agreed or who refuse to do necessary tasks that have to be done but which they do not like? How to identify the weakest link or to take up the slack in a chain of teleworkers? What about those teleworkers who almost always are behind schedule and succeed in postponing deadlines? Selection and appraisal procedures are available to cope with these and other similar crucial questions.

Tables 5.3 and 5.4 summarize some of the work-related settings and personal traits that are currently considered to optimize the selection of competitive teleworkers getting the job done better and faster. These characteristics are drawn from an analysis of published literature (Gray, Hodson and Gordon, 1993; Moorcroft and Bennett, 1995; Nilles, 1994) and in-depth interviews with managers and out-of-the-office employees and associates with a minimum experience of two years with telecommuting agendas.

The success of teleworking is largely dependent on finding the right candidates and on identifying the right managers. It necessitates raising the vested interest and awareness among volunteers of all the implications and added responsibilities derived from teleworking. It requires a special kind of manager ready to develop specific criteria and strategies to compensate for the perceived loss of control over their teleworking subordinates.

The beaten track

Telework is not up for grabs. It requires an approach in two steps: this seems to be a Janus cloth. It requires the selection of adequate managers ready to supervise a network of virtual employees spread out across a wall-less workplace. It also

Table 5.3   Work-related facets inside telecommuterland

Job characteristics	• Information-based tasks • Feedback from the job itself • In touch by telecommuting • High performance requires concentration • Scheduling control and flexibility • A fragmentary organization of services and outputs • Remote access to expertise • Location of the independent working environment • High degree of autonomy and responsibility
Workplace circumstances	• Balance between work and domestic responsibilities • Suitable storage space for equipment • Suitable care for child or elderly person • Family acceptance of home working • Permanent location • Security for equipment and work in progress • Health and safety measures • Temperature and light control • Access to ISDN outlets

Table 5.4   Occupational profiles identified among competent teleworkers

Expert knowledge	• Familiarity with computers in general to solve emergencies • Deep knowledge of issues which are the main subject of the product/service • A competent user of e-mail, discussion lists and word-processing systems
Skills	• Interpersonal networking skills, such as active listening, reading and writing • Able to express a technical problem in non-technical words • Managerial and decision-making skills • Written communication skills • Time and task management skills
Attitudes	• High motivation for autonomy and flexibility at work • Task orientation to concentrate on outputs and goals • Patient to understand users complaints • Awareness to detect in advance signs of strain and stress • A flexible mood to deal with tense emotional discussion on-line • Initiative and willingness to comprehend problems and simplify solutions • High need for achievement to meet deadlines with distinction • Not a 'workaholic' • Innovative mind in problem-solving
Personality	• Emotionally stable and mature to maintain a goodwill climate • Introversion to think over problems in an impersonal and distant manner • Receptive and open minded to foster good communication networks • Independent and persuasive to attract early adopters • Self-control and pragmatism to set priorities in work schedules • Self-sufficiency and reliability in handling tasks without face-to-face dialogues

requires the selection of adequate candidates ready to perform regularly a very thorough piece of work out-of-the-office.

There seems to be a certain agreement that managers and teleworkers should be recruited only among volunteers (Wright and Oldford, 1995). Managers who are used to having subordinates on a string, paying a lot of attention to time spent on tasks, show themselves reluctant to become involved in the supervision of unseen subordinates. In a similar manner employees who make a mountain out of a molehill or who need regular face-to-face contacts to think they are on the right track rarely ask to participate in a telework programme.

Another common aspect is that both managers and teleworkers cannot be newcomers into the firm. A period of adjustment to the internal culture is essential to create a climate of mutual trust and loyalty. Managers and future teleworkers recruited from other companies or sectors must work within the firm's premises to overcome the mindset which is not compatible with principles, concepts, processes, procedures and facts in force within the hosting organization. In a similar vein, people looking for their first job (young starters in the labour market) must be hired and stay during the probation period in the premises of the firm and under the supervision of the manager that will take care of them when they become enrolled in the teleworking program.

Only qualified managers and employees must be considered adequate candidates for launching a telework programme. Daily use of information technologies requires a background of expert knowledge, resourcefulness as well as abstract reasoning or intelligence. From 1975 to 1979 the first author of this paper was employed in the role of assistant to the personnel manager of a national bank that took over a savings bank. It was the time of the introduction of informatics in the Spanish banking system. In the national bank cashiers and accountants with a minimum of one year of experience in the job were selected to participate in a training programme to use a delayed computerized system to keep books by double entry. Only experienced employees with a high score in factor g (measured by Cattell and Cattell's (1977) scale 3) were accepted for this workshop in the national bank. Employees with a similar experience in the savings bank were enrolled in the same programme, but the high score in the factor g scale was not a requisite (their scores were made available because the scale was administered during the workshop but without a cut-off purpose). A follow-up during the first month after the end of the workshop showed that experienced personnel with a high score in g submitted a significantly ($p < 0.05$) lower number of questions and doubts to external monitors and consultants than experienced personnel with a low score in g. Abstract reasoning favoured (high score in factor g) getting to the heart of the matter in information technologies applied to banks' accounting. There was logic to what they did. Concrete reasoning (low score in factor g) favoured the submission of a whole series of very specific questions and detailed cases during the period of transfer of training. These findings were never published; they belong to an internal report on the cost–benefits of psychological testing in human resources management.

Task-centred managers who are used to negotiating and fixing goals with sub-ordinates come in handy. It means that the least preferred co-worker (LPC) scale is an adequate instrument in so far as low LPC managers value task achievement and task success (Fiedler, 1978). However, an overly controlling supervisor is soon perceived negatively. Positive or negative climates spread out quite rapidly because teleworkers are enabled to leave messages on electronic bulletin boards and because they are used to communicating with those above as well as below in the hierarchy (PATRA, 1995). The ability to fix feasible objectives and encourage involvement is also another requisite for managers to be assessed psychologically by using situational tests.

Teleworkers enrolled in situations illustrated by some of the examples introduced in earlier sections of this chapter meet the typical profile described in Table 5.4.

A large majority of these traits and behavioural patterns are capable of being assessed using psychological, situational and work sample tests. Group exercises must be reformulated and performed on an on-line and a long-distance basis. The *Sixteen Personality Factor Questionnaire*, 5th edn. (Cattell, Cattell and Cattell, 1993) is a conventional and updated tool to assess, for instance, the personality dimensions outlined in Table 5.4.

Another aspect that cannot be set apart is the detection of teleworkers and managers who have become addicted to on-line services. Chapman *et al.* (1995) identify the following indicators of this syndrome:

- logging on quite often during the day regardless
- excessive irritation if the connection system fails
- very keen on writing on-line messages
- fond of on-line interpersonal and friendly contacts
- logging on for the late item before stopping work.

Conventional approaches in the domains of occupational and health psychology allows us to deal successfully with these symptoms.

Disabled people may find teleworking the panacea for working condition constraints as well as stereotypes. On-line services are a safeguard to prevent the presence of prejudiced intruders and supply a safe conduct to travel through the net around the world without restrictions. Employers supporting equal opportunities of employment for disabled people have here the Golden Fleece indeed.

Candidates in distress as a consequence of severe conflicts in their marriage, who have a very delicate child or elderly person to care for in their personal surroundings, or candidates who cannot afford a room at home devoted almost exclusively to out-of-office activities are not suitable for this form of employment. This is also the case as far as 'workaholics' are concerned.

Getting the knack of teleworking

Conventional procedures in the domain of personnel selection and appraisal can be tailored to compensate for the perceived loss of control. Tables 5.3 and 5.4 illustrate the basic issues concerning selection. As far as appraisal is concerned, often teleworking starts on a trial basis. Several criteria have been identified to enable careful monitoring.

Setting clear objectives to be reached in periodic spot checks

Progress report dates enable blocks to be removed. They introduce a sort of remote 'hands-on' management control by specifying the end-results expected. In this way, teleworking frees up a manager's time because supervision focuses solely on overall direction and supervision. Teleworkers have to perform the assignment in a satisfactory manner fixed by the objectives. Managers and teleworkers interact in the decision-making process that allows them to fix objectives in work schedules and to negotiate the amount of work given and expected. Managers have a clear idea about the work that is performed, but not so much the process by which it is carried out.

Specifying the teleworkers' range of discretion

It is convenient to make provision concerning the use or non-use of employer-owned equipment and furniture for private purposes. Currently the employer supplies and maintains all the necessary equipment, whereas the teleworker provides and maintains a room solely for the tasks to be performed. Teleworkers are invited to satisfy occupational health and safety requirements. There are expenses such as telephone, electricity, heating and air conditioning which are reimbursed totally or partially. The employer gets the benefit of saving in office costs and teleworkers may get the benefit of subsidies in their home costs. A process-oriented management is absent: this fact is balanced by letting every teleworker know what constraints exist (Evans, 1995).

Trusting every teleworker

Remote incumbents are held accountable for their assignments but also they are ready to participate in determining the standards by which they will be judged. Providing feedback and assessment of performance favours a climate of long-distance cooperation and legitimacy. Teleworkers are quasi-entrepreneurs with an output-oriented management focus.

Encouraging initiative and independence

Telecommuting provides substantial freedom and discretion for teleworkers in scheduling their work and in determining the procedures to be used in carrying it out. However, often teleworkers try to push decisions or problems back upward to their supervisor. They know they are the only persons to analyse the true cause 'in situ'. During the initial phase they feel that they cannot come up with appropriate explanations and solutions. They call on the supervisor or on peers for guidance as soon as the incident occurs. Keeping in touch is an important aspect, but creating a dependence might be dysfunctional.

Devising a foolproof way to stay in touch with each teleworker

Social isolation is a major barrier. Often teleworkers feel they are left out in the cold. On-line conferences and networking allow staff to air their ideas, problems and suggestions with peers, supervisors and clients. On-line newsletters, discussion lists, newsgroups and e-mail loops are other options to ward off the inevitable isolation of working alone. From time to time it is convenient to organize face-to-face meetings or encounter groups to maintain the contact that exists in the conventional workplace.

Table 5.5 lists some areas of concern identified by the European Foundation for the Improvement of Living and Working Conditions (Moorcroft and Bennett, 1995). Most of them can be easily remedied or overcome by strategic redesign and planning.

Table 5.5   Areas of concern in teleworking

For the employee	For the employer
Loss of employee status, protection, benefits and pay	Remote management, control, logistics and communication
Social and professional isolation	Security and confidentiality of information and systems
Reduced career opportunities	
Less interesting work and increased monotony	Team and company identity and loyalty
	Costs
Loss of the homework distinction	Time required to plan and implement
An increase in strain and stress	Child/elder-care to ensure an adequate and undisturbed work time
Increased home-related costs	
Health and safety standards and the monitoring of their implementation	Start-up costs
	Running costs
Child/elder-care	
Employee representation/union membership	

Source: Moorcroft and Bennett (1995): reproduced by permission.

New employees are rare among telecommuters, which means that selection procedures are thought less important and worthwhile than appraisal procedures. Mainly younger candidates with high qualifications and expertise in very specific domains are hired as home telecommuters. They are enrolled for project-based tasks and activities that do not require a detailed knowledge of internal policies and procedures.

Senior employees are quite common among telecommuters. Organizations do accept teleworkers who are accustomed to coping with the internal structures and production systems. This means that the appraisal procedures of well-known employees receive further attention than selection procedures applied to new hires. By engaging them in telecommuting, it is another way of realizing that this is just a different mode of working. A follow-up of e-mail usage reflects the degree of efficiency attained when exchanging messages with managers and the perception of contact between people-centred managers and their teleworking subordinates. Entrepreneurs in virtual firms and managers in real firms do not care about how the product was developed, only about its quality. Teleworking employees or associates learn what must be done, and when and how well it must be done.

GENDER DIFFERENCES

New applications of advanced telecommuting technologies to other areas in contemporary society are an everyday occurrence. The European Foundation for the Improvement of Living and Working Conditions has sponsored a case study review of experiences available in a very specific domain: telehealth and telemedicine (Gott, 1995). The elderly, the young, pregnant women and the disabled are the potential users and the main beneficiaries of these changes, enabling them to lead better and healthier lives. It means that several health-care services supplied to outpatients will launch the idea of virtual ambulatory care centres or of virtual welfare centres.

It will depend on the introduction of advanced technologies into the home. The availability of an integrated system such as the integrated services digital network (ISDN) and the integrated broadband communication will allow the video transmission of images of the home-based worker and of the supervisor located at the main office. This kind of visual access may correct the feeling of isolation in the job among teleworkers.

Women and men perceive and use computer-mediated communication as well as voice and video telephony systems quite differently (Moran, 1993). For instance, at home women tend to become second call users of personal computers because there is almost no software accommodated to their domestic interests. The telephone is seen as a social lifeline by women and as a functional instrument by men. Both try to keep in touch with colleagues in the network, but women tend to reduce psychological distance by being friendly and communicative, whereas men tend to maintain the psychological distance by being short, brusque and curt. The telework carried out by men at home is considered part and parcel of a main job, whereas it is viewed as part and parcel of the daily grind by other household members when it is done by women. This is one of the consequences of enhancing or reducing the psychological distance in the job. Probably, the development of telehealth and telemedicine services will increase the caring work of women. The idea of an 'electronic home' seems to be a male-oriented concept as a direct consequence of the lack of female involvement in its design. Commercial surveys show evidence that women in general are less likely to buy or work on-line. Follow-ups of people hitting or joining Home Pages in the World Wide Web show that currently only one out of four visitors is female.

Fairness issues in personnel decisions will remain important under the framework of these new forms of employment. Differences in validity coefficients and in differential predictions might appear again. This old debate about personnel psychology will continue.

FINAL REMARKS

As has been discussed in this chapter, the appearance of more and more advanced technological applications is causing a true revolution in organizational contexts and in consumer behaviour.

Telework, telecommuting and virtual firms are good examples of such unavoidable change. New technology-supported working environments emerge, and with them new ways of conceiving the job and the organization itself. From this perspective alternative paradigms for the study and structuring of organizations are also being explored in an attempt to integrate legal, social and individual implications, and flexibilize working procedures in order to catch up with such developments. In fact, one of the points discussed in this chapter has been the need for different criteria in the selection and appraisal of teleworkers. Along these lines, paradigms such as business process re-engineering (COBRA Project, 1994) seem to offer a perspective of change that can cope with the dramatic changes that technology is originating, but more time and extra research work are required before coming to definite conclusions.

Telework is also attracting criticism, however. The intensive use of information technologies can cause three symptoms. The first is physical: headaches, deteriorating vision and back problems. The second is psychological: anxiety and depression. The third has to do with the disintegration of social communities built around a job and the social codes associated with the workplace. The concurrence of the three symptoms questions the validity of telework as a consolidated conception of the job.

It is precisely in this sense that, along the lines of recent EU-funded projects (cf. Practice Project, 1994), the introduction of telework should be contemplated as a gradual process. Initial experiences are designed and performed in order to gather critical factors for success, specific for each organization, which will therefore guide extensive and effective implementation.

It is convenient to end this chapter with a touch of scepticism and irony. During the twentieth century information technology has rarely followed its oracles' prophecies to the letter. Each discovery opens up new horizons, but followers only make a path if they walk through the wood of expectations.

Sports are broadcast through the radio and the TV and at the same time crowd the media and the stadia during a terrible winter. The bride and the groom trapped in a traffic jam when they leave for their honeymoon listen to the sportscaster. One of them likes football, the other dislikes it. Built-up and fashionable areas in US cities are wired to cable television, whereas one of the appealing features of some smart residential neighbourhoods in EU cities is that houses are not connected to cable television. The Open University has been improved by TV and video production media, but many university students still live on campus because they prefer to keep in touch with professors or classmates and because they have a gift for flirtation. There are groups of researchers used to spending their days reading ancient pieces of scrolls or parchments and to transmit scanned images and articles over modem or fax. They are experienced scribes in old and new information technologies. Both, in some way, shall coexist.

REFERENCES

ATTICA Project (1994). *Analysis of Constraints to the Development of Telework in the European Community Area.* Commission of the European Communities.

Auerbach Report (1993). La Paradoja de la Productividad en Tecnologías de la Información. *Chip*, **Julio-Agosto**, 30–34.

Avgerou, C. and Cornford, T. (1993). A review of the methodologies movement. *Journal of Information Technology*, **8** (4), 277–286.

Bailey, D.S. and Foley, J. (1990). Pacific Bell works long distance. *Human Resources Magazine*, **35** (8), 50–52.

Beniger, J.R. (1990). Conceptualizing information technology as organization, and vice-versa. In J. Fulk and C. Steinfeld (eds.), *Organizations and Communication Technology*. Newbury Park, CA: Sage.

Blanch, J.M. (1990). Categorías sociolaborales e innovación tecnológica. In J.M. Peiró, *Trabajo, Organizaciones y Marketing Social*. Barcelona: PPU.

Burns, B. (1992). *Managing Change: A Strategical Approach to Organizational Development and Renewal*. London: Pitman Publishing.

Cattell, R.B. and Cattell, A.K.S. (1977). *Tests de factor 'g'*. Madrid: TEA.

Cattell, R.B., Cattell, A.K. and Cattell, H.E. (1993). *Sixteen Personality Factor Questionnaire*, 5th edn. Champaign, IL: Institute for Personality and Ability Testing.

Chapman, A.J., Sheehy, N.P., Heywood, S., Dooley, B. and Collins, S.C. (1995). The organizational implications of teleworking. In C.L. Cooper and I.T. Robertson, *International Review of Industrial and Organizational Psychology*, Vol. 10. Chichester: John Wiley.

Coates, J.F. (1994). Going to work: What a waste of time and money. In CompuServe Telework Europa Forum, File name: towork.txt.

COBRA Project (1993). *Business Restructuring and Teleworking: Current Practice*. Deliverable 1, IT&T Action Plan for Teleworking, Commission of the European Communities.

COBRA Project (1994). *Business Restructuring and Teleworking: Corporate, Social and Policy Issues*. Deliverable 4, IT&T Action Plan for Teleworking, Commission of the European Communities.

Damodaran, L. (1991). Toward a human factors strategy for information technology systems. In B. Shackel and S. Richardson (eds.), *Human Factors for Informatics Usability*. Cambridge: Cambridge University Press.

Davies, R. (1995). Telecommuting: Culture, social roles and managing telecommuters. *International Journal of Career Management*, electronic document at this URL address: http://www.mcb.co.uk/services/conferen/hrn/ijcm/ijcmcon1.html Virtual Conference Centre, File name Telecom.htm.

Dawnson, W. and Turner, J. (1989). *When She Goes To Work She Stays at Home*. Canberra: Department of Employment, Education and Training.

Di Martino, V. and Wirth, L. (1990). Telework: A new way of working and living. *International Labour Review*, **129** (5), 529–554.

Evans, A. (1995). Working at home: A new career dimension, *International Journal of Career Management*, electronic document located at this URL address: http://www.mcb.co.uk/services/conferen/hrn/ijcm/ijcmcon1.html, Virtual Conference Centre, File name Reading2.htm.

Fiedler, F.E. (1978). The contingency model and the dynamics of the leadership process. In L. Berkowitz, *Advances in Experimental Social Psychology*. New York: Academic Press.

Gordon, G.E. (1988). The dilemma of telework: Technology versus tradition. In W.B. Korte, S. Robinson and W.J. Steinle, *Telework: Present Situation and Future Development of a New Form of Work Organization*. Amsterdam: North-Holland.

Gott, M. (1995). *Telematics for Health: The Role of Telehealth and Telemedicine in Homes and Communities*. Oxford: Radcliffe Medical Press.

Gray, M., Hodson, N. and Gordon, G. (1993). *Teleworking Explained*. Chichester: John Wiley.

Grover, V. and Goslar, M. (1993). Towards an empirical taxonomy and model of evolution for telecommunication technologies. *Journal of Information Technology*, **8**, 167–176.

Heilmann, W. (1988). The organizational development of teleprogramming. In W.B. Korte, S. Robinson and W.J. Steinle, *Telework: Present Situation and Future Development of a New Form of Work Organization*. Amsterdam: North-Holland.

IBM Europe (1994). Turning the office inside out. In CompuServe Telework Europa Forum, File name: ibmtw.asc.

Kaye, A.R. (1992). *Collaborative Learning Through Computer Conferencing. The Najaden Papers*. NATO ASI Series vol. 90. Berlin: Springer-Verlag.

Kinsman, F. (1987). *The Telecommuters*. Chichester: John Wiley.

Layzell, P. and Loucopoulos, P. (1989). *Systems Analysis and Development*. Lund: Chartwell-Bratt.

Mitchell, H. (1994). Networking and Open Electronic Networking, in CompuServe Telework Europa Forum, File name: oenmta.txt.

Mitchell, H. (1995). Teletrade and Electronic Commerce, in CompuServe Telework Europa Forum, File name: ttrade.txt.

Moorcroft, S. and Bennett, V. (1995) *European Guide to Teleworking: A Framework for Action.* Loughlinstown House, Ireland: European Foundation for the Improvement of Living and Working Conditions.

Moran, R. (1993). *The Electronic Home: Social and Spatial Aspects.* A Scoping Report. Luxembourg: Office for Official Publications of the European Communities.

Nickerson, R.S. (1981). Why interactive computer systems are sometimes not used by people who might benefit from them. *International Journal of Man–Machine Studies,* **15,** 469–483.

Nilles, J.M. (1994). *Making Telecommuting Happen: A Guide to Telemanagers and Telecommuters.* New York: Van Nostrand Reinhold.

Olson, M. (ed.) (1989). *Technological Support for Work Group Collaboration.* Hillsdale: Lawrence Erlbaum Associates.

PATRA (1995). *Psychological Aspects of Teleworking in Rural Areas.* Final Report, CEC/DGXIII, Contract 02004, located at CompuServe, Telework Europa Forum, File name PATRA10.ZIP Hypertext Document for Windows.

Peiró, J.M. (1984). *Psicologia de la Organización.* Madrid: UNED.

Peiró, J.M. (1990). *Organizaciones: Nuevas perspectivas psicosociológicas.* Barcelona: PPU.

Peiró, J.M. and Prieto, F. (1994). Telematics and organizational processes. In E. Andriesen and R. Roe, *Telematics and Work.* Hillsdale, NJ: Lawrence Erlbaum.

Perrow, Ch. (1970). *Organizational Analysis: A Sociological View.* Belmont, CA: Wadsworth.

Practice Project (1994). *Code of Practice for Telework in Europe.* Project T1021, Commission of the European Communities.

Pratt, J.H. (1984). Home teleworking: A study of its pioneers. *Technological Forecasting and Social Change,* **25,** 1–14.

Prieto, F., Martí, C., Peiró, J.M. and González-Romá, V. (1990). Desarrollo tecnológico de los procesos de telecomunicación y su incidencia sobre dimensiones estructurales de las organización. In J.M. Peiró (ed.), *Trabajo, Organizaciones y Marketing Social.* Barcelona: PPU.

Prieto, J.M. (1989a). Incertidumbre laboral percibida a traves de las nuevas formas de empleo y autoempleo, *Informació Psicologica,* **38,** 36–41.

Prieto, J.M. (1989b). New ways of employment and self-employment. In B.J. Fallon, H.P. Pfister and J. Brebner (eds.), *Advances in Industrial and Organizational Psychology,* pp. 285–293. Amsterdam: Elsevier Science Publishers.

Prieto, J.M. (1993). The team perspective in selection and assessment. In H. Schuler, J.L. Farr and M. Smith, *Personnel Selection and Assessment: Individual and Organizational Perspective.* Hillsdale, NJ: Erlbaum.

Prieto, J.M. and Martin, J. (1990). New forms of work organization. *The Irish Journal of Psychology,* **11** (2), 170–185.

Qvortrup, L. (1993). Flexiwork and telework centres in the Nordic countries. Trends and perspectives. Paper presented at the ECTF International Seminar Flexiwork Policy in the European and Nordic Labour Markets, Helsinki, 18–19 May 1993.

Simón, C. (1995). A systematic approach for the analysis, design and implementation of telecommunications-supported training (TST) systems. Unpublished PhD. Thesis, Open University, UK.

Simón, C. and Zorkoczy, P. (1991). Towards an architecture of technology-based training systems. Paper presented at the II International Conference Corporate Training and Effective Performance, University of Twente, September 1991.

TelePrompt Project (1994). *Telework and Telework Training.* EC Comett Programme.

Warburton, R.G. (1993). *Designing Object-Oriented User Interfaces Using User Driven Design.* KNOW HOW Consultancy and Services, IBM Applications Development and Solutions Center, IBM UK Ltd.

Woodward, J. (1958). *Management and Technology.* London: HM Stationery Office.

Wright, P.C. and Oldford, A. (1995). Telecommuting and employee effectiveness career and managerial issues. *International Journal of Career Management,* electronic document located at http://www.mcb.co.uk/services/conferen/hrn/ijcm/ijcmcon1.html Virtual Conference Centre File name: Reading1.htm

Zorkoczy, P. (1989). *Development of Instructional Technology Architecture and Associated Strategies*, Technical Report n. 25. Milton Keynes: The Open University, Centre for Electronic Education.

Zorkoczy, P. (1991). *Developments Coming from Telecommunications and Training-related Services*. Proceedings of the TBT'91 Workshop, DELTA Programme, Commission of the European Communities.

PS

An electronic version of this chapter is available online in the following URL address:

http://www.ucm.es/OTROS/Psyap/libros/telework/

Chapter 6

Assessment in a Technological World

PAUL G. W. JANSEN

Department of Business Administration, Faculty of Economics and Econometrics, Free University of Amsterdam, De Boelelaan 1105, 1081 HV Amsterdam, The Netherlands

INTRODUCTION

Information is considered to be the fifth production factor, in addition to land, capital, labour and management. Information technology is becoming one of the most critical means of production for all enterprises. In a recent organizational survey on the current competencies in business, participants identified a number of challenges facing their organizations. The investigator concludes that the 'challenges are so numerous and of such a magnitude that the overriding management issue was seen to be the development of more flexible and adaptable organizations' (Coulson-Thomas, 1991, p. 46). Large-scale application and sound management of information technology (IT) were mentioned as the most important means for coping with the external developments.

This chapter concentrates on the impact of IT on processes of personnel selection and assessment. Although it is an update of Jansen (1989), it can be read independently of that study. To quote Scott Morton (1991, p. v), who edited a volume of research directed at the impact of new information technologies (IT) on organizations, we will use 'a very broad definition of IT, including computers of all types, both hardware and software; communication networks, from those connecting two personal computers to the largest public and private networks; and the increasingly important integrating of computing and communication technologies, from a system that allows a personal computer to be connected to a mainframe in the office to globe-spanning networks of powerful mainframe computers'. By 'IT' we mean all technologies which are directed at the collection, storage, compilation, revision, editing, processing, and communication of

International Handbook of Selection and Assessments, Edited by N. Anderson and P. Herriot.
© 1997 John Wiley & Sons Ltd.

information. 'Information technology can be defined as the hardware and software that is used to collect, transmit, process and disseminate data in an organization' (Laudon and Turner, 1989).

In the next section we will present a brief overview of current IT developments. In the third section, seven general trends in organizations and work in which IT plays a dominant part are studied. In the final section we will discuss seven corresponding general trends in assessment procedures and systems.

CHANGES IN TECHNOLOGY

Developments in IT

Benjamin and Blunt (1992) verified to what degree predictions made by Benjamin in 1982 about IT development in the 1990s have been realized. What has come true is that:

- Work stations are as prevalent as telephones
- IT investments as percentage of turnover have increased by at least 50%

What specifically has *not* come true is that:

- IT applications for different functions have been integrated

Benjamin and Blunt go on to predict that in the near future:

- Electronic mail will be omnipresent, with integration of image, voice and text
- Managers who are responsible for IT organizations will have to acquire abilities for planned or controlled change; for IT to have success in the coming decennium, changes will have to be *managed*

It has become apparent that every IT application is in itself an organizational complication because:

- The centroid of knowledge, and thus of power, is transferred
- The dimension of time is modified
- It facilitates new ways of organizing

Successful implementations of IT systems are scarce because they do not represent a neutral instrument but have their own dynamic impact on the organization.

Applications of IT

This becomes apparent with applications of IT, where we face the dilemma that as applications get more and more entangled and integrated, complexity and costs will increase, but in cases of separate, independent applications, problems of consistency and coordination arise, and consequently costs will still rise accordingly as the organization increases in size.

In general, IT applications can be grouped into four categories:

1. *Control* systems: these control business processes in a real-time way, e.g. an accounting system which operates on the basis of weekly reports, or production process control systems in chemistry plants.
2. *Information collection and processing* systems: e.g. computers, printers, terminals, microfilm, archive systems, distributed databases, text processing, xerographic systems, interactive (video)systems.
3. *Personal support* systems: e.g. electronic agendas, expert systems, telework, management information systems.
4. *Communication* systems: e.g. telephone, telex, facsimile, teleconferencing, image processing, electronic data interchange, electronic mail.

Current trends are, first, to integrate the four types of applications (e.g. telematics, multimedia applications), and second, to 'de-individualize' (in particular the second and third type of systems). We are witnessing a development to 'group support systems', systems which support collaborative group work. In the latter case, of course, research is warranted especially into the cultural requirements and limits of 'Shared Information Technology' (see, for example, Kydd and Jones, 1989).

Innovation cycles for personal computers (PCs) and corresponding software are still accelerating. Since the introduction of the PC by IBM in 1981, two additional PC generations have already passed by (categorized by type of micro processor). As a consequence, software generally is lagging behind. It is, however, important to stress that the main technological advances in IT do not relate to advances in increased speed or memory capacity, but to increased modularity, flexibility, applicability and reusability of hardware and software environments (Boynton, 1993, p. 60).

Therefore accurate forecasting of forthcoming technological changes still remains difficult. It is possible to a limited degree to predict incremental changes in existing technology (such as faster levels of the PC), but it is almost impossible to predict at present still unknown breakthroughs in technology, let alone their impact on functionality. Thus, although the importance of 'technology monitoring' is increasing, is still does a bad job of actual forecasting (Boyd, 1992, pp. 16–17).

Roach (1991) argues that in the United States, the large amount of investment in IT in the service sector (e.g. banking, retail and wholesale trade) has not led to a corresponding increase in productivity. In the realm of services, technology 'connects' machines, but so far it has done little to install productive synergy among people (in contrast to manufacturing where technology year after year has given rise to more efficient ways to production). Until now, IT has been severely *under*-used in services because it has not been accompanied by appropriate changes in working habits: 'The challenge facing services is primarily managerial' (Roach, 1991, p. 91). But we are on the verge of a change in this. In the next section we will describe a number of general IT-related trends which will have a large impact on service organizations or staff departments in the coming years.

CHANGES IN FUNCTIONAL CONTEXT AND CONTENT

Rising standards of living, the improving educational level of the workforce and the growing complexity of all the respective markets 'surrounding' a company (e.g. the consumer market, the financial market, the labour market, but also the 'political market') have the effect of making the environment of a company much more complicated—and also increasingly *unpredictable*. Organizations are becoming interweaved with other organizations. Narrow connections to external suppliers and customers are arising. As the *velocities* of diverse 'turnarounds' within an organization accelerate, the speed of various processes increases, and the time for research, production, and sales is shortened. Far-reaching decisions have to be made on a basis of uncertain or incomplete information. Moreover, industrial corporations are being restructured according to principles of lean production, of the 'learning organization' (Senge, 1990), and of total quality management.

Organizations are being created that are *dynamically stable* and IT, and especially management of information is going to play an important role in this context (Boynton, 1993). Future organizations will be characterized in the following terms: networked, integrative, flat, flexible, small, vision-based and team-oriented (Bancroft, 1992, p. 249). Job definitions will be flexible, decisions will be made at numerous levels, power will be shared, improvement will be continuous, and learning will be viewed as work (Bancroft, 1992, p. 254).

In view of all this, we distinguish the following general trends in organizations and work:

- Unpredictability of future functions
- Increasing velocity
- Permanent change

In addition we envisage four other developments.

Fourth trend: Knowledge-driven companies

Modern organizations will move from being energy-based or energy-driven to being information-based or knowledge-driven (Boyd, 1992; Roos and Von Krogh, 1992). Industries are becoming more dependent on advanced knowledge than on energy. This means that 'individual abilities will continue to be critically important to their organizations' (Boyd, 1992, p. 11). Examples are the pharmaceutical, genetic engineering, ceramic, aerospace, and telecommunications industries. Although, because of the application of new technologies, the number of people employed in these industries is tending to decrease, the remaining workers have a proportionally larger influence on the organization's final performance. 'Most firms already are, or soon will be, competing on competencies' (Roos and Von

Krogh, 1992, p. 423; see also Sparrow, Chapter 17 in this volume). This implies that a firm's particular competencies have to be both *assessed* and *managed*.

Adler (1986, p. 20) concludes that 'the life-long learning idea is not just another passing fad; it reflects the changing nature of technology'—which parallels the conclusion in Jansen (1989, p. 96) that 'psychological abilities that are critical to "education permanente" within the function are required'. Finally, Bancroft (1992, pp. 243–244) also mentions life-long learning, growing diversity, increased entrepreneurship, and greater intellectual skill as implications of IT from the perspective of the workforce. This implies further trends.

Fifth trend: Upgrading of function content

In Jansen (1989) we gauged the effects of computerization on functions in two categories: *informatics* and *automation* (the same distinction can be found in Scott Morton, 1991, and Zuboff, 1988). Informatics (information science) relates to the situation whereby more and more workers are called upon to handle information: to collect information, to prepare information for others, to reason with information, and make decisions based on information.

Automation, on the other hand, means that either the production process itself or the control over production is automated. In the first case, controlling tasks remain a human 'prerogative'. Automation can lead to monotonous vigilance tasks, brought about by the necessity of having to perform simple operations very close together in a short time. But this is not necessary; ample evidence exists for the reverse outcome of automation. Because of this, Jansen (1989) concluded that there is no one-to-one, direct translation of technological innovation into working conditions; it depends on management practices.

The same conclusion, that the impact of IT on jobs is decided by management practices, is reached by Roach (1991), and it can also be found in a recent overview by Yates and Benjamin (1991). They state that IT aimed at reducing costs will very probably tend to deskill jobs. This is reinforced by the traditional engineers' norm of 'perfect' machine performance. According to this, the sophisticated IT equipment should be 'protected' against its users. 'Idiot-proof is still very often the engineer's implicit norm' (Adler, 1986, p. 12). But applications made in order to increase organizational effectiveness tend to increase job scope. Depending on how IT is used, that is, how it is *managed*, it may enhance or deskill functions. Ostermann (1991) addressed the same topic. IT in the hands of a manager with Tayloristic perspective will lead to deskilling jobs, but in the hands of a manager with a socio-technical or 'empowerment' style, it will lead to enlarged employee creativity in the interaction between employee and new technology. He refers to a study of circuit board design. Whereas it appeared in fact to be possible to let a relatively unskilled employee design a board using Computer Aided Construction technology, far better results were obtained when the new technology was made a tool in the hands of skilled workers.

As a result of a systematic survey, Adler (1986) concluded that the general impact of new technologies on jobs had had an *upgrading*, not a de-skilling effect. This is reinforced by the fact that the increasing sophistication of IT, handling IT in itself becomes a major skill that enriches the job. The 'corporation of the 1990s' (Scott Morton, 1991) asks for general problem-solving skills, for abstract intellectual functioning.

For example: Telework

Telework refers to an employee who works, for at least 20% of the working hours, at a fixed place that is geographically separated from the location of the employer, but who remains 'on line' connected to the company via IT applications (via a 'life line'). Weijers, Meijer and Spoelman (1992, p. 1049) recently published a study about telework in The Netherlands, according to which experiences with telework in the UK are the same as in The Netherlands. They estimate that about 25% of all jobs in The Netherlands could be done through telework. Weijers, Meijer and Spoelman stipulate, however, that telework should be 'part of a larger set of arrangements towards a flexible organization of work' (1992, p. 1049). They also point out that telework gives birth to two quite different groups of functions: on one hand the work of the well-educated professionals, but on the other hand the typing and data entry jobs of the not-so-well educated (mostly female) workers. In both cases, the company consists of a very flexible, decentralized network, i.e. it does not have some kind of central head office.

The professionals report an increase in autonomy and flexibility; functions which are experienced, at the same time, as more stringent job requirements. They also mention an increase in motivation. The data typist work is characterized by an increase in social isolation and income uncertainty because of flexible 'min–max' contracts. Nevertheless, organizations report increases in productivity for both groups from 20% up to 40%. The impact of telework on professional jobs can, generally, be characterized as 'doing the reading, writing, problem solving, puzzling and thinking at home'. About two days a week are spent at the office to meet colleagues and to discuss the results obtained at home. Staff meetings become more important; they also tend to become more formal and structured. A general finding is that informal contacts do not deteriorate but become more efficient; they tend to 'get organized'.

Sixth trend: Interface management

Organizations react to the outburst of complexity and structural lack of control by implementing decentralization strategies. Davidson and Davis (1990) describe the emergence of another form of organizing brought about by the advent of the information society. *Not* a company which, like a box of bricks, is built from fixed functional cells, in which employees are 'locked in'. *But* a set of flexible tasks, a set of dynamic teams, a network the boundaries of which will be such that what is inside and what is outside the department becomes blurred. Intermediary layers and media are eliminated. 'Horizontal systems cut laterally across functions and departments so that process capabilities can be combined and recombined to support rapid and flexible product and service delivery' (Boynton, 1993, p. 69). Small business units are created which are closer to their *own* business environment. The new structures are linked to each other by a fine-drawn information network.

Hierarchical management is replace by 'horizontal management'. In order to increase output and commitment, employees are 'brought to the market'. Ritual, bureaucratic behaviour is 'rooted out' by opening up the organization in this way. But there is no *one* market: employees have to manage a complex set of interfaces with different environments—with their 'subordinates', with external or internal customers, with financial stakeholders, with suppliers, with political institutions and so on. All of these critical working situations are characterized by the necessity to *negotiate*. They represent a shift from hierarchical, vertical directing to horizontal adaptation and fine-tuning. It is not possible any more to 'get things done in/through people', to 'influence others in their course of action' (Moses and Byham, 1977) by invoking expert or hierarchical *power*. People have to be convinced, i.e. treated on an equal level. Output of the many interface situations which comprise the work of every employee should be both *contract* and *commitment*.

At present, this appears to be a difficult task, especially for managers who have been raised in a hierarchical organization, and who, in part, have relied on information knowledge as a source of their power. Essential components of interface management are:

• Having a general survey to determine what is effective in which situation
• Managing the bombardment of information, caused by informatics and the exponential increase of interfaces
• Stating clear goals to which employees feel committed
• Coaching instead of supervising, as control loses its status as the essence of managerial work
• Training of employees on the job; this means that a manager should possess professional job skills as well as being able to transfer them to employees
• Acceptance of global training needs, both for managers and for employees.

Stress on output

Emphasis on the output from the multitude of interfaces confirms the need for standardization of output as the mechanism of work coordination (Mintzberg, 1983). But this requires a clear functional structure: Where am I in the organization? Who is my customer? Who am I working for? This is one of the reasons for the 'flattening' of the organization described in the earlier section on 'interface management', i.e. re-engineering the work towards a simpler structure. Increased stress on output is complicated by the trend towards 'upgrading of functionality', which in turn involves professionalism, i.e. standardization of skills, as the coordinating mechanism. In particular, this professional and organizational (cultural) standardization is directed to the *style* of delivering the product or services to customers, that is to the style of 'interface management'. Since (as is also acknowledged in modern marketing theory) companies are competing on such professional and organizational *values*, in effect this style *is* the very product.

Organizations are beginning to realize that customers are literally buying *the way* in which they get their products or services delivered. In this manner, the co-ordinating mechanisms of standardization of output and of skills become equivalent—which increases the management problems described in the discussion on interface management.

In the next section we will investigate how current selection and assessment procedures cope with these seven trends. See Figure 6.1 for an overview.

CHANGES IN ASSESSMENT TECHNIQUES AND PROCEDURES

Classification of assessment procedures

There are numerous procedures for assessing a person's performance or potential. When we assume that present behaviour is the best predictor of future behaviour, these methods can be ordered according to two leading questions which, in our opinion, a user of assessment *should* ask him or herself when designing an assessment procedure (cf. Jansen, 1991). The first is:

1. Does the present function of the candidate include tasks which are a sample of the function for which the candidate is to be assessed? That is, can the prior function, in terms of concrete sets of behaviour, be compared to the function at issue?

GENERAL TRENDS IN

Organizations and work	Selection and assessment
1. Unpredictability of future functions $\longrightarrow$	Assessment of general characteristics
2. Increasing velocity $\longrightarrow$	More efficient and faster assessment; computerized testing
3. Permanent change $\longrightarrow$	Assessment of dynamic criteria
4. Knowledge-driven companies $\longrightarrow$	Assessment of learning potential
5. Upgrading of functionality $\longrightarrow$	Abstraction and self-assessment
6. Interface management $\longrightarrow$	Situational assessment
7. Stress on output $\longrightarrow$	Utility of selection and assessment

Figure 6.1 Trends in organizations and work, and corresponding trends in selection and assessment

Suppose question 1 is affirmed. Then obviously the next question is:

2. Is it possible to acquire this already existing function information in a reliable, valid, efficient, and ethical way?

When this question is also answered in the affirmative, a set of assessment techniques for *recording past behaviour* is indicated. Examples are the application letter (or form), references, performance appraisal, and a biographical questionnaire by means of which a detailed inventory is made of specific elements of past behaviour. Comparable to the latter instrument is the accomplishment record (Hough, 1984): a precise and written documentation of what someone *really* has been able to accomplish in their previous function (i.e. a record of past job successes). The most important instrument belonging to this category is, however, the traditional interview in which the candidate *tells* the assessor *about* his or her experiences.

But when the first question is answered with *no*, one has to resort to procedures which *evoke* with the candidate their behaviour vis-à-vis the function at issue. The same route is indicated when the answer to the second question is negative. In both these cases, assessment procedures should aim at letting the candidate demonstrate, in controlled circumstances, critical behaviours of the future function. These methods first generate actual ('present') behaviour, which is subsequently assessed.

To this category there belong two types of instruments. First, those which are based on either a 'written' simulation of job behaviour—the mental test (invoking relevant cognitive behaviours by paper-and-pencil means)—or a 'verbal simulation'—the situational interview (asking the candidate what he or she would actually do or say when confronted with . . .). And second, those in which 'real life' behaviour is generated: the assessment centre method. Using these distinctions, various techniques for assessing persons can be classified according to the scheme depicted in Figure 6.2.

Figure 6.2 is, generally, self-explanatory. Note that the interview is considered both a recording and a generating instrument. It focuses both on past behaviour and on the (present) way the candidates behave in the interview itself in accordance with a number of problem situations presented to them. Many of the difficulties in conducting a selection interview that is both effective and appealing to candidates are to be attributed to this double layer of letting the candidates talk about their past behaviour and having to consider this talking in itself as some kind of situational exercise.

Having classified assessment instruments and procedures in this way, we can now turn to a discussion of the impact of the seven organizational trends on assessment and selection (cf. Figure 6.1).

First trend. Unpredictability of future functions: Assessment of general characteristics

The number and nature of interfaces cannot be planned beforehand. Therefore assessment will increasingly be oriented towards 'meta-criteria' such as the ability to learn, the motivation for change and, even, being amused at dynamic

Does the present function include tasks which are a sample of
the function for which the candidate is to be assessed?

|No |Yes

↓   ↓

Techniques for   ←——— No ——— Is it possible to acquire the
invoking functional   information on present function
behaviour   performance in a reliable, valid,
                                    efficient and ethical way?

↓   ↓   ↓   Yes

Real   Verbal   Written   ↓
life
         ↓
      Situational   Techniques for recording
      interview   past function behaviour

                                            ↓

Assessment   Mental test   Interview
centre   Personality   Application letter
Interview   questionnaire   Biographical
                                   questionnaire
                                   References
                                   Accomplishment
                                   record
                                   Performance
                                   appraisal

└————————————————┘   └————————————————┘
Focus on present behaviour   Focus on past behaviour

Figure 6.2   Classification of assessment procedures according to two leading questions

unpredictability. This is reinforced by the fact that several studies have shown
that between two and four factors typically underlie assessors' ratings (see e.g.
Thornton and Byham, 1982; Shore, Thornton and McFarlane Shore, 1990). The
latter are, as a result of such empirical analyses of assessment centre results, in
favour of 'grouping assessment dimensions into broad interpersonal- and
performance-style categories' (Shore, Thornton and McFarlane Shore, 1990, p.
111). These general or *meta-dimensions* embrace being:

- Intelligent (in several senses: analytical, creative, social, practical—'problem
  solving', *intellectual competencies*)
- Socially oriented and capable (interpersonal sensitivity/effectiveness: 'interpersonal skills', *interpersonal competencies*)
- Independent and strong (decisive, resistant: 'leadership', *adaptability and resilience competencies*)
- Ambitious (motivated, involved, committed)
- Operationally competent (productive, effective, systematical: 'planning and organizing', *results orientation competencies*) graduates

The terms in quotes stem from the study by Shore, Thornton and McFarlane Shore. Similar 'supra competencies' are reported by Dulewicz (1989); they have been printed in italics.

These are just general categories, in a language that fits the company's management style. For example, the very same quartet of meta-dimensions (competencies) is used, with different denotations in each case, by three of the largest Dutch corporations (Royal Shell, Philips, Royal PTT Nederland) to assess the career potential of young academic graduates (Van Wees and Jansen, 1994). Note that, in these examples, the use of meta-criteria does not imply that person assessment takes place in a vague, impressionistic way. The general, dimensional ratings are firmly rooted in a basis of concrete behaviour, reliably observed in relevant (sample-valid) situational exercises.

It is extremely important for psychologists not only to formulate those criteria, but also to keep them tied both to a *behavioural basis*, and to what is known in psychological science. Every manager will subscribe to the need for 'creativity', 'adaptive thinking' and 'abstract reasoning'. But there is a lot of disagreement about what this means *in practice*, and what contribution can be expected from these competences to 'daily business'. Until now, psychology has been only moderately successful in translating existing theories of intelligence and personality *processes*, for instance the 'triarchic theory of intelligence' (Sternberg, 1985) or the 'Big Five of personality' (Barrick and Mount, 1991), into workable assessment procedures (and development procedures as well on account of the fourth general trend). It will be a challenge for psychologists to deal effectively and professionally with the problems of clients who ask for general meta-criteria, while at the same time not succumbing to the temptation to use all kinds of vague, impressionistic assessment instruments and dimensions.

Second trend. Increasing velocity: More efficient and faster assessment

A general trend with respect to selection of job applications, which can be observed especially with respect to assessment centre implementations, is that organizations are demanding that they should be more simple, less time-consuming and thereby less costly (see also the seventh general trend). Assessor training programs taking three days or longer are difficult to 'sell'. In the same way, it is becoming less acceptable for assessment centre end meetings to last several days. For the future, an important challenge to psychologists is the need to simplify assessment procedures, in time and costs, without lowering standards of validity, reliability and ethics. One means to this end is, for instance, reducing the number of dimensions to be weighed in an assessment centre. The remaining dimensions then are more of a general, 'meta-'nature, in accordance with the first (but also with the third and fifth) general trend.

Computerized testing

As described by Jansen (1989, p. 104; see also Burke, 1992) computerized testing started in the early 1960s. Initially, computers were used to score and interpret standard psychological tests. Later on, new scoring models, based on item response theory instead of on classical true score theory, were applied. In addition, extra information on testing behaviour (e.g. latencies) was recorded. Jansen concluded that 'it is still uncertain what will be the general impact of computerized testing on the design and implementation of instruments of personnel selection. Partly, this is caused by a, still, relative lack of experience with real world applications'. The latter still holds true. In Europe, acceptance and general application of computerized testing in normal selection settings seems to take longer than expected. Other reviewers also state that computerized testing has not yet lived up to its expectations (see Bartram, 1989; Burke and Normand, 1987; Skinner and Pakula, 1986).

Recently, a special issue of the German *Journal for Work and Organizational Psychology* was devoted to 'computer-assisted assessment' (Ottawa, 1993). In his introduction (p. 108) the guest-editor concluded that for practical, large scale applications, advantages still seem to be limited to:

1. *Easier processing of large numbers of candidates.* It seems that, at present, computerized assessment serves two aims: to increase efficiency and heighten effectiveness. Mostly only the first is realized, in the form of less test-taking time and more accurate estimation of personal ability. With respect to the second, test builders generally confine themselves to the statement that validity is not lowered by computerizing. An often neglected third aim is greater acceptability, because the test is 'individualized'.
2. *Avoiding the appearance of school exams.* This was also mentioned by Jansen (1989) as an important 'corporate image argument' in favour of computerized testing. With the rise of new computer technology, it may be culturally necessary to abandon 'old-fashioned' paper-and-pencil tests and to resort to computerized testing, although from a scientific or rational point of view nothing may be gained by this. Computerized testing may not yield better predictions of job success and it may be a lot more expensive, but it does send the message to job applicants that the company is really 'high tech'.

By using computerization, it is possible to design the test in such a way that it adapts itself to the testee. An essential for this kind of 'tailoring' is of course an external criterion, e.g. a required level of accuracy of the estimation of the subject's capacity, or the establishment of that item difficulty at which the testee eventually attains a score of 50% correct. At present, tailored testing takes two forms.

In the case of *adaptive testing*, the items exist already, in the form of a large bank, from which items are sampled in such a way that the external criterion is attained in an efficient way. Necessary for this application are:

- A well stocked bank (entailing a big prior investment)
- An algorithm for computing fast and reliable estimates of the person's ability
- A criterion for estimation error, i.e. a measurement model

In the case of *dynamic testing*, however, items are constructed 'on the spot'. The test does not consist of preconceived, fixed format items, but is equivalent to a procedure for constructing items. The computerized test consists of an item-building algorithm by which concrete items are generated for the candidate being tested. In the latter case, the flexibility of the test in adapting itself to the present candidate is its major asset. Necessary in this case are:

- An item-generating algorithm for the construction of the item content, both according to a pre-established format and to comply with a pre-established level of difficulty
- A criterion for estimation error

In the opinion of this author, real progress will be made in computerized testing when program designers do not have to concentrate any more on the *way* the test is administered, but instead can redirect their attention to test content, and to scoring models. Computerizing the *dynamic interplay* between candidate and test should be considered 'clerk's work'; it is not the essence of computerized *assessment*.

An example of a successful computerization of the test administration process alone, is the system 'Personal Question Manager' (PQM) built by the Institute of Applied Organizational Research of Royal PTT Nederland (Hoekstra and Boekhoudt, 1993). It is distributed by one of the largest testing service organizations in The Netherlands. PQM is not a specific application. It is an empty 'shell' in which all types of concrete computer interactions—e.g. mental tests, attitude questionnaires, telephonic inquiries, checklists (for instance used in routine equipment checks, or annual medical controls), performance appraisal, and self-assessment—can be implemented. The typical interaction situation is that, first, a question or problem situation is presented on a display, and second, the candidate has to give an answer or make some choice. Depending on the response, the next question or situation is presented. The core of PQM consists of a very flexible editor for text, graphic materials (also video images), results processing, data storage, and reporting. By using PQM in that way one is able to implement, in a very short time, every type of interaction wanted.

A system such as PQM restores to the psychologist the responsibility for the *content* of the system, that is the responsibility for

- designing new item materials

and

- developing corresponding scoring models

both of which have been neglected in many computerized assessment initiatives.

In general, it appears that the transition from isolated pioneering and pilot applications of computerized testing to large-scale implementations in normal day-to-day assessment activities is slow. In The Netherlands the general situation at present is that all large private assessment organizations are involved in computerized testing. But it is still not a 'mainstream' activity. Computerized assessment is reserved for special clients, and not yet directed to the mass market.

Some reasons for this are:

1. Managers, personnel advisers, psychologists and assessees still seem to be 'afraid' of technology.
2. Computerized assessment brings back the flavour of professionalism it was starting to abandon. In the circumstances of computerization, managers have the feeling that they are again, 'alienated' from assessment procedures.
3. Budget for computerization generally is low. Companies do not want to spend much money on this—although they are still prepared to invest a lot of money both in new technology (e.g. computerization of offices) and in other assessment implementations, e.g. the assessment centre, which are more appealing.
4. Computerized testing follows the common curve in acceptance of (very) new technologies or of diffusion of innovation. The start is very slow, followed by a gradual increase in use, but then suddenly, at the point of about 40% 'market share', a sudden 'burst' of implementations occurs. As Bartram (1989, p. 369) puts it: 'Throughout history, the initial impact of any new technology tends to have been constrained by the difficulty people have divorcing themselves from ways of thinking related to the old technology.' In our view, acceptance of computerized assessment will increase when managers are more inclined to *actually use* IT in their daily work.
5. Initiatives in computerized testing are mainly directed to incorporating the administrative part of the test-taking process into the computer. But as was stipulated above, applied psychologists, managers, and testees, are (rightly) mainly interested in test *content*.

By putting the 'hardware of psychology into the computer' it will become more accepted that interpretation of test results is not the preserve of psychologists any more, but is done either by personnel officers, or by the candidates themselves (see the fifth general trend for a discussion of the latter). Because of this 'democratization' of psychological assessment techniques, in the near future the task of a psychologist will consist of instrument construction and validation, of transference of testing knowledge and practices, and of advising personnel officers or counselling candidates.

Third trend. Permanent change: Assessment of dynamic criteria

The most interesting features of computerized assessment are:

- The possibility of tailored testing
- The possibility of avoiding the limitations posed by traditional paper-and-pencil media

An example of the latter would be performing interactive situational exercises on a PC. J. Funke (1993) studied computer-based situational exercises (e.g. the in-basket). Because job requirements are becoming ever more complex (see earlier sections), the simulations obviously cannot be true replications of future work. Sample validity has therefore to be ascertained at a higher, more abstract level of function requirements. Funke argues that what counts in a technological world is the ability to learn quickly, adequately and permanently (the same was stipulated by Jansen, 1989, pp. 101–102). In this respect, it is pointed out that it is not so much the participants in a management game who undergo a learning experience, but the constructors of the game! In the same way, assessment of computerized situational exercises should be directed at learning abilities: at the ability (a) to construct models for seemingly fuzzy problems with many variables, and (b) to put these hypotheses to an empirical test. An example of using computer-based procedures to assess candidates' analysis and solution *processes* of this kind of complex dynamic problem is presented by U. Funke (1993).

The general turn from studying output measures to process attributes in assessment, stimulated both by (extra-) organizational developments and by computerization, was preceded by developments in formal test theory which started some 25 years ago but which never really permeated to practical applications. Or as Moser and Schuler (1989, p. 282) put it: 'With regard to measurement and testing situations in organizations, so far these *probabilistic* models have almost no importance. The classical test theoretical model is still dominant.' There is a whole body of severely underused, 'modern' item response theory especially suited for these kinds of assessment situations (see e.g. Guion and Ironson, 1983). In this respect Ottawa's complaint (1993, p. 108), about test theory lagging behind this trend of 'dynamising' in applications, is not correct.

Another consequence of the turn to dynamic criteria is that basic motivational processes become more important. Organizations, but also individual employees, want to know what motivates people. At present, the best possible instrument for assessing employee motivation is still the interview. And because the motivation interview has to be well conducted, it will remain a prerogative of psychologists. In some companies already, it is customary to probe basic motivational processes of employees around mid-life, in order to prevent early obsolescence. Not only on account of recurring technological innovations, but also in respect of the demographic trend towards an ageing workforce, assessment of motivation for permanent learning is becoming compulsory (cf. Rosen and Jerdee, 1989; Waskel, 1991; Welford, 1976).

Fourth trend. Knowledge-driven companies: Assessment of learning potential

Central to the proposed classification in Figure 6.1 are first the notion of functions overlapping in tasks, and second the difference between recording past behaviour and evoking actual or present behaviour. Another distinction that comes into use when the candidate's observed behaviour has to be weighed according to some pre-established norm, is that between taking either the present or the future as a norm. That is, one can assess either *performance*—what counts is present mastery of the variety of problems posed—or *potential*—what counts is the assessed potential to attain future performance standards later on, in due time.

At present, the trend is clearly towards assessing for potential instead of assessing for performance. This is caused by the societal, technological, and organizational developments described earlier. These make it very difficult, if not impossible, to predict what specific kinds of function skills will be needed even in the near future. What are needed instead are 'dynamic criteria' such as awareness of the necessity to learn, flexibility, trainability and eagerness for personal development. For instance, instead of performance-oriented assessment centres we see potential-oriented development centres (Goodge, 1991; Griffith and Allen, 1987; Iles, Robertson and Rout, 1989). The same trends can be observed in the domain of computerized assessment. In Jansen (1989, p. 101f.) we argued that the classical intelligence test is, in particular, suitable for assessment of the ability to pick up complex and new mental tasks fast, i.e. it can be a good indicator of 'fluid intelligence'.

The shift from performance to potential, however, has implications for the evaluation of assessment results. For example, when an in-basket is used to assess the current *performance* level of a candidate, it is necessary to eliminate all kinds of disturbances having to do with the candidate not being accustomed to this kind of selection technique. Research has revealed that in-basket performance improves on replication, but that this exercise effect wears out after the second in-basket (Brannick, Michaels and Baker, 1989). Therefore, an efficient means for assessing the 'real' performance level is to apply an in-basket twice (preferably two parallel forms), and to base the assessment result on the second outcome. But when the aim is to assess *potential*, the difference between the second and first in-basket achievements can be taken as indicative of learning potential.

It is important to remark here that this shift to dynamic, future-oriented criteria does not imply that past behaviour cannot be taken any more as a basis for making predictions about future behaviour. Instead, it involves a transformation in the evaluation of past performances. The recording procedures in assessment will increasingly become oriented towards more abstract criteria such as 'general style of functioning', and 'modes of behaviour'. And this of course has implications for invoking either sample validity or construct validity as a priori indicators of the effectiveness of assessment.

Fifth trend. Upgrading of function content: Abstraction and self-assessment

Adler (1986) identifies three qualitative changes in types of skill: new type of task responsibility, new degree of task abstractness, and new levels of task interdependence. Manual tasks become procedural. Higher order conceptual processes dominate. Workers must have a general understanding of the organizational information flow and of computer system operations. The net effect is an abstraction of tasks.

This is visible for instance in the class of computing functions. Benjamin and Blunt (1992) predict that it will remain a hybrid: maintenance of infrastructure and adviser for higher level management. The trend is to stimulate management of IT by appointing IT directors (Coulson-Thomas, 1991). They should excel in technical, as well as in business, organizational, and advisory competences. With respect to programming, the age of the laborious 'monk work' seems to be coming to an end. In the future, programs will be constructed from 'semi-manufactured articles' or ready-made 'objects'. The work of a programmer thereby acquires a 'synthetic' quality.

Another consequence of the upgrading of functionality is a shift in responsibility from the manager to the employee (also conditioned by the 'flattening' of organizations). In the domain of assessment this will reinforce an already visible movement toward self-assessment. Employees are, and feel, responsible for their own careers, for keeping their knowledge and ability levels up to date. In correspondence with the fourth general trend, they regularly invite feedback on their behaviour, on account both of 'real work' in the past, and of performance generated by, say, situational exercises in an assessment centre, and on account of, for example, self-report instruments (for instance a behavioural questionnaire). *Employees become more curious about how they are doing, and what this implies for what they will be doing in the future.* Accordingly, we move to the complex situation that employees want to play an active part in the interpretation of information which refers both to their past and their present performance, which is phrased in general, 'abstract' terminology, and which should comply with trainability-oriented or potential development criteria. Because of this, the need for career guidance by a professional psychologist will increase.

Still another consequence of increased career curiosity and commitment has already been discussed under the label 'democratization' with respect to the second general trend. Psychologists will have to become more open, and will have to make their instruments transferable either to staff such as personnel officers or to the candidates themselves. For example, in The Netherlands several 'do-it-yourself' books of such a clear and explicit 'cookery book' nature have appeared recently (cf. Jansen and de Jongh, 1993; Van der Maesen de Sombreff, 1990, 1993). In these publications, the authors try to reconcile scientific standards with practical feasibility.

Sixth trend. Interface management: Situational assessment

When work becomes equivalent to effectively handling a multitude of interfaces, a trend towards 'situational assessment' is indicated. Employees grow either by learning to handle *more and essentially different* interface situations, or by learning to cope with the *same* situation (e.g. dealing with a customer), taking into account different norms of effectiveness (e.g. either qualitative or quantitative criteria).

A number of authors argue that the assessment centre is a predictively valid instrument because it probes, via a limited number of critical job samples, the candidate's *mastery of essential functional tasks*, of critical job elements (see Goodge, 1988; Neidig and Neidig, 1984; Norton, 1977; Sackett and Dreher, 1982, 1984). In accordance with the second and seventh trends toward more simple assessment procedures, these authors in effect propose 'task-based assessments' in which candidates get feedback on their overall effectiveness in dealing with specific, critical job situations. By using only meta-dimensions this type of very situation-specific assessment can be aligned with the first general trend. Generally, task-based or situational assessment (not only in the form of an assessment centre, but also implemented in a situational interview, or a biographical inventory, or a procedure for performance appraisal) requires less time (for assessor training and for the final meeting), and produces results which are both more easily fed back to the candidate, and lend themselves much better for training and development purposes.

Seventh trend. Stress on output: Utility of selection and assessment

In close correspondence with the second general trend, organizations increasingly want to have insight into the cost-effectiveness of assessment—not only with respect to the application of, for example, a mental test in the case of entrance selection of academic graduates, but also regarding development-oriented assessment of senior personnel, and with respect to the training programme itself. As an illustration, some doctoral dissertations have recently appeared in The Netherlands, written by professional psychologists (all working 'in the field') about the utility of selection (Van der Maesen de Sombreff, 1992) or of training (Van Sandick and Schaap-Neuteboom, 1993). These studies (based on the work of Schmidt *et al.*, 1979, and Schmidt, Hunter and Pearlman, 1982) were directed at existing, frequently used assessment or development instruments and procedures. In both cases, satisfying results were obtained. The attention devoted to these studies by the general public (e.g. in the form of newspaper articles and interviews in the popular press), demonstrates the current appeal of the 'language of money'. This trend will certainly continue.

CONCLUSION

Confidence in the short-term fruits of among IT has decreased considerably the past few years, particularly among managers. Costs have been increasing steadily, while revenues have not yet become visible. IT was too widely regarded as a means of rationalizing existing business processes or functions. The life-cycle of such a technically-oriented IT seems at its end. A new 'breed' of IT, of an intrinsically service-oriented nature, is on the way, paralleled by a shift from software-driven functions in computing, to functions based on providing consultancy. The introduction of IT tends to be accompanied by a rethinking or re-engineering of the entire business process (this was one of the main topics of the second European Congress on IT, 1992). Compared to the previous review made by Jansen (1989), progress has been made in the realms of technology and assessment. The use of (personal) computers, both to process and to communicate (share) information, has become widespread in managerial and general office functions. Functions, and organizations, are modifying themselves.

With respect to computerized assessment, professional psychologists will have to make the same 'turn'. From the adage 'automation is equivalent to reorganization', we can infer that computerized assessment means rethinking the total assessment process, *including* the position of the psychologist him/herself. In a technological world of value-driven, competency-based companies, assessing the asset of current competencies that will 'prevail' in the near future will become increasingly important, both for individual employees and for the organization. And because of continual change, this assessment will have to take place on a periodic basis. It is in this respect that computerized assessment will become important, and even indispensable. But it will be implemented as a means of *repeated* self-assessment, both of the mix of current *competencies*, and of the dynamics of the *function* and its surroundings.

ACKNOWLEDGEMENT

The author is grateful to Srini Durvasala for his comments.

REFERENCES

Adler, P. (1986). New technologies, new skills. *California Management Review,* **24** (1), Fall, 9–28.
Bancroft, N. H. (1992). *New Partnerships for Managing Technological Change.* New York: Wiley.
Barrick, M. R. and Mount, M. K. (1991). The Big Five personality dimensions and job performance: A meta-analysis. *Personnel Psychology,* **44**, 1–26.
Bartram, D. (1989). Computer-based assessment. In P. Herriot (ed.), *Assessment and Selection in Organizations* (pp. 369–390). New York: Wiley.
Benjamin, R. I. and Blunt, J. (1992). Critical IT issues: The next ten years. *Sloan Management Review,* Summer, 7–19.
Boyd, C. W. (1992). *Individual Commitment and Organizational Change.* New York: Quorum Books.
Boynton, A. C. (1993). Achieving dynamic stability through information technology. *California Management Review,* **35** (2), Winter, 58–77.
Brannick, M. T., Michaels, Ch. E. and Baker, D. P. (1989). Construct validity of in-basket scores. *Journal of Applied Psychology,* **74**, 957–963.
Burke, M. J. (1992). Computerized psychological testing. In N. Schmitt and W. C. Borman (eds), *Personnel Selection* (pp. 203–239). San Francisco: Jossey-Bass.
Burke, M. J. and Normand, J. (1987). Computerized psychological testing. Overview and critique. *Professional Psychology,* **18**, 42–51.
Coulson-Thomas, C. (1991). Directors and IT, and IT directors. *European Journal of Information Systems,* 1(1), 45–53.
Davidson, W. H. and Davis, S. M. (1990). Management and organization principles for the information economy. *Human Resource Management,* **29**, 365–383.
Dulewicz, V. (1989). Assessment centres as the route to competence. *Personnel Management,* **21** (11), November, 56–59.
Funke, J. (1993). Computergestützte Arbeitsproben: Begriffsklärung, Beispiele Sowie Entwicklungspotentiale (Computer-based work samples: Concepts, examples, and future developments). *Zeitschrift für Arbeits- und Organisationspsychologie,* **37** (3), 119–129.
Funke, U. (1993). Computergestützte Eignungsdiagnostik mit komplexen dynamischen Szenarios (Computer-based personnel selection with complex dynamic scenarios). *Zeitschrift für Arbeits- und Organisationspsychologie,* **37** (3), 109–118.
Goodge, P. (1988). Task-based assessment. *Journal of European Industrial Training,* **12**, 22–27.
Goodge, P. (1991). Development centres: Guidelines for decision makers. *Journal of Management Development,* **10**, 4–12.

Griffith, P. and Allen, B. (1987). Assessment centres: Breaking with tradition. *Journal of Management Development*, **6**, 19–29.

Guion, R. M. and Ironson, G. H. (1983). Latent trait theory for organizational research. *Organizational Behavior and Human Performance*, **31**, 54–87.

Hoekstra, H. A. and Boekhoudt, M. (1993). *PQM (Personal Question Manager)*. Royal PTT Nederland/PTT Research ITB, Assessment & Human Resources. The Netherlands: Groningen.

Hough, L. M. (1984). Development and evaluation of the 'accomplishment record' method of selecting and promoting professionals. *Journal of Applied Psychology*, **69**, 135–146.

Iles, P., Robertson, I. and Rout, U. (1989). Assessment-based development centres. *Journal of Managerial Psychology*, **4**, 11–16.

Jansen, P. G. W. (1989). New technology and selection. In P. Herriot (ed.), *Assessment and Selection in Organizations* (pp. 93–107). New York: Wiley.

Jansen, P. G. W. (1991). *Het beoordelen van managers. Effectiviteit van assessmentcenter methoden bij selectie en ontwikkeling van managers* (Appraising managers. Effectiveness of assessment center methods for selection and development of managers). Baarn, The Netherlands: Nelissen.

Jansen, P. G. W. and Jongh, F., de (eds) (1993). *Assessment centers: Een open boek* (Assessment centers: An open book). Utrecht, The Netherlands: Het Spectrum/Marka.

Kydd, C. T. and Jones, L. H. (1989). Corporate productivity and shared information technology. *Information & Management*, **17**, 277–282.

Laudon, K. C. and Turner, J. (1989). *Information Technology and Management Strategy*. Englewood Cliffs, NJ: Prentice-Hall.

Maesen de Sombreff, P. E. A. M. (1990). *Testwijzer. Het gebruik van psychologische tests bij personeelsselectie* (Testwise. The use of psychological tests in personnel selection). Assen/Maastricht, The Netherlands: Van Gorcum.

Maesen de Sombreff, P. E. A. M. (1992). Het rendement van personeelsselectie (The profit of personnel selection). Doctoral dissertation. Groningen, The Netherlands: State University of Groningen.

Maesen de Sombreff, P. E. A. M. (1993). *De testgids* (The test guide). Amsterdam, The Netherlands: VNU/BPA.

Mintzberg, H. (1983). *Structure in Fives: Designing Effective Organizations*. Englewood Cliffs, NJ: Prentice-Hall.

Moser, K. and Schuler, H. (1989). The nature of psychological measurement. In P. Herriot (ed.) *Assessment and Selection in Organizations* (pp. 282–305). New York: Wiley.

Moses, J. L. and Byham, W. C. (1977). *Applying the Assessment Center Method*. New York: Pergamon Press.

Neidig, R. D. and Neidig, P. J. (1984). Multiple assessment center exercises and job relatedness. *Journal of Applied Psychology*, **69**, 182–186.

Norton, S. D. (1977). The empirical and content validity of assessment centres versus traditional methods for predicting managerial success. *Academy of Management Review*, **2**, 442–453.

Osterman, P. (1991). The impact of IT on jobs and skills. In M. S. Scott Morton (ed.), *The Corporation of the 1990s. Information Technology and Organizational Transformation* (pp. 61–91). New York: Oxford University Press.

Ottawa, H. (ed.) (1993). Themenheft Computerunterstützte Diagnostik (Special issue computer-assisted assessment). *Zeitschrift für Arbeits- und Organisationspsychologie*, **37** (3), 108–149.

Roach, S. S. (1991). Services under siege—The restructuring imperative. *Harvard Business Review*, September–October, 82–91.

Roos, J. and Krogh, G., von (1992). Figuring out your competence configuration. *European Management Journal*, **10** (4), December, 422–427.

Rosen, B. and Jerdee, T. H. (1989). Retirement policies: Evidence of the need for change. *Human Resource Management*, **28** (1) Spring, 87–103.

Sackett, P. R. and Dreher, G. F. (1982). Constructs and assessment centre dimensions: Some troubling empirical findings. *Journal of Applied Psychology*, **67**, 401–410.

Skacett, P. R. and Dreher, G. F. (1984). Situation specificity of behaviour and assessment centre validation strategies: A rejoinder to Neidig and Neidig. *Journal of Applied Psychology*, **69**, 187–190.

Sandick, A. S., van and Schaap-Neuteboom, A. M. (1993). Rendement van een bedrijfsopleiding. (Profit of a company training). Doctoral Dissertation. Zaandam, The Netherlands: Albert Heijn Opleidingen.

Schmidt, F. L., Hunter, J. E., McKenzie, R. C. and Muldrow, T. W. (1979). Impact of valid selection procedures on workforce productivity. *Journal of Applied Psychology*, **64**, 609–626.

Schmidt, F. L., Hunter, J. E. and Pearlman, K. (1982). Assessing the economic impact of personnel programs on workforce productivity. *Personnel Psychology*, **35**, 333–347.

Scott Morton, M. S. (ed.) (1991) *The Corporation of the 1990s. Information Technology and Organizational Transformation*. New York: Oxford University Press.

Second European Congress on Information Technology (1992). Organized by Heliview Marketingservice BV and KPMG Klynveld Management Consultants. Noordwijk (The Netherlands)/Frankfurt (Germany).

Senge, P. (1990). *The Fifth Discipline/Heart and Practice of the Learning Organization*. New York: Doubleday.

Shore, T. H., Thornton, G. C. III and McFarlane Shore, L. (1990). Construct validity of two categories of assessment center dimension ratings. *Personnel Psychology*, **43**, 101–116.

Skinner, H. A. and Pakula, A. (1986). Challenge of computers in psychological assessment. *Professional Psychology*, **17**, 44–50.

Sternberg, R. J. (1985). *Beyond IQ: A Triarchic Theory of Human Intelligence*. Cambridge: Cambridge University Press.

Thornton, G. G. III and Byham, W. C. (1982). *Assessment Centers and Managerial Performance*. New York: Academic Press.

Waskel, Sh. A. (1991). *Mid-life Issues and the Workplace of the 90s: A Guide for Human Resource Specialists*. Westport, CT: Quorum Books.

Wees, L., Van and Jansen, P. G. W. (1994). Dual ladder 'in balance'. *International Journal of Career Management* (in press).

Weijers, Th., Meijer, R. and Spoelman, E. (1992). Telework remains 'made to measure'. The large-scale introduction of telework in The Netherlands. *Futures*, **24** (December), 1048–1055.

Welford, A. T. (1976). Thirty years of psychological research on age and work. *Journal of Occupational Psychology*, **49**, 129–138.

Yates, J. and Benjamin, R. I. (1991). The past and present as a window on the future. In M. S. Scott Morton (ed.), *The Corporation of the 1990s. Information Technology and Organizational Transformation* (pp. 61–91). New York: Oxford University Press.

Zuboff, S. (1988). *In the Age of the Smart Machine: The Future of Work and Power*. New York: Basic Books.

Chapter 7

Selection and Training of Expatriate Employees

SAMUEL ARYEE

Department of Management, School of Business, Hong Kong Baptist University, 224 Waterloo Road, Kowloon, Hong Kong

INTRODUCTION

Progress in the fields of telecommunication and transportation, among others, has accelerated the integration of national economies with the consequent creation of a global economy. The competitive pressures that arise from a global economy have meant that for many organizations, setting up overseas subsidiaries has become a strategic option in their efforts to create and sustain competitive advantage. A critical requirement in the competitiveness of globalizing firms is the effective utilization of human resources in order to respond to the opportunities and challenges of expatriate assignments. A major challenge facing many globalizing firms, however, is the retention of expatriate employees in overseas subsidiaries with retention failure rates reported to be between 16% and 40% (Baker and Ivancevich, 1971; Stenning, 1979; Misa and Fabricatore, 1979; Tung, 1981). Such high retention failure rates are not limited to expatriate employees of globalizing firms, but generally, to various personnel who work and live in a foreign culture for a significant duration such as technical assistance personnel, Peace Corps volunteers and military personnel. Perhaps more so for globalizing firms than for other governmental organizations, retention failure rates in expatriate assignments constitute a significant financial impact as these firms seek to allocate resources to respond to the challenges of the global economy.

The consensus in the extant literature is that expatriate retention failure stems from the practice of using domestic staffing policies in staffing the overseas subsidiaries (Dowling and Schuler, 1990; Stone, 1991; Black, Gregersen and

International Handbook of Selection and Assessment, Edited by N. Anderson and P. Herriot.
© 1997 John Wiley & Sons Ltd.

Mendenhall, 1992). For many globalizing firms, therefore, the need to attune their staffing policies to the realities of the foreign environment may entail confronting such issues as:

1. How can the best people be selected to go abroad to work in a foreign environment?
2. How should they be trained?
3. Once selected, how can a cultural transition be made?
4. What do the nationals of one country working in another country need in order to be effective, productive workers in the new environment? (Korth, 1985, p. 440).

Efforts to minimize expatriate selection failure have, consequently, focused on developing more culture-sensitive selection and training practices. The selection and training practices of globalizing firms are, as in the domestic context, embedded in what Herriot (1992) describes as the psychometric subculture of selection with its managerialist concerns of productivity and cost–benefit utility.

Given its managerialist orientation, whether applied in the domestic or overseas context, the psychometric approach to selection tends to neglect the employee's subjective perception of his/her relationship with the organization and the mutuality of interest. An increasingly important concept that captures this mutuality is the concept of psychological contract. A psychological contract refers to an individual's beliefs regarding terms and conditions of a reciprocal exchange arrangement between that person and another party and can be described as transactional or relational. Transactional contracts involve specific monetizable exchanges between parties over a specific time period, the acquisition of people with specific skills to meet present needs at highly competitive wage rates, and the absence of long-term commitments. In contrast, relational contracts are reciprocal obligations involving both monetizable and non-monetizable exchanges, open-ended, governed by values of good faith and fair dealing and the motivation to sustain the relationship over time (Rousseau, 1989; Rousseau and Parks, 1993). At the core of both transactional and relational contracts is the notion of unwritten expectations on the part of both employees and employers regarding the nature of their exchange.

Recently, the employment relationship has been observed to be undergoing changes, and these changes take a variety of forms. Rousseau (1990) noted that in the face of competitive pressures, some organizations have moved to a more transactional contract in order to achieve maximum flexibility in work force utilization, while others have adopted strong cultures which emphasize long-term employment in exchange for loyalty and 'buy in' to the organization's culture and value (relational contract). Guzzo, Noonan and Elron (1994) suggested that expatriate employees experience broad, relational psychological contracts because virtually all parts of their daily lives are open to employer influence which defines both tangible and less tangible aspects of the contract. They suggested that the less tangible aspects of the contract should include the expectations of employees regarding their careers and centrality to the strategic core of the business while working abroad.

Consistent with its psychometric underpinnings, the primary focus in the expatriate selection and training literature are the needs of the globalizing firm. Given the expansive and therefore relational nature of the contract between globalizing firms and their expatriate employees, the position in this chapter is that in staffing their overseas subsidiaries, globalizing firms must not only be concerned with their needs, but also with those of their expatriate employees. For example, globalizing firms must be concerned with the extent to which an expatriate assignment will facilitate the career goals of the expatriate employee. The suggestion in this chapter, therefore, is for globalizing firms to adopt a social negotiation approach (Herriot, 1992) to staffing their overseas subsidiaries. Inherent in a social negotiation approach is the recognition that the employment relationship or, as in this context, the expatriate assignment, can and should satisfy the needs of both the globalizing firm and the expatriate employee. To this end, the selection procedures should provide opportunities for the expectations of both parties to be revealed, discussed and negotiated upon (Herriot, 1992). Such an orientation to the selection process would ensure a mutually satisfactory relational contract between the expatriate employee and his/her globalizing firm.

A mutually satisfactory relational contract is consistent with the model of work adjustment proposed by Lofquist and Dawis (1969) and applied to selection and retention in international contexts (Newman, Bhatt and Gutteridge, 1978). The model conceptualizes tenure or, as in this context, competence retention, as a function of both perceived satisfactoriness of the individual's job performance and individual job satisfaction. Perceived satisfactoriness of the individual's job performance is a function of the correspondence between his/her abilities and the ability requirements of the job. In the context of our discussion, such abilities and competencies might include knowledge of foreign markets, cultural values and norms, and the administration of product lines across regional barriers which are of increasing value to the globalizing firm (Mendenhall, Dunbar and Oddou, 1987). Given the broad relational contract expatriate employees experience (Guzzo, Noonan and Elron, 1994), it is our view that individual satisfaction and therefore competence retention is dependent upon both (1) organizational career development programmes that facilitate the career growth of expatriates (Feldman and Thomas, 1992; Tung, 1988) and (2) the fulfilment of the individual's expectations regarding an employer's responsibility for personal and family wellbeing (Guzzo, Noonan and Elron, 1994) or what Newman, Bhatt and Gutteridge (1978) describe as life satisfaction issues.

Competence retention has long been practised by the diplomatic service whereby diplomatic service personnel are regularly rotated through foreign assignments. Competence acquired from foreign assignment rotations are retained in the service when personnel are recalled home and, as experts in specific geographical areas, are charged with the responsibility for formulating policies for these areas. Application of the diplomatic service model of competence retention in globalizing firms would suggest a recognition of the expatriate assignment as an integral part of the globalizing firm's human resource development strategy. To this end, competence acquired by the expatriate employee as a result of his/her multiple expatriate assignments should be critical to building up organizational competencies and as a result facilitate the expatriate employee's career progression on returning to corporate headquarters (Tung, 1988; Mendenhall, Dunbar and Oddou, 1987).

Given the importance of a global perspective and cross-cultural skills in the increasingly competitive global economy, globalizing firms will have to design innovative ways of managing the expatriation process and of retaining competencies developed by their repatriated employees (while on expatriate assignment) if they are to successfully compete in the global economy.

NATURE AND CONTEXT OF EXPATRIATE ASSIGNMENTS

Since the vast majority of expatriate employees are managerial and/or professional employees, they not only have to respond to the domestic problems of motivation, leadership and productivity, but also many of these expatriate employees are commonly exposed to levels of responsibility far greater than would be true of their domestic colleagues. A model of the expatriate employee's network of relations developed by Rahim (1983), which implicitly defines the nature of the expatriate assignment, is depicted in Figure 7.1. Inherent in the model is experienced role conflict on the part of the expatriate employee. Rahim (1983) identified three sources of such role conflict. First, the expatriate employee is expected to conduct the operations of the subsidiary within the constraints imposed by the local or host governments. Role conflict may stem from the possible incompatibility between globalizing firms and host governments about ideologies, objectives and policies. A second source of conflict is the expectation that the expatriate employee act as a link between corporate headquarters and the subsidiary. This role requires the expatriate employee to implement objectives and policies formulated by corporate headquarters which may contradict the expatriate employee's way of handling local problems, thereby resulting in conflict. A final source of role conflict experienced by the expatriate employee stems from the long arm of the laws and regulations of the home government which may constrain the operations of the overseas subsidiaries. Since these laws and regulations may not necessarily be compatible with those of the host government, the expatriate employee may be caught in the middle of conflicting governmental regulations. As Torbiorn (1985) observed, the conflicts inherent in the expatriate assignment may be influenced by organizational norms, in terms of parent–company expectations of the manager, and by the set of cultural norms that the expatriate employee holds in relation to other cultural and organizational norms that may be represented by other role-senders. Given that an expatriate employee will have to live and work in a different sociocultural context, the nature of an expatriate assignment is jointly determined by organizational and cultural norms.

Although there is no commonly accepted definition of culture, Kluckhohn and Kroeberg's (1952) definition has gained widespread currency. They defined culture as consisting of patterns of behaviours that are acquired and transmitted by symbols over time, which become generally shared within a group in order to serve as a cognitive guide or blueprint for future actions. A major implication of

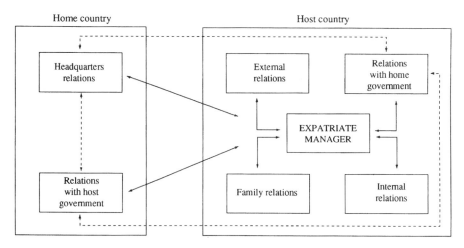

Figure 7.1   Manager relations between the expatriate manager and other parties interested in international business. *Source:* Rahim (1983); reproduced by permission.

culture is that for individuals seeking to live and work in a foreign culture, they have to acquire the 'cognitive guide or blueprint' of the host country nationals if they are to function effectively in that context. Stenning (1979) suggested that acquisition of the 'cognitive guide or blueprint' of the host country nationals will enhance the likelihood of the individual (expatriate employee) making iso-morphic attributions concerning the causes and intentions of the behaviour of host country nationals. The ability to make isomorphic attributions as a result of acculturation on the part of the expatriate employee (Mendenhall and Oddou, 1985) is particularly important given research evidence that the effectiveness of a specific managerial behaviour is contingent upon the cultural context in which it is performed (Black and Porter, 1991).

The nature and context of an expatriate assignment have implications for the definition of expatriate success. As indicated by the reasons for expatriate reten-tion failures, such as difficulties with one's family situation and difficulties in understanding a dissimilar culture (Tung, 1981), overseas success entails more than job success or performance. Given the multiplicity and complexity of factors that are 'in play', the task of developing valid criteria for overseas success has been noted to be immensely difficult (Kealey and Ruben, 1983). In an attempt to resolve the criterion problem in the expatriate or cross-cultural literature, Kealey and Ruben (1983) proposed a three-dimensional conceptualization of overseas success or effectiveness. They described the first dimension as professional effec-tiveness, defined as the possession of technical skill and knowledge resulting in the capacity to perform daily tasks, duties and responsibilities on the overseas job. The second dimension was defined in terms of personal family adjustment, which they described as the ability to be happy and personally satisfied with the over-seas situation, and this feeling of satisfaction must include family members if they should be present. The third dimension was defined in terms of intercultural interaction, which describes an interest in and capacity for interaction with nationals of the host culture. Kealey and Ruben's (1983) three-dimensional conceptualization of overseas success has recently been reinforced by Black and Mendenhall's (1990) indicators of the effectiveness of cross-cultural training. If cross-cultural skill development is treated as being conceptually synonymous with intercultural interaction, then the indicators of cross-cultural training effectiveness (performance adjustment and cross-cultural skill development) identified by Black and Mendenhall (1990) provide support for Kealey and Ruben's (1983) attempt to resolve the criterion problem in the expatriate selection literature.

EXPATRIATE SELECTION CRITERIA

An implication of the work of Kealey and Ruben (1983) and that of Black and Mendenhall (1990) is the growing recognition of overseas or expatriate success as a multidimensional construct. An on-going task for practitioners and researchers alike has been the identification of expatriate selection criteria or predictors of expatriate success. On the basis of an extensive review of the extant literature on expatriate success, Tung (1981) identified 18 selection criteria and grouped them into four broad categories: (1) technical competence on the job; (2) personality traits or relational abilities; (3) environmental variables and (4) family situation. In her study of 80 MNCs, Tung (1981) found that the extent to which each of the components of the criteria were used was contingent upon the level of the job assignment. She identified four job levels: (1) chief executive officer; (2) functional head; (3) trouble shooter and (4) operative. For example, Tung (1981) reported that 'communicative ability' was important for chief executive officer but not for the other job assignments, while such criteria as 'maturity and emotional stability' and 'technical knowledge of the business' were perceived by respondents to be important for all job categories. However, in a recent study that examined the importance ratings of factors perceived to contribute to expatriate success among a nationally heterogeneous sample of expatriate employees, Arthur and Bennett (1995) reported that contrary to Tung's (1981) earlier findings, importance ratings were not influenced by job type (managerial/non-managerial). Instead, the importance ratings were influenced by organizational type (service; communication, transportation and utility; manufacturing/production) such that expatriated employees in service organizations ascribed more importance to relational and psychosocial factors. A contingency orientation has not been a trend in the expatriate selection literature.

In spite of the seeming variety of expatriate selection criteria found in the extant literature (Mendenhall and Oddou, 1985; Ronen, 1989), there appears to be some consensus among the criteria. On the basis of the work of Tung (1981) and of Mendenhall and Oddou (1985), Ronen (1989), whose classification of expatriate selection criteria appears to enjoy widespread acceptance (Arvey, Bhagat and Sales, 1991), summarized expatriate selection criteria and used rational methods to identify the underlying dimensions of these criteria. As shown in Table 7.1, Ronen (1989) identified five broad categories, namely job factors, relational dimensions, motivational state, family situation and language skills.

Table 7.1 Categories of attributes of success

Job factors
- Technical skills
- Acquaintance with host-country and headquarters operations
- Managerial skills
- Administrative competence

Relational dimensions
- Tolerance for ambiguity
- Behavioural flexibility
- Non-judgementalism
- Cultural empathy and low ethnocentrism
- Interpersonal skills

Motivational state
- Belief in the mission
- Congruence with career path
- Interest in overseas experience
- Interest in the specific host-country culture
- Willingness to acquire new patterns of behaviour and attitudes

Family situation
- Willingness of spouse to live abroad
- Adaptive and supportive spouse
- Stable marriage

Language skills
- Host-country language
- Non-verbal communication

Source: Ronen (1989); reproduced by permission.

Given the widespread acceptance of Ronen's categories of attributes of success, the rest of this section will be devoted to a more detailed discussion of these attributes. First, job factors have traditionally been considered a major factor in expatriate selection (Miller, 1973; Torbiorn, 1982). Research by the International Orientation Resources cited in Teagarden and Gordon (1995) found that 90% of all companies base their expatriate selections on a candidate's technical expertise. Ronen pointed out that although competency in the functional area should be considered an initial requirement in the selection process, other job factors such as managerial skills, particularly administrative competence, should also be taken into consideration when selecting an expatriate employee.

Relational dimensions, as categorized by Ronen (1989), encompass properties that range from deeply rooted personality characteristics (such as extroversion or emotional stability) to a more transient socialized value system (such as ethnocentrism) to incidental behaviour resulting from the interaction of the individual with immediate environmental conditions (courtesy, initiative, interest in locals) (Ronen, 1989, p. 431). Relational skills have been noted to be particularly important if the expatriate employee is going to have considerable contact with host nationals (Tung, 1981; Ruben and Kealey, 1979).

The third selection criteria is motivational state, which Ronen (1989) defined in terms of belief in the mission, congruence with career path, interest in overseas experiences, interest in specific host-country culture and willingness to acquire new patterns of behaviour and attitudes. Given that expatriate assignments are not generally integrated into organizational career paths, many employees of globalizing firms have been rather reluctant to accept expatriate assignments. Feldman (1991) reported that expatriate employees who perceive their assignment to have career implications were more successful than those who did not. Hall and Gudykunst (1989) observed that a high achievement motivation and a positive orientation to an expatriate assignment increased the likelihood of expatriate retention.

In view of the consistent finding in the literature that expatriate retention failure stems from the inability of the spouse and children to adjust to living in a foreign culture, the fourth selection criteria identified by Ronen (1989) is the family situation of the expatriate. In addition to assessing the willingness of the spouse and children to live abroad, other factors to be considered should include the personal characteristics of the spouse, his/her career situation and the educational needs of the children. Hawes and Kealey (1981) reported that spouse's effective communication with host country nationals was directly linked to expatriate retention in overseas assignments. The effective adjustment of the spouse and children to living overseas will serve a social support function for the expatriate employee, because it provides the resilience that the expatriate employee needs to face the stress and challenges of daily life (Ronen, 1989).

The final selection criteria is language skills. Communication theorists (Hammer, Gudykunst and Wiseman, 1978) not surprisingly note the importance of fluency in the host country's language as a prerequisite for effective communication, and therefore a cognitive dimension of intercultural effectiveness. Zeira and Banai (1981), cited in Ronen (1989) report that managers from European host-country organizations prefer locals as top executives but will accept expatriates if they are fluent in the local language and are sensitive to the silent (non-verbal) language.

While researchers have made considerable progress in identifying the selection criteria for an expatriate assignment, Ronen (1989) noted the difficulty of establishing the relative importance of each category. Against this backdrop, Torbiorn (1982) noted the impossibility of finding anyone possessing all the selection criteria, particularly as some are contradictory. Globalizing firms therefore use either compensatory or non-compensatory strategies in selecting an employee for an expatriate assignment. In a compensatory strategy, the globalizing firm focuses on a single important criterion, such as technical ability, because it compensates for non-possession of the other skills. In a non-compensatory strategy, on the other hand, a potential expatriate is evaluated on a number of criteria and is expected to possess some of the criteria before being sent overseas. Given the limited empirical research on the effectiveness of the selection criteria, a non-compensatory strategy represents a lower risk strategy. In a recent study, Teagarden and Gordon (1995) reported a significant correlation between the use of non-compensatory selection strategy and their three success measures of lower rate of early returns, greater market share attainment and a higher percentage of managers accomplishing objectives.

CROSS-CULTURAL TRAINING OF EXPATRIATES

As a component in an integrative attempt on the part of globalizing firms to enhance expatriate retention rates, expatriate or cross-cultural training supplements as well as reinforces the perceived predictors of expatriate success. An assumption underlying cross-cultural training is the view that although cultures are universal, there are distinct differences between cultures that create difficulties in the interaction of individuals from different cultural backgrounds. Since these difficulties stem primarily from the inability of the interacting individuals to make isomorphic attributions, cross-cultural training aims to develop cultural awareness of, and sensitivity to, the values and beliefs of the host culture. As a learning process, cross-cultural training aims to teach individuals perceptual skills (rules for interpreting their environment) and behavioural skills (rules for comporting themselves within it).

Brislin (1979) suggested a three-fold classification of pedagogical approaches to cross-cultural training:

1. The cognitive information-giving approach, which is exemplified by area studies and cultural orientation programmes aimed at providing trainees with factual information about a specific country.
2. The 'affective' approach, which emphasizes the learning of information and skills with the aid of such techniques as cultural assimilators and role playing. Typically, this approach helps trainees to recognize their own values, to analyse contrasts with other cultures and ultimately apply the insights gained to improve the effectiveness of interaction.
3. The behavioural/experiential or immersion approach, which uses such techniques as sensitivity training, field experience and simulations.

The objective is to provide trainees with opportunities to engage in specific behaviours, review the behaviours critically, abstract some useful insight from the analysis, and apply the results in a practical situation. Given the diversity of training situations and expected outcomes, an emerging trend in the literature is the focus on situational contingencies that influence the choice or selection of a specific training method. Situational contingencies noted to be relevant in the choice of training method and rigour are culture novelty, degree of interaction and degree of job novelty (Tung, 1982; Black and Mendenhall, 1991).

CROSS-CULTURAL TRAINING EFFECTIVENESS

It has been reported that only 30%–45% of managerial employees sent on expatriate assignments receive cross-cultural training (Dunbar and Katcher, 1990). The apparent lack of enthusiasm for cross-cultural training on the part of corporate elites has been attributed to their perception that such training is ineffective in enhancing cross-cultural interactions. Black and Mendenhall's (1990) review of 29 published studies and Desphande and Viswesvaran's (1992) meta-analysis of over 20 empirical studies both provided evidence to attest to the positive effect of cross-cultural training on cross-cultural skills development, cross-cultural adjustment and job performance.

IMPLICATIONS FOR RESEARCH AND PRACTICE

When expatriate assignments are considered as a strategy for developing a pool of managerial talent, the view in this chapter is that globalizing firms should adopt a social negotiation approach which, unlike the psychometric approach, considers both the interests of the firm and the expatriate employee in the selection process. The role of selection in the expatriation process can be more fully realized when a number of human resource management issues have been addressed.

First, in light of the recognition of interest in an overseas assignment, or motivational state in general, as a selection criterion, it would be useful if researchers were to focus on understanding factors that influence an interest in overseas assignments. In a recent study, Aryee, Chay and Chew (1996) found that receptivity to an expatriate assignment was influenced by personal characteristics and organizational relocation policies. The effect of organizational relocation policies on receptivity to an expatriate assignment was found to be contingent upon the cultural similarity or dissimilarity of the country of relocation from one's own country. Given the paucity of research in this area, future research should further explore this issue in terms of both cultural similarity/dissimilarity and level of economic development of the country of relocation.

Secondly, there is a need for research that addresses the issue of conceptualization and operationalization of expatriate success and selection criteria. Quite often the indicators of success have been discussed in terms of the selection criteria, although in recent times there is a growing recognition of the multidimensionality of expatriate success (Black and Mendenhall, 1990). Such selection criteria as adaptability, maturity, sensitivity and stability have not been operationalized consequently, making it difficult to empirically establish the extent to which they predict expatriate success. Related to the selection criteria is the impossibility of finding prospective expatriate employees who possess all the attributes. While a compensatory vs. a non-compensatory approach was noted earlier, a recent suggestion is the development of a weighting system, since not all the criteria would be equally relevant for all types of expatriate jobs. The culture and job profile suggested by Mendenhall and Oddou (1986) appears to address the issue of which factors should be considered in the selection of prospective expatriates.

A third issue for researchers is the validation of the different methods of selection. Black, Gregersen and Mendenhall (1992) observed that globalizing firms tend to use a very limited range of selection methods. While validation of the selection methods constitutes a fundamental research task, it is equally important to examine the factors that inhibit globalizing firms from utilizing the available findings on how to select candidates for expatriate assignments. A probable way forward in expatriate selection may lie in Black, Gregersen and Mendenhall's

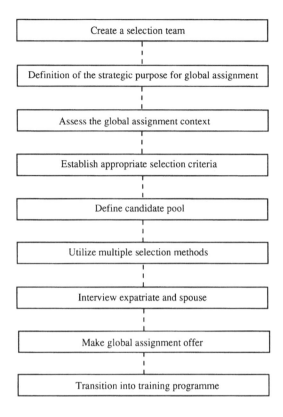

Figure 7.2   Global assignment selection process. *Source:* Black, Gregersen and Mendenhall (1992); reproduced by permission.

(1992) proposed model for systematizing the selection process shown in Figure 7.2.

In addition to its strategic orientation, two innovative features of the model are the proposed use of (a) a selection team and (b) multiple selection methods. Hixon (1986) suggested the institutionalization of a selection board or team made up of successfully repatriated employees empowered to review and approve, by consensus, all selection decisions. The rationale for the use of multiple selection methods stems from the principle of converging evidence which suggests that the more differing sources of information one has available on a particular candidate, the more reliable the resulting assessment (Kealey and Ruben, 1983).

Fourthly, the relationship between a relational psychological contract as suggested by the social negotiation approach to selection and competence retention should be empirically investigated. Specifically, researchers should empirically and conceptually identify policies that define a relational contract as opposed to a transactional contract, and examine their relative effectiveness in enhancing competence retention. In an initial research effort, Guzzo, Noonan and Elron (1994) found that expatriates' specific and general assessments of their employers' practices and support mediates the relationship of employer practices to retention-relevant outcomes (p. 625).

From a practitioner perspective, an implication of a social negotiation approach to the selection and training of expatriate employees is the integration of the human resource functions to ensure a comprehensive and effective management of the expatriation process. An integrative human resource orientation to the management of expatriates should first focus on the appraisal of the performance of expatriate employees not only to validate the selection criteria but also to ascertain the extent to which required competencies are being acquired by expatriate employees. While acknowledging the difficulty of expatriate performance appraisal, Gregersen, Black and Hite (1995) suggested three ways in which globalizing firms could design accurate expatriate performance appraisal: (1) identify the strategic goals for the expatriate assignment; (2) identify the specific uses for performance appraisal and (3) incorporate the unique contexts of expatriate assignments into the design of expatriate performance appraisals.

Secondly, expatriate assignments should be integrated into the globalizing firm's career or human resource development system, as has been repeatedly suggested (Tung, 1988; Mendenhall, Dunbar and Oddou, 1987). This implies that firms may have to stop the practice of hurriedly selecting an expatriate employee to resolve a staffing crisis in an overseas subsidiary, particularly as competencies acquired during the expatriation should fit into the strategic intent of the globalizing firm. An implication of such an orientation is that international experience should be considered a prerequisite for advancement into the top management ranks of globalizing firms.

REFERENCES

Arthur, W. and Bennett, W. (1995). The international assignee: The relative importance of factors perceived to contribute to success. *Personnel Psychology*, **48**, 99–114.

Arvey, R.D., Bhagat, R.S. and Sales, E. (1991). Cross-cultural and cross-national issues in personnel and human resources management. Where do we go from here? In G.R. Ferris and K.M. Rowland (eds.), *Research in Personnel and Human Resources Management*, Vol. 9, pp. 367–407. Greenwich, CT: JAI Press.

Aryee, S., Chay, Y.W. and Chew, J. (1996). An investigation of the willingness of managerial employees to accept an expatriate assignment. *Journal of Organizational Behavior*, **17**, 267–283.

Baker, J.C. and Ivancevich, J.M. (1971). The assignment of American executives abroad: Systematic, haphazard or chaotic? *California Management Review*, **13**, 39–44.

Black, J.S. and Mendenhall, M. (1990). Cross-cultural training effectiveness: A review and theoretical framework for future research. *Academy of Management Review*, **15**, 113–136.

Black, J.S. and Mendenhall, M. (1991). A practical but theory-based framework for selecting cross-cultural training methods. In M. Mendenhall and G. Oddou (eds.), *International Human Resource Management*, pp. 177–204. Boston, MA: PWS-Kent.

Black, J.S. and Porter, L.W. (1991). Managerial behaviours and job performance: A successful manager in Los Angeles may not succeed in Hong Kong. *Journal of International Business Studies*, **22**, 99–113.

Black, J.S. Gregersen, H.B. and Mendenhall, M. (1992). *Global Assignments: Successfully Expatriating and Repatriating International Managers*. San Francisco: Jossey-Bass.

Brislin, R.W. (1979). Orientation programs for cross-cultural preparation. In A.J. Marsella, G. Tharp and T.J. Ciborowski (eds.), *Perspectives on Cross-Cultural Psychology*, pp. 287–304. Orlando, FL: Academic Press.

Desphande, S.P. and Viswesvaran, C. (1992). Is cross-cultural training of expatriate managers effective: A meta analysis. *International Journal of Intercultural Relations*, **16**, 295–310.

Dowling, P.J. and Schuler, R.S. (1990). *International Dimensions of Human Resource Management*. Boston, MA: PWS-Kent.

Dunbar, E. and Katcher, A. (1990). Preparing managers for foreign assignments. *Training and Development Journal*, September, 45–47.

Feldman, D.C. (1991). Repatriate moves as career transitions. *Human Resource Management Review*, **1**, 163–178.

Feldman, D.C. and Thomas, D.C. (1992). Career issues facing expatriate managers. *Journal of International Business Studies*, **23**, 271–294.

Gregersen, H., Black, S. and Hite, J. (1995). Expatriate performance appraisal: Principles, practices and challenges. In J.O. Selmer (ed.), *Expatriate Management: New Ideas for International Business*, pp. 173–195. Westport, CT: Quorum Books.

Guzzo, R.A., Noonan, K.A. and Elron, E. (1994). Expatriate managers and psychological contract. *Journal of Applied Psychology*, **79**, 617–626.

Hall, P.H. and Gudykunst, W.B. (1989). The relationship of perceived ethnocentrism in corporate cultures to the selection, training, and success of international employes. *International Journal of Intercultural Relations*, **13**, 183–201.

Hammer, M.R., Gudykunst, W.B. and Wiseman, R.L. (1978). Dimensions of intercultural effectiveness: An exploratory study. *International Journal of Intercultural Relations*, **2**, 382–393.

Hawes, F. and Kealey, D.J. (1981). An empirical study of Canadian technical assistance. *International Journal of Intercultural Relations*, **5**, 239–258.

Herriot, P. (1992). Selection: The two subcultures. *European Work and Organizational Psychologist*, **2**, 129–140.

Hixon, A.L. (1986). Why corporations make haphazard overseas staffing decisions. *Personnel Administrator*, **31**, 91–94.

Kealey, D.J. and Ruben, B.D. (1983). Cross-cultural personnel selection criteria, issues, and methods. In D. Landis and R.W. Brislin (eds.), *Handbook of Intercultural Training: Issues in Theory and Design*, Vol. 1, pp. 155–175. New York: Pergamon Press.

Kluckhohn, C. and Kroeberg, A.L. (1952). *Culture: A Critical Review of Concepts and Definitions*. New York: Vintage Books.

Korth, C.M. (1985). *International Business Environment and Management*, 2nd edn. Englewood Cliffs, N.J.: Prentice-Hall.

Lofquist, L.H. and Dawis, R.W. (1969). *Adjustment to Work*. New York: Appleton.

Mendenhall, M. and Oddou, G. (1985). The dimensions of expatriate acculturation: A review. *Academy of Management Review*, **10**, 39–47.

Mendenhall, M. and Oddou, G. (1986). Acculturation profiles of expatriate managers: Implications for cross-cultural training programs. *Columbia Journal of World Business*, **21**, 73–79.

Mendenhall, M., Dunbar, E. and Oddou, G. (1987). Expatriate selection, training, and career pathing: A review and critique. *Human Resource Management*, **26**, 331–345.

Miller, E. (1973). The international selection decision: A study of managerial behavior in the selection decision process. *Academy of Management Journal*, **16**, 234–252.

Misa, K.F. and Fabricatore, J.M. (1979). Return on investment of overseas personnel. *Financial Executive*, **47**, 42–46.

Newman, J., Bhatt, B. and Gutteridge, T. (1978). Determinants of expatriate effectiveness: A theoretical and empirical vacuum. *Academy of Management Review*, **4**, 655–661.

Rahim, A. (1983). A model for developing key expatriate executives. *Personnel Journal*, **62**, 312–317.

Ronen, S. (1989). Training the international assignee. In I.E. Goldstone (ed.), *Training and Development in Organizations*, pp. 417–453. San Francisco: Jossey-Bass.

Rousseau, D.M. (1989). Psychological and implied contracts in organizations. *Employee Rights and Responsibilities Journal*, **2**, 121–139.

Rousseau, D.M. (1990). New hire perceptions of their own and their employer's obligations: A study of psychological contracts. *Journal of Organizational Behavior*, **11**, 389–400.

Rousseau, D.M. and Parks, J.M. (1993). The contracts of individuals and organizations. In L.L. Cummings and B.M. Staw (eds.), *Research in Organizational Behavior*, Vol. 15, pp. 1–43. Greenwich, CT: JAI Press.

Ruben, I. and Kealey, D.J. (1979). Behavioral assessment of communication competency and the prediction of cross-cultural adaptation. *International Journal of Intercultural Relations*, **3**, 15–17.

Stenning, B. (1979). Problems of cross-cultural contact: A literature review. *International Journal of Intercultural Relations*, **3**, 269–313.

Stone, R.J. (1991). Expatriate selection and failure. *Human Resource Planning*, **14**, 9–18.

Teagarden, M.B. and Gordon, G. (1995). Corporate selection strategies and expatriate manager success. In J.O. Selmer (ed.), *Expatriate Management: New Ideas for International Business*, pp. 17–36. Westport, CT: Quorum Books.

Torbiorn, I. (1982). *Living Abroad: Personal Adjustment and Personnel Policy in the Overseas Setting.* New York: John Wiley.

Torbiorn, I. (1985). The structure of managerial roles in cross-cultural settings. *International Studies of Management and Organization*, **15**, 52–74.

Tung, R. (1981). Selecting and training personnel for overseas assignments. *Columbia Journal of World Business*, **16**, 68–78.

Tung, R. (1982). Selection and training procedures of US, European, and Japanese multinationals. *California Management Review*, **25**, 57–71.

Tung, R. (1988). Career issues in international assignments. *Academy of Management Executives*, **2**, 241–244.

Zeira, Y. and Banai, M. (1981). Attitudes of host-country organizations towards MNC's staffing policies: A cross-country and cross-industry analysis. *Management International Review*, **21**, 38–47.

Chapter 8

Selection of Military Staff

N. M. HARDINGE

Defence Evaluation and Research Agency, Centre for Human Sciences, Farnborough, Hampshire GU14 6TD, UK

INTRODUCTION

Bearing arms and operating in certain hostile environments is the principal task of the Armed Services and this sets it apart from other occupations. In wartime and in peace, there are also many other military tasks which have civilian equivalents such as maintenance and training, logistic support, procurement and administration. However, even in peacetime, Service careers are very different from those of most civilian occupations. A wide range of tasks, such as fighter pilot, submarine captain, tank commander, etc., are high risk and stressful. Unlike civilian occupations, the Services cannot readily recruit into their core ranks in mid-career. Therefore they need to attract enough people into the Service, to train them and to retain those they need. The organization also makes particular demands. Service personnel are required to be highly mobile and to move as directed to new jobs and locations. Many aspects of lifestyle are predetermined, e.g. uniforms, accommodation, social and recreational activities. In many ways the Services offer a complete lifestyle. Compatibility with that lifestyle is a major consideration in Service selection. The military develop their own assessment procedures to select the personnel who can best cope with Service training, military jobs and the military way of life. It is of note that, although many tasks require combat skills, these have traditionally been developed by training rather than by selection.

PRESSURES FOR CHANGE

For several decades there has been a trend to civilianize many of the 'second-line' functions. The fall of the Berlin Wall has also had significant effects on the size,

International Handbook of Selection and Assessment, Edited by N. Anderson and P. Herriot.
© 1997 John Wiley & Sons Ltd.

role and structure of the Armed Services and this is impacting upon selection and appraisal procedures. The Services have been greatly reduced and many more functions have been civilianized. The US Services are reducing from 2 174 000 personnel in 1987 to 1 453 000 by 1999. In 1984, the UK armed strength was 326 000; in 1994 it was down to 254 000, and is expected to be 210 000 by the year 2004. There is now a much greater emphasis on operations other than war, such as humanitarian relief and peacekeeping. In such operations the Services expect to work as part of a coalition force, operating in a wider range of roles and in different geographical areas. Other, broader social changes have altered personnel policies in the Armed Services. These have affected the rights of individuals, have influenced the position of minority groups, and have reduced many of the differences between Service and civilian life-styles including the loss of some sense of job security.

Within many Western nations (such as the United Kingdom, the United States and Canada) there has been a steady move away from conscription towards all-volunteer forces. In all-volunteer forces, reserves and auxiliaries play a key role in maintaining defence capability. The United Kingdom may need to draw more extensively on reservists to support its future activities and it is therefore revising its associated legislation. Selection, training and broader human factors policies may also need to be refined. Most other European countries rely on a cadre of career personnel and a much larger body of conscripts. For example, 85% of Sweden's wartime air force will be provided by conscripts and reserves. National factors such as force structure, type of education, job design, career patterns and demographic trends will shape the selection and assessment procedures that are used. In the 1940s the selection principles that had been developed for civilian careers guidance and assessment were adopted and modified for the Armed Services. Some of the main tenets still apply: giving candidates as much information as possible to encourage their co-operation and self-selection; using interviews, based upon structured biographical questionnaires because of their inclusiveness and acceptability; employing assessment batteries which incorporate both measures of general ability to match training demands and of specific abilities to support allocation; regarding interests, educational proficiencies and previous experience as being at least as relevant as test scores to selection and allocation decisions. There has been continuous development and exchange of techniques since then. Assessment tests have changed in response to the changing military requirement. They have also changed in response to external educational developments and entry standards; and allocation procedures have altered in order to get the best out of the available manpower. Recruitment, assessment, retention, pay and training policies have all been significantly affected by the social changes and there has been a significant focus on gender-free and culture-fair methods of assessment.

The nature of many essential tasks has changed and this requires changes in the content of test batteries. Operating tasks, such as flying and driving, are changing from continuous psychomotor skills to parallel information-processing skills. They have become dominated by the need to handle high information workloads, assign priorities and make rapid choices. Equally, the skill requirements for technicians have substantially altered. The manual skills of rectification and repair have been displaced by cognitive skills of systems diagnosis and troubleshooting. After reviewing the job content and training of its airman engineers, the British Royal Air Force (RAF) found that it needed two mechanics for every technician where previously it had needed two technicians for each mechanic. The British Royal Navy (RN), with its particular need to reduce the manning of ships at sea, has combined the jobs of operators and mechanics to produce operator-maintainers for a wide range of systems. This requires fewer numbers, provides greater job satisfaction and retention, but requires higher ability personnel. In its latest change, of the Warfare Branch, it is using tests of specialized abilities (technical understanding, fault diagnosis, numerical reasoning and mechanical knowledge) to identify the candidates with the potential for these new jobs.

CHANGES IN SELECTION AND APPRAISAL POLICIES

The military are becoming more accountable to outside bodies for their personnel practices; transatlantic and European nations are subject to increasing legislation to safeguard individual and minority interests. In the United States, there is significant legislation to protect individual liberties; Congress requires, for instance, a regular review and update of the Service test batteries. In the United Kingdom, many exemptions covering Health and Safety at Work, liability to compensation, and employment practices have been removed. Personnel and selection matters are frequently raised by questions in the UK Parliament. The Parliamentary Defence Committee and the National Audit Office now play a more active role in Service matters. A number of rulings by the European Parliament have had a significant impact on personnel policies in the European Services. The United Kingdom, in particular, has revised many of its policies and presently it is examining its position on sexual orientation in the Forces. The stimulus is not entirely external as the UK Services set themselves performance indicators for achievement in a variety of personnel functions.

Gender differences

For both demographic and social reasons, efforts have been made to broaden the manpower base in most Western nations. More women have been recruited, more jobs have been opened to women, and combat roles have been opened to them. These changes affect volunteers: if conscription were required, an issue to be addressed is the acceptability of women being drafted into combat roles. Most nations still exclude women from some situations (e.g. on ships or in tanks in combat zones). In America, they are excluded from aircraft or ships on combat missions; Canada aims for full integration (except on submarines); Belgium, Denmark and Norway have no combat limitations. France and Greece exclude women from combat units; Germany accepts women as voluntary medical officers only; Italy and Spain completely exclude women from the military. In the United Kingdom, having first integrated selection and then training, the separate women's Services (the Women's Royal Naval Service, the Women's Royal Army

Corps and the Women's Royal Air Force) were subsequently abolished and al-most all jobs are now open to them. They can serve as fighter pilots and on ships, but are excluded from serving in tanks, certain posts in the Infantry and Royal Armoured Corps and artillery units and as naval clearance divers. Where posts are open to women, equality in selection has been a matter of some priority. Psychometric tests are routinely monitored for gender fairness. There are usually slight, predictable differences in line with the findings of Anastasi (1968). In the UK Army, for example, males do better on the spatial rotation tests and females better on the verbal tests. There are, however, no significant differences in the Army's composite scores. There are, however, significant gender differences in terms of physique and physical fitness. Most Services deal with differences by using separate norms for assessment. The British Army has developed new gender-free physical fitness tests which are role-related and are based upon generic military tasks and specified performance standards. These were intro-duced in April 1996 (Rayson, Holliman and Bell, 1994). Hendy (1990) describes attempts to derive anthropometric requirements for female aircrew from a de-tailed analysis of cockpit geometry and task requirements. Establishing fair selec-tion methods is only the first step towards equal treatment. The integration of women into the fighting forces represents a longer-term commitment. Efforts are taken to monitor training, postings and appraisal procedures and equal oppor-tunities. Management initiatives to obviate sexual harassment and abuse of auth-ority have been developed; however, the next stage, that of managing diversity within the Services' tight-knit groups and teams, will also need to be addressed.

Ethnic differences

In the United States, the population mix is rapidly changing. In 1990, racial and ethnic minorities made up 25% of the population; by 2020 they are expected to form almost 40%. This is expected to impact upon the effects of enlistment standards on participation, on the differential effects of downsizing, on the staffing of highly technical jobs and upon training requirements. Even where the population mix is not a factor, changing social views on fair treatment have wrought significant changes. A UK Army sponsored study of ethnic differences (Peat Marwick McLin-tock, 1989) examined all aspects of recruitment and selection including: applicants' perceptions, contact with the Services, recruitment, initial contacts, testing, the med-ical examination and interviews. Their extensive list of proposals formed the basis of a subsequent development programme. The recommendations included changes to the psychometric tests to ensure that they incorporated simpler instructions, more everyday language, measurement of trainability rather than knowledge of technical terms, gradations of difficulty, regular revisions, etc. New tests have been introduced which require only a knowledge of the alphabet, familiarity with num-ber sequences up to 10 and a reading age of 11 years but which, nevertheless, provide an effective screening device. Also, pre-test booklets, which describe the tests and give trial items, are usually used. The recommendations also addressed the recruiters' assessment of personal qualities. It was felt that some of the criteria concerned (e.g. school marks, work history, participation in team sports, and reserve and cadet experience) might hinder ethnic minority candidates who have different backgrounds. Cross-cultural awareness training was recommended for recruiters involved in selection interviews. Both the RN and RAF have also reviewed their recruitment and selection procedures to minimize ethnic differences. One study (Wilson, Eitelberg and Foder, 1993) found that ethnic minorities were proportionately under-represented in the UK, New Zealand, Canadian and Australian forces, but were appropriately represented in the US armed forces. The US have several successful affirmative action programmes and are refining techniques for revealing institutional discrimination in their promotion systems.

Adjustment to educational trends

Military selection tests identify the candidates most likely to succeed in training, and most previous ability tests have been a mixture of basic aptitude and knowledge. As educational patterns have changed, the tests have had to be revised. Whereas the US armed services vocational aptitude battery (ASVAB) is revised annually, most European tests are revised when a change in educational syllabus or job content requires it. The tests therefore are revised to address changes in measurement standards and the educational syllabus to accommodate the introduction of new technical information and terms, and to reflect changing standards in vocabulary, etc. In the United Kingdom, changes such as the introduction of a national curriculum and the widespread adoption of national vocational qualifications in lieu of more traditional academic qualifications will affect selection procedures. In many cases candidates with recognized educational qualifications would be accepted by the Services even if they did not achieve the normal selection test score. In other cases a recognized educational qualification is an essential prerequisite to selection. To increase the manpower base or to meet political pressures to rely on less exclusive criteria, some Services are developing new screening devices. As well as test scores, these might use factors such as employment record, age, educational record, years of schooling, etc. As educational qualifications have moved away from fixed syllabuses and external assessment towards locally determined content and local assessment, the predictivity of some educational qualifications has changed and there has also been a parallel requirement for a pre-screening stage of testing which could screen out candidates who have too little chance of success in the full selection process.

Conditions of service

Service terms and conditions of service are under review in the United Kingdom. The Betts Report (Betts, 1995) recommends that officers are no longer selected for a full career but are selected for a short-term contract with the option to extend to a second engagement by mutual agreement and then to a third. It advocates longer postings, a reduced number of ranks, and a move towards performance-related pay by decoupling rank and pay. In addition, it recommends rationalization of the trade structure and a regular review of job evaluations. Such changes would have profound effects for Service selection and appraisal systems. One concern is that such moves towards commercial terms and conditions would affect the military ethos.

Methods of assessment and appraisal

Appraisal systems are being reviewed in a number of countries. Work in the United States is driven by legislative initiatives and the Services' need to be able to demonstrate its compliance. Also, techniques which will enable them to select the best personnel to retain for re-engagement are being considered. This is leading towards assessments which are broader-based than measures of job performance and which combine assessments of effort and leadership, discipline and bearing with selection test scores and assessments of first-tour performance. Similarly, a Canadian review of its assessment devices emphasized that a multi-dimensional construct of performance (which included job performance, professionalism, management of subordinates and fitness/appearance) was more effective than simpler, dual factor models. In the United Kingdom, downsizing means that there will be fewer top jobs in the Services, with officers from a relatively broader range of military backgrounds competing for them. The Army is therefore examining the need for changes in its approach to appraisals. It aims to identify the core competencies for top jobs, to determine if these have changed and if current appraisal systems are adequate to cater for them. Competency-based assessment procedures are being widely introduced into Service selection and appraisal. The RAF is using this approach to assess performance in Initial Officer Training and the RN to assess performance on its Warfare Officers Courses. The New Zealand Forces are also revising their appraisal system to include core competencies and performance indicators.

RECRUITMENT AND SELECTION OPERATIONS

The scale of operations means that military recruitment and selection is a year-round activity conducted by full-time staff at dedicated assessment centres. All nations would wish to maintain the recruitment infrastructure necessary to provide for rapid expansion and mobilization if needed, but recruitment organizations are being drastically reduced and reorganized in line with general force reductions. Within each nation the different Services also have separate recruitment and selection organizations and operate slightly different policies. Only Canada has an integrated defence force and uses a single selection system. Where each of the UK Services once had a separate nation-wide network of recruiting offices, these are being reduced and reorganized into 40 tri-Service Armed Forces Careers Offices (with a small number of additional satellite Army offices). It is also considering making use of civilian careers services. Its test-development resources have been integrated and it is beginning to develop a tri-Service pre-filtering test. For non-officer selection, the United States administer their Armed Services Vocational Aptitude Battery (ASVAB) to about 600 000 applicants annually, in 65 military entrance processing stations and about 700 mobile-team

sites. US Services share test procedures but maintain separate recruiting operations; the Australian Services share recruiting facilities but have separate testing arrangements; and Canada has a single selection system to match its
integrated force structure. The Services tend to use different approaches to
select officers and other ranks. Typically, an assessment centre procedure is
used for officer selection, with each Service having its own centre; a simpler
process of sequential screening is used for other ranks in a wide range of locations. Appraisal tends to be continuous and very decentralized, conducted as
part of the line-management function. In some cases, significant training courses
are used as a vehicle for appraisal, and the value of introducing assessment
centre procedures for mid-career assessment is under consideration. The development and evaluation of the tests and procedures that are used by the
military tend to be centrally monitored. Different nations use different levels of
civilian specialist (i.e. psychologist) support. Psychologists are widely used to
develop and support the selection system. Many nations include them as members of the selection board. Only a few nations—Belgium and Australia are
among them—use civilian psychologists to make independent selection decisions. One or two nations (e.g. Canada and Australia) have a cadre of Service
psychologists. In reviewing officer selection, Jones (1991) identified four principal approaches which he ordered in terms of chronology and degree of psychologists' involvement. These are given in Table 8.1.

Table 8.1 Principal approaches to military selection

Approach	Assessment technique	Nation or armed force
Academic qualifications and personal record	Academic examinations Application forms Reference reports Interviews, etc.	Egypt France Spain US Military Academies USSR
Paper and pencil Psychological instruments	Aptitude tests Biodata Interest inventories, etc.	Spain Reserved Officers US Armed Forces Reserve Officer Training Corps and Officer Candidate Schools
Assessment centres	Situational tests Aptitude tests Interviews, etc.	Australia India New Zealand Pakistan United Kingdom
Construct-orientated psychological assessment	As assessment centres + Peer assessment Personality inventories Psychologists' assessments	Belgium Denmark Germany Israel Netherlands Canada

Adapted from Jones (1991).

ASSESSMENT CENTRE PROCESS

Officer selection procedures aim to identify both leadership qualities and specialist or professional abilities. The assessment centres use a panel to evaluate educational qualifications, psychometric tests, biodata, interviews, reference reports and performance in group exercises. Group exercises are a particular feature of this procedure; they are based on the belief that the personal qualities that are crucial to success as an officer can best be assessed by observing individuals interacting with others. It is an extended process (two or three days at least) and whilst it is manpower intensive and costly, it provides good levels of prediction. In a study of the Canadian Navy's assessment centre, Rodgers and Johnson (1987) found a correlation of 0.42 between the overall assessment and assessments of practical leadership shown in training. They also report the following correlations between the component predictors and the criterion: assessor's rating of biographical information 0.34, peer assessment 0.26, leaderless group discussions 0.25, chairman's assessment 0.25, interview board 0.24 and group task 0.16. For the UK Royal Navy, Jones (1984) found correlations of 0.39 between overall assessments and assessments of officer-like qualities in initial training. Drakely (1986) found correlations ranging from 0.28 to 0.51 between assessments and training criterion measures produced up to five years later. McLaughlan (1994) recently conducted an extensive review of the selection procedure of the British Army. He found that the assessment centre was trying to apply absolute selection standards and was allowing the system to run short of people. Given the very high validity coefficients obtained by the process, he accepted that the system should meet manning requirements and should simply take the best available. The assessment centre approach is used where the skills to be identified are felt to be rare and imprecise. With a central panel making the assessments, trade-offs can be made between an individual's strengths and weaknesses (as revealed by the different selection devices); satisfactory levels of reliability and validity can still be achieved and utility analyses have demonstrated their cost-effectiveness (Jones, 1988).

ACADEMIC QUALIFICATIONS AND PERSONAL RECORD

The United States does not use selection boards for commissioning because of the high throughput and costs. Most candidates enter the officer corps via some form of training, either from their university-based Officer Training Corps or their Officer Candidates School and selection is determined by academic qualifications and personal record. The Scholastic Aptitude Test (SAT) and American College Test provide widely accepted, standardized measures of academic qualification. The personal record typically includes aspects such as recommendation, biographical factors and extra-mural activities. Sections of the SAT yield correlations in the range of 0.32–0.40 with academic performance at the US Military Academy; test scores combined with personal record and other data raises this to 0.50 (Butler and McCauley, 1987). The United States is, however, examining the applicability of assessment centres.

SEQUENTIAL PROCESS

The selection of other ranks is usually much briefer and cheaper. Psychometric tests, biodata and interviews are used, together with educational qualifications where they are available. Typically, the selection process is organized as a series of hurdles, with minimum standards required in each part, and the stages are sequenced for greatest efficiency. Usually a candidate would first be asked to complete a biographical questionnaire (giving age, qualifications, family background, school or employment record, job preferences, etc.). The next step would be a series of computer-based or paper-and-pencil aptitude tests). Candidates would then be interviewed. Clearly unsuitable candidates would be rejected; those marginally below the minimum test standard would be counselled to try again. Candidates meeting the minimum standards would be interviewed in more depth. The questionnaire and interview data would be recorded and rated by the selector and would provide the principal means of assessing qualities and motivation. Unsuccessful candidates should be given some form of careers advice (in so far as the selectors have the time and are able to advise on other careers). Successful candidates have the medical test to look forward to. After a candidate has passed the medical, employers' references will be called for. (These are used late in the sequence because not all employers take kindly to an individual leaving his or her job.) The proportion of candidates excluded at each stage of the process will be strongly influenced by the number of vacancies in the Service and the number of applicants. Test standards will be adjusted up and down—within narrow limits—in response to changes in the recruiting climate.

APPRAISAL PROCESS

All military services have extensive and formalized systems of performance assessment (probably to support and compensate for the pattern of short postings). Reports are completed annually, and again after changes in boss, job or unit. Appropriate training and development needs are highlighted then. The Services have patterns of career and training development for the officers in each specialization. These are not fixed, but usually there is a series of recognized courses and valued postings that develop individual skills and experience and also provide a basis for assessment and career decisions. Often Service careers will develop in one of two directions: as a specialist or as a more general manager or policymaker. High flyers are usually identified early on and will be steered towards a series of high-profile postings. The general aim is to provide wide experience and increasing responsibility as a preliminary to staff college and to the higher positions of policy-making or senior command that generally follow. Whilst attendance at junior staff college is usually widely available for all officers and is sometimes mandatory, selection for senior staff college is much tougher. The usual criteria will include completion of the junior staff course, recommendation by commanding officers, completion of written examinations and subsequent vetting on the basis of past performance reports. The military has developed a highly standardized and very comprehensive system of reporting and assessment. The Australian Forces are considering the introduction of behaviourally anchored rating scales to correct an upward drift in gradings. This kind of drift in appraisals is observed in other nations (e.g. the United Kingdom and the United States) and the meta-analytic studies of Hunter and Hunter (1984) and of Vineberg and Joyner (1982) revealed that Service appraisals yield lower correlations than those found in civilian organizations. New types of question are being considered for appraisal. These couch questions in terms of problem situations; individuals are asked to prioritizie them and also to select the best and worst of a set of solutions to a given problem.

THE TOOLS USED FOR ASSESSMENT AND APPRAISAL

Aptitude tests

Changes in models of human abilities and in selection technology are significantly affecting the structure and content of aptitude tests. Traditionally assessment is based on paper-and-pencil tests with the items ordered in terms of difficulty and a set testing time allowed. Individual performance, therefore, is usually a function of power and speed. In such tests the two factors are strongly intercorrelated, but there is no way of assessing how candidates might have traded speed against accuracy. Reliability and validity, and to some extent gender and culture-fairness, are engineered by using a battery of tests each of which addresses a different area of knowledge or cognitive functioning (typically numerical, verbal, spatial, or mechanical and reasoning). The simple use of minimum scores determines acceptability for the Service: often a profile of minimum test scores in each test is used to determine allocation. Test batteries would be similar in composition for both officers and other ranks and would reflect general reasoning ability or educability rather than any generic task structures. However, there would be additional aptitude tests for special duties (e.g. aircrew) and the United Kingdom is currently developing tests for specializations such as RN aircrew, fighter controller, air traffic controller and bomb disposal. The typical structure, therefore, would be very similar to their equivalents in the public sector (e.g. the US general aptitude test battery (GATB) and differential aptitude tests (DAT)). The similarity between the key cognitive constructs measured by different test batteries such as these is well established (Hunter, 1986). Sperl, Ree and Steuck (1992) showed the similarity between the factors measured by the ASVAB and the equivalent test for officers (the armed forces officer qualifying test). The test battery currently being developed for UK Army officers is based on much the same factors as those used in the battery for selecting soldiers. Armstrong et al. (1988) validated the ASVAB against membership in civilian organizations. Only a lack of criterion data prevented them from conducting a full validation using job performance measures. Ree and Earles (1990) showed that a variety of metrics of general ability can be derived from the

ASVAB and all will predict training performance effectively. They found inter-correlations between 14 different estimates of general mental ability ranging from 0.93 to 0.99. On the other hand, special aptitudes derived from ASVAB had little extra to offer in predicting training performance. Hunter and Hirsh (1987) showed that military tests and civilian tests are equally effective in predicting training success in their respective domains. Summarizing over 500 military studies involving nearly 500 000 personnel, various predictors yielded an average validity of 0.62. In their review, which linked selection and appraisal to a number of different areas in work and organizational psychology, they concluded that job knowledge provides a correlation of about 0.80 with performance; that cognitive composites do not predict any better than general cognitive ability (0.75); and that specific aptitude tests do not add to the prediction given by general cognitive ability except in a handful of jobs. Rather than reflecting an assumed structure of human abilities, current models now place assessment into the broader context of task and criterion variables. Performance requirements would be placed into ability domains, and any of a variety of tests might be utilized to produce a composite to measure it. The composition of the UK Army's test battery has been revised and, although it contains subtests which reflect the previous Army tests, it largely identifies general ability and trainability with working memory in line with Christal's model (Kyllonen and Christal, 1988). Whilst the subtests utilize numbers, letters, words and spatial patterns, they have a very low knowledge content and are strongly correlated with the processes of working memory, fluency in encoding and comparison, and semantic figural and numerical reconstruction.

Work sample tests

Most simulator-based tests represent some form of work sample. Because of the time and cost involved, they tend to be used for complex jobs such as aircrew. Aircrew typically have been selected by a battery of discrete psychomotor and cognitive tests, but the benefits of low-cost simulation and the high validity of work-sample tests now make simulator-based tests a more attractive option. The Canadian automated pilot selection system (CAPSS) uses a simulator to deliver five hours of simple, representative flying tasks (Spinner, 1990). This is expected to increase the prediction of success in the primary flying training stage from 0.29 to between 0.40 to 0.50 and to provide a 13% improvement in the pass rate. The finding that work samples predict measures of job performance almost completely, supports the wider use of work-sample tests and encourages the development of research programmes such as the US learning abilities measurement program (LAMP) which uses work samples as key criteria. Robertson and Downs (1989) use work samples to measure trainability and they have identified two performance variables in trainability tests: task performance and learning from feedback. The significant development in work-sample and trainability testing is the focus on identifying the processes of learning, the way that these change over time and the way that individual abilities can best be matched to learning requirements.

Interviews

All the Services use interviews as a significant part of the selection process. The intrinsic unreliability of the interview is minimized by using highly structured interviews, by using standard assessment forms and rating scales, by intensive training and by using Service personnel as, effectively, full-time selectors. The major part of the selection process depends on this one procedure but, because it is manpower intensive, there is surprisingly little monitoring of individual interviews or of the interview process. The RN regularly monitor and coach their interviewers. This process will probably become much more common as part of initiatives to ensure gender- and culture-fairness. Assessing the validity of the interview is easier because it can be based on the rating scales used, and consistent but low correlations (between 0.17 and 0.25) can be found between interview assessments and wastage in early training (Smith, 1992).

Biodata

Despite their effectiveness (Rothstein *et al.* (1990) indicate validity coefficients of about 0.35) surveys suggest that biodata measures are used infrequently in the US and UK civil sectors (Hammer and Kleiman, 1988; Smith & Abrahamsen, 1992). Biodata have been more widely used in the military, usually as a screening device, and sometimes as part of the assessment centre's battery of selection measures. The RN have used biodata measures for some time as a screening device. Their Professional Achievement Predictor, which is largely based on educational qualifications, correlates 0.50 with success in professional examinations for officers and is currently being renormed and reweighted. Numerous US instruments have been developed: for screening Marine Corps recruiters and drill instructors (Urban and McDaniel, 1989), Air Officer trainees (Barrett, 1989), and for reducing attrition of soldiers in their first enlistment (Walker, White and Schroyer, 1989). McDaniel (1989) found biodata scales corelated 0.19 with premature discharge from the US National Guard.

Assessment scales

McLaughlan's (1994) study of British Army officer selection found that only nine of its 20 assessment dimensions were needed and that five of these could account for 77% of the variance in predicting final board mark. The dimensions could be organized into five factors (roughly equating to influence; interpersonal relations; practical ability; intellect; energy). The use of behaviourally anchored rating scales was also recommended. Despite the findings of Hunter and Hunter (1984) on Service appraisals, Schmidt, Ones and Hunter (1992) report comparable reliabilities for performance ratings provided by Service personnel and civilians. For measures of overall performance, they report a median single-rater reliability of 0.66; the mean single-rater reliability for supervisors trained in the use of behaviourally anchored rating scales ranged between 0.51 and 0.68. Dobson and Williams (1989) examined the validity of assessments in selecting British Army officers; The validity for predicting job performance was 0.33 and for predicting specialized Army training grades was 0.31. Vance, Coovert and MacCullam (1988) examined the predictive value of self, peer and supervisor ratings by correlating them with objective measures of task performance. They found that all three methods could provide equally valid predictions, but that the validity of the predictions provided by each method was related to type of task. Other work has examined the relative effect that factors such as training and supervisor support have on job performance and has identified the influence of moderators such as length of experience and job complexity (McDaniel, Schmidt and Hunter, 1988, Vance, Coovert and MacCullam, 1989). Such findings should influence the design of future assessment scales.

Personality tests

The Services aim to reflect the broad spectrum of the wider society, but there is no doubt that they do have particular values and attitudes. Neil (1984) showed that RAF officer entrants have a distinct personality profile. Traditionally, personality differences (viewed as team or leadership qualities) have been assessed by interview and group exercises. The process of selecting personalities who will fit into the organizational ethos is now widely reflected in the way that commercial organizations use personality tests to select employees who match a company culture or set of corporate values. The UK Services already use personality tests to screen personnel for special duties. For the purposes of general selection, they rely on interview assessments, references, weighted application blanks and, in the case of officer selection, group exercises. The lower reliability and validity of personality tests has meant that they have not been able to add anything useful to the predictive power of the selection process so far. However, the Dutch Army replaced group exercises in 1981 with measures of personality derived from personality tests, biodata and interviews, and the United Kingdom is examining the utility of personality tests in several areas. The RN, for instance, is trialling a trait self-description personality questionnaire with officer applicants and trainees. Australia is assessing the utility of personality measures for initial selection and potential senior officer identification. Some nations believe that basic soldiering skills and discipline provide a sound basis for peace-keeping roles; others believe that military and peace-keeping roles require different temperaments and therefore see personality tests as especially relevant for screening for peace-keeping (Aschenbrenner, 1989).

NEW DEVELOPMENTS

Important advances have been made in several areas of testing, namely in the development of constructs of mental abilities, trainability tests, techniques of test construction and computer-based testing (CBT) applications. More significantly, these are being drawn together to produce entirely new test systems and to bridge the gaps between the theory of individual differences and other areas of work and organizational psychology.

Computer-based testing

First developments in computer-based testing (CBT) seem to focus on the organizational benefits of translating paper-and-pencil tests into a machine format. CBT can provide benefits such as reduced testing time; lower error rates in scoring; improved test security; ease of test revision; and application of new scoring techniques (see Alkhadher, Anderson and Clarke, 1994). Subsequent developments use the computer as a platform for adaptive testing, for developing new types of test item or new kinds of test.

Computer adaptive testing

The US ASVAB takes 3.5 hours to administer and there is a long delay in obtaining the scores for applicants at the mobile sites. Administering the ASVAB by computer could reduce testing time to one day and would substantially reduce costs. It would also allow the incorporation of new types of test item. A computer-assisted screening test (CAST) (see Sands and Gade, 1983) has been introduced in the Army to replace a pencil-and-paper screen (the armed forces qualifying test—AFQT). Using 10 work knowledge and five arithmetical reasoning items, CAST takes 5–10 minutes to administer. It correlates 0.82 with AFQT scores. It is used to give selectors the probability of an applicant's succeeding in each of the (three) levels of qualification. After its introduction, the numbers taking the full ASVAB were reduced by more than half. The production of test items in these tests is by selection from a pool of pre-written items which have been trialled and graded for difficulty. The UK British Army recruit battery (BARB) is a computer-based system which uses software algorithms for the real-time generation of items of specified difficulty. This system provides an excellent platform for developing and implementing adaptive testing. As the testing period is only one hour and scoring is real time, this is not a development priority in the United Kingdom.

New types of test item

The UK Micropat system (Bartram, 1987) exploits CBT to provide new forms of dynamic test item. It addresses tracking skills, the way individuals respond to new instructions and control laws, how they trade-off speed and accuracy, information scheduling, etc. Used for the selection of helicopter aircrew, it measures decision-speed, risk-taking, and time-sharing skills and adds significantly to predictions provided by the previous aircrew test battery's measures of tracking, spatial abilities and reasoning. For selecting pilots for the Army Air Corps, inclusion of Micropat scores increases prediction of outcome in flying training, especially at the later stages. For example, it increased prediction in basic flying training from 0.34 to 0.55 and in advanced flying training from 0.21 to 0.58. The tests also offer improved prediction for RN observers (navigators) and appear to tap different ability domains, an additional benefit which should be very valuable in classifying individuals as pilot or observer. Bartram suggests that Micropat not only measures performance; it also measures response style, i.e. the way in which a task is performed. It would be interesting to see if individual differences in risk-taking/avoidance and in speed/accuracy trade-offs would relate not just to system management requirements in training but also in operational stages. Rate of learning was correlated with subsequent performance to see if this provided improved predictive validity in aircrew selection, but none was found.

Matching tests with abilities

Recent developments in military selection research have been enriched by the different types of measurement proposed by different models of mental ability. Kyllonen and Christal (1990) suggested that working memory capacity was the key determinant of performance, the g factor, in a variety of ability tests. Others (Bejar, 1986) have identified the cognitive factors that contribute to the difficulty in performing certain representative tasks, and they have derived models for predicting performance of them. From such models, Irvine, Dann and Anderson (1990) have produced computer algorithms to develop test items of controlled difficulty. They have also drawn these separate developments together to construct a new test system. They constructed, a priori, a new test battery which provides an effective measure of general ability by incorporating selected tasks which cover four of Carroll's second-order factors (Carroll, 1993). Using performance models of these tasks, they then produced software algorithms to generate test items which would provide effective score characteristics, in line with item-response theory. This provided the basis for a new selection test battery for the UK Army (BARB) which was introduced in 1992. BARB represents significant developments in terms of test content, construction and administration. Items are generated at the time of testing, using software algorithms to define the level of difficulty of the items presented. Each candidate therefore takes a unique test—but all tests are of equal difficulty. The instructions are screen-delivered; responses are made by use of a touch screen and the tests are automatically scored in real time. Six of the BARB subtests produce highly correlated measures of working memory based upon letter-checking, number manipulation, spatial rotation, logical inference, semantic identity and alphabet manipulation. These are combined to provide a general trainability index (GTI). A seventh test measures time estimation (see Irvine, Dann and Anderson, 1990). The variability in content from test to test is measured by getting candidates to take a subtest twice in the same test session. The 'test–retest reliabilities', using what amount to parallel versions, are very high (in the region of 0.74 to 0.89). Tested over 28–35 days, this form of test–retest yielded a correlation between GTIs of 0.88 (Tapsfield, 1993). Although the test is strongly biased towards working memory and is somewhat biased towards speeded aspects of performance, paper-and-pencil versions of BARB correlate very highly with conventional, education-based, selection tests and have proved to be very effective predictors of success in a range of different kinds of training course (Collis and Irvine, 1991).

Matching abilities with tasks and training

European validity studies tend to be small scale but have typically used a variety of criteria. In comparison, the criteria for many US validity studies were based on declarative knowledge. More recent studies, however, have used job performance criteria. The LAMP project specifically set out to generate work-sample tests as a criterion. Kyllonen examined task demands and information-processing requirements in order to design assessment tests that are closely related to learning requirements. He suggests that four basic aptitudes (processing speed, memory capacity, declarative knowledge and procedural skill) can account for individual differences in learning and he goes on to relate these differences to the requirement for different kinds of instruction (Kyllonen *et al*, 1991). The LAMP tests produced correlations of 0.5–0.75 with measures of learning and yielded an incremental validity of 0.20 to that of the ASVAB. The connection between measurement and learning is important because the effective criterion for most military selection tests is some form of training performance; the research programme also provides an important bridge between the domains of assessment and instructional theory.

Matching ability measures to performance assessments

The US Army's Project A also used CBT as a platform for developing new types of test item (e.g. speed of reaction, perceptual processing, memory, psychomotor abilities). These tests, together with ASVAB scores and measures of interests and of temperament, were related to a variety of performance measures which reflected different aspects of job performance. Of the numerous ability tests, spatial ability added to the prediction of technical proficiency and general soldiering that is provided by ASVAB's measure of general cognitive ability (with an incremental validity of only 0.02–0.03). Factor analysis identified six ability and five criterion domains for a wide range of military jobs. Using this structure, McHenry *et al.* (1990) describe the results of correlating a set of 74 assessment scores with performance for a selection of nine jobs (see Table 8.2). Schmidt, Ones and Hunter (1992) describe Project A as probably the largest and most expensive selection research project in history, and its principal benefits lie not in the production of new tests, but in its systematic study of the relationships between abilities and performance measurement. These should be of widespread interest and the reader is referred to the special issue of *Personnel Psychology* which contains eight more articles describing the programme.

Project A demonstrated that job performance is multidimensional in nature and, despite the convergence of cognitive ability measures and their high correlation with performance, other types of measure are needed. The predictors of technical proficiency were quite different from those for effort and leadership and personal discipline; also, even within this one organization, different mixes of skills, interests and temperament were needed to optimize prediction of technical proficiency in the different jobs. The study showed that basic cognitive abilities were a very effective predictor of who *can* perform a job and that the measures of temperament and interest help identify who *will* perform the job.

Table 8.2 Mean validity for composite scores within each predictor domain for nine military occupations

	Predictor domain					
	General cognitive ability	Spatial ability	Perceptual–psychomotor ability	Temperament/personality	Vocational interest	Job reward preference
Core technical proficiency	0.63	0.56	0.53	0.26	0.35	0.29
General soldiering proficiency	0.65	0.63	0.57	0.25	0.34	0.30
Effort and leadership	0.31	0.25	0.26	0.33	0.24	0.19
Personal discipline	0.16	0.12	0.12	0.32	0.13	0.11
Physical fitness and miliatry bearing	0.20	0.10	0.11	0.37	0.12	0.11

Adapted from McHenry *et al.* (1990).

Numerous small-scale UK studies have demonstrated the long-term stability of selection measures. More recent US studies (Schmidt *et al.* (1988), the Office of the Assistant Secretary of Defence (1990)) also showed that differences between higher and lower ability personnel persisted over many years.

Matching people with jobs

The British Army recruit battery (BARB) derives its robust measure of *g* from the homogeneity of the criterion tasks. Such efficiency is not enough, however. Other ability components or factors are needed to make satisfactory allocation decisions. By reworking ASVAB data sets, Alley and Teachout (1992) showed that using a differential placement model could result in performance gains of one-third of a standard deviation above current assignment procedures. Johnson and Zcidner (1989) indicate how using new ASVAB composites for allocation purposes would provide significant additional utility. Groben, Darby and Skinner (1990) describe the development of new methods for classifying and assigning Air Force recruits in their GATES project. Measures of job characteristics, person characteristics and selection standards are utilized to provide outputs that meet the objectives of alternative (efficiency and effectiveness) assignment strategies. The different assignment measures that are used under each heading include the following:

Efficiency (job fill)
- Casual time
- Minority fill
- Gender representation
- Unfilled training places

Effectiveness (job fit)
- Technical school performance
- Expected job performance
- Expected productive capacity
- Expected job satisfaction

The GATES model can be used to examine the relationship between job fit and job fill under given recruiting conditions and to assess the effect of new composites, job restructuring or new quotas. In the United Kingdom, verbal and numeracy abilities are heavily relied upon to guide allocation decisions; therefore, item generation theory is being used to augment BARB with appropriate subtests. An alternative approach would be to combine measures of personality and motivation with BARB scores, and Collis and Beard (1994) have demonstrated that this gives much improved differentiation. A third approach is to develop person–job matching techniques to optimize the fit between individuals and jobs when groups need to be allocated. Hobson (1995) describes how RAF jobs have been fitted into a framework of performance and ability domains. For each branch, a profile is produced of the job requirements, expressed in terms of five ability domains (spatial ability, attentional capacity, psychomotor, mental speed and reasoning). Candidates' test scores are weighted to produce a score in each of the domains and the candidate's profile is matched to the job profile.

A PEEK INTO THE FUTURE

Some of the developments that were predicted (Hardinge, 1989) have come about, such as the widening of the manpower base and the development of new computer-based tests. Improvements in testing general ability meant that there was not a greater emphasis on specialized ability tests as had been expected. The significant political and social changes that have taken place make some of the views about appraisal now seem complacent. So what will happen next? The trend towards reducing Service differences will continue and there will be further reductions in the differences between military and civilian ways of life. Social pressures will continue to establish the rights of individuals in the military; sexual orientation will probably move up the agenda. The emphasis will shift from selection to training and appraisal in order to promote gender- and culture-fairness and also as an organizational response to the need to adapt to change. Competency-based assessment and appraisal systems will become almost universal; formalized appraisal at various career points will be much more common. Such developments should foster the fairer treatment of minority groups. Hopefully as attitudes and policies mature the focus will be more on accepting differences and managing diversity. We will have stopped trying to find better measures of ability and will be looking for a better match between the individual's unique combination of physical, cognitive and affective functions and the organization's training and job requirements. Allocation models will be a major concern. There will be a strong emphasis on profile matching techniques and on 'intelligent' computer-based test reports, and individual counselling will play a bigger part in career decisions.

AUTHOR NOTE

The views expressed are those of the author and do not necessarily represent those of the Ministry of Defence.

REFERENCES

Alkhadher, O., Anderson, N. and Clarke, D. (1994). Computer-based testing: A review of recent developments in research and practice. *Work and Organisational Psychologist,* **4** (2), 169–187.

Alley, W.E. and Teachout, M.S. (1992). Differential assignment potential in the ASVAB. Presentation at Annual Meeting of American Psychol. Assoc. 100t, Washington DC. In Landy, F.J. and Shankster, L.J. (1994). Personnel Selection & Placement. *Annual Review of Psychology,* Vol. 45, 261–296.

Anastasi, A. (1968). *Psychological Testing,* 3rd edn. London: Collier–Macmillan.

*Aschenbrenner, H. (1989). *Proceedings of the NATO Workshop on Psychological Fitness.* Bonn: Ministry of Defence.

Armstrong, T.R., Chalupsky, A.B., McLaughlin, D.H., Dalldorf, M.R. (1988). Armed Services Vocational Aptitude Battery: Validation for Civilian Occupations, Brook Air Force Base, Texas. Air Force Human Resources Laboratory.

Barrett, L.E. (1989). Cognitive versus non-cognitive predictors of Air Force Officer training. 1989 Annual Convention of the American Psychological Association, New Orleans, Louisiana.

Bartram, D. (1987). The development of an automated testing system for pilot selection: The Micropat Project. *Applied Psychology: An International Review,* **36** (3), 279–298.

Bejar, I.J. (1986). Analysis and Generation of Hidden Figure Items: A Cognitive Approach to Psychometric Modelling. Report RR-86-20. Princeton, NJ: Educational Testing Service.

Betts, M. (1995). The Independent Review of the Armed Forces' Manpower, Career, and Remuneration Structures: Managing People in Tomorrow's Armed Forces. Report to Secretary of State for Defence. London: HMSO.

Butler, R.P. and McCauley, C. (1987). Extraordinary stability and ordinary predictability of academic success at the US Military Academy. *Journal of Educational Psychology,* **79,** 83–86.

Carroll, J.B. (1993). *Human Cognitive Abilities: A Survey of Factor Analytic Studies.* Cambridge University Press, New York.

Collis, J.M. and Beard, C.A. (1993). The use of personality and vocation measures for allocation of Royal Naval ratings: some preliminary indicators of validity. SP(N) Report TR315. London. Ministry of Defence.

*Collis, J.M. and Irvine, S.H. (1991). The Plymouth ABC Battery for RN/WRNS Ratings and RM Other Ranks Under Training; Validity and Reliability Studies; Summary Report. SP(N) Report TR271. London: Ministry of Defence.

Dobson, P. and Williams, A. (1989). The validation of the selection of male British Army officers. *Journal of Occupational Psychology,* **62,** 313–325.

Drakely, R.J. (1986). Royal Navy Officers' selection scores and success beyond initial training. Paper presented at 26th Annual Conference of Military Testing Association, Munich, 5–9 November.

Groben, Capt J., Darby, M. and Skinner, J. (1989). Generic Assignment Test and Evaluation (GATES). Armstrong Laboratory Human Resources.

Hammer, E.G. and Kleiman, L.A. (1988). Getting to know you. *Personnel Administration,* **34,** 86–92.

Hardinge, N.M. (1989). Personnel Selection in the Military. In P. Herriot (Ed) *Assessment and Selection in Organizations*. London: John Wiley.

Hendy, K.C. (1990). Aircrew/cockpit compatibility: A multivariate problem seeking a multivariate solution. Paper presented at NATO Aerospace Medical Panel Symposium on Recruiting, Selection, Training and Military Operations of Female Aircrew, Tours, France, April 1990. AGARD Conference Proceedings No. 491.

Hobson, C.J. (1995). Pilot Selection Process: Rational Weight Study, DRA Customer Report DRA/CHS/CR95/5031T-001/8.0.

Hunter, J.E. (1986). Cognitive ability, cognitive aptitudes, job knowledge and job performance. *Journal of Vocational Behaviour*, **29**, 340–362.

Hunter, J.E. and Hirsh, H.R. (1987). Application of meta-analysis. In C.L. Cooper and I.T. Robertson (eds.), *International Review of Industrial and Organisational Psychology*. London: John Wiley.

Hunter, J.E. and Hunter, R.F. (1984). Validity and utility of alternative predictors of job performance. *Psychological Bulletin*, **96**, 72–98.

Irvine, S.H., Dann, P.L. and Anderson, J.D. (1990). Towards a theory of algorithm-determined cognitive test construction. *British Journal of Psychology*, **81**, 173–195.

*Johnson, C.D. and Zeidner, J. (1989). The economic benefits of predicting job performance, Institute for Defence Analysis Paper P-2241, IDA Washington, US.

Jones, A. (1984). Royal Navy officer selection: Developments, current procedures and research. Paper presented at 26th Annual Conference of Military Testing Association, Munich, 5–9 November.

Jones, A. (1988). Estimation of the utility of an assessment centre against training and operational outcomes. Paper presented to the British Psychological Society Occupational Psychology Conference, Manchester.

Jones, A. (1991). Psychologists and military officer selection. In R. Gal and A.D. Mangelsdorff (eds.), *Handbook of Military Psychology*. London: John Wiley.

Kyllonen, P.C. and Christal, R.E. (1988). Cognitive Modelling of Learning Abilities: A Status Report of LAMP (AFHRL-TP-87-66). Manpower and Personnel Division, Airforce Human Resources Laboratory, Brooks Air Force Base, Texas, USA.

Kyllonen, P.C. and Christal, R.E. (1990). Reasoning ability is (little more than) working memory capacity? *Intelligence*, **14**, 389–433.

Kyllonen, P.C., Tirre, W.C. and Christal, R.E. (1991). Knowledge and processing speed as determinants of associative learning. *Journal of Experimental Psychology: General*, **120** (1), 57–79.

McDaniel, M.A. (1989). Biographical constructs for predicting employee suitability. *Applied Psychology*, **74**, 464–470.

McDaniel, M.A., Schmidt, F.A. and Hunter, J.E. (1988). A meta-analysis of the validity of methods for rating training and experience in personnel selection. *Personnel Psychology*, **41** (2), 283–314.

McHenry, J.J., Hough, L.M., Toquam, J.L., Hanson, M.A. and Ashworth, S. (1990). Project A validity results: The relationship between predictor and criterion domains. *Personnel Psychology*, **43**, 335–354.

McLaughlan, Brig. I.W. (1994). The Review of the Potential Officer Selection System. Report for the Adjutant General. London: Ministry of Defence.

Neil, G.W. (1984). Officer Selection: The Role of Personality. Research Note 20/84. Research Branch HQ RAF Support Command, RAF Brampton, Huntingdon, Cambs.

Office of the Assistant Secretary of Defense, Force Management and Personnel (1990). Report to the House Committee on Appropriations. Joint Service efforts to link enlistment standards to job performance. Washington DC: Off. Assist. Sec. Defense.

*Peat Marwick McLintock and Mass Observation (1989). Ethnic Minority Recruitment to the Armed Services, vols. 1–3.

Rayson, M.P., Holliman, D.E. and Bell, D.G. (1994). Physical Selection Standards for the British Army: Phase 3 Development of Physical Selection Tests and Pilot Study. Report DRA-CHS-WP-94006. Centre for Human Sciences, Defence Research Agency, Farnborough, UK.

Ree, M.J. and Earles, J.A. (1990). Relationships of General Ability, Specific Ability, and Job Category for Predicting Training Performance. Brooks Air Force Base, TX: Air Force Human Resources Laboratory.

Robertson, I.T. and Downs, S. (1989). Work-sample tests of trainability: a meta-analysis. *J. Appl. Psychol.*, **74**, 402–410.

Rodgers, M.N. and Johnson, V.W. (1987). Predicting performance at basic officer training with the Naval Officer Selection Board. Paper presented at 29th Annual Conference of Military Testing Association, Ottawa, 19–23 October.

Rothstein, H.R., Schmidt, F.L., Erwin, F.W., Owens, W.A. and Sparks, C.P. (1990). Biographical data in employment selection: Can validities be made generalizable? *Journal of Applied Psychology*, **75**, 175–184.

Sands, W.A. and Gade, P.A. (1983). An application of computerised adaptive testing in U.S. Army recruiting. *Journal of Computer Based Instruction*, **10**, 87–89.

Schmidt, F.L., Hunter, J.F., Outerbridge, A.N. and Goff, S. (1988). Joint relation of experience and ability with job performance: test of three hypotheses. *J. Appl. Psychol.*, **73**, 46–57.

Schmidt, F.L., Ones, D.S. and Hunter, J.E. (1992). Personnel selection. *Annual Review of Psychology*, **43**, 627–670.

Smith, S.J.E. (1992). An Evaluation of the Personal Qualities Assessment Profile (PQAP). Army Personnel Research Establishment Report 92R023. APRE, MOD, Farnborough, Hampshire GU14 6TD, UK.

Smith, M. and Abrahamsen, M. (1992). Patterns of selection in six countries. *The Psychologist*, **5**, 205–207. British Psychological Society.

Sperl, T.C., Ree, M.J. and Steuck, K.W. (1992). Armed services vocational aptitude battery and air force qualifying test: Analyses of common attributes. *Military Psychology*, **4** (3), 175–188.

Spinner, B. (1990). Predicting success in basic flying training from the Canadian Automated Pilot Selection System (Working Paper 90-6). Willowdale, Ontario: Canadian Forces Personnel Applied Research Unit.

*Tapsfield, P.G.C. (1993). The British Army Recruit Battery: Test–Retest Reliability. HAL Technical Report 5–1993 for Army Personnel Research Establishment, MOD, Farnborough, UK.

Urban, G.D. and McDaniel, M.A. (1989). Factor and cluster analyses of the special assignment battery. Paper presented at 97th Annual Convention of the American Psychological Association, New Orleans, Louisiana.

Vance, R.J., Coovert, M.D. and MacCullum, R.C. (1988). Construct models of task performance. *Journal of Applied Psychology*, **74** (3), 447–455.

Vance, R.J., Coovert, M.D. and MacCullum, R.C. (1989). Construct validity of multiple job performance measures using confirmatory factor analysis. *Journal of Applied Psychology*, **73** (10) 74–80.

Vineberg, R. and Joyner, J.N. (1982). Prediction of Job Performance: Review of Military Studies. Alexandria, VA: Human Resource Organisation.

Walker, C.B., White, L.A. and Schroyer, C. (1989). Implementing the US Army's assessment of background and life experiences (ABLE). Paper presented at 97th Annual Convention of the American Psychological Association, New Orleans, Louisiana.

*Wilson, Cdr F.P., Eitelberg, M.J. and Fodor, Lt Cdr D.B. (1993). Ethnic Participation in the Militaries of TTCP Countries. Willowdale, Ontario: Canadian Forces Personnel Applied Research Unit.

References preceded by an asterisk are not available outside the Ministry of Defence.

Chapter 9

Selection for a Profession: A Case Study

ROBERT WOOD

Pearn Kandola Occupational Psychologists, Oxford, UK

GRAHAM HAMER

Inns of Court School of Law, London, UK

CHARLES JOHNSON

Psychometric Research & Development Ltd, St Albans, UK

TIM PAYNE

Pearn Kandola Occupational Psychologists, Oxford, UK

TRAINING FOR THE BAR

In the United Kingdom there are two branches of the legal profession with separate vocational training arrangements. *Solicitors* are lawyers to whom clients have direct access. In representing clients in courts they instruct *barristers* whose prime focus is as specialist advocates, and to whom clients have access only via solicitors.

The training of advocates is divided into three stages. The first stage is known as the academic stage. It is concerned primarily with acquiring knowledge of the central areas of law, and is achieved by completing a legal degree or conversion course for graduates from other disciplines. (At the outset, all students join one of the four Inns of Court. These function, in effect, as professional associations.) Students then take a one-year vocational stage, called the Bar Vocational Course. Finally, there is a one-year period in what is called *pupillage*, where the newly qualified advocate works under the supervision of an experienced advocate. The

International Handbook of Selection and Assessment, Edited by N. Anderson and P. Herriot.
© 1997 John Wiley & Sons Ltd.

pupillage is carried out in 'chambers', which are the offices from which the experienced advocates work.

Pupillage can be thought of as an apprenticeship. During the second six months the 'pupil' is allowed to appear in court for the first time. At the end of this period he or she is able to apply for a 'tenancy', which gives a permanent place in chambers, and means that the new advocate has become fully part of the independent practising Bar.

It is only a small profession in the United Kingdom, with less than 400 new entrants taken on each year. It follows that some selection has to take place at one or more points in the system. This chapter is concerned with an attempt to introduce selection at the point of entry to the vocational stage of the training process, the Bar Vocational Course.

ORIGINS OF THE FIRST SELECTION PROCESS

The Council of Legal Education (CLE) is responsible for overseeing the Bar Vocational Course. The course is run at the Inns of Court School of Law (ICSL) on behalf of the Bar Council. People wishing to be advocates must complete this course successfully if they are to progress further. The course was introduced in 1989–90. (From 1997 it is to be taught by other institutions as well as the ICSL.)

Until 1991, all applicants satisfying the stipulated academic requirements were admitted to the course. However, rapidly increasing numbers of applicants (see Table 9.1) made it necessary to introduce an interim means of limiting the numbers on the course pending the development of a considered selection process by the Bar Council. The interim system used in 1992 and 1993 selected applicants on the basis of their first degree results, since there appeared to be a clear correlation between degree performance and success on the course. But there was unease that academic results alone were not enough to justify selection to a course of vocational training. It was said that using degrees alone was likely to disadvantage mature students and those from ethnic minorities, who historically had achieved poorer degree results than others. Out of these submissions came pressure to change the selection process.

Table 9.1   Applications to the Inns of Court School of Law

Year	Applications	Registrations
1986–87	946	754
1987-88	942	749
1988–89	1071	806
1989–90*	1075	845
1990–91	1175	899
1991–92	1368	1076
1992–93†	1655	1037
1993–94†	1981	1033

* New Bar Vocational Course introduced.
† Interim selection system.

For the 1994 selection process the Bar Council asked the CLE, on the basis of professional advice, to introduce an ability test into the process so that, as they put it, at least one element of the process would be indisputably age-blind, colour-blind and gender-blind. The other elements were the results of the Advanced (A) level school-leaving examinations taken at age 18 in the United Kingdom (in the United Kingdom A levels are a pre-requisite for university entry) and a scored application form. It was also proposed that borderline candidates be interviewed. However, this proposal was thrown out on the grounds that it was not appropriate to use an additional selection element for borderline candidates only, when that element had not been used in making decisions about making offers to the other applicants. With interviews likely to prove the least reliable means of predicting performance on the course, the objections were given additional force.

THE SELECTION PROCESS—MARK I

In outline, the process which it was planned to implement (Mark I) was as follows:

- All applicants would be required to complete and return an application form. This would request factual information, some of which would be scored.
- All applicants would be required to take a critical reasoning test.
- Each applicant would be assigned a score based on the scored part of the application form and on his/her performance on the test.
- On the basis of this score, approximately the top 800 applicants would be offered conditional places.
- All offers of places would be conditional on joining an Inn of Court, satisfactory completion of the academic stage, and payment of fees.
- The candidates ranked immediately below those offered places would be included on a waiting list and would be offered places in the order in which they were ranked should any candidates already accepted drop out.
- The remaining applications would be rejected.
- A Central Selection Board (CSB) would be set up to supervise the selection procedure.
- The CSB would ensure that appropriate equal opportunities monitoring be carried out at all stages of the selection procedure.

Development of the original process

The Bar Vocational Course covers a range of knowledge and skills, assessed by a variety of means. Apart from options that are studied only in the third term and involve a combination of skills and substantive law knowledge, there are three broad areas on the course which are assessed:

1. Knowledge subjects (Evidence, Civil Litigation, Criminal Litigation)—these are assessed by the use of multiple choice tests.

2. Written skills (Opinion Writing, Drafting)—these are assessed with a mixture of marked practical training exercises, both seen and unseen.
3. Oral skills (Advocacy, Conference, Negotiation)—these are assessed by a mixture of seen and unseen practical training exercises.

The purpose of the selection process was to find people who would be able to meet the standards set down for passing this course.

Development work on the process had been carried out by an academic occupational psychologist. The test the CLE was advised to use was the Watson–Glaser, or Critical Thinking Appraisal (CTA). On the face of it, the Watson–Glaser was a good choice, indeed almost a compelling choice, given what was available. It consists of five sections, all of which require the application of analytical reasoning skills. The sections are: Inference, Recognition of Assumptions, Deduction, Interpretation, and Evaluation of Arguments. As a set of mental tools, what else would an advocate need?

As part of the development work, 109 of the students taking the 1991–92 Vocational Course were recruited to sit the Watson–Glaser. Subsequent analysis concluded that the Watson–Glaser was a good predictor of success on the Vocational Course, although a disappointingly small number of ethnic minority students volunteered to take the test. The 109 also completed a draft version of the application form. A further group of 106 students from the 1992–93 course took the Watson–Glaser and completed a revised version of the form.

The analysis of the consolidated data from the two groups of students confirmed the Watson–Glaser as a good predictor of performance in the Vocational Course assessments, with an overall correlation coefficient of 0.49. However, when looked at as a predictor of different elements assessed on the course, it ranged between 0.13 and 0.52, the highest correlations being with the multiple choice tests used to test knowledge of evidence, and civil and criminal procedure, and the lowest for the oral examinations. Thus, there was some evidence of discriminant validity, and also some of the convergent validity, albeit moderated through a format factor.

The analysis also showed that average A-level performance was another strong predictor, stronger than the Watson–Glaser, because it produced similar correlations with the multiple choice examinations, but higher with the oral and written examinations.

Unfortunately, the analysis was contra-indicative of the predictive validity of the other elements it had been planned to score, that is to say, those on the application form. This created a number of problems:

(a) The number of usable categories on the application form fell from six to one, i.e. A levels.
(b) Only A levels had been validated as a predictor and no other academic qualifications were to be scored (given the decision to exclude degree class). However, some 15% of applicants had not taken A levels but had gained a variety of other qualifications.

(c) A provisional analysis of the A-level scores threw up evidence of dispropor- tionate impact on ethnic minority applicants (so the problem it was hoped had disappeared with the exclusion of degree class had reappeared).

On the basis of the regression equations he derived, the psychologist advising proposed using the following formula to arrive at an overall applicant score:

$$\text{Total score} = 1.4 \times \text{CTA total (out of 80)} + 10.85$$
$$\times \text{A-level average}[1] \text{ (maximum 5)} + 221.71 \text{ (constant)}.$$

This would put the scores on a range of 221–388 (rounded off).

Although expressing considerable reservations about the process as it stood, the psychologist felt, on balance, that even with the problems that had surfaced, the process as a whole was better than the previous interim arrangements. Even so, he felt it necessary to write a further letter expressing his anxieties about the process as it stood and drawing attention to reservations he had expressed to the Bar Council's Selection Working Party in October 1992, when reasons of cost had been given for abandoning more elaborate selection tests.

In essence, the position was that no one was happy with the procedure, but all the available alternatives were worse.

Subsequently, however, a further problem presented itself. The Watson–Glaser is commercially available, albeit through qualified psychologists. Although the psychologist advising had been satisfied that the Psychological Corporation's security arrangements were adequate, and that potential candidates would not be able to gain access to the test, evidence came to light to indicate that this confi- dence was misplaced. It emerged that two institutions had obtained copies of the test and one appeared to have given its students part of an American version of the test. The Watson–Glaser, which was planned to be at the centre of the process, was thus called into question. As it happens, subsequent analysis by ourselves found no cause for concern. However, the moral of the story is: never use an off- the-shelf product for a public assessment event.

The CSB had not yet met and was in no position to address the serious prob- lems that were arising. Accordingly, it fell to the CLE to rescue the 1994 selection process. It immediately sought professional advice, and asked two of us (Wood and Johnson, who were already working for the Bar Council) to work together to ensure that a fair and workable system would be in place to select students for entry to the 1994–95 Vocational Course.

Attempts to rescue the Mark I process

It was known that the Watson–Glaser and A-level results would do a good job in predicting the multiple choice course tests, and to a lesser extent, the written course exercises, but definitely not the oral course exercises. It had been expected that the application form would have helped out here, but it had apparently collapsed. However, there had been a development on this front. One of us (Johnson) had been asked by the Bar Council to see if there was any way to salvage the application form. He suspected that potentially useful predictors of performance on the course were being masked by the fact that some examinations correlated very poorly with others. In particular, using only total examination score as a criterion would be inappropriate, since this score was dominated by the multiple choice tests taken during the course.

Johnson realized that reanalysis in terms of the three groups of examinations— written, oral, and multiple choice—might throw up items on the application form predictive of examination performance, which might then be combined into a usable application form score. The emphasis was properly on items which correlated best with oral examination performance, since there was already adequate coverage of the other elements. Enough items emerged to enable a formula to be produced to arrive at an application form score. The score itself was most predictive of performance on the oral examinations (Negotiation, Conference Skills, Advocacy). After a check that the formula cross-validated on another sample, it was possible to say that the application form had been salvaged.

However, there did not seem to be enough information on candidates, especially information about personal attributes like perseverance which are usually predictive of further achievement. Sending out for references would have been an easy way to obtain this sort of information, but there was no confidence that referees would reply in time. It was decided instead to send out what was called a 'supplementary' application form. In constructing this form we went back to the research work which had informed the design of the Bar Vocational Course (Johnston and Shapland, 1990). Seven questions were formulated with the aim of eliciting information about some of the skills areas identified in the research as being important in the work of the junior Bar. The form was sent out to students before Christmas with an explanatory letter and a request that it should be returned by mid-January 1994. The forms were then double marked 'blind' by a team in accordance with a marking scheme approved by the CSB, which by that time had begun to hold regular meetings and was beginning to get to grips with the problems with which it had been presented.

Elements of the process

The Mark I selection process was approved by the CSB in February 1994. The elements comprised:

(a) a *multiple choice score* (Watson–Glaser scored out of 80);
(b) an *academic score*, based in most cases on average A-level performance, which had been taken out of the application form (maximum possible score 5);
(c) an *application form score* calculated from various 'tick box' items on the form (maximum possible score 29); and
(d) a *supplementary application form score* representing the marked answers to the seven questions asked on the supplementary form (maximum possible score 35).

The actual selection mechanism involved setting minimum levels in each of these four elements and requiring candidates to meet those levels in *each* of the four elements. This approach to selection—a rejection of the usual method of *compensation*—mirrored exactly the Vocational Course assessment system in which, for example, a very strong performance in the knowledge-based multiple choice tests cannot compensate for significant weakness in written skills. In other words, students have to meet the standard in all aspects of the work. The correlations between the elements are, in fact, quite low in practice, so a lot is being asked of students. In what was going to be a highly competitive selection situa ion, it was thought that a lot might also be asked of candidates.

The selection method used a series of sweeps through the data with each of the four element levels being lowered at each sweep until a sufficient number of candidates had been selected to meet the entry target. At each sweep the score levels were progressively lowered. Although elements (a)–(c) had been validated in the original trialling, element (d) had not been so validated; in fact, had not been validated at all. To make some allowance for this, a lower level was always set for the supplementary form score. In the event, only the very lowest scorers on this form were eliminated, and nearly all of those had failed on one or more of the other elements. This progressive sweeping method bears some similarity to the 'sliding band' method discussed by Cascio *et al.* (1991).

The use of what is known as a *conjunctive scoring model* (Green and Wigdor, 1988) in a live assessment event is, we think, quite novel. No other examples have come to light. On the other hand, the use of *disjunctive* models, whereby exceeding the threshold is required in only one or perhaps two designated elements, and compensation is allowed in the rest, is quite common, at least in education. In the occupational sector, however, fully compensatory models are not so common. It is far more likely that candidates for jobs will be eliminated serially through a series of screens; in other words, a progressive disjunctive model.

The selection mechanism was implemented exactly as described. A total of 882 candidates were offered places; in addition, 40 were placed in the first waiting list band and 28 in the second.

Outcry against the Mark I process

The publication of the results created a tremendous outcry and the CLE found itself attacked from all sides: by the rejected applicants, by the universities, by the media, by the Inns of Court, and by the Bar Council. Several hundred appeals were received. It is instructive to consider the reasons for the reaction because they could certainly be present in other professional entry situations:

1. Applications for entry to the course reached their peak in precisely the year in which full selection was being introduced. So, for the first time ever there were going to be more losers than winners, with well under half the applicants being offered a place.
2. The universities teaching the students had not been consulted or involved in devising the selection process. Moreover, since references had not been used and degree classifications played no part, they had no input whatsoever into the process.

3. Changes to the process as originally published, e.g. the supplementary application form, had reduced the confidence of applicants and their supporters in the selectors.

4. All successful selection processes must reach a level of acceptability with applicants and engender a belief from them that the selection elements and criteria were appropriate. This was not the case here; the Watson–Glaser attracted particular hostility. The comment was frequently made: 'What has such a test got to do with being a barrister?' (What had been so self-evidently face valid to the planners was not so obvious to these applicants.) There were also serious flaws in the operation of the Watson–Glaser which candidates did not know about (see below).

5. Rather than rally behind the process, members of the profession became some of its most vocal critics.

6. The failure to use degree classification was a major weakness, although the motives for excluding degree (worries about fairness) were honourable. The Bar Council had been keen that applicants should know the result of their applications as early as possible so they would be able to plan their futures and, in particular, to give them as much time as possible to raise the fees for the course. However, most of the law degree students would not know their results until late June or July with the course due to start in September. It was not felt to be fair to use degree classification for some applicants but not others, hence the use of A levels (or their equivalents) and the ignoring of evidence of degree performance even if present. There was also a desire to avoid the complications of conditional offers based on a degree yet to be obtained. But, in not using degree classification, the system was forgoing the use of what was known to be the best overall predictor of performance on the course.

7. The decision not to allow compensation between elements of the process created a significant presentational problem, although again it was done for good reasons. And, of course, at certain points the decisions to reject could look rather arbitrary: someone with a distinguished academic career, a good Watson–Glaser score, a good supplementary application form score, and an Inns scholarship, could be rejected because of, it was said, 'failing to tick a few boxes on the application form'; an otherwise strong candidate might be 0.01 short of what was required in A-level average to get an offer. These examples could be multiplied.

8. The process lacked any point where human judgement was exercised in respect of any individual applicant. While this might be thought to be a desirably objective and universalistic approach, and we certainly thought so, it created considerable hostility among applicants and their supporters.

9. A key aspect of the work of many barristers involves presenting material orally, and yet the selection process contained no direct measure of this sort of ability. Applicants often complained they had not had the chance 'to put their case'.

The weaknesses in the process as implemented, and the vociferousness of the criticism, became too great for nothing to be done. The CLE and the Bar Council therefore agreed to act together to try, for the second time, to rescue the selection process. Evidently, degree classification had to come back in somewhere. This was done by allowing compensation where candidates had scored below the offer standard in one element only. Those who had obtained upper second class honours degrees were allowed to compensate for failure in either the A-level element or the application form element, but not in both. Those who had not yet completed their degrees were made conditional offers on the basis of achieving the offer standard. Those with first class honours were allowed to compensate for failure in any single element. Conditional offers were also made on this basis to those who had not completed their degrees.

These amendments to the process were expected to bring in a further 250 students, the most which the Vocational Course could accommodate. The CLE and the Bar Council resolved to make no further concessions to the criticisms and to resist any further attempts to break the process. The inevitable legal challenge was successfully fought, although not before a full hearing had been held before the Visitors to the Inns of Court which found in the CLE's favour. However, even having won this battle, it was clear that the process would have to be completely revised for the following year.

THE SELECTION PROCESS—MARK II

The CSB, in devising its new process (Mark II), was not under the same restraint about costs as the Bar Council's original working party had been. While not exactly presented with a blank cheque, the prime directive to the Board was to produce an acceptable, successful process. As a start, it decided to go back to first principles, back to the work of Johnston and Shapland (1990). Their research with junior advocates had indicated that a successful advocate would need to possess, in some combination or other, the following qualities or KSAs:

- Intellectual ability
- Interpersonal skills
- Presentational skills
- Personal coping skills
- Motivation

The CSB took the identification of the five qualities as being central to its task and, with the help of its professional advisers, sought appropriate means of assessing these qualities in applicants.

The experience with the Watson–Glaser

The first thing the CSB had to do was decide what to do about the Watson–Glaser. What had actually happened there?

The maximum raw score on the Watson–Glaser is 80. As many as 570 of 2243 applicants, or 25%, scored 70 or more. This represents extreme bunching at the top of the distribution and means that most of these applicants were not properly measured. An even more striking statistic is that out of the 100 top scoring applicants 97 were men. The difference between males and females approached half a standard deviation. Both the bunching and the sex difference should have been spotted at trialling.

That was not all. Whereas 30% of male applicants scored 70 or more, as did 18% of female applicants, for those who nominated themselves as being from ethnic minorities the figure was 5%. Looking at scores of 55 or less, the figure for males was 14%, for females 20%, but for ethnic minorities 50%. The difference represents a full standard deviation, consistent with differences reported on similar comparisons with ability tests (Schmitt and Noe, 1986). What was going on?

For the first 16 items of this test the choice is between five options. Thereafter, and for the remaining 64 items, the choice is between two or three options, mostly two—true or false. The opportunity for guessing—informed or otherwise—is therefore always present. That in turn lowers the reliability of the test for any application. Now opportunities for guessing favour risk-takers and there is evidence (Grandy, 1987) that rather than attempting every question, which is clearly the most rewarding test-taking strategy, women will be more inclined to leave a blank, which of course gains no credits at all. Inspection of the answer sheets in this case confirmed the tendency of women, even the higher scoring women, to omit or fail to reach questions. This effect may not wholly explain the disparity between male and female scores, but it goes some way to doing so, and it is something users of the Watson–Glaser must be aware of.

Concerning applicants who designated themselves as belonging to ethnic minorities, two things can be said. Most of them were women, so the omitting effect was present and may even have been amplified. There is also evidence that, for whatever reason, ethnic minority test-takers in the United Kingdom have struggled with speeded tests (Wood, 1993); the same has been reported of black job-seekers in the United States doing the GATB (Hartigan and Wigdor, 1989).

It should also be borne in mind that the percentage of ethnic minority applicants was well in excess of what would have been predicted from their representation in the population at large, or even an academic population. That, coupled with their marked over-representation among the very lowest scorers, suggests that there were too many ethnic minority applicants who entered with very little chance of success, a point made by the Barrow Report (Barrow *et al.*, 1994).

Originally, the CSB might have expected to use the Watson–Glaser in a very hard-edged way to choose people strictly in a top-down fashion, but once it saw the results it knew this was not an option. Instead, the Watson–Glaser was used in a bottom-up way, employing as low a cutoff score as could reasonably be defended. Even so, and this follows from the figures presented, the Watson–Glaser still fell heavily on the ethnic minority applicants. For women, the effects were much mitigated simply because the cutoff had fallen so low and most women scored in the middle of the distribution. The lesson there is not to automatically lower the cutoff until there is an understanding of the distribution as a whole.

One further point is that had a compensatory scoring model been used instead, as was urged in the aftermath of Mark I, then the effect on ethnic minority, female and indeed mature applicants would have been even more severe than was the case with the conjunctive scoring model, the reason being the huge influence of the Watson–Glaser, and to a lesser extent A levels, and the advantages these gave to young white males. Incidentally, the application forms produced the least disproportionate impact, and that has been true in the two years since.

Direct measures replaced the Watson–Glaser

It was clear that the Watson–Glaser had to go, and also that the whole process had to be looked at. It could have been argued that there was still a case for a multiple choice ability test to predict performance on the multiple choice knowledge tests used on the Vocational Course, but the experience with the Watson–Glaser had been so chastening that the argument was never pursued. In any case, other elements, particularly degree class, were expected to predict multiple choice course performance.

In the event, the Watson–Glaser was replaced by a combination of written exercises and an oral assessment. The professional advisers had argued all along for direct measures, and now the decision was taken to bear the cost.

The written exercises are targeted on key intellectual capabilities that advocates need to possess (summarizing, drafting, formulating an advice). The exercises are double marked, blind; another rarity in a mass selection event.

The oral test concentrates on the quality of candidates' presentational skills, and their ability to think on their feet. This exercise, in particular, has represented a huge undertaking, and one which may be unique. We have come across nothing like it in the literature. Where else have 1500 applicants been given a five minute oral assessment by two assessors with all evidence videotaped for possible future reference?

ELEMENTS OF MARK II

The selection process Mark II materialized as follows:

- An application form
- Degree classification
- Performance in an oral test
- Performance in three written tests

The application form was gathered in first. The oral and written tests were taken on the same day in December. Which each candidate took first was decided randomly.

The application form

The application form seeks a range of detailed information. It asks for details of degrees and postgraduate qualifications either gained or being taken. There are two sections asking for information about work and other related experience. The remainder of the form concentrates on eliciting evidence around: intellectual ability, manifested in ways other than degree classification; experiences in dealing with people; experiences where presentation and advocacy skills have been demonstrated, although not necessarily in a legal context; personal coping skills; motivation and commitment to a career at the Bar. In addition, two referees are asked to verify what the applicant has written and, if they cannot, to so indicate on the form.

Detailed rubrics and notes accompanied the form, giving examples of the type of evidence that would be admissible, that is to say, concrete examples, not general statements or opinions. The scoring system allocates marks for the factual content of the answers, not their style. As with the written tests, the forms were double marked, blind; an unusual thing to do with application forms, but again indicative of the desire to ensure fair treatment.

In its structure, the form was a direct successor of the supplementary application form, although the scoring system was completely revamped. More importantly, it built on the original application form, so that the validity of items that had been salvaged, which were, by and large, the most valid items, was conserved in the Mark II version. A reasonable expectation would be that the validity of the form is at least as good as, if not better, than the original form.

The oral test

An important aspect of advocacy is the ability to communicate orally, and win someone round to your point of view. While such skills are developed in the training offered on the Vocational Course, it is vital that at selection those seeking to practise at the Bar show signs—let us put it no stronger than that—of being able to offer a coherent argument orally. Here was an element that was completely missing from the Mark I selection process, and its inclusion was welcomed, not least by the applicants themselves, for whom it tended to validate the whole process.

The oral test involves the delivery, before two assessors, of a five minute oral presentation, followed by two questions. The assessors comprise one lay person, usually someone connected with the law, and a qualified advocate. They are required to arrive at a consensus rating of performance on five dimensions—content, structure, presentation, persuasiveness, and response to questions—using a five-point behaviourally anchored scale for each. Training is given to assessors before each selection event, and performance is monitored throughout the eight days of the event. Assessor pairs are reconstituted every two days, although always keeping the lay person and the professional, the point being to try to contain and neutralize marker error as much as possible.

Candidates are given a choice of one from a possible six topics, and 15 minutes to prepare. The choice of topics is randomized so that after every 15 minute slot a fresh list of topics appears. In order not to give any undue advantage, the topics are not legally based and candidates are not expected to provide detailed factual information. The two questions at the end are chosen from a list drawn up beforehand. All of this was explained in the familiarization notes that went out to applicants well in advance of the event, and also included sample topics. Thus, the opportunity to practise was there, and applicants were urged to do so.

Reliability trials were held before implementation, and checks were also made on assessors' ratings during and after the event. Rater agreement on the weakest performers, which mattered most given the selection ratio, was always good. The evidence for the validity of the oral tests rests on the similarity between the test, and the scoring method, and the oral exercises staged during the Vocational Course.

The written tests

The written tests supply a direct measure of an applicant's ability in summarizing material, drafting and giving advice. Again, the tests assume no legal knowledge or specific legal skills. Applicants are allowed 2½ hours to complete the tests under invigilated conditions.

To ensure that candidates would not know which topics they were going to get, *eight* parallel forms were devised, and the choice rotated every half-day session. Such a large number of forms would appear to be unique in public examining, but then the circumstances demanded it. Public examinations are nearly always organized so that all candidates sit the examinations simultaneously. Here it was not possible, hence the elaborate arrangements.

The texts for the summarizing exercises were taken from newspapers and periodicals, with candidates required to condense 1100 or so words down to 170. The drafting exercises invited candidates to frame rules for fictitious games, such as 'fierce juggling' and 'ultimate polo'. The advice tests comprised dilemma scenarios, such as whether a student should spend limited funds on travel to India, or on buying a computer; or which school a mother should send her two children to. The familiarization notes offered sample questions, and scoring criteria, so that applicants would know what to expect.

Training was given to raters before both selection events. Rater agreement was checked during and after the events. Raters invariably agreed on who the weakest performers were, and what score should be given, and where they did not, one of us moderated the scores. Evidence for the validity of the written tests rests on their obvious relevance to the three constructs, and on close point-to-point correspondence between the tests and the written exercises students undertake on the Vocational Course (test construction was overseen by ICSL lecturers, and the dilemma scenarios were written by one of the lecturers).

The selection mechanism

The process is competitive, and how well applicants score collectively, in conjunction with the entry numbers target, determines the minimum score required to achieve an offer. Each of the four selection elements is allocated a score with the maximum number of points available for each element being:

- Application form   20 points
- Degree classification   35 points

- Performance in oral test   20 points
- Performance in written tests   25 points

Points are allocated for degree classification as follows:

First class honours   35 points
Upper second class honours   23 points
Lower second class honours[2]   11 points

The raw scores are adjusted statistically to allow each element to contribute in the above proportions (i.e. the scores are standardized). These scores are then aggregated into a total score, on which candidates are ranked. At this point, decisions about offers can be made. In cases where degrees have not yet been completed, applicants are made offers conditional upon gaining a particular degree classification.

The decision to allocate the greatest weighting to degree classification reflects the preeminence of intellectual skills in the work of an advocate, and also the fact that degree class was already known to be the best overall predictor of performance on the course. As for the application form, if it was to count at all, it would need to be weighted at parity, or near parity, with the written and oral elements.

The CSB sought to gain wide acceptance for the new process, both from within the Bar world and outside. The Chair of the CSB, a former High Court judge, consulted widely, including a number of legal academics and careers officers. The new process was presented to the CLE at a full day meeting. This meeting was also attended by representatives from the Bar Council and the Inns of Court and it endorsed the new process.

The revised process was launched in September 1994, with a view to selecting students for entry to the course in September 1995. It was run exactly as designed and none of the procedures required any significant revision. The process was used again for selection for entry to the 1996–97 course, again without significant modification.

RESULTS FROM THE 1996 SELECTION PROCESS

Table 9.2 shows some summary data for the 1996 process. Evidently, the biggest difference between white and ethnic minority applicants was on the written tests. Whenever these comparisons are made, and there is disproportionate impact, it is invariably comprehension and production of the English language which is at the root of it.

The white–ethnic minority difference on the oral test is not so great, which is what would be expected. People for whom English is not the first language get on better speaking the language than writing it.

Table 9.3 shows correlations between the elements for the whole entry. They are sufficiently low to indicate that the elements were picking up different attributes, as planned. As such, they constitute evidence for discriminant validity. Negative correlations for gender mean that men did slightly better than women.

Table 9.2   Means and standard deviations (in parentheses) on the four assessment elements for white and ethnic minority applicants: 1996 process

		Whites (N = 1039)	Non-whites (N = 338)
Application form	(A)	10.25 (4.34)	9.52 (4.47)
Written tests	(W)	13.79 (5.19)	9.46 (5.76)
Oral test	(O)	10.66 (4.49)	8.18 (4.56)
Degree	(D)	20.55 (7.10)	15.79 (6.31)
Total (out of 100)		55.26 (13.26)	42.95 (13.46)

Table 9.3   Correlations between the four elements and gender: 1996 process

	A	W	O	D
A	—	—	—	—
W	0.14	—	—	—
O	0.25	0.32	—	—
D	0.15	0.29	0.24	—
Gender	0.00	−0.04	−0.12	0.02

The only gender difference of any size was on the oral test, actually one mean point difference, which, with a pooled standard deviation of approximately 14, is insignificant.

It should be noted that these results are moderated by degree status, and maybe also by other correlated effects, such as age. By degree status is meant whether the applicant is already in possession of a law degree, or is still awaiting the result (it will be recalled that in Mark II offers are conditional upon getting a certain degree class). To give an illustration of the moderating power of degree status, the difference between whites and ethnic minorities on the written tests (where the biggest difference is found overall) reduces from a mean difference of 5.10 points, for those with degrees, to 3.66 for those awaiting degrees. On the oral test, the corresponding reduction is from 2.86 to 2.13, still about half a standard deviation.

SO WAS MARK II SUCCESSFUL?

There are a number of points which might be made in answer to this question:

• The process was widely praised by academics and careers officers, and appears to have been fully accepted by the profession. Certainly, there was none of the fuss surrounding the Mark I event.

- The process proved very acceptable to applicants. Anecdotal reports suggest that they particularly like the oral test for its obvious relevance. The process therefore gained the acceptability that had been missing in the previous year.
- There was a substantial drop in applicants from the all time high of 2290 (the 1994 entry) to 1456 (the 1995 entry). The precise reasons for this can only be guessed at, although it was part of a wider pattern of falling demand for places on legal conversion courses and vocational courses for solicitors. It might also be speculated that having an appropriate selection process did lead to some significant self-selection by potential applicants. There was no doubt that candidates not possessing at least budding speaking skills would find the oral test daunting. However, it might be supposed that such people are precisely the ones who should not be seeking a career as an advocate. In that respect, the oral test served as a realistic job preview.
- Another aspect of the drop in applicants was that there was not very much selection going on for the 1995 entry, though rather more for the 1996 entry. As a consequence, there was less disproportionate impact on those groups who had experienced it in 1994.

SUMMARY

In this case study of selecting into a profession, it transpired that the acceptability of the process was the over-riding requirement. This led to some improved measurement practice (replacement of indirect by direct measures) and greater attention to fairness (double and blind marking, use of referees). It also forced the reinstatement of a measure—degree classification—about which there had been adverse impact worries, although, after reinstatement, it was only partially determining of the selection outcome, whereas before it had been wholly determining. One casualty was a decision mechanism based on simultaneously exceeding cut-offs on each of the elements of the process—the *conjunctive* scoring model. It was sacrificed in favour of the usual adding of scores together, the *compensatory* scoring model, which is so irresistible to lay people, but which, even when scores had been standardized, caused more adverse impact on ethnic minorities, females and mature students owing to the preponderance of young, white males among high scorers on the Watson–Glaser.

It can be said of the Mark II selection process that in the end it demonstrated fitness for purpose, although at a price. By any standards this is an expensive selection process. Even so, after all the difficulties along the way, it is perhaps disappointing that for reasons entirely unconnected with the efficacy of the process, it will have been used for two years only, and then abandoned. It has been abandoned because from 1997 training for practice as an advocate is to be shared among several UK institutions, who apparently will be free to devise and implement their own selection arrangements. Quite what these arrangements will be remains to be seen. Perhaps (and this is most probable) they will rely heavily on degree result, as in the past. Whether the problem of acceptability we have highlighted here will be diffused because there is no longer a single selection authority, is not clear. If pressure is exerted for a selection process which has proved its acceptability, then it is not so much abandonment, as mothballing.

END NOTES

1. A-level average was calculated by allocating 5 points for an A grade, 4 points for a B grade, etc. the points being summed and divided by the number of subjects taken.
2. This is the minimum level acceptable under the Bar regulations.

REFERENCES

Barrow, J., Deech, R., Larbie, J., Loomba, R. and Smith, D. (1994). *Equal Opportunities at the Inns of Court School of Law*. London: Council of Legal Education.

Cascio, W.F., Outtz, J., Zedeck, S. and Goldstein, I.L. (1991). Statistical implications of six methods of test score use in personnel selection. *Human Performance*, **4**, 233–264.

Grandy, J. (1987). *Characteristics of Examinees Who Leave Questions Unanswered on the GRE General Test Under Rights-Only Scoring*. ETS Research Report, 87–38. Princeton, NJ: Educational Testing Service.

Green, B.F. and Wigdor, A.K. (1988). *Measuring Job Competency*. Washington, DC: National Academy Press.

Hartigan, J.A. and Wigdor, A.K. (1989). *Fairness in Employment Testing: Validity Generalization, Minority Issues, and the General Aptitude Test Battery*. Washington, DC: National Academy Press.

Johnston, V. and Shapland, J. (1990). *Developing Vocational Legal Training for the Bar*. Sheffield: Faculty of Law, University of Sheffield.

Schmitt, N. and Noe, R.A. (1986). Personnel selection and equal employment opportunity. In C.L. Cooper and I. Robertson (eds.), *International Review of Industrial and Organizational Psychology*. New York: John Wiley.

Wood, R. (1993). *Assessment and Testing: A Survey of Research*. Cambridge: Cambridge University Press.

Chapter 10

Tacit Knowledge and Job Success

ROBERT J. STERNBERG

Department of Psychology, Yale University, P.O. Box 208205, New Haven, CT 06520-8205, USA

TACIT KNOWLEDGE AND JOB SUCCESS

There is good evidence to suggest that measures of general intelligence (so-called 'g') provide the single best predictor of job success across jobs (e.g. Ree and Earles, 1993; Schmidt and Hunter, 1993). Thus, if we were to consider in a single analysis welders, lathe operators, high-level executives, nurses, and accountants, among other jobs, we would probably find conventional measures of intelligence to be about as good as or better than any other single measure. But measures that are highly predictive of success *across* jobs are not necessarily particularly predictive *within* jobs.

There is no mystery as to why scores on conventional tests might be much more successful across than within jobs. Consider three reasons why there might be such a difference. First, the range of IQs across jobs is very large, whereas within jobs it may be relatively small. For example, the difference in IQ between an average assembly-line worker and an average actuary is likely to be larger than the difference in IQ between the top and bottom quartiles or possibly deciles within each of these jobs. Restricting range of IQ will lower correlations across jobs.

Second, although IQ may matter to some extent for most jobs, within a given job other factors might be much more important. For example, no matter what your IQ, you will not succeed as a surgeon, actuary, watchmaker, or professor of French literature without a lot of knowledge about your area of specialization. Additionally, the surgeon and watchmaker have to be able to work well with their hands, albeit in different ways. Moreover, you will not succeed as a football or basketball player without a lot of athletic talent as well.

International Handbook of Selection and Assessment, Edited by N. Anderson and P. Herriot.
© 1997 John Wiley & Sons Ltd.

Third, many industrial psychologists agree that there is more to intelligence than IQ, and certainly more to human abilities than IQ. Modern theories of intelligence define intelligence more broadly than did many theories in the past. For example, Gardner (1983) speaks of intelligences not typically captured by the IQ, such as musical, bodily-kinesthetic, interpersonal, and intrapersonal. Sternberg (1985) also speaks of aspects of intelligence that are not measured by conventional intelligence tests, such as the creative and practical aspects. And certainly, the creative abilities that are so important in many jobs are hardly measured at all by conventional intelligence tests.

There are a priori motivations for seeking tests for prediction of job success that are not just IQ tests. These motivations stem from the differences between the characteristics of the kinds of problems people face in jobs and the kinds of problems faced on typical tests of intelligence and related abilities. More than 20 years ago, Wason and Johnson-Laird (1972) found that content played an important part in reasoning—that the skill with which people think does not just depend on the form of the problem. And since then, many other investigators have found the context in which problems are solved is also of critical importance (see, for example, Ceci, 1990; Rogoff and Lave, 1984; Sternberg and Wagner, 1986). Consider how test problems and real-life problems differ from each other.

Conventional test problems are formulated by others, are well-defined, have all information provided from the beginning, have only one supposedly correct answer, usually have only one method of obtaining the correct answer, are disembedded from ordinary experience, and are of little or no intrinsic interest to the test-taker. Problems on the job, in contrast, emphasize recognition and formulation of just what the problems are, are usually ill-defined, require information seeking, have multiple 'correct' solutions, have multiple methods of obtaining these solutions, require use of prior experience, and are highly motivating for the job incumbent faced with the problem.

Within jobs, therefore, we find a need for measures that will predict job success in a way that goes beyond IQ. We have proposed such measures (Sternberg and Wagner, 1993; Sternberg, Wagner and Okagaki, 1993; Wagner and Sternberg, 1985, 1986; Williams and Sternberg, in press), which we proceed to describe here. These measures are of construct called 'tacit knowledge'.

The concept of tacit knowledge

Tacit knowledge, a construct first introduced by Polanyi (1976), is the knowledge that you need to succeed in an endeavor, that is not formally taught, and that often is not even verbalized. It is knowledge typically acquired on the job or in the situation where it is actually used. Tacit knowledge is typically informal, in that it is not actually a part of any discipline that is formally taught anywhere, although in theory, tacit knowledge can be verbalized and taught (in which case we still refer to it as 'tacit knowledge' even though strictly speaking it is no longer tacit). Tacit knowledge also differs from more formal knowledge in that there is often resistance to its revelation. For example, a company whose stated promotion policies encourage innovation but whose true promotion policies reward conformity, or perhaps membership in certain groups, is not likely to want these facts to be known. Thus, tacit knowledge is often not readily available for the asking, but must be inferred simply by spending time in an environment and carefully observing what is happening in that environment.

Theoretical basis for understanding and assessing tacit knowledge

Tacit knowledge can be understood or measured under the rubric of a number of different theories of abilities or attainments. We have used the triarchic theory of human intelligence (Sternberg, 1985, 1988) as the basis for our investigation of tacit knowledge. In particular, the processes for acquisition of tacit knowledge (described below) correspond to the components of knowledge acquisition in the theory, and more generally, measures of tacit knowledge assess one aspect of practical intelligence.

In the triarchic theory, a distinction is made between adaptation to existing environments, shaping of existing environments to transform them into different environments, and selection of wholly new environments. Adaptation involves changing oneself to suit the existing environment. Shaping involves changing the environment to suit oneself. And selection involves finding a new environment that suits one better than the environment one is in. Measures of tacit knowledge can assess any of these three aspects of practical intelligence. In most of our work, measures of tacit knowledge have assessed adaptation. But in new work currently under way on measuring tacit knowledge for leadership (Horvath, Williams, Forsythe, McNally, Wattendorf, and Sternberg, 1993) we have begun constructing assessments of tacit knowledge for shaping the environment through leadership activities.

Acquisition of tacit knowledge

According to Sternberg (1985), three main processes are used in the acquisition of tacit knowledge: selective encoding, selective comparison, and selective combination. Selective encoding is used when a person extracts pieces of relevant information from a multitude of informational inputs. Thus, when a person is new on the job, he or she may be bombarded by stimuli, but only a fraction of these will be relevant to success on the job. The good selective encoder separates the wheat from the chaff. For example, a lawyer needs to figure out which of the many principles of law are relevant to a particular case; a doctor needs to figure out what tests to perform to make a diagnosis, given a set of symptoms; a real-estate salesperson needs to figure out what kind of house a client truly can afford, usually without directly asking a person his or her income.

Selective comparison is used when a person relates new information to old information already stored in memory. A lawyer looks for past precedents, a doctor for old cases that shed light on new ones. But people in jobs must beware of drawing analogies that go too far. For example, if an executive notes that his coercive ways of getting compliance in an old organization seem as if they can be carried over to his job in a new organization, he is using selective comparison, but not necessarily correctly. Tacit knowledge can be wrong. For example, the executive who makes this selective comparison may be misreading the environment, and using tacit knowledge that will ultimately lead to his downfall.

Selective combination is used when a person puts together information in a way so as to make sense of it. 'Putting 2 and 2 together' is a way of saying that a person is doing selective combination. For example, a person who notices that people with large offices have several attributes in common—longevity with the company, good relations with the boss, and a history of successes in generating products—would have used selective combination to figure out how to get a large office. The clinical psychologist uses selective combination in taking cues from longer conversations with a client and trying to put them together to form a diagnosis. Again, the combination of information may be right or wrong, and therefore predict either success or failure.

Kinds of tacit knowledge

The categories of tacit knowledge one uses depend to some extent on the particular job to which tacit knowledge is applied. But a taxonomy that we have found useful in the past (e.g. Wagner and Sternberg, 1985, 1986) distinguishes between tacit knowledge about self, others, and tasks, on the one hand, and local versus global tacit knowledge, on the other.

Tacit knowledge about the self refers to knowledge about how to organize and motivate yourself to work effectively. For example, knowing how to avoid procrastination would be an example of tacit knowledge about the self. Tacit knowledge about others refers to knowledge about how to manage and get along with subordinates, colleagues of equal rank, and those in senior positions in the organizational hierarchy. For example, knowing what you can and cannot say to your boss would be an example of tacit knowledge about others. Tacit knowledge about tasks refers to knowledge about how to get a job done. For example, knowing what criteria to count in deciding whether to award a contract would require tacit knowledge about the task of awarding contracts.

Local tacit knowledge is the kind that is used to get through the day. For example, knowing what to say to an employee who has just given her third excuse for not finishing an assignment would be an example of tacit knowledge. Global tacit knowledge is used to make decisions that involve your career as a whole. For example, knowing when to move to another company because upward advancement is blocked in your own company would be an example of global tacit knowledge.

The form of tacit knowledge

We believe that tacit knowledge takes the form of condition–action sequences. That is to say, it takes the form: If A, then B, where A may be compound. For example, it may be the case that if you observe your boss in a bad mood and you have observed that when he is in a bad mood he is best left alone, then you should say nothing to him if at all possible. This formalism of the condition–action sequence has several implications.

First, tacit knowledge is procedural as opposed to declarative. In other words, it is knowledge about what to do when. It is not merely knowledge about what happens in a given place, but rather, about what to do, given what happens.

Second, tacit knowledge is practical—it is knowledge for use in an actual organization or everyday situation. Whereas formal knowledge of the kind taught in courses may or may not be applicable on the job, tacit knowledge always is.

Third, in order for tacit knowledge to be exploited effectively, you need to know both the procedures (actions) and their link to the environment (when and where to use them). It is not enough to know what to do—you have to know when and where to do it, and when and where not to.

Much of tacit knowledge is scripted (Schank and Abelson, 1977). In other words, it is part of a script or schema people follow in certain situations. Examples of scripts in business would be attending a dinner party with superiors, telling an employee he is fired, interviewing for a new job, and encouraging a secretary to arrive earlier at the beginning of the working day.

MEASURING TACIT KNOWLEDGE

Note several features that the items we have developed have in common. First, each is a job-relevant scenario, in which the examinee says what she would do if faced with the situation described in the scenario. Often, the form of response is to give a rating from 1 to 9 as to how desirable a course of action would be. But the examinee may be asked to fill in a blank with one or more desirable courses of action. The advantage to the rating procedures is that it gives a uniform set of data across subjects. The advantage of the fill-in procedure is that the examinee needs to think of the option or options for himself, rather than having these options provided for him.

Second, each scenario is relatively job-specific. Although you could make parallel scenarios for other jobs (and we have), the scenario is described in terms of the job for which the test is constructed. In this sense, tests of tacit knowledge are in opposition to IQ tests, which are designed to be general across jobs.

Third, the options vary in plausibility. Some are designed to be plausible and good, others plausible but not so good, and still others simply implausible. Examinees have to recognize which options are better and which are worse.

Fourth, there are no 'objectively correct' answers. What is correct in one job might be incorrect in another, and what might be correct in one company might be incorrect in another. Thus, tacit-knowledge items not only have to be created for particular jobs; they have to be keyed in terms of the culture of a given organization.

Fifth, tacit-knowledge tests can be used for selection, placement, or instructional purposes. When used for instruction, non-optional answers become a basis for learning how better to handle difficult, job-related situations.

Sixth, even test-takers with no formal on-the-job experience can take tacit-knowledge tests, because such tests measure tacit knowledge acquired not only in a specific job, but in life, in general. We have found, for example, that college students with no business experience can attain respectable, although not 'impressive' scores.

Finally, tacit-knowledge tests do not have to be paper-and-pencil in format. The paper-and-pencil simulation is easy to administer and score, but does not measure performance in 'real time'. Simulations can also be done in real time. For example, we have created tacit-knowledge measures for sales (see Sternberg, Wagner, and Okagaki, 1993) in which an examinee makes a phone call and tries to 'sell' a product to the examiner at the other end of the line. The examiner raises various objections. The test-taker is scored in terms of speed, content, and sincerity of tone of voice in the conversation. Examples of tacit-knowledge items are shown in Table 10.1.

Construction of tacit-knowledge tests

Although the details may differ across occupations, the general procedures for creating tests of tacit knowledge are roughly the same. First you typically do a literature review through which you try to extract the tacit knowledge necessary for a job as specified in the extant literature of a job. Often, books by people actually in the job detailing their experiences at work are more useful than scientific studies, which tend to be high on quantitative results but often low on qualitative content that constitutes tacit knowledge.

Second, you interview successful people in the field for which you plan to devise the test of tacit knowledge. You construct an interview designed to elicit as much of their tacit knowledge as possible. No one question will elicit all of this tacit knowledge. Asking them about their toughest situations, their greatest successes, mistakes from which they have learned, observations of others, and best advice to new people in the field are all ways of digging up what they know about their jobs. A good interview is done in person, and in a relaxed, non-evaluative setting.

As part of the second step, it is useful also to interview people whom you have identified as not particularly successful at the job. In this way, you can learn about 'wrong' tacit knowledge, or tacit knowledge that doesn't work. As distractors (weak responses) are made of such tacit knowledge, the comments of people who are less than successful can be as helpful as the comments of the more successful. Obviously, you do not tell the people whom you are interviewing in what group they fall!

How do you identify more and less successful people? Probably the most effective way is through nominations. You ask people who are respected in the job to nominate the two groups of people. In some fields, it is possible to identify groups on the basis of objective measures of work (e.g. number of publications, citation rates of publications, number of yearly sales or sales income, tips, books sold, etc.). There is no one measure that captures all aspects of success, so using a variety of criteria is essential.

Third, you combine the results of the literature review and the interviews and any other sources of data you may have to construct tentative scenarios plus answer options (should you choose to use answer-option format). You should

Table 10.1   Scenarios for Measuring Tacit Knowledge

MANAGING SELF

You are concerned that you habitually put off completing disagreeable tasks and wish to improve this aspect of your work-related performance. Upon further examination, you think that your problem is one of procrastination—being unable to start tasks you need to get done on a given day. You have asked for advice about dealing with this problem from several friends in the company who seem to be especially productive when it comes to completing tasks. Rate the quality of the following pieces of advice that you have been given:

- Wait to begin a given task until you really wish to do it
- Spend some time considering just what it is you dislike about a particular task and then try to change that aspect of it
- Get rid of all distractions (perhaps by taking the task into a conference room) so that there is nothing else you can do but the task you must complete
- Force yourself to begin the day by spending 15 minutes on the task, in the hope that once you have started you will keep on it

MANAGING OTHERS

You have just learned that detailed weekly reports of sales-related activities will be required of employees in your department. You have not received a rationale for the reports. The new reporting procedure appears cumbersome and it will probably be resisted strongly by your group. Neither you nor your employees had input into the decision to require the report, nor in decisions about its format.

You are planning a meeting of your employees to introduce them to the new reporting procedures. Rate the quality of the following things you might do:

- Emphasize that you had nothing to do with the new procedure
- Have a group discussion about the value of the new procedure and then put its adoption to a vote
- Give your employees the name and number of the director responsible for the new procedure, so that they may complain to that individual directly
- Promise to make their concerns known to their superiors, but only after they have made a good faith effort by trying the new procedure for six weeks
- Since the new procedure will probably get an unpleasant response anyway, use the meeting for something else and inform them about it in a memo
- Postpone the meeting until you find out the rationale for the new procedure

MANAGING TASKS

You are responsible for selecting a contractor to renovate several large buildings. You have narrowed the circle to two contractors on the basis of their bids and, after further investigation, you are considering awarding the contract to the Wilson & Sons Company. Rate the importance of the following pieces of information in making your decision to award the contract to Wilson & Sons:

- The company has provided letters from satisfied former customers
- The Better Business Bureau reports no major complaints about the company
- Wilson & Sons' bid was $2000 less than the other contractor's (approximate total cost of the renovation is $325 000)
- Former customers whom you have contacted strongly recommend Wilson & Sons for the job

Note: Examinees rate the quality of each piece of advice on a 1 (low) to 9 (high) scale.

construct scenarios that sample the job widely, rather than ones that all sample a relatively narrow slice of the job. The broader the sampling of jobs, tasks, and decisions, the more valid your questionnaire is likely to be.

Fourth, you show the questionnaire to experts of various types for their comments. The expert groups might include people you interviewed, other successful people you didn't interview, scholars in a given field, psychologists who could comment on the quality of the items from the standpoint of test construction, and so on. Soliciting feedback can save you the hassle of later finding out that you have a lot of bad items.

Fifth, you do a formative evaluation of the questionnaire on people in the job. Here, you actually try out the items, and maintain only those items that discriminate between successful and unsuccessful people in the job (see section below on scoring).

Sixth, you revise the questionnaire on the basis of the formative evaluation of a concurrent validity study. Items or options that do not distinguish the more from the less successful in the job are dropped. Some items will be modified to make them clearer. Other items may be added. Eventually, you produce a revision. If the revision is a large departure from the earlier version, you will probably want to do a second formative evaluation.

Seventh, you do a summative evaluation. This stage is the final one in testing out the questionnaire. You choose your samples of successful and unsuccessful people with care. You test for reliability and validity of items and of the test as a whole. In assessing reliability, you should look at both internal-consistency reliability and test–retest reliability. In assessing validity, you need to consider both convergent and discriminant validity, meaning that you need to choose criteria against which to evaluate the questionnaire that represent things that the measure should correlate with (e.g. measures of job success) and also things that the measure should not correlate much with (e.g. IQ—if the correlation were high, you wouldn't need the tacit-knowledge measure). In assessing validity, a variety of criteria of job success should be used, as no one criterion fully captures all aspects of job success.

Eighth, you collect normative data and other statistics that you will need to be able to use your test on future samples. Through such data you learn what good and not-so-good scores are, and how to evaluate scores at every point in-between.

One issue you do not have to worry about in a test of this kind is the issue of 'faking'. The test is a test of knowledge, not of personal preference. We ask what the best course of action would be, not what the examiner would necessarily do in the situation. There may thus be a gap between knowledge and action. But our goal is to measure the former, not the latter.

Scoring tacit-knowledge measures

Because there is no 'objectively' correct answer to a tacit-knowledge item, scoring procedures need to be created that capitalize on the unique feature of the items— that there are better and worse items as a function of the job and the context in which it is done. There are three main scoring methods that we have used.

The first and probably most easily used is the measure of distance against one or more expert profiles. A group of top-notch experts serves as a normative group, and then the tests of other people are scored against the average answer profile(s) of the experts. Where there are various kinds of expertise or various contexts in which the job is done, individual questionnaires might be scored against alternative or even multiple profiles of expert responses. Scoring can be done using either a distance measure or a correlation. The former kind of measure looks at the distance between expert responses and examinee responses, and is scale-dependent. The latter kind of measure looks at the degree of similarity between expert and examinee patterns of response, and is scale-independent.

The second type of scoring is based on statistical correlations between directions of item responses and group membership. If you have, say, an expert and a novice group, you score an item positively if the experts tended to give higher mean responses to the item than did the novices, whereas you score the item negatively if the experts gave lower mean responses. Note that in this scoring system, you only look at direction of responses of experts relative to novices, not at the magnitude of the difference. You would use this type of scoring system when you believe that the magnitudes of the differences are not likely to be reliable.

The third type of scoring is based on a rules-of-thumb approach. Here, you identify the pieces of tacit knowledge you wish to measure. You then set up item responses that either represent these pieces of tacit knowledge, or else that represent distorted or weakened versions of these pieces of tacit knowledge. You then score as correct responses based on the pieces of tacit knowledge, or take a difference score between ratings for the 'good' pieces of tacit knowledge versus ratings for the distorted or weakened pieces of tacit knowledge.

The role of values

Tests of tacit knowledge highlight an aspect of testing that is left in the background in conventional testing or indeed in other conventional selection methods, namely, the role of values. What constitutes a better or worse response in a tacit-knowledge test depends upon the values of the people keying the test. Behaviour that one company may value for advancement—for example, success at any cost—may be devalued in another company. It is for this reason that tacit-knowledge tests should be keyed for a given job and job context.

The importance of values for these tests seem like a disadvantage to tacit-knowledge tests in comparison with other tests. I would argue, however, that values play an important part in *all* testing. The only question is whether their role is obvious. In conventional intelligence testing, we typically value speed of information processing, the ability to work with abstractions that have little or nothing to do with real-world problems, the ability to play the multiple-choice testing game, obedience to an examiner, and so on. There is no such thing, really, as a value-free test. Even biologically based tests set up values. There are many biological indices that could be measured, and in choosing certain ones over others, we are inevitably valuing some kinds of functioning over others.

There is nothing shameful about allowing a role of values in testing, because there is no such thing as a value-free test. The problem arises when people begin to think that they have devised measures that are value-free. What has really happened is that the people are so blind to their own values that they do not realize how these values are realized through the tests. Often, the test-constructors will then go ahead and impose these values on other cultural or societal groups, simply assuming that any right-minded culture would value the same things they do. The evidence, however, is that cultures differ in what they value (see, for example, Berry, 1984; Laboratory of Comparative Human Cognition, 1982; Rogoff and Lave, 1984). To the extent, then, that tacit-knowledge tests highlight the role of values, they are highlighting a reality that applies to all testing, not just tacit-knowledge testing.

FINDINGS FROM TACIT–KNOWLEDGE STUDIES

We have done a number of tacit-knowledge studies, using measures such as our *Tacit Knowledge Inventory for Managers* (Wagner and Sternberg, 1991). Some, but not all, of these studies are summarized in Sternberg, Wagner, and Okagaki (1993; see also Sternberg and Wagner, 1993; Wagner, 1987; Wagner and Sternberg, 1985, 1986. Here are some of the main findings of those studies.

First, tacit knowledge tends to increase with experience on the job. In other words, people who have been in a job longer tend to have more tacit knowledge than those who have not been in the job as long. But the relation is not always linear, possibly due to cohort effects. It may be that certain tacit knowledge grows out of date, so that very late in one's career, up-to-date tacit knowledge relevant to a job decreases. Moreover, some people who have been in a job longer have less tacit knowledge than other people who have been in the job for less time. The important variable appears to be not amount of time in the job per se, but what the person has learned from being in the job.

Second, scores on tests of tacit knowledge in different fields tend to be positively correlated with each other. We do not have much data on this relation, but the data we have for academic psychology and business—two very different fields—suggest a correlation of about 0.6. In other words, there is some overlap between tacit knowledge of different occupations, but it is far from complete.

Third, tacit-knowledge measures are good although far from perfect predictors of actual measures of job performance. We have used multiple measures of job performance over several different careers, and have found correlations typically in the range of 0.3 to 0.4. These correlations, although not stunningly high, are consistently statistically significant and suggest overlap between tacit knowledge and success. The correlations must also be viewed in light of the limited reliability of measures of success. We do not correct correlations for unreliability, or restriction of range, for that matter.

Fourth, tacit-knowledge measures typically show very small positive correlations with measures of IQ and other measures of ability (such as the subtests of the *Armed Services Vocational Aptitude Battery*—ASVAB). In our studies, the correlations have not been statistically significant, although their direction tends to indicate a very weak relation. These results, of course, make sense. In the triarchic theory, the same processes are applied to each aspect of intelligence. What differs is the context in which they are applied. Intelligence tests are fairly decontextualized, whereas tacit-knowledge tests are highly contextualized. Thus, we would expect a weak correlation between the two types of measures.

It might be argued that the correlation between the two types of measures would be much stronger in samples that show the full range of IQ (mean of 100, standard deviation of 15 or 16). None of our samples is of this kind. But we do not believe that such samples are realistic with respect to assessment of tacit knowledge on the job. The reason is that there are probably few jobs in which you find the full range of IQ. For example, it would be the rare business executive with an IQ of 80, or the rare assembly line worker with an IQ of 140. That is not to say that examples of such anomalies do not exist—only that they are rare.

Fifth, different aspects of tacit knowledge are themselves correlated with each other. When we have measured tacit knowledge of self, others, and tasks, as well as local and global tacit knowledge, we have found a generally positive pattern of intercorrelations, suggesting that people who are higher in one kind of tacit knowledge also tend to be higher in other kinds of tacit knowledge. These correlations are modest to moderate (about 0.3), although they would probably be higher were subscale reliabilities higher. It should be noted, however, that although the subscales of tacit knowledge correlate with each other, they do not correlate with IQ.

Sixth, tacit knowledge seems to be distinct from variables with which one might expect it to be confounded. In one study, we used hierarchical regression to look at the prediction of performance on a managerial simulation from conventional measures of intelligence, personality, styles of thinking, and interpersonal orientation. The prediction due to the tacit-knowledge measure was significant even when this measure was entered as the last variable in the prediction equation. The score on the tacit-knowledge test was also the single strongest predictor of success in the managerial simulation, thus indicating significant incremental validity to the procedure.

It has been suggested that tests of tacit knowledge are nothing more than tests of job knowledge (Schmidt and Hunter, 1993). We don't agree, based on our comparison of tacit-knowledge tests with other tests. However, we certainly do not claim that tests of tacit knowledge are qualitatively different from anything that has ever been used before. They overlap with tests of utilization of informal job knowledge, and they certainly overlap with the kinds of skills measured by in-baskets and assessment centers. Whatever one wishes to call the type of test we are using, we believe it is a useful type of test.

Seventh, when people are asked to respond to tacit-knowledge questionnaires with responses for the ideal job context rather than for the actual context, correlations with external variables are about the same as when they respond for the actual contexts. In other words, it doesn't appear much to matter whether people answer for the way they think things are or for the way they think things should be—at least from a correlational point of view.

Eighth, tacit knowledge differs as a function of the level of a given job. Thus, when one talks about managers, one should talk about the level of management in order fully to assess tacit knowledge. The problems that top-level executives deal with are rather different from those dealt with by middle managers.

Finally, tacit knowledge can be taught (Sternberg, Okagaki, and Jackson, 1990). Ideally, a questionnaire measuring tacit knowledge would be used as an entry device for assessing tacit knowledge, and would then be followed up by a program that would train people and help them build upon the tacit knowledge they already have. We have done such training at the secondary-school and college levels, and are currently designing a program that will provide training in tacit knowledge for leadership.

Limitations of tacit–knowledge tests

Although we obviously believe in the utility of tacit-knowledge tests, it is proper in closing to emphasize that they should constitute only one element in a selection or assessment program. A full program would look as well at broad aspects of intelligence (such as analytic, creative, and practical aspects), personality, formal knowledge, styles of thinking, motivation, and experience. We believe that tacit-knowledge measures are a useful, but not sole component in a successful program for measuring potential for success on the job.

REFERENCES

Berry, J. W. (1984). Towards a universal psychology of cognitive competence. In P. S. Fry (ed.), *Changing Conceptions of Intelligence and Intellectual Functioning* (pp. 35–61). Amsterdam: North-Holland.

Ceci, S. J. (1990). *On Intelligence . . . More or Less*. Englewood Cliffs, NJ: Prentice-Hall.

Gardner, H. (1983). *Frames of Mind: The Theory of Multiple Intelligences*. New York: Basic Books.

Horvath, J. A., Williams, W. M., Forsythe, G. B., McNally, J. A., Wattendorf, J. and Sternberg, R. J. (1993, June). *Tacit Knowledge in Military Leadership*. Report to the Army Research Institute. New Haven, CT: Yale University.

Laboratory of Comparative Human Cognition (1982). Culture and intelligence. In R. J. Sternberg (ed.), *Handbook of Human Intelligence* (pp. 642–719). New York: Free Press.

Polanyi, M. (1976). Tacit knowledge. In M. Marx and F. Goodson (eds), *Theories in Contemporary Psychology* (pp. 330–344). New York: Macmillan.

Ree, M. J. and Earles, J. A. (1993). *g* is to psychology what carbon is to chemistry: A reply to Sternberg and Wagner, McClelland, and Calfee. *Current Directions in Psychological Science*, **1**, 11–12.

Rogoff, B. and Lave, J. (1984). *Everyday Cognition: its Development in Social Context*, Cambridge, Mass.: Harvard University Press.

Schank, R. C. and Abelson, R. P. (1977). *Scripts, Plans, Goals, and Understanding*. Hillsdale, NJ: Erlbaum.

Schmidt, F. L. and Hunter, J. E. (1993). Tacit knowledge, practical intelligence, general mental ability, and job knowledge. *Current Directions in Psychological Science*, **1**, 8–9.

Sternberg, R. J. (1985). *Beyond IQ: A Triarchic Theory of Human Intelligence*. New York: Cambridge University Press.

Sternberg, R. J. (1986). *Intelligence Applied: Understanding and Increasing your Intellectual Skills*. San Diego, CA: Harcourt Brace Jovanovich.

Sternberg, R. J. (1988). *The Triarchic Mind: A New Theory of Human Intelligence.* New York: Viking.

Sternberg, R. J., Okagaki, L. and Jackson, A. (1990). Practical intelligence for success in school. *Educational Leadership,* **48**, 35–39.

Sternberg, R. J. and Wagner, R. K. (eds) (1986). *Practical Intelligence: Nature and Origins of Competence in the Everyday World.* New York: Cambridge University Press.

Sternberg, R. J. and Wagner, R. K. (1993). The *g*-ocentric view of intelligence and job performance is wrong. *Current Directions in Psychological Science,* **2** (1), 1–4.

Sternberg, R. J., Wagner, R. K. and Okagaki, L. (1993). Practical intelligence: The nature and role of tacit knowledge in work and at school. In H. Reese and J. Puckett (eds), *Advances in Lifespan Development* (pp. 205–227). Hillsdale, NJ: Lawrence Erlbaum.

Wagner, R. K. (1987). Tacit knowledge in everyday intelligent behavior. *Journal of Personality and Social Psychology,* **52**, 1236–1247.

Wagner, R. K. and Sternberg, R. J. (1985). Practical intelligence in real-world pursuits: The role of tacit knowledge. *Journal of Personality and Social Psychology,* **49**, 436–458.

Wagner, R. K. and Sternberg, R. J. (1986). Tacit knowledge and intelligence in the everyday world. In R. J. Sternberg and R. K. Wagner (eds), *Practical Intelligence: Nature and Origins of Competence in the Everyday World* (pp. 51–83). New York: Cambridge University Press.

Wagner, R. K. and Sternberg, R. J. (1991). Tacit knowledge: Its uses in identifying, assessing, and developing managerial talent. In J. Jones, B. Steffy and D. Bray (eds), *Applying Psychology in Business: The Manager's Handbook* (pp. 333–344). New York: Human Sciences Press.

Wason, P. C. and Johnson-Laird, P. N. (1972). *Psychology of Reasoning: Structure and Content.* London: B. T. Batsford.

Section 2

Business Change and Psychological Responses

As we argued in our editorial chapter, changes in their social, economic, and technological context are forcing organizations to view assessment and selection as an essential part of their overall response in their effort to survive and grow. While organizational responses have been highly visible, personnel psychologists' contributions have been strangely muted. Rather, they have been viewed as technicians, while HR professionals have seized their opportunity to be involved in the direction of the business. This generalization is probably more true of the United States and the United Kingdom than of some other countries. The issue comes down to the fundamental one of clients and stakeholders; how prominent a stakeholder are organizations for US and UK psychologists?

Allan Williams and Paul Dobson rightly place these strategic issues at centre stage in Chapter 11. Their concern, they say, 'is with the implications for selection of strategic choice and change, and with the role that selection can play in promoting and enabling strategic change'. They admit that their approach is more theoretical and normative than descriptive, but their objective is to encourage organizations 'to align strategic choice and change with the role and design of selection systems . . . so as to achieve their strategic objectives more effectively'. Using the strategic directions of innovation, quality enhancement, and cost reduction, Williams and Dobson demonstrate clearly that different employee behaviours and different jobs are critically important for each of these directions to be taken successfully. Given this context of strategic change, operational criteria regarding successful current performance need to be supplemented by visionary and transformational criteria. The former are those necessary for successful future job performance, the latter for enabling change to happen.

This distinction is followed up by Marise Born and Paul Jansen in Chapter 12. They concentrate on radical organizational change, where there is a 'fundamental change in the perspective or framework from which reality is perceived'; a change in organizational culture, in other words, which involves the prioritization of new values rather than merely the reordering of existing ones. The importance of personal characteristics is stressed; both in those who exercise transformational leadership and in their followers. The former may need an absence of certain characteristics as well as the presence of others; the latter will certainly need to be hardy, stable and calm. Where such conditions of organizational turnaround exist, Born and Jansen suggest that many traditional features of selection procedures are inappropriate. Realistic job previews may be more valuable than job analyses, for example.

These strategic considerations take us right back to the classic psychometric issue: the criterion problem, authoritatively addressed for this volume initially by Bob Guion (Chapter 13). We have to ask constantly by what outcomes should the success of a selection procedure be assessed? Guion concentrates on job-related criteria, and emphasizes that in this sense a criterion is a variable to be explained or predicted, as in the phrase 'criterion-related validity'. He argues that the choice of criterion is vital, since it may serve a variety of purposes. 'A criterion valued from a marketing perspective may complement, conflict with, or simply differ from one valued from a production perspective—or from a public relations perspective'. This is a refreshingly far cry from the assumption that the criterion measure chosen is unimportant compared with the validity coefficient obtained. The purpose of criterion is not to evaluate a test; that is putting the cart before the horse. It is rather to focus attention on what is important to the organization to predict, understand or change. This chapter performs a vital function in demonstrating the changes in fundamental scientific assumptions that are necessary if the dominant paradigm is to adapt (or, as Kuhn would suggest, be overthrown).

Moving this issue nearer the day-to-day concerns of selection practitioners, in Chapter 14 Wieby Altink, Coert Visser and Michiel Castelijns explore the development of organizational criteria. They consider why we should need criteria in any case and the role that criteria can play in the recruitment and selection process. Their focus is squarely on practical issues and concerns, but also emphasizes the relationships between criteria and the wider organization. The authors ably illustrate that even the criteria of any selection system cannot feasibly stand in isolation from, nor be sensibly detached from, the wider HR strategy of an organization.

Given that the strategic emphasis of many organizations over the past two decades has been to bring down costs by increasing productivity, it is hardly surprising that psychologists have developed utility theories in order to persuade organizations of the productivity benefits to be derived from using valid selection methods. Equally surprising (or perhaps not) is the finding that actual usage of methods by organizations is negatively correlated with both their validity and their utility. After a clear account of utility theory, John Boudreau, Michael Sturman and Timothy Judge go on to ask in Chapter 15 the important question of why this should be so. They argue that utility formulae have not been applied to the typical organizational situation, where there are usually several selection methods being used in a system, and where criteria are frequently multiple rather than single. Furthermore, selection is not typically top-down, as utility theory assumes, and some of the costs of changing selection systems may have been ignored. Again, the real issue is about stakeholders: Is the task to set up a theory of what could be true in an entirely different world? Or is it to collaborate with practitioners to help them define and address their problems?

According to Kevin Murphy (Chapter 16), meta-analysis and validity generalization, like utility analysis, have the potential 'to help professionals and practitioners become more highly informed and sophisticated consumers of the extensive body of research that bears upon the practical problems they are called upon to solve'. After an equally lucid exposition of the basics and current developments in meta-analysis and validity generalization, Murphy too addresses the question of why this potential has yet to be realized; why, in fact, organizational use of selection instruments is in inverse proportion to their validity as discovered by meta-analysis. Technical answers to this question include the fact that we are not sure how much of the variability between studies is due to situational differences in the taking of the measurements; and the differing quality of the research studies that go into the meta-analytic pot. Extravagant claims have been made for what is after all only a sophisticated statistical tool that enables us to summarize different research investigations. However, while these considerations give researchers pause for thought, do they really impinge upon practitioners? Perhaps the reasons lie elsewhere, for example in the irrelevance of the criterion measures employed to organizations' current strategic concerns.

In a landmark chapter (Chapter 17), Paul Sparrow outlines the use of competencies as an alternative framework for relating the human resource needs of present-day organizations to their selection and assessment processes. Particularly in the area of management, where it is hard to specify tasks and conduct a traditional job analysis, competencies present a useful alternative to more traditional forms of assessment. Sparrow distinguishes management competencies (knowledge, skills, and attitudes) from behavioural competencies (behavioural repertoires which people input into a work context) and from organizational competencies (those resources and capabilities that the organization has which are linked to its business performance). The benefits for organizations of using competency analysis are enumerated at length in this chapter; benefits as assessed by practitioners rather than researchers. Not least amongst them is a common language about people which can be used across the different HR systems. Sparrow echoes Williams and Dobson's concern with future rather than present HR requirements and with the need to manage the processes of organizational change. His suggestions for establishing the competencies of the future will be of great interest to practitioners. It is interesting to note that competencies have been found useful by practitioners and have been researched by HR academics; traditional psychologists have tended to ignore them.

Finally, in Chapter 18, Kevin Murphy and Nathan Luther address a highly specific area of assessment which nevertheless has very general lessons to teach us about our role as applied psychologists. This is the topic of testing for honesty, integrity and deception. Small-scale theft and huge cases of corporate corruption can ruin organizations from the least to the greatest; from the 30% of small businesses that go bankrupt through employee theft to Barings and Deutsch Morgan Grenfell, rocked by fraud on a grand scale. So large is the cost of workplace dishonesty that any method that addresses the problem is likely to have considerable appeal. In a scrupulous review of the evidence, Murphy and Luther show that while most of the better known behavioural methods perform at little better than chance levels, integrity questionnaires do predict overall performance and counterproductive behaviour satisfactorily. The issue, however, is: Should organizations use even the valid measures? If we perceive our role as technologists, then we will leave that decision to others. If we are more than technologists, then we will be drawing the organization's attention to the possible costs of introducing integrity tests. Among such costs the authors cite negative effects on employee morale, labour relations, and attractiveness to recruits. As they observe, you can attempt to deal with the problem by changing the people or changing the situation or the system; the latter may have greater pay-offs.

PETER HERRIOT
August 1996

Chapter 11

Personnel Selection and Corporate Strategy

ALLAN P. O. WILLIAMS AND PAUL DOBSON

Centre for Personnel Research and Enterprise Development, City University Business School, Frobisher Crescent, London EC2Y 8HB, UK

In this chapter we consider the relationship between an organization's strategy and the characteristics of its selection systems. Our basic thesis is that different strategies have different implications for the nature, role and importance of human resource management (HRM) and selection. Our concern is with the implications for selection of strategic choice and change and with the role that selection can play in promoting and enabling strategic change.

A cautionary note at the outset. Whilst we have drawn upon available evidence in justifying our arguments, much of this chapter is theoretical rather than descriptive. This may give the impression that we are over-emphasizing the importance of the rational and optimal in organizational decision-making, and under-emphasizing the role of the emergent (Mintzberg, 1988), the satisficing (March and Simon, 1958), and the powerful (Pettigrew, 1973). We recognize the importance of these latter factors, but our primary purpose in this chapter is to introduce conceptual frameworks that will encourage organizations to align strategic choice and change with the role and design of selection systems (and other HRM activities) so as to achieve their strategic objectives more effectively.

This chapter is in five sections. First, we explore the nature of organizational strategy and its relationship to HRM strategies and the manpower delivery system. Next we look at the implications of strategic choice and then strategic change for HRM and selection. Fourth, we consider the role of selection in strategic change and present a framework for 'strategic personnel selection', and finally we draw some conclusions.

International Handbook of Selection and Assessment, Edited by N. Anderson and P. Herriot.

THE NATURE OF ORGANIZATIONAL STRATEGY

There are many different definitions of strategy. Several American writers, as J. G. Smith (1990) has pointed out, have equated strategy with competitive advantage. Whilst this is understandable from the position of American technical supremacy (at least until recent years) and mass home markets, it is perhaps unnecessarily narrow. Broader definitions emphasize strategy as a programme or plan for determining and realizing organizational goals. Chandler (1962) provides a fairly typical definition. He defines strategy as:

> ... the determination of the basic long-term goals and objectives of an enterprise, and the adoption of courses of action and the allocation of resources necessary for carrying out these goals.

A more recent definition is provided by Johnson and Scholes (1993, p. 10):

> Strategy is the direction and scope of an organization over the long term: ideally, which matches its resources to its changing environment, and in particular its markets, customers or clients so as to meet stakeholder expectations.

These definitions need to be tempered by Mintzberg's (1988) argument that an organization's strategy is often emergent rather than the outcome of systematic planning.

Corporate, business and functional level strategies

As a number of writers have pointed out—for example Purcell (1989) and Miller (1992)—organizational strategy can usefully be viewed from a number of perspectives:

- first, from a corporate perspective where the concern is with the kinds of businesses in the portfolio, the relationships between them, how they are controlled, and the levels of investment
- second, from a business level perspective where concern turns more to competitive strategy and the product/market mix
- third, from a functional level where strategy is concerned with the functional contribution to the attainment of business goals.

HRM strategies are functional level strategies designed to promote internal functioning and capability and negate external threats and seize external opportunities in order to attain business goals. This relationship is shown in Figure 11.1.

Traditionally, business strategy has been dominated by operational, financial and marketing approaches and HRM (or perhaps 'personnel' would be the more appropriate label) has played a reactive role in the analysis, choice and implementation of business and corporate strategy. In more recent times, however, with increasing rates of change in the environment and the increasing board-level status and professionalism of the function, more proactive models and roles have

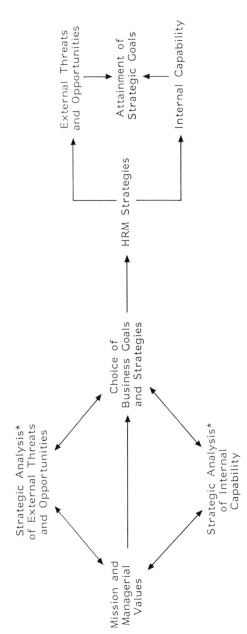

Figure 11.1   HRM strategies facilitating the attainment of business goals

been adopted. Thus, increasingly, HRM is likely to make an input into strategic analysis in terms of, for example, demographic change and internal competencies, and to be more actively involved in strategic choice. Similarly, HRM strategies have become more proactive in promoting strategic change and in developing internal capability in order to increase strategic options for an uncertain future.

Selection in context: the manpower delivery system

Recruitment, selection, training and development are HRM systems designed to facilitate the attainment of organizational goals. The outputs of the recruitment system form inputs to selection, and the latter's outputs form the inputs for training. Change in the nature of recruitment, training and development possess implications for selection. The interconnectedness of recruitment, selection, training and development suggests that it is wise to view selection as part of a larger system of manpower delivery.

The manpower delivery system is charged with providing the organization with the right people in the right jobs at the right time. In order to do this it has to employ methods to close the gap between manpower demand on the one hand and manpower supply on the other, utilizing the professional and financial resources at its disposal. Changes in the demand system (typically sparked by environmental change or poor organizational performance) result in strategic change or organizational redesign, a consequent change in manpower requirements and a gap between supply and demand, that are likely to require the realignment of the manpower delivery mechanisms. Changes on the supply side of the equation, that result from demographic or societal change, are also likely to require change in the nature of manpower delivery. Of course, organizations do not change automatically nor necessarily as planned. A schematic representation of the manpower demand and delivery systems is shown in Figure 11.2.

Snow and Snell (1993) have suggested that three different models of manpower delivery can be distinguished. These are the provision of manpower for existing jobs, for envisaged future jobs, or for jobs which cannot be prescribed. The third model, whose purpose is to increase the strategic capability of the organization rather than to match determinable manpower requirements, requires the organization to consider its stock of knowledge, skills and abilities and to select or develop individuals to add to this stock thereby increasing its ability to respond to unknown future scenarios. Relatedly, Prahalad and Hamel (1990) argue that long-term competitive advantage is gained from developing and nurturing a portfolio of core competencies within the organization rather than treating the organization as a portfolio of discrete businesses.

IMPLICATIONS OF STRATEGIC CHOICE FOR HRM AND SELECTION

Strategic choice and the related organizational and job design decisions have significant implications for the nature of selection in an organization. It appears unwise to view selection in isolation from other HRM activities, so we will first

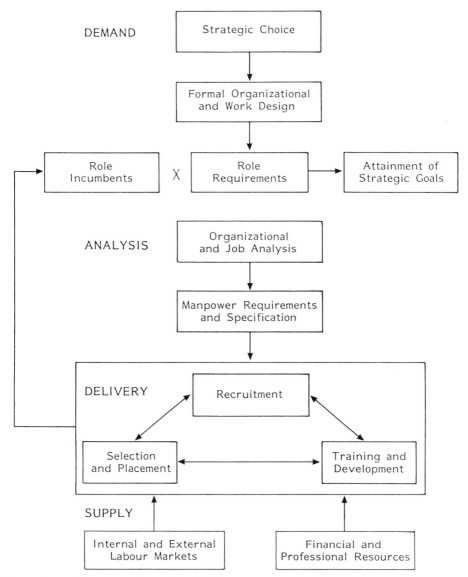

Figure 11.2   Manpower demand and delivery systems

tease out the implications of corporate and business level strategic choice for manpower delivery and HRM in general and then consider the more specific implications for selection.

Consequences of business maturity and portfolio planning decisions

Products have a life cycle of birth, growth, maturity and decline. Related to this is the accumulated experience curve (Hamermesh, 1986) which suggests that

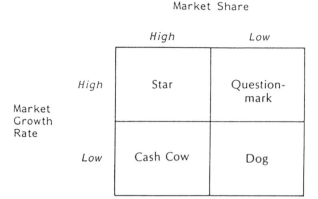

Figure 11.3   The Boston Consulting Group model

average costs will decline as the accumulated experience of selling, producing, engineering and financing a product increases. In theory, therefore, companies with the highest market share will have the greatest accumulated experience, lowest costs and highest profits. These ideas lay behind the development of portfolio planning which essentially is concerned with switching investment from mature and declining businesses into those with potential so that they can enter the market early and achieve a strong competitive position. The best-known system is that developed by the Boston Consulting Group (1970) which categorizes businesses into four groups (as shown in Figure 11.3) according to their market share and market growth rate.

- Question-mark businesses compete in rapidly growing markets with the aim of moving up the experience curve ahead of the competition. Growth in new markets is difficult to predict and gaining experience in situations of uncertainty can be problematical. These businesses are therefore characterized by uncertainty and require substantial investment in excess of their own profitability.
- Star businesses are rapidly growing and whilst they require high levels of investment their dominant position in the market often allows them to generate sufficient profits to finance further growth. They are characterized by growth, development, change and a positive outlook.
- Cash Cow businesses are mature and can take full advantage of their accumulated experience. They require only modest investment and generate large profits and a positive cash flow. They are characterized by stability, profitability, moderate levels of investment, and formalization.
- Dog businesses operate in a declining market with declining profitability. Costs are pared down to the minimum to squeeze out any remaining value and are likely to be disinvested. Threat, tight financial control and zero investment are typical characteristics.

Whilst Hendry and Pettigrew (1992) have suggested that the relationship between the product life cycle and HRM is not a simple one, we can hypothesize that businesses at different stages of development will have different implications for HRM and selection. Question-marks are unlikely to invest to a significant extent in a formal HRM function. Key people are likely to be known or head-hunted rather than to be identified through professionally developed internal procedures. As the business increases its market share the organization needs to be developed. Stars are likely to engage more actively in the process of developing and retaining people. A rudimentary HRM function is likely to appear, and with it the beginnings of formalized recruitment selection and training procedures. People and their development grow in importance. In the early stages of growth an organization's needs centre on recruitment; as it matures, activities like career development are likely to become more prominent. Cash Cow organizations are likely to be large and formalized with well-developed and sophisticated HRM functions. It is here that we are likely to find a large specialist staff engaged in recruitment, selection, training, succession planning, performance appraisal and so on. The declining markets of the Dog businesses are accompanied by reduced investment. Training budgets are likely to be cut, the HRM function delayered as the organization pares itself back to the operating core. Kochan and Barocci (1985) illustrate the above relationships as in Table 11.1.

Baird and Meshoulam (1988) present a similar analysis where the programmes of activities, professional skills and the management of HRM needed in order to be effective are related to the stage of development of the organization. Baird and Meshoulam do, however, take one further step in suggesting that HRM skills, activities and management also need to be integrated with one another.

Table 11.1   Relationships between the product cycle and aspects of HRM

	Introduction	Growth	Maturity	Decline
RECRUITMENT SELECTION AND STAFFING	Attract best technical/ professional talent	Recruit adequate numbers and mix of qualified workers Succession planning: manage rapid internal labour movements	Encourage sufficient turnover to minimize layoffs and provide new openings . Encourage mobility as reorganization shifts jobs around	Plan and implement workforce reductions and reallocations
TRAINING AND DEVELOPMENT	Define future skill requirements and begin establishing career ladders	Mould effective management team through management and organization development	Maintain flexibility and skills of an ageing workforce	Implement retraining and career consulting services

Consequences of financial control versus organic growth strategies

Goold and Campbell (1987), in their study of 16 diversified UK companies, identified a group of companies operating corporate policies which appear to have significant implications for HRM and selection. They termed these companies 'financial control companies' as opposed to 'strategic planning companies'. In other words, because of the short-term view of the stock markets these companies emphasized short-term profit performance focused more on financial performance than competitive position and tended to expand through acquisition rather than market share. Individuals who meet their targets are rewarded, others tend to be replaced. For example, the Hanson Trust has cut on average 25% of labour costs out of acquired companies (Porter, 1987). BTR, another member of the financial control group identified by Goold and Campbell, acquired the major Australian company ACI in 1988. Within three months the whole of the human resource planning department at head office was closed down. No opportunity was given for the director of human resource planning to present a human resource strategy (Purcell, 1989). These types of companies do not grow their people or their organizations and are readily prepared to disinvest.

Unfortunately for HRM these companies are very successful in financial terms and are well liked by the capital markets for they produce the best all round financial performance. They substantially outperform the industrial average, with high profitability ratios and growth rates (achieved by acquisitions) (Goold and Campbell, p. 161).

The approach of these financial control companies can be usefully contrasted with a notable statement by the Confederation of British Industry (1989):

> Individuals are now the only source of sustainable competitive advantage. Efforts must be focused on mobilising their commitment and encouraging self development and lifetime learning.

Whilst it is important to distinguish between financial performance and competitive advantage given that the reviews of the relationship between levels of people investment and organizational performance, for example between investment in training and education and performance (Keep and Mayhew, 1987), are inconclusive, this statement by the CBI would appear to be little more than an article of faith. We argue below that in many circumstances people are critical for business success but this is likely to apply to only a proportion of an organization's employees—those with low substitutability, demanding role requirements, high role impact and high role performance—and even the financial control companies look after their key employees. What does appear likely is that the continued success of the portfolio approach will bring more sharply into focus the dilemma: profitability or people? It will become increasingly clear that in many instances people-orientated values represent a moral stance, not a route essential to organizational survival or profitability.

Consequences of competitive strategic decisions

A number of typologies of competitive strategy and their implication for HRM have appeared in the literature. Schuler and Jackson (1987) categorize strategies as being focused upon either innovation, quality enhancement or cost reduction. This is shown in Table 11.2.

Sonnenfeld and Peiperl (1988) relate the strategic types of Miles and Snow (1978) to differences in emphasis upon external recruitment or internal development and differences in the criteria used for assignment, reward and excommunication. Thus, for example, 'prospector' organizations select on the basis of expertise and recruit externally at all levels, they place very little emphasis upon training, and reward, promote and retire staff on the basis of job performance. In contrast, 'defenders' recruit externally largely at junior levels and emphasize the development of staff with rewards and advancement tending to be based upon group contribution, corporate service and loyalty.

Impact of strategic choice on the criticality of people

Different business strategies appear to have differing implications for the significance of people in the organization. There is a fundamental question here for organizational psychology, HRM and management practice and yet few appear to have addressed it directly: under what circumstances are people critical success factors? The success of financial control companies suggest that the 'people' variables (e.g. leadership style, job motivation, organizational commitment) may not be as critical as we would like to think, at least not in terms of profitability over the short-term. In contrast, Prahalad and Hamel (1990) have argued that, rather than treat the organization as a collection of strategic business units to be developed or disinvested according to market conditions, long-term product leadership is gained from viewing the organization as a portfolio of core competencies and taking steps to develop and utilize the core competence carriers over the long-term. They view these embedded skills as a key corporate resource.

We cannot pretend to be able to fully answer the question of the criticality of the human resource. But we can make an initial attempt from a normative perspective at identifying some of the contingencies that may (or should) influence an organization's level of investment in its people and adoption of an organic growth approach.

Figure 11.4 suggests that the criticality of people varies as a function of the product of an individual's role requirements, role impact, substitutability and job performance; i.e.

$$\text{Criticality} = f\,(\text{Requirements} \times \text{Impact} \times \text{Substitutability} \times \text{Performance})$$

Most of these factors reflect strategic considerations such as the nature and maturity of the business, market competition and environmental uncertainty, and design contingencies such as degree of formalization and division of labour. Strategic choice and change and consequent organizational and job design decisions influence role requirements and role impact, substitutability, and the level and likely variability of job performance. In short, strategic choice influences the criticality of people to business success and, as we shall see, the potential value of selection.

Whilst not exhaustive, such factors should have some influence upon when an organization is likely to find it cost-beneficial to invest in selection and in people

Table 11.2 Three business-level strategies and their HRM implications

Strategy	Employee role behaviour	HRM policies
INNOVATION	A high degree of creative behaviour Longer-term focus A relatively high level of cooperative, interdependent behaviour A moderate degree of concern for quality A moderate concern for quantity An equal degree of concern for process and results A greater degree of risk-taking A high tolerance of ambiguity and unpredictability	Jobs that require close interaction and coordination among groups of individuals Performance appraisals that are more likely to reflect longer-term and group-based achievements Jobs that allow employees to develop skills that can be used in other positions in the firm Compensation systems that emphasize internal equity rather than external or market-based equity Pay rates that tend to be low but that allow employees to be stockholders and to have more freedom to choose the mix of components that make up their pay package Broad career paths to reinforce the development of a broad range of skills
QUALITY ENHANCEMENT	Relatively repetitive and predictable behaviours A more long-term or intermediate focus A moderate amount of cooperative, interdependent behaviour A high concern for quality A modest concern for quantity of output High concern for process Low risk-taking activity Commitment to the goals of the organization	Relatively fixed and explicit job descriptions High levels of employee participation in decisions relevant to immediate work conditions and the job itself A mix of individual and group criteria for performance appraisal that is mostly short-term and results-orientated A relatively egalitarian treatment of employees and some guarantees of employment security Extensive and continuous training and development of employees
COST REDUCTION	Relatively repetitive and predictable behaviour A rather short-term focus Primarily autonomous or individual activity Moderate concern for quality High concern for quantity of output Primary concern for results Low risk-taking activity Relatively high degree of comfort with stability	Relatively fixed and explicit job descriptions that allow little room for ambiguity Narrowly designed jobs and narrowly defined career paths that encourage specialization expertise and efficiency Short-term results-orientated performance appraisals Close monitoring of market pay levels for use in making compensation decisions Minimal levels of employee training and development

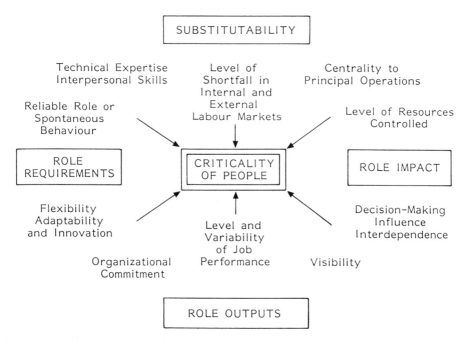

Figure 11.4   Factors affecting the criticality of employees

issues such as the development of employees' expertise or interpersonal skills, above-average compensation, and to promote job involvement and organizational commitment.

Of course such an analysis is normative, and under these circumstances it makes sense to invest in people. Actual investment in people is also likely to reflect management values and philosophy and crucially the organization's cash position. Cash-rich organizations can afford to invest in people. Under conditions of financial constraint it is too frequently that HRM budgets get cut.

The corollary is that there are types of organizations, and different parts of an organization, where the contribution of employees to organizational performance is less significant. For example, in a typical machine bureaucracy (the job is prescribed, deskilled, routine and controlled) and where individuals can easily be replaced from the labour market. In these situations there is little value to be gained in investing in people, or in developing the organization to encourage high levels of motivation and commitment. Indeed the basic principles of Taylorism were an attempt to reduce the criticality of people to business performance.

Impact of strategic choice on the utility of selection

As we have already observed, there would appear to be general differences across organizations in the extent to which they invest in their people and perceive

Table 11.3   Utility formula of Schmidt *et al.* (1979)

Incremental utility relative to random selection is:

$$\Delta \; Utility = T \, [\, (N_s) \, (SD_y) \, (r_{xy}) \, (\bar{Z}_x) \,] - [\, (C) \, (N_{app}) \,]$$

where:

N_s = number of applicants selected
N_{app} = number of applicants
T = length of tenure in years
C = cost of method 1
r_{xy} = validity of method 1
SD_y = 'dollar' value of one standard deviation difference in criterion level
$\bar{Z}_x$ = average standardized predictor score of those selected

employees to be a critical success factor. This relates to the utility of HRM (as opposed to specifically the utility of selection) but is likely to have implications for selection in the availability of HRM expertise, the allocation of budgets, and the utility of selection itself. As an organization's investment in people increases, so too does the value of selecting the right people (see also Boudreau, Sturman and Judge, 1994).

Selection is likely to be influenced by the perceived costs and benefits to the organization of investing in its people. This is likely to represent, at best, enlightened self-interest rather than people-orientated values. Consequently the extent to which selection methods are seen as cost-beneficial in a particular situation is likely to influence their use in identifying and choosing employees.

The equation in Table 11.3 gives the utility formula of Schmidt *et al.* (1979) for calculating the incremental utility of a selection device relative to random selection.

The following factors impact upon the utility of a selection method: variation in criterion performance; absolute salary levels; number of individuals selected; the selection ratio; length of tenure; validity and cost of method. To this we can add the costs of training and development. Thus, other things being equal, the potential value of selection to an organization increases: as there is an increase in the variability of performance between job incumbents; the dollar value to the organization of the incumbents' job performance increases; as training and development costs increase; as the number selected increases; as the number of applications increase (job openings held constant); as the average length of tenure of job incumbents increases; as the validity of the methodology increases; as the costs of selection decrease. Most of these factors, and consequently the potential value of selection, vary with strategic choice.

Variation in job performance is likely to be greater when jobs are complex, uncertain, changing and are difficult to prescribe; for example, organizations that are developing in a competitive environment and following an innovative business strategy. On the other hand, mature or declining traditional industries with an adequate supply of labour, high division of labour and formalization are likely to result in less variation in criterion performance. Of course it should be remembered that there are variations within organizations as well as between them. Typically jobs increase in uncertainty, complexity and autonomy as one moves to consider more senior positions. Other things being equal, the utility of selection increases at more senior levels and amongst cash-rich companies that pay staff above-average pay levels for their industry.

Training and development costs increase with the extent of the shortfall in required skills and characteristics and with the complexity of the target job. Thus, organizations such as the armed forces, police, clearing banks, airlines make major investments in training because trained army officers, police, bank managers or pilots do not normally exist in the labour market. When these jobs are complex and require high levels of expertise and management skills such as leadership, communication or problem-solving skills, then the required investment in training is likely to be costly and long-term. In such cases it is clearly of utility for these career-based organizations to select the right people, and to retain their services, through rewards and career management. These in turn increase the associated costs and consequent value of selection.

The size of business units and the design of jobs within them is a strategic design issue. Such decisions increase the utility of selection when they result in larger numbers of individuals being required. Selection is likely to be of greater value to large homogeneous organizations and to increase under a policy of expansion and growth. Likewise the cultivation of a positive corporate image may increase the utility of selection if it results in the organization having to process larger numbers of applicants.

The impact upon utility of strategic type and change does appear to create difficulties for dollar-based utility analysis. It raises doubts over the specific applicability of the Schmidt *et al.* (1982) 40–70% rule, and upon the feasibility of the Rational Estimate methodology.

Schmidt *et al.* appear to have over-generalized their conclusions regarding the relationship between salary and value of output. For example, Johnson and Scholes (1984, p. 106) report statistics which suggest that within a sector there are differences in added-value per employee over time, differences in added-value between sectors, and differences between nations. More recently, Escover (1994) suggested (but admittedly provided little evidence) that the added value of employees is greatest at the bottom and top of the organization and considerably less in middle management. Our own analysis in terms of criticality would suggest, for example, that typically poorly paid boundary roles such as hotel receptionists and chambermaids, restaurant waiters and bank clerks may well add relatively more value than that reflected by their salary.

Numerous factors would appear to moderate the relationship between the cost of an individual's input and the value of their output. For example, recruitment from the external labour market, job evaluation schemes and performance-related pay and promotion may serve to strengthen the link. Recruitment from an internal labour market, national salary and bargaining structures, rewards and advancement based upon tenure and loyalty may serve to weaken the link. These factors reflect differences between organizations in terms of strategic type and choice; for example, between Miles and Snow's 'prospectors' and their 'defenders', and between many private and public sector organizations.

The 40–70% rule further assumes that the differences between employees in terms of the value of the outputs from their jobs is normally distributed. In many cases this is not so. For instance, many jobs are technologically determined (e.g. machine paced).

Consequently, estimates of selection utility may well be inaccurate when the 40% rule is applied in situations where there is reason to believe that the value of the output and salary are not strongly linked or criterion performance is not normally distributed. Further, Rational Estimate methodology stretches credibility when applicants are being selected for future jobs the nature and output value of which are largely unknown.

In these situations either Rational Estimate needs to be developed to reflect the specific circumstances, or where this is inappropriate, selection utility is perhaps better estimated on the basis of financial savings in providing an equivalent service rather than in terms of the increased value of the outputs (see Eaton *et al.*'s 1985 Superior Equivalents technique) or dollar-based utility estimates abandoned altogether in favour of utility as an estimate of the increase in average performance that is likely to result from the use of the selection method.

Impact of strategic choice on selection criteria

Strategy and design represent the demand system and influence the manpower requirements in terms of the skills and characteristics required of job incumbents. Organizations following different strategies, or operating different design options, will possess different manpower requirements. Organizations operating in different sectors are likely to seek different skills and characteristics and use different selection dimensions and methods. For the most part the specific implications are straightforward and require no further explanation. Two strategic developments are, however, worthy of a little amplification; namely the requirement for a more innovative workforce, and the increasing internationalization of business.

Greater effort is likely to go into the development of psychometric tests and simulation exercises to help in the process of building up a flexible and innovative workforce. Although there are a number of situational and organizational factors that impact upon flexibility and innovation (West and Farr, 1990), investigations into the personal characteristics of creative and innovative individuals may be of potential value in selection. These have involved attempts either to identify and measure a creativity trait (e.g. Guilford, 1959) or to isolate the personality traits related to creative production. Some of the traits frequently held to be associated with creativity are desire for autonomy, social independence, high tolerance of ambiguity, a propensity for risk-taking and anxiety. Kirton's (1976) Adaptation–Innovation Inventory is an example of an instrument that is designed to help in the process of selecting and developing individuals with respect to these characteristics. But even if we were able to measure creativity reliably, and select more creative individuals, this is unlikely to have much benefit for the organization unless work and organizational factors support creative production.

The increasing internationalization of business and mobility of the workforce across national boundaries, especially in the European Union (EU), has implications for selection. It is an increasingly common occurrence that non-nationals apply for jobs especially at the more senior levels. For example, it is becoming increasingly common for candidates from other EU countries to apply for jobs in the UK, and vice versa. Given the impact of language differences upon maximum performance and, in particular, typical performance measures, their use may be of questionable fairness in these cases. With typical performance measures the difficulty is not in translating the items into the native language, but rather in the interpretation of typical behaviour across cultures. Is 'Being the centre of attention at a social event' as much indicative of being extroverted in Italy or Greece as it is in the UK? McCulloch (1993) suggests culturally based norms and the use of experienced test developers fluent in both languages as a way of overcoming this problem. However, one is left with the doubt of whether or not cultural differences undermine the validity of the construct despite equivalence in meaning.

Multinationals also have the problem of selecting international managers—i.e. those who work abroad. The appropriate dimensions of assessment are, in addition to language proficiency or learning aptitude, likely to include an interest in and experience of other cultures and evidence of easy adaptation, as well as personal circumstances. Even when multinationals devolve selection to local units, difficulties are likely to be encountered. As Shimmin (1989) reports, there are considerable variations in acceptable and legal practice between European countries.

IMPLICATIONS OF ENVIRONMENTAL AND STRATEGIC CHANGE FOR HRM AND SELECTION

Figure 11.5 outlines the effects of environmental change on strategy and organization as seen by McKinley and Starkey (1988).

McKinley and Starkey view strategic change as resulting from change in the organization's environment. Thus, for example, organizations need to embrace the potential benefits of new technology, respond to changes in material or labour supply, the impact of new legislation, and so on, if they wish to remain competitive. Equally, strategic choice influences the nature of the organization's environment. Choice over the market to enter, and the positioning of products and services in that market, have significant implications for the rate at which the organization will have to respond in order to be successful. For example, those organizations entering highly competitive markets will need to respond rapidly to changing customer requirements and competitor initiatives.

It is important to distinguish between change which is predictable and change which is not. Thus, Snow and Snell's three models of staffing, to which we referred earlier, relate to increasing rates of change in an organization's

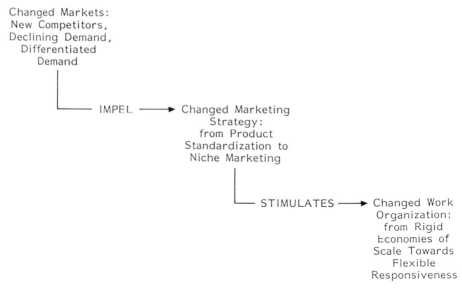

Figure 11.5   Impact of environmental change upon strategy

environment: stability, predictable change, and change which is largely unpredictable being foreseeable only over the short term. Increasing rates of change cause increasing uncertainty, shortening time horizons, and an increasing need for responsiveness and flexibility.

Impact of change on the criticality of people

People are more of a critical success factor for companies operating in a turbulent environment. Kotter and Schlesinger (1979) and many others have pointed out that there are a number of alternative strategies for implementing change but that it is typically easier if you have people with you. Change, it would seem, increases the criticality of employees. Increasing rates of change make the future less predictable and jobs and roles less able to be prescribed. A competitive environment which requires continual product innovation, shorter product life cycles and re-positioning of products in the market requires changing skills and employee commitment and support.

Impact of change on selection criteria

Sparrow (1994) suggests that at any particular point in time we can think about and classify competencies in relation to a particular organization as being stable (i.e. always likely to be required, such as reasoning ability among managers), emerging (i.e. will become more relevant if the organization continues to pursue a particular strategic path), declining (less important now than they were), or transitional (important only during a period of transition). In selecting individuals we now have to consider not only the operational criteria that will be used in judging their job performance, but also the visionary criteria that have been identified as likely to give the organization a competitive edge in the future, and transformational criteria that are necessary for enabling the change to happen. We can characterize these three types of criteria as follows, with their relationship shown schematically in Figure 11.6.

- *Operational criteria*—These refer to the attributes that are required for successful current job performance such as the abilities, knowledge, interpersonal skills and the beliefs and values (e.g. loyalty to the organization, cost consciousness) that are required to meet current job demands.
- *Visionary criteria*—These refer to the attributes that are hypothesized necessary for successful future job performance (e.g. managing greater complexity, managing more proactively, using information technology as a transformational force).
- *Transformational criteria*—These refer to the attributes that are required to enable change to happen (e.g. envisioning, teambuilding, conflict management, persuasiveness): the competencies for change rather than the changing competencies (Sparrow and Bognanno, 1993; Sparrow, 1994).

We shall illustrate the use of visionary and transformational criteria when discussing the role of selection in strategic change.

Impact of change on the balance of power between employer and job applicants

The development of technology and increasing specialization in the workplace is going to place increasing demands for professional and technical expertise. Herriot (1989a) has suggested this may well shift the balance of power towards employees, requiring organizations to adopt more of a selling frame of reference in their recruitment and selection policies. Of course, individuals with relatively unique and sought-after skills and expertise have always possessed this power of negotiation. It is predicted that in future increasingly large numbers of employees will possess relatively non-substitutable expertise and be in a position to negotiate with employers on their conditions of employment. This is less likely to be the case in stable mature organizations where the provision of expertise through

Figure 11.6 Relationship between three types of criteria (developed from Beckhard and Harris, 1987)

traditional agencies (e.g. education and professional bodies) is likely to keep pace with requirements. It is the organizations providing specialist products and services, and those forced to make continual improvements in the process of manufacture, where demand is likely to outstrip supply.

A shift in the balance of power towards the applicant may have an effect on the choice available to an organization with respect to methods of assessment. Evidence and commonsense suggest that applicants differentiate between methods with respect to fairness (Iles and Robertson, Chapter 27 in this volume). In a particular situation the most valid method may not be perceived as the most fair. Thus, applicants may react adversely to the use of methods that review studies (e.g. Reilly and Chao, 1982; Hunter and Hunter, 1984; Schmitt *et al.*, 1984) have shown to be among the most valid single predictors of performance and/or tenure—for example, biodata and peer evaluations. On the other hand they may be more attracted to the time-consuming and expensive assessment-centre method. This method may make them feel exhausted at the end of one or two days, but they are likely to be impressed by the thoroughness of the procedure, by the increased opportunities they are given to display relevant behaviours, and by the potentially rich learning outcomes it affords.

Impact of change on the identification of selection criteria

If jobs and their component tasks change at an increasing rate, then employees are likely to perform a number of related but different jobs during their working life. Task-based job analysis techniques which assume stability and are based upon the analysis of the current job are likely to become less useful. In such a situation, person specifications and selection criteria require input from some method of future scenario development and analysis (Williams *et al.*, 1991).

Impact of change on the evaluation of validity, utility and fairness

As Herriot (1992) has pointed out, an increasing rate of change does create a problem for the traditional psychometric approach to selection. Increasing rates of change will require the manpower delivery system to become more closely linked with future strategic focus, to be more responsive and to adopt shorter time frames. The traditional approach to predictive validation and the evaluation of fairness and utility will become increasingly problematical. It is likely that in many organizations predictive validation will become unfeasible and greater reliance and faith will be placed upon validity generalization conclusions. There is likely to be an increase in the use of the concurrent paradigm and in the use of content and synthetic validation methods, and where predictive validation is used it is likely to target performance criteria over a much shorter time period.

The use of visionary criteria is also problematical when it comes to assessing the validity, utility and fairness of the selection and assessment methods used. Here, neither the predictive nor the concurrent approach is likely to be possible for the job requirements are envisaged rather than operational. Organizations will need to take considerable care in justifying their use in cases of adverse impact.

Impact of change on assessors' criteria-in-use

Akkerman (1989) has pointed out that there is frequently only partial overlap between the formal criterion of prediction and the criterion-in-use. Thus when we investigated the selection of Army officers, whilst there did exist a formal statement of the criterion—namely 'to identify those who after training would be able to lead a platoon in battle'—it seemed likely that those actually making selection decisions were more concerned with success in training at Sandhurst (Dobson and Williams, 1989). In times of rapid change one can envisage difficulties for such 'criteria-in-use'. This problem may be compounded in those organizations that have traditionally used target role incumbents as assessors. If jobs change radically, such an option will not be available because individuals experienced in the target role will not exist. In the future there may be dangers in organizations, such as a national diplomatic service, relying on the criteria-in-use of retired senior personnel in the process of selection.

Signs and samples for the future

An increasing rate of change is likely to result in an emphasis upon the identification of training and retraining potential rather than the assessment of behavioural repertoires. The UK competency frameworks which tend to emphasize observable behaviours are situation-specific, and because of their limited generalizability would appear to be unsuited to times of rapid change. Sparrow and Bognanno (1993), in discussing the BP competency framework, suggest that organizations will need to re-identify and reclassify competencies every two to three years.

Interestingly, the US approach tends to emphasize inferred personal characteristics which have far greater generalizability. Increased rates of change may well result in a renewed concern with the kind of person being selected: a concern with signs rather than samples of behaviour. It would seem likely that there will be an increase in the use of inferred characteristics as dimensions of assessment in order to assess the kind of person being selected and what they are capable of doing in the future. It is to be hoped that this will not result in the wholesale abandonment of the use of observation of behaviour in real and simulated situations in favour of written measures of typical performance. It is noticeable that the British armed forces, which for some time have had to identify training potential, have emphasized intelligence and personality as dimensions of assessment that are inferred in part from behaviour observed in simulation exercises.

Changing career patterns within organizations which will require individuals to adapt to a number of different roles and job demands during their career are likely to signal renewed emphasis on measures of general cognitive ability. According to Weschler (1958), 'Intelligence is the aggregate or global capacity of the individual to act purposefully, to think rationally and to deal effectively with his environment'. Measures of such an entity would appear to be relevant to a future of organizational uncertainty.

ROLE OF SELECTION IN PROMOTING AND ENABLING STRATEGIC CHANGE

Strategic change will typically require the organization to revise its person specifications, dimensions and methods of selection in order to provide for future manpower requirements. In aligning selection to strategy in this way, selection can act as a significant agent for change. When not aligning itself selection can present a significant obstacle to change. It is noticeable that many of the organizations with sophisticated and longstanding selection procedures (e.g. the British Army— Dobson and Williams, 1989) possess strong cultures that appear to be resistant to change. In determining who is and who is not a member of an organization, selection systems are potentially powerful cultural agents. When used to promote strategic change they can be powerful change agents.

Role of selection criteria in change

Selection in determining who is and who is not a member of the organization influences the composition of the organization in terms of skills, values and other personal attributes. The selection criteria used in many ways prescribe not just the future competencies of employees but also the future competencies of the organization itself. In using visionary criteria future manpower requirements can be met, in using transformational criteria the organization becomes more able to initiate and respond to change whatever the nature of that change may be.

In the late 1980s we undertook an investigation of organizational culture change involving a series of case studies (Williams, Dobson and Walters, 1993). Organizations used a combination of methods to implement strategic cultural change, and selection played a key role. The prospect of privatization led East Midlands Electricity (a public utility organization) to select sales-orientated professionals and moved them into key positions in their attempt to change from an engineering to a more sales and customer focused organization; they also increased their sales staff by 63% over five years. Fifteen or so years ago the building societies (mutual benefit organizations originally created to provide loans to enable house purchase from savers' funds) competed amongst themselves and operated a cartel with respect to interest rates paid on investments and interest rates charged on mortgage loans. High interest rates and general deregulation brought the clearing banks in more direct competition with the building societies. The need to become more commercially orientated led Abbey National into a number of changes, including an increase in their recruitment of business graduates.

Before recruiting a new workforce in their Southampton plant, Toshiba had a clear idea of the strategic values or culture they intended establishing. Self-selection played an important part in their recruitment. In order that potential employees had the right expectations, they took care in wording their recruitment literature so as to promote cooperation on the shopfloor (e.g. they referred to assembly-work operators rather than to specific jobs or trades). They also used a Realistic Job Preview (RJP) to screen attitudes and values of potential employees towards being a member of a 'clockwork' organization—an organization where reliable and cooperative role behaviour was considered a key element of strategy. This Japanese approach of using recruitment and selection as key factors in establishing a planned culture was also used by Nissan in the UK (Wickens, 1987; Garrahan and Stewart, 1992).

Operational criteria are usually based around known job requirements. Visionary criteria are based on envisaged future job requirements. Transformational criteria, on the other hand, may be concerned with relatively unknown future scenarios. Whilst rarely mentioned in traditional OD texts the use of transformational criteria in selection, placement and development can make a significant contribution to an organization's renewal processes and the development of the learning organization (Lippitt, 1982; Pearn, Roderick and Mulrooney, 1995).

BP (Sparrow and Bognanno, 1993) and NatWest (Cockerill, 1989) are good examples of how major companies can try to ensure they have the basic raw material in senior management to cope with a scenario where the only certain fact is that the future will be impregnated by change! BP's transformational criteria were based upon their own competency framework of Open Thinking, Personal Impact, Empowering and Networking. The work of Schroder (1989) provided NatWest with an attractive and practical model. The model provides a competency-based strategy for selecting and developing managers, and for building the teams that new organizational structures demand for coping with the rapidly changing environments characteristic of the information age. Schroder's work suggests what managers have to do to be able to react and capitalize on high levels of change. Moreover, assessment centre techniques are available to assess the extent to which individuals have or need to develop the eleven competencies in the model. The competencies include three *cognitive* (information search, concept formation, conceptual flexibility), three *motivating* (interpersonal search, managing interaction, developmental orientation), three *directional* (self-confidence, presentation, impact), and two *achieving* (proactive orientation, achievement orientation). Operational definitions of these competencies, and justification for their inclusion, are provided by Schroder. Schroder stresses that these competencies represent managerial behaviour leading to excellent and not merely adequate performance.

Other taxonomies of managerial competencies for coping with unprecedented future turbulence have been put forward (e.g. Morgan, 1989; Dale, 1990). Schroder's is one of the more persuasive from the empirical perspective. Whether competencies are used as criteria or not, such frameworks do possess the potential to integrate action across selection, training and appraisal activities and link them to a desired future state; i.e. they are both coherent and appropriate.

Selecting the leaders for strategic change

In selecting the future leaders of the organization, selection can make a significant contribution to the recruitment of new ideas and recipes promoting new strategic directions. As Schein (1984) has pointed out, leaders are particularly key in the creation and change of organizational culture. Tichy and Devanna (1990) argue that organizations need the characteristics of transformational leaders in order to cope effectively with change. Coulson-Thomas (1990) reports the use of facilitating directors at Rank Xerox. The power of newly appointed Chief Executive Officers (CEOs) makes them key players in the process of strategic change. Three good reasons for this include:

- They are sufficiently free of the organization's cultural influences to be able to see problems and opportunities in a fresh light.
- Their learning experiences in another culture enable them to consider alternative models.
- The circumstances of their appointment may build up expectations in others that they are there to initiate change.

In our study of organizational culture change there were a number of examples of the importance of leader selection in promoting change. This was most obvious in the selection of CEOs. There were examples of new CEOs being brought in because of financial crises or deteriorating market share. Sometimes the main criterion for bringing in a particular person was because he or she had successfully demonstrated a particularly relevant skill in another company. Sometimes the main criterion seemed to be that the individual appointed had the necessary vision and force of personality to assess and drive through whatever changes were needed.

Integrating HRM, selection and organizational requirements

Noel Tichy (1983), amongst others, has argued that in order to be effective business strategy should be made contingent upon the nature of the organization's environment and an analysis of the organization itself; then organizational design and functional strategies and operations are aligned to promote the attainment of strategic goals. In order to be effective in meeting present strategic requirements, or in promoting and enabling future strategic change, not only does selection need to be vertically integrated with these requirements, but also it needs to be horizontally integrated with other HRM activities. As Hendry and Pettigrew (1992) suggest, HRM activities need to be both coherent and appropriate. Organizations that take this fully into account when introducing systematic selection procedures, or when planning changes to existing systems, are potential models of good practice of the 'strategic personnel selection' approach. A conceptual framework for strategic personnel selection is given in Figure 11.7.

Organizational requirements largely reflect the nature of the organization's environment, and the turbulence and amount of uncertainty of this environment would appear to have particular implications for the role and criteria of HRM in general and selection more specifically. As Hendry and Pettigrew (1992) have suggested, many organizations need to adopt HRM policies and practices which enable continual proactive change. This requires organizations and HRM to focus

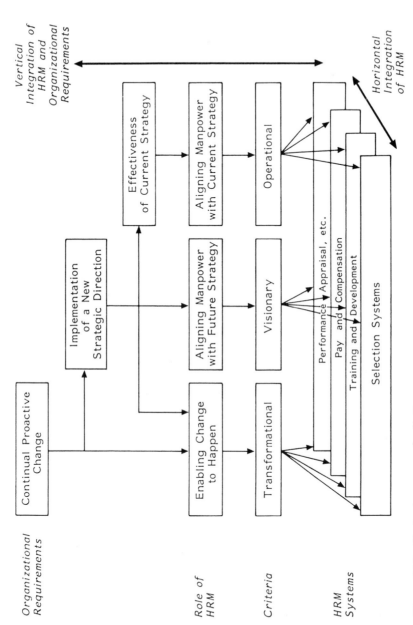

Figure 11.7 Strategic personnel selection

on the future and how the transition from the present to the desired future state is to be managed. In order for selection to be effective it needs to consider the scenario where it is not just concerned with meeting manpower requirements of current job performance but also with future job demands and the attributes necessary to enable the change to happen.

CONCLUSIONS

We have argued for a better understanding of the mutual interactions between business strategic choice and change and HRM/personnel strategies. We have tried to show that strategic choice and change affect personnel selection in a number of ways, including: the levels of resources and expertise within HRM and consequently the likely validities, fairness and effectiveness of operational systems; the relative emphasis given to external recruitment and selection as against internal development of staff; the role that selection plays in the more traditional approach of matching applicants to prescribed profiles as opposed to the more proactive approach of increasing strategic capability and forces for change; the selection criteria and methods used; the criticality of different groups of employees within the organization and consequently the utility of selection; the ease or difficulty of evaluating selection systems, with consequences for developing effective operational systems.

We hypothesize that where HRM strategies in general and selection specifically are coherent and aligned to current and future business strategy, personnel selection will make a significant contribution to organizational performance. Strategic personnel selection, as we have called this approach, will help the organization to cope with and adapt to change, ensuring that it has the right people and leaders for the future.

We conclude on a cautionary note. The problem for organizational psychologists and other management consultants is not so much to convince management of the power of HRM and personnel selection systems and methods in formulating and achieving strategic objectives, but to get them to apply the relevant knowledge by adopting the 'good practices' that are followed by a minority of organizations. We have implicitly or explicitly highlighted some of the factors that will facilitate or inhibit the realization of the theoretical benefits of strategic personnel selection. Awareness of these factors is the first step in their control. They include:

- Management needs to understand the complex implications of organizational strategy for HRM in general and for selection in particular (see Tables 11.1 and 11.2). Moreover, the concept of the criticality of people needs to be explored in the process of developing organizational strategy (see Figure 11.4).
- A well-communicated and understood organizational strategy should facilitate the effective coordination of the demand and delivery systems (see Figure 11.2), and enable appropriate selection systems and methods in the latter to contribute successfully towards the achievement of strategic goals (see Figure 11.1).
- Strategic personnel selection requires as much attention being given to the proactive visionary criteria of tomorrow as to the reactive operational cri-

teria of today (see Figure 11.6). Increasing rates of change and concern with future strategic capability are going to place further strain on traditional frameworks, on methods of job analysis, and on the estimation of the validity and utility of selection systems.

- The enhanced bargaining power of some categories of applicants, and the accelerating rate of change, are going to exacerbate the perennial problems of selection—cultural, political and economic forces inhibiting the use of certain valid methods of assessment; the criterion problem; the mismatch between the time necessary to validate selection procedures and the time for critical situational variables to change.

In this chapter we have purposefully not elaborated on the validity and use of different methods of assessment in relation to particular criteria, since these topics are already well aired in the literature (e.g. Cook, 1988; Herriot, 1989b). Managers and practitioners should nevertheless be concerned with some of the findings in this area—several surveys have shown that the most valid methods are not necessarily those in common use (Robertson and Makin, 1986; Shackleton and Newell, 1991). CEOs and their teams of supporting managers need to develop appropriate cognitive models to ensure that the gap between theory and practice with respect to selection methods is not perpetuated in the use of HRM and selection systems for the formulation and achievement of strategic objectives.

REFERENCES

Akkerman, A.E. (1989). Criteria and individual assessment. In M. Smith and I. Robertson (eds) *Advances in Selection and Assessment*. Chichester: John Wiley.

Baird, L. and Meshoulam, I. (1988). Managing two fits of strategic human resource management. *Academy of Management Review*, **13**(1), 116–128.

Boston Consulting Group (1970). *The Product Portfolio Concept*, Perspective no. 66. Boston, MA: Boston Consulting Group.

Boudreau, J.W., Sturman, M.C. and Judge, T.A. (1994). Utility analysis: what are the black boxes, and do they affect decisions? In N. Anderson and P. Herriot (eds) *Assessment and Selection in Organizations: First Update*. Chichester: John Wiley.

Chandler, A.D. (1962). *Strategy and Structure*. Cambridge, MA: MIT Press.

Cockerill, T. (1989). The kind of competence for rapid change. *Personnel Management*, **21**(9), 52–56.

Confederation of British Industry (1989). *Evaluating Your Training: Matching Outcomes to Needs*. London: CBI.

Cook, M. (1988). *Personnel Selection and Productivity*. Chichester: John Wiley.

Coulson-Thomas, C. (1990). Developing Directors. *European Management Journal*, **8**(4), 488–499.

Dale, G. (1990). Management proven in the marketplace. *Conference on Identifying and Applying Competencies within your Organization*. London: Resource Ltd.

Dobson, P. and Williams, A.P.O. (1989). The validation of the selection of male British Army Officers. *Journal of Occupational Psychology*, **62**(4), 313–325.

Eaton, N.K., Wing, H. and Mitchell, K.J. (1985). Alternate methods of estimating the dollar value of performance. *Personnel Psychology*, **38**, 27–40.

Escover, J.L. (1994). The value measure. *Management Decision*, **32**(1), 12–14.

Garrahan, P. and Stewart, P. (1992). *The Nissan Enigma*. London: Mansell.

Goold, M. and Campbell, A. (1987). *Strategies and Styles: the Role of the Centre in Managing Diversified Corporations*. Oxford: Blackwell.

Guilford, J.P. (1959). Traits of creativity. In H.H. Anderson (ed.) *Creativity and its Cultivation*. New York: Harper.

Hamermesh, R.G. (1986). *Making Strategy Work: How Senior Managers Produce Results*. New York: John Wiley.

Hendry, C. and Pettigrew, A. (1992). Patterns of change in the development of human resource management. *British Journal of Management*, **3**, 137–156.

Herriot, P. (1989a). *Recruitment in the 1990s*. London: Institute of Personnel Management.

Herriot, P. (1989b) (ed.). *Assessment and Selection in Organizations*. Chichester: John Wiley.

Herriot, P. (1992). Selection: the two subcultures. *European Work and Organizational Psychologist*, **2**(2), 129–140.

Hunter, J.E. and Hunter, R.F. (1984). Validity and utility of alternative predictors of performance. *Psychological Bulletin*, **96**, 72–95.

Johnson, G. and Scholes, K. (1993). *Exploring Corporate Strategy*. Englewood Cliffs, NJ: Prentice-Hall.

Keep, E. and Mayhew, K. (1987). The assessment: education training and economic performance. *Oxford Review of Economic Policy*, **4**(3), 219–230.

Kirton, M.J. (1976). Adaptors and innovators: a description and measure. *Journal of Applied Psychology*, **6**, 622–629.

Kochan, T.A. and Barocci, T.A. (1985). *Human Resource Management and Industrial Relations: Text, Readings and Cases*. Boston, MA: Little Brown.

Kotter, J.P. and Schlesinger, L.A. (1979). Choosing strategies for change. *Harvard Business Review*, March–April.

Lippitt, G.L. (1982). *Organizational Renewal: a Holistic Approach to Organization Development*, Englewood Cliffs, NJ: Prentice Hall.

March, J.G. and Simon, H.A. (1958) *Organizations*, New York: Wiley.

McCulloch, S. (1993). Recent trends in international assessment. *International Journal of Selection and Assessment*, **1**(1), 59–61.

McKinley, A. and Starkey, K. (1988). Competitive strategies and organizational change. *Organization Studies*, **9**(4), 555–571.

Miles, R.E. and Snow, C.C. (1978). *Organizational Strategy, Structure, and Process*. New York: McGraw-Hill.

Miller, P. (1992). Integrating strategy and human resource management. In B. Towers (ed.) *The Handbook of Human Resource Management*. Oxford: Blackwell.

Mintzberg, H. (1988). Opening up the definition of strategy. In J.B. Quinn, H. Mintzberg and R.M. James (eds) *The Strategy Process: Concepts, Contexts and Cases*. Englewood Cliffs, NJ: Prentice-Hall International.

Morgan, G. (1989). *Riding the Waves of Change: Developing Managerial Competencies for a Turbulent World*. Oxford: Jossey-Bass.

Pearn, M., Roderick, C. and Mulrooney, C. (1995). *Learning Organizations in Practice*. Maidenhead: McGraw-Hill.

Pettigrew, A.M. (1973). *Politics of Organizational Decision-Making*. London: Tavistock.

Porter, M.E. (1987). From competitive advantage to corporate strategy. *Harvard Business Review*, May–June.

Prahalad, C.K. and Hamel, G. (1990). The core competence of the corporation. *Harvard Business Review*, May–June.

Purcell, J. (1989). The impact of corporation strategy on human resource management. In J. Storey (ed.) *New Perspectives on Human Resource Management*. London: Routledge.

Reilly, R.R. and Chao, G.T. (1982). Validity and fairness of some alternative employee selection procedures. *Personnel Psychology*, **35**, 1–62.

Robertson, I.T. and Makin, P.J. (1986). Managerial selection in Britain. *Journal of Occupational Psychology*, **59**, 45–57.

Schein, E. (1984). *Organizational Culture and Leadership*. Oxford: Jossey-Bass.

Schmidt, F.L., Hunter, J.E., McKenzie, R.C. and Muldrow, T.W. (1979). Impact of valid selection procedures on work-force productivity. *Journal of Applied Psychology*, **64**, 609–626.

Schmidt, F.L., Hunter, J.E. and Pearlman, K. (1982). Assessing the economic impact of personnel programs in workforce productivity. *Personnel Psychology*, **35**, 333–347.

Schmitt, N., Gooding, R.Z., Noe, R.A. and Kirsch, M. (1984). Meta-analyses of validity studies published between 1964 and 1982 and the investigation of study characteristics. *Personnel Psychology*, **37**, 407–422.

Schroder, H. (1989). *Managerial Competence: the Key to Excellence.* Iowa: Kendall/Hunt.

Schuler, R.S. and Jackson, S.E. (1987). Linking competitive strategy with human resource management practices. *Academy of Management Executive*, **1**(3), 207–219.

Shackleton, V. and Newell, S. (1991). Management selection: a comparative survey of methods used in top British and French companies. *Journal of Occupational Psychology*, **64**(1), 23–36.

Shimmin, S. (1989). Selection in a European Context. In P. Herriot (ed.) *Assessment and Selection in Organizations.* Chichester: John Wiley.

Smith, J.G. (1990). *Business Strategy*, 2nd edn. Oxford: Blackwell.

Snow, C.C. and Snell, S.A. (1993). Staffing as Strategy. In N. Schmitt *et al.* (eds) *Personnel Selection in Organizations.* San Francisco, CA: Jossey-Bass.

Sonnenfeld, J.A. and Peiperl, M.A. (1988). Staffing policy as a strategic response: a typology of career systems. *Academy of Management Review*, **13**(4), 588–600.

Sparrow, P. (1994). Organizational competencies: creating a strategic behavioural framework for selection and assessment. In N. Anderson and P. Herriot (eds) *Assessment and Selection in Organizations: First Update.* Chichester: John Wiley.

Sparrow, P. and Bognanno, M. (1993). Competency requirement forecasting: issues for international selection and assessment. *International Journal of Selection and Assessment*, **1**(1), 50–58.

Tichy, N. (1983). *Managing Strategic Change: Technical, Political and Cultural Dynamics.* New York: John Wiley.

Tichy, N. and Devanna, M.A. (1990). *The Transformational Leader.* Chichester: John Wiley.

Weschler, D. (1958). *The Measurement and Appraisal of Adult Intelligence.* London: Baillière, Tindall & Cox.

West, M.A. and Farr, J.L. (eds) (1990). *Innovation and Creativity at Work: Psychological and Organizational Strategies.* Chichester: John Wiley.

Wickens, P. (1987). *The Road to Nissan.* London: Macmillan.

Williams, A.P.O., Dobson, P. and Walters, M. (1993). *Changing Culture: New Organizational Approaches*, 2nd edn. London: Institute of Personnel Management.

Williams, A.P.O., Woodward, S., Brooke, C. and Reynolds, R. (1991). *Future IT Role and Skill Needs in City-oriented Organizations.* London: City University Business School.

Chapter 12

Selection and Assessment During Organizational Turnaround

MARISE PH. BORN

Department of Work and Organizational Psychology, Vrije Universiteit, Amsterdam, The Netherlands

PAUL G. W. JANSEN

Department of Business Administration, Faculty of Economics and Econometrics, Vrije Universiteit, Amsterdam, The Netherlands

INTRODUCTION

A general characteristic of organizations is their changeability and motion. Organizations are constantly on the move—when they are looking for new markets or are improving products, when they are reacting to changing circumstances, when they are trying to survive. Organizational movement, however, has intensified strongly (cf. Jansen and Van Wees, 1994; Rousseau, 1995). Mergers and acquisitions are taking place both more often and more globally. Having taken on a large scale at the end of the 1980s, mergers and expansions have entered a turbulent phase over the last few years (cf. Hogan and Overmyer-Day, 1994). Major changes are happening in core products and core structures as a result of stronger competition and technological change, increasingly shorter product life cycles, more awareness of the natural environment, increasing interdependence among the economies of different countries, and political turbulence. Organizational turnarounds follow each other at a seemingly exponential pace.

The character of the change varies—from choosing another location (e.g. Swedish companies physically have been locating in other countries because of restricted markets at home, Western-owned companies have been locating in

International Handbook of Selection and Assessment, Edited by N. Anderson and P. Herriot.
© 1997 John Wiley & Sons Ltd.

developing countries), to merging and taking over (e.g. owing to the development of a single European market); from expanding by deciding for other products, other markets, to appointing new top level management, etc. Often these changes happen in combination. Restructuring the organization and introducing a new organizational culture with an accompanying competency profile for the personnel are two of the consequences—and so, frequently, are losses of jobs (see Sparrow, Chapter 17, and Jackson, Chapter 31, in this volume).

The severity of the change ranges from quite predictable and gradual transitions to violent crises which might even threaten the existence of the organization. As we shall see (in the section on types of major change), the severity can be indicated by the type of learning involved (cf. Jansen and De Jong, 1996).

The worldwide increased mobility of organizations is mirrored by an increased mobility of workers and society, and a faster pace of life in general.

This chapter addresses the following issues. The second section deals with major changes that are characteristic of the 1990s in the conditions outside of and within organizations. The next section focuses on the impact of organizational turnaround on selection and assessment. The fourth section, on the other hand, discusses the impact of assessment and selection on (facilitating) turnaround. The final section contains several concluding observations.

TYPES OF CHANGES

This section takes up two themes. First, attention is given to five clear trends of organizational turnaround that have an impact on the field of human resource management. These five are:

- internationalization
- merging and taking over
- societal changes in the competency-profile
- development of HRM-policies to cope with permanent change
- reduction of government influence.

Secondly, three more general types of change are discussed according to which the various turbulences can be classified.

Five trends

Businesses go international and global

One of the main trends, on which relatively much research is done, is the growing internationalization of organizations and industries. There is, for instance, the growing importance of organizations of the 'international community' (the IMF, the World Bank, and the United Nations), and national industries 'go international' more and more. These developments have boosted a new international direction within the domain of human resource management (HRM), visible in the establishment of new human resources institutes, like, for example, the foundation of the 'Institute for International Human Resources' in 1991 as an offshoot of the American Society for Human Resource Management (SHRM), and the foundation of an international section of the Dutch Foundation for Personnel Management in October 1994 in The Netherlands. A journal exclusively addressed to issues of International HRM, the *International Journal of Human Resource Management*, was first published in 1991.

What impact does the internationalization of an organization have on the management of its human resources? Hollinshead and Leat (1995) reproduce a typology by Adler and Ghador (1990) in which HR approaches depend on three phases in multinational development, the ethnocentric, the polycentric, and the geocentric.

- In the *ethnocentric phase* the assumption is that tried and tested approaches to management can be extended from the country of origin to sites in other countries. Staffing procedures are controlled from the centre and local labour may be recruited.
- In the *polycentric phase* the assumption is that the best thing to do is to place local managers and workers to formulate policies that most realistically reflect local needs. The focus is on decentralization and autonomy of sites. Local staff are recruited and executives are expatriated.
- In the *geocentric*, and according to Hollinshead and Leat probably most successful phase, local and international strengths are combined. National demarcation is ignored, especially for recruitment at managerial levels, and local needs are responded to flexibly but are also transcended.

It can be assumed that most international endeavours at present are in the ethnocentric or the polycentric phases. This present state can be recognized in the attempt by Frölich (1995) to give an impression of the daily difficulties of personnel managers dealing with an international taskforce. Frölich discusses 10 major issues that emerged from interviews with heads of the international personnel management departments of 25 large international Dutch companies. The following are the main issues:

- There is great difficulty in recruiting highly qualified local personnel (commercial top managers) in foreign countries. The foreign local labour market is unknown to the organization; the organization is relatively unknown to the local labour market.
- Turnover under local personnel abroad is high. Many key positions of the business establishments abroad are held by expatriates. Possibilities for local personnel to rise to higher positions therefore are limited.
- There is a shortage of personnel with international experience. Organizations' international expansion often occurs faster than predicted. A consequence is that an 'experience gap' develops within an organization, and that managers with experience are sought for in vain.

- There is a threatening shortage of personnel wanting to work abroad. One of the main reasons for the shortage is the 'dual career' family situation of many personnel.
- The sites abroad experience a lagging behind in their information supply in comparison with the home business. Direct contact is impeded because of the larger distance.
- The level of competence of expatriates returning to the home base often no longer fulfils the job requirements. Because of the haste in making the arrangements for sending out personnel abroad, frequently selection of personnel is a matter of coincidence. That is, personnel who are 'free to go' at the moment the decision has to be taken, will go, while no further thought is given to the career planning of the employee so that problems are postponed.
- Differences between terms of employment and labour contracts (salary, etc.) among expatriates and between expatriates and local employees are viewed as unjust and arbitrary. The more nationalities, divisions, etc. come into the picture, the more the necessity for good coordination is felt.
- Existing knowledge at home is not utilized to introduce the best working methods at the sites abroad. The interviewees see loss of local autonomy experienced by the local management abroad as the main cause.
- Division of the tasks of human resource management between a central and a local part often remains unclear. Centralized decisions and control often become impossible and undesirable.
- International human resource management at home often lacks knowledge in time on developments in international regulations and law.

From these ten points of difficulty it can be seen that complexity, ambiguity and potential conflict accompany personnel issues during internationalization. Several of the points concern the problematic issue of *expatriation*. This matter has been given considerable attention in the HRM literature and forms the main topic of the chapter by Aryee (Chapter 7 in this volume).

A last issue regarding the trend of internationalization is its *politicization* of selection and assessment. The World Bank in Washington, DC, may serve as an example of a pure form of international business as the employed workers at the Bank come from 150 different countries. Weenink (1995) sketches the increasing outside political pressure under which the World Bank has to operate. Criticism from outside pressure groups on the World Bank's policy, and power changes between political parties in funding countries, imply that financial support of the World Bank is constantly a point of discussion. Political issues affect selection and assessment activities to a large extent. Owing to agreements between the 178 member countries of the World Bank, the 'issue of nationality distribution' is one of the leading principles in selecting personnel. Each of the donor countries should be represented among the personnel employed. This leading political principle of not underrepresenting or overrepresenting countries may overshadow the aim of selecting the best candidate. The 'gender issue' only complicates this matter. Traditionally, the World Bank has been a men's bastion. In the recruitment and career planning of personnel, managers' policy in improving the representation of women is being judged.

The politicization tendency of personnel selection and placement issues is recognizable in international bodies in general, e.g. in intergovernmental European Union bodies. Also, it is recognizable in the representation of personnel in power positions after two or more original organizations have gone through a *merger*.

Continuing mergers and takeovers

The flood of mergers and takeovers in the 1990s has not as yet ended. Amalgamations in the world of finance and banking, in the media, and in the world of entertainment bring about larger and larger businesses.

The personnel issue here is the issue of 'who fits in, and where?'. Gilkey (1991) discusses the matter of 'boundary delineation' when businesses blend: 'Since conflicts inevitably arise as the company defines its new identity, it is not possible to determine easily who is and who is not meeting the new criteria' (p. 354). In contrast to stable organizational policies, where membership is clearly defined by means of traditionally used selection procedures, personnel now come in from separate firms into a new merge with roles and relationships that are unclear and insecure in the beginning. Placement and outplacement will form the main issues. To prevent morale declining, it is essential to provide for quick clarity in the role and situation of each employee, e.g. within two months after the merger approval. The answer to the question who will be staying and what will their status be, has to be given fast and clearly. Issues of job security should be addressed promptly and realistically.

Paradoxically, the most loyal long-term employees sometimes are the ones who offer greatest resistance in the new environment. Their attachment to a particular group has to make way for new attachments, which can be a difficult process. A lack of clarity during transition management may lead to 'survivor's guilt'— employees staying may sense that their survival during the turnaround has been something arbitrary and even gained through the misfortune of others (see Jackson, Chapter 31 in this volume). Such emotions may (temporarily) impair performance and lead to a sense of being an accomplice in a brutal power play. Sound transition planning is needed to prevent such effects.

In sum, it is the *procedure* through which personnel issues are handled that needs much attention. Clear-cut and timely communication is essential to the success of the merge.

Societal trends: the competency-profile changes

Interesting research has been done by Moelker (1992) in The Netherlands. The focus was on the question: To what extent has the competency-profile, as required in written newspaper advertisements, changed over the years? The question was asked: In what way are the qualifications of the labour force changing to keep pace with the demands of industry? To answer the question, Moelker collected a sample of 5346 advertisements from three Dutch national daily newspapers from editions published on six Saturdays over the period from 1955 to 1990. He found that the importance of experience and education increased over this period. Moreover, there was a striking rise in the importance of socio-normative qualifications (defined as general competencies, e.g. 'flexibility', 'creativity', 'willingness to cooperate') in comparison with skills and knowledge qualifications. The most asked-for competencies in 1990 were communicative qualities, leadership qualities, independence, flexibility and intelligence.

In the 'future prediction' research of Daniels and Duijzer (1989), using the delphi method, these same five competencies were predicted to be the most important in the year 2000, with flexibility becoming the number one competency. This trend can, for example, be recognized in the reorganization plan of 1995 of the oil multinational Shell: Shell wants to bring about more achievement directedness, flexibility, and a combination of teamwork and individual responsibility among personnel. The aim is to have a faster and more flexible operating organization.

Moelker offers the 'differentialization/generalization' hypothesis to explain the changed competency-profile. The idea is that tasks have become more and more *differentiated* within occupational roles—a trend clearly opposite to Taylorian splitting up of tasks between occupational roles. Occupational roles consist of many more tasks than they used to in the past; Moelker's study shows that the number of tasks mentioned in the advertisements has indeed increased over the years. To integrate the growing diversity of tasks of an occupation, and to account for the changing identity of tasks, more abstract *general* competencies are necessary. Socio-normative qualifications, together with higher required educational levels, nowadays can be seen as generalized competencies and as such meet the necessity of shifting from one task to another faster and more easily. This need for more general competencies is still continuing—it will only grow to accommodate the business demands in the boom of turnarounds.

Explicit business HRM policies: coping with permanently changing environments

Businesses are actively developing HRM strategies for an increasingly changing environment. The 1990s can be described as an unstable environment where there is a scarcity of suitably skilled people and high interdependence between employees. Owing to demographic trends—shortages of younger workers and a gradually ageing workforce—shortages within certain categories of staff (e.g. technical/specialist) can be expected, whereas at the same time the higher level of competition causes greater and higher quality demands.

Rousseau (1995) calls the business strategy of the 1990s 'the strategy of the *responsive organization*'. Where there are increasingly shorter product life cycles, the interdependence between employees will increase and teamwork between and within organizational units will be accentuated. Rousseau notes the tendency within teams to train managers as well as peers in performance appraisal and giving feedback. Several team-oriented organizations commonly use peer appraisal; peers will be better informed about individual contributions than the leader.

To increase the responsivity to dynamic environments, Hollinshead and Leat (1995) see the necessity to formulate increased *flexibility and commitment of personnel* as the broader policy goals for HRM. Citing Guest (1988), Hollinshead and Leat imply that personnel management should be concerned with more than good selection, training and communication. Not only should personnel selection contribute to high quality of work, but it also should focus on the potential for attitudinal commitment to the organization.

Reduced government influence: deregulation and continuing privatization

The need to reduce overheads, owing to financial factors in the Western world, and the rise of capitalism in former communist countries, have the same implication, namely privatization of businesses. The major impact in the domain of HRM often is loss of jobs. Moreover, in former communist countries a total change of (top) management has often taken place and party members have been replaced. During communism, political attitudes and affiliations were more of an influence in selection than were knowledge and skills. Also, disciplinary measures were lacking (for example, there were no sackings). In nearly all cases, privatization mostly implies more organizational freedom regarding personnel decisions: a more flexible use of financial incentives and promotions, as well as disciplinary actions, cause more differentiation in the personnel reward system.

Three general types of major changes

At a more abstract level, the various described turbulences within and surrounding an organization can be classified according to three general levels of change (Golembiewski, Billingsley and Yeager, 1976):

- *alpha change*: a change in the level of an 'existential state' given both a constant measuring instrument and a constant conceptual domain;
- *beta change*: changes in both the level of an 'existential state' and recalibration of the measuring instrument, while the conceptual domain remains unchanged;
- *gamma change*: reconceptualization of the entire domain, fundamental change in the perspective or framework from which reality is perceived.

For instance, when only the circumstances change without a modification in the way employees perceive and interpret the organization and its environment, we speak of an alpha change (e.g. a takeover, or replacement of the CEO). However, if employees, in reaction to some kind of alpha change, are inclined to employ other levels of the same criteria for the individual interpretation of the organizational context, we speak of a beta change (e.g. finding the existing, 'traditional' criterion of quantity of production *more* important and consequently judging the organization from that point of view). Finally, it is possible that the very 'interpretational scheme' of the employees involved in a beta change is modified (e.g. stressing quality instead of quantity, or perceiving the work as a service business instead of as mass production). Essential in the latter case, which is denoted as a gamma change, are changes in values, in culture, in what the organization and its employees feel to be important. The latter change can be at stake, e.g. in mergers where to a great extent a new organization emerges from the original ones.

Crucial to this and other models (see, for example, Argyris and Schön, 1978, for a reduction to two levels of change or learning, or Porras and Silvers, 1991, for an elaboration to four levels of change) is the distinction between a variable and its environment, i.e. between that what is measured (the 'existential state') and the system in which the measurement takes place (consisting of the measurement instrument and the context of the act of measurement, i.e. the aim of the measurement). An example will make this distinction clear. Consider the following problem (taken from an actual assessment centre In-Basket):

In order to accomplish something in which another department of your organization is involved, you have already tried several times to use the official communication channels. So far you have not succeeded. However, you happen to know someone who works in that department, and who would be able to help you to get 'the thing done'. What would you do?

Generally, managers solve this problem by directly contacting the former acquaintance and solving the problem in this informal and direct 'hands-on' way. Only a few managers use quite a different approach. According to these, mostly top-level, managers the real problem is that the communication channels in this organization obviously are blocked. By directly contacting the former acquaintance, this problem will only be reinforced. In the second type of solution, the nature of the problem has changed. What the second type of manager does is to *reframe* the problem (and by that they in fact perform a gamma type of change). This suggests a point that is confirmed by research: effective managers 'read' a problem situation in order to determine (in this order):

1. the *criterion* that 'really' is at stake,
2. the *demand cues* of the situation,
3. the *skill mix* that is needed to solve the problem.

This means that ineffective managers are not sufficiently able

1a. To *frame* the problem: What type of problem do I really have here? A social problem, or a commercial problem, or a technical problem, or maybe not a problem at all?

Having answered the first question:

2a. To *read* the problem: What kind of behavior is asked of me?

Having answered the second question:

3a. To *use* the skills which are needed with regard to *this* problem. Am I competent enough in view of what (I think that) is asked of me?

The first question deals with the context of management, the second and third with 'states' within a given context. Clearly, turnaround managers mainly will have to deal with framing problems, i.e. with sense-making and re-interpreting changed circumstances—gamma-type changes.

IMPACT ON ASSESSMENT AND SELECTION

In this section we first report on research that has been done on personal requirements for managing a turnaround effectively, and managing personnel having to 'deal with' turnarounds. In the preceding section we argued that, in general, a turnaround implies that leaders are required to be effective in another way. That implies that other competencies, maybe even quite another style of leadership, are needed. Secondly, the impact on procedures of personnel assessment and selection will be dealt with.

Content of leadership dimensions

Transformational leadership

There is much evidence that the characteristics of the *personality* of the (top-level) manager can be determining for the *performance* of the total organization (Slater, 1989; Smith, Carson and Alexander, 1984). Especially in the case when a turbulent situation requires beta or gamma types of changes, it appears that personal characteristics can have a decisive influence. However, this research also shows that especially low-quality gamma types of reactions of, in particular top-level, managers can lead to a rapid 'self-destruction' of the organization.

A manager who proceeds according to the principles of the 'path goal' theory of leadership (House, 1971), that is who

- clarifies means–end expectations and
- is able to generate satisfying outcomes to employees

is denoted as a *transactional leader*.

In contrast to this type of leader we also find in the literature the notion of the *transformational* leader. In a famous article by Zaleznik (1977), functional–organizational management becomes completely equivalent to transactional management, and personal leadership to transformational management. Some characteristics of transformational leaders are (Bryman, 1992; Koopman and House, 1995):

- Leaders have a 'vision'; they are able to formulate their goals and tasks in an idealistic way.
- They very strongly believe in themselves.
- Leaders put very high demands both on themselves and on employees. Thus, leaders are 'authoritarian' in the sense that they load the weight of their work-related tasks onto employees.

- Leaders are communicatively very strong, and in that way are able to 'empower' employees. Merely by a leader's inspiring presence employees feel stronger and are able to deliver better performances.
- Typical personal characteristics are 'compelling' eyes and outstanding oratorical abilities. Often leaders are perceived as handsome.

Where transactional leaders are oriented towards the behavior and the performance of employees and aim to comply with *existing* goals of both organization and employees, 'charismatic and transformational leadership theories focus on the followers: their emotional responses to the leader' (Fiedler and House, 1994, p. 102). A transformational leader wants to *change* the goals of the organization and of its employees. As a consequence, transformational leadership effects both high performance and high satisfaction levels among employees (Fiedler and House, 1994, p. 106). That is the reason why, in general, employees have strong positive feelings about transformational leaders. These leaders are able (or are perceived to be able) to fulfil a number of important emotional needs of employees. All of this, of course, makes a transformational leader an important change-agent in the event of major turnarounds. The explicit integration of the two research lines on transactional and transformational leadership is presently the subject of study (cf. Koopman and House, 1995).

A special case of transformational leadership is the *charismatic leader*. In situations of crisis a person emerges with a radical solution who attracts a number of very loyal followers and realizes his mission in a successful way. House, Spangler and Woycke (1991) conclude, after a study into the leadership motive of American presidents, that personality and charisma really do have an effect. In spite of societal and organizational restraints, there appears to remain a sometimes considerable opportunity for the personality of the leader. Since the 1980s the concept of the charismatic leader has also been studied in the context of organizations. As was stated in the introductory section, the main reason for this is that the internal and external turbulence of organizations has increased to a level where the reaction time of the organization is less than the rate of change. In such a case, only an a priori anticipation to *expected* changes makes it possible to cope with turbulence. Needed for this is a type of leadership that 'ensures' that employees want and are able to think and act more or less in an autonomous way. Charismatic leadership has been suggested as the answer to this need (the terms 'charismatic' and 'transformational' are often used as synonyms; see, for example, Fiedler and House, 1994, p. 102f).

Personal characteristics of the 'turnaround leader'

Theories about 'charismatic leadership' risk succumbing to the (fatal) attraction of the 'great man theory of leadership' (Wrightsman, 1972, p. 491). According to that theory, *everything* depends on this 'great man'. In fact, the power of 'great men' is determined by both the mastery and adequate application of situationally specific skills, and some general dispositions. And in addition, by being in the right place at the right time. Nevertheless, the study by House, Spangler and Woycke (1991) discussed above shows that the *influence of personal characteristics is not to be underestimated*. The personality of top-level managers can have an important effect on organizational behavior and organizational effectiveness (Miller and Toulouse, 1986). For that reason empirical research into 'leadership traits' has proliferated over the last few years. In this section we discuss a number of recurring findings from this research.

What are the personal characteristics necessary to manage a turnaround effectively? Research by Tichy and Devanna (1986, in Yukl, 1994, p. 360f) shows that leadership during turnaround should be *aware of the need to change*. Especially when changes in the organizational environment are gradual and the organization is still prosperous, leaders often do not recognize the threats to their organization. Environmental awareness and *persuasiveness in convincing* management to carry through a (major) transformation is an essential leadership asset. In carrying through a major turnaround, the leader needs to inspire the workers. Tichy and Devanna found that, in contrast to the single visionary entrepreneur starting a new business, the presence of one visionary leader is not enough for turnarounds in large organizations to be successful. A group of key people in the organization should support the ideas for change; the ideas should be common property.

In institutionalizing organizational change, Tichy and Devanna found that effective leaders had the following attributes:

- they saw themselves as change agents,
- they were *prudent risk-takers*, believed in people and were *sensitive* to their needs (cf. Tjosfold, 1984, 1990),
- they had a set of core values to guide their behavior,
- they were flexible and *open to learning* from experience,
- they had *cognitive* skills and believed in disciplined thinking and the necessity for careful analysis of problems (this is confirmed by results from studies by Janis, 1989, and Hunter and Rothstein Hirsch, 1987), and
- they were *visionaries*.

The characteristic of *prudent risk-taking* is confirmed by the overview of McClelland and Boyatzis (1982), which suggests that effective turnaround management requires *high levels of activity inhibition* and *self-control* in order to stick to agreed-upon procedures, not to react to incidents and to proceed steadily in a way that is acceptable to all parties involved in the process. This does not preclude the situation in which immediate action is necessary before acceptance is obtained. In such cases acceptance, i.e. commitment, has to be obtained after the fact. But also in these cases, the above-mentioned characteristics are needed.

A related study is research by Kilduff and Day (1994), which shows that career mobility is enhanced by being able to 'self-monitor'. Persons who are high on 'self-monitoring' are very sensitive to what others expect of them, so they are very sensitive to role expectations. Since they are so sensitive to external cues, to a high degree they react in a situationally specific way. However, persons who are low on 'self-monitoring' are almost exclusively internally guided in their behaviors by the peculiarities of their own affective and emotional situation.

Finally, Lewin and Stephens (1994, p. 190) stress the importance of the factor 'openness' in the sense of having both broad interests and a high level of moral reasoning.

Hogan, Curphy and Hogan (1994) conclude, after a review of research into the personality of effective leaders, that these are characterized by a mixture of all the Big Five personality factors (cf. Barrick and Mount, 1991):

- They are responsible, possess personal integrity, are achievement oriented and possess internal work norms (conscientious).
- They have social prominence, are dominant, sociable, oriented to status, assertive, energetic, verbally fluent, decisive, and risk-prone (extrovert).
- They are diplomatic, cooperative, show empathy, are friendly and socially easily approachable, give social support, and have a basic trust in other people (agreeable).
- They are self-confident, emotionally controlled, possess self-acceptance, independence, stress-resistance, and have an internal locus of control (stable).

Only the factor openness is not present in this overview, which underlines the still unclear evidence about the contribution of this factor to effectiveness as a turn-around leader.

Janis (1989) hypothesizes which *lack of personality characteristics* might cause failure of effective leadership during organizational periods of crisis. A failure in leadership may be the consequence of:

- Underestimating the importance of a threat leading to the simple cognitive rule 'continue business-as-usual', caused by a lack of conscientiousness and of openness and by a cool, calm coping style and by chronic optimism.
- Over-reacting to a threat by, cognitively, experiencing inherent difficulties in solving the problem and a lack of time to find a high quality solution, caused by chronic low self-confidence/efficacy and chronic pessimism in solving the problem.
- Over-reacting to a threat by experiencing affiliative difficulties in gaining acceptance of the policy chosen, experiencing the threat of retaliation, and loss of social support in the organization, caused by a strong need for social approval, a strong need for power and status, a high dependency on a cohesive group of fellow executives, and beliefs about the readiness of other powerholders in the organization to inflict retaliation.
- Over-reacting to information that might cause personal constraints by following self-serving, egocentric rules. Strong personal motives or strong emotions may be aroused. Janis seeks the causes for this type of reaction in a lack of conscientiousness, negativism/ambivalence towards the organization, a low stress tolerance, a lack of perceived control, an externalized anger-coping style and chronic hostility towards opponents.

Another important personality factor of leadership is *locus of control*. This refers to the degree to which someone believes either that he or she is in control of his or her behavior, that he/she is 'in charge' of his/her behavior ('internal' locus of control), or that he/she is under the influence of the environment ('external' locus of control), so that things 'just happen' to him/her. Locus of control would be predictive of task-orientedness, stress-resistance, the ability to take calculated risks, and intrinsic motivation. Top-level managers who are high on the internal locus of control are more effective than their colleagues who are more externally controlled.

There is some debate about whether locus of control is either a general personal disposition, or depends purely on the situation. Boone and De Brabander (1993), for instance, take a dispositional stance, stating that persons can be characterized by 'generalized control expectancies' as a result of fundamental and stable individual differences. But Hodgkinson (1993) agrees to a situational concept of locus of control. According to this author, it is necessary to distinguish different, situationally specific, 'strategic control expectancies'. In that case, locus of control would not be a stable personal characteristic because it is influenced by work experiences.

With respect to the motive pattern of leaders, Lord and Maher (1991) mention a high *need for achievement*, i.e. they are keen to achieve personal successes by their own efforts. Fiedler and House (1994, pp. 103–105) discuss a number of studies from which it appears that transformational leaders are high on both the need for achievement and the *need for power*, i.e. they want to personally influence others in their behaviors. According to Winter (1993, p. 533) several years of leadership research have yielded the following picture of managers who are high in need for power. They (both men and women!) are confrontational in cases of negotiation, and competitive, but at the same time also charismatic and able to create an inspiring working climate. Finally, House and Baetz (1979) report that effective leadership requires both motives.

To really be effective, the leader must also be able to translate these, and other, general dispositions into situationally specific behaviors, i.e. into specific competencies and skills (Arnold, Robertson and Cooper, 1991, p. 228). For instance, it appears that at high management levels, where one does not achieve personal success 'of one's own' but exclusively works through others, a high need for achievement impedes being effective as a manager. But in technical–professional and lower management positions, being high on need for achievement correlates with successful leadership (Spangler and House, 1991, p. 3).

The various leadership characteristics discussed so far correspond to the attributes by which persons are recognized as 'leaders' in their environment. Thus, interestingly, attribution of leadership takes place by perception of personal characteristics that, generally, also appear related to actual effectiveness as a leader (Lord and Maher, 1991). And, it also appears that leaders primarily fail because of 'an overriding personality defect' (Hogan, Curphy and Hogan, 1994, p. 499), which can be described by adjectives such as arrogant, revengeful, unreliable, insensitive, overambitious, over-controlled and compulsive.

Procedures of selection and assessment during turnarounds

Classic personnel selection and assessment (e.g. as described by Guion, 1991) basically presupposes several placid and stable circumstances—circumstances that are virtually non-existent in phases of organizational turnarounds.

First, personnel decisions are classically described as job-oriented and not person-oriented, i.e. it is an existing job that is thought necessary to be filled and for which people are to be hired. On the contrary, during turnarounds one often has to decide where already hired people are to be placed. Such placement decisions will be more difficult and diverse.

During turnarounds, where many staff will have been sacked by the necessity of downsizing (see Jackson, Chapter 31 in this volume) the remainder of the staff will often be doing twice the work. For these members of staff it is likely that work role ambiguity, role conflicts and status problems will appear. In general, high demands combined with little control will be the outcomes for the survivors of a merger or takeover. Under such pressures, personnel react differently. The following personality characteristics have been found to relate to the way work pressures are handled: *hardiness, neuroticism,* and *type A/type B personality* (see, for example, Buunk and De Wolff, 1988, for an overview). Hardiness comprises the feeling that one controls external events, that one has a deep feeling of involvement and goal-directedness, and that one is flexible in adjusting to unexpected changes. The work-output of hardy personnel will suffer less during organizational change. The same can be said for personnel with a stable, non-neurotic personality. Personnel with type A behavior (characterized by, for example, excitability, impatience, lack of time and competitiveness) seem to be influenced by work stress more than personnel with type B behavior (more patient and calmer).

In terms of a *person–environment fit,* more hardy, stable and type B-like personalities fit better into the pressurized conditions of organizational turnaround. These findings imply that under stressful turnaround circumstances not only regular assessment of, for instance, knowledge and skills, is needed, but also personality assessment. Personality questionnaires and role-playing exercises in which time pressure, role ambiguity and role conflict are simulated, are methods that can be used here.

A final remark is that effect of type A/type B is mitigated by the type of effect accompanying the type A/type B behaviors. Type A behavior may be accompanied by positive arousal (enthusiasm, vitality) but also by negative arousal (nervousness, irritability) (Cooper and Marshall, 1978; Maes, 1986; Spence, Helmreich, and Pred, 1987). In the latter case, the effect of stressors will be more severe.

Secondly, during turnaround the position of *top management* in many cases is questioned, often resulting in its (partial) replacement, and in replacement of the CEO. The overview by Bedeian (1987) of research between 1975 and 1985 shows that replacement of top management can be a necessary condition for a constructive reaction to an imminent fall of the organization. New management can bring a new set of organizational values. The new managers are not committed to old behavioral repertoires that are not successful; they bring in their own 'antecedents' in the form of personality, intelligence and ambition.

The issue here is a politically complex one of (re)placement of management, reaching beyond the technical aspects of personnel selection and into political bargaining matters. Ideal turnaround leadership characteristics have been discussed in the section on leadership dimensions; the question remains: To what extent can such leadership be attained? The result of a merger of two companies, for instance, can be a troublesome compromise between both companies. Such a compromise may, for instance, contain an equal sharing of management positions between the two former businesses and a team of two CEOs. In general, the resulting agreement will reflect the power relationship between the partners of a merger or takeover. A strong and stable company taking over a weak one has the ability to impose its own management and thus its own culture on the other company. The difficulty for the players in the field is to prevent power issues from overriding their efforts towards high quality management.

As is mentioned in the next section, assessment procedures (assessment centers) may help to develop a homogeneous set of organizational innovative values among top management. As a lead for such assessment exercises, Farr and Ford's model of individual motivations to change (Farr and Ford, 1990) may be used. An individual's motivation to change is seen by this model as affected by four factors: the perceived need for change, one's self-efficacy, the perceived payoff from change, and one's technical knowledge. By trying to influence these four factors, management can be stimulated to adapt the new values.

Thirdly, within personnel management, predictions and selection decisions generally are thought to be dependent upon well-executed job analyses in which the components of the job are identified and described and from which a clear-cut description of required competencies can be deduced. During turnarounds, on the other hand, it can very well be that the job for which one engages personnel does not as yet exist. In that case, *job analysis* is more adequately defined as a— perhaps difficult—*planning process*.

Fourthly, in many occupations and industries traditions have developed with respect to typical or accepted means of recruiting and selecting. For instance, the recruitment of executives traditionally brings with it the expenditure of large sums of money on consultants or search forms to determine the suitability of candidates (cf. Rynes, 1991). When turnarounds become the order of the day, existing traditions should be questioned and existing recruitment and selection techniques might need to be used differently. For example, one of the techniques that is more important during phases of turnaround is the *realistic job preview*, because this type of interview is directed towards employee retention rather than employee attraction. Employee retention is an important goal for organizations-in-change: commitment to an organization, notwithstanding the turbulence it is going through, becomes an essential target. Rynes (1991) poses several hypotheses raised to explain the strength of the realistic job preview. One of these is the 'commitment hypothesis': people develop stronger commitment to organizations that give them the information they need to make fully informed job choices. The result is self-selection and better work adjustment. Another hypothesis described is the 'coping hypothesis': 'realistic information allows new hires to devise anticipatory strategies for dealing with problems likely to arise on the job' (Rynes, 1991, p. 423).

Finally, the general view is that personnel selection should be evaluated by job-relevant criteria, but these are quite difficult to define when what will be done is still unclear. Therefore, very specific sample ('situational') validity no longer works during turnarounds. That is to say, the very change of functions, job tasks, organizational structure and cultural aspects implies that prediction and selection can no longer rely so much on the content and sample validity of assessment instruments. Instead, validity information of (assessment center) instruments is to be based on some sort of construct validity, or some sort of 'generalized sample validity'. In this regard, one can pose the question whether very specific situations can be pointed out which are and will be important anyhow during turnaround, e.g. 'having to deal with unexpected circumstances', 'having to deal with ambiguity', 'having to work in (new and changing) teams' or 'having to deal with permanent change'. In our view, such situational descriptions are so abstract in character that they in fact are generalized constructs—to be translated into required qualifications and competencies like stress tolerance (see the first point in this section), flexibility and openness.

General qualifications—e.g. flexibility, stress tolerance, intelligence, cooperation, and openness—are valued during turnaround. These general personal qualifications form the best fit to turnaround environments. Classic personality and intelligence tests may be suited to measure these qualifications on an individual level. The *assessment of groups* (assessment centers) forms a necessary addition, in which qualifications can be measured at the group level instead of individually. At the group level individual qualifications, for instance, can be translated into—concerning cooperation—team support and team building, and—concerning openness, flexibility and intelligence—goal change and goal emphasis.

FACILITATING TURNAROUND: USING ASSESSMENT PROCEDURES

Existing assessment techniques can be used in specific ways to stimulate organizational change. Some techniques fit in very well. Next to the already mentioned use of realistic job previews, some examples are:

- *Peer rating.* In the context of performance appraisal, rating by one's team instead of by one's manager becomes an important technique. By changing and increasing interdependencies between organizational units, a manager will not be able to manage an 'overview' of an individual's performance. A side-effect of peer rating is an increased commitment of the worker to the team (cf. Rousseau, 1995).
- The installation of *new procedures* for personnel *appraisal* in order to condition a new style of management, and introduction of an *assessment center* with the explicit target of creating commitment and 'educating' top-level managers in the new set of business values and the future vision of the company (cf. Jansen and Van Wees, 1994; see also Fletcher, Chapter 28 in this volume).
- *More extensive personnel feedback* and appraisal techniques *per se*. In chaotic periods clarifying expectations are important, so that people receive a benchmark against which to operate. Guidelines on how to succeed and help to identify career paths stimulate employees' confidence in and identification with their employer.

CONCLUSION

We have seen that five trends can be connected with organizational turnaround: internationalization and globalization of organizations, mergers and takeovers, societal changes in the competency-profile of applicants, active organizational HRM policies to cope with a permanently changing environments, and government deregulation.

The overall effect of these trends is a tendency towards the requirement of a more general competency-profile for personnel, containing qualifications like intelligence, organizational commitment, independence and communicative competencies.

At a more abstract level, the strength of organizational turbulence can be classified into so-called alpha, beta or gamma change. Gamma change is the most fundamental change, implying a total reconceptualization of organizational reality.

Turnaround managers often will have to deal with a re-interpretation of reality. Transformational leadership is suggested as an effective way of leading turnaround. Environmental awareness, persuasiveness, internal locus of control and prudent risk-taking, among other things, have been found to be important personality factors of leaders of organizational change.

Turnaround issues of assessment and selection will more explicitly revolve around placement decisions, attempts to capture requirements of future jobs, and the retention of personnel by turning attention to organizational commitment. Assessment and selection techniques that will be relevant during turnaround are realistic job previews, peer rating, assessment centers to condition a new style of management, and extensive personnel feedback.

REFERENCES

Adler, N.J. and Ghador, F. (1990). Strategic human resource management: A global perspective. In R. Pieper (ed.), *Human Resource Management: An International Comparison.* Berlin: De Gruyter.

Argyris, C. and Schön, D. (1978). *Organizational Learning: A Theory of Action Perspective.* Reading, MA: Addison Wesley.

Arnold, J., Robertson, I.T. and Cooper, C.L. (1991). *Work Psychology. Understanding Human Behavior in the Work Place.* London: Pitman.

Barrick, M.R. and Mount, M.K. (1991). The Big Five personality dimensions and job performance: A meta-analysis. *Personnel Psychology,* **44**, 1–26.

Bedeian, A.G. (1987). Organization theory: current controversies, issues, and directions. In: C.L. Cooper and I.T. Robertson (eds.), *International Review of Industrial and Organizational Psychology,* Chichester: John Wiley.

Boone, C. and de Brabander, B. (1993). Generalized vs. specific locus of control expectancies of chief executive officers. *Strategic Management Journal,* **14**, 619–625.

Bryman, A. (1992). *Charisma and Leadership in Organizations.* Newbury Park, CA: Sage.

Buunk, A.P. and de Wolff, Ch.J. (1988). Sociaal psychologische aspecten van stress op het werk [Social-psychological aspects of stress at work]. In P.J.D. Drenth, Hk. Thierry and Ch.J. de Wolff (eds.), *Nieuw Handboek Arbeids- en Organisatiepsychologie [New Handbook Work and Organizational Psychology],* pp. 3.8-1–3.8-50. Deventer: Van Loghum Slaterus.

Cooper, C.L. and Marshall, J. (1978). Sources of managerial and white collar stress. In: C.L. Cooper and R. Payne (eds.), *Stress at Work,* pp. 81–105. New York: John Wiley.

Daniels, J.J.M.C. and Duijzer, G. (1989). *Persoonskenmerken van de Arbeidskracht in 2000; Een Delphi Onderzoek. [Biographical Characteristics of Labourers in 2000; a Delphi research].* Onderzoeksverslag [Research report]. Amsterdam: Universiteit van Amsterdam.

Farr, J.L. and Ford, C.M. (1990). Individual innovation. In M.A. West and J.L. Farr (eds.), *Innovation and Creativity at Work*, pp. 63–80. Chichester: John Wiley.

Fiedler, F.E. and House, R.J. (1994). Leadership theory and research: A report of progress. In: C.L. Cooper and I.T. Robertson (eds.), *Key Reviews in Managerial Psychology*, pp. 97–116. New York: John Wiley.

Frölich, J. (1995). De business issues in internationaal personeelsmanagement [The business issues in international personnel management]. *In-, door- en uitstroom van personeel [In, through, and out flow of personnel]*, **2** (4/5), 17–22.

Gilkey, R. (1991). The psychodynamics of upheaval: Intervening in merger and acquisition transitions. In M.F.R. Kets de Vries (ed.), *Organizations on the Couch*, pp. 331–360. San Francisco, CA: Jossey-Bass.

Golembiewski, R.T., Billingsley, K. and Yeager, S. (1976). Measuring change and persistence in human affairs: Types of change generated by OD designs. *Journal of Applied Behavioral Science*, **12**, 133–157.

Guest, D.E. (1988). *Human Resource Management: Is It Worth Taking Seriously?* London: First annual Sear lecture at the London School of Economics.

Guion, R.M. (1991). Personnel assessment, selection, and placement. In M.D. Dunnette and L.M. Hough (eds.), *Handbook of Industrial and Organizational Psychology*, 2nd edn, vol. 2, pp. 327–398. Palo Alto, CA: Consulting Psychologists Press.

Hodgkinson, G.P. (1993). Doubts about the conceptual and empirical status of context-free and form-specific control expectancies: A reply to Boone and De Brabander. *Strategic Management Journal*, **14**, 627–731.

Hogan, R., Curphy, G.J. and Hogan, J. (1994). What we know about leadership. Effectiveness and personality. *American Psychologist*, **49** (6), 493–504.

Hogan, E.A. and Overmyer-Day, L. (1994). The psychology of mergers and acquisitions. In C.L. Cooper and I.T. Robertson (eds.), *International Review of Industrial and Organizational Psychology*, Vol. 9, pp. 247–281. Chichester: John Wiley.

Hollinshead, G. and Leat, M. (1995). Human Resource Management. An International and Comparative Perspective. London: Pitman.

House, R.J. (1971). A path goal theory of leadership effectiveness. *Administrative Science Quarterly*, **16**, 321–338.

House, R.J. and Baetz, M.L. (1979). Leadership: Some empirical generalizations and new research directions. In: B.M. Staw (ed.), *Research in Organizational Behavior*, Vol. I. Greenwich, CT: JAI Press.

House, R.J., Spangler, W.D. and Woycke, J. (1991). Personality and charisma in the U.S. presidency: A psychological theory of leader effectiveness. *Administrative Science Quarterly*, **36**, 364–396.

Hunter, J.E. and Rothstein Hirsch, H. (1987). Applications of meta-analysis. In: C.L. Cooper and I.T. Robertson (eds.), *International Review of Industrial and Organizational Psychology*, pp. 221–258. New York: John Wiley.

Janis, I.L. (1989). *Crucial Decisions*. New York: The Free Press.

Jansen, P.G.W. and de Jong, R.D. (1996). Implementing organizational change: Six steps and a case. In: M. Prokop (ed.), *The 1996 Annual: Developing Human Resources*. San Diego, CA: Pfeiffer & Company.

Jansen, P.G.W. and van Wees, L.L.G.M. (1994). Conditions for internal entrepreneurship. *Journal of Management Development*, **13** (9), 34–51.

Kilduff, M. and Day, D.V. (1994). Do chameleons get ahead? The effects of self-monitoring on managerial careers. *Academy of Management Journal*, **37**, 1047–1060.

Koopman, P.L. and House, R.J. (1995). Charismatisch leiderschap in organisaties [Charismatic leadership in organizations]. In R. van der Vlist, H. Steensma, A. Kampermann and J. Gerrichhauzen (eds.), *Handboek Leiderschap in Arbeidsorganisaties [Handbook of Leadership in Work Organizations]*, pp. 39–52. Utrecht: Lemma.

Lewin, A.Y. and Stephens, C.U. (1994). CEO attitudes as determinants of organization design: An integrated model. *Organization Studies*, **15** (2), 183–212.

Lord, R.G. and Maher, K.J. (1991). *Leadership and Information Processing. Linking Perceptions and Performance.* Boston, MA: Unwin Hyman.

Maes, S. (1986). Gezondheidspsychologie: de rol van gedrag in gezondheid en ziekte [Health psychology: The role of behavior in health and illness]. *Gedrag & Gezondheid [Behavior and Health]*, **14** (2), 49–56.

McClelland, D.C. and Boyatzis, R.E. (1982). Leadership motive pattern and long-term success in management. *Journal of Applied Psychology*, **67**, 737–743.

Miller, D. and Toulouse, J.M. (1986). Chief executive personality and corporate strategy and structure in small firms. *Management Science*, **32** (11), 1389–1409.

Moelker, R. (1992). Zou hij onze nieuwe werknemer kunnen zijn? [Could he be our new employee?], Academic Dissertation. Erasmus Universiteit, Rotterdam.

Porras, J.I. and Silvers, R.C. (1991). Organization development and transformation. *Annual Review of Psychology*, **42**, 51–78.

Rousseau, D. (1995). *Psychological Contracts in Organizations.* Thousand Oaks, CA: Sage.

Rynes, S.L. (1991). Recruitment job choice, and post-hire consequences: A call for new research directions. In M.D. Dunnette and L.M. Hough (eds.), *Handbook of Industrial and Organizational Psychology*, 2nd edn, vol. 2, pp. 399–444. Palo Alto, CA: Consulting Psychologists Press.

Slater, S.F. (1989). The influence of managerial style on business unit performance. *Journal of Management*, **3**, 142–165.

Smith, J.E., Carson, K.P. and Alexander, R.A. (1984). Leadership: It can make a difference. *Academy of Management Journal*, **27**, 765–776.

Spangler, W.D. and House, R.J. (1991). Presidential effectiveness and the leadership motive profile. *Journal of Personality and Social Psychology*, **60**, 1–17.

Spence, J.T., Helmreich, R.L. and Pred, R.S. (1987). Impatience versus achievement strivings in the Type A pattern: Differential effects on students' health and academic achievement. *Journal of Applied Psychology*, **72**, 522–528.

Tichy, N.M. and Devanna, M.A. (1986). *The Transformational Leader.* New York: John Wiley.

Tjosfold, D. (1984). Effects of leader warmth and directiveness on subordinate performance on a subsequent task. *Journal of Applied Psychology*, **69**, 422–427.

Tjosfold, D. (1990). Making a technological innovation work. *Human Relations*, **43**, 1117–1131.

Weenink, H.C. (1995). De Wereldbank en Internationaal HRM [The World Bank and International HRM]. *In-, Door-, en Uitstroom van Personeel [In, Through, and Out Flow of Personnel]*, **2** (4/5), 77–90.

Winter, D.G. (1993). Power, affiliation, and war: Three tests of a motivational model. *Journal of Personality and Social Psychology*, **65**, 532–545.

Wrightsman, L.S. (1972). *Social Psychology in the Seventies.* Belmont, CA: Wadsworth.

Yukl, G. (1994). *Leadership in Organizations*, 3rd edn. Englewood Cliffs, NJ: Prentice-Hall.

Zaleznik, A. (1977). Managers and leaders, are they different? *Harvard Business Review*, **55**, 67–78.

Chapter 13

Criterion Measures and the Criterion Dilemma

ROBERT M. GUION

Bowling Green State University, Bowling Green, OH, USA

Set aside the many meanings that the word 'criterion' can have. Ignore (for this chapter) its use in such terms as 'criterion-referenced measurement'. Limit its meaning here to its use in the phrase, 'criterion-related validity'. So limited, a criterion is a variable to be explained or predicted, analogous to the dependent variable in a psychological experiment.

Even in that limited sense, ambiguity remains. Some criteria are construct-related, others are job-related; many are both. Some people call for a third category which I will call candidate-related, i.e. criteria of candidate well-being (see, for example, Drenth, 1989, p. 9; Schuler, Farr and Smith, 1993). Construct-related criteria are used in hypotheses about construct validity; they are explicitly relevant to the theory of the construct. Job-related criteria are measures of job behavior or performance (or results) important to an organization; they may be predicted from test scores, and the predictions enable specific organizational improvements. Predictor scores and job-related criteria are different, not redundant, constructs (Austin and Villanova, 1992, p. 838). This chapter focuses on job-related criteria, but the issues it discusses apply also to defining and measuring candidate-related criteria such as job satisfaction or stress avoidance.

Job-related criteria (from here on, simply criteria) classify or quantitatively measure performance, behavior, events, or outcomes deemed important to the organization, or to parts of it, and to decisions to be made. They are measures by which we can gauge the goodness of various interventions, from employee selection procedures to work place redesign to organizational development programs. They represent values. The world, we were told as children, is full of a number of things, and some are more important than others. Choosing a criterion to explain

International Handbook of Selection and Assessment, Edited by N. Anderson and P. Herriot.
© 1997 John Wiley & Sons Ltd.

or predict or ultimately to improve is (or should be) saying, in effect, 'this is important; improving it is valuable in this organization'. A criterion may be effectiveness in doing a job or task. It may be a pattern of behavior considered a prerequisite to effectiveness (e.g. planning before acting) or a source of ineffectiveness (e.g. perseveration in old ways when conditions have changed), behavior making a generally good work environment (e.g. helping others; Borman and Motowidlo, 1993), or to desired (or unwanted) results of behavior (e.g. production, scrap, new business, loss of customers)—in short, a variable or condition important enough to be predicted, improved, or corrected. Unfortunately, researchers and organization human resources specialists alike continue to pick and to use criterion measures with remarkably little thought a half century after Jenkins (1946) complained of researchers assuming that criteria were God-given or 'just to be found lying about'.

Maybe some would argue that criterion choice matters little, if at all. They might, perhaps, point to meta-analyses, particularly of selection test validities, where validity generalizes despite the variety of criterion measures reported. On the other hand, I argue that it matters a great deal, and that it matters increasingly as organizations increasingly recognize diverse constituencies and diverse areas for improvement or correction. A criterion valued from a marketing perspective may complement, conflict with, or simply differ from one valued from a production perspective—or from a public relations perspective. Business organizations of an earlier time may have operated solely according to internal values, but today's business environment requires considering the interests and concerns of a variety of publics. A decision that improves production at a unit level may also have external consequences, such as environmental effects, or effects on community employment levels; a decision leading to individual improvement may have external consequences on workers' families. It is important to consider the variety of possible outcomes of interventions so that unwanted outcomes can be anticipated, and corrective action taken, before they become problems. It is equally important to understand the individual and group behavior patterns that lead to important outcomes so they may be encouraged or changed.

CRITERION MEASURES FREQUENTLY USED

Behavior or performance can be observed and rated. Events can be recorded and counted. Results of performance can be counted or weighed or compared with standards. The counts and ratings and comparisons traditionally are accepted as givens, with 'obvious' organizational value. The variety is great.

Measures of performance effectiveness

The *Principles for the Validation and Use of Personnel Selection Procedures* define performance as 'the effectiveness and value of work behavior and its outcomes' (Society for Industrial and Organizational Psychology (SIOP), 1987, p. 39). Only behavior leading to valued outcomes is effective under this definition;

performance criteria quantify the effectiveness of work behavior for achieving organizational or job goals. Other definitions have been offered (e.g. Campbell *et al.*, 1993), but this one is commonly meant in discussions of the kinds of criterion measures, and their problems, described in this section.

Performance records

Records generally show results. In a manufacturing job, they may show the amount of production and maybe some aspects of quality (e.g., rejected production resulting in scrap or rework). In police work they may include, among other entries, arrest records, commendations, or disciplinary actions. Sales work may be assessed in dollar volume of sales, or perhaps the number of independent sales made. These results of job behavior are important enough to the employing organization that records about them are kept, and they provide criteria.

Often, however, they are not as useful as might be thought; they are merely 'lying about'. Too often the record reports results not controlled by the person's individual performance; only a combination of several less-than-satisfactory indicators may be acceptable as a record of individual sales outcomes. Landy and Farr (1983, p. 45) cited studies of sales performance using several (as many as 36) recorded indicators in complex indices of sales effectiveness, including such facets of performance as gross sales, average amount of sales, returns or cancellations, and some ancillary outcomes that facilitated or inhibited sales.

Records often yield contaminated data. The production of machine workers may be contaminated by machine differences; sales records may depend on characteristics of the territory, such as income level of the residents or the number and skills of competing sales persons; the number of documents entered into a computer depends on the complexity of the documents. Users of criteria developed from apparently objective data in the records need to be alert to the possible flaws in the data, influences not controllable by the worker's own behavior. It is bad science, and it is bad practice, to accept the records without question.

Performance tests

A problem with records is that the behavior and conditions creating the recorded numbers are not standard; conditions underlying one person's record may have differed in critical ways from those affecting someone else's. Performance testing is a standardized approach for assessing proficiency. Many kinds of performance tests have been used. They may be cognitive or non-cognitive, or paper and pencil, oral, or 'hands-on'; response options may impose anywhere from severe to minor constraints on responses. Performance can be described with a single, overall score or a set of component scores—or with a satisfactory–unsatisfactory dichotomy or as points along a scale. Scores might be relatively objective. A score on a machine set-up test might be the time required to do it. The pounds of pressure required to break a weld might be a score. Or one might program a computer to count the number of corrections made in a sample word-processing task. The variety of scoring possibilities is almost unlimited—but ratings predominate.

Work samples are common performance tests. They systematically sample or simulate job content and are administered under standard conditions. Either the work process, the resulting product, or both may be observed and scored. In a flight test for a pilot's license, the check pilot evaluates how well each of several required maneuvers is performed; the work process is evaluated. Some work samples result in products, whether 'hard copy' in using a word processor or a set of soldered connections in a piece of electronics, and it may be that only the product is 'scored'.

Work samples and simulations are *abstractions* of work actually done on a job; they are created by incorporating certain limited features of actual job demands. They may be faithful reproductions of actual assignments, or sanitized simulations of critical components, or the extreme abstraction of measuring isolated job skills free from the constraints of literal job content. Even the least abstraction, the reproduction of real tasks, involves choosing the most important sorts of assignments. Another general characteristic of work samples, whether process or product is scored, is that the measure of performance is usually based on ratings. Ratings are often criticized as criteria, but it is inconsistent to complain about ratings as criteria and then less critically advocate performance tests instead. Moreover, simulation is commonly assumed to match job behavior, but it is not a safe assumption. In the sanitized context of a simulator, examinees may enjoy taking a risk that would not be taken in actual work settings.

Work sample development, like most criterion development, begins with job analysis. Some things identified in job analysis will not be considered important for criterion purposes; choices must be made. Distinguishing a 'job content universe' from a 'job content domain' (Lawshe, 1975), I once described the choices as a four-step procedure (Guion, 1979):

1. A complete job analysis identifies a job content universe.
2. The part of the universe to be assessed defines a job content domain.
3. Related assessment possibilities (including scoring methods) define a test content universe.
4. The choices among them define the test content domain.

The job domain for a criterion work sample or other performance test is itself a sample of the job content universe and the sampling should be done with care. It should include important or critical tasks, preferably those that many but not all examinees will do well (so that differentiation occurs throughout the range of proficiency). Some choices are less obvious: Should domain definition include rarely performed tasks? Is it more important to predict performance on tasks that must be routinely performed or the relatively rarely demanded proficiency in handling unusual situations that may arise?

Performance testing should perhaps be used more often, but despite the virtues of standardization, its value as a criterion can be overstated. Performance tests usually describe proficiency when the person is doing his or her best. If what is valued is actual day-to-day performance, not a hypothetical 'can do' but a realistic 'does do', performance test scores may be inappropriate criteria. Reliability is a particularly vicious problem in scoring performance tests. All possible procedural safeguards for reliability should be built into the scoring system. A detailed scoring key or protocol should be developed, preferably by (or with the help of) job experts who have assisted in developing the tests. Scorers should be thoroughly trained to use it; they should know what to look for, and how to evaluate specific components. When possible, scoring should be done by two or more independent observers; degrees of score differences that are excessive should be defined, and the procedures for reconciling differences should be clear. These are not easy requirements.

Portfolios and 'authentic' assessment

By the early 1990s, the phrase 'authentic performance assessment', had become popular. Arising in educational assessment, the term refers to a variety of procedures ranging from arithmetic tests that require the examinee to develop the answers without the hints present in multiple choice items to wholly unconstrained portfolios of the work the examinee considered his or her best. The idea needs more careful thought than it has been given. What is 'authentic' (or not) in assessment is unclear. It is hard to imagine an inauthentic or unreal assessment, but it is easy to imagine an invalid assessment. However, the term does not seem to refer to validity. It seems to refer to the similarity of the stimulus content of the assessment to the stimulus content of the tasks to be performed and to the absence of constraint on responses. In this sense, authenticity in performance assessment is little more than a popular term for fidelity of simulation.

Perhaps probationary performance is an authentic criterion, but the assumption requires critical thinking. The content of probationary assignments may differ from that in later assignments. Moreover, performance on even a well-designed probationary period, with rotation of basic tasks, is usually assessed by methods that differ from performance as such—usually by ratings that introduce a high level of authenticity-threatening abstraction.

The contemporary icon in 'authentic' assessment rhetoric, i.e. portfolio assessment, identifies a wider problem. A portfolio is a collection of accomplishments. Commercial artists in a large advertising agency may collect examples of their recent work. Managers may develop portfolios of documents describing plans, programs, or results of specific managerial actions from which their performance may be assessed. Portfolios might include collections of documented real-world performance such as awards, production records, commendations or disciplinary actions, and so on. They may turn to records, including selected information from personnel files.

The concept of a portfolio, however, differs from a personnel file, because it is personally selective and therefore even less standardized. The individual worker chooses to include items that are favorable and to exclude those that are not. The emphasis is on content that is 'best' rather than 'all' or 'representative'. It is a measure of maximum, not typical, performance, and it therefore has questionable authenticity if authenticity implies 'day in, day out performance'. Moreover, even if it should reflect daily performance, it can be contaminated if those previously identified as 'high potential' people are given high-profile assignments where merely satisfactory performance is automatically viewed more positively than excellence in performance of routine assignments.

Performance ratings

Supervisors are often asked questions like:

1. On the whole, how effective is the ratee's work? (Responses may be scaled from 'excellent' to 'poor'.)
2. How does the ratee's rate of production compare with others? (A response scale may be used, with categories ranging from 'in the top 5%' to 'in the bottom 5%', or ratees may be ranked in order; other items might ask about quality, consistency, or other aspects of performance.)

Ratings can be made in different forms. Most are graphic rating scales, in a variety of guises as suggested in Figure 13.1. Others include various personnel comparison schemes, checklists based on Thurstonian or Likert methods of attitude scale measurement (or derivatives of them), and scales with behaviorally-based anchors stemming from Behaviorally Anchored Rating Scales (BARS) (Smith and Kendall, 1963). Conventional wisdom suggests that choices among these have little influence on the resulting assessments.

But, conventional wisdom can be questioned; format *can* matter. A frequently overlooked feature of the article introducing BARS (Smith and Kendall, 1963) was its brief mention of the final rating form. It required raters to record actually-observed behavioral examples to support the ratings given. To put this feature in context, review the original BARS rating method:

1. Rating dimensions were defined by groups of potential raters, in their own terms (not those used by psychologists).
2. General statements were written for the meaning of each dimension at high, satisfactory, or low performance levels.
3. Examples of behavior that might be 'expected' (i.e. typical) of specific ratees were developed and edited for each dimension.
4. Other groups of potential raters 'retranslated' the behavioral examples, assigning them to the dimensions.
5. Examples consistently and correctly assigned to the dimensions for which they were written were scaled; those with little variance in scale values were retained for possible use.
6. Vertical, graphic rating scales were drawn and points on them anchored by scaled examples.

Raters could mark an anchored point or any other along the scale, but the point chosen as the rating had to be documented by reporting an actually observed example of the ratee's behavior, an example thought to fit in with the scaled examples at that point. The effect of using such a requirement has not yet been studied adequately.

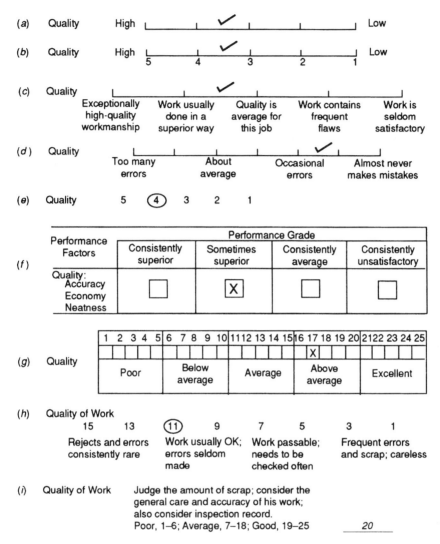

Figure 13.1 A variety of graphic rating scale response forms (from Guion, 1965, Figure 4-1).

From early work with graphic rating scales to the more modern choices emphasizing behaviorally-based ratings, it has been the practice to ask raters to rate workers on different scales, e.g. each worker might be rated on dependability, work accuracy, and speed of production. The literature on performance rating has been choked with stuff about halo effects, commenting on the lack of independence among ratings of things that ought logically to be independent; ratings of independent dimensions in assessment center observations have long been known to be more highly correlated within exercises than the correlations between ratings of the same dimensions within exercises. Along comes Fletcher

(1995), demonstrating the same thing for performance ratings over time: ratings of presumably independent dimensions in the same year correlate more highly than ratings of any one dimension across different rating periods. With such findings, it is justifiable to ask, even derisively: What is measured by the ratings?

Recent years have seen much research on the cognitive processes of raters. Much of it has been interesting and some of it has been useful. Nevertheless, a growing skepticism about the practical merit of such research seems to have resulted in decreased efforts along these lines. Part of the skepticism is based on the persistent use of inappropriate research samples and designs, such as college sophomores reading narrative vignettes, or viewing video tapes, rather than supervisors rating people with whom they have worked and will continue to work for relatively long periods of time. Another basis for skepticism is that the research has produced so few hypotheses testable in actual work places. Whatever the reason for the decline in this research area, it is important to recognize that it originally stemmed from dissatisfaction with ratings as criteria, that it attempted to come to an understanding of the sources of dissatisfaction and invalidity, and that its demise leaves us pretty much as we were, lacking confidence in supervisory ratings as criteria.

Behavioral measures

Most performance measures, including ratings, assess results of behavior at work. Focusing more narrowly on the behavior that produces the results may lead to understanding of results-oriented criteria. Moreover, behaviors may themselves *be* the results of interest, especially when they are important to the organization in a broader sense than the usual idea of performance effectiveness.

Long ago, Wallace (1965) argued that behavior that enhances or inhibits effectiveness is a better criterion than a presumably objective, directly relevant measure of effectiveness—and certainly better than a global rating. The argument still holds. An example in sales work compared sales volume with indicators of 'canvassing'—leaving one's desk to go out to look for prospective buyers. Sales volume (or corresponding measures of productivity in other jobs) depends on many influences not under the individual sales person's control. But what one does (e.g. sitting in one's chair versus actively prospecting for customers) may be one influence that the individual does in fact control. Moreover, as Wallace argued, and as Thayer (1992) reiterated, learning to predict such behavioral criteria can lead to a better understanding of the more global performance outcomes and to interventions that enhance them. Predicting appropriate and useful behavior may lead to better employee selection than can be achieved with poorer predictions of outcomes, even those of greater relevance to the employing organization. It is a bitter paradox that employment psychology has spent so much effort on the improvement of predictors without a corresponding effort to understand the criteria it seeks to predict (Thayer, 1992).

Some explicit behaviors have direct organizational relevance in ways different from, but as important as, performance effectiveness. At an individual level, behaviors like showing up for work rather than being absent, staying on the job rather than quitting, or praising the organization rather than belittling it in inter-actions with outsiders are examples. Corresponding examples at work unit levels include unit absenteeism, turnover, and public relations effects. Special attention in recent years has been given, particularly at unit levels, to criteria such as inven-tory shrinkage (as a euphemism for theft) and broader constructs like 'coun-terproductive behavior'. These, too, need better understanding as a prologue to better prediction, but they are important variables in their own right.

Like records and ratings, behavioral observations and counts are flawed and poorly understood. For example, we seem to have had some peculiar ideas about the reasons for absence. For years absence was considered avoidance of work, with no recognition of the element of choice a worker faces between going to work and such competing forces as applying for a mortgage, tending a sick child, or going fishing. More recent treatments have examined attendance or absence more as cognitive conflict, perhaps (in the older language) approach–approach rather than approach–avoidance conflict (e.g. Hackett, Bycio and Guion, 1989). In measuring absence as a criterion, each instance may be classified as either avoidable or un-avoidable; such distinctions are laudable attempts to avoid mere event-counting and to ensure that the resulting measure makes organizational or psychological sense. The attempt may not succeed. Sickness is often classified as an unavoidable absence, for example, but its effect on attendance is inconsistent. Among the nurses studied by Hackett, Bycio and Guion (1989), minor illness was the most commonly cited reason for absence, but responsibility to co-workers could override the physi-cal malaise and lead an individual nurse, faced with a specific situation, to go to work. When the nursing staff in the person's unit is at full strength, the illness probably leads to absence; when the unit is short-handed, the conscientious nurse drags off to work (with, it is hoped, due regard for possible contagion!).

In that example, which constitutes a measurement flaw or error, the attendance or the absence? If absenteeism is seen as work avoidance so that one assigns sickness to an 'unavoidable absence' category, then does not the attendance of the sick nurse constitute a measurement error? It is not a random error if it is a deliberate (if misguided) display of conscientiousness, but it is nevertheless an error according to the operations used to deal with sickness. If one sees attend-ance as a measure of conscientiousness, then it is a measurement error to count as not conscientious the absence from a hospital ward because of contagious illness that can infect the patients. The point, of course, is that the behavioral count, the criterion measure, surely implies *something*, but that the inferences drawn from it are, at best, less than perfectly valid.

Similarly, we do not know the psychological meaning of turnover, accident rates, or institutionalized patterns of theft by employees. Yet such criteria are used in blissful ignorance either because (remembering Jenkins) they are considered God-given or happen to be conveniently available.

Criterion measures: A critical commentary

All of these examples of criteria, commonly used or not, are necessarily flawed, and the most pervasive flaw is their absence of meaning. To be blunt, after a half-century of complaining, we still do not know what we are doing when we choose and measure a criterion. Too many psychologists, for too long, resisted the notion of validity as important to criteria, or the notion of criteria as constructs. The values that valid criterion measurement should reflect are rarely articulated; they may not even be considered in making the choice. Criterion choices are too often based on convenience, habit, or copying what others have used, not on what *should* be measured— the construct. Rare is the evidence of serious thought about the construct to be measured, although since the seminal article by Binning and Barrett (1989) it has begun to be heard frequently. Only by defining the construct to be represented by a criterion measure can the flaws of contaminating sources of variance be identified and reduced and the value of specific interventions be properly assessed.

THE CRITERION PROBLEM

It is popular to bemoan 'the criterion problem', usually referring to the difficulty in finding a satisfactory criterion measure. The problem is deeper. The 'criterion' has been considered a yardstick for judging whether a test is useful. For this purpose, practicality requires practical criteria: production, accidents, scrap rates, and other things that affect profit or loss. Such criteria are not always available or, if available, trustworthy. Ratings are common, but not fully trusted.

Psychometric methods have been applied in developing criterion measures: attitude measurement for rating forms, test development procedures like item analysis, factor analysis, or reliability analysis are common, even though they do not solve the criterion problem. The psychometric concept of validity, however, has long seemed to confuse people when applied to criteria. Finding criteria to validate criteria seems unending and futile to them, leading inexorably to an unmeasurable ultimate criterion. Concepts of content and construct validity have only lately been applied to criteria, and only with confusion. Psychometric solutions to the criterion problem gave way to emphases on cognitive processes in ratings (Feldman, 1981; Landy and Farr, 1980), but cognitive research and its elusive search for accuracy in rating merely evaded the validity question. In short, the background of thinking about criteria is dominated by ideas that seemed good at one time but later went out of style as not very satisfying (see Austin and Villanova, 1992, for an historical background).

The 'problem' in brief

I think the 'criterion problem' is, at root, persistence in going at things backwards. It stems from the idea that the purpose of a criterion is to evaluate a test or other intervention. From that view, one begins with an idea for an intervention and then hunts for a way to evaluate it. As the aphorism has it, it places the cart ahead of the horse. It is far more sensible to begin with something important to predict or understand or change, and then to think of ways to do so, i.e. to form hypotheses with the 'something important' cast as a dependent variable (or, if you must, as a criterion) and consider a variety of possible correlates, causes, or predictors.

With the cart properly placed, the criterion problem is one of clarification and understanding. Thayer (1992) asked: 'Do we understand our criteria?' We must reply: 'Rarely, if at all.' Improved prediction can be expected where there is a firm understanding of the event, condition, or variable to be predicted. It is hard to develop or evaluate measurement of a construct we cannot define conceptually.

Thoughts of criterion constructs

Defining criterion constructs is an exercise in theory development. A theory of a construct is not necessarily big, impressive, or scholarly; it is a clarification of thinking. It may help to use and modify some psychological constructs already available; they may require fine-tuning to fit local needs but can be helpful way-points. Suppose that organizational analysis suggests problems of irresponsibility. A theory of a criterion construct might start with a set of desired behaviors: coming to work despite conflicting demands, helping newcomers, accepting overtime or unpleasant but necessary assignments, or keeping records accurately. These things seem to fit psychological theories of conscientiousness; the construct may eventually be defined as conscientious behavior in the work place, and a modest 'network' of expected correlates (or expected non-correlates) might be included among the implications of the construct.

Measurement operations flow from the construct (not vice versa). Depending on the local definition, a criterion composite might include letters of commendation (e.g. letters from the public praising something done by a police officer or by a truck driver), attendance, accidents, quitting, completion of training, or thoroughness of inspection of one's own work. Data analysis, similar to test item analysis, can shed light on the internal consistency of such a composite, and correlations of composite scores with other variables can identify contaminants and theoretically sensible sources of variance—in short, provide evidence of the meaning to be inferred from the measures. This is called construct validity.[1]

A theory of job performance

Campbell *et al.* (1993) proposed a theory of job performance as cognitive, motor, psychomotor, or interpersonal *behavior* controllable by the individual, relevant to organizational goals, and scalable (at least conceptually) in terms of proficiency—surely an important criterion construct. Their concept differs from the SIOP definition; it explicitly excludes work outcomes, effectiveness, and productivity. In this sense, their view is congruent with the call by Dachler (1989) for greater attention to the kinds of processes through which results are achieved. They do not consider performance unidimensional. In their view, the true rank order of employees on one proficiency component is not likely to be their rank order on another.

Three determinants of performance proficiency in their theory help sharpen performance constructs:

- *declarative knowledge*, factual knowledge and understanding of things one must do;

Table 13.1 A proposed taxonomy of higher order performance components (adapted from Campbell *et al.*, 1993)

1. *Job-specific task proficiency*
   Proficiency in the performance of the job's central substantive or technical tasks.

2. *Non-job-specific task proficiency*
   Proficiency in general tasks performed by virtually everyone in an organization or in a group of related jobs within the organization.

3. *Written and oral communication task proficiency*
   Proficiency in tasks requiring use of language, whether formal oral or written presentations to a group or interpersonal communication.

4. *Demonstrating effort*
   Consistency of effort, expending extra effort as needed, and persistence in working even under adverse conditions.

5. *Maintaining personal discipline*
   Avoidance of negatively valued behavior: alcohol and substance abuse at work, violating laws or rules, excessive absenteeism, etc.

6. *Facilitating peer and team performance*
   Supporting and helping peers and acting as a de facto trainer; facilitating group functioning by example, by keeping focus on goals.

7. *Supervision/leadership*
   Influencing subordinate performance by setting goals, teaching, being a good model, and appropriate use of reward or punshiment.

8. *Management/administration*
   Management functions broader than direct supervision.

- *procedural knowledge*, skill in knowing how to do them; and
- *motivation*, the direction, degree and persistence of effort in doing them (Kanfer and Ackerman, 1989, provide background).

The theory also proposes eight 'general' factors shown, modified and abbreviated, in Table 13.1.

Not all of these apply to any given job; most jobs, for example, lack a management component (as defined), although a management-like construct may be seen as a form of personal discipline. Some jobs require only elementary communication skills, and people who work alone have no team performance component. But one or more of these eight components can provide a framework for defining more narrowly defined constructs of local interest. Note that performance is not merely doing assigned tasks. Being on time, staying rather than quitting, working overtime as needs arise, helping others, avoiding work group conflicts, justifying trust, or providing a good model for others—all of these can help define constructs conceptually and operationally.

Such behavior can define the context in which work is done. Borman and Motowidlo (1993) referred to these as 'contextual criteria', different from task or job performance in four ways:

(a) they define the work environment,
(b) they are common to all (or most) jobs in an organization;
(c) they are more motivational than cognitive; and
(d) although desired, they are less likely to be explicitly required.

Even with task performance, defining a criterion construct as a proficiency has advantages over simply accepting output measures, even if output is the working definition. Defining the construct permits a more complete evaluation of the measurement. If counted output is supposed to reflect certain job-specific task behaviors, such as specific job skill, then the validity of the count, *for that purpose*, is compromised to the extent that it is subject to influences not under individual control. Such variables are contaminants; they undermine the construct validity of the criterion measure.

Trainability and adaptability

Of many possible criterion constructs, give special thought to trainability and adaptability, constructs of response to change. Speed of learning to perform a new set of job tasks is an important construct and becoming more important, especially where people must frequently adapt to changed technology or assignments. Change happens, in organizations and in their environments; adaptability to change should be a more common criterion construct.

Organizations grow and adapt by changing. Criteria should be defined to promote *effective* change, including maintaining useful stability in the face of change. Innovation should be rewarded, but it should also be evaluated. The construct of effective change does not refer to mindless adulation of change for its own sake nor to the idea that every innovation is to be pursued enthusiastically. New ideas sometimes solve problems; sometimes they create new ones, and some simply do not work. Nevertheless, people who imagine and develop new ideas to change products, services, or ways of doing things are valuable to organizations and to society, and the criteria by which they are hired, promoted, trained, and managed should encourage them.

Emphasis on change requires changed perspectives on job analysis. Results of job analysis tend to describe a job as it is being done; criteria inferred from it may perpetuate existing behaviors and standards. Procedures that successfully predict or encourage them maintain the status quo. Avoiding criteria that merely reinforce the way things are requires an intelligent recognition of the inevitability and desirability of change.

CHOICES IN FORMING CRITERION CONSTRUCTS

Refining criterion constructs requires some judgments and choices. The three choices described here are presented as dichotomies, which is, of course, an oversimplification. Nevertheless, the dichotomies can help to identify considerations in defining the 'theory of the construct'.

Consider again the pair of questions presented earlier: 'On the whole, how well does the ratee do his or her job?' and 'How does the ratee compare with others?' Two choices are illustrated by these questions: (a) the choice between one global, overall criterion versus several narrow and more specific ones, and (b) the choice between normative (relative) inferences versus notions of absolute performance. A third is illustrated if either question is preceded by, 'When this ratee is working at his or her best, . . .' This is the choice between typical and maximum performance. Even when other choices must be made, these seem central.

Criterion dimensionality

Performance on many jobs can be assessed on several different, independent factors. Moreover, criteria other than task performance can also have important implications for personnel decisions. Researchers and managers can simultaneously and independently consider a variety of criteria. On the other hand, meta-analysis seems to have demonstrated that precisely defined criterion dimensions are unnecessary. In fact, most validation research has used only a single, overall criterion.

Even where independent criteria are measured, a common practice combines them into a single composite, assigning nominal weights to the components. Nominal weights (desired weights) are based on organizational value judgments, assumed importance to performance, estimated cost of error, or intuition. Effective weights are computed contributions to composite criterion variance. They are rarely the same. Nominal weights influence effective weights, but so also do differences in variability among components, intercorrelations, and even reliabilities (Guion, 1991; Richardson, 1941).

An analytical approach to organizational and job functioning favors multiple, independent criteria. Single, global criteria may make more sense from two perspectives. One is the perspective of practicality. The other is the perspective of a synthesizing approach to organizational understanding. Dachler (1989), writing from this perspective, called for a holistic assessment of people in the selection process but also for a concept of success that is both holistic and developmental. My position tends to be analytical, but my position should not blind readers to the dynamic implications of a more holistic view.

Choosing for understanding

Using a single composite criterion is like the proverbial ostrich, a way to avoid finding that different components may be predicted or understood by different variables. Different criteria, if important, should be predicted independently. I advocated this long ago (Guion, 1961) and still do. Doing so risks predicting that an applicant might do well on one criterion and poorly on another, a prospect some find frightening. Actually, standardized predictions can be combined just as criterion components are, and doing so can help decision-makers to understand better what they are doing. Dunnette (1963) was also impatient with insistence on a single, overall criterion. Calling for a higher priority for understanding than for prediction, he called for a model of personnel selection decisions that would take individuality of candidates into account along with the situations that might make some considerations more compelling than others. His call should be heeded at last. It can promote scientific understanding of which apparent differences in job behavior actually make a difference in influencing organizational effectiveness.

Choosing for practicality

It is often argued that a single, overall criterion is more practicable than explorations among multiple criteria. Foreshadowing meta-analysis, Schmidt and Kaplan (1971) pointed to both economic and psychological uses of criteria. They favored the single composite ('regardless' of correlations among components) for economic constructs and examination of individual components for the sake of psychological understanding.

The argument that the more inclusive overall construct is also more practicable rejects the Jenkins (1946) assumption that validity depends on the specific criterion used: 'It is now clear that for criteria of overall job performance . . . and tests of cognitive ability, this assumption is incorrect . . . there are no documented cases of an aptitude or ability test being valid for one such criterion measure but not for another (i.e., zero validity)' (Schmidt, Ones and Hunter, 1992, p. 656).

I have three objections to this view. First, the absolute notion that only a zero coefficient is not valid ignores the fact that validity using one criterion component can be greater than validity for another. Secondly, the generalization applies to cognitive tests and proficiency criteria; it may not apply to other kinds of criteria (e.g. contextual criteria), or to specific categories of performance criteria studied too infrequently to contribute much to a meta-analysis.

The third objection is more important. The quotation continues to treat a criterion as something picked up solely for the purpose of validating a test, thus missing the point; it continues to place the cart in front.

In short, the choice remains. If it is plausible that predictors of one criterion differ substantially from those of another, then scientific caution requires explicitly different hypotheses for the different components. If the presumption is wrong, then the error will be found if the predictors for the different hypotheses turn out to be the same. If only the inclusive criterion is used (i.e. the assumption that differences do not matter), then the assumption cannot be tested and found wrong.[2]

Practicality is in the eye of the beholder. 'Practical' for design engineers may differ from the views of production engineers, and both may differ from marketing or human resources managers. Differences in views of practicality may require different predictive hypotheses, each with a different criterion (Villanova, 1992). Currently, the pendulum on this issue favors overall criteria, but it appears to be swinging again. The growing interest in 'good citizenship' (Organ, 1988), such as willingness to help colleagues, or to put in extra time, is apparent in practical selection research aimed mainly at 'bad citizenship' and in the growing interest in integrity testing (Goldberg *et al.*, 1991; O'Bannon, Goldinger and Appleby, 1989). Predictions of such criteria that are inconsistent with predictions of job performance may force renewed attention to multiple criteria.

Table 13.2   A simplex matrix of correlation coefficients

Variable	1		2		3		4		5		6		7
1	r_{11}	>	r_{12}	>	r_{13}	>	r_{14}	>	r_{15}	>	r_{16}	>	r_{17}
2			r_{22}	>	r_{23}	>	r_{24}	>	r_{25}	>	r_{26}	>	r_{27}
3					r_{33}	>	r_{34}	>	r_{35}	>	r_{36}	>	r_{37}
4							r_{44}	>	r_{45}	>	r_{46}	>	r_{47}
5									r_{55}	>	r_{56}	>	r_{57}
6											r_{66}	>	r_{67}
7													r_{77}

Dimensionality over time

Criterion dimensionality over time has been controversial (Austin, Humphrey and Hulin, 1989; Barrett and Alexander, 1989; Barrett, Caldwell and Alexander, 1985; Hulin, Henry and Noon, 1990). Ghiselli (1956) called it 'dynamic dimensionality'; a related concept is validity decay over time. The latter is based on simplex correlation matrices (Humphreys, 1960), as illustrated in Table 13.2.

In my view, the evidence for changes in validity over time, including decays, seems stronger than the evidence for stability, but I suspect the vehemence of the debate is unwarranted. Most of the evidence either way is based on cognitive tests predicting global performance criteria; at least one study has shown that a cognitive test predicts better than does a measure of achievement motivation in the short run but that the relative advantage reverses in the long run (Helmreich, Sawin and Carsrud, 1986). This, I believe, is very close to Ghiselli's notion of dynamic criteria. Before taking a general position on validity decay, I want evidence from many matrices, with varying independent variables as well as criteria, investigating the generality, and the limits of the generality, of the simplex.

Normative measures vs. standards

Psychological measurement traditionally uses the standard deviation of a normal distribution as its unit. Most test scores, for example, are interpreted either in terms of standard score differences from the mean or in terms of the percentage of those in a norm group having a lower score. So are most criteria, including most ratings. The problem with normative criteria is that the best people in one group may not measure up to the poorest in another.

The alternative is to set a standard level of criterion performance and to measure individual performance in units above or below the standard. Setting a standard is difficult but possible when performance is measured objectively, with well-defined units (e.g. typing speed in standard words per minute). The problem with standard-setting is that it may not be possible when measurement scales are subjective and ambiguous. A rating of 'meets or exceeds standard' does not do it.

Despite the problems, the choice should be considered at the construct level. Normative constructs are sensible for ordinary jobs, where performance levels do not differ with dramatically different consequences. They seem questionable for others.

Typical vs. maximum performance

Should the criterion construct reflect what a person *can* do under desirable or optimal circumstances, or what the person *will* do under typical circumstances? In an interesting field experiment, Sackett, Zedeck and Fogli (1988) used standard-content grocery carts to test the abilities of supermarket checkout clerks to record prices of items quickly and accurately, i.e. to measure how quickly and accurately they *can* do the job when it is carefully standardized. They also had computerized records of speed and accuracy in non-standardized, daily work, measuring how quickly and accurately the same clerks had been working routinely. The two measures were poorly correlated. Can-do and will-do performance are not highly related; and one must decide which construct is more useful in a given situation.

From an organizational point of view, it is probably more immediately useful to measure typical rather than maximum performance. Workers tend to develop an habitual pace and way of working, and this habit is likely to be more important in most jobs than the pace or methods that may be demonstrated in extraordinary situations. If this dichotomy is considered carefully, it can have many valuable implications. We tend to think of criteria in the context of those interventions that can be called personnel decisions—e.g. selection, promotion, or training decisions. These are largely matters of ability assessment. The everyday, routine performance of a worker may be influenced (just as maximum performance is) by the worker's abilities; it may also be influenced by the worker's motivation, general activity level, attitudes toward the job and organization, job design, supervisor's practice—in short, the whole host of topics in the broad field of industrial and organizational psychology and management practice. A stronger focus on typical behavior, if managers and researchers will emerge from their own routine cocoons, suggests a wider range of plausible interventions for improvements or corrective actions.

Nevertheless, there are many situations where maximum performance may be the more important criterion construct. Police work, for example, is often said to consist of long periods of boredom, in which performance is routine and perfunctory, interrupted by moments of panic, in which performance had better be the best possible. The same can be said of most protective service occupations or others in which emergency actions must at times be taken.

A CONCLUDING COMMENT

Whether at the construct level or the measurement level, some statistical concepts need to enter into criterion choice. One is probable criterion variance. Why try to predict performance on a task that everyone does about equally well (or poorly)? Criterion constructs worth pursuing are likely to be those with wide individual differences. They may also be those with low mean levels of performance, especially when the variance around low means is small. This consideration implies a standard of acceptable performance, but even if one cannot be cleanly defined, the criterion may be justified because of a general impression within an organization that its overall level is inadequate. In choosing a criterion, one should have reason to believe that its variance is too high or that its mean level is too low.

The statement is presented in statistical terms, but its implication is organizational, not statistical. These are the considerations that make managers and researchers decide that the criterion is organizationally (or scientifically) important enough to work on. This decision should be the starting point.

The 'criterion problem' is not simply the problem of finding an acceptable way to measure job performance (or some aspect of it). It is not even a problem of choosing from available measures. And it is certainly not a problem of finding measures to justify selection or other intervention procedures already decided on. It is a problem of identifying, at a construct level, the behaviors, events, or outcomes that should be predicted and subsequently changed, and of developing the best possible hypothesis about the actions that can be taken to effect such change.

The criterion dilemma facing us is whether to continue with the cart in front, thereby holding to tradition, or to break with that tradition and put the horse in front.

ENDNOTES

1. In discussing criterion constructs, we must not lose sight of practical matters like reducing absenteeism, or other unwanted events or variables. If these things are important to an organization, and if they are predictable, then the relevant research should be done. But managers and researchers alike should ask why the successful prediction was possible—should seek understanding, which implies the ability to define a more fundamental criterion construct.

2. Responding to a statement in the *Smithsonian* to the effect that no litmus test exists for distinguishing positions grounded in scholarship from those grounded in ideology, Doering (1992, p. 14), said, 'there *is* a simple and reliable test. Scholarship admits the possibility of error.' My view is that a hypothesis that can be shown to be wrong is preferable to one that is more likely to hide error.

REFERENCES

Austin, J.T., Humphreys, L.G. and Hulin, C.L. (1989). A critical reanalysis of Barrett, Caldwell, and Alexander. *Personnel Psychology*, **42**, 583–596.

Austin, J.T. and Villanova, P. (1992). The criterion problem: 1917–1992. *Journal of Applied Psychology*, **77**, 836–874.

Barrett, G.V. and Alexander, R.A. (1989). Rejoinder to Austin, Humphrey, and Hulin: Critical reanalysis of Barrett, Caldwell, and Alexander. *Personnel Psychology*, **42**, 597–612.

Barrett, G.V., Caldwell, M.S. and Alexander, R.A. (1985). The concept of dynamic criteria: A critical reanalysis. *Personnel Psychology*, **38**, 41–56.

Binning, J.F. and Barrett, G.V. (1989). Validity of personnel decisions: A conceptual analysis of the inferential and evidential bases. *Journal of Applied Psychology*, **74**, 478–494.

Borman, W.C. and Motowidlo, S.J. (1993). Expanding the criterion domain to include elements of contextual performance. In N. Schmitt and W.C. Borman (eds.), *Personnel Selection*, pp. 71–98. San Francisco, CA: Jossey-Bass.

Campbell, J.P., McCloy, R.A., Oppler, S.H. and Sager, C.E. (1993). A theory of performance. In N. Schmitt and W.C. Borman (eds.), *Frontiers in Industrial and Organizational Psychology: Personnel Selection*, pp. 35–70. San Francisco, CA: Jossey-Bass.

Dachler, H.P. (1989). Selection and the organizational context. In P. Herriot (ed.), *Assessment and Selection in Organizations: Methods and Practice for Recruitment and Appraisal*, (pp. 45–69. Chichester: John Wiley.

Doering, P.F. (1992). [Letter to the editor]. *Smithsonian*, **23**(3), 14.

Drenth, P.J.D. (1989). Introduction to Section 1: The context. In P. Herriot (ed.), *Assessment and Selection in Organizations: Methods and Practices for Recruitment and Appraisal*, pp. 9–12. Chichester: John Wiley.

Dunnette, M.D. (1963). A note on *the* criterion. *Journal of Applied Psychology*, **47**, 251–254.

Feldman, J.M. (1981). Beyond attribution theory: Cognitive processes in performance appraisal. *Journal of Applied Psychology*, **66**, 127–148.

Fletcher, C. (1995). New directions for performance appraisal: Some findings and observations. *International Journal of Selection and Assessment*, **3**(4) (Special issue).

Ghiselli, E.E. (1956). Dimensional problems of criteria. *Journal of Applied Psychology*, **40**, 1–4.

Goldberg, L.R., Grenier, J.R., Guion, R.M., Schrest, L.B. and Wing, H. (1991). Questionnaires Used in the Prediction of Trustworthiness in Pre-employment Selection Decisions: An A.P.A. Task Force Report. Washington, DC: American Psychological Association.

Guion, R.M. (1961). Criterion measurement and personnel judgments. *Personnel Psychology*, **14**, 141–149.

Guion, R.M. (1965). *Personnel testing*. New York: McGraw-Hill.

Guion, R.M. (1979). *Principles of work sample testing: III. Construction and evaluation of work sample tests*. TR-79-A10. Alexandria, VA: United States Army Research Institute for the Behavioral and Social Sciences.

Guion, R.M. (1991). Personnel assessment, selection, and placement. In M.D. Dunnette and L.M. Hough (eds.), *Handbook of Industrial and Organizational Psychology*, 2nd edn, pp. 327–397. Palo Alto, CA: Consulting Psychologists Press.

Hackett, R.D., Bycio, P. and Guion, R.M. (1989). Absenteeism among hospital nurses: An idiographic-longitudinal analysis. *Academy of Management Journal*, **32**, 424–453.

Helmreich, R.L., Sawin, L.L. and Carsrud, A.L. (1986). The honeymoon effect in job performance: Temporal increases in the predictive power of achievement motivation. *Journal of Applied Psychology*, **71**, 185–188.

Hulin, C.L., Henry, R.A. and Noon, S.L. (1990). Adding a dimension: Time as a factor in the generalizability of predictive relationships. *Psychological Bulletin*, **107**, 328–340.

Humphreys, L.G. (1960). Investigations of the simplex. *Psychometrika*, **25**, 313–323.

Jenkins, J.G. (1946). Validity for what? *Journal of Consulting Psychology*, **10**, 93–98.

Kanfer, R. and Ackerman, P.L. (1989). Motivation and cognitive abilities: An integrative/ aptitude treatment interaction approach to skill acquisition. *Journal of Applied Psychology*, **74**, 657–690.

Landy, F.J. and Farr, J.L. (1980). Performance rating. *Psychological Bulletin*, **87**, 72–107.

Landy, F.J. and Farr, J.L. (1983). *The Measurement of Work Performance*. New York: Academic Press.

Lawshe, C.H. (1975). A quantitative approach to content validity. *Personnel Psychology*, **28**, 563–575.

O'Bannon, R.M., Goldinger, L.A. and Appleby, G.S. (1989). *Honesty and Integrity Testing: A Practical Guide*. Atlanta, GA: Applied Information Resources.

Organ, D.W. (1988). *Organizational Citizenship Behavior: The Good Soldier Syndrome*. Lexington, MA: Heath.

Richardson, M.W. (1941). The combination of measures. In P. Horst (ed.), *The Prediction of Personal Adjustment*, Bulletin No. 48, pp. 379–401. New York: Social Science Research Council.

Sackett, P.R., Zedeck, S. and Fogli, L. (1988). Relations between measures of typical and maximum job performance. *Journal of Applied Psychology*, **73**, 482–486.

Schmidt, F.L. and Kaplan, L.B. (1971). Composite vs. multiple criteria: A review and resolution of the controversy. *Personnel Psychology*, **24**, 419–434.

Schmidt, F.L., Ones, D.S. and Hunter, J.E. (1992). Personnel selection. *Annual Review of Psychology*, **43**, 627–670.

Schuler, H., Farr, J.L. and Smith, M. (1993). The individual and organizational sides of personnel selection and assessment. In H. Schuler, J.L. Farr and M. Smith (eds.), *Personnel*

Selection and Assessment: Individual and Organizational Perspectives, pp. 1–5. Hillsdale, NJ: Erlbaum.

Smith, P.C. and Kendall, L.M. (1963). Retranslation of expectations: An approach to the construction of unambiguous anchors for rating scales. *Journal of Applied Psychology*, **47**, 149–155.

Society for Industrial and Organizational Psychology (1987). *Principles for the Validation and Use of Personnel Selection Procedures* 3rd edn. College Park, MD: SIOP.

Thayer, P.W. (1992). Construct validation: Do we understand our criteria? *Human Performance*, **5**, 97–108.

Villanova, P. (1992). A customer-based model for developing job performance criteria. *Human Resources Management Review*, **2**, 103–114.

Wallace, S.R. (1965). Criteria for what? *American Psychologist*, **20**, 411–417.

Chapter 14

Criterion Development: The Unknown Power of Criteria as Communication Tools

Wieby M. M. Altink, Coert F. Visser and Michiel Castelijns

Adviesbureau Psychotechniek Utrecht B.V., Utrecht, The Netherlands

INTRODUCTION

Much has been written about the development of criteria: the standards against which personnel are hired and appraised. We know that criteria should reflect the relevant tasks and responsibilities in the job and organization, that they should meet certain psychometric standards and, moreover, that they should not result in unfair discrimination (against races, gender, etc.). Many tools have been developed to derive criteria that fulfil these purposes. However, less attention has been paid to the process by which criteria are formulated. This process offers many opportunities to communicate with organization members about the goals of the organization and the required and desired performance (see also Anderson and Ostroff, Chapter 20 in this volume).

In our opinion, criterion development is not just a manner of applying a psychometric 'recipe', as many textbooks still seem to suggest. Criterion development is an activity by which important aspects of behaviours, competencies and achievements are communicated throughout the organization. Should not all organization members (employees, managers, personnel officers, consultants) work with these important issues that motivate and direct performances within organizations? Why not then pay more attention to their role in the process of criterion development?

This chapter gives some examples that, we hope, trigger ways of thinking about how to develop criteria and the opportunities to involve organization members in this process. You might achieve the same result that a manager of one of our client organizations described in the following way: 'Now I understand why I should

International Handbook of Selection and Assessment, Edited by N. Anderson and P. Herriot.
© 1997 John Wiley & Sons Ltd.

discuss these measures with the members of my team—they simply reflect the goals to which we are heading!'

WHY CRITERIA?

The question 'Why should we develop criteria?' seems redundant in the case of selection and appraisal procedures. Criteria, or concrete measures of performance, define how a candidate fulfils and—in the case of selection—will perform in a certain job. It is a known fact: criteria play a double role. They formulate in a specific manner what individuals have to do, and they also give standards against which we can evaluate whether these goals have been reached. Criterion development follows upon the process of job analysis. First we state which tasks have to be performed, specify the necessary skills hereto and then we construct specific standards that are necessary to measure, lead, coach and evaluate performance.

To give an idea of what criteria are, we show some examples in Figure 14.1. These examples, which we encountered in our practice as external human resource management consultants, show in addition that we sometimes have to deal with behaviours and performances that are not easily described, measured or predicted. Criteria might be formulated on a more abstract or concrete level. They may sometimes concern tasks, competencies, behaviours or capacities and personality requirements. The level of abstraction and the constructs to which criteria refer depend on the specific purpose for which criteria are developed and also on several psychometric considerations. However, a central feature of criterion constructs is that they can be transformed into observable skills, behaviours and habits, which can be communicated about with employees to observe, predict and evaluate performance and (future) achievements.

CHANGES IN ORGANIZATIONS AND THEIR ENVIRONMENTS AND THE WAY THEY AFFECT THE CRITERIA TO BE CHOSEN

Many organizations are experiencing drastic changes in their environments. Technological developments make new products possible. As a consequence of the increasing speed of technological developments product cycles are getting shorter and shorter. New markets are emerging as well as new customer needs and demands. Unfortunately, it is no longer sufficient to be competitive in one's own national market; world class competitiveness is the new aim in order to achieve sustained success. Workers today are generally more highly skilled and better educated than before. They put different demands on organizations. They have less tolerance for hierarchy, they demand high quality of work and the opportunity to develop themselves, to have a meaningful role and to enjoy their work.

Organizations have to be able to adapt to and to cope with the new organizational environments and market demands which are getting stricter and different. Goals which many organizations set have to do with achieving higher quality, higher speed, lower costs, dependability and adaptiveness (Flood, Gannon and

Criterion	Description
Productivity	Products made/delivered within a certain timespan
Oral communication	Messages communicated to others in a clear and understandable way
Client service	Number of complaints by clients; acquired contacts within a certain timespan
People management	Motivation/productivity of personnel, creation of 'team spirit', skills that relate to enhancing individual and team performances

Figure 14.1   Examples of criterion constructs and descriptions

Paauwe, 1995). Finding the right sources of *competitive advantage* is an important quest. Nowadays human resources management (HRM) is seen as probably the major source of competitiveness (Pfeffer, 1994; Flood, Gannon and Paauwe, 1995). Human resources are valuable, scarce, difficult to copy and difficult to substitute. Also there are several sources of *competitive parity*. They imply developments that organizations have to keep up with in order to keep up with their competitors. Examples are applying new technologies, flattening organization structures and making processes more simple and flexible.

Several drastic changes in work are occurring related to the above-mentioned changes. There are changes related to technological developments. The work place of today is getting informed. New jobs or roles emerge in the development of new technology. New tasks emerge in the application of new technology as well. However, there is also a process going on of sub-tasks, tasks and jobs disappearing. Knowledge-intensive applications like computers and robots replace human work to some extent. Here there is a parallel with *Fordism*, the mechanization of human work. Also emerging are new ways of communicating. Of course there is the 'electronic highway'. People can communicate easily with each other even though they may be far apart. Teleworking is also a new possibility.

The need for different ways to manage people leads to major changes in organizations too. Human resources are seen as a major factor for achieving company success. Organizations put more emphasis than before on developing a strategic HRM. Making sure that the work force is valuable is a major concern. The development of individuals within organizations is too. People demand development opportunities on the one hand; they can be made more valuable for organizations on the other hand. Another way of improving HRM practices is to improve the consistency of different elements, like selecting people, appraising, developing and rewarding them. Line managers being given the responsibility for these HRM tasks. Topics that get much attention are the flexible work force, broader tasks, more investment in training and development, self-management and empowerment, management by objectives, output-oriented appraisal, flexibility in rewards and raising the internal and external mobility of employees.

There are also some structural changes in the way work is designed. First, there is a process of revision of labour division and simplification of work processes going on (Visser, Altink and Algera, Chapter 21 in this volume). Secondly, there is a tendency to cluster people into teams. Teams can be more flexible than individuals and are more capable of dealing with complex problems. Many organizations throughout the world are experimenting with self-managing teams (Wellins, Byham and Dixon, 1994). Temporary assignments and project work is another trend. To be very flexible and get fast results people from different disciplines work together with a specific assignment until the desired results have been achieved.

As a result of all these changes, there are some new demands on people. High priority is put on aspects like *knowledge* and the permanent development of knowledge. A bigger emphasis on *intellectual skills* and *capabilities* will be inevitable. *Adaptiveness* is another criterion which will be relevant due to changing work content and contexts. People have to be willing and capable of broadening their skills. *Cooperativeness* is a requirement because of the emphasis on teamwork. Workers have to be ready to commit and adapt to team goals. On the other hand, people have to be able to work independently. Employees have to be *self-managing*. They are responsible for achieving the results they have committed themselves to. A more intensive co-operation and new ways of communicating places higher demands on *communicative skills*. To be more self-managing, more *knowledge about business processes* is required. Orientation toward *adding value* to organizational goals as well as an orientation toward *innovation* will be necessary to meet new market demands.

These developments clearly make the use of criteria important.

PROCEDURES FOR CRITERION DEVELOPMENT

Because of their importance, work and organization psychologists have paid much attention to the development of criteria throughout the years. Algera and Greuter (1989) discuss aspects that have to do with theoretical and conceptual points of view. For instance, they discuss such issues as 'Should criteria be defined in terms of behaviours, capacities or performances?'; 'Should we formulate an overall criterion that reflects all performances, or should we apply several criteria that are more or less independent from each other?' In addition they discuss the research around criterion development, pointing out the relevance of more meta-analytic research that indicates the relevance of job criteria against single jobs and jobs overall (see also Landy and Rastegary, 1989; Guion, Chapter 13 in this volume).

Nevertheless, nowadays a major problem for criterion development is that jobs are no longer clearly 'visible', and task activities are rapidly changing. Think, for instance, about work in the IT or health care sectors. Both types of job activities could be recognized clearly in the 1980s. Nowadays these jobs are changing rapidly, and will continue to change in the coming years. From a 'specialized role' workers are asked to perform a more 'broad' role: they have to service clients and they should have knowledge about many issues beside their own specialism. The project work now typical of many jobs is one of the best examples of these developments. Criterion development not only relates to the derivation and description of important job performances, but also to questions like: 'What is the difference in performance between types of job?'; 'Do these differences relate to the content of the work activities, or to the organization in which work is performed or the market and clients that are served?'

Looking at the knowledge available to tackle the above issues, we think that the work of organizational psychologists, and the work of other authors in the field of criterion development, form a sound basis for a discussion about the status of criteria within organizations. These authors have described major principles that relate to the definition and measurement of criteria. A summary of these is given by the performance modelling approach introduced by Greuter (1989). A design procedure is presented by which psychometric pitfalls can be overcome, and which provides direction to the development of adequate criteria for selection and appraisal. This procedure is described in Figure 14.2. It states that you first have to define the problem that is the goal of criterion development (e.g. in the case of selection, the prediction of future work performance of applicants; in the case of appraisal, evaluation of performance of personnel). The second step directs you to defining requirements, such as predictive validity, practicality, and utility. Then you define relevant criterion variables and you formulate the instruments that enable you to predict/evaluate the performance level on these criterion variables. The steps considering structure, form and parameters (steps 4, 5 and 6 in Figure 14.2) relate to the combination of the scores obtained in the process of selection/appraisal. This can be an algebraic function or a more 'clinical' model (see also Cascio, 1992).

In deriving criteria, a clear vision on the design procedure seems inevitable. The simple reason for this is that we do not develop criteria 'in a vacuum': we have a special purpose. Sometimes this purpose may be more 'widespread': in some

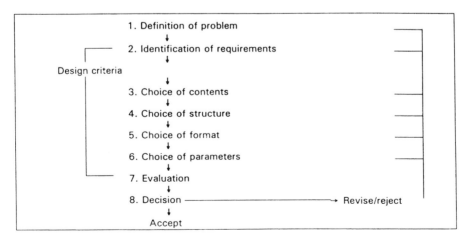

Figure 14.2 Developing performance models. *Source:* Greuter (1989)

cases we would have to develop criteria that serve several purposes (as for instance job redesign, training, coaching, development and change). Sometimes criterion development may be directed to specific objectives, as for instance the hiring of minority members, appraisal of certain performances, etc. As Greuter states, the design cycle has the advantage that 'it stipulates why required attributes are relevant for adequate job performance' (Greuter, 1989, p. 175). This comment is, in our opinion, extremely important because performance and achievements can only be guided when all organization members understand which direction has to be followed, what they have to do to achieve their own—or team—goals, and the measure against which they will be evaluated.

Unfortunately, the procedures for the development of criteria do not give specific guidance when we have to derive criteria for jobs that are less stable with regard to the content of work activities. In fact we often see that the process of criterion development does not go any farther than the identification of general requirements that give little opportunity to coach and direct performance. Criteria, then, may still be useful to predict and evaluate performance and achievement, but they are often remote from the actual job experiences of employees and managers. In such a case there is clearly a risk of criteria 'existing' but not being 'alive' and shared by those who are concerned.

We elaborate on this last issue in the next section, because we think that the changing nature of work asks for another view on criterion development.

PSYCHOMETRIC AND ORGANIZATIONAL CONSIDERATIONS

As we have already noted, there seems to be a feeling that we know how to develop criteria, but we are also aware that we might not tackle all the difficult issues in formulating adequate criteria. To illustrate this attitude: the personnel officers and managers that we speak to are seldom enthusiastic about criterion development. They see criterion development as a task that has to be done and which leaves little room for innovation. Moreover, because it is not easy to define criteria in an unambiguous way, practitioners (but also researchers) make do with a formulation of those behaviours that *can* be measured, instead of the behaviours that *should* be measured (Akkerman, 1989).

In addition, the number of publications about criterion development is decreasing. Our literature scan through several important journals revealed only articles in which criterion measures are evaluated against certain types of jobs, or general articles that describe how we may 'technically' develop criteria. In this regard the conclusions that Landy and Rastegary (1989) draw from their meta-analysis still hold: most studies pay attention to idiosyncratic criteria and less attention is paid to the way in which criteria are actually derived and developed. The recent discussion about behavioural competencies (see Chapter 17) gives new insight, but has not yet led to a clear statement of how criteria should be developed, so that they actually work.

We believe that it is important to realize that the discussion about criteria has—up to now—been a purely psychometric one (think about the statement of the

Reliable measurable	Should measure behaviours and outcomes in an objective manner
Content valid	Rationally related to the job performance activities
Defined specific	Cover identifiable behaviours and outcomes
Independent	Important behaviours and outcomes should be included in a comprehensive criterion
Non-overlapping	Criteria should not overlap
Comprehensive	No important behaviours or outcomes should be omitted
Accessible	Criteria should be phrased and named in a way that is comprehensible
Compatible	Criteria should fit in with an organization's goals and culture
Up to date	Criteria should be regularly reviewed in response to organizational change

Figure 14.3   Some requirements for criteria

manager in our introduction). Requirements are set for criteria: they should be relevant (cover job and tasks), give opportunities for the management of performance (concrete, non-deficient, motivating) and be adequately measurable (reliable, valid and acceptable for all—free from unfair discrimination). In addition to this, other requirements may be set, like the requirement that criteria should be 'up to date': they should be regularly reviewed in response to organizational change (see Figure 14.3).

To think that these psychometric requirements make up the total of the process of criterion development seems mistaken, however. Criteria are the foundation of procedures of selection, appraisal, development, job redesign and, last but not least, organizational change and development. Therefore they constitute concepts that can be used to organize employees, to direct their attention, and to lead their performance. They are also concepts to direct managers toward their task, which—in our opinion—can be made more stimulating by giving them the tools to discuss work with employees in a constructive way.

To achieve this broader perspective it is vital to introduce organizational practices in the process of criterion development. For example, if the organization is using the method of goal-setting to motivate and reward performances, then a similar type of procedure could be applied to develop criteria for selection. The advantage is that expectations are clearly communicated in the first encounter between organization and candidates. When the organization consists mainly of professionals, having a high level of expertise in performing their jobs, it might be more fruitful to apply a procedure by which principles of self-management are introduced in the derivation of criteria. In this instance opportunities are made to delegate performance management. In sum, the way in which procedures for criterion development are applied should be in line with the goals of the organization and its common managerial practices. This does not imply that we would like to throw away psychometric considerations in the process of criterion development. Relevance can easily be combined with psychometric soundness, as we will illustrate by some examples that we encountered in our consulting practice. These will be discussed next, after the introduction of a general model that summarizes how to combine psychometric procedures for developing criteria with procedures for communication about criteria within organizations.

CRITERIA IN RELATION TO ORGANIZATION PERFORMANCE

Do you recognize the following? You ask your boss, or the personnel officer, for a clear-cut description of the *criteria* against which you will be measured. Mostly, at least in our experience, the response is a 'glazed look'. The term, or name, 'criterion' is often exclusively limited to the language of work and organizational psychologists. 'Subtle' distinctions are even made between conceptual and operational criteria. Conceptual criteria define behaviours and performances at a rather abstract level, while operational criteria describe behaviours and performances at a rather abstract level, while operational criteria describe behaviours and performances that are concretely measurable. What we mean by these terms is often not understood by others, though. In fact, criteria are often taken to mean those aspects on which an employee is hired or the instruments by which his or her performance will be predicted (predictors and instruments).

Nonetheless, when you ask your manager, or personnel officer, or employee to state which goals are important in the (or their) work, they come up with very specific statements. So, criteria are recognizable in practice, simply because people have to run a factory, or an organization, or do a job. In fact, criteria reflect what has to be done in a job, a team or organization. The point is to find the right way to communicate about criteria and, subsequently, to define them in an objective and unambiguous way. The latter is extremely important because nowadays jobs are often not easily recognizable (Bridges, 1994). However, this does not mean that criteria will cease to exist. Criteria for group performance may differ from criteria for individual performance, but they still exist. The reason for this is simply that performance has to be managed/guided/predicted within organizations, and this cannot be done except by the use of criteria. The person(s) who are performing these management tasks might change though. For instance, self-managing teams may formulate their own criteria. Even more, they might apply their own criteria instead of the criteria that their manager has set. Clearly, there is more need, but also opportunity, to discuss criteria.

It is a reality: criteria change over time, and are not fixed. Criteria have become more and more matters of discussion—and this situation will only be more the case in the future. For instance, the criteria named in Figure 14.1 are nowadays designed in a totally different manner. Client service means that you should have insight into your product/service, should have 'content' knowledge and that you should be up-to-date regarding your experience with the products of competitors. A simple criterion like 'oral communication' is nowadays formulated somewhat as follows: can give insights in a clear manner, knows what he or she is talking about, shows 'sensitivity' and knows how to trigger the motivation of others. In sum, criteria are intertwined with organizational goals, and change over time, sometimes very rapidly. One of our major client organizations changed the criteria for their total work force (in total about 4000 employees) within a timespan of a couple of months, simply because an organizational change was needed owing to international market competition.

How can we develop criteria in a changing situation and still preserve the psychometric qualities that criteria should meet? In this case we think that it is useful to refer to the fact that criteria can be defined at more than the individual levels of analysis: for instance, at the level of organizational change and development and at the level of measurement and prediction. We summarize this point of view in Figure 14.4. In this figure we indicate which roles criteria can have and which requirements should be made for their development in each of the phases. In fact, this model should be seen as an elaboration on the design cycle of Greuter, but this time with an exclusive focus on the process that is followed.

1. First, there should be a clear goal (this speaks for itself, but we still encounter situations in which criteria are formulated from an objective that is different from that which they actually have to fulfil). At this stage we should not worry about psychometric requirements too much. More important is the discussion

Goals of criteria	Definition	Measurement	Communication
Goals for organization (development and change)	Organizational level	Tasks derived from organizational goals	Acceptable for management and employees
	General/relevant/ recognizable	Reflect organizational products/services	Goal-directing
Means to enhance performance (motivating and rewarding)	Job/group level or project team	Performance: objective/fair	Clear procedure; acceptable (comments are possible)
	Relationship to reward	Possibility for concrete feedback	Direction of performance
Behaviour development and coaching	Career paths, relationships between tasks	Behavioural clusters that indicate relationships	Win–win situation
	Communication about training/ education	Should direct development	Relationship between past, present, and future should be clear
Instruments for measurement of criterion performance	Operational	Psychometric requirements	Relationship of task to measurement clear
	To be connected at selection/appraisal procedures	Relationship to development/ appraisal	Opportunity for self-selection

Figure 14.4 Criterion development within the content of organizational activities

that we start about criteria. An applicable tool is to think about criteria in terms of 'metaphors' (examples are 'relationship directed'; 'drive'; 'insight'). We define activities that relate to the business of the organization and that reflect in a clear-cut way the products or services that have to be delivered, as well as the relationship with our clients and competitors. In fact, this stage implies image-building as well. We advise that a connection is made at this point with the public relation activities of the organization. The reason is that the new criteria will become more visible to all. It goes without saying that an integrated vision about management and performance is needed in this phase, or will have to be developed.

2. In the next stage we proceed to a rough specification: Which methods or procedures do we intend to choose for evaluation or prediction of performance? To what extent is the participation of other organizational members in the criterion development necessary in order to obtain commitment? Are there sustaining facilities to improve job performance available? In this stage it becomes important also to think about issues like objectivity, reliability, validity and fairness. For instance, if it is the case that an organization has appointed few members of minority groups, it is important to discuss how these groups could be integrated into the organization. Perhaps other facilities should be provided first, in order to enhance the job performance of these groups? We often see that employees cannot meet their standards simply because resources are lacking. In this instance we are not referring only to materials, machinery, etc. but also to managerial practices by which feedback is given on performance and successes and failures are discussed. Such omissions are most easily detected by starting up a communication structure between employees and managers.

3. Thereupon we go to the phase in which we pay attention to the development of behaviours and competencies. This implies of course that we have to specify the relationship with education and training, and courses that are available/ offered. In this phase it is important to think about issues like trainability, possibilities for coaching on the job, etc. Our experience is that this phase is often neglected, simply because another department will take care of this issue. If criteria are being developed that will be used throughout the organization, this issue should be tackled in this phase because otherwise measurements may be constructed that prevent employees from developing their skills. If future developments are difficult to predict for the organization, then it still seems useful to discuss several scenarios. Clarity is needed, even if only some possible future directions are described, to ensure that employees are aware of their future performances and react cooperatively to changes.

4. Finally, we define the criteria that will be applied in selection and appraisal procedures. At this point matters such as psychometric soundness become important, because concrete instruments have to be constructed that measure criterion performance. At this stage communication with workers/candidates and their (future) managers becomes more and more vital. Operational measurements should leave enough room for a clarification of mutual expectations and involvement. For instance, the issue of 'self-selection' should be

addressed at this stage by choosing adequate tests and questionnaires. In this phase it is important that operational measures are chosen that are flexible. This means that if job activities are likely to change, it is useful to construct criterion measurements that lend themselves for revision. Our experience is that measurements at a concrete level are easy to adapt when they refer to a more general criterion that describes performances that will be needed in the next five years. Trying to develop criteria that last at least ten years is no longer possible nowadays. This mistake should therefore be avoided in the operational phase.

COMMUNICATION ABOUT CRITERIA: EXAMPLES AND PROCEDURES

Too many procedures for criterion development start from the implicit assumption that a procedure for job analysis will reveal relevant criterion measurements. Mostly, however, organization members first want to deliberate about criteria in order to achieve commitment. Or, they simply want to discuss important changes and development first. Then a process is needed in which a communication tool is derived within the organization, or with help of external consultants, to discuss the types of behaviour and competencies needed today and in the future. We now present some short cases that illustrate procedures that might be applied in these instances.

Case 1: Developing criteria in order to rebuild an organization

A large (international) organization within the financial services sector asked us to develop a procedure by which graduate trainees might be hired. The key point was that they were encountering more competition from other organizations. In the past they had hired many technically competent people, but in the future more emphasis should be laid on commercial and managerial skills. The several decentralized units each claimed, however, that their own situation was 'unique' and that specific criteria should be formulated for them. In this Dutch situation regional differences relate to urban circumstances (high work load, many international clients, diversity in services) versus rural circumstances (local clients, lower work load, more social talk needed to convince clients, etc.). In short, the common stereotypes: urban versus rural.

First we discussed some general skills that were required by all employees within this organization. These skills were communicated by means of the use of the CIT method (see Visser, Altink and Algera, Chapter 21 in this volume). Thereupon our advice was to apply an assessment-centre method that would be performed with managers from the organization (coming from several decentralized units). This method had to be sustained by other communication procedures though. Therefore we devised a training programme for assessors. The advantage was that all managers involved met each other in an informal way which made it possible to communicate about relevant goals for performance. In fact, the training of assessors was used to communicate the criteria and to discuss them. It emerged that the supposed 'cultural diversity' between the several units was in fact minimal, and all managers agreed to the general criteria.

This example shows that training sessions can be a good tool to communicate about criteria and discuss descriptions of required and desired performance. The result now is that managers feel committed to the new personnel hired and the development of their professional and commercial skills. Issues such as whether decentralized units should apply local criteria have been discussed at the first stage in which the goals of the organization were communicated through the organization. Now a development centre is being implemented and procedures of reward are tied to the new goals. In fact, the process of criterion development has been more important to the goal of achieving organizational change than the actual definition of criteria.

Case 2: Developing criteria for 'growth'

Again the case study is set in a large organization, in this case in the transport sector. The organization went through a reorganization because of bad financial results and severe market competition. The task was to develop a selection and appraisal procedure.

Because the organization had paid less attention to the development of personnel and all personnel had very specific skills relating to a particular type of business, we formulated criteria for 'growth'. We defined a set of behavioural descriptions that made clear which skills, behaviours and performance were needed throughout a particular career path. This set of criteria was communicated by means of instruments and procedures. This procedure was followed because the organization concerned possessed a rather bureaucratic structure and therefore it was impossible to 'skip' certain departments and managers.

Nevertheless, the concrete instruments yielded a stimulating discussion at short notice. The reason for this was simply that employees and managers knew that something had to be changed in order to ensure the survival of their organization. Giving them a concrete goal that was derived from the future vision gave relief. The total organization became involved in the issue of career management. The criterion set became a central issue in deciding which type of employee could join the 'new' organization in the future, and in offering concrete tools for the development of employees. In addition to this it also became clear why some employees were less able to meet future goals. In fact, they experienced this themselves during the process of criterion development and raised no objections to the specification of the new criteria: they already knew themselves that they could not meet the new standards and that it would be more realistic to head for another type of job.

In this example the discussion about criteria started after having formulated a set of behaviours and performance that relate to career management paths. This procedure was inevitable because the criterion set defined in a clear and concrete way which goals had to be followed for the future. By formulating them in terms of development the criterion set became a tool that sustained reorganization procedures. Managers could discuss at a concrete level which methods were available to retain and develop employees. Outplacement of employees became more acceptable as well, because the criteria were clearly formulated and concretely measurable. They made it clear for individuals why they could no longer belong to the 'future organization', and specified in addition which possibilities they had for retraining and accepting other positions in the national workforce.

Case 3: Development of criteria for management development purposes

The last case applies to a medium sized organization that supplies manufactured goods. This organization felt that something had to be done about the development of their managers. The market asked for the development of new products.

In this instance we applied the procedure of 'work conferences'. We organized a meeting with managers to brainstorm several ideas and to work out their own ideas about innovation activities. At these conferences we applied such techniques as SWOT analysis, creative thinking, etc. In fact, we offered them concrete means to sustain the process of organization and management development.

This procedure yielded several new criteria, formulated at a concrete level, which could be used for the development of managers and the organization. Moreover, all managers stated that they would actively sustain and buy into these criteria. The descriptions and instruments that we formulated were discussed at a workshop and are now used to direct management behaviour. The next step will be to formulate criteria for employees that managers will discuss themselves by means of the method of work conference.

This case exemplifies the fact that managers are not always unwilling to look at their own performance. They know that setting clear goals is not always easy and they realize that their approach can have strong and weak points. Because organizational development asks much from the creativity of managers, it is more fruitful to have them participate in this process rather than replacing them by others unfamiliar with the company's business.

It is not the abstraction level of the definition of criteria, nor the fact that we define task performances, behaviours, personality requirements, etc. The simple fact is that we discussed criteria and connected them to the situation in which organizations and employees and managers find themselves. This grounding in organizational reality enabled us to connect the task of criterion development of important issues like organizational change, development of members and the skills of managers and employees.

Of course, we have to choose the relevant procedure for deriving criterion measures (Algera and Greuter, 1989; Greuter, 1989). Work-oriented procedures are best applied when there is a clear goal for the organization in a time-span of about three to five years. Worker-oriented methods—when we rely more heavily on less predictable person-skills—are preferable if jobs change rapidly (within a time span of about two to three years). An extremely important issue is whether organizations will stay in change, or some kind of equilibrium will be reached. This, simply because deriving criteria is a time-consuming business (costly) and relevance is still not easy to detect. Relevance refers to matters that do not directly relate to selection or appraisal businesses, for instance adherence with organizational goals, integration of selection and development practices, etc.

A FINAL COMMENT: THE CHANGING ROLE OF THE PROFESSIONAL

Clearly, our role in deriving criteria changes as well. We cannot rely solely on our psychometric procedures and have to integrate this procedure with other activities. These activities relate particularly to the process of criterion development. We discuss below some considerations relating to our role.

First, it is important to define what role we have to take in criterion development. For instance, can we manage all parties involved? This question relates to aspects like the organization members with whom we are on speaking terms. Also, there is a question about power within the organization: Who is our direct counterpart, who is our adviser, and who are our clients? This concerns the first introductory phase. Sometimes we will have to give up the task of criterion development simply because the organization is not ready for a commitment. In such a case we had better investigate performance issues and think about a new strategic point of view.

In other instances we can use such methods as:

- Training: by means of training we can disseminate relevant issues to the organization and its members.
- Methods of teambuilding: goals can be set clearly and interaction between team members will be increased.
- Methods concerning the process of development of criteria: we are actively involved in organizational change methods by our discussions with those concerned.

In fact we have become process facilitators and do not solely take the role of psychometric expert. This implies that other competencies are needed to be successful in this new role. Skills like strategic reasoning, persuasiveness and networking are important in this respect. In fact, in the business of human resource management consultancy interpersonal styles and methods of communication are essential. However, when we look at the education programmes for work and organizational psychologists, we often see that courses that foster these skills have been abolished owing to a reduction in study time. As a consequence students who aim to work in this area will have to acquire these skills by means of post-academic courses and training programmes.

In adddition to this, we think that it is vital that work and organizational psychologists use new and modern methods for job analysis and criterion development. With respect to this, we still find too often that work and organizational psychologists who work in the field of personnel selection pay more attention to the diagnosis of skills and capacities of employees than to the analysis of job characteristics and requirements. Our experience is that nothing is more important to selection than an adequate definition of the job and the criterion performances. As we tried to demonstrate in this chapter, the activities of work and organizational psychologists may generate a process that fosters organization development. So, certainly there is a market for work and organizational psychologists to prove their knowledge and competencies.

Perhaps we are advocating a role that leaves too much room for organizations and team members to interfere in the process of criterion development. Nevertheless, we think that their ideas should be integrated into the process of criterion development. Developing criteria means building up performance and communicating about performance. The process by which we give shape to this is of the utmost importance. Criterion development is not a matter of applying a simple 'recipe'. Criteria relate to the new direction that organizations, managers and employees take, and relate to innovation activities. This leaves ample room for content experts to disseminate their ideas.

ACKNOWLEDGEMENTS

We owe much gratitude to Dr Martin Greuter who set out the major principles on criterion development in his chapters in the previous edition of this Handbook. Although his illness prevented him from writing the update of his chapters, his ideas are elaborated on by those who worked closely with him. We hope that our contribution reflects some of the enthusiasm that Martin created by his work and studies.

REFERENCES

Algera, J.A. and Greuter, M.A.M. (1989). Criterion development and job analysis. In P. Herriot (ed.) *Assessment and Selection in Organizations*. Chichester: John Wiley.

Akkerman, A. (1989). Criteria and individual assessment. In M. Smith and I. Robertson (eds.), *Advances in Selection*. Chichester: John Wiley.

Bridges, W. (1994). *Job Shift: How To Prosper in a Workplace Without Jobs*. Reading, MA: Addison-Wesley.

Cascio, W.F. (1992). *Applied Psychology in Personnel Management*. Englewood Cliffs, NJ: Prentice-Hall.

Flood, P.J., Gannon, M.J. and Paauwe, J. (1995). *Managing Without Traditional Methods*. Reading, MA: Addison-Wesley.

Greuter, M.A.M. (1989). Performance modelling for personnel selection. In P. Herriot (ed.), *Assessment and Selection in Organizations*. Chichester: John Wiley.

Landy, F.J. and Rastegary, H. (1989). Criteria for selection. In M. Smith and I. Robertson (eds.), *Advances in Selection*. Chichester: John Wiley.

Pfeffer, J. (1994). *Competitive Advantage Through People, Unleashing the Power of the Work Force*. Boston, MA: Harvard Business School Press.

Wellins, R.S., Byham, W.C. and Dixon, G.R. (1994). *Inside Teams*. San Francisco, CA: Jossey-Bass.

Chapter 15

Utility Analysis: What Are the Black Boxes, and Do They Affect Decisions?

JOHN W. BOUDREAU, MICHAEL C. STURMAN AND TIMOTHY A. JUDGE

Center for Advanced Human Resource Studies, New York State School of Industrial and Labor Relations, Cornell University, Ithaca, New York 14853-3901, USA

Suppose we could calculate for a manager the return on investments in human resource management (HRM) programs, such as testing, training, compensation, and performance appraisal. Further, what if such calculations were based on accepted scientific research about the effects of such programs, and could be expressed in terms of financial and economic considerations (such as interest rates and taxes) to make them comparable to the calculations routinely carried out by analysts in such areas as marketing, finance, and manufacturing operations? Suppose further that the vast majority of evidence from studies using such methods had shown that the payoff from HRM programs was extremely high, often exceeding 100% even with very conservative assumptions. For example, one such study (Rich and Boudreau, 1987) calculated the return from using a computer programing ability test (the Programmer Aptitude Test, PAT) instead of traditional interview ratings to select replacements for a group of 201 computer programers. The analysis suggested that using the PAT would produce an incremental return of US$2.77 million over an 11-year period, for an additional investment of $10 per applicant, or about US$5811. A return-on-investment of over 400 times the initial investment. Moreover, the analysis suggests that there is less than a 2% chance that using the test will lose money, and the chance of seeing a net return of over one million US dollars is greater than 40%.

Such tools not only exist, they have been available to managers for over four decades, and the techniques to implement them have been the subject of intensive

International Handbook of Selection and Assessment, Edited by N. Anderson and P. Herriot.
© 1997 John Wiley & Sons Ltd.

discussion and research during the last 15 years. In industrial and organizational psychology, these tools are called 'utility analysis'. Results of utility analysis suggest that in many situations it is possible to express the effects of HRM programs in monetary units and, moreover, the payoff from such programs seems extraordinary even under the most conservative of assumptions. As a result, one might expect to see HRM executives among the most respected within organizations, budgets for HRM programs expanding as organizations realize the value of such programs, and a general recognition of HRM programs as key components of organizational profitability. Yet, those who work within and consult with organizations know that such a renaissance for HRM programs has not been forthcoming. Organizations persist with activities (such as the unstructured employment interview) that research has shown to produce low returns, and many HRM decisions continue to be made informally, without the use of financial analysis.

Utility analysis has been described as 'a family of theories and measures designed to describe, predict, and/or explain what determines the usefulness or desirability of decision options, and to examine how information affects decisions' (Boudreau, 1991, p. 621). Utility analysis (UA) evolved to provide tools for better describing and communicating the impact of HRM and industrial psychology interventions on organizational goals. Most UA research has been based on an implicit assumption that such communication would be aimed toward managers, who control the resources necessary to implement such interventions. Previous research has noted the need to move beyond developing new measures of utility parameters, and to focus on the role of UA information in managerial decision processes (Boudreau, 1989, 1991). Yet there remains a lack of research exploring these issues. In this chapter, we attempt to explicate some of these underlying assumptions and suggest how future UA research may fruitfully test them. We focus specifically on areas where the practice of human resource management seems to diverge from the implied behaviors of UA theory. These deviations provide potential clues about how to enhance the accuracy and usefulness of UA models, and suggest new directions for future UA research and practice.

The themes developed in this chapter relate to UA applications in training, compensation, performance assessment, and internal staffing. However, for simplicity and exposition, we will use the external selection model as our guiding framework. External selection is the focus of a significant proportion of UA research, so using this model will relate our themes to a large body of literature. Using the external selection model, this review will attempt to 'open up the black boxes' of four fundamental UA processes:

1. The relationship between predictors and criteria, represented by r, the correlation coefficient.
2. The nature of the criteria, represented by SD_y.
3. The nature of the selection process, represented by $\bar{Z}_x$.
4. The nature of the implementation process, represented by C.

Figure 15.1 depicts the distinction between the traditional and proposed frameworks. The traditional framework focuses primarily on the new selection intervention and its ability to predict performance, assumes the predictor scores will be used in a system of top-down hiring (the highest-scoring applicants gets the first job offer, followed by the next-highest scorer, and so on), and focuses on a one-dimensional measure of performance. The proposed model suggests that new interventions are usually combined with those currently being used, that predictor information is often used in ways that diverge from a top-down selection system, and that the notion of performance must include multiple dimensions or aspects.

SELECTION UTILITY: AN EXAMPLE

An example will help to clarify the meaning and usage of selection utility parameters, and highlight some of the points to be addressed here. The example will

Traditional UA Framework:

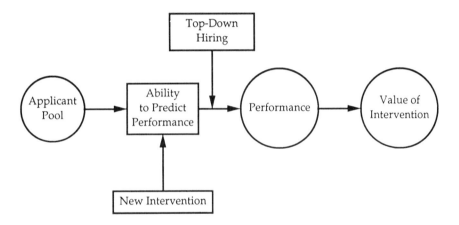

Proposed UA Framework:

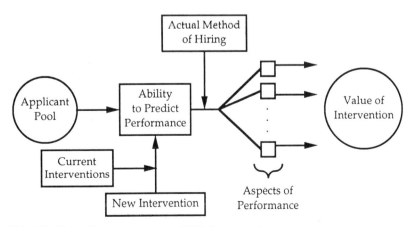

Figure 15.1   Traditional versus proposed UA framework

Table 15.1   Example application of selection utility analysis

Quantity of Person-Years Affected

11-year analysis period
5-year application of the selection system
201 existing employees
LEVG (Projected leverage based on past separation patterns) = 963
DF_{LEV} (Discount factor, discount rate of 15%, 11-year analysis) = 0.519

Factors Affecting the Value of Quality Change in Job Performance per Person Year

Selection ratio (the proportion of applicants who are hired) = 0.398
$\bar{Z}_x$ (the average Z-score on the predictor, of those hired) = 0.97
r_{INT} (the expected validity of the interview) = 0.14
r_{PAT} (the expected validity of the Programer Aptitude Test) = 0.73
SD_y (the value of a one-standard-deviation difference in job performance) = US$15 888
1-TAX (the proportion of increased profits retained after taxes) = 0.61

Factors Affecting the Costs of Implementing Selection Systems

N_a (Quantity of future applicants tested or interviewed) = 765
DF_{COST} (Discount Factor, 15% discount rate over 5 years) = 0.761
C_{INT} (Cost of the interview, per person) = US$634
C_{PAT} (Cost of PAT, per person) = US$644
1-TAX (the proportion of increased profits retained after taxes) = 0.61

Utility Calculation

Utility		= {[LEVG	× DF_{LEVG}	× $\bar{Z}_x$	× SD_y	× r	]-[C_{INT}	× N_a	× DF_{COST}]}	× 1-TAX
US$ 432 651	INT	= {[963	× 0.519	× 0.97	× US$15 888	× 0.14]-[US$634	× 765	× 0.761]}	× 0.61
US$3 201 248	PAT	= {[963	× 0.519	× 0.97	× US$15 888	× 0.73]-[US$644	× 765	× 0.761]}	× 0.61
US$2 768 597	DIF	= {[963	× 0.519	× 0.97	× US$15 888	× 0.59]-[US$10	× 765	× 0.761]}	× 0.61

Note: Calculations based on Rich and Boudreau (1987)

illustrate the utility model application of Rich and Boudreau (1987), which incorporated many of the features that have been suggested by researchers, and provides a detailed report of its application. The present example will focus only on those parameters discussed in this paper.

The example of Table 15.1 shows that the value of improved selection is determined by three main factors: (a) the *quantity* of employees and years affected by improved selection; (b) the value of the change in *quality* attributed to the program, and (c) the *costs* of implementing the program. Rich and Boudreau (1987) provide detailed summaries of the derivation of these factors.

For our purpose, the following points are most important. The quantity of employees and years affected is a function of anticipated hiring and separation patterns, and has a great deal to do with the projected value of improved selection. In this example, these hiring and separation patterns suggest that 963 person-years of performance are affected by selection in this group of 201 programers. The quality of the performance change is a function of $\bar{Z}_x$, which reflects how choosy the organization can be when hiring. In this case, the organization acquires applicants in the top 39.8% of the distribution, producing an average standardized test score ($\bar{Z}_x$) of 0.97, or almost one standard-deviation higher than if only average applicants were acquired. Quality is also a function of the *validity*, or strength of the relationship between the predictor (x) and job behaviors, this relationship symbolized by the correlation coefficient, *r*. In this case, research suggests that the typical unstructured interview has a validity of 0.14, while the PAT has a validity of 0.73. The product of $\bar{Z}_x$ and r predicts the average standardized level of job behaviors we can expect, using the selection device, but this value is not in dollar terms. To translate standard scores into dollars, utility analysis typically adds a factor (SD_y) reflecting the dollar value of a one-standard-deviation difference in job behaviors. In this case, a managerial survey was used to estimate the value of SD_y to be \$15 888 per person, per year (see Rich and Boudreau, 1987 for details of the estimation process). Finally, the cost of improved selection depends on the cost of selecting each individual, and on the number of applicants that must be examined to generate the selection information. In this case, the interview costs US\$633, and the PAT is assumed to add an additional US\$10 to that process (based on previous estimates by other researchers). After accounting for the organization's cost of capital (the discount rate) and tax obligations, Table 15.1 shows that the payoff to both selection devices is substantial, but the PAT produces an extremely high return on investment.

Understandably, such values have aroused great controversy among both researchers and practicing managers (see Boudreau, 1989, 1991 for reviews). There has been a suggestion that such large values must be unrealistic, and heated debate about the proper method of estimating the parameters of the model. Beyond questions of accuracy, however, are larger issues: Is the utility model an appropriate representation of the actual selection issues faced by managers? Is utility information useful in communicating the value of improved selection to managers interested in financial consequences? Why does it appear that utility analysis is used only by a very limited number of practicing managers? While this chapter cannot provide definitive answers to these questions, we propose to highlight some of the issues that bear on these questions, and to suggest directions for future research that should be useful for enhancing our understanding of the value of improved selection, as well as helping practicing managers better employ these tools in their work.

MULTIVARIATE VALIDITY OVER TIME: THE BLACK BOX OF *r*

The validity or correlation coefficient forms the basis for all UA models. Indeed, frustration with the ability of the validity coefficient to adequately communicate the magnitude of organization consequences from employee selection was what originally led to the search for more complete utility models (Boudreau, 1983, 1991). As the example of Table 15.1 shows, even a predictor with relatively low validity and high cost (such as the interview with a validity of 0.14 and a cost of US\$634 per applicant) can produce handsome payoffs. In the 1950s, early utility-analysis researchers proposed that managers did not seem to understand the value of such predictors, or the value of increasing predictor validity, and speculated that dollar-valued utility calculations might communicate better.

Virtually all UA models have incorporated the validity coefficient, but it usually has been treated as a bivariate correlation between a single predictor and a single criterion (usually performance appraisals, as discussed later). However, evidence suggests that organizations construct their selection processes by using multiple predictors. Virtually every organization uses reference checks, some form of application blanks, and employment interviews (Gatewood and Feild, 1994; Milkovich and Boudreau, 1994), while a smaller proportion of organizations also use ability tests or biographical data. US and Japanese manufacturers are famous for implementing lengthy and detailed selection processes using multiple predictors, especially for team-oriented production processes (e.g. Bowen, Ledford and Nathan, 1991). Thus, when organizations consider implementing new predictors, such as cognitive ability tests or work samples, it seems likely that such methods will be *added* to the existing group of predictors, rather than being applied separately (Sturman and Judge, 1994). The information of greatest value to decision makers is the incremental validity new selection devices would produce if added to the existing group of predictors. The selection costs associated with the final selection procedure should reflect all of the costs involved in using all procedures, and the validity of the selection procedure should reflect the multivariate combined validity of both the previous and newly-added predictors. The need to consider multiple predictors has been noted before (Jones and Wright, 1992), but has not yet been explicitly incorporated into the UA framework. The resulting utility values under the reasonable assumption of multiple predictor usage may be quite different from those produced under the tenuous assumption that each predictor will be used individually.

For example, using data from Rich and Boudreau (1987), and applying the one-cohort selection utility model of Brodgen, Cronbach, and Gleser (B-C-G), the univariate validity of the interview was 0.14, and the univariate validity of the Programer Aptitude Test (PAT) was 0.73. The single-device utility of the interview was $431 744 and the single-device utility of the PAT was $3 198 258. The implication of such a calculation is that the organization could achieve $3 198 258 in increased value per cohort by abandoning the interview and using only the PAT. However, organizations seem unlikely to abandon the interview, so the most appropriate comparison is between the combination of the interview and the PAT, versus the interview alone. The formula for the multiple correlation of two predictors (Nunnally, 1978, pp. 176–177), suggest that if the two procedures are combined, the multiple correlation will differ depending on the intercorrelation between the two predictors. If we assume a range of correlations (0.00, 0.25, 0.50, or 0.75) between the PAT and interview, we obtain different multiple correlations for the predictor combination (0.74, 0.73, 0.77 and 0.95, respectively). This result, combined with a cost level that reflects the combined costs of the two predictors, suggests utilities for the predictor combination of $3 024 175, $2 972 715, $3 165 209, and $4 011 408, respectively (Sturman and Judge, 1994). Thus, the incremental utility of combining the two predictors is somewhat lower (6–7%) than the utility of substituting the more-valid predictor for the interview, at moderate intercorrelation levels. Only when the two devices are highly correlated does it make sense to keep both. Using a model that acknowledges predictor intercorrelations provides a more accurate picture of the consequences of maintaining the interview as part of the selection process. Because it is rare for organizations to exclude interviews from their selection processes, such a model also provides a more accurate utility estimate.

Acknowledging the possibility of adding new predictors to old ones requires information about intercorrelations among predictors, which may be absent from validation and validity generalization data. Moreover, in actual selection situations, it appears that decision makers incorporate additional factors into their deliberations, beyond the typical selection dimensions of knowledge, skills, and ability. Individual dispositions and personality have been shown to relate to important employee behaviors (Judge, 1992). Actual selection strategies and decisions may incorporate such dispositions, as is evident from research on the characteristics recruiters look for in job applicants (Bretz, Rynes and Gerhart, 1993). We need more research on the interrelationships between dispositions and other more traditional predictors, and on the reaction of organizational decision makers to using dispositional information and multiple predictors in their selection decisions. UA models that incorporate such information may be seen as more credible by decision makers familiar with the multiple-predictor reality of employee selection. To date, we have little evidence of how decision makers perceive the additive value of multiple predictors, or whether they can effectively use information about multiple-predictor relationships to make better selection strategy decisions.

Practicing managers might well consider whether they tend to simply add new predictors to old ones. As we have seen, such a practice may waste resources if a higher level of predictability could be attained by simple substitution of a new predictor for an old one.

Temporal validity variations

Validity may vary over time (Hulin, Henry and Noon, 1990), though evidence is mixed and sparse regarding predictive relationships between criteria and job-performance measures (Barrett, Alexander and Doverspike, 1992). The traditional UA model that uses one validity value for all future periods may mis-state the actual value of a predictor whose validity changes. In the worst case, if validity declines over time, then a utility calculation based on constant validity values may significantly overstate the actual value of predictors. We do not know if managers consider this possibility when considering new selection systems. Managers may have experience with temporal shifts in the relative performance of individuals over time (Hofmann, Jacobs and Gerras, 1992). For example, they may know of cases where the initial differences in performance are significantly reduced as employees gain experience, causing validity to decline as the lower-performing employees improve to the level of the initially-higher performers. Managers may consider such shifts in their decisions. Utility models and values that presume stable relative performance levels within each hired cohort, and thus stable validities, conflict with this experience. Future UA research could profitably explore the degree to which such temporal variations affect utility estimates, and the degree to which they affect decision makers' judgments about the value of selection strategies.

MULTIDIMENSIONAL CRITERIA: THE NATURE OF SD_y

Both managers and researchers have focused on SD_y as a key factor in the credibility and usefulness of utility analysis. As the example of Table 15.1 indicates, the level of SD_y has profound effects on the dollar values produced, and for almost 15 years there has been a spirited debate about the best way to estimate this parameter, with a variety of alternative measures suggested. Boudreau (1991) reviewed the research investigating alternative methods of estimating the standard deviation of performance in dollars (SD_y), and the question of whether it can be estimated accurately. To date, there is little consensus on the proper measurement method, though Boudreau suggested that the minimum value of SD_y necessary to communicate the value of improved selection is often much less controversial. In Table 15.1, the minimum value of SD_y needed to justify using the PAT instead of the interview is US$1059 per person, per year, which is approximately half of the *lowest* estimate provided by any manager in the Rich and Boudreau (1987) study. It is not our present purpose to add to the debate about the relative accuracy or appropriateness of various approaches of estimating SD_y. Rather, we would like to focus attention on a neglected aspect of the issue, the multidimensionality of employee value.

Boudreau (1991) pointed out that UA has its roots in multiattribute utility analysis (MAU), which offers tools and theories for making decisions with multiple and conflicting outcomes (Bazerman, 1990). Undoubtedly, criteria for employee selection are multidimensional. Virtually any introductory HRM textbook recognizes that performance ratings are not the only criterion for employee selection (e.g. Milkovich and Boudreau, 1994). Absenteeism, trainability, flexibility, likelihood of separation, and 'fit' between the individual's characteristics and those needed for long-term organizational success are also commonly valued outcomes of selection (Judge and Ferris, 1992). Yet, virtually all UA applications presume a univariate criterion, y, which reflects the dollar value of individual employee performance. Some research has investigated the judgment processes underlying SD_y. Bobko, Karren and Parkington (1983) noted that sales managers reported using pay as an anchor for their estimates of 'overall worth'. Burke and Frederick (1984) found that supervisors of sales managers reported using five dimensions in judging employee value: (a) management of recruiting, training, and motivating personnel; (b) amount of dollar sales achieved; (c) management of sales coverage; (d) administration of performance appraisal; and (e) forecasting and analyzing sales trends. Burke (1985) found that supervisors of clerical workers followed job evaluation dimensions in their judgments, with salary-related factors most frequently used. Even these investigations focus primarily on job-specific performance behaviors, despite the fact that an individual's value to an organization realistically goes beyond their current performance in a particular job.

Can multivariate criteria be represented by single-criterion validity?

A complete value criterion would include not only job performance, but also the level of withdrawal behaviors, speed with which new tasks are learned and applied, relationships with co-workers, ability to perform in a variety of future work situations, and 'fit' with the cultural and behavioural norms of the organ-ization (Bowen, Ledford and Nathan, 1991; Judge and Ferris, 1992). The per-ceived value of an individual or group is likely to depend on the individual making the judgment, and these differences in perceived value may differ in ways that are not simply random, as suggested by research which compares the performance ratings of supervisors, co-workers, and subordinates (Harris and Schaubroeck, 1988). Though each may provide valid performance assessments, the results of each assessor may differ from the others. Moreover, meta-analytic studies have suggested that supervisory ratings explain less than 50% of the variance in objective results (Heneman, 1986), so both objective and subjective measures are needed to fully represent performance criteria. Typically, SD_y is estimated by having experts place a dollar amount on the 'overall value' of employees, which some might argue will automatically incorporate all the rel-evant performance dimensions. Previous efforts to detect the dimensions used by decision makers in making an overall SD_y estimate are helpful in testing this argument, but they fail to reflect the fact that different performance dimensions may have different relationships to each other, and may relate very differently to particular predictors.

Even when UA researchers estimate SD_y with methods that reflect multiple criterion dimensions, they typically measure validity (r) as the correlation be-tween a predictor and one criterion (such as performance ratings) to reflect a multidimensional estimate of employee value. Yet performance ratings are used for many purposes, non-performance factors are often reflected in performance ratings as a way to achieve organizational goals, and managers frequently have little faith that performance ratings truly reflect differences in employee value (Murphy and Cleveland, 1991; Oppler *et. al.*, 1992). There is also evidence that withdrawal behaviors may covary and may form a single common construct (Judge and Hulin, 1994). Maximum and typical performance levels may not be highly correlated (Sackett, Zedeck and Fogli, 1988). It would appear fruitful to consider alternatives to the tradition of using a validity coefficient based on per-formance ratings to represent the relationship between a selection strategy and the multiple dimensions of employee performance. It would also be fruitful to investigate whether UA estimates are more or less influential depending on how decision makers perceive the dimensionality of employee value. For managers, the question is whether one trusts a measure of r that reflects only job perfor-mance ratings as the criterion, or a measure of SD_y that may not reflect multiple performance perspectives, multiple performance dimensions, or the value of indi-viduals beyond their current job assignment. Even considering the effects of these omissions, the utility values that have emerged are so large that one could argue they are sufficient to establish the fact that improved selection is worth the invest-ment in almost all cases. Yet, organizations persist in using selection systems that do not reflect research, and utility analysis models remain rare in organizations. To date, we have little evidence on whether decision makers discount the cred-ibility of utility values because they presume that computed values reflect a very limited set of criteria, and that effects of selection on other criteria may offset those included in the calculation.

Using employee movement to represent multiple criteria

The fact that employees are unlikely to spend their entire career with the same organization, let alone in the same job, has been well publicized by the popular business press. UA concepts can reflect the effects of employee recruitment, separations, and movement between jobs (Boudreau, 1991). Thus, employee movement consequences of selection alternatives can be represented by the effects of movements on employee performance in other positions, the quality and quantity of recruits, and/or the quality and quantity of those leaving and staying in the job. For example, the traditional utility model presumes that all employees hired, regardless of their quality, will remain on the job for the same amount of time. Thus, selection mistakes due to lower-validity predictors are assumed to plague the organization for up to ten years in some analyses. A more realistic assumption might be that such selection mistakes will be weeded out through attrition, thus increasing the value of the workforce even with less-valid selection, and reducing the difference between more and less-valid selection systems.

Much debate focuses on the notion of 'fit' as a long-term measure of the value of an individual to the organization, including multiple criteria of value and encompassing multiple possible future roles (Bowen, Ledford and Nathan, 1991; Judge and Ferris, 1992). It appears that recruiters and interviewers consider the broader concept of 'fit' in their deliberations (Bretz, Rynes and Gerhart, 1993). Other evidence also suggests that applicants choose jobs based on their perceived fit with the organization's values and other attributes (Judge and Bretz, 1992). Thus, utility models that encompass phenomena such as recruitment, separations, and internal movement may better reflect the long-term value of individual fit with the organization. To date, little research has explored the relative accuracy and value of such models, or their attractiveness to decision makers. While such models are undoubtedly more complex than simple single-job utility models (Hunter, Schmidt and Coggin, 1988), no evidence exists to suggest whether such models are viewed as more credible due to their complexity, or less credible due to their inability to incorporate more realistic phenomena.

Multi-attribute utility analysis to define criteria

Extending UA models to reflect movement patterns beyond selection encompasses more of the performance domain, but such utility models still treat performance in any particular work role as a univariate phenomenon. To fully address the issue of multidimensional performance in a given work role requires that the diverse performance elements be combined. One might treat each element as a separate performance measure, calculating utility for each of several performance elements. Certain utility parameters would be the same for all elements, such as the number of applicants, the number of selected employees, the selection ratio, and the cost of the predictor(s). However, for each performance criterion, the validity of the predictor(s) may vary. Similarly, the SD_y value for each criterion may be different, depending on the amount of discretion afforded by the work role on that dimension, the value of that dimension to the organization, and the variability among applicants and employees in their capability to exhibit that performance dimension. Encompassing multiple performance dimensions in this way requires little modification of existing models. It merely combines several single-criterion models into an overall utility estimate by adding the individual utility estimates for each performance dimension.

However, such an additive approach is likely to produce misleading results depending on the correlations among the criteria. Performance elements may conflict (e.g. effort devoted to individual selling may detract from helping co-workers and vice versa). If maximizing one performance dimension detracts from the other or, as in the case of typical and maximal performance, if two performance dimensions are uncorrelated, then the sum of the utilities based on them may not accurately reflect the true utility of their combination. What is needed is an approach to estimating SD_y that allows decision makers to consider multiple performance criteria, yet still obtains an overall utility value reflecting the combination of those criteria. Techniques for estimating overall utility functions from disparate criteria have been available for several decades, generally described as Multi-Attribute Utility (MAU) estimation techniques (Dawes, 1982; Huber, 1980). Such approaches attempt to determine the relative importance and trade-offs between multiple criteria in estimating the overall utility level. We know little about the relative weights decision makers place on different performance dimensions, how different performance dimensions relate to each other, and how these relationships affect the perceived relative value of different employees. Future research might fruitfully examine these questions. The anwers will have implications not only for UA research, but also for research on job evaluation and performance assessment.

Moreover, such research is likely to shed light on the ways in which different constituents evaluate employee value. Many organizations are undergoing fundamental changes in the way they organize and assign responsibility for decisions, including flatter structures and decentralized decision power (see Sparrow, Chapter 17 in this volume, for instance). Such reorganization may mean that very different constituents will make decisions about the use of selection strategies or other human resource programs. The key constituency for UA information in organizations of the future may be teams, task forces, or subordinates, rather than supervisors or top managers. We have little data regarding how work groups define employee value, or whether such definitions differ significantly from those of more traditional supervisors. However, it seems likely, given the necessary interaction inherent in work groups, that interpersonal fit may have even greater value in term-based organizations (Bowen, Ledford and Nathan, 1991). Virtually all existing UA research reflects criteria from the perspective of the supervisor rather than the work group. Utility values calculated from the perspective of the supervisor may not reflect the criteria used by work groups in judging performance (Neuman, 1991). For managers, the key issue may not be whether human resource professionals understand the value of improved selection, but whether teams, task forces, and quality-improvement networks can understand it.

Combining multiple predictors and criteria

If the outcomes of selection strategies are affected by multiple criteria and multiple predictors, UA models should consider how to simultaneously encompass the effects of both. The 'black boxes' of both the correlation coefficient and SD_y contain complex relationships when multiple criteria and multiple predictors are involved. The utility framework proposed here suggests that actual organizations typically face selection strategy choices in which the consequences depend on multiple predictor–criterion relationships and differentially weighted criterion dimensions. Examining the utility consequences of such situations requires much more extensive information about both the predictor and the criterion space. We need information about predictor interrelationships and their relative ability to predict several different criteria (see Figure 15.1). We also need information on criterion interrelationships and their relative importance in determining overall employee value (Alliger and Janak, 1989). Such information may help explain why predictors that appear to offer high utility within the single-predictor, single-criterion model may be somewhat less attractive when viewed in combination with other predictors and criteria. If the interview is used to assess global traits that may contribute to many criteria, and if new predictors are likely to be combined with the interview in any practical selection system, a multivariate criterion and predictor utility model may offer an explanation for the resilience of the interview compared to such apparently superior predictors as work samples and cognitive ability tests.

THE BLACK BOX OF $\bar{Z}_x$

A third utility 'black box' involves the average standardized predictor score of the selected group. As Table 15.1 shows, this parameter reflects the 'choosiness' with which applicants are selected based on their predictor scores. Typically, it is assumed to reflect a single predictor, and selection of applicants from the top down, in order of their predictor scores, until all vacancies are filled. Recognizing the existence of multiple predictors means that this parameter may best be considered a predictor composite, weighted to achieve maximum predictability. Existing utility models do not generally proceed from this perspective, but it is relatively simple to consider the variable x as a weighted composite of predictors with each individual's x-score representing the value of that composite. It seems plausible that managers conceive of the selection process in this way, with several predictors interacting to form a composite from which selection decisions are made.

A more significant limitation of existing utility models concerns the classic assumption that applicants are scored on the predictor (or composite), are ranked from the top down on those scores, job offers are made in order of predictor scores, and applicants accept all job offers. Such assumptions are convenient because they make the calculation of $\bar{Z}_x$ a simple transformation of the normal distribution, for which there are available tables of values (Naylor and Shine,

1965). Research has addressed the possibility that applicants reject job offers which, depending on the relationship between applicant qualifications and rejection patterns, reduces the effective value of $\bar{Z}_x$ (e.g. Murphy, 1986; Rich and Boudreau, 1987). Others have examined the utility effects of modifying a top-down selection strategy to enhance the racial and/or gender composition of the accepted group (Schmidt, Mack and Hunter, 1984).

Each of these modifications provides insights into the degree to which deviations from top-down hiring affect the traditional selection utility model. While some organizations undoubtedly do rank applicants and offer jobs according to those rankings, we believe that deviations from the top-down strategy are likely to be the rule, rather than the exception, and can occur for many reasons other than organizational attempts to reach diversity goals or to offset the effects of candidates rejecting offers. Decision makers seldom will be content simply to make selection decisions based on the top-down scoring of a particular selection device, especially a cognitive ability test. Selection strategies have many goals beyond obtaining high-quality employees. Interviews, for example, may be intended to communicate organizational goals, to present a certain image to applicants, or to involve certain organizational constituents in the selection process. Evidence from employee recruiting suggests that recruiter behaviors and characteristics are interpreted by applicants as indicators of organizational characteristics (Rynes, Bretz and Gerhart, 1991), so organizations may adopt recruiting, screening, and selection techniques based on these characteristics rather than on the ability to select the best candidates.

Even when decision makers attempt to use selection devices purely to identify the best quality candidates, there are likely to be deviations from the typical top-down strategy. Evidence from the decision-making literature suggests that people tend to ignore base rates, overweigh vivid information, and overestimate their ability to make accurate probabilistic judgments (Bazerman, 1990). These tendencies may make decision makers reluctant to adopt a simple top-down hiring strategy, even when such a strategy is statistically likely to yield the highest quality pool of new hires. For example, if a cognitive ability test is added to a selection system that previously involved only interviews, the highest utility strategy may be to ignore the interviews and select using a top-down ranking based on test scores. Yet organizations persist in relying heavily on unstructured interviews, and we can assume that the results of interviews are used in combination with test scores. We have little evidence regarding how actual selection decision makers combine different types of selection information to make decisions. If the top-down approach is not adopted, perhaps decision makers mistakenly place too much weight on vivid interview information or fail to realize the fallibility of interview impressions.

Previous research has examined whether applicant characteristics influence selector willingness to offer jobs, but this research generally has focused on personal characteristics such as race, or objective qualifications such as academic credentials (e.g. Lin, Dobbins and Farh, 1992; Macan and Dipboye, 1990; Olian, Schwab and Haberfeld, 1988). Future research might profitably examine how decision makers combine information from different selection methods. When decision makers participate in one or more selection activities (such as interviews), their behaviors may not conform to the classic utility model assumption of top-down selection. If decision makers 'believe in' the validity of the interview and/or find the idea of 'testing' dehumanizing or otherwise inappropriate, they may choose to ignore test scores in favour of interview impressions. The classic utility model portrays the *potential* utility of tests when used rigorously, but it does not reflect the *actual* utility of tests interjected into situations where decision makers are unprepared to use them. The 'marginalist' approach (Jones and Wright, 1992), through which decision makers apply techniques with the lowest marginal cost first and progress to higher-cost techniques only as needed, may not describe actual decision behavior. Thus, the true effect of selection strategies is achieved only after the selection information is filtered through the cognitive behavior of decision makers. Even the most valid and least costly strategy may have low utility if its results are given too little weight when actual selection decisions are made.

Future utility research could fruitfully examine how decision makers react to the availability of different kinds of selection information. It would be interesting to know whether involving decision makers in the selection process increases their willingness to use selection information, or whether compelling evidence (such as utility analyses showing that top-down selection based on test scores is lucrative) can convince decision makers to alter their traditional practices. As noted earlier, much research on decision making has documented the biases exhibited when making decisions and using information. There is ample evidence that linear models outperform human decision makers across a variety of situations (Dawes, 1982), so we would expect utility models to be capable of outperforming human decision makers in selection (when accuracy in predicting job performance is the criterion). Yet there is also evidence that decision makers fail to adopt potentially lucrative human resource strategies due to various cognitive limitations (e.g. Florin-Thuma and Boudreau, 1987). To date, there has been little integration between this research and the use of selection information.

Is maximizing organizational performance the true objective?

One additional reason why decision maker behaviors may deviate from utility-analysis prescriptions is the possibility that utility analysis describes a model in which one strives to increase organizational performance. An alternative possibility is that organizational decisions are directed at very different objectives, such as individual political advancement, or that they occur through a random process called a 'garbage-can' model (Huber, 1982). For example, decision makers may persist in using unstructured interviews precisely *because* such techniques have low validity and thus maintain ambiguity in the selection process. Such ambiguity may provide a power base for those professionals who are recognized as successful in achieving good results in such a 'mysterious' process. If such results could be achieved simply by using test scores, the powerful selection 'experts' might well lose their organizational power. While admittedly a somewhat cynical view, this perspective seems plausible, at least in some situations. Thus, future research might examine the possibility that utility analysis is resisted not because the managers are irrational or do not understand the models, but because the managers' criteria are very different from those suggested by utility analysis.

ACTUAL BARRIERS TO ADOPTING NEW INTERVENTIONS, THE FULL COSTS, *C*

The classic utility model reflects the incremental costs of new selection devices in the parameter *C*. These costs can be expressed in terms of the number of applicants, the number of hires, or the total program. The cost term in utility models virtually always reflects only the costs of actually administering and scoring selection procedures. This often ignores some very real costs which are likely to affect the value of improved selection strategies. Some organizations will be required to increase the pay and/or benefits of workers hired under a new selection strategy. Economic theory predicts that unless an organization adjusts wages to reflect increased qualifications, it will be difficult to attract the most qualified workers (Cascio and Morris, 1990; Jones and Wright, 1992). Becker (1989) has discussed several scenarios through which the apparent benefits of selection may be reduced due to increased remuneration obligations or because of decrements in quality caused by a failure to increase remuneration commensurate with increased qualifications. We have little research to suggest how applicant qualifications interact with organizational rewards, but it seems plausible that utility models which ignore the need to adjust rewards for qualifications may overstate utility levels. On the other hand, substantial evidence suggests that variability in rewards for a given job is not large enough to reflect all variability in employee value (Bishop, 1987). Thus, the cost adjustment necessary to attract better-qualified employees may be less than the increase in value they afford the organization. Still, wages and benefits are not the only factors affecting organizational attractiveness. Other organizational attributes may require adjustment to attract desired applicants to the organization. The decision to select more rigorously may entail changes in the organizational features most likely to be valued by the more qualified applicants (Wanous *et al.*, 1992; Williams and Dreher, 1992), and these changes likely entail costs. Furthermore, recent research suggests that use of some selection instruments (e.g. drug tests or stress tests) may be more costly to organizations because they are perceived as unfair by applicants, decreasing job seekers' willingness to accept a job offer from organizations using these instruments (Judge *et al.*, 1994; Smither *et al.*, 1993).

The costs of implementing new selection strategies may be much higher than previously suggested because previous calculations did not include the resources necessary to convince decision makers to use selection information most efficiently. Organizations develop routines and customs, and adopting new HR programs may frequently challenge these routines and customs. A hidden cost may well be the effort and resources necessary to 'unfreeze' the organization, so that it is prepared even to consider new approaches. This sort of organizational inertia may be costly to oppose (Boudreau, 1984; Jones and Wright, 1992). It may be difficult to attain high potential utility because key decision makers will simply not use new methods. Those who do implement new HR programs are likely to encounter costs of convincing, training, and communicating with key constituents in order to gain acceptance. Typical costs might include training managers or employee teams on the benefits of new selection processes, employee communications explaining the need for new processes and their divergence from processes used before, and support systems (such as computer systems and databases) to ease implementing and using new procedures. There also may be required changes in recruiter behaviors to attract high-quality applicants. To date, we have little information about the actual and perceptual barriers to implementing new selection systems and the costs of covering them. Both the subjective and objective costs of surmounting resistance to change are likely to affect actual utility applications, though they remain absent from most UA discussions.

MAKING PROGRESS THROUGH PRACTITIONER–RESEARCHER COLLABORATION

UA research provides models that identify some of the variables that affect selection utility, but the focus on model development and parameter measurement has left large gaps in our understanding of whether important assumptions are met, and whether information from such models is likely to be used by decision makers. If UA models are to achieve widespread use, future research must shed light on these issues to guide the further development of new UA models, and to provide assistance in presenting UA information to key stakeholders. We believe that UA models can improve communication and understanding of the value of selection, and can lead to better decisions about investments in improved selection, as well as other HR programs. However, the apparent lack of widespread adoption of UA, and the potentially damaging tendency for managers to fail to adopt valuable HR interventions, suggests a need for a more collaborative approach to future understanding. Both researchers and practitioners must play a role, if future UA model developments are to illuminate the questions posed here.

First, HR professionals should calculate UA values, even using simple traditional models. While published reports suggest that such values are high, we do not yet know if this is generally true. Numerous UA studies during the last 15 years, and the example of Table 15.1, suggest an extraordinary potential for lucrative returns to HR investments. However, we have little evidence that selectors are aware of such possibilities. If they begin to implement even simple UA models, such calculations will increase their understanding of the models. This will undoubtedly lead to questions, which will provide the kernels of future research. In this chapter, we have suggested that selection practitioners may wish to focus on the following questions:

1. Does the actual selection system use multiple predictors, instead of only single predictors? Do recruiters combine information from different predictors? If so, collaborative research to determine the relationships among predictors, and their relative ability to predict different criteria, may be useful.

2. Do recruiters consider only a single performance criterion, or does an employee's value to an organization depend on multiple factors, assessed from multiple perspectives? If HR practitioners believe that UA models are limited by a single-criterion focus, then collaborative research can help to identify the multiple criteria, multiple performance assessors, as well as the effects on UA values of considering multiple predictor–criterion relationships. Also relevant here is the question of whether recruiters require that UA models acknowledge the movement of employees between positions. If so, researchers and practitioners could fruitfully collaborate to identify what movements are most critical to determining employee value, and how to incorporate those movements into the model in a way that is credible and useful to managers.
3. How do recruiters actually use selection information? Is a top-down hiring approach realistic, or do the practical demands of selection require that other approaches be used? Researchers and practitioners could work together to identify and describe how selection information is actually used, and then to determine if moving toward a top-down strategy is valuable. Such research could also provide selectors with useful information on how the information from multiple selection devices is combined and used by decision makers. Theories can suggest the sort of biases that are most likely to occur, and collaborative research could examine their occurrence and effects. If information is actually used in a non-optimal way, opportunities for training may be uncovered. There may also be potential here for 'expert systems' that can incorporate the technology of UA within automated systems that free the recruiter from the burdens of computation and technical understanding. Some UA research has used computer technology in this way (e.g. Rich and Boudreau, 1987), but to date we have little information about how such systems might work with practicing recruiters. Also relevant here is the question of whether the 'rational' approach of UA models is even realistic. Research is needed to clarify the true purposes served by selection systems, and the degree to which they confer personal, expert or political power on certain groups.
4. What are the true costs and resources necessary to change selection systems, and are they accurately reflected in the UA calculations? The example in Table 15.1 reflects the suggestion by many psychologists that improved testing will require only minimal investments (such as $10 per test). Are such suggestions realistic? If not, what are the key implementation costs, and how can they better be reflected in future utility models?

In summary, we continue to believe that UA research has the potential to help recruiters make better HR decisions, and to communicate the impact of those decisions more effectively. However, to achieve that potential requires research that focuses less on improvements to the traditional utility model, and more on examining whether that model fits the reality of HR decisions in actual organizations. Such research requires that HR managers and researchers work together. HR managers must strive to understand the UA framework, to help direct research that will make it as useful as possible. HR researchers must see practitioners not merely as subjects providing estimates of UA parameters, but as the recipient of UA information, and as the source of information to help improve UA models. Such collaborations have great potential to realize the potential for UA models in the future.

REFERENCES

Alliger, G. M. and Janak, E. A. (1989). Kirpatrick's level of training criteria: Thirty years later. *Personnel Psychology*, **42**, 331–342.

Barrett, G. V., Alexander, R. A. and Doverspike, D. (1992). The implications for personnel selection of apparent declines in predictive validities over time: A critique of Hulin, Henry, and Noon. *Personnel Psychology*, **45**, 601–617.

Bazerman, M. (1990). *Judgment in Managerial Decision Making*, 2nd edn. New York: John Wiley.

Becker, B. E. (1989). The influence of labor markets on human resources utility estimates. *Personnel Psychology*, **42**, 531–546.

Bishop, J. H. (1987). The recognition and reward of employee performance. *Journal of Labor Economics*, **5**, S36–S56.

Bobko, P., Karren, R. and Parkington, J. J. (1983). Estimation of standard deviations in utility analysis: An empirical test. *Journal of Applied Psychology*, **68**, 170–176.

Boudreau, J. W. (1983). Effects of employee flows on utility analysis of human resource productivity improvement programs. *Journal of Applied Psychology*, **68**, 396–407.

Boudreau, J. W. (1984). Decision theory contributions to HRM research and practice. *Industrial Relations*, **23**, 198–217.

Boudreau, J. W. (1989). Selection utility analysis: An agenda for future research. In M. Smith and I. Robertson (eds), *Advances in Personnel Selection and Assessment* (pp. 227–258). London: John Wiley.

Boudreau, J. W. (1991). Utility analysis for decisions in human resource management. In M. D. Dunnette and L. M. Hough (eds), *Handbook of Industrial and Organizational Psychology*, 2nd edn (vol. 2, pp. 621–745). Palo Alto: Consulting Psychologists Press.

Bowen, D. E., Ledford, G. E., Jr and Nathan, B. R. (1991). Hiring for the organization, not the job. *Academy of Management Executive*, **5**, 35–51.

Bretz, R. D., Rynes, S. and Gerhart, B. (1993). Recruiter perceptions of applicant fit: Implications for individual career planning and job search behavior. *Journal of Vocational Behavior*, **43**, 310–327.

Burke, M. J. (1985). An investigation of dimensions employed and percentile ordering effects in estimating performance standard deviations in dollars for clerical occupations. Unpublished manuscript.

Burke, M. J. and Frederick, J. T. (1984). Two modified procedures for estimating standard deviations in utility analyses. *Journal of Applied Psychology*, **71**, 334–339.

Cascio, W. F. and Morris, J. R. (1990). A critical reanalysis of Hunter, Schmidt, and Coggin's (1988) 'problems and pitfalls in using capital budgeting and financial accounting techniques in assessing the utility of personnel programs'. *Journal of Applied Psychology*, **75**, 410–417.

Dawes, R. M. (1982). The robust beauty of improper linear models in decision making. In D. Kahneman, P. Slovic and A. Tversky (eds), *Judgment under Uncertainty: Heuristics and Biases* (pp. 391–407). Cambridge, UK: Cambridge University Press.

Florin-Thuma, B. C. and Boudreau, J. W. (1987). Performance feedback utility in a small organization: Effects on organizational outcomes and managerial decision processes. *Personnel Psychology*, **40**, 693–713.

Gatewood, R. D. and Feild, H. S. (1994). *Human Resource Selection*, 3rd edn. Hinsdale, IL: Dryden Press.

Harris, M. M. and Schaubroeck, J. (1988). A meta–analysis of self–supervisor, self–peer, and peer–supervisor ratings. *Personnel Psychology*, **41**, 43–62.

Heneman, R. L. (1986). The relationship between supervisory ratings and results-oriented measures of performance: A meta-analysis. *Personnel Psychology*, **39**, 811–826.

Hofmann, D. A., Jacobs, R. and Gerras, S. J. (1992). Mapping individual performance over time. *Journal of Applied Psychology*, **77**, 185–195.

Huber, G. P. (1980). *Managerial Decision Making*. Glenview, IL: Scott, Foresman & Company.

Huber, G. P. (1982). 'Decision support systems: Their present nature and future applications. In G. R. Ungson and D. N. Braunstein (eds), *Decision Making—an Interdisciplinary Inquiry*. Belmont, CA: Wadsworth Publishing Company.

Hulin, C. L., Henry, R. A. and Noon, S. L. (1990). Adding a dimension: Time as a factor in predictive relationships. *Psychological Bulletin*, **107**, 328–340.

Hunter, J. E., Schmidt, F. L. and Coggin, T. D. (1988). Problems and pitfalls in using capital budgeting and financial accounting techniques in assessing the utility of personnel programs. *Journal of Applied Psychology*, **73**, 522–528.

Jones, G. R. and Wright, P. M. (1992). An economic approach to conceptualizing the utility of human resource management practices. In G. R. Ferris and K. M. Rowland (eds), *Research in Personnel and Human Resources Management* (vol. 10, pp. 271–279). Greenwich, CT: JAI Press.

Judge, T. A. (1992). The dispositional perspective in human resources research. In G. R. Ferris and K. M. Rowland (eds), *Research in Personnel and Human Resources Management* (vol. 10, pp. 31–72). Greenwich, CT: JAI Press.

Judge, T. A., Cable, D. M., Blancero, D. and Johnson, D. E. (1994). Effect of selection systems on job choice decisions. Working paper, Cornell University.

Judge, T. A. and Bretz, R. D., Jr. (1992). Effects of work values on job choice decisions. *Journal of Applied Psychology*, **77**, 261–171.

Judge, T. A. and Ferris, G. R. (1992). The elusive criterion of fit in human staffing decisions. *Human Resource Planning*, **15**, 47–68.

Judge, T. A. and Hulin, C. L. (1994). Job satisfaction and subjective well-being as influences on employee withdrawal. Working paper, Center for Advanced Human Resource Studies, Cornell University.

Lin, T., Dobbins, G. H. and Farh, J. (1992). A field study of race and age similarity effects on interview ratings in conventional and situational interviews. *Journal of Applied Psychology*, **77**, 363–371.

Macan, T. H. and Dipboye, R. L. (1990). The relationship of interviewers' preinterview impressions to selection and recruitment outcomes. *Personnel Psychology*, **43**, 745–768.

Milkovich, G. T. and Boudreau, J. W. (1994). *Human Resource Management*, 7th edn. Homewood, IL: Richard D. Irwin.

Murphy, K. M. (1986). When your top choice turns you down: The effect of rejected offers on the utility of selection tests. *Psychological Bulletin*, **99**, 133–138.

Murphy, K. R. and Cleveland, J. N. (1991). *Performance Appraisal: An Organizational Perspective*. Boston, MA: Allyn & Bacon.

Naylor, J. C. and Shine, L. C. (1965). A table for determining the increase in mean criterion score obtained by using a selection device. *Journal of Industrial Psychology*, **3**, 33–42.

Neuman, G. A. (1991). Autonomous work group selection. *Journal of Business and Psychology*, **6**, 283–291.

Nunnally, J. C. (1978). *Psychometric Theory*. New York: McGraw-Hill.

Olian, J. D., Schwab, D. P. and Haberfield, Y. (1988). The impact of applicant gender compared to qualifications on hiring recommendations: A meta-analysis of experimental studies. *Organizational Behavior and Human Decision Processes*, **41**, 180–195.

Oppler, S. H., Campbell, J. P., Pulakos, E. D. and Borman, W. C. (1992). Three approaches to the investigation of subgroup bias in performance measurement: review, results and conclusions. *Journal of Applied Psychology*, **77**, 201–217.

Rich, J. R. and Boudreau, J. W. (1987). Effects of variability and risk in utility analysis: An empirical test and simulation. *Personnel Psychology*, **40**, 55–84.

Rynes, S. L., Bretz, R. D. and Gerhart, B. (1991). The importance of recruitment in job choice: A different way of looking. *Personnel Psychology*, **44**, 13–22.

Sackett, P. R., Zedeck, S. and Fogli, L. (1988). Relations between measures of typical and maximum job performance. *Journal of Applied Psychology*, **78**, 482–486.

Schmidt, F. L., Mack, M. J. and Hunter, J. E. (1984). Selection utility in the occupation of US park ranger for three modes of test use. *Journal of Applied Psychology*, **69**, 490–497.

Smither, J. W., Reilly, R. R., Millsap, R. E., Pearlman, K. and Stoffey, R. W. (1993). Applicant reactions to selection procedures. *Personnel Psychology*, **46**, 49–76.

Sturman, M. C. and Judge, T. J. (1994). Utility analysis for multiple selection devices and multiple outcomes. Working paper, Cornell University.

Wanous, J. P., Poland, T. D., Premack, S. L. and Davis, K. S. (1992). The effects of met expectations on newcomer attitudes and behaviors: A review and meta-analysis. *Journal of Applied Psychology*, **77**, 288–297.

Williams, M. L. and Dreher, G. F. (1992). Compensation system attributes and applicant pool characteristics. *Academy of Management Journal*, **35**, 571–595.

Chapter 16

Meta-analysis and Validity Generalization

KEVIN R. MURPHY

*Department of Psychology, Colorado State University, Fort Collins,
Colorado 80523, USA*

The very substantial volume of research in the areas of selection and appraisal is both a blessing and a curse. On the one hand, there are a large number of studies that bear on many, if not most of the important scientific and practical questions in this area. On the other hand, the sheer volume of this research makes the task of extracting some meaning from the mound of data and findings a formidable one. Narrative literature reviews are clearly useful and important, but it is difficult to adequately summarize trends in the research literature with a verbal summary of study outcomes. Meta-analysis provides a set of tools that can be extremely useful in summarizing and understanding the substantial body of research in personnel selection and assessment. Furthermore, these methods can contribute substantially to both research and practice.

Suppose you were to study the effectiveness of a newly-developed test. A simple examination of the raw data from that study might give you an overall sense of the meaning of your data, but it would be much better to compute a variety of statistics, which would help you both to describe the data at hand and to make some inferences about its meaning. Meta-analysis takes the results of each study on a particular topic (e.g. the validity of paper-and-pencil tests as predictors of overall job performance) as a unit of analysis, and involves computing familiar statistics both to describe the overall trends in the body of research reviewed and to draw some conclusions about the meaning of those findings. Although specific applications and methods of meta-analysis are still the topic of controversy (Algera *et al.*, 1984; James, Demaree and Mulaik, in press; Schmidt *et al.*, 1985), the basic procedures, assumptions, and findings of meta-analysis are increasingly accepted and used by both researchers and practitioners.

International Handbook of Selection and Assessment, Edited by N. Anderson and P. Herriot.
© 1997 John Wiley & Sons Ltd.

Meta-analysis is useful in developing and testing theories (Schmidt, 1992), but its most important contribution may be in the application of research to real-world problems. There are substantial gaps between research and application in areas such as personnel selection and assessment (cf. Dunnette, 1990); meta-analysis provides one set of tools that can be useful in closing those gaps. Personnel research can be thought of as a resource that, if properly used, will contribute to the quality and success of practitioners' efforts. Meta-analysis has the potential to help professionals and practitioners become more highly informed and sophisticated consumers of the extensive body of research that bears on the practical problems they are called upon to solve.

Consider the case of a human resource professional who is asked whether a cognitive ability test might be a useful part of an organization's personnel selection. There are literally thousands of studies of the validity of tests of this type and this research is both relevant and useful in making such a decision. In the past, the sheer volume of this research stood as an obstacle to its application; it is virtually impossible to read, synthesize, and apply such a large number of studies. A meta-analysis of these studies would answer two key questions: (a) in general, how well do tests of this type predict future performance or success, and (b) does the validity of this type of test vary, depending on the job, the organization, the specific test used, and so on? Knowing the answers to these two questions would certainly help the professional make a sound recommendation.

METHODS OF META-ANALYSIS

There are a number of methods of quantitatively summarizing the outcomes of multiple studies, any or all of which might be referred to as meta-analysis. For example, Rosenthal (1984) developed methods of combining the p values (i.e. probability that experimental results represent chance alone) from several independent studies to obtain an estimate of the likelihood that the particular intervention, treatment, or other ploy has some effect. Glass, McGaw and Smith (1981) developed methods of combining effect size estimates (e.g. the difference between the experimental and control group means, expressed in standard deviation units) from multiple studies to give an overall picture of how much impact treatments or interventions have on key dependent variables. Schmidt and Hunter (1977) developed methods of combining validity coefficients (i.e. correlations between test scores and criterion measures) from multiple studies to estimate the overall validity of tests and other selection methods.

Validity generalization (VG) analysis represents a specific method of meta-analysis that is very common in the areas of personnel selection and assessment. In fact, VG methods are so common in this particular area that the terms validity generalization and meta-analysis will be used almost interchangeably in this chapter. However, it is useful to keep in mind that VG methods represent one somewhat specialized application of meta-analysis, and although they are ubiquitous in personnel research, these particular methods are virtually unknown in other areas of research where meta-analyses are now common.

Validity generalization; the basic rationale

Many validity studies feature small sample sizes and/or unreliable criteria. (As will be documented in a later section, sample sizes appear to be larger in more recent research than in studies from the 1950s through the early 1970s.) Because sampling error leads to random variations in study outcomes and measurement error artificially lowers (i.e. attenuates) validities, it is reasonable to expect that validity coefficients from different studies will *seem* to vary randomly from study to study and will generally *seem* small. However, the effects of sampling error and unreliability are both relatively easy to estimate, and once the effects of these statistical artifacts are taken into account, you are likely to conclude that the actual validity of the test or assessment procedure studied is probably both larger and more consistent than a simple examination of the observed validity coefficents would suggest.

For example, suppose that there are 100 studies of the validity of structured interviews as predictors of job performance, and in each study the reliability of the performance measure is 0.70 and N (i.e. the sample size) is 40. If the average of the observed validity coefficients is 0.45, the formula for the correction for attenuation suggests that the best estimate of the validity of these interviews is probably closer to 0.54 (i.e. 0.45 divided by the square root of 0.70). Thus, a simple correction for measurement error suggests that the interviews are probably more valid than they seem on the basis of a quick examination of the validity studies themselves.

Because each validity coefficient comes from a fairly small sample, it is natural to expect some variability in study results; this variability can be estimated using a well-known formula for the sampling error of correlation coefficients (Hunter and Schmidt, 1990). For example, if the standard deviation of the validity coefficients coming from these 100 studies is 0.18, it is likely that about 66% of this variability is due to simple sampling error. On the basis of sampling error alone, you would expect a standard deviation of 0.12, given an N of 40 and a mean observed validity of 0.45 (see Hunter and Schmidt, 1990, for a detailed discussion of the formulas used to make such estimates).

There are a number of meta-analytic procedures that go beyond the simple corrections described above, incorporating corrections for range restriction, differences in criterion reliability across studies, and the use of dichotomous criteria. Several variations on the basic model proposed by Schmidt and Hunter (1977) were reviewed by Burke (1984). Hedges (1988) and Raudenbush and Bryk (1985) discussed applications of Bayesian models in meta-analysis. Hedges and Olkin (1985) elaborated a general statistical model for meta-analysis that includes as a special case a variety of procedures similar to those developed by Schmidt and Hunter. James, Demaree and Mulaik (in press) discussed in detail the structural models that underlie VG procedures (see also James *et al.*, 1992). Finally, Thomas (1990) developed a mixture model that attempts to describe systematic differences in validity among specific subgroups of validity studies.

Although the results of various meta-analytic approaches do not always agree, these methods lead to similar general conclusions about the validity of selection tests, interviews, assessment centres, and so on (Schmidt, 1988). In particular, it seems highly likely that test validities are generally both larger and more consistent across situations than the results of many individual validity studies would suggest (Hartigan and Wigdor, 1989; Schmidt, 1992; see, however, Murphy, 1993). Indeed, given the nature of much of the available validation research (i.e. small N, unreliable measures, range restriction), this general finding is virtually a foregone conclusion, even though it directly contradicts one of the most widely-held sets of assumptions in personnel psychology—i.e. that validities are generally small and inherently unstable.

Applications of validity generalization

The methods developed by Schmidt and Hunter have been widely applied. For example, Schmidt (1992) noted that 'meta-analysis has been applied to over 500 research literatures in employment selection, each one representing a predictor–job performance pair' (p. 1177). The most frequent application of these methods has been in research on the relationship between scores on cognitive ability tests and measures of overall job performance; representative examples of this type of validity generalization analysis include Pearlman, Schmidt and Hunter (1980), Schmidt, Gast-Rosenberg and Hunter (1980) and Schmidt, Hunter and Caplan (1981). However, applications of meta-analysis and validity generalization analysis have not been restricted to traditional test validity research. Hunter and Hirsch (1987) reviewed meta-analyses spanning a wide range of areas in applied psychology (e.g. absenteeism, job satisfaction). Recent applications of meta-analytic methods have included assessments of the relationship between personality traits and job performance (Barrick and Mount, 1991), assessments of race effects in performance rating (Kraiger and Ford, 1985) and assessments of the validity of assessment centre ratings (Gaugler *et al.*, 1987). Finally, Hom *et al.* (1992) have combined meta-analysis with structural modeling to assess the appropriateness of several competing theories of turnover in organizations.

VALIDITY GENERALIZATION AND THE CONSISTENCY OF VALIDITIES

The most significant controversies in the area of validity generalization concern the consistency of validity across jobs, organizations, or situations. Suppose that you examined 75 studies of the validity of spatial ability tests as predictors of job performance, and found that the validity coefficients were all of similar magnitude, and did not vary more than you would expect on the basis of the statistical characteristics of your set of 75 studies (e.g. you would expect some variability in study outcomes on the basis of sampling error alone). Is that a sufficient basis for concluding that the validity of spatial ability is constant across settings? Does this guarantee that a new test that you devise will also show this same level of validity? Does your answer change if there are more studies, or even multiple meta-analyses that yield approximately the same results? Much of the technical literature in the area of validity generalization is concerned with questions of this sort.

Validity generalization vs situational specificity

One potential source of confusion in VG analysis is the relationship between validity generalization and the consistency of validity across jobs, organizations, or situations. In the VG literature, the existence of substantial variability in the level of validity across situations (after correcting for statistical artifacts) is referred to as situational specificity. If the correlation between test scores and job performance truly depends on the job, organization, or the situation, validity is said to be situationally specific. Validity generalization, on the other hand, refers to the classification of tests or other assessment devices as 'valid' or 'not valid'. If a test demonstrates at least a minimal level of validity in a sufficiently wide range of situations, validity is said to generalize. If a test cannot be consistently classified as 'valid', validity generalization fails.

Validity generalization is most relevant to the practical application of tests or other assessment devices. If it can be shown that tests are at least minimally valid in virtually all setttings where they have been applied, it seems reasonable to conclude that they will also be at least minimally valid in other settings which are similar to those studied in the existing body of validation research. When validity generalization has been established for a test or class of tests, the fear that a particular test (or tests similar to those included in the validity generalization studies) will be *completely* useless in a new situation is probably not a realistic one.

Situational specificity, on the other hand, is most relevant to scientific theory and research, although it also carries practical implications. If it can be shown that the *level* of validity of a test or class of tests is consistent across jobs, organizations, situations, this implies that the relationship between the construct(s) measured by the test and performance does not depend on features of the job, or situation, in which the test is used. This demonstration of cross-situational consistency aids in establishing, testing and applying theories of human behavior in organizations (Schmidt, 1992).

The processes involved in testing the validity generalization and situational specificity hypothesis are illustrated in Figure 16.1. In both cases, you start by calculating the mean and variance of the observed distribution of validities. Next, you correct for unreliability, range restriction, and other statistical artifacts that might affect the mean of the validity distribution, and correct for sampling error, variation across studies in range restriction and unreliability, and other statistical artifacts that might affect the variance of the distribution of validities (see Hunter and Schmidt, 1990, for formulas and sample calculations). At this point, the two processes diverge.

The situational specificity hypothesis involves a comparison between the observed variance in validities and the variability expected solely on the basis of sampling error and other artifacts. If the variability expected on the basis of statistical artifacts is as large, or nearly as large, as the observed variability in validities, the situational specificity hypothesis is rejected. Schmidt, Hunter, and their colleagues have suggested a '75% rule', where the situational specificity

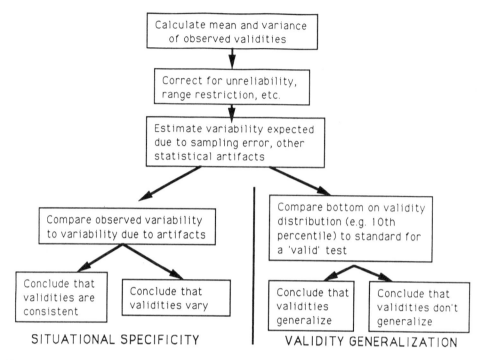

Figure 16.1   Assessing situational specificity versus validity generalization

hypothesis is rejected if the variability expected on the basis of statistical artifacts is at least 75% as large as the observed variance in validities. Several aspects of the situational specificity hypothesis, including this decision rule, will be discussed in detail in sections that follow.

The procedure for determining validity generalization is quite different. After applying corrections for unreliability, sampling error, and so on, the test of validity generalization involves comparing the bottom of the corrected validity distribution (e.g. the value at the 10th percentile of the corrected distribution) to some standard which represents a minimal level of validity (e.g. a validity coefficient of 0.00, or 0.10). For example, if the value at the 10th percentile of a corrected validity distribution was greater than 0.10, proponents of validity generalization would conclude that you could be 90% confident that the test would be at least minimally valid in essentially all new applications.

For example, Gaugler *et al.* (1987) conducted a meta-analysis of assessment centre validities. Part of their analysis focused on correlations between assessment centre ratings and measures of job performance. Their review included 44 validity coefficients of this type, from 29 separate studies. The mean and the standard deviation of these validity coefficients were 0.25 and 0.15, respectively. After correcting for sampling error, unreliability, and other statistical artifacts, Gaugler *et al.* (1987) reported that: (a) the best estimate of assessment centre validity was given by a corrected mean validity of 0.36; (b) the corrected validities varied substantially across studies (i.e. a corrected standard deviation of 0.14);

and (c) 90% of the corrected validities were greater than 0.18. This set of results led them to conclude that the assessment centre method was at least minimally valid in virtually all reported applications (i.e. assessment centre validity generalized), but that the level of validity was *not* consistent across studies, suggesting that characteristics of the jobs, organizations, assessment exercises, or whatever could substantially affect the validity of assessment centre ratings.

In principle, there is no necessary relationship between tests of situational specificity and tests of validity generalization. The most common finding, at least in the area of ability testing, has been that validities are both: (a) generalizable, in the sense that such tests appear to be at least minimally valid predictors in virtually all settings; and (b) consistent, in the sense that the level of validity is reasonably comparable across settings (Hunter and Hirsch, 1987; Hunter and Hunter, 1984; Schmidt, 1992). However, as Figure 4.2 and Gaugler *et al.*'s (1987) analysis illustrate, it is also possible to conclude that validities are generalizable, but not consistent. That is, tests might show *some* validity in virtually all settings, but might be substantially more useful in some jobs, organizations, or other applications than in others.

Figure 16.2 suggests two other possibilities, neither of which has yet been encountered in the area of personnel testing. First, it is possible for validities to be consistent but not generalizable, which would be the case if all validity values were near zero. If all corrected validities are indeed near zero, the conclusion that the test was simply invalid as a predictor of performance would generalize quite nicely across situations. Finally, validities might be neither consistent nor generalizable. This would occur in the unlikely case where tests sometimes showed negative validities, sometimes showed positive validities, but showed no general trend in one direction or the other.

On the whole, it is easier to demonstrate validity generalization than to demonstrate consistent levels of validity across situations. Mean validities are reasonably high for most structured selection procedures (see Hunter and Hunter, 1984; Reilly and Chao, 1982; Wiesner and Cronshaw, 1988), which means that the lower bound of the validity distribution is almost always greater than zero, 0.10, or whatever other standard is used to define minimal validity for this class of tests and assessment procedures. Demonstrations of situational specificity, on the other hand, are typically more difficult and controversial.

SITUATIONAL SPECIFICITY

		Consistent	Not Consistent
Validity Generalization	Valid	validities range from 0.35 to 0.50	validities range from 0.10 to 0.70
	Not valid	validities range from 0.00 to 0.05	validities range from -0.20 to 0.25

Figure 16.2   Possible outcomes of tests of situational specificity and validity generalization

Implications of validity generalization and situational specificity

Demonstrations of validity generalization have become commonplace in several areas of personnel research. For example, there have been a large number of meta-analyses of the validity of cognitive ability tests as predictors of performance, examining validity studies in a wide range of jobs, organizations, and settings, and they have consistently demonstrated validity generalization (Hunter and Hirsch, 1987; Schmidt, 1992). As a result, there is now a presumption that well-developed cognitive ability tests will show at least *some* correlation with job performance in virtually all jobs, organizations, or other settings. Thus, if your intent is to determine whether a well-developed ability test will show any validity whatsoever in a new application, there is probably no point in conducting a validity study; the accumulated body of validation research provides a clear basis for assuming that cognitive ability tests will show at least minimal validity as predictors of performance in virtually any job.

In most settings, however, it is not enough to know whether validity is greater than zero; it is often important to have some idea of how well a particular type of test, interview protocol, or assessment technique is likely to work in a particular setting. Questions about the *level* of validity (as opposed to its presence or absence) involve tests of situational specificity. One way to appreciate the importance of situational specificity is to consider the implications of rejecting the specificity hypothesis. Suppose you knew that the validity of a test was typically in the 0.40–0.45 range, and further, you were presented with clear evidence that the validity of this test did *not* vary across a wide range of jobs, organizations, and other settings. As a practical matter, you would be able to predict with considerable accuracy the validity of this test in a new setting (i.e. the correlation between test scores and job performance measures collected in a new job or setting should also be approximately 0.40–0.45). The rejection of situational specificity would also be important to the development and testing of theories of job performance, because it would imply that the relationship between the constructs measured by the test and job performance was invariant over jobs, organizations, and settings.

If the validity of tests or assessment procedures *does* vary across the jobs, organizations, and settings, this complicates the task of the personnel psychologist or the personnel manager, because it may not be possible to predict with complete accuracy how a test will function in a new setting. Thus, if your interest is in the level of validity you can reasonably expect in a new setting, assessments of situational specificity are likely to be more important than simple demonstrations of validity generalization.

DIFFICULTIES IN ASSESSING SITUATIONAL SPECIFICITY

For most of the history of personnel selection research, it was assumed that tests, interview protocols, or other assessment procedures that were valid predictors of performance in one setting might be useless in other, apparently similar settings. Although there have been few attempts to develop a compelling theory for *why* tests might be highly valid in some settings and not in others (James *et al.*, 1992), the data seemed compelling, and for many years it was believed that no matter how well the test worked in other settings, a new validity study would be needed whenever the test was introduced into a new situation.

Validity generalization research suggests that much of the apparent variability in levels of test validity is probably due to sampling error and other statistical artifacts, and that the evidence of true situational specificity (i.e. the hypothesis that a test if in fact more valid in some settings than in others) is weak. Schmidt, Hunter and their colleagues have gone further, claiming that the validity of cognitive ability tests is essentially constant, at least within some very broad groupings of jobs (Hunter and Hirsch, 1987; Schmidt *et al.*, 1993). For example, Schmidt, Hunter and Raju (1988) claimed that validity generalization 'studies have concluded that there is no situational specificity for cognitive ability tests' (p. 666). The only potential moderator of test validity that has been accepted by some VG researchers is job complexity; ability tests seem to show higher validities in more cognitively-demanding jobs (Gutenberg *et al.*, 1983; Hunter and Hunter, 1984; Murphy, 1989). With this potential exception, Schmidt, Hunter and their colleagues have made a strong claim for the invariance of cognitive test validities over situations.

The claim that there is no situational specificity is controversial; questions regarding this claim can be grouped under three main headings: (1) the power of VG procedures to detect validity differences; (2) the role of sample size in tests of situational specificity; and (3) the lack of useful models to explain how situational variables might or might not moderate validity.

Power to detect variability in validities

Validity generalization models test the situational specificity of validity by comparing the observed variation in validities to the amount of variability one would expect on the basis of statistical artifacts such as sampling error. For example, if the observed variance in validities is no larger than the variance expected on the basis of sampling error, it might be reasonable to conclude that there is little or no real variability in validities, and that the observed variance *is* in fact due to sampling error. The situational specificity hypothesis is rejected if the observed variance in validities is not much larger than the variance one would predict as a result of statistical artifacts.

A frequent criticism of validity generalization procedures is that they are biased in favor of the hypothesis that validity is consistent. In part, this criticism has to do with the statistical minutiae of various VG formulas (see James *et al.*, 1992, for a statistical critique of current VG formulas). The broader issue, however, relates to the statistical power of VG procedures to detect true differences in test validity across jobs, organizations, or situations. In this context, power refers to the probability that VG procedures will detect true and meaningful differences in validity. Research on the statistical power of VG procedures suggests that this probability can be disappointingly low.

The statistical power of VG procedures is affected by a number of variables; the two that have received the most attention are the number of studies included in the meta-analysis (k) and the number of subjects included in each study (N). Many validity generalization studies, particularly in the area of cognitive ability testing, include large numbers of studies (i.e. large k), most of which are based on small samples (i.e. small N). Osburn *et al.* (1983) found that the power of VG procedures was unacceptably low for detecting small to moderate differences in true validity when the average N was less than 100. Sackett, Harris and Orr (1986) found that when there were small differences in true validity (e.g. differences of 0.10 in actual test validity over situations), power was low regardless of N or k. They also reported that power was unacceptably low for detecting larger differences in true validity (e.g. 0.20) when N or k was small. These studies suggest that when the actual level of test validity varies by as much as 0.10–0.20 over situations, VG procedures may nevertheless lead one to conclude that validity is constant across situations. Ashworth *et al.* (1992) note another problem with meta-analyses that include only a few studies (i.e. small k). The conclusions of these meta-analyses can be substantially affected by the so-called 'file-drawer effect', where the existence of a small number of studies that failed to find any evidence of validity (and hence remained in the file drawer) could undermine meta-analytic claims for the generalizability or consistency of validity.

The inability of some VG procedures to reliably detect validity differences in the 0.10–0.20 range is not necessarily a serious problem; in many contexts, one might argue that differences that small, even if detected, would not constitute meaningful variation in validity. However, a study by Kemery, Mossholder and Roth (1987) suggests that VG procedures can show low power even in situations where validity differences are large. Their study considered the situation in which a test has essentially no validity in most applications, but has a high level of validity (e.g. 0.60) in some. They found low levels of power for detecting validity differences in situations where as many as 10–30% of the true validities were 0.60 (and the rest were 0.00).

Schmidt, Hunter and Raju (1988) criticized research on the power of VG procedures on several grounds. Their most telling criticism is a practical one, i.e. the fact that multiple meta-analyses of areas such as the validity of ability tests have led to converging results. While any single meta-analysis may exhibit low levels of power, if several independent analyses lead to the same conclusions about situational specificity, it is hard to dismiss those conclusions as a statistical fluke. Nevertheless, the research reviewed here suggests that considerable caution must be observed in rejecting the hypothesis of situational specificity, particularly on the basis of a meta-analysis that includes a small number of studies, or that is made up primarily of small-sample studies. In particular, the research reviewed here suggests that considerable caution must be used in interpreting tests of situational specificity when the average N is less than 100–200, or when k is less than 15–20.

The role of sample size in tests of situational specificity

Schmidt (1992) suggests that approximately 80–90% of the variability in ability test validities is due to statistical artifacts. While this figure seems impressive, it does not by itself tell you much about situational specificity. A close analysis of VG studies shows that the percentage of variance accounted for by statistical artifacts is strongly affected by the sample sizes of validity studies, and that figures such as 80% of the variance accounted for are found only when VG methods are applied to small-sample studies (McDaniel *et al.*, 1986; Murphy, 1993; Schmitt *et al.*, 1984).

A comparison of meta-analyses of small-sample studies versus large-sample studies leads to two important conclusions. First, because of sampling error, the *amount* of variability in test validities depends substantially on *N*. Validities obtained from large-sample studies tend to be relatively consistent across situations, whereas (because of sampling error) small-sample validities vary substantially across situations. Extensive and unsystematic variability in test validities across situations seems to be restricted to small-sample validity studies. Second, the *percentage* of variance due to statistical artifacts such as sampling error varies inversely with *N*. In meta-analyses based primarily on small samples, sampling error alone often accounts for 70–80% of the variance in test validities. In VG analyses that include larger samples, the percentage of variance accounted for might be as small as 15–30% (McDaniel *et al.*, 1986; Schmitt *et al.*, 1984).

It seems clear that decision rules defined in terms of the percentage of variance accounted for are deficient. If *N* is small (e.g. less than 100), the percentage of variance accounted for by statistical artifacts will tend to be large. If *N* is large (e.g. greater than 200), the percentage of variance accounted for by artifacts will be small. If *N* is large enough, this percentage will tend to zero, and can even appear to become negative (i.e. when the corrected variance in validities is larger than the observed variance: see Murphy, 1993). In the long run, the percentage of variance accounted for by statistical artifacts (particularly sampling error) might turn out to be little more than a roundabout estimate of the number of subjects included in the studies analyzed.

Lack of a situational model

The belief that test validities across situations was long part of the common wisdom of personnel researchers; the belief that validities do *not* vary across situations seems to now be part of that common wisdom. Given all of the attention that has been devoted to situational specificity, both by its advocates and its critics, there have been remarkably few attempts to articulate just how situational variables might affect validity, which situational variables might be important, or even what exactly constitutes a situation (James, Demaree and Mulaik, in press; James *et al.*, 1992). Gutenberg *et al.* (1983) suggested that validities would be higher for more jobs with more complex information-processing demands than for simpler jobs. Murphy (1989) suggested that validities might be higher when organizations were in a turbulent environment, where new tasks, technologies, and responsibilities were constantly being added, than when the environment was stable and the process of production was routine. More recently, James *et al.* (1992) articulated how the restrictiveness of an organization's climate might affect the validities of tests.

Restrictive climates are characterized by highly structured work environments, an emphasis on standardization, formalization, and control, and extensive centralization of authority. Non-restrictive climates are characterized by decentralization, autonomy, innovation, and a relative lack of structure. James *et al.* (1992) predicted that tests will be more useful predictors of performance in non-restrictive than in restrictive environments. Similar predictions have been made by other researchers (e.g. Kemery, Mossholder and Roth, 1987; Murphy, 1989).

James *et al.* (1992) note that the effects of variation in organizational climate, situational constraints on performance, and similar strains on the validity of tests will be obscured by traditional VG procedures. In particular, these situational characteristics may lead to substantive effects that are dismissed as statistical artifacts in VG procedures, and are 'correct for'. For example, they note that an important goal of restrictive climates is to reduce differences in employees' output, which means that there should be less true variability in performance in restrictive than in non-restrictive climates. This range restriction is not a statistical artifact, and any 'correction' for the fact that some climates restrict variance in output whereas others enhance this variance would be misleading and inappropriate.

Similarly, James *et al.* (1992) note that the reliability of the criterion (here, the performance measure employed) should be substantively affected by the restrictiveness of the climate. If there are small true differences in performance in restrictive climates, it follows that the reliability of performance measures will also tend to be small. In contrast, performance measures should be relatively reliable in non-restrictive climates, where there are meaningful differences in performance to measure. The net result is that there should be variability in criterion reliabilities as a function of the restrictiveness of the situation. Once again, VG procedures that correct for this variability will produce misleading results. This variability is not a statistical artifact unrelated to 'true validity', but rather is a meaningful source of validity differences across climates that vary in their restrictiveness.

Suppose that you used the same test to predict performance in four large organizations, two of which were characterized by highly restrictive climates and two by climates that put no restrictions on individual variation, innovation, or change. In the first two organizations, you would expect little variability in performance, which implies low reliability and low validity (both because of low reliability and range restriction). In the second two organizations, you would expect larger variation in performance, more reliable performance measures, and larger validities. Traditional VG procedures would lead you to regard the differences in validity across situations as the result of a set of statistical artifacts (i.e. differences in range restriction and unreliability across organizations), and would lead you to correct for those artifacts. In this case, statistical corrections would lead to the misleading conclusion that the 'true validity' of the test was the same in all four organizations. This conclusion is correct only in the trivial sense, where 'true validity' is defined in terms that have no relationship to the contexts in which the tests are actually used. In this example, the tests really are more valid and useful in some contexts than in others, and analytic procedures that lead to the conclusion that there are no differences in test validity are simply misleading.

James *et al.* (1992) called for systematic research on potential moderators of validity, with particular attention to identifying the *processes* by which validities might be altered as situational variables change. During the long period when situational specificity was assumed, there was virtually no serious attempt to explain *why* validities might vary. James *et al.* (1992) present a clear example of how such a theory might be developed, and how this theory might provide an alternative explanation of substantive phenomena that are dismissed in VG analyses as statistical artifacts.

Are validities situationally specific?

It is difficult to draw a firm set of conclusions from the research on the situational specificity of test validities. On the one hand, the available data do not provide strong support for the hypothesis of situational specificity. In the absence of any compelling theory to explain why validities might vary, personnel researchers have used the apparent instability of validity coefficients across situations as their main source of evidence for situational specificity. In many cases, however, the variability in test validities is not substantially larger than that which would be expected on the basis of sampling error, and this variability in test validities is not an adequate basis for inferring true situational specificity.

On the other hand, the available body of evidence and research is not sufficient to support the conclusion that there is *no* true variability in validity coefficients. There are both logical and analytic problems with VG procedures that make it difficult to accept the strong conclusions of Schmidt, Hunter and their colleagues regarding situational specificity (Hartigan and Wigdor, 1989; James, Demaree and Mulaik, in press; James *et al.*, 1992). First, arguments based on the percentage of variance accounted for by statistical artifacts are ambiguous at best. Second, VG procedures can treat real and meaningful situational differences as statistical artifacts, and without justification correction for their influence. Finally, the data base may not be sufficient to provide strong tests of the assertion that validity is constant across situations. Despite the fact that there are hundreds of validity studies in some meta-analyses, many of these studies have (until recently) employed small samples and poorly-measured criteria. At this point, we simply cannot say with confidence whether or not test validities vary across jobs, organizations, or settings. This may have implications for both research and practice, as will be outlined below.

CONTRIBUTIONS AND CHALLENGES OF META-ANALYSIS AND VALIDITY GENERALIZATION

Meta-analytic methods have made a number of contributions to research in the behavioral sciences. Virtually every meta-analysis published has provided some useful information about the domain being analyzed. However, the most significant contributions of meta-analytic methods are probably not in what they tell us about the particular research domains summarized, but rather in how they have changed the way in which we use existing research and the way in which we design ongoing research.

The technical literature on meta-analysis and validity generalization suggests that a number of significant methodological challenges still need to be faced, and that methodological advances may change many of the conclusions reached by early meta-analyses (Hedges, 1988; James, Demaree and Mulaik, in press; Schmidt *et al.*, 1993). However, the most significant questions regarding meta-analytic methods are not likely to involve their statistical details, but rather to revolve around the limitations imposed by the quality of the data base analyzed and by attempts to group highly diverse tests, assessment procedures, and performance measures into meaningful meta-analyses.

Improving the use of research

Meta-analysis and validity generalization methods have given researchers and practitioners both the tools and the encouragement to systematically examine the huge base of empirical research that is the foundation for our current practices in selection and assessment. The body of research on topics such as ability testing is too large and varied to be sensibly integrated in a narrative review. No matter how skillful the reviewer, it is virtually impossible to make valid inferences and to avoid invalid ones without the aid of some set of quantitative methods. As was noted at the beginning of this chapter, the meta-analyst's task is similar to the task you face every time you collect data on more than a handful of participants—i.e. to make sense of that data. Meta-analytic methods provide statistical tools that closely parallel the familiar statistics routinely computed in individual studies. Some meta-analytic methods are considerably more complex than the familiar statistics used every day in primary research (Hedges and Olkin, 1985), but the basic concepts are simple, familiar, and useful.

The rapid growth of meta-analysis has made the primary research literature more accessible and more useful to current researchers and practitioners. The availability of careful meta-analyses in many important areas provides both researchers and practitioners with accessible and accurate summaries of major findings and research trends that were virtually impossible to obtain twenty years ago. One possibility is that the judicious use of meta-analysis will improve both science and practice, by providing a clearer picture of the meaning of the accumulated research in particular areas (Schmidt, 1992). Critics of some meta-analytic methods (e.g. James, Demaree and Mulaik, in press) remind us that the incautious use of these techniques may do more to impede the progress of science and practice than to advance it, and their warning is well taken. However, if kept in their proper perspective, these methods are likely to improve the way in which we use the existing body of research on selection and assessment to guide and inform our current efforts.

Improving the quality of research

Perhaps the most lasting and important message of validity generalization research is that validation studies based on small samples and unreliable measures are simply a bad idea. On the whole, these studies are more likely to mislead and misinform us (e.g. to suggest that validity varies substantially over situations, when the real culprit is sampling error) than to provide new and useful knowledge. It is clear that studies of this sort will not disappear overnight (Sedlmeier and Giferenzer, 1989), but there is also evidence that VG research has encouraged the use of larger samples, better measures, and more carefully designed studies in examining the validity of the tests and assessments used in selection and appraisal. For example, Schmitt *et al.* (1984) reviewed validity studies published between 1964 and 1982. The average sample size of these studies is substantially larger than the sample sizes cited in earlier VG research. For example, many early validity generalization analyses featured average sample sizes of approximately 60–75 (see Table 1 in McDaniel *et al.*, 1986), whereas in the Schmitt *et al.* review, the average N ranged approximately around 600–750, depending on the criterion.

There has never been a good reason to do validation studies with small samples, poor measures, and so on, but until the advent of VG research, this point was not driven home with sufficient force to actually affect the quality of validation research. It is now clear that validity studies of this type are worse than useless, in the sense that they take time, energy and resources, but they are very unlikely to tell you anything about the validity of the test or assessment method being studied. If VG research does indeed encourage future researchers to design better studies and to stop relying on small samples, it will have made a contribution that has more lasting value than the substantive findings of the many meta-analyses that have been published over the last 15 years.

The quality of the data base

There has been a continuing debate in meta-analytic circles over the advisability of including or excluding studies from meta-analyses on the basis of their quality. On the one hand, it is widely believed that you will learn more from a small number of well-designed studies than from the cumulative results of many poorly-designed ones. Hedges and Olkin (1985) summarized this position with the statement, 'We believe that no statistical procedure can perform the magic of extracting valid and reliable conclusions from data of poor quality' (p. 14). On the other hand, there are no widely accepted indices of study quality, and the studies one meta-analyst might decide to discard as useless, other meta-analysts might regard as perfectly acceptable.

Hunter and Schmidt (1990) advocate including as many studies as possible in meta-analyses. While there are some strong reasons for attempting to include all studies (e.g. the lack of clear rules for including some studies and excluding others), meta-analyses that attempt to be comprehensive are only as good as the studies reviewed. Advocates of meta-analysis recognize that the ultimate solution to this issue is to develop better studies, not better methods of meta-analysis

(Hedges and Olkin, 1985; Hunter and Schmidt, 1990). However, there is less consensus on what to do about the frequently poor quality of existing bodies of research.

There are several variables that might contribute or detract from the quality of a set of studies, and from the meta-analysts' ability to draw valid conclusions from those studies. First, as noted above, samples may be so small that sampling error has massive effects on the results of individual studies. On the whole, this problem might not prove a fatal limitation to the meta-analyst. If there are enough studies sampled from the same population, using the same sets of predictor and criterion variables, it should be possible to predict how much variance in study outcomes is likely to be due to sampling error, and to estimate the mean validity and the non-sampling-error variance in test validities. A more difficult problem may be caused by the operationalization of key constructs in the studies reviewed. As will be noted in the section below, if studies vary considerably in terms of what they actually measure, and how well they measure it, it may be difficult to draw any sensible conclusions about the meaning of the parameter estimates that are obtained from a meta-analysis.

Can we sensibly combine validities from diverse sources?

All meta-analyses involve combining the results of separate studies to estimate a population effect. For example, a VG analysis of studies correlating some measure of quantitative ability with some measure of job performance might be used to estimate the overall relationship between these two constructs, and to determine whether this relationship is consistent over situations, jobs, organizations, and so on. The statistical models underlying meta-analytic procedures (e.g. Hedges and Olkin, 1985) treat each study as if it were randomly sampled from the same population, and involve applying well-known rules of inference from such samples to the populations they represent. The question that is rarely faced in meta-analysis is whether studies that use different tests, assessment methods, performance measures, can be sensibly combined, and if so, what the average validity coefficient coming from such a heterogeneous set of studies might tell us.

Returning to the example above, if all studies of quantitative ability and job performance used comparable measures, under comparable circumstances, determining the average validity coefficient means might be a simple task. However, a typical VG analysis is likely to include a wide range of measures of both the predictor and criterion, ranging from well-validated tests to home-grown assessments that have 'quantitative' or 'job performance' in the title. The subjects involved in different studies will range from new employees to seasoned veterans in any of a variety of jobs. The assumption that all of these tests and assessments measure the constructs of quantitative ability and performance equally well (except for differences in random measurement error), and that the subjects are randomly sampled from a population of interest is unlikely to be true. At best, the population actually sampled from might be described in terms such as 'workers in a variety of jobs and settings assessed with tests having "quantitative" in the title, and evaluated on whatever measure of "job performance" happens to be available.' It is not clear whether inferences about that population are really useful. However, if this is the population actually sampled, there is no statistical ground for making inferences about the 'true correlation' between the constructs of quantitative ability and job performance on the basis of traditional VG procedures.

In principle, there would be nothing to stop you from doing a grand meta-analysis of the relationship between all X variables and all Y variables studied in the social and behavioral sciences. Indeed, given the sample sizes typical in this research (e.g. Sedlmeier and Gigerenzer, 1989) it is likely that a large proportion of the variability in the r_{xy} values (for randomly chosen Xs and Ys) reported in all behavioral science research will probably be due to sampling error! The problem with this sort of meta-analysis is that its results would be impossible to interpret. The same general problem is, however, faced in all meta-analyses. Whenever studies that are nominally similar (e.g. 'quantitative' and 'job performance' in the title) are grouped together, there will be some ambiguity in describing exactly what the 'population validity' estimated on the basis of that set of studies truly means. As a rule of thumb, it will probably be easier to interperet the results of meta-analyses that combine validity studies of relatively standardized tests or assessments (e.g. commercially published cognitive ability tests) than those that combine studies of tests or assessment procedures that are highly diverse (e.g. selection interviews, work sample tests, simulations).

In the long run, improving the quality of research and selection may be the key to addressing the problem of aggregation. As long as we are forced to rely on sets of studies that appear to be similar, but that in fact may be measuring a variety of different constructs or processes, we will never find the task of interpreting meta-analyses an easy one. As the quality of research improves, the task of extracting meaning from the cumulative results of our research studies is likely to become easier. First, the basic problem that motivated VG research in the first place (i.e. small and inconsistent validities due to statistical artifacts) will solve itself if the quality of our research improves. Second, questions about the meaning of meta-analytic estimates obtained from a motley collection of studies will become less complex as studies adopt better and more comparable measures, better data collection designs, and larger, more carefully assembled studies. As long as we continue to rely on studies of poor quality (no matter how many there are), our ability to extract meaning from the data will forever be limited. If the results of VG studies can help to encourage better research, the lasting contribution of these techniques will be assured.

Can meta-analysis improve both science and practice?

Proponents of meta-analysis and validity generalization claim that these methods represent a key to advancing both science and practice in areas such as selection and assessment (Hunter and Schmidt, 1990; Schmidt, 1992). This claim has some merit, as long as those who conduct and read meta-analyses keep the limitations of these techniques firmly in mind. The first and most serious limitation of these methods is that a meta-analysis is no better than the base of research articles that it summarizes (Hedges and Olkin, 1985). Second, these methods are still evolving, and the extravagant claims of early meta-analysts no longer seem credible (Hartigan and Wigdor, 1989). Finally, meta-analysis is nothing more than a statistical tool, and while it can tell us many useful things, it is unlikely to provide the final answers to the scientific and practical concerns of human resource scientists and professionals.

With these caveats firmly in mind, it is nevertheless clear that meta-analysis and validity generalization can contribute substantially to both science and practice. As noted earlier, these techniques provide practical and precise methods of summarizing the existing body of research, and can serve as an indispensable aid to researchers and practitioners. In particular, they provide a reasonable way of incorporating existing research to help frame and address scientific and practical problems. This chapter has focused on validity generalization, but the potential contributions of meta-analysis extend far beyond the narrow bounds of validity research. It is difficult to imagine a scientific or practical problem in personnel selection and assessment that has not been addressed, at least indirectly, in a number of prior studies. Meta-analyses provide a method of summarizing this research, and of identifying the range of problems that have or have not been solved by previous studies. By providing an efficient method of summarizing the vast array of relevant studies, meta-analyses give both researchers and practitioners a sound scientific base for starting their work. A meta-analysis will not answer every scientific or practical question, but it provides a valuable starting point for structuring both research and practice.

AUTHOR NOTES

Correspondence regarding this chapter should be sent to Kevin R. Murphy, Department of Psychology, Colorado State University, Fort Collins, CO 80523, USA. I appreciate the thoughtful input of several colleagues, including Michael Burke and George C. Thornton III.

REFERENCES

Algera, J. A., Jansen, P. G., Roe, R. A. and Vijn, P. (1984). Validity generalization: Some critical remarks on the Schmidt–Hunter procedure. *Journal of Occupational Psychology*, **57**, 197–210.
Ashworth, S. D., Osburn, H. G., Callender, J. C. and Boyle, K. A. (1992). The effects of unrepresented studies on the robustness of validity generalization results. *Personnel Psychology*, **45**, 341–361.
Barrick, M. R. and Mount, M. K. (1991). The big five personality dimensions and job performance. *Personnel Psychology*, **44**, 1–26.
Burke, M. J. (1984). Validity generalization: A review and critique of the correlational model. *Personnel Psychology*, **37**, 93–113.
Dunnette, M. D. (1990). Blending the science and practice of industrial and organizational psychology: Where are we and where are we going? In M. Dunnette and L. Hough (eds), *Handbook of Industrial and Organizational Psychology*. Second edn (vol. 1, pp. 1–27). Palo Alto, CA: Consulting Psychologists Press.

Gaugler, B., Rosenthal, D., Thornton, G.C. III and Bentson, C. (1987). Meta-analysis of assessment center validity. *Journal of Applied Psychology*, **72**, 493–511.

Glass, G. V., McGraw, B. and Smith, M. L. (1981). *Meta-analysis in Social Research*. Beverly Hills, CA: Sage.

Gutenberg, R. L., Arvey, R. D., Osburn, H. G. and Jenneret, P. R. (1983). Moderating effects of decision-making/information processing job dimensions on test validities. *Journal of Applied Psychology*, **68**, 602–608.

Hartigan, J. A. and Wigdor, A. K. (1989). *Fairness in Employment Testing: Validity Generalization, Minority Issues, and the General Aptitude Test Battery*. Washington, DC: National Academy Press.

Hedges, L. V. (1988). Meta-analysis of test validities. In H. Wainer and H. Braun (eds), *Test Validity* (pp. 191–212). Hillsdale, NJ: Erlbaum.

Hedges, L. V. and Olkin, I. (1985). *Statistical Methods for Meta-analysis*. New York: Academic Press.

Hom, P. W., Carnikas-Walker, F., Prussia, G. E. and Griffeth, R. W. (1992). A meta-analytical structural equations analysis of a model of employee turnover. *Journal of Applied Psychology*, **77**, 890–909.

Hunter, J. E. and Hirsch, H. R. (1987). Applications of meta-analysis. In C. L. Cooper and I. T. Robertson (eds), *International Review of Industrial and Organizational Psychology*. (pp. 321–357). Chichester, UK: Wiley.

Hunter, J. E. and Hunter, R. F. (1984). Validity and utility of alternative predictors of job performance. *Psychological Bulletin*, **96**, 72–98.

Hunter, J. E. and Schmidt, F. L. (1990). *Methods of Meta-analysis: Correcting Error and Bias in Research Findings*. Newbury Park, CA: Sage.

James, L. R., Demaree, R. G. and Mulaik, S. A. (in press). A critique of validity generalization. In B. R. Gifford and L. C. Wing (eds), *Report of the National Commission on Testing and Public Policy*. Boston, MA: Kluwer-Nijhof.

James, L. R., Demaree, R. G., Mulaik, S. A. and Ladd, R. T. (1992). Validity generalization in the context of situational models. *Journal of Applied Psychology*, **77**, 3–14.

Kemery, E. R., Mossholder, K. W. and Roth, L. (1987). The power of the Schmidt and Hunter additive model of validity generalization. *Journal of Applied Psychology*, **72**, 30–37.

Kraiger, K. and Ford, J. K. (1985). A meta-analysis of race effects in performance ratings. *Journal of Applied Psychology*, **70**, 56–65.

McDaniel, M. A., Hirsch, H. R., Schmidt, F. L., Raju, N. and Hunter, J. E. (1986). Interpreting the results of meta-analytic research: A comment on Schmitt, Gooding, Noe, and Kirsch (1984). *Personnel Psychology*, **39**, 141–148.

Murphy, K. R. (1989). Is the relationship between cognitive ability and job performance stable over time? *Human Performance*, **2**, 183–200.

Murphy, K. R. (1993). The situational specificity of validities: Correcting for statistical artifacts does not always reduce the trans-situational variability of correlations coefficients. *International Journal of Selection and Assessment*, **1**, 158–162.

Osburn, H. G., Callender, J. C., Greener, J. M. and Ashworth, S. (1983). Statistical power of tests of the situational specificity hypothesis in validity generalization studies: A cautionary note. *Journal of Applied Psychology*, **68**, 115–122.

Pearlman, K., Schmidt, F. L. and Hunter, J. E. (1980). Validity generalization results for tests used to predict job proficiency and training success in clerical occupations. *Journal of Applied Psychology*, **65**, 373–406.

Raudenbush, S. W. and Bryk, A. S. (1985). Empirical Bayes meta-analysis. *Journal of Educational Statistics*, **10**, 75–98.

Reilly, R. R. and Chao, G. T. (1982). Validity and fairness of some alternate employee selection procedures. *Personnel Psychology*, **35**, 1–67.

Rosenthal, R. (1984). *Meta-analysis Procedures for Social Research*. Beverly Hills, CA: Sage.

Sackett, P. R., Harris, M. M. and Orr, J. M. (1986). On seeking moderator variables in the meta-analysis of correlational data: A Monte Carlo investigation of statistical power and resistance to Type I error. *Journal of Applied Psychology*, **71**, 202–210.

Schmidt, F. L. (1988). The problem of group differences in ability test scores in employment selection. *Journal of Vocational Behavior*, **33**, 272–292.

Schmidt, F. L. (1992). What do data really mean? Research findings, meta-analysis, and cumulative knowledge in psychology. *American Psychologist*, **47**, 1173–1181.

Schmidt, F. L., Gast-Rosenberg, I. and Hunter, J. E. (1980). Validity generalization results for computer programmers. *Journal of Applied Psychology*, **65**, 643–661.

Schmidt, F. L. and Hunter, J. E. (1977). Development of a general solution to the problem of validity generalization. *Journal of Applied Psychology*, **62**, 643–661.

Schmidt, F. L., Hunter, J. E. and Caplan, J. R. (1981). Validity generalization results for two groups in the petroleum industry. *Journal of Applied Psychology*, **66**, 261–273.

Schmidt, F. L., Hunter, J. E., Pearlman, K. and Hirsch, H. R. (1985). Forty questions about validity generalization and meta-analysis. *Personnel Psychology*, **38**, 697–798.

Schmidt, F. L., Hunter, J. E. and Raju, N. S. (1988). Validity generalization and situational specificity: A second look at the 75% rule and Fisher's z transformation. *Journal of Applied Psychology*, **73** 665–672.

Schmidt, F. L., Law, K., Hunter, J. E., Rothstein, H. R., Pearlman, K. and McDaniel, M. D. (1993). Refinements in validity generalization procedures: Implications for the situational specificity hypothesis. *Journal of Applied Psychology*, **78**, 3–14.

Schmitt, N., Gooding, R. Z., Noe, R. D. and Kirsch, M. (1984). Meta-analyses of validity studies published between 1964 and 1982 and the investigation of study characteristics. *Personnel Psychology*, **37**, 407–422.

Sedlmeier, P. and Gigerenzer, G. (1989). Do studies of statistical power have an effect on the power of studies? *Psychological Bulletin*, **105**, 309–316.

Thomas, H. (1990). A likelihood-based model for validity generalization. *Journal of Applied Psychology*, **75**, 13–20.

Wiesner, W. H. and Cronshaw, S. F. (1988). A meta-analytic investigation of the impact of interview format and degree of structure on the validity of the interview. *Journal of Occupational Psychology*, **61**, 275–290.

Chapter 17

Organizational Competencies: Creating a Strategic Behavioural Framework for Selection and Assessment

PAUL R. SPARROW

Management School, Sheffield University, Sheffield, UK

WHAT ARE COMPETENCIES?

Management competencies represent an increasingly popular approach to human resource management (HRM). There has been an evolution in the content and focus of HRM within most organizations that has made the topic more popular. Consider the nature of HRM in the Midland Bank, as seen by Nigel Barrett, the Head of Human Resource Development. Figure 17.1 demonstrates a number of points found in the academic literature. In Midland Bank the personnel issues in the 1970s were all about industrial relations, performance and administration. By the 1980s additional responsibilities focused on training and development, culture change and rewards (pay for performance). In the 1990s, HRM will be dominated by the need to redesign the organization, to resource a broad set of competencies, and to adopt a human resource planning process to tie the various HRM activities together. And why do they need tying together? Figure 17.1 symbolizes the HRM system as a series of 'cog wheels'. At different times in the process of change, different 'cogs' have to be turned faster than others. For example, bringing about a change may demand that most attention is devoted to issues of culture first, then redesigning the organization and work structure, then identifying and resourcing the appropriate competencies and so forth. In most organizations each 'cog' has been set up under different circumstances to meet different pressures. They have their own history and send out different signals or reinforce conflicting

International Handbook of Selection and Assessment, Edited by N. Anderson and P. Herriot.
© 1997 John Wiley & Sons Ltd.

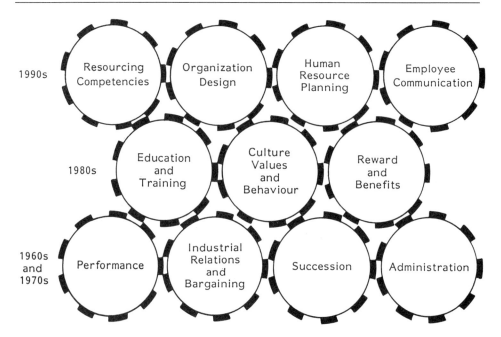

Figure 17.1 The historical development of HRM in the Midland Bank (reprinted with kind permission of Nigel Barrett, Head of Human Resource Development, Midland Bank)

behaviours. The pay system tells you to behave one way, the career system assesses another set of criteria, both of which have little to do with the espoused culture, and seem not to be considered in recruitment. A survey of US Chief Executives found that only 26% expected to be able to implement their strategy in line with their intention (Heyer and Lee, 1991) because of such conflicting signals from their HRM systems. The process of aligning the total HRM system takes several years. Finding an approach that brings consistency and coherence to the behavioural signals sent out by each of the HRM systems, whilst also reflecting the strategic needs of the business, has become an urgent task.

The language of 'competency' in the singular, and 'competences' or 'competencies' in the plural has become one of the 'big ideas' in HRM, on a par with management by objectives, total quality management (TQM) and empowerment (Connock, 1992). A number of organizations have focused significant parts of their HRM systems around sets of competencies for managers (Boam and Sparrow, 1992; Dale and Iles, 1992; Fletcher, 1992; Iles, 1992; Salaman, 1992; and Spencer and Spencer, 1993). They have attempted to define a series of effective individual behaviours, usually in the context of superior organizational performance. This context-specific specification of effective individual behaviours is then operationalized in order to choose the right people to join the organization, appraise and manage their performance, assess their career readiness or potential and diagnose appropriate development actions. Couched in terms of behaviours—what people actually do as opposed to what they say they do—

competencies have proved an attractive way of linking effective performance to the strategic direction of the business whilst maintaining sensitivity to the sharp end of operational practice. Moreover, the approach, popular in US and British organizations, is being transferred into other countries in the Asia/Pacific region (Armstrong, 1991; Glass, 1990; Macleod and Wyndham, 1991, and Murdoch, 1992), Scandinavia (Hansson, 1988) and continental Europe (Hooghiemstra, 1990).

However, there has been little critical consideration of what these organizations are really identifying and this is dangerous. If organizations use an inappropriate identification process they risk building and integrating critically important HRM systems on a bed of shifting sand. So what exactly are competencies, or what should they be? Three different concepts developed over the 1980s and 1990s. They are used quite interchangeably, resulting in considerable confusion amongst practitioners and psychologists alike. Table 17.1 makes some critical distinctions. They reflect three different perspectives on the nature of management skills and three different levels of analysis—all of which are important.

The first (vocational competence) approach considers the skills needed to handle the more specific, routine tasks that reflect what the role of management actually does across all organizations. The second (behavioural competency) approach focuses more on the nature of managerial resourcefulness (Kanungo and Misra, 1992) and what individual managers need in order to cope with the non-specific, discretionary requirements of being a manager. The third (strategic competence) picks up the most important context-specific aspects of organizations and seeks to identify the corporate-level skills that are needed by the total pool of human resources or capital in the organization. In this chapter I shall argue that from a HRM perspective, a combination of the second and third concepts is the most appropriate approach to the topic of management competency.

GENERIC VOCATIONAL COMPETENCES AND BEHAVIOURAL COMPETENCIES

The first source of discussion about competency came from the management educationists and trainers. After the stream of influential national publications and reports in the early 1980s attacking Britain's poor comparative track record of training and management education, it became apparent that it was necessary to go back to basics and reconsider the essential nature of what managers need to do, and therefore what the nation should be developing. This model developed specifications of outcomes, knowledge, skills and attitudes that had to be learned, based on analyses of job roles and responsibilities. It presents a task-orientated picture of competence, a common denominator for all organizations, indicating what is of particular relevance to a specific industry. This model is used to specify occupational standards of performance or expectations of workplace performance. In the UK it has formed the core of developments in the Management Charter Initiative (MCI) and National Vocational Qualifications (NVQs). The approach has not been very successful, with around 43% of those organizations that have adopted a competency route using this task-orientated approach. However, 85% of these organizations reported that they

Table 17.1   Three concepts of individual and organization competences and competencies

Element of definition	What are management competences?	What are behavioural competencies?	What are organizational competences?
DESCRIBE . . .	Knowledge, skills and attitudes (and a few personal behaviours)	Behavioural repertoires which people input to a job, role or organization context	Resources and capabilities of the organization linked with business performance
IDENTIFIED THROUGH . . .	Functional analysis of job roles and responsibilities	Behavioural event investigation techniques	Market analysis methods. Strategic and business planning evaluation
WHICH FOCUS ON . . .	Task-centred analysis of jobs which reflect expectations of workplace performance	Person-centred analysis of jobs that reflects effectiveness	Internal resources (such as tangible technical or capital assets as well as strategic management skills)
AND INDICATE . . .	Areas of competence (fields of knowledge) which a person must demonstrate effectively	What people need to bring to a role to perform to the required level	What makes the organization more successful than others, i.e. long-term and fixed sources of competitive advantage
PERFORMANCE CRITERION BASED ON . . .	Entry (threshold) standard, i.e. wide reach into broad range of management jobs	Characteristics of superior (excellent) individual performance, i.e. more senior management levels	Superior records of innovation, learning, quality and other long-term business criteria
APPLIED TO . . .	Generic Vocational Education and Training standards across organizations and occupations, i.e. common denominators	Tailored excellent behaviours to integrate all areas of HRM, i.e. reinforce distinguishing characteristics	Marketing and product strategies, selection of best economic rent-generating activities, underlying business processes
LEVEL OF ANALYSIS . . .	Occupation and sector based on sample of key jobs	Job level, or across the management hierarchy	Organization level and underlying business process

Table 17.1   (*cont.*)

Element of definition	What are management competences?	What are behavioural competencies?	What are organizational competences?
OWNERSHIP . . .	Competence owned by national institutions and organizations and granted to individuals	Competency held by the individual and brought to the organization	Competence held by the organization and jointly developed by individuals
ASSESSMENT ONUS . . .	Accreditation of past activities to grant professional status	Identification of potential to ensure best internal resourcing decisions	Articulation of key success factors and unique proprietary know how
INDIVIDUAL MOTIVATION . . .	Externally transferable achievement and qualification	Internally rewardable achievement and recognition	Organizationally-sustainable employment and security

would not use the information for promotion decisions, 91% were negative about its usefulness for recruitment, and 70% felt it had not influenced the way they trained and developed managers (*Personnel Management*, 1990). Whilst having some merit in specifying minimum standards of performance and providing small or poor practice organizations with an immediate guide to management effectiveness, the model is seen as bureaucratic, cumbersome and unrelated to the practical world. It appears to offer few attractions to those organizations that are trying to integrate their total HRM system around competencies and does not pick up the organization-specific and in-house nature of management skills.

A second, more widely adopted model, originated at the McBer Corporation and Harvard Business School (Boyatzis, 1982). This model views competencies as 'soft skills' that are associated with underlying characteristics (such as motive, trait, skill, aspect of one's self-image, social role or body of knowledge) of superior individual performance in an occupational role. There has been considerable confusion about what is meant by the term 'competency'. What psychological constructs do competencies tap? Are there generic competencies or are they all organization-specific? Are they learnable (developable) or discriminative (selectable)?

In the ensuing debate Woodruffe (1991) made a useful distinction between 'areas of competence' or fields of knowledge (i.e. aspects of the job which a person must perform effectively) and 'competencies' which are aspects of the person that enable them to develop particular areas of competence. In other words, competencies should be viewed as behavioural repertoires (sets of behaviour patterns) which some people can carry out more effectively than others. A behavioural competency includes all those behaviours that individuals input into a broad organizational context (ranging from success in an individual job, a role or career stream, or within the organization as a whole given its structure and strategic purpose) in order to perform well. They involve an implicit performance criterion (excellence) and are expressed in terms of performance outputs—i.e. what is achieved and produced from a situation by managing it effectively. The validity of the approach lies in its use of 'criterion samples', i.e. people who have clearly had success in their jobs. It also lies in the identification only of those behaviours that are causally related to a successful outcome. Competencies have to include a 'causal intent' that generates action towards the desired outcome. A characteristic is not a competency unless it predicts something meaningful in the real world (Spencer and Spencer, 1993). A behavioural competency is therefore defined as 'an underlying characteristic of a person which results in effective and/or superior performance in a job' (Boyatzis, 1982). However, since behaviour without intent is not a source of competency, competencies are comprised of a series of elements:

1. *Bodies of knowledge:* i.e. what the employee needs to know in order to achieve the goals the job specifies. Information in specific content areas.
2. *Skills:* i.e. what the employee has to possess in order to do the job. The ability to perform a physical or mental task and demonstrate a sequence of behaviour that is functionally related to a performance goal and can be applied to a range of situations.
3. *Attitudes and values:* i.e. what the employee needs to display in connection with achieving the tasks. Attitudes that predict behaviour in the short or long term.
4. *Traits:* i.e. characteristic or quality of a person that is associated with effectiveness. Physical characteristics and consistent responses to situations or information.
5. *Motives:* i.e. drive or thought that is related to a particular goal. The things a person consistently thinks about or wants that cause a desired action or goal.
6. *Self-image:* i.e. the understanding an individual has of him or herself in the context of values held by others.
7. *Social roles:* i.e. the perception of social norms and behaviours that are acceptable and the behaviours that a person needs to adopt in order to fit in.

In his pioneering work, Boyatzis (1982) studied 2000 managers holding 41 different jobs in 12 (mainly Anglo-Saxon) organizations. He recognized that using a post hoc labelling process meant that competencies drew upon a variety of individual attributes such as personality traits, skills and abilities. He distinguished between 'threshold' management competencies which usually means the minimally acceptable level of work, and 'superior' management competencies, defined as the level achieved by one person out of ten. Identification of these behavioural competencies—whether against such an explicit performance criterion or a less well defined one—relies on one or more of a range of job analysis techniques (such as repertory grids, critical incidents, structured skills questionnaires, observations, diaries, and behavioural event interviews) used to gather data from a neutral or blind stance (tapping the employee's constructs of 'effective' performance without specifying what sort of criteria the organization believes are most appropriate) or a values-driven stance (specifying performance criteria that the organizational culture or strategy suggest are most appropriate). It is the relevance (causal link to performance) of the behaviours identified and the quality and consistency of the rules applied to govern the way in which they are expressed that makes the competency approach so potentially powerful.

The labels used to make the list of behaviours more palatable (and more traditionally assessable by psychologists) are actually of less importance (Sparrow and Bognanno, 1993). Why? Because the labelling process is post hoc. It is merely a tool for reducing potentially hundreds of effective behaviours into simpler labels and a shorthand to convey the essence of effective behaviour, based on three options:

- Mathematical clustering in which behaviours rated on a series of dimensions are grouped on the basis of a factor analysis or similar technique and competency labels attributed to describe and make sense of the grouped behaviours
- Interpretation by trained psychologists, grouping behaviours along traditional grounds (frequently distinguishing between analytical, interpersonal and results achievement attributes)
- Allocation of behaviours to labels that have some other purpose or meaning within the organization (for example, to support statements of culture or mission)

Many of the problems raised by these approaches to clustering and naming of competencies—such as the need to consider issues of congruence and appropriate naming—have been discussed by Ferguson and Cox (1993) in the context of exploratory factor analysis. Because the resultant competencies and behavioural indicators tap a wide range of psychological sources (personal traits, motives, attitudes, skills and aptitudes) and summarize these root sources at a descriptive level, many practitioners will find that when used as part of an assessment centre, there is considerable overlap between labels based on 'competencies' and the more traditional concept of work-related 'dimensions'. Where the job analysis has been based on competency-based approaches, the two are one and the same thing. However, many assessment centres use work-related 'dimensions' which have been derived through a different methodology or maintain a clear division between the separate elements of bodies of knowledge, attitudes, personality traits and so forth. It is the composite nature of behavioural competencies that supporters claim makes them lie at the heart of effective performance across a wide range of tasks and management fields. This composite and strong behavioural description of competencies necessarily places a premium on selection and assessment techniques that focus upon observable behaviour, although psychologists will often use traditional psychometric instruments as one source of evidence.

APPLICATION OF BEHAVIOURAL COMPETENCIES

Not surprisingly, behavioural competencies have been applied to a wide range of HRM policies and practices. A review of the management literature and conference proceedings suggests that considerable benefits have been reported from the use of behavioural competencies in the areas of recruitment and selection, career development, performance appraisal and management, and the management of change (see Table 17.2). These benefits are either specific improvements to the content of HRM in these areas, or general improvements associated with the process of identifying, articulating and communicating the behavioural model of effectiveness. The methodological rigour of competency profiles is difficult to assess from most reports. The benefits outlined in Table 17.2 are based on the reports (either to other practitioners through conferences or to an academic audience through journal papers) of personnel professionals. Psychologists tend to ignore such evidence—sometimes with good reason, sometimes without good reason. It is beyond the scope of this chapter to review the supporting evidence behind these benefits, but a few observations are needed. Some benefits are self-evident to practitioners and would be applicable to any job or person specification (whether competency-based or otherwise). Many of the benefits claimed by practitioners do not need supporting through independent study since they are based on accepted practice or tenets of occupational psychology. This observation applies to many of the 'process benefits', such as higher ownership of the final profile amongst line managers as a result of their involvement in the design of the competency study, provision of information and subsequent interpretation of the study findings. These are benefits related to the 'consulting process' and form the basis of much organizational development work. A number of other benefits arise from the 'behavioural description' element of the competency approach. For example, more accurate and consistent rating has long been claimed for behaviourally-anchored scales, as has the benefit of behavioural information to improve skills training and enable detailed interpersonal feedback. Many of the 'behavioural' benefits form the tenet of much historical work in occupational psychology. However, hidden amongst such practitioner benefits there are many as yet untested claims—for example, more effective succession planning, better decisions about the organization structure, and more appropriate self-selection. Empirical investigation of such claimed benefits is now being carried out (see for example Mabey and Iles, 1993; Robertson, Iles, Gratton and Sharpley, 1991) but it will be many years before the impact of the competency-based approach on the more strategic aspects of HRM can be assessed. Indeed, the fact that competency-based approaches are being used in conjunction with a myriad of other organizational changes makes systematic assessment of benefits even more problematic. It is for such reasons—as well as the obvious danger of variable methodology and skill in the competency identification process—that some authors have strongly criticized the competency approach. Indeed, a number of clear weaknesses in the approach exist. Some of these criticisms are developed in the next sections.

Despite this debate about the validity of claimed benefits, competency-based approaches to recruitment and selection have been reported in the UK by several organizations such as Cadbury Ltd, Shell, Safeway, Prudential, and National Provincial. Application in the area of career development has been even more widespread, including organizations such as BAT Industries, British Rail, British Petroleum, British Telecom, Cadbury Schweppes, Glaxo, IBM, Kent County

Table 17.2   The HRM content and process benefits associated with well-designed competency approaches

HRM Content Benefits

RECRUITMENT AND SELECTION
- Visible and agreed set of standards for systematic assessment
- More rigorous job analysis process to defend against equal opportunities legislation
- Reduces variable practice by individual selectors and assessment on irrelevant characteristics
- More sophisticated and flexible targeting of applicants, e.g. women returners, untried labour pools, freedom from previous norms
- Conveying of relevant information to assist self-selection in adverts or assessment centre exercise design
- Enhancement of application form design to focus on more important aspects of previous experience
- More informed initial screening and sifting decisions based on targeted questionnaires
- Informed choices about the types of assessment tools best used in the selection procedure to ensure adequate coverage of competencies
- Provision of information for situational interviews to assess potential

CAREER DEVELOPMENT
- Promotes career restructuring by identifying real 'career bridges' or 'break-points' as opposed to the status quo, i.e. results in more cross-functional movement and technical to professional moves
- Informs decisions about the underlying number of vertical hierarchies in the structure
- Standards set for progression based on behavioural sets and not the individual
- Career decisions made on the basis of future potential not just current competency
- Facilitates succession planning
- Strengths and weaknesses provide a referent for planned development

PERFORMANCE MANAGEMENT
- Provides a guideline for decisions about grading in job evaluation
- Provides a framework under which objectives for the appraisal system may be developed and set
- Broadens appraisal systems to consider 'how well it is done' measures as well as the more traditional 'what is achieved' measures
- Facilitates the development of behaviourally-anchored rating scales or language ladders for more accurate performance management assessment
- Concentrates the appraisal interview discussion on performance and effectiveness
- Provides a language for feedback on sensitive and emotive issues

HRM Process Benefits

- Involvement of line managers in the identification process and design of assessment tools results in higher ownership of the results
- Forces a link between the strategic direction and recruitment criteria
- Identification process creates a shared understanding of the types of people needed in the organization
- More informed decisions about the most appropriate resourcing decision, i.e. buy, make or design out the competencies
- Provides a language for self-development and self-assessment and a basis for coaching and training
- Generates useful information to help build successful teams
- Represents a tool for developing the business culture, forcing clearer articulation of the strategy, or consideration of how new structures or business processes may actually work

Council, Manchester Airport, Midland Bank, the National Health Service, National Westminster Bank, Shell UK, Tesco Stores and W. H. Smith.

More recently, with the advent of prolonged economic recession and a need to reinvigorate pay-for-performance systems, competencies have also been applied in a performance management setting in organizations such as the Automobile Association, BSS Ltd, Boots the Chemists, First Direct, Manchester Airport, Nationwide Building Society, and the Wellcome Foundation. There are numerous other organizations who have not reported their models in either the academic or practitioner literature.

A fourth, and more testing, application of behavioural competencies has been in management change programmes. Organizations are beginning to appreciate that the process of labelling behavioural indicators into strategically-meaningful titles provides a language and forum for capturing cultural changes (Iles, 1992; Mabey and Iles, 1993; Mills and Friesen, 1992; Sparrow and Bognanno, 1993). However, adopting competency frameworks can produce quite shocking insights into the organization. Consider the following example. A division of a large pharmaceutical organization reduced its workforce from 2500 to 1200, with a fall in management posts from 160 to 60. A long period of historical business decline was followed by a radical restructuring of businesses, sale of non-core activities and investment in remaining divisions. Existing staff were invited to forward themselves for a reselection process driven by a series of new competencies that had been identified as important for the future organization. They were not being assessed for jobs or positions in the new structure, but for the blend of competencies required by the whole organization. Placement of the survivors would be a later decision. Initially expecting the selection decision to be one of weeding out some poorly-skilled individuals and then making difficult choices between the remaining pool to fill the few vacancies, the assessors actually found that they could not even fill the 60 posts from the original pool of candidates. The management workforce, even when reduced from 160 to 60, were severely deficient in many competency areas. Only 16% of the surviving managers scored over the halfway mark on the leadership competencies, and the people management competencies were equally poor. The inferred level of competency was based on the traditional assessment centre approach, in which trained assessors provided ratings of performance on a series of exercises (in this case situational interviews, group exercises, an in-tray and psychometric tests) and a final overall rating for each competency was agreed in the 'wash-up' session of the assessment centre. The new managing director recognized, through the use of the competency approach, that the new 'delayered' organization with its 'empowered' managers simply would not be 'competent' enough. The competency framework challenged decades of recruitment and selection practice and the historical climate and culture of the old organization (which had penalized initiative, decision-making and responsibility and designed out the need to deal with employees on an interpersonal level, thereby creating anything but competent managers). Interesting changes occurred from an equal opportunities perspective as well. Many female managers scored significantly better than their male counterparts. In the new structure they found themselves in charge of managers who for years had been their bosses. In the face of such challenges the organization did not revert to its old ways, but put in place a wide-ranging HRM strategy in order to address the competency issues of the new structure.

A CHANGING CONTEXT FOR COMPETENCIES: NEW RESOURCING EQUATIONS

Organizations face a host of complex problems that carry significant implications for the type of human resources needed and represent an overwhelming force for change. The pressures for change are only going to increase. Consider the future business environment for Europe (Sparrow and Hiltrop, 1994). The drive towards a more flexible and responsive organization has increased the number of people operating at the boundary of the organization in part-time or contract relationships. Mergers and acquisitions, strategic alliances, privatization, and deregulation are redrawing the economic space across Europe, resulting in changes in national ownership and a wave of rationalization and 'downsizing'. Only 25% of East German jobs in existence before unification are expected to survive the process, yet West Germany can satisfy total East German demand for goods simply by running one extra half-day shift a week (Sparrow and Hiltrop, 1994). France has planned levels of privatization twice the value of the UK programme. Over 85% of the Fortune 1000 organizations downsized their white-collar workforce from 1987–91 at massive cost. IBM has spent one-third of all the profits it has ever made in its history on restructuring. Nor are the gains that clear. In a study of 1468 downsizings, the US Society of HRM found that in 50% of cases productivity remained the same or got worse. Although downsizing treats only the symptom of organizational problems (too many people) as opposed to the cause (the amount of work and the way it is done) it is having a pervasive impact on the nature of skills, competencies and HRM. As the quality differential between North American and European countries and other areas erodes, there is also increasing pressure on labour costs. German labour costs are 50% higher than those in the US, 70% higher than Japan, seven times higher than Singapore and twelve times higher than Mexico. Future age dependency ratios make social security systems unsustainable. In 1970 in France there were three people in work to support every non-active person. By 2010 the ratio falls to 1.7 to 1.0, and by 2020 the ratio in the EU as a whole will be one to one. In this changed and more competitive business context, organizations fear that there will be a continued decline in the overall level of employment. They are unable increasingly to provide life-long employment, are shifting towards more flexible patterns of employment, and concentrating on the development of their internal labour markets. Although demographic shortages created a shift from a buyers' to a sellers' market for some, future competitive pressures on productivity and expectations of continued 'downsizing' mean that for the majority of individuals entry into organizations is becoming a more gradual, selective and phased process.

Not only are resourcing equations for organizations changing irrevocably but, for the survivors, the shape of work is changing. There are business pressures for

Table 17.3   The HRM implications of flat structure organizations (after Mills and Friesen (1992))

	Hierarchical structure	Cluster structure
RECRUITMENT	Carried out by supervisor and personnel function	Devolved to member of the team cluster
	Assessment centres and realistic job previews developed to test technical skills	Testing on the basis of ability to fit into the group and perform in the environment immediately
	Low immediate costs (automated process) but high indirect costs (expensive supervision or staff turnover)	Higher immediate costs (multiple interviews) balanced by lower staff turnover and improved productivity
	Assess technical work skills and learning ability	Assess social skills and interaction ability
MANAGERIAL CONTROL	Confidence in performance based on willingness of subordinate to carry out directives	Confidence in performance based upon competency (knowledge and professionalism) of team
REWARDS AND INCENTIVES	Strong reliance on direct benefits	More power given to indirect benefits around opportunity, growth and development
	Compensation fixed by rank and determined by length of service, teamwork and/or productivity	Rewards given on the basis of knowledge, performance, quality
	Pay grades set on analysis of carefully designed 'comparison' jobs	Tighter link between pay and performance
CULTURE	Used to control and define behaviours	Used as a means of communicating and influencing behaviours
CAREER MANAGEMENT	Advancement through rank	Advancement through leaving the team
	Perception of greater promotion opportunity	Recognition of career plateaux
	Career reward through climbing ranks	Career reward through successive Projects, i.e. broadened scope of work, greater opportunities for diversity and challenge, wider networks of contacts
PERFORMANCE APPRAISAL	Personnel function driven performance criteria	Senior-manager designed performance criteria

Table 17.3   (*cont.*)

	Hierarchical structure	Cluster structure
	Clear defined job descriptions. Appraisal measures based on achieving set outputs	Appraisal measures that are not all job-specific, i.e. can earn a good rating in several different ways to encourage multiple skill use
	Limited sources of information. Supervisor focus	Varied sources of information. External focus

Source: Reprinted from *European Management Journal*, **10**(2), D. Q. Mills and B. Friesen, 'The learning organisation', 146–156 © 1992, with kind permission from Pergamon Press Ltd

higher quality design of products and delivery of service. Rules and formalization are reducing as organizations attempt to overcome functional, product and national boundaries. Total quality management (TQM) programmes require a deeper understanding of internal customer–supplier relationships. Technical changes in products, business processes and information systems have resulted in the redesign of much managerial work, with complete business outputs and processes being 're-engineered'. Decision support systems continue to erode the difference between technical and general managers, and in general there is more information, knowledge (and therefore power) at lower levels of the organization. Based on the experiences of British Petroleum, Mills and Friesen (1992) have outlined the HRM implications of the shift towards 'delayered' and 'downsized' organizations (see Table 17.3).

In this business environment, whilst employee behaviour is the most direct way in which strategies are implemented, employees must also have quite prescriptive competencies in order to exhibit these behaviours. In thinking about these competencies we need to distinguish between human resources as individuals (who have associated behavioural competencies and characteristics) and human resources as the total pool of human capital within the organization (who need to show a behavioural reflection of the strategic competences of the organization). Rather than just focusing on specific management practices and tools and the way these align individual employee behaviour with strategic goals, HRM strategists (and psychologists) need to focus on the competency of the total pool of human capital within the organization as the resource that makes up competitive advantage (Wright and McMahan, 1992). Individual employee behaviour has to be analysed in the context of organization competencies. Why? Because management skills are increasingly organization-specific. In the UK, this has been evidenced by a rejection of generic competence approaches in favour of individually-tailored behavioural approaches (*Personnel Management*, 1990), as argued earlier. Few organizations see the benefit of generic competence descriptions because they see them as overly-bureaucratic, unspecific and irrelevant to the 'way we do things around here'. Different organization structures, growth paths and unique career paths have reinforced the development of organization-specific skills.

CRITICISMS AND CHALLENGES TO THE SELECTION AND ASSESSMENT PARADIGM

There has been a parallel debate within the field of industrial psychology over problems with the traditional selection and assessment paradigm. European organizations appreciate that survival now depends on the quality of their people and a conscious and specific direction of their HRM systems in both the short and long term (Boerlijst and Meijboom, 1989). The selection and assessment of people—indeed the whole range of decisions to be made about resourcing the organization—provides a powerful basis for influencing and organizing human behaviour in line with its strategic direction. Assessment for such resourcing decisions involves '. . . collecting and processing relevant information in a systematic and reliable manner with a view to realising and maintaining adequate matching between the organisation and its surroundings' (Boerlijst and Meijboom, 1989, p. 26).

There are two contrasting perspectives on selection. Meta-analysis and validity generalization studies probably represent the most important methodological innovation in psychology within recent decades (Schuler and Guildin, 1991). Research on meta-analysis and validity generalization has challenged the beliefs of many psychologists about the importance of many situational variables (a key element of the competencies-based approach) in limiting the validity of historical empirical studies (Schmidt and Hunter, 1977). By estimating the magnitude of systematic errors across validity studies and determining more realistic assessments of true situational variation, most meta-analytic studies have revealed impressive results. On the one hand, then, work on validity generalization suggests that there is substantial transfer in the predictive validity of general cognitive, perceptual and psychomotor abilities for both job proficiency and training success for a wide range of jobs. Moreover, the job components or synthetic validity approach assumes that those jobs with particular activities in common share similar requirements, general skills and abilities and common links to selection predictors. Therefore, the validity of most existing psychological tests only alters with large changes in job content (McCormick and Ilgen, 1987). However, different task requirements do moderate test validities and (especially in managerial jobs) generalizable cognitive abilities as measured by general mental abilities tend to be relatively less important (Smith and Robertson, 1989).

Therefore, many psychologists are now seeking new ways of collecting information about management competencies and better methods of matching this to the organization's needs. This has become necessary because selection and assessment in European organizations in the 1990s is concerned with problems of change—both change in the business environment and change in the perspectives held by managers on the nature of organization and the meaning and practice of employee recruitment and selection. In this period of change it is argued, many currently accepted assumptions in recruitment, selection and assessment will need to be reassessed because they emerged from experiences steeped in organization systems, structures and styles that are rapidly disappearing. Ultimately, it is a matter of judgement as to whether psychologists believe that the underlying job components and tasks in managerial jobs have been changed sufficiently—or made specific to each organization—by recent efforts at empowerment, delayering, the creation of new organizational forms and competitive arrangements. At what point do the rules of the past no longer apply?

In the field of selection we are likely to see the development of more complex tools and techniques, a need to tolerate greater ambiguity of performance criteria, and a challenge to many of the methods that have made sense to those managers who constructed the old organizations. This challenge will reduce the meaning and usefulness of many traditional methods of recruitment and selection. The field has come under criticism on three counts:

- Selection tools and techniques seem to have hit a (not high enough) ceiling in terms of their predictive validity (de Wolff, 1989)
- The validity of the performance criteria traditionally used to consider the choice of selection methods is being questioned
- There are a number of methodological problems even with some of the most predictive selection and assessment tools

Snow and Snell (1992) point out that the challenge to organizations in the future is to create flexibility and adaptability in their workforces. In order to cope with the increasingly dynamic and competitive business environment, rapid strategic response, and close monitoring of implementation throughout the workforce, organizations need to adapt recruitment and selection systems in order to resource a new set of skills. The topic of selection and assessment has shifted from a paradigm of matching past performance to a defined job towards one of estimating a person's probable adaptability and ability to learn new skills and tasks (Shimmin, 1989). Organizations are faced with three strategic selection choices:

- Select for short-term proficiency and accept the possibility of high levels of turnover if employees cannot cope with change
- Select for longer term adaptability to change, but accept that there will be limited knowledge of future changes and therefore some difficulties in assessing 'adaptability'
- Follow a path of continuous modifications as the future unfolds, with numerous changes to selection systems (where reliance is on the external labour market) or vocational training systems (where reliance is on an internal labour market)

The majority of competency-based approaches fall into the second category, but view longer term adaptability to change from a highly situational perspective. Another challenge comes from the call for a more judicious, strategic and targeted approach to competencies seen in the literature on existing assessment centre practice. Crawley, Pinder and Herriot (1990) argue that despite the emphasis on management competencies, the exact status of the construct is still not clear. A number of difficulties exist with the traditional assessment centre approach, mainly concerned with the limited ability of managers to handle complex assessment decisions driven by multiple competencies or dimensions. Jones *et al.* (1991) note that the validity achieved by assessment centres is surprisingly low given the validity of their component parts. Payne, Anderson and Smith (1992) reported that the predictive power of assessment centres was only equivalent to or lower than common alternatives such as work sample tests, situational interviews or cognitive ability tests, and in practice 85% of assessors' decisions could be correctly identified and predicted from the test battery scores alone. In a study of assessment centres for a financial services organization, Israel *et al.* (1993) found a fall in validities against criterion measures of career potential from 0.56 in 1985 to 0.36 by 1988. Research in the late 1980s and early 1990s has demonstrated that the correlation between overall assessment ratings (OARs) and a variety of criterion measures is frequently low. Managers seem incapable of accurately assessing cross-situational abilities from most exercises, often frequently being unduly influenced in their rating of specific criteria by the general task performance of the candidate. The design of exercises to assess critical management roles and the creation of exercise-specific behavioural frameworks, scales and checklists have helped to counter this problem to some extent, but serve to add to the cost and complexity of the approach (Iles, 1992). Even when assessment centres use only ten dimensions and competencies, many assessors tend to rely on perhaps only three of these dimensions in making their OAR, and frequently attach greater weight to the lower validity predictors. Suggested solutions are to reduce the number of dimensions in order to reflect only higher order constructs, to reduce the memory load and to improve their relation to specific outcomes in the organizations (Klimoski and Brickner, 1987). Even these modifications do not always improve overall validity of assessment centres (Jones *et al.*, 1991). Clearly, as psychologists we need to accept that it may be more important to forgo our preference for completeness of behavioural description and focus instead on the changing relevance of management competencies and the use of business-sensitive mechanisms to prioritize their assessment.

CONCEPTS OF FUTURE COMPETENCIES

To make matters more difficult, the nature of competencies is changing. As the topic of management competencies has been raised to the top of the strategic agenda, there has been a shift in thinking about their nature. An empirical study of eight UK organizations found that their ability to compete rested on their capacity to comprehend the competitive forces at play, how these had changed over time, and the ability of the organization to mobilize and manage the resources necessary for the chosen response (Whipp, 1991). HRM is linked to the process of competition through the issue of learning, with the ability to learn faster than competitors seen as the only sustainable advantage. Therefore '. . . the ability of the organization to reconstruct and adapt its knowledge base (made up of skills, structures and values) should be a key task for managers' (Whipp, 1991, p. 189).

The strategic HRM literature now points to the need to educate, mobilize and then integrate managers into the strategic change process. The nature of the relationship between organizations and their managers has evolved over recent years. In the past, managerial competency was equated with the possession of specific skills and abilities, but it now rests in '. . . the development of attitudes, values and "mindsets" that allow managers to confront, understand and deal with a wide range of forces within and outside their organizations' (Morgan, 1989). Organizations can no longer continue to drive through the rear-view mirror, analysing what they and other excellent organizations already do. Pedler, Burgoyne and Boydell (1991) note that the competencies identified by many organizations are orientated to the skills needed to allow the organization to continue doing what it is already doing. If such competencies are used as part of a human resource development strategy they only serve to reinforce and fix the current or historical ways of doing things, dragging the cloak of the old business into the new. If a competency framework creates too much homogeneity amongst managers it may reduce the potential for novel ideas and viewpoints to emerge. Psychologists have recently focused on the importance of cognitive diversity in top teams in order to facilitate strategic implementation (Bantel and Jackson, 1987; Sparrow, 1994).

Therefore, a more proactive, future-orientated approach, intended to anticipate likely strategic changes and the position of the organization and its members to address these challenges, is required (Boam and Sparrow, 1992). The paradox is that the need to understand a new competency typically comes at a time when the job holders' knowledge of the competency is at its lowest. Identifying such competencies is an educational and values-driven process, rather than the more traditional job analysis process favoured by psychologists. It has become common to build in a learning element to future-orientated competencies, either by recognizing aspects of learning (such as creativity, mental agility and balanced learning habits) as specific competencies to be assessed, or recognizing future forecasting as a competency, and incorporating the behaviours and skills associated with reading the future (such as spotting major 'fracture lines' and discontinuities) into corporate profiles. It is also important that such competency frameworks are treated as templates against which whole teams may be assessed and resourced. Individuals are unlikely to have strengths against more than three or four of these competencies. An examination of some competency models in use by leading organizations reinforces the 'super-human' nature of their competency frameworks. It also reveals four different assumptions about the most appropriate performance criteria for future-orientated competencies:

1. *Reacting to and capitalizing on change:* Schroder (1989) derived a set of 11 high performance competencies based on complex experimental simulations of team performance and assessment centre experiences. They have been applied to managers operating in dynamic, high change (unknown) turbulent environments in decentralized organizations. National Westminster Bank adopted this approach in an attempt to improve customer service and create the desired organizational changes. These competencies highlight the cognitive and interpersonal dimensions of adaptability. Information search, concept formation, conceptual flexibility, interpersonal search, managing interaction and personal

impact have all been operationalized by National Westminster for assessment purposes at senior levels in the organization.

2. *Enabling organization change to happen:* in other situations, the challenge faced by organizations is the need to create a central resourcing policy in businesses that face very different strategic scenarios. British Petroleum defined effective performance as the ability to implement change, no matter what the change might be. The competencies for change highlighted by British Petroleum were driven, and labelled, according to a series of culture change dimensions (Sparrow and Bognanno, 1993). They included behavioural indicators under the heading of open thinking, networking, empowering and personal impact, although there was some overlap with the National Westminster criteria, particularly in the area of conceptual flexibility, information search skills and interpersonal reach.

3. *Sustaining a competitive advantage:* a more traditional approach, for example that adopted by Cadbury Schweppes, concentrates on the skills and behaviours associated with strategic planning and thinking. These competencies highlighted the importance of adaptability, decisiveness, innovation, leadership, risk taking, and strategic vision.

4. *Being effective in a turbulent world:* Shell Canada focused on a series of characteristics or competences at the organizational level which facilitate the comprehension and management of complexity and uncertainty. The competencies identified included building bridges and alliances, reframing problems, scanning, forecasting, identifying fracture lines, visioning, empowering, skills of remote management, creativity, learning and innovation (Morgan, 1989).

It is immediately apparent that these criteria include a range of behavioural competencies as defined earlier, and other generic competences which include fields of knowledge and culturally appropriate actions. There is a thin line between intuitive deduction about future competencies and simple speculation about 'desirable' organizational characteristics (such as the need to create a learning organization, fewer organizational layers, a reduction of internal boundaries and greater levels of empowerment). Any proven link between such organizational characteristics and individual performance becomes difficult to justify on conventional grounds. The search for validity is transferred from searching for the predictive validity that lies at the heart of many selection systems focused around job systems, to a search for:

- Content validity of the behavioural indicators (i.e. their relevance to individual and organizational effectiveness or their motivational power when used as the cornerstone of a resourcing policy)
- Construct validity of the assessment dimensions that may be used to assist resourcing decisions

Arguments and support for, and confidence in the competency approach, become based on an act of faith and belief in the reliability of the various competency identification and forecasting methodologies (such as behavioural event investigation, repertory grids, critical incidents, organizational climate surveys and so forth).

This 'act of faith' is also now steeped in a business logic, which is being provided for psychologists by the strategic management writers and theorists.

STRATEGIC COMPETENCES AT THE ORGANIZATIONAL LEVEL

The third source of discussion about competency has emerged from strategic management writers and theorists (Barney, 1991; Fiol, 1991; Grant, 1991; Hamel and Prahalad, 1991; Klein, Edge and Kass, 1991; Mahoney and Panadian, 1992; Reed and DeFillippi, 1990). Strategy is difficult to plan in the 1990s because of rapid discontinuous change and intense competition. Traditionally, strategy considers the organization's internal resources—the assets, capabilities, organizational processes, firm attributes, information and knowledge that enable the organization to conceive of and implement its strategies (Barney, 1991). The selected strategy generates above normal rates of return (economic rents) because the chosen internal resources are scarce, protected by collusive agreements, demonstrate entrepreneurial insight into an uncertain or complex environment, or are organization-specific (Mahoney and Panadian, 1992). In order to provide some fixed points to help deal with high levels of turbulence, strategists are attempting to translate the strategic capabilities of organizations into underlying competences (Grant, 1991) and as management skills have become organization-specific, then the concept of 'organization-level' skills and capabilities becomes a central source of differential and sustainable competitive advantage. Many organizations have found that their historical cost and quality advantages have been eroded as new competitors have entered the market, innovations in technology have spread rapidly throughout the sector, or alternative national 'business systems or logics' have proved more effective at creating these advantages (for an empirical investigation of the changed basis of competition in the UK, see Pettigrew and Whipp, 1991). As these cost and quality advantages lose their potency, Hamel and Prahalad (1991) stress the importance and exploitation of 'core competences' (viewed as static attributes which senior managers need to seek out in order to capitalize on opportunities). Whilst Hamel and Prahalad (1991) view organization-level competences as distinctly technical, marketing or strategic capabilities, Grant (1991) builds on this view by examining what lies beneath such organization competences (such as the ability to innovate and the development of a learning organization). He sees organization competences and capabilities as a meshing together of organization resources such as the skills of individual people, leadership, and more tangible assets such as capital resources, brand reputation and patents held. Similarly, Klein, Edge and Kass (1991) view 'corporate skills' as strategic combinations of individual (human) competencies, hard organizational factors (such as equipment and facilities) and soft organizational factors (such as culture and organization design). The focus is shifting more towards the individual and soft organizational factors. The richer the connection between the capabilities and skills of the organization's human resources, the distinctive areas of high performance and technical know-how of the organization, and the dominant logic or mental models of the top management teams, then the more effective the strategy will be (Reed and DeFillippi, 1990; Sparrow, 1994). Klein, Edge and Kass (1991) conclude that as product life-cycles shorten and skill development life-cycles lengthen '. . . the skillbase must therefore be actively managed as the mainstay of competitive strategy'.

The strategists are viewing management skills in the context of strategic key success factors—evidenced by the organization's behaviour and the skills of the total pool of human resources—and based on the possession of core corporate-level skills, coherence across these skills, and unique 'know-how'. Whilst the definition of these strategic competences is clearly distinguishable from the concept of behavioural competencies, there is a meeting of the minds between strategists, HRM practitioners and psychologists. The core competences considered in the strategic management literature impact management competencies in two ways. First, there must be a behavioural reflection of the specific technical and marketing capabilities they tend to describe; second, there must be a set of conceptual abilities that are associated with the identification, modification and management of strategic competences. This is what most organizations want to see tapped by the behavioural competencies identified by psychologists.

A LIFE-CYCLE PERSPECTIVE ON ORGANIZATIONAL-LEVEL COMPETENCIES

In linking organizational-level competencies to behaviours observed at the individual level there is a critical distinction between identifying competencies for change—and analysing changing competencies (Boam and Sparrow, 1992; Sparrow and Bognanno, 1993). Organizations take a dynamic and changing view about what constitutes effective performance and as they move through different business environments, or themselves mature, the relevance of any one competency is bound to alter. This perspective fits into the third selection option identified by Shimmin (1989) and discussed earlier in this chapter. Rather than creating generic lists of competencies associated with 'coping with change' or 'making change happen' a more sophisticated picture of competencies for the organization (or career stream, or individual job) is needed. We need to create a behavioural reflection of both the individual management competencies and the strategic competences of the total pool of human resources. This requires a flexible framework that reflects the changing relevance of competencies in the present and future, assesses their utility, boils down the considerable number of dimensions and behavioural indicators into a manageable and powerful framework, and enables psychologists to target the selection of competencies for assessment purposes (thereby overcoming some of the problems with assessment centres discussed earlier).

When the relevance of competencies at the organizational level is considered over time, there are *four* different categories of competency (see Figure 17.2). The competencies and behavioural indicators within each category vary from organization to organization, and across industrial sectors (Boam and Sparrow, 1992). Some competencies may be termed *emerging*. Whilst not particularly relevant to the organization and its jobs at present, the strategic path the organization is pursuing places a greater emphasis on them in the future. They reflect an articulated view of future pressures on the individual manager (such as changes to corporate culture, the workings of a new delayered structure, the implications of a redesigned business process) and seek to provide behavioural indicators associated with these pressures. Other competencies may be *maturing*. Having played an important part of organizational life (and the jobs within it) in the past, they are becoming less relevant in the future due to a shift in strategy, or the designing out of the competency through technology or work structuring. They may still be relevant to existing performance management systems, but need to be designed out of recruitment and potential identification systems. A third category may be termed *transitional*. Neither currently important, nor implied by the strategic plan, change can only be achieved or managed smoothly by placing greater emphasis on them. The 'competencies for change' identified by organizations such as British Petroleum, Cadbury Schweppes, National Westminster and Shell should really be viewed as transitional competencies. They represent an integral part of the change process and so are highly relevant. Other (hopefully transitional) competencies at the individual level might include the requirement to demonstrate a high capacity to live with uncertainty, manage stress, cope with pressure and manage conflict. A fourth category of competency may be termed *stable* or *core*. These are enduring competencies that will remain as important tomorrow as they are today. They lie at the heart of effective performance despite the current or forthcoming flavour of the business plan, strategic direction or management of change programme. These pick up what is particular about the industrial sector (public versus private, scientific versus marketing, long business cycle versus short business cycle), the existing culture, or indeed the strategic competence of the total pool of people. They also reflect some of the generic aspects of the role of being a manager.

In thinking about—and classifying—competencies as being stable, emerging, declining or transitional, it becomes easier to understand the need to attach a 'shelf life' to any competency profile, match the wide range of behavioural

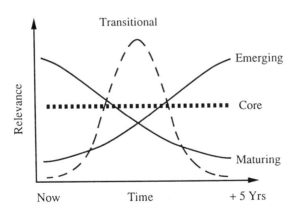

Figure 17.2 The changing relevance and life-cycle of organizational-level behavioural competencies

indicators to the desired type of application, and make prioritizing decisions for assessment tools and techniques. Clearly, the relative focus or weighting that can be given to a competency will change in proportion to the speed of change within the business environment and nature of the job. However, the more forward-looking the profile is the longer its shelf life. It is impossible to put a finite figure in years, months and days on any profile, but experience indicates that organizations only need to reidentify and reclassify competencies every two to three years or so.

There is a need to develop a flexible package of competency requirement fore-casting techniques. In extending the shelf life of a competency profile and moving beyond generic 'competencies for change' we also need to help organizations create powerful distillations of 'effective behaviours'. This requires careful defini-tion and manipulation of the performance criterion used in traditional job analysis techniques, i.e. what does 'effective' performance really mean in an organizational and strategic context? It might involve the use of visioning workshops to articu-late major business changes in structure, process and culture, top team building programmes, competitive and best practice analysis, and simulation of new tech-nologies, all as part of an educative process. Technical and business, rather than psychological, knowledge becomes critical in such an identification process, as do forecasting techniques that incorporate defensible hypotheses about the organiza-tion's future. Psychologists need to become involved in what is an educative and broadening process, yet still be able to identify the behaviours (as opposed to nice sounding words) that are relevant in such a context.

IMPLICATIONS OF ORGANIZATION-LEVEL COMPETENCIES FOR PSYCHOLOGISTS

Such organization-level behavioural competencies have profound implications for HRM. Psychologists have traditionally identified a taxonomy of skills based on the abilities of individuals, profiled specific jobs along this taxonomy, and then made resourcing decisions. Once organizations build HRM strategies around competencies, then the competency, not the individual, becomes the unit of anal-ysis, especially once this competency becomes a behavioural reflection of the strategic capabilities of the organization. Organizations will make more sophisti-cated resourcing decisions intended to design themselves around these higher level 'competencies'. Only then will they audit the skills and abilities of their people. Resourcing decisions that may be informed by the identification and knowledge of organizational level competencies include:

- The selection or deselection of people (or units of their time) on the basis of the relevance of their competency to the task or to the team
- Large-scale development programmes to close competency gaps with competitors
- Designing out of the need for competencies that are time-consuming to develop through technology or work structuring

- Contracting out of under-developed competencies (through choices and assessments of partners in alliances or joint ventures, or the practice of executive leasing)

It seems likely that the field will develop this way given developments in both HRM strategy and the business environment. The question is, will psychologists be able to inform organizations and guide their efforts, or will organizational practice supersede our ability to contribute? Will organizational competencies be identified by line managers and internal staff—with the associated risk of lax methodology and limited consideration of the assessment task? As assessment psychologists we have to ask ourselves about our own competencies. Perhaps the best guidance is to consider some of the characteristics that have helped personnel managers make the transition to a more strategic HRM role. In addition to traditional consultancy, job analysis interview and process management skills, the areas of competence noted in Table 17.4 are important. To what extent, however, are these picked up by professional training schemes for psychologists?

There is time to close the gap. For the competency approach to develop in a more strategic direction there is a potentially huge research agenda for industrial psychologists. The most important methodological and research developments should include:

- An audit of existing practice, the levels of integration of HRM systems actually achieved and the perceived benefits and problems

Table 17.4 Fields of competence required to identify organizational competencies

Perception and understanding of the connections between the business and HRM needs in the sector the client organization operates

Diagnostic skills to audit and take stock of the existing skill base of the client organization in the light of anticipated business and technological changes

Ability to identify and advise on the business opportunities afforded by the existing skill base of the client organization, creating a business case for why human resources are a perceived source of competitive advantage

Preparedness to initiate new styles and patterns of HRM activity in the client organization in advance of business changes

Cultural understanding to be able to preserve what is valuable from clients' previous missions and values, meet new task requirements and be sensitive to individual satisfaction and career needs

Knowledge of the power base of the personnel management function and the overarching information, commercial and financial policies of the client organization

Sensitivity to the changing internal situation in the client organization during major periods of change

Political skills to identify the internal and external forces of change, and ability to audit a wide range of HRM policies and procedures from a behavioural perspective

Recognition of the range of pressure points within HRM that can be brought to bear in a strategic change situation, and that may be improved by the adoption of a competency framework

- Examination of international practice, and clarification of the variation in behavioural indicators of competencies from one country to another
- The building up of a repertoire of future-orientated data collection techniques
- Development of methods to weight competencies in terms of their relevance, development time, and the depth of talent pool
- Identification of methods to determine 'fracture lines' between competencies, i.e. when behavioural indicators represent significantly new demands that should be used to structure careers or organizations.

As organizations and HR directors emerge from the current chaos in the business environment—as the downsizings continue and the problems these create come to the fore, as complete business processes are 're-engineered'—then they will be looking for ways to reintegrate the organization and its HRM systems. Helping organizations to create broad selection and assessment systems based around organizational-level behavioural competencies may offer an attractive way forward.

REFERENCES

Armstrong, A. (1991). Management skills and performance audit. *Asia Pacific Human Resource Management*. Summer, 25–39.

Bantel, K. and Jackson, S. (1989). Top management and innovation in banking. Does the composition of top teams make a difference? *Strategic Management Journal*, **10** (Special Issue), 107–124.

Barney, J. (1991). Firm resources and sustainable competitive advantage. *Journal of Management*, **17** (1), 99–120.

Boam, R. and Sparrow, P. R. (eds) (1992). *Designing and Achieving Competency: A Competency-based Approach to Managing People and Organisations*. London: McGraw-Hill.

Boerlijst, G. and Meijboom, G. (1989). Matching the individual and the organization. In P. Herriot (ed.), *Assessment and Selection in Organizations: Methods of Practice for Recruitment and Appraisal*. London: John Wiley.

Boyatzis, R. (1982). *The Competent Manager*. New York: John Wiley.

Boerlijst, R. (1992). Building on competence: The effective use of managerial talent. In G. Salaman (ed.), *Human Resource Strategies*. London: Sage.

Connock, S. (1992). The importance of 'big ideas' to HR managers. *Personnel Management*, **21** (11), 52–56.

Connor, K. R. (1991). A historical comparison of resource-based theory and five schools of thought within industrial organisation economics: Do we have a new theory of the firm? *Journal of Management*, **17** (1), 121–154.

Crawley, B., Pinder, R. and Herriot, P. (1990). Assessment centre dimensions, personality and aptitudes. *Journal of Occupational Psychology*, **63** (3), 211–216.

Dale, M. and Iles, P. (1992). *Assessing Management Skills: A Guide to Competencies and Evaluation Techniques*. London: Kogan Page.

Ferguson, E. and Cox, T. (1993). Exploratory factor analysis: A user's guide. *International Journal of Selection and Assessment*, **1** (2), 84–94.

Fiol, C. M. (1991). Managing culture as a competitive resource: An identity-based view of sustainable competitive advantage. *Journal of Management*, **17** (1), 191–211.

Fletcher, S. (1992). *Competence-based Assessment Techniques*. London: Kogan Page.

Glass, P. (1990). Skills required for effective performance by hospital managers. *Asia Pacific Human Resource Management*, February, 24–40.

Grant, R. M. (1991). The resource-based theory of competitive advantage: Implications for strategy formulation. *California Management Review,* **33** (3), 114–135.

Hamel, G. and Prahalad, C. K. (1991). Corporate imagination and expeditionary marketing. *Harvard Business Review,* **69** (4), 81–92.

Hansson, J. (1988). *Creative Human Resource Management: Competence as Strategy.* Stockholm: Prisma.

Heyer, S. and Lee, R. (1991). Rewiring the corporation. *Journal of Business Strategy,* **12** (4), 40–45.

Hooghiemstra, T. (1990). Management of talent. *European Management Journal,* **8** (2), 142–149.

Iles, P. (1992). Centres of excellence? Assessment and development centres, managerial competence, and human resource strategies. *British Journal of Management,* **3** (2), 79–90.

Jones, A., Herriot, P., Long, B. and Drakeley, R. (1991). Attempting to improve the validity of a well-established assessment centre. *Journal of Occupational Psychology,* **64** (1), 1–21.

Kanungo, R. N. and Misra, S. (1992). Managerial resourcefulness: A reconceptualisation of management skills. *Human Relations,* **45** (12), 1311–1332.

Klein, J., Edge, G. and Kass, T. (1991). Skill-based competition. *Journal of General Management,* **16** (4), 1–15.

Klimoski, R. and Brickner, M. (1987). Why do assessment centres work? The puzzle of assessment centre validity. *Personnel Psychology,* **40** (2), 243–260.

Mabey, C. and Iles, P. (1993). The strategic integration of assessment and development practices: Succession planning and new manager development. *Human Resource Management Journal,* **3** (4), 16–34.

Macleod, G. and Wyndham, J. (1991). Developing the competent manager. *Asia Pacific Human Resource Management,* Winter, 69–78.

Mahoney, J. T. and Panidian, J. R. (1992). The resource-based view within the conversation of strategic management. *Strategic Management Journal,* **13** (2), 363–380.

McCormick, E. J. and Ilgen, D. (1987). *Industrial and Organisational Psychology,* 8th edition. London: Routledge.

Mills, D. Q. and Friesen, B. (1992). The learning organisation. *European Management Journal,* **10** (2), 146–156.

Morgan, G. (1989). *Riding the Waves of Change: Developing Managerial Competencies for a Turbulent World.* Oxford: Jossey-Bass.

Murdoch, V. J. (1992). Assessment centres: Through the glass brightly. *Asia Pacific Journal of Human Resources,* Spring, 29–41.

Payne, T., Anderson, N. and Smith, T. (1992). Assessment centres, selection systems and cost effectiveness: An evaluative case study. *Personnel Review,* **21** (4), 48–56.

Pedler, M., Burgoyne, J. and Boydell, T. (1991). *The Learning Company: A Strategy for Sustainable Development.* London: McGraw-Hill.

Personnel Management (1990). Management Charter Initiative has had little impact so far. *Personnel Management,* **22** (1), 14.

Pettigrew, A. and Whipp, R. (1991). *Managing Change for Competitive Success.* Oxford: Basil Blackwell.

Reed, R. and DeFillippi, R. J. (1990). Causing ambiguity, barriers to imitation, and sustainable competitive advantage. *Academy of Management Review,* **15** (1), 88–102.

Robertson, I. T., Iles, P. A., Gratton, L. and Sharpley, D. (1991). The impact of personnel selection and assessment methods on candidates. *Human Relations,* **44** (9), 963–982.

Salaman, G. (ed.) (1992). *Human Resource Strategies.* London: Sage.

Schmidt, F. L. and Hunter, J. E. (1977). Development of a general solution to the problem of validity generalisation. *Journal of Applied Psychology,* **68**, 407–414.

Schroder, M. (1989). *Managerial Competence: The Key to Excellence.* Dubuque, Iowa: Kendall and Hunt.

Schuler, H. and Guildin, A. (1991). Methodological issues in personnel selection research. In C. L. Cooper and I. T. Robertson (eds) *International Review of Industrial and Organizational Psychology,* vol. 6. Chichester: John Wiley.

Shimmin, S. (1989). Selection in a European context. In P. Herriot (ed.) *Assessment and Selection in Organizations: Methods and Practice for Recruitment and Appraisal.* London: John Wiley.

Smith, M. and Robertson, I. (eds) (1989). *Advances in Selection and Assessment*. Chichester: John Wiley.

Snow, C. and Snell, S. (1992). Staffing as strategy. In N. Schmitt and W. Borman (eds) *Personnel Selection*, vol. 4. San Francisco, CA: Jossey Bass.

Sparrow, P. R. (1994). The psychology of strategic management: Emerging themes of diversity and cognition. In C. L. Cooper and I. T. Robertson (eds) *International Review of Industrial and Organizational Psychology*, vol. 9. London: John Wiley.

Sparrow, P. R. and Bognanno, M. (1993). Competency requirement forecasting: Issues for international selection and assessment. *International Journal of Selection and Assessment*, **1** (1), 50–58.

Sparrow, P. R. and Hiltrop, J. M. (1994). *European Human Resource Management in Transition*. London: Prentice-Hall.

Spencer, L. M. and Spencer, S. M. (1993). *Competence at Work: Models for Superior Performance*. London: John Wiley.

Tziner, A., Ronen, S. and Hacohen, D. (1993). A four-year validation study of an assessment centre in a financial corporation. *Journal of Organizational Behaviour*, **14** (3), 225–237.

Whipp, R. (1991). Human resource management, strategic change and competition: The role of learning. *International Journal of Human Resource Management*, **2** (2), 165–191.

Wolff, C. J. de (1989). The changing role of psychologists in selection. In P. Herriot (ed.), *Assessment and Selection in Organizations: Methods and Practice for Recruitment and Appraisal*. London: John Wiley.

Woodruffe, C. (1991). Competent by any other name. *Personnel Management*, **23** (9), 30–34.

Wright, P. and McMahan, G. (1992). Theoretical perspectives for strategic human resource management. *Journal of Management*, **18** (2), 295–320.

Chapter 18

Assessing Honesty, Integrity, and Deception

KEVIN R. MURPHY AND NATHAN LUTHER

Department of Psychology, Colorado State University, Fort Collins, CO 80523-1876, USA

INTRODUCTION

Honesty in the workplace is a topic that has attracted increasing attention among organizational researchers. Research suggests that workplace dishonesty, including theft, fraud, embezzlement, etc., is widespread and costly. Estimates of the amount lost per year to employee theft vary widely; in the United States alone, employee theft is thought to account for losses of \$20–50 billion (Moore, 1988). Employee theft is cited as one of the primary reasons for up to 30% of all small business failures in the United States, and losses from corporate corruption and white-collar crime are thought to exceed \$100 billion (Murphy, 1993).

Theft and embezzlement are not the only causes for concern over workplace dishonesty. Résumé fraud appears to be common (McKee and Bayes, 1987); substantial discrepancies between application blanks and reports from employers in areas such as previous position held, previous salary, duration of employment, and reasons for leaving are frequently reported. Employers are also increasingly concerned about issues ranging from substance abuse (Normand, Lempert and O'Brien, 1994) to industrial espionage (Fennelly, 1989). Corporate illegal activity seems rampant, with several major scandals in investment companies, banks, and corporations in recent years (for a review of research linking corporate corruption to management characteristics, see Daboub *et al.*, 1995). As a result, a great deal of attention has been devoted to efforts to reduce or control workplace dishonesty.

This chapter examines the use of tests and other assessment methods in predicting and assessing dishonesty and deception in job applicants and/or incumbents.

International Handbook of Selection and Assessment, Edited by N. Anderson and P. Herriot.
© 1997 John Wiley & Sons Ltd.

We consider both pre-employment screening methods and methods that might be used in investigating dishonesty and deception among job incumbents. In preparing this chapter, we conducted an intensive literature search for international research on the use of measures of honesty in personnel management, and contacted personnel management organizations in several countries where integrity tests, polygraphs, graphology, or other measures thought to provide information about honesty, are known to be used. The use of (and research on) these methods in the workplace appears to be much more common in the United States than elsewhere, and with very few exceptions, the studies cited in this chapter come from American sources.

We start this chapter with a discussion of what the various methods used to assess or predict honesty in the workplace actually measure. Next, we review measures that are used to predict future dependability in work settings, including:

1. integrity tests,
2. other self-reports, and
3. graphological analyses.

We then review methods that are used to detect or infer deception in specific contexts, including:

1. polygraph analyses,
2. voice stress analyses,
3. drug and alcohol tests, and
4. assessments of behavioral cues to deception.

Finally, we discuss issues that organizations should consider before deciding whether to use such tests and assessments in dealing with workplace dishonesty.

WHAT IS BEING ASSESSED?

The tests and assessment techniques listed above are all designed to provide information about honesty, but they differ substantially in their focus. It is useful to distinguish first between deception and integrity or dependability. Measures of integrity/dependability are used to make inferences about an individual's past or future behavior. For example, integrity tests are typically used to forecast future workplace dishonesty (sometimes on the basis of admissions of previous misdeeds). Similarly, integrity interviews, application blanks, and a variety of self-report measures are used to make predictions about an individual's likely level of honesty and dependability. These inferences might be based on information about past behavior, or on measures of specific traits and attributes thought to be relevant to workplace honesty, but in all cases the focus is on predicting future behavior rather than drawing inferences about the truthfulness of specific claims or statements.

Although the terms honesty, integrity, and dependability are often used interchangeably in this literature, a useful distinction can be drawn between them. Honesty refers to a particular respect for truthfulness, whereas integrity and dependability imply slightly broader conceptions, including a willingness to comply with rules, internalized values, norms and expectations. Tests that are used to infer future behavior in the workplace are likely to draw upon this broader conception rather than focusing narrowly on honesty *per se*.

Assessments of deception are designed to determine whether an individual is telling or withholding the truth in a particular context. For example, polygraph examinations are structured to support inferences about whether a subject's responses to a specific set of questions are truthful. Similarly, voice stress analyses are designed to determine whether answers to specific questions are truthful. Drug and alcohol tests are used to determine whether individuals are withholding information about their use of alcohol, drugs, or other substances of abuse. In all these cases, these tests are used to draw inferences about the probability that individuals are attempting to deceive or withhold information from the examiner.

The distinction between tests of deception and predictions of future honesty is often blurred in practice. For example, it is common practice in many US firms to use drug or alcohol tests in pre-employment screening.[1] These tests may do little more than indicate whether an individual has ingested alcohol or drugs within the last few hours to days, and might be more suited to detecting and deterring deception (e.g. in determining whether drugs or alcohol were involved in an accident) than to predicting whether a job applicant is likely to be a good prospect for employment. In general, tests or assessment methods that provide valid information about deception in specific contexts might nevertheless prove useless in predicting future dishonesty (Ben-Shakhar and Furedy, 1990; US Congressional Office of Technology Assessment (OTA), 1983). Similarly, measures of integrity or dependability may provide little information about the truthfulness of a specific statement or claim.

ASSESSING INTEGRITY

Assessments of integrity involve an inference about the likelihood of future workplace dishonesty, based on past behavior, expressed attitudes, or some set of traits or attributes. This category of assessments includes integrity tests as well as a number of alternative self-report measures. Graphologists also claim to be able to make valid inferences about future behavior, on the basis of structural analyses of handwriting samples.

Integrity tests

Although paper-and-pencil integrity tests have been in existence since at least the 1950s, their widespread use is relatively recent. O'Bannon, Goldinger and Appleby (1989) report that in the 1980s these tests were used by 10%–15% of all US employers, concentrated in the retail sales, banking, and food service industries, and that over 2.5 million tests are given by over 5000 employers each year. There are several reasons to believe that the current figures for integrity test use are even higher; these include increasing awareness of the cost and extent of employee theft and increasing evidence of the validity of several widely distributed tests.

Although the individual tests differ in a number of specifics, there are a number of features common to virtually all integrity tests. In particular, integrity tests usually include items that refer to one or more of the following areas: (a) direct admissions of illegal or questionable activities, (b) opinions regarding illegal or questionable behavior, (c) general personality traits and thought patterns thought to be related to dishonesty (e.g. the tendency to constantly think about illegal activities), and (d) reactions to hypothetical situations that may or may not feature dishonest behavior.

A distinction is usually drawn between tests that inquire directly about integrity, asking for admissions of past theft, or asking about the degree to which the examinee approves of dishonest behaviors, and tests that indirectly infer integrity on the basis of responses to questions that are not obviously integrity-related. Several authors (e.g. Sackett, Burris and Callahan, 1989) refer to the former as 'overt' tests, and to the latter as 'personality based' tests. The labels 'clear purpose' and 'veiled purpose' (or 'disguised purpose') are also used; these labels might be preferable because they highlight the fact that the purpose of testing is sometimes obvious and sometimes hidden from examinees.

Examples of tests usually classified as either clear-purpose or veiled-purpose integrity tests, together with descriptions of dimensions measured by the tests (in some cases, these refer merely to the labels attached to scale scores reported) are presented in Table 18.1; detailed descriptions of the dimensions measured by 43 integrity tests are presented in O'Bannon, Goldinger and Appleby (1989). As the table suggests, the distinction between clear-purpose and veiled-purpose tests is not always a simple one (O'Bannon, Goldinger and Appleby, 1989; US Congressional Office of Technology Assessment (OTA), 1990). Many clear-purpose tests include items, scales, etc. that are not obviously related to honesty, and many veiled purpose tests contain items that might alert the respondent to the true purpose of the test.

Although these tests may measure a number of distinct factors, there is evidence that a general honesty factor may pervade many of these tests (Harris and Sackett, 1987; Ones, Viswesvaran and Schmidt, 1993). One implication is that the choice of a specific test might not be critical; several well-researched tests seem to provide overlapping measures, at least with regard to the general honesty/integrity dimensions measured.

Validity of integrity tests

Sackett and his colleagues have conducted several reviews of research on the reliability, validity, and usefulness of integrity tests (their latest review is Sackett, Burris and Callahan, 1989; see also Goldberg *et al.*, 1991; OTA, 1990). Ones, Viswesvaran and Schmidt (1993) conducted a large-scale meta-analysis that quantitatively summarized the outcomes of multiple validity studies; Table 18.2 lists

Table 18.1 Examples of integrity tests

Test	Scores reported	Remarks
Reid Report	Honesty attitude, social behavior, substance abuse, personal achievements, service orientation, clerical/math skills	Measures both attitudes and direct admissions
Stanton Survey	Honesty attitude, admissions of previous dishonesty	Measures both attitudes and direct admissions
Hogan Reliability Index	Score from Hogan Personality Inventory (HPI)	HPI is a general-purpose personality scale; reliability index one of many scores reported
PDI Employment Inventory	Productive behavior, tenure	Measures attitudes, self-description

mean observed and corrected validities for both job performance and counter-productivity criteria. Although each review raises different concerns, and several reviews lament the shortcomings of research on the validity of integrity tests, the general conclusion of the more recent reviews is positive. Earlier reviews of research on integrity tests were sharply critical, but it appears that both the research and the tests themselves have improved, partly as a result of the earlier criticism. There is now a substantial body of evidence showing that integrity tests have some validity for predicting a variety of criteria that are relevant to organizations. This research does not say that tests of this sort will eliminate theft or dishonesty at work, but it does suggest that individuals who receive poor scores on these tests tend to be less desirable employees.

In discussing validity evidence, it is important to identify the specific criteria used in different studies. Some studies have validated integrity tests against measures of counterproductive behavior, whereas others have validated these tests against measures of general job performance. For example, scores on integrity tests show average correlations of 0.21 and 0.33 with measures of job performance and counterproductivity, respectively (correcting for unreliability and a

Table 18.2 Integrity test validities reported in Ones, Viswesvaran and Schmidt's meta-analysis

Criterion	Mean observed r	Corrected r^*
Job performance	0.21	0.34
Supervisory ratings	0.21	0.35
Production records	0.22	0.28
Counterproductive behavior	0.33	0.47
Theft	0.36	0.52
Broad counterproductivity	0.32	0.45

* Values are corrected for unreliability and range restriction.

variety of statistical artifacts, the estimated population correlations are 0.34 and 0.47, respectively; Ones, Viswesvaran and Schmidt, 1993). These two criteria are clearly not independent; employees who engage in a wide variety of counter-productive behaviors are unlikely to be good performers. Nevertheless, there are important differences between the two criteria and, more important, differences in the validity of integrity tests for predicting the two.

Other self-report methods

Integrity tests represent the most widely used and most controversial method of using self-reports to assess or infer honesty or integrity. There are a variety of other methods, ranging from those that use information from the application blank to infer integrity to those that are designed to assess psychopathology. As with integrity tests, the rationale behind all these methods is that information provided by the individual may help to indicate an overall likelihood to either engage in or avoid various types of dishonest behavior.

Biographical data

Self-report methods are usually used to assess a person's attitudes, beliefs, values, etc. Although not technically a self-report, the application blank that virtually all applicants fill out represents a method of obtaining information from the respondent that might be used in inferring his or her integrity. Several authors (e.g. McDaniel, 1989) have suggested that the weighted application blank might be used to infer honesty. Rosenbaum (1976) applied this technique to predict theft in the retail industry. This study suggested higher levels of theft for individuals who: (a) held a large number of previous jobs, (b) had an out-of-town vs. local address, (c) were at their present address for a relatively short time, (d) had few dependants, (e) did not own an automobile, and (f) did not want relatives contacted in the case of an emergency. It is well known that individuals with loose ties to the organization or the community are more likely to steal than individuals with longstanding connections (Hollinger and Clark, 1983); several of the items identified by Rosenbaum (1976) seem to relate to this theme.

McDaniel (1989) studied the validity of biographical measures obtained from background investigations. Although conceptually similar in many ways to the biographical data obtained from application blanks, background investigations often concentrate on negative information, such as drug use, criminal convictions, or bad credit history. He found that a number of background factors, including school suspension, drug use, quitting school, poor grades and failure to become involved in extracurricular activities, and previous contacts with the legal system were all significantly correlated with unsuitable discharges from the military.

The use of biographical data to predict theft and infer integrity has many advantages. This type of data can often be verified, which reduces the likelihood of faking, and this method is highly unobtrusive. Job applications are virtually universal, and it is quite possible that an individual will never find out that his or her application is used to infer integrity. There are, however, a variety of problems inherent in this approach. First, weighted application blanks can be openly discriminatory, particularly if factors such as race, gender, or income are directly entered into the equation. Secondly, the weights may be unstable, especially if they were originally estimated in small samples. Thirdly, this approach lacks face validity. That is, the relevance of many of the items on an application blank for predicting integrity is not always obvious, and even if this method leads to valid decisions, there may be substantial problems with the acceptance of decisions based on weighted application blanks.

Personality tests

Lewicki (1983) reviewed research on a variety of personality characteristics that may be related to lying, including an individual's stage of moral development, level of Machiavellianism, and internal vs. external locus of control. Ego strength and field dependency are thought to be related to ethical behavior in managers (Murphy, 1993).

Conscientiousness is one of five facets that defines the most widely accepted taxonomy of personality (Digman, 1990; McCrae and Costa, 1985). A number of paper-and-pencil tests of integrity and honesty include scales labeled 'Dependability', which is thought to be one aspect of conscientiousness. An analysis by Barrick and Mount (1991) suggests that conscientiousness is also related to a number of objective and subjective measures of job performance. Other personality dimensions are important in some jobs, or are related to specific performance measures (Hough *et al.*, 1990, review research on personality as a predictor of performance in the military), but the dimension of conscientiousness is potentially unique in its broad relevance.

Conscientiousness seems to be a critical component of most paper-and-pencil tests of integrity. Most veiled-purpose tests directly measure conscientiousness, or some closely related personality construct (Sackett, Burris and Callahan, 1989). Overt integrity tests are not necessarily designed to measure this personality characteristic, but even these tests are probably influenced by the respondent's level of conscientiousness. Highly conscientious individuals are probably less likely to commit illegal or questionable acts, which means that they simply have less to admit when responding to tests that call for admission of past thefts, crimes, or other questionable behaviors.

Measures used to assess psychopathology

There is an increasing interest in screening employees for various forms of psychopathology, using instruments such as the Minnesota Multiphasic Personality Inventory (MMPI). In part, this is a continuation of an earlier tradition in which inventories such as the MMPI and the California Personality Inventory, as well as projective devices such as the Rorschach Inkblot Test were used in an attempt to detect delinquency and criminality (Hollinger and Clark, 1983).

Although assessments of psychopathology do not always deal directly with integrity, they are very likely to deal with related concepts, such as problems in dealing with authority, emotional stability, responsibility, and the like. The use of MMPI subscales in screening for integrity is increasingly common, especially in police departments and in the security and nuclear power industries (Lowman, 1989). To date, however, there is little evidence that this test can validly predict honesty in the workplace (OTA, 1990). More generally, there is little compelling evidence that pre-employment screening for psychopathology will have a notice-able impact on honesty, theft, etc. in the workplace (Lowman, 1989). Pre-employment screening for psychopathology is both useful and important, but it does not appear to provide a valid substitute for integrity tests or other reason-ably valid methods of inferring honesty or dishonesty.

Graphology

Another technique that is sometimes used to assess honesty is handwriting anal-ysis, or graphology. The underlying theory is that various characteristics of a person's handwriting provide information about his or her personality, including traits such as honesty or loyalty. Although there are serious questions regarding the validity of assessments provided by this technique (Ben-Shakhar, 1989), it is widely used, especially in Israel (Ben-Shakhar *et al.*, 1986) and France (Ben-Shakhar and Furedy, 1990). In the United States, over 2000 employers are thought to use graphology in pre-employment screening (Murphy, 1993).

The graphologist's method

Graphology involves an examination of a number of specific structural charac-teristics of a handwriting sample (e.g. letter shapes and sizes), which are used to make inferences about the writer. Computerized systems for handwriting anal-ysis exist, but most graphological analyses are still done by individual grapholo-gists. Although this technique was originally used for forensic purposes (e.g. determining whether a document is a forgery), it is now widely used as a method of personality assessment. Graphologists typically insist that the sample must be spontaneous, and that handwriting samples which involve copying text from a book, or writing a passage from memory, will not yield a valid reading. The writing sample requested by a graphologist is often a brief autobiographical sketch, or some other sort of self-description (Ben-Shakhar, 1989; Ben-Shakhar *et al.*, 1986).

Graphologists claim that neither the content nor the quality of the writing sample (e.g. fluency, clarity of expression) influence their assessments, and that their evaluations are the result of close examination of the features of letters, words, and lines in the sample. There are several reasons to believe that this claim is false, and that even if graphologists try to ignore the content of the writing sample, their assessments are nevertheless strongly influenced by that content. First, several studies have shown that when the same biographical passages are examined by graphologists and non-graphologists: (a) their assessments of indi-vidual examinees tend to agree, and (b) graphologists are no more valid in their assessments than non-graphologists (Ben-Shakhar *et al.*, 1986; Ben-Shakhar, 1989).

Because non-graphologists presumably do not attend in a systematic way to the graphological features of the writing, but rather to the content of the stories, their ability to make assessments that are similar to and every bit as good as those made by professional graphologists strongly suggests that both groups are attending to the same material—i.e. the content of the writing samples. Indeed, Ben-Shakhar *et al.* (1986) showed that predictions based solely on the content of the writing sample (this study used a simple unweighted linear model to combine information from the various passages in each description into a prediction) were more valid than those obtained from professional graphologists. Secondly, when the content of passages is not biographical in nature (e.g. meaningless text, or text copied from some standard source), graphologists seldom make valid predictions.

One interesting trend in the use of graphology is that this technique, unlike polygraphs or integrity tests, is quite often used in assessing candidates for middle- and upper-management positions. There are a variety of potential explanations for this. First, graphologists claim that their method provides information about a broad spectrum of personality traits. Whereas polygraphs and integrity tests focus mainly on honesty, graphology supposedly reveals a number of personality traits that are thought to be critical to success (honesty is only one of these). Secondly, graphology is less invasive than the polygraph or some integrity tests. The candidate being assessed may not even know that his or her handwriting sample will be evaluated by a graphologist (thus raising some of the same privacy-related issues as raised by the administration of voice stress analysis over the phone), although applicants are often informed of this fact. In any case, graphology supposedly has broad range of application, and the assessment of honesty is only a small part of what graphologists claim to do.

Validity of graphological analysis

In evaluating graphology, there are two separate questions that might be asked. First, how valid and reliable are the general predictions produced by a graphological analysis? For example, if graphology is used in personnel selection, then we might ask the graphologist to predict who is more or less likely to perform well on the job. Secondly, how accurate are the specific assessments of particular personality traits? If graphology is used to measure specific traits, such as integrity, then we might ask whether this method provides valid measures of that trait.

There is evidence that graphologists can make somewhat valid predictions of a job applicant's overall performance, but it is also clear that non-graphologists who examine the same material make equally valid predictions (see Ben-Shakhar, 1989, for a review of the relevant research). This research suggests that there is little to be gained from attending to the purely graphological aspects of the writing sample.

The available evidence also casts doubt on graphologists' ability to make even the most general assessments of individuals, or at least to do a better job than non-graphologists, given the same materials. This suggests that assessments of specific characteristics such as honesty and integrity via graphoanalysis will not be successful. There is little, if any, empirical research that adequately assesses the accuracy of specific assessments made by graphologists (e.g. assessments of a candidate's honesty), but given the generally dismal track record of graphologists in making global predictions, there is very little reason to believe that their more specific predictions will be any better. While there is some evidence of temporal stability and inter-rater agreement in graphological analyses (Tziner, Chantale and Cusson, 1993), evidence for the validity of graphological assessments is limited, at best.

TESTS OF DECEPTION

Several methods have been used to assess deceptiveness in work settings, including polygraph examinations, voice stress analysis, drug and alcohol tests, and behavioral assessments. Descriptions of each method and research on the validity and usefulness of each are presented below.

Polygraph examinations

It is often assumed that deception is stressful, and that a number of physiological and behavioral cues might indicate that the individual is attempting to deceive. The use of such methods to detect deception has a long and varied history, going back almost 3000 years. Ben-Shakhar and Furedy (1990), Kleinmuntz and Szucko (1984) and Lykken (1981) all describe the ancient use of physical signs such as blushing, accelerated heartbeat, and dryness of the mouth as indicators of deception.

Sometimes referred to as a 'lie detector', the polygraph is an apparatus used to measure and record the physiological responses of an individual under interrogation. Typically, this apparatus includes sensors or devices that measure heart rate, blood pressure, respiration rate and palmar sweating. The use of a polygraph typically requires that electrodes, blood pressure cuffs, and sensors to measure respiration rate be attached to the examinee, and that physiological reactions that accompany answers to various questions be recorded. The theory behind this technique is that the physiological data provide information that helps the examiner determine whether or not the subject is deceptive in his or her answers to specific questions.

Although the polygraph is used in criminal and security-related investigations in a number of countries, its use in organizations (particularly for pre-employment inquiries) is a uniquely American phenomenon (Ben-Shakhar and Furedy, 1990; Lykken, 1981). In the early 1980s, approximately one million polygraph examinations were given per year, nearly three-quarters of those in employment settings (Lykken, 1981). The use of the polygraph in organizations declined dramatically after 1988, when a federal law severely restricted the use of the polygraph in employment settings. However, prior to that law the polygraph was widespread; some organizations are still pressing for legislation to overturn the existing restrictions on the polygraph.

Techniques in polygraph examination

All polygraph examinations require examinees to respond to a number of questions that are either relevant or irrelevant to the issue under investigation. In describing the various techniques used to construct a polygraph examination to investigate an incident such as the theft of an expensive tool, it is useful to distinguish between three types of questions:

1. relevant questions—questions that are directly relevant to the incident in question (e.g. did you steal the tool?),
2. control questions—questions that are irrelevant to the investigation, but that would probably prove stressful to examinees (e.g. have you stolen anything from your last employer?), and
3. irrelevant questions (e.g. do you own a foreign car?).

There are many methods that are used in constructing a set of questions for a polygraph examination. For example Lykken (1981) describes: (a) the Lie Control Technique, in which questions designed to elicit deceptive answers (e.g. have you ever done anything illegal?) serve as controls, (b) the Truth Control Technique, in which answers regarding a fictitious incident serve as controls, (c) the Positive Control Technique, in which each relevant question is used as its own control, and subjects are instructed to answer twice to each question, once telling the truth and once telling a lie (presumably, stress is higher when the subject lies), and (d) the Relevant Control Technique, in which both irrelevant and potentially relevant questions are asked. In all cases, differences in reactions to relevant, irrelevant, and control questions are used to infer deceptiveness.

The Guilty Knowledge Technique, which is used to determine whether the examinee has knowledge of the event that would only be available to the guilty party, has shown the most consistent evidence of validity in detecting deception. Returning to the example of an investigation of a stabbing incident, you might ask 'Was the victim's shirt brown?', 'Was the victim's shirt blue?', etc. and instruct the individual to answer all questions negatively. Presumably, the individual who has guilty knowledge will react differently to the question that actually taps that guilty knowledge than to other questions.

In general, research on the polygraph suggests that the Guilty Knowledge Technique is both the most valid and the least utilized method of polygraph investigation (Ben-Shakhar and Furedy, 1990; OTA, 1983). One reason for the rather infrequent use of this method is the fact that until recently many polygraph examinations were conducted as part of pre-employment screening. Because the polygraph was often used for general inquiries about job applicants' trustworthiness rather than for investigations of specific incidents, the Guilty Knowledge Technique often could not be applied. Control Question Techniques are still the most common, although this method has come under increasing criticism because of the limited validity of comparisons between relevant and control questions (Ben-Shakhar and Furedy, 1990).

Validity evidence

In general, polygraph examinations have shown some evidence of validity in criminal investigations (OTA, 1983; Raskin, 1988); validity is highest when the Guilty Knowledge Technique is used, and is substantially lower when the more common Control Question Techniques are used (Ben-Shakhar and Furedy, 1990; Lykken, 1981; OTA, 1983). The difference between the two techniques is especially stark in terms of false positive rates (i.e. percentage of non-deceptive subjects who 'fail' to polygraph examination). Ben-Shakhar and Furedy (1990) summarize results from comparable studies using the two techniques, and show that the Control Question Technique has a false positive rate more than triple that of the Guilty Knowledge Technique (15.4% vs. 5%). The reliability and validity of the polygraph investigation declines so dramatically when one moves from investigations of specific events to a general evaluation of a job applicant's character that pre-employment polygraph examinations are unlikely to provide a basis for valid decisions (Ben-Shakhar and Furedy, 1990).

Voice stress analysis

In addition to the polygraph, other mechanical methods, and in particular voice stress analysis, have been suggested as a method of detecting deception. Although the exact methods used by different voice stress analysts vary, the conceptual underpinnings of this method are relatively consistent. Voice stress analysts believe that there are discernible patterns of voice production, sometimes referred to as microtremors in the voice, that indicate deception. A number of electronic devices have been developed to measure these voice characteristics, and voice stress analysts have used the charts produced by these devices to assess deception in a variety of criminal and organizational settings.

Proponents of voice stress analysis point to many potential advantages of their method, especially as compared with the polygraph. First, voice stress analysis appears to be less subjective than the polygraph. Polygraph examinations include extensive interviews, behavioral examinations, etc. in addition to the data that are obtained from the machine itself, and it is highly likely that polygraph examiners are affected by this information. Voice stress analyses do not involve these complex procedures; this method is often completely unobtrusive (i.e. the person being assessed might not be aware of the fact, which may raise ethical questions about informed consent). As a result, voice stress analysts appear to rely more on the output of their machines, and less on other verbal or behavioral information obtained during the analysis. Secondly, voice stress analysis is substantially less intrusive and intimidating than a polygraph examination, because voice stress analysis does not entail physically connecting an individual to a machine; voice stress analysis can even be carried out over the phone (Waln and Downey, 1987).

Reliability and validity evidence

Although proponents of this method claim high levels of accuracy, empirical research on the accuracy and validity of voice stress analysis has been far from encouraging. First, the reliability of this method is highly suspect (Hovarth, 1979; Waln and Downey, 1987). The agreement between readings of the same voice stress charts by independent analysts is generally low, and correlations between the same interviews in their original form and recordings of those interviews that had been transmitted over the telephone are also low (Waln and Downey, 1987). Secondly, the validity of judgments made on the basis of voice stress analysis appear to be questionable (Lykken, 1981). For example, Hovarth (1979) showed approximately chance level of success in identifying deception in mock crime situations. Similarly, a study by O'Hair and Cody (1987) showed that voice stress analyses were unsuccessful in detecting spontaneous lies in a simulated job interview. Voice stress analysis may be more successful in detecting real crimes or other non-trivial deceptions, where the level of stress is presumably higher, but even here the evidence of validity is rather thin.

Ultimately, the evaluation of voice stress analysis boils down to the same set of issues that underlie the evaluation of the polygraph—i.e. the presence or absence of some unique physiological reaction to deception. It seems clear that there are identifiable physiological markers for stress (although there are substantial individual differences in reactions to stress), but this does not mean that there are reliable physiological indicators of deception. Some people who give completely honest answers will nevertheless feel a great deal of stress when being interrogated. Most researchers accept Kleinmuntz and Szucko's (1984) assertion that there are no unique physiological correlates of lying. Mechanical methods that measure stress reactions will not provide adequate measures of deception; some individuals find deception stressful, but others do not.

Drug and alcohol testing

As part of a nationwide campaign against drug abuse that began in the 1980s, employee drug testing grew from a relative rarity to a common practice in the United States (Normand, Lempert and O'Brien, 1994). Large-scale alcohol testing is a more recent phenomenon. A federally mandated program now requires preemployment alcohol tests for all safety-sensitive jobs in the US transportation industry. This program alone will require more than 1.25 million tests per year.

Although drug and alcohol tests are not used to infer overall integrity, they are used to deter and detect one type of counterproductive behavior that is thought to be extremely costly in the workplace—i.e. substance abuse. There are some paper-and-pencil tests that are used to measure or infer substance abuse (Crown and Rosse, 1988), but the most common methods involve biological tests to detect the presence of drugs in the system. The overwhelming majority of these tests are conducted prior to employment, and failure can disqualify the applicant for employment.

The most common method of drug and alcohol testing involve the use of breath or urine samples (breath tests are used only in alcohol testing), although blood, hair, or saliva samples might be used (Butler, 1993; Normand, Lempert and O'Brien, 1994). All these methods test for the presence of drug metabolites in the system, which would indicate somewhat recent drug usage. Metabolites of some drugs, such as marijuana, may stay in the system for up to three weeks, but for many drugs the presence of metabolites indicates drug use within the last few hours or days. Significantly, none of the widely used pre-employment testing methods provides direct information about (a) drug or alcohol use at work, or (b) drug impairment at work.

Validity evidence

Public discussions of employee drug testing often focus on the possibility that drug tests will make false positive errors—i.e. that they will indicate that a non-user has drugs in his or her system. Personnel specialists often focus on a different set of questions—i.e. whether the results of drug tests have any relevance for safety, absenteeism, productivity, and other behaviors at work. In discussing research on employee drug tests, it is useful to separate these two distinct meanings of the term 'validity'. That is, the question of whether employee drug tests provide valid information about the presence or absence of drugs in the system is quite distinct from the question of whether people who fail drug tests are likely to be less safe, less productive, etc. than those who pass.

There is clear evidence that when appropriate procedures for collecting and analyzing specimens are followed, drug tests are highly accurate, and the likelihood of false positives is minimal (Normand, Lempert and O'Brien, 1994; Normand, Salyards and Mahoney, 1990). Similarly, alcohol tests (particularly those using breath or blood samples) are highly accurate in detecting the presence of alcohol in the bloodstream (Butler, 1993). However, even when the test gives an accurate reading, it is important to remember that these tests do not measure either substance abuse or impairment at work. Bioassay methods test for specific by-products or metabolites of one or more illicit drugs, but say nothing more than whether an individual has recently used a specific substance (Dubowski, 1986; Normand, Lempert and O'Brien, 1994). Individual differences in patterns of both drug use and drug impairment are substantial, and the implications of pre-employment drug or alcohol tests (or of periodic tests given to current employees) for substance abuse or impairment on the job are not necessarily clear.

Although there are a number of shortcomings in many studies of the criterion-related validity of employee drug tests, there is growing evidence that the results of employee drug tests are related to a number of job-relevant criteria, including absenteeism, involuntary turnover, and perhaps overall job performance (Normand, Lempert and O'Brien, 1994; Normand, Salyards and Mahoney, 1990). However, the relationships between the results of drug tests and these criteria appear to be both weak and inconsistent. To date, there is virtually no evidence relating the outcomes of pre-employment alcohol tests to criteria such as job performance, absenteeism, or safety.

Behavioral cues to deception

As noted earlier in this chapter, it has long been believed that there are a number of behaviors that indicate deception, ranging from sweating and halting speech to an unwillingness to look another person in the eye. Interviewers are sometimes trained to recognize these behaviors, and to use them to infer deception. For example, in describing the 'integrity interview', Buckley (1989) suggested that the repeated observations of the following behaviors might indicate attempts to deceive: (a) hesitancy in answering, (b) sudden movement of the upper or lower body away from the examiner, (c) grooming or cosmetic gestures, such as arranging clothing or jewelry, or adjusting and cleaning glasses, and (d) hiding hands or crossing arms or legs. Johnson (1987) described a more subtle system, which involves observing the eye movements of the subject. This system is based on the belief of researchers in neurolinguistic programing that the direction of eye movements indicates the type of mental activity the subject is engaging in. For right-handed subjects, looking to the left is thought to indicate that you are searching your memory whereas looking to the right is thought to indicate thoughts about the future. Therefore, if you ask a person about incidents in the past (e.g. theft from previous employers) and he or she looks to the right (i.e. thinks about the future rather than the past), this might indicate deception. Claims about the relationship between direction of gaze and deception are not accepted in the scientific community; for a review of research on neurolinguistic programing and its interpretation, see Druckman and Swets (1988).

Unfortunately, the literature and lore concerning the behavioral cues to deceptoin represents a jumble of intuition, folk tales and well-established facts. Researchers have attempted to identify behavioral correlates of deception, with only partial success. Examples of behavioral correlates of deception that have been identified in the research literature (e.g. Ekman, 1975; Ekman and O'Sullivan, 1991) are presented in Table 18.3. Although all these behaviors are correlated with deception, the correlations appear to be weak. That is, these behavioral indicators may allow a skilled observer to do better than chance in detecting deception, but do not allow a high degree of accuracy.

Studies on the detection of deception through the observation of behavioral cues such as those listed in Table 18.3 have consistently shown the exact pattern of results described above—i.e. an ability to detect deception that is only slightly better than chance (DePaulo *et al.*, 1989). For example, a recent study (Ekman and O'Sullivan, 1991) asked police officers, judges, FBI and CIA polygraph examiners, and US Secret Service agents to attempt to detect deception in a realistic

Table 18.3 Some behavioral cues associated with deception

1. Verbal
    - hesitation in speaking
    - higher pitch
    - speech errors

2. Non-verbal
    - increased blinking
    - frequent swallowing
    - fast or shallow breathing
    - self-manipulative behaviors—e.g. rubbing or scratching
    - more masking smiles, fewer enjoyment smiles

laboratory task. Only Secret Service agents performed better than chance. Ekman's (1975) research suggests why this is the case. He suggests that there are few behaviors, if any, that are universal indicators of deception, noting that 'no clue to deceit is reliable for all human beings . . .' (p. 97). His extensive program of research suggests that many individuals show consistent behavioral cues when they lie, but that the specific behaviors that indicate deception vary from person to person. One person might usually sweat and hesitate in speaking, while another might change his or her pitch. If the behaviors that indicate deception are indeed idiosyncratic, it may be pointless to train interviewers, supervisors, or others to look for the signs of deception—these signs might be completely different for each potentially deceptive person.

One reason that behavioral cues provide only weak evidence of deception is that most behaviors are multiply determined (i.e. there are several causes for behavior), and contextually-dependent (i.e. the same behavior may mean different things in different contexts). This means that deception might prompt different behaviors in the same person at different times, and that the same behavior that is prompted by deception in one context might indicate something else (e.g. stresses that have nothing to do with deception) in another. While behavioral cues provide some weak evidence of truthfulness, the age-old belief that a weak handshake, an unsteady gaze, a dry mouth, etc. indicate deception is such an oversimplification that it will be wrong more often than right.

SHOULD ORGANIZATIONS ADOPT TESTS OF HONESTY AND DECEPTION?

The assessment of honesty, integrity, and deceptiveness in organizations involves a number of potential costs and benefits. A complete discussion of the utility of the measures discussed above is beyond the scope of this chapter (see Murphy, 1993; O'Bannon, Goldinger and Appleby, 1989; Ones, Viswesvaran and Schmidt, 1993; Sackett, Burris and Callahan, 1989 for discussions of various facets of this cost-benefit analysis), but it is worthwhile highlighting the major issues an organization should consider in deciding whether to employ such measures. The problem of workplace dishonesty is so large and costly that virtually any method that promises to address the issue is likely to have considerable appeal. The research reviewed above suggests that some of these methods do indeed show evidence of validity (specifically integrity tests and drug and alcohol tests), and that they might be useful *if applied appropriately*.

To be useful, tests of honesty or deception must be sensibly matched to specific organizational decisions. For example, integrity tests do show adequate evidence of validity in predicting both overall job performance and counterproductive behavior, which is consistent with their use in pre-employment screening. In contrast, drug and alcohol tests are often used in making personnel selection and classification decisions. These tests can indicate whether an individual has used a specific substance within the last few hours or days, but they may not reveal anything else. The use of a drug or alcohol test to predict future suitability for employment is at best a substantial inferential leap.

There are several potential drawbacks to applying these testing and assessment techniques in organizations. First, many job applicants and incumbents find these methods offensive and objectionable (Normand, Lempert and O'Brien, 1994; O'Bannon, Goldinger and Appleby, 1989). These tests are likely to be viewed as evidence that management distrusts applicants and incumbents (Murphy, 1993), as invasions of privacy (Stone and Stone, 1990), and as arbitrary, capricious and untrustworthy bases for making important decisions. This last concern is often well-founded. Most of the techniques reviewed here (i.e., graphological predictions, workplace polygraph examinations, voice stress analyses, inferences based on behavioral cues) show little evidence of validity, and their continued use in organizations has little scientific justification. Even when specific tests or testing techniques show adequate validity, their use may be deeply controversial, and the negative effects of these tests on employee morale, labor relations, the firm's ability to attract the best applicants, etc. might outweigh the benefits associated with the use of valid tests or assessment techniques (Murphy, 1993). Secondly, the use of these tests and assessments may be restricted by law, contract, or custom. As we note below, tests of integrity and deception can be controversial even in the most favorable environments, and it may be impossible to use these tests, even if the organization reaches the conclusion that their use might be desirable.

Use of these tests and assessments in the workplace is, at present, largely an American venture. Although all of these methods have found application in other countries, both the use of these tests in the workplace and research on such testing applications has centered on the United States. American corporations seem to have shown more willingness to venture into controversial testing areas than their counterparts in other industrialized countries. We speculate that the controversies that have surrounded this type of testing will be considerably more intense in countries where the rights and prerogatives of job applicants and incumbents are given more attention than in the United States, and we suggest that organizations that have not yet employed such methods proceed very cautiously in adopting tests or assessments of honesty, integrity and deception.

There are two broad strategies for controlling employee theft and similar acts of dishonesty:

1. change the person, or
2. change the situation (Murphy, 1993).

Testing is an attempt to change the type of person who is hired, by screening out individuals who are thought to present undue risks. There are a number of strategies for changing the situation, ranging from increasing security to reducing employees' opportunities to engage in dishonest behavior. One potential pitfall of relying on tests and assessments is that they will lead organizations to ignore important situationally-oriented methods of dealing with dishonesty. There is always a temptation to believe that a new test or assessment of integrity or deception will 'solve' the problem of dishonesty, and disregard situationally-oriented interventions that might contribute substantially in reducing employee theft, misuse of resources, corporate corruption, etc. The best programs for dealing with dishonesty are likely to include both person-oriented and situation-oriented methods, and testing should always be considered (if it is considered at all) in the context of other organizational efforts to deal with workplace dishonesty.

Person-oriented interventions (e.g. integrity tests) may do little to address the systemic causes of workplace dishonesty. For example, corporate corruption usually involves many people working in concert to achieve dishonest ends, and it is likely that the existence of such corruption is the result of flaws in the system rather than flaws in a few individuals. Research shows that corporate wrongdoing is usually in part a function of the characteristics of the organization (particularly its top management; Daboub *et al.*, 1995), and programs designed to reduce corporate dishonesty by screening out a few high-risk individuals may be worse than useless. The danger inherent in concentrating on the individual is that it may lead to the situational causes of dishonest behavior being ignored. If the 'bad apples' are weeded out from an essentially dishonest workgroup, their replacements might also be corrupted by the group, and might turn out to be just as bad. Perhaps the most important lesson from surveys of research on honesty in the workplace (e.g. Murphy, 1993) is the need to match the intervention to the problem. Individually oriented interventions, such as tests and assessments of honesty or deceptiveness, have their place in addressing individual instances of dishonesty, but they are not appropriate choices when the problem is with the system rather than with the individuals in the system.

ENDNOTE

1. As we note in our final section, most of the techniques discussed in this chapter are both more common and more readily accepted in the United States than in the United Kingdom or Europe. Negative reactions on the part of applicants or incumbents may far outweigh the benefits of using some of the techniques described here.

REFERENCES

Barrick, M.R. and Mount, M.K. (1991). The big five personality dimensions and job performance: A meta analysis. *Personnel Psychology*, **44**, 1–26.

Ben-Shakhar, G. (1989). Non-conventional methods in personnel selection. In P. Herriot (ed.), *Assessment and Selection in Organizations*. Chichester: John Wiley.

Ben-Shakhar, G., Bar-Hillel, M., Bilu, Y., Ben-Abba, E. and Flug, A. (1986). Can graphology predict occupational success? Two empirical studies and some methodological ruminations. *Journal of Applied Psychology*, **71**, 645–653.

Ben-Shakhar, G. and Furedy, J.J. (1990). *Theories and Applications in the Detection of Deception*. New York: Springer-Verlag.

Buckley, J.P. (1989). The integrity interview: Behavioral analysis interviews for job applicants. *The Investigator*, **5** (3), 9–12.

Butler, B. (1993). *Alcohol and Drugs in the Workplace*. Toronto: Butterworths.

Crown, D.F. and Rosse, J.G. (1988). A critical review of the assumptions underlying drug testing. *Journal of Business and Psychology*, **3**, 22–41.

Daboub, A.J., Rasheed, A.M.A., Priem, R.L. and Gray, D.A. (1995). Top management team characteristics and corporate illegal activity. *Academy of Management Review*, **20**, 138–170.

DePaulo, P.J., DePaulo, B.M., Tang, J. and Swaim, G.W. (1989). Lying and detecting lies in organizations. In R. Giacalone and P. Rosenfeld (eds.), *Impression Management in the Organization*, pp. 377–396. Hillsdale, NJ: Erlbaum.

Digman, J.M. (1990). Personality structure: Emergence of the five-factor model. *Annual Review of Psychology*, **41**, 417–440.

Druckman, D. and Swets, J.A. (1988). *Enhancing Human Performance: Issues, Theories and Techniques*. Washington, DC: National Academy Press.

Dubowski, K.M. (1986). Recent developments in alcohol analysis. *Alcohol, Drugs, and Driving*, **2** (2), 13–46.

Ekman, P. (1975). *Telling Lies: Clues to Deceit in the Marketplace, Politics, and Marriage*. New York: Norton.

Ekman, P. and O'Sullivan, M. (1991). Who can catch a lie? *American Psychologist*, **46**, 913–920.

Fennelly, L.J. (1989). *Handbook of Loss Prevention and Crime Prevention*, 2nd edn. Boston, MA: Butterworth.

Goldberg, L.R., Grenier, J.R., Guion, R.M., Sechrest, L.B. and Wing, H. (1991). *Questionnaires Used in the Prediction of Trustworthiness in Preemployment Selection Decisions*. Washington, DC: American Psychological Association.

Harris, M.M. and Sackett, P.R. (1987). A factor analysis and item response theory analysis of an employee honesty test. *Journal of Business and Psychology*, **2**, 122–135.

Hollinger, R.C. and Clark, J.P. (1983). *Theft by Employees*. Lexington, MA: D.C. Heath.

Hough, L.M., Eaton, N.K., Dunnette, M.D., Kamp, J.D. and McCloy, R.A. (1990). Criterion-related validities of personality constructs and the effect of response distortion on those validities. *Journal of Applied Psychology*, **75**, 581–595.

Hovarth, F. (1979). The effects of differential motivation on detection of deception with the Psychological Stress Evaluator and the galvanic skin response. *Journal of Applied Psychology*, **64**, 323–330.

Johnson, K.L. (1987). How to interview for the truth. *Manager's Magazine*, **62**, 28–29.

Kleinmuntz, B. and Szucko, J. (1984). Lie detection in ancient and modern times: A call for contemporary scientific study. *American Psychologist*, **39**, 766–776.

Lewicki, R.J. (1983). Lying and deception: A behavioral model. In M. Bazerman and R. Lewicki (eds.), *Negotiating in Organizations*. Beverly Hills, CA: Sage.

Lowman, R. (1989). *Pre-employment Screening for Psychopathology: A Guide to Professional Practice*. Sarasota, FL: Professional Resource Exchange.

Lykken, D.T. (1981). *A Tremor in the Blood: Uses and Abuses of the Lie Detector*. New York: McGraw-Hill.

McCrea, R.R. and Costa, P.T., Jr (1985). Updating Norman's 'adequate taxonomy': Intelligence and personality dimensions in natural language and questionnaires. *Journal of Personality and Social Psychology*, **49**, 710–721.

McDaniel, M.A. (1989). Biographical constructs for predicting employee suitability. *Journal of Applied Psychology*, **74**, 964–970.

McKee, T.E. and Bayes, P.E. (1987). Why audit background investigations. *Internal Auditor*, **44** (5), 53–56.

Moore, R.W. (1988). Unmasking thieves: From polygraph to paper. *Journal of Managerial Psychology*, **3**, 17–21.

Murphy, K.R. (1993). *Honesty in the Workplace*. Pacific Grove, CA: Brooks/Cole.

Normand, J., Lempert, R. and O'Brien, C. (1994). *Under the Influence?: Drugs and the American Workforce*. Washington, DC: National Academy Press.

Normand, J., Salyards, S.D. and Mahoney, J.J. (1990). An evaluation of preemployment drug testing. *Journal of Applied Psychology*, **75**, 629–639.

O'Bannon, R.M., Goldinger, L.A. and Appleby, J.D. (1989). *Honesty and Integrity Testing: A Practical Guide*. Atlanta, GA: Applied Information Resources.

O'Hair, D. and Cody, M.J. (1987). Gender and vocal stress differences during truthful and deceptive information sequences. *Human Relations*, **40**, 1–13.

Ones, D.S., Viswesvaran, C. and Schmidt, F.L. (1993). Comprehensive meta-analysis of integrity test validities: Findings and implications for personnel selection and theories of job performance. *Journal of Applied Psychology*, **78**, 679–703.

Raskin, D.C. (1988). Does science support polygraph testing? In A. Gale (ed.), *The Polygraph Test: Lies, Truth and Science*, pp. 96–110. London: Sage.

Rosenbaum, R.W. (1976). Predictability of employee theft using weighted application blanks. *Journal of Applied Psychology*, **61**, 94–98.

Sackett, P.R., Burris, L.R. and Callahan, C. (1989). Integrity testing for personnel selection: An update. *Personnel Psychology*, **42**, 491–529.

Stone, E.F. and Stone, D.L. (1990). Privacy in organizations: Theoretical issues, research findings, and protection mechanisms. In G. Ferris and K. Rowland (eds.), *Research in Personnel and Human Resources Management*, Vol. 8, pp. 349–411. Greenwich, CT: JAI Press.

Tziner, A., Chantale, J. and Cusson, S. (1993). *La Sélection du Personnel*. Laval, Québec: Éditions Agence D'Arc.

US Congressional Office of Technology Assessment (1983). *Scientific Validity of Polygraph Testing: A Research Review*. Washington, DC: Government Printing Office.

US Congressional Office of Technology Assessment (1990). *The Use of Integrity Tests for Pre-employment Screening*. Washington, DC: Government Printing Office.

Waln, R.F. and Downey, R.G. (1987). Voice stress analysis: Use of telephone recordings. *Journal of Business and Psychology*, **1**, 379–389.

Section 3

Personnel Selection and Assessment

The chapters that comprise Section 3 of this Handbook focus sharply upon the changing nature and practice of selection and assessment in organizations. Building on Sections 1 and 2, which discuss in more general terms the changing context within which selection and assessment procedures operate, the contributions in Section 3 discuss the specific ways in which recruitment procedures are developing in response to these environmental drivers. But organizational change is, as many personnel psychologists will testify, far from smooth in its progress, and its multi-dimensional trajectory often raises unexpected problems and issues along the way. So, it appears, is undoubtedly the case in relation to organizational selection and assessment procedures. The seven contributions in Section 3 illustrate vividly the tensions inherent between theory and practice, between state-of-the-art assessment methodologies and the realities of organizational practice, and between the needs of individuals, work teams and organizations. The chapters span the whole gamut of issues from theoretical model-building, to forging conceptual and empirical links between HR systems, to the on-going use of long-standing and ubiquitous assessment procedures including job analysis and interviews, to models of personality assessment, to the emergent challenges of selecting for teamwork and future potential.

In Chapter 19 Ben Schneider, Amy Kristof-Brown, Harold Goldstein and D. Brent Smith consider the vexed question of person–organization (P–O) fit. As a mushrooming area of recent research, these authors do not purport to offer a comprehensive but a selective review of the literature. They overview the historical development of research into P–O fit and establish valuable links with earlier studies into person–environment fit. They then proceed to explore both the advantages and disadvantages of P–O fit for individuals and organizations and, as the authors conclude: 'There may be a dark side to good fit.' Excessive P–O fit, it is now well established, can stifle work role innovation and critically restrict the range of strategic responses available to an organization. Not surprisingly, the authors caution against going overboard in efforts to use selection procedures to maximize P–O fit; they do, nevertheless, describe in detail the principles of applying P–O fit to selection processes. Their chapter serves as an apposite reminder that although 'people make the place', too many highly similar individuals are unlikely to make for a good place of work.

Not unrelated to this theme is Chapter 20 by Neil Anderson and Cheri Ostroff. Here, the authors attempt to integrate two disparate fields of research and practice: selection and socialization. They argue that the two are essentially parts of the same process of organizational entry, yet have been falsely separated. Whilst selection has traditionally focused upon person–job fit, socialization has been more concerned with person–organization fit. The two, it is argued, are better conceptualized as elements in a single process that occurs over time. They propose the concept of 'socialization impact' to suggest that selection methods, by design or default, begin the pre-entry socialization of prospective employees. The authors argue for five domains of socialization impact—information provision, preferences, expectations, attitudes, and behaviour. They conclude by restating their case that selection techniques are not just 'predictors' of job performance, but also 'affectors' of subsequent behaviour.

Coert Visser, Wieby Altink and Jen Algera (Chapter 21) set their sights squarely upon the viability of conducting thorough job analysis in the rapidly changing context of work organizations. Exposing many of the difficulties inherent in traditional job analysis procedures, the authors pose real-life problems for the continued use of job analysis in a work environment in which many jobs are unstable and continuously evolving. In common with the editorial chapter to this Handbook which argues the need for 'bimodal prediction', i.e. predicting both the composition of the work role and person–work role fit, Visser, Altink and Algera state quite categorically that '. . . human resources management today requires a fundamentally new way of analysing work'. This begs the question: What would such procedures be? In response, the authors indeed examine in some detail the ways in which future-oriented job analysis can be done. Specifically, they consider the use of Critical Incidents Technique (CIT), the Position Analysis Questionnaire (PAQ), and the Work Profiling System (WPS). In conclusion, they posit a number of major challenges for job analysis to remain viable in the future. As traditionally the foundation stone upon which selection procedures are built, this contribution highlights the challenge of changing circumstances to selection practice in organizations. It seems that even job analysis, held for so long by selection researchers and practitioners to be sacred and quintessential, demands to be updated if it is to remain an effective component of recruitment and selection procedures in the future.

Staying with this theme of the implications of the changing nature of work for selection and assessment practice, in Chapter 22, Robert Dipboye re-opens the file on an old favourite—the selection interview. He provides a comprehensive and persuasive case for the wider use of structured interviews. Since it is now well established that structured interview formats are more valid and reliable than their unstructured counterparts, Dipboye tackles the intriguing dilemma of why they are not used more frequently by organizations. He first identifies five types of structured interview—Situation Interviews (SI), Highly Structured Interviews (HSI), Patterned Behaviour Description Interviews (PBDI), the LIMRA structured interviewing guide, and the multimodal interview. He then considers the myriad of ways in which interviewers 'go wrong' in their task, some related to the social skills of information gathering, others to the cognitive skills of information processing. The author then proceeds to describe a variety of strategies for improving the interview process, including standardization, rating forms, and interviewer training. Finally, and perhaps most crucially, he describes six reasons why structured interviews are not more widely practised—concerns about recruiting, the personal needs of the interviewer, considerations of P–O fit, procedural and distributive justice, personal power maintenance by interviewers, and the symbolic and ritualistic functions of interviews. This chapter therefore incorporates the concerns of both researchers and practising interviewers; the moral of this contribution surely being that psychometric considerations alone will not persuade recalcitrant organizations to upgrade and improve their selection practices.

In Chapter 23, Gerald Matthews likewise targets a popular method of candidate evaluation, but in this case it is personality assessment. He ably reviews an expansive range of developments in research into the Big Five model of the structure of personality. Matthews critically evaluates the basis and development of the Big Five model in the opening sections of his contribution. Next, he applies the model to the strictures of assessing personality in occupational contexts, concluding that issues of band width and fidelity are less of a primary concern than that of demonstrating incremental criterion validity across different selection scenarios. Matthews then moves on to consider response bias, ipsative and normative approaches to personality assessment, and concludes with a brief discussion of the implications for practice. Since personality is increasingly taking centre stage in candidate assessment, this review and discussion is timely and should prove useful in translating some of the 'hot issues' currently being addressed by personality researchers into the pragmatic concerns of selection practitioners.

Michael West and Natalie Allen (Chapter 24) contribute the penultimate chapter of Section 3. Their topic, selecting for teamwork, is becoming a primary aim in organizational selection procedures, where project teams and matrix structures are the in vogue methods of work organization. These authors indeed commence their chapter by acknowledging this increasing prevalence of teamwork in organizations. They go on to define what is meant by the 'team', and then to establish the knowledge, skills and abilities (KSAs) found by recent research to be predictive of effective team membership. In the second half of their chapter, West and Allen extend this review to the composition of effective work teams, of necessity an important concern in establishing appropriate criterion dimensions for team selection. To conclude, the authors proffer a number of especially important directions for future research and practice. In so doing they highlight the importance of conceptualizing selection processes in relation to other organization procedures and support mechanisms for teamwork.

As the concluding chapter to Section 3, in Chapter 25 Tony Keenan encapsulates many of the fundamental challenges to any selection system attempting to cope with changing conditions, but he also raises again the mountain of difficulties faced by practitioners under such circumstances. His area of concern, the selection of graduates, is notoriously problematic, at least in the United Kingdom, and the chapter at several points reaffirms the difficulties in selecting for this level of organizational entry. In response, the author proposes ways in which a heavily modified procedure could be established, using common assessment methods, to predict longer-term potential. Such proposals are not merely esoteric; they respond to the day-to-day concerns of graduate recruiters charged with the near-impossible task of predicting potential up to 15–20 years in the future. Keenan aptly concludes his chapter, and indeed this Section, by noting that the resources expended in selection should not ideally be decided by short-term cost concerns, but by the long-term payback of selecting graduate staff with real potential for senior management positions in an organization.

NEIL ANDERSON
August 1996.

Chapter 19

What Is This Thing Called Fit?

Benjamin Schneider

Department of Psychology, University of Maryland, College Park, MD, USA

Amy Kristof-Brown

College of Business Administration, University of Iowa, Iowa City, IA, USA

Harold W. Goldstein

Department of Psychology, New York University, New York, NY, USA

D. Brent Smith

Department of Psychology, University of Maryland, College Park, MD, USA

INTRODUCTION

The intellectual history of those who study the nature of human behavior in work organizations can generally be traced to one of two theoretical paradigms. These paradigms posit very different origins or determinants of behavior in organizations. Where one paradigm focuses on the attributes of individuals behaving in organizations, the other concentrates on the attributes of the organizations in which people behave. Those scholars who study the attributes of individuals in organizations (e.g. ability, personality) implicitly believe that these attributes are fundamental for understanding behavior at work and, indeed, for understanding organizational effectiveness. Scholars with this individual focus have been called 'personologists'.

At the other extreme are scholars who are engaged in the study of organizational attributes (e.g. reward systems, culture) as the primary determinants of behavior in organizations. In fact, the majority of the research and theory in the

---

International Handbook of Selection and Assessment, Edited by N. Anderson and P. Herriot.

organizational sciences flows from this emphasis on the situational bases of behavior and many subfields have emerged emphasizing the situational control of
behavior (e.g. Total Quality Management (TQM), job enrichment). Scholars in this
tradition have been referred to as 'situationists'.

Rarely have the two ends of this individual–organizational continuum
achieved rapprochement. One exception to the exclusive focus of personologists
and situationists is represented by the small group of researchers who study
person–organization (P–O) fit.[1] We say 'small group of researchers' because,
although almost everyone pays lip service to the Lewinian dictum that behavior
is the result of some combination of personal and environmental variables, only
a small group of scholars actually conduct research simultaneously employing
concepts and collecting data from both these sources. People who believe in fit
attribute the observed behavior of people to an index of the degree to which
there is similarity, overlap, convergence, correspondence, compatibility, or like-
ness between a set of attributes of people and a set of attributes of the setting
(Edwards, 1991). Research on P–O fit posits that when good fit exists, positive
outcomes are usually (but not always, as we will see) predicted for individuals
and organizations, while poor fit is usually (but not always) assumed to yield
less effectiveness for both.

A central goal of the present chapter is to explore the implications of the P–O
fit paradigm for its conceptual and practical implications regarding the whole
personnel selection endeavor. To accomplish this goal, we first provide a brief
historical introduction to the study of P–O fit. We then review some of its
contemporary theory and research, with particular emphasis being given to
contrasting outcomes of P–O fit for individuals and organizations. This focus on
outcomes at two levels of analysis illuminates a contradiction regarding the
consequences of good fit—a contradiction we address. Finally, we sketch the
implications of this review of P–O fit theory and research for the traditional
steps in the personnel selection process. No attempt is made to provide a complete review of the growing literature on P–O fit, as reviews of this nature are
available elsewhere (cf. Edwards, 1991; Judge and Ferris, 1992; Karren and
Graves, 1994; Kristof, 1996; O'Reilly, Chatman and Caldwell, 1991; Schneider,
Goldstein and Smith, 1995).

P–O FIT: AN HISTORICAL INTRODUCTION

P–O fit is a close relative of the more generic person–environment (P–E) fit. P–E fit
research in psychology has a long history tracing its empirical roots to Murray's
(1938) need-press theory. Need-press theory proposes that when people's needs
fit the environment (the 'press') in which they find themselves then positive
affective outcomes will follow. P–E fit theory, in turn, represents one form of
person–environment psychology (PEP; cf. Walsh, Craik and Price, 1992). PEP is
the most generic term for an approach that rests on the fundamental assumption,
influenced by Lewin's (1935) writings, that behavior must be understood as a joint
function of personal attributes and environmental attributes.

Two kinds of PEP theory and research exist, those of the P–E fit model and those of the P × E model. A few examples from each of these literatures will make these distinctions clear.

P–E fit research

Typical of PEP research of the P–E fit variety is that of Moos and his colleagues. Swindle and Moos (1992) conceptualize persons in terms of their profile of goals and their strategies to reach their goals, while the environment is conceptualized in terms of the degree to which it is stressful or benign so far as goal achievement is concerned. In their research, the person (i.e. goals) and the environment (i.e. stressful/benign) are operationalized along numerous commensurate dimensions and the fit of the person profile to the environmental profile is used as a correlate of individual outcomes. Fit, not the personal goals nor the environmental attributes, is the conceptually interesting predictor. Similarly, Pervin (1984) conceptualizes environments in terms of the profiles of opportunities they afford individuals for goal gratification (he uses the term 'affordance' to connote what a particular situation affords in terms of goal attainment). In both Swindle and Moos (1992) and Pervin (1984, 1992), data about both the P and the E are derived from persons; the environment is, therefore, the phenomenological environment.

Other researchers within the P–E fit framework argue for methodological separation of the person variables and the environmental variables and continue to view fit in terms of profiles of person and environmental variables.[2] In this regard, perhaps the most well-known and well-researched P–E fit theory is that proposed by Holland (1985) for understanding individuals' vocational adjustment and satisfaction. Holland's theory proposes that persons are satisfied with and adjust most easily to vocations when those vocations they join fit their own career-relevant personality type (a hexagonal model containing six vocational personality types yielding a six-dimensional profile). Hundreds, if not thousands of studies now support his conceptualization utilizing different measures of career-relevant personality (the Vocational Preference Inventory; the Self-Directed Search) and of career environments (proportions of persons with particular career interests in an environment; job analysis codings of the jobs in a work environment) (see Holland, 1985, for a complete description of these measures).

P × E research

The second stream of PEP research emerged from Lewin's (1935) dictum that behavior is some function of P and E, in interaction. Although Lewin did not specify the nature of the function [he claimed that behavior = $f(P,E)$], considerable research in what has come to be called interactional psychology is associated with the algebraic interaction of P and E (see Endler and Magnusson, 1976; Magnusson and Endler, 1977; Walsh, Craik and Price, 1992, for reviews). The P × E formulation is known more commonly as the moderator variable approach to person and environment theory and research. In this approach the situation is thought to moderate or alter the relationship between a person variable and some criterion, or some person variable is thought to moderate the effects of the situation on individual behavior.

Hackman and Oldham (1980) provide an example of the P × E or moderator variable approach. They proposed that jobs high in motivating potential will be most satisfying to people with high growth need strength; this would be a case where P is hypothesized to moderate the relationship between E and B.

For purposes of the present chapter, research of the moderator variable form (P × E) will not be addressed. We chose to ignore this literature for several reasons. First, in the truest sense of the word 'fit', the interactional model just does not *fit*. Frequently, if not always, either P or E is indexed by a single variable so fit is not an issue; the issue is the degree to which either P moderates the E–B relationship or E moderates the P–B relationship. Secondly, in the organizational sciences, and especially in personnel selection, there is scant research at all employing the algebraic interpretation of the Lewinian dictum (for an exception see articles on ability × situation interaction research by Schneider, 1978a, 1978b).[3]

In summary, P–O fit theory and research falls within a class of research generically called P–E fit research which is a variant of the still more generic world of research called person–environment psychology (PEP). Within PEP there have been two streams of research. One stream of research, P–E fit research, has focused on multiple dimensions of P and E simultaneously and the degree to which they fit. The second kind of research has been of the P × E variety in which single dimensions of P and E are studied simultaneously through algebraic interactions (also known as moderator variable research). The P–E fit model of PEP research and theory will be the focus of the present paper. Additionally, it is important to note that although we are discussing the concept of P–O fit, we recognize that there are other equally interesting types of fit including person–group fit, person–vocation fit, and person–job fit. Kristof (1996) distinguishes between fit at these various environmental levels and clarifies the differences between these multiple types of congruence. Although these other types of fit may also be relevant determinants of individual and organizational outcomes, in this chapter we will our focus to fit with organizational level variables.

In the review that follows we concentrate on recent P–O fit theory and research emphasizing our observation that the overwhelming majority of research on fit (both P–E and P–O) has used various indices of individual affect as outcome criteria: adjustment, satisfaction, commitment, and turnover. Little of the research on P–O fit has concerned productivity or other indicators of work performance and this is especially true for indicators of *organizational* effectiveness.

CONTEMPORARY P–O FIT THEORY AND RESEARCH

By what logic should selection processes attempt to fit a person with an organization to yield positive consequences? Or, why is fit desirable? There are two streams of scholarship that provide answers to these questions. The first stream emerged from person–environment psychology briefly described earlier. In PEP theory the rationale invariably held that the fit of a person to an environment would be good for the person. Implicitly, and in many cases explicitly (e.g. Pervin, 1992; Swindle and Moos, 1992), the environment is seen as affording individuals the chance to gratify their needs when the environment fits the needs they have. In this research tradition the criterion of interest has been individual affect, primarily individual adjustment and satisfaction or stress reduction.

The most complete recent examples of P–O fit research relevant for individual satisfaction and commitment were conducted by Chatman (1989, 1991) and her colleagues (O'Reilly, Chatman and Caldwell, 1991). They designed a measure of organizational culture in which culture was operationalized as 54 values that organizations might enact (e.g. innovative, fair). Incumbents use the Q-sort methodology to sort the 54 values into a values profile that represents the organization's culture. The same 54 values are given to persons hired for the organization who produce a new sorting of the values, this time in terms of self-description. The research that follows relates each person's value profile to the profile of the organization he or she joins using the index of P–O fit as a predictor of subsequent outcomes. In two studies (Chatman, 1991; O'Reilly, Chatman and Caldwell, 1991) the P–O fit index has been shown to predict satisfaction, commitment, turnover and, to some degree, individual performance—over periods as long as two years. Chatman and her colleagues also demonstrated that P and O alone are not predictive of these outcomes; it is the *fit* of P and O that is valid.

Other research of this kind, reminiscent of the work of Pervin (1984), has employed person, environment and criterion data collected from the same people. For example, Parkington and Schneider (1979) studied the fit of persons to their perceived environment as a correlate of job stress and job dissatisfaction. They asked bank branch employees to respond to 16 issues regarding the way they thought customers should be served and, for those same 16 issues, the way they believed their management thought customers should be served. They then calculated the fit of employee beliefs about service delivery to employee beliefs about management across the 16 issues and showed that the poorer the fit for individuals the more role ambiguity and conflict they experienced and the more dissatisfied they were.

Note that in this line of research, like research in PEP in general, the criteria relate to individual consequences, primarily affective ones. This is not surprising since much of the research tradition in psychology has been concerned with individual adjustment and satisfaction (Walsh, Price and Craik, 1992). Usually, but not always, high levels of fit are thought to yield positive consequences; the exception, of course, is when the situation is conceptualized in negative terms in the first place. For example, a good fit of people with a Type A personality (Rosenman and Friedman, 1959) to a high stress environment is associated with negative individual consequences such as stress and burnout (Matteson and Ivancevich, 1982).[4]

In recent years, a second stream of research on P–O fit theory has emerged that focuses on organizational effectiveness rather than individual effectiveness and affect. As such, theory and research of this stream has typically conceptualized the organization in terms of requirements and conceptualized fit as the degree to which individuals fit what the organization requires.

Bowen, Ledford and Nathan (1991) present the most clearly articulated conceptualization of this issue. They propose that organizations should recruit and select people who fit the organization. The organization in this case is conceptualized in terms of culture which, in turn, is linked to the strategic imperatives of the firm. Bowen, Ledford and Nathan thus move from a concern for individual adjustment and satisfaction to organizational effectiveness, arguing that employees should bring values, attitudes, and personalities that will help promote effectiveness for a specific organization.

Bowen, Ledford and Nathan do not argue that there are 'good' and 'bad' values and personalities in the abstract. Rather, there are 'good' and 'bad' personalities and values for particular organizations. For Bowen, Ledford and Nathan, fit can be achieved with all types of people, but each organization must identify, through organizational analysis, what it requires in terms of worker personality and values and then develop measures to select such persons. They suggest that the profile of values used by Chatman (1991) and O'Reilly, Chatman and Caldwell (1991), described earlier, is one such measure to use as a basis for making hiring decisions.

Bowen, Ledford and Nathan do not deny the importance of selecting individuals whose knowledge and abilities fit the requirements of a job. Their emphasis on selection for the organization is an emphasis *beyond* selection for a job. Their logic is that selection for the organization provides firms with increased flexibility in moving people from job to job because they will bring with them the right personality or values for the organization. Moreover, in a time when organizations are committed to flattened hierarchies, self-managed teams, and other processes that decrease immediate contacts with supervisors, selecting people for self-control and self-management skills becomes increasingly important. In such an environment, people who fit the culture will have the personal qualities that will provide them with appropriate direction in the absence of an immediate boss; the culture can exercise control over behavior best for people who have the 'right stuff' (meaning people who fit the culture in terms of values and/or personality). An additional benefit of focusing on fit in terms of psychological variables is that these variables do not discriminate on the basis of demographic characteristics. Therefore, rather than selecting people who fit demographically into an organization (i.e. all white males), the focus turns to selecting people of all demographic backgrounds who share similar values, personalities, or beliefs.

It is important to reiterate that Bowen, Ledford and Nathan (1991) do *not* suggest eliminating traditional methods used to select people for job-relevant knowledge and skills. They simply recommend incorporating P–O fit criteria to better predict long-term job performance, potentially in multiple jobs within the organization. They do not provide empirical evidence to support their proposal, but their logic rests on the presumption that a good fit of people to the organization's culture will be beneficial for organizational effectiveness.

Argyris (1957), Hambrick and his colleagues (Hambrick and Mason, 1984; Hambrick and Brandon, 1988), and Schneider (1987) would support Bowen, Ledford and Nathan's focus on organizational level outcomes, but would disagree with the presumption that organizational effectiveness would result from good P–O fit. Argyris (1957) has argued that too much of the 'right type' is dangerous for organizations. In an early study of organizational climate, Argyris discovered that the climate of a bank was dominated by a 'right type' and that this domination was a cause of stultification and lack of organizational innovation.

Hambrick and his colleagues have similarly proposed that good fit in top management teams (TMTs) will have negative consequences for organizational effectiveness. They conceptualize the issue somewhat differently from Argyris but with similar conclusions. They argue that TMTs must *collectively* have a profile of values and visions that fit the needed strategic direction of the firm. However, because no one member of the team can have all of the values and vision required for effective strategy implementation, no one member can be expected to fit all the strategy demands; the collective TMT must fit those demands. Moreover, excessive fit among members of the TMT will doom the organization to a narrow vision, poor implementation of the necessary strategy, and a general lack of firm competitiveness.

Schneider (1983, 1987) has proposed a similar framework for understanding the negative consequences of good fit. The logic of his attraction–selection–attrition (ASA) framework is that, over time, organizations naturally attract, select and keep people who are homogeneous with respect to type. This happens, he argues, because people are naturally attracted to similar others and, if they are dissimilar, they leave the organization (for empirical support see Bretz, Ash and Dreher, 1989). This combination of selective attraction to organizations, followed by formal and informal selection based on fit, and finalized by attrition of those who do not fit, yields a conformity in the outlook of organizational members that renders organizations incapable of adapting to environmental changes. Thus, Schneider proposes that homogeneity narrows the perspectives from which the larger environment can be viewed. This, in turn, yields incomplete information about the necessary changes the organization must make to effectively adapt to the environment (Schneider, Goldstein and Smith, 1995).

Note that in Argyris', Hambrick and his colleagues', and Schneider's efforts the criterion has changed from individual adjustment and satisfaction to organizational effectiveness. These writers believe that what is good for the individual in terms of satisfaction and adjustment might be bad for the organization in terms of adaptability and capacity for change. Good fit may produce satisfaction for individuals, as well as a host of other seemingly positive organizational outcomes such as harmony, cooperation, low interpersonal conflict and cohesiveness (cf. Guzzo and Shea, 1992). Those interested in organizational effectiveness, however, have begun to question whether these individually positive outcomes may, simultaneously, inhibit organizational effectiveness. Indeed, one wonders if Argyris, Hambrick and his colleagues, and Schneider might argue for abandoning satisfaction, harmony and cohesiveness in favor of tension, conflict, and dissatisfaction, because these seemingly uncomfortable consequences may in turn yield organizational effectiveness. Burke and Deszca (1982), for example, have shown that people with Type A personalities prefer work climates characterized by high performance standards, spontaneity, ambiguity and toughness—variables usually associated with stress—yet the research on Type A personality people consistently shows they are effective. Moreover, it is possible that situations with high performance standards, spontaneity, ambiguity and toughness are the ones in which they will be most effective. A curvilinear relationship most likely exists in this case—one in which either too much or too little of the organizational characteristics would be detrimental to performance.

Argyris, Hambrick, and Schneider might claim that, for P–O fit research to be relevant for organizational effectiveness, the implicit assumptions underlying P–O fit research must be revisited. These assumptions are that (a) a goal of fit is individual adjustment and satisfaction as well as the organizational harmony and cohesiveness that follow, and (b) that only positive outcomes are associated with P–O fit. They would argue that these assumptions may be true as far as they go but they are inadequate so far as long-term organizational effectiveness is concerned.

In summary, we have shown that the consequences following from P–O fit may not always be positive; individuals may feel comfortable while their organizations fail. As Schneider, Smith and Goldstein (1994) have recently put it: There may be a dark side to good fit. This dark side may be that good fit results in a narrowing of the perspective from which information in the environment is perceived (Hambrick and Mason, 1984), and a reduction in the ability to sense and adapt to change in the environment (Schneider, 1987). In a time of increasingly rapid environmental change perhaps selecting for good P–O fit is not such a good idea. Most likely, a balance needs to be struck between the issues that yield individual satisfaction and cohesiveness among organizational members and the breadth of perspective and flexibility required for organizational success. We begin such a discussion in the following section.

STRIKING THE BALANCE

It is one thing to say a balance should be struck and another to say *how* this should be accomplished. We have only recently begun struggling with this balancing act, so our proposals and thinking are in preliminary form. In developing these thoughts, especially with relevance to personnel selection, we have been guided by the following assumptions:

1. Individuals' satisfaction in organizations is a worthwhile goal because the satisfaction that people experience is related to the quality of their life. Furthermore, individuals' satisfaction is related indirectly to such organizational effectiveness outcomes as stress and turnover (Dawis, 1992; Ironson, 1992), both of which can be costly. Unfortunately, high levels of individual satisfaction may also get reflected in inflexibility and low adaptability, yielding organizational ineffectiveness.

2. Cohesiveness, unity of purpose, cooperation, and harmony are positively related to effectiveness in the short run. Miller's (1991) insightful research into organizational decline reveals quite clearly that organizations can become successful through facilitation of these outcomes. What yields the demise of successful organizations over the long run, Miller argues, is continued internal perseverance in refining what yielded success in the first place that, in turn,

yields an inability to look outward for the information that signals the need to change.

3. The people make the place (Schneider, 1987). The qualities of the people in an organization largely define organizational design. Structure, technology, and culture are a consequence of the people in an organization. As such, the qualities of the people hired are critical for the short- and long-term effectiveness of organizations.

In our deliberations about the issue of why good fit may or may not be desirable for individuals and organizations, we have sketched a series of additional questions to be answered: Good fit for whom, on what, and when? (Schneider, Smith and Goldstein, 1994).

Good fit for whom?

Bowen, Ledford and Nathan, and Hambrick and his colleagues, may both be correct. It may be useful for organizations to hire for the culture *and* to hire for diversity of perspective. For example, good P–O fit may be detrimental for persons in decision-making positions, yet beneficial for persons in non-decision-making roles. Thus, perhaps strategic long-term decision-making requires persons with breadth of perspective, making it important to fill TMT positions with diversity of values, competencies, and inclinations. Among members of the TMT this diversity will generate certain conflicts, certain ambiguities, and a degree of turmoil which, evidence shows (e.g. Bourgeois, 1985; Grinyer and Norburn, 1975), will serve the long-term interests of the organization. That is to say, diversity of perspectives in the TMT will result in an expansiveness in the variety of issues considered in implementing strategy as the organization proceeds into the future. Conversely, for positions in which strategic decision-making is not a fundamental job demand, hiring people for their agreement on the abstract goals and purpose of the organization should be useful.

Although we have answered the question of 'Good fit for whom?' by creating a distinction between TMT members who engage in decision-making and other employees, this distinction is rarely so straightforward. In an era of flattened hierarchies and increasing reliance on self-managing teams, more employees are becoming involved in organizational decision-making. For example, Manz and Sims (1993) in their book *Business Without Bosses*, list 17 specific responsibilities of self-managing teams. At least half of these activities—including analyzing quality problems, setting team goals, and preparing annual budgets—rely heavily on decision-making capabilities. Therefore, as with TMTs, the long-term best interests of the firm are most likely served by team members (who will be engaged in large amounts of decision-making) bringing a diversity of perspectives to the workplace.

Good fit on what?

Regardless of the strategic direction in which a firm might move, we believe it is important for everyone in the business to share a global vision of the organization.

For example, suppose an organization was in a service business and the quality of the service delivered served as a benchmark for activities throughout the firm. TMT members would need to have different perspectives on what service quality requires (with human resources managers thinking about selection, training, and compensation and operations managers thinking about facilities, efficiencies, and cost containment) but everyone throughout the organization would need to share the service quality vision and contribute to the maintenance and enhancement of the service quality culture (Schneider and Bowen, 1995). As noted in response to the 'for whom?' question, TMT members must have a diversity of perspectives with regard to tactics but share a common vision with others in the corporation; this is the spillover of the 'for whom?' into the 'on what?' question. Thus, in the service quality example, we actually addressed *two* issues when describing what organizational members must bring to the organization in terms of fit: low fit of TMT members (and other key decision-makers) to each other with regard to perspective, and simultaneously good fit for everyone across the firm with regard to the service quality value.

The issues on which there should be differences and simultaneously similarity will vary from organization to organization. There is no one best model because organizations function in such different kinds of environments (e.g. with regard to turbulence, industry, legal constraints, and so forth). Even two companies, each in the same industry, can be successful with different value perspectives in their TMT members and different shared members' values between the organizations. However, regardless of the shared values concerning long-term identity (one bank may decide to achieve quality through technology and another through establishing warm and friendly relationships with customers), the TMT must be peopled by individuals who differ in their perspective on how these strategies can best be implemented.

Some have argued that the identity of organizations with regard to cultural issues (like service quality) is set in motion early by the founders of organizations (Schein, 1992; Schneider, 1987). The message here is that deeply rooted cultures will be very difficult to change and that, to bring about change, new people will most likely be required—people who bring with them the new values and personality required for the new culture. Through personnel selection it is possible to contribute to the changing of a culture, but only if the focus in staffing moves from achieving a specific job match to attracting, selecting and keeping the kind of people who will *make* the new place (Bowen, Ledford and Nathan, 1991). Schneider's (1987) ASA framework suggests that this process will not be an easy one, as people who do not fit the culture of an organization are more likely to leave than to change it; it is an issue of balance. That is to say, the newcomers must be similar enough to incumbents so that they empathize with the present but different enough to provide the impetus for change. Such people, put in positions of power and authority and accompanied by other types of change interventions (such as restructuring, new reward systems, intensive retraining, and/or organization development projects), can become a sustaining mechanism for a new organizational culture (Schein, 1992).

Good fit when?

It is possible that good fit is beneficial early in a company's history but that fit after the initial burst of success can be dangerous to its long-term health. For example, we noted in discussing Miller's (1991) work that homogeneity early in an organization's history yielded the cohesiveness and cooperation required for success but that, later on, this very cohesiveness that was associated with homogeneity narrowed the vision and the ability to adapt to change required as the environment changed. As Denison (1990, pp. 79–80), in his book on the relationship between culture and bottom-line organizational performance, put it:

> . . . a strong, consistent culture is an asset to an organization in the short term, but over the long term, particularly when an organization's environment changes rapidly, that consistency can compromise an organization's ability to adapt effectively.

We thus propose that TMT diversity of perspective must be of special concern shortly after the initial burst of success in an organization when cohesiveness and cooperation have helped to achieve early goals, people are feeling good about themselves and each other, and the future looks brightest. It is at this point when diversity of perspective can offset complacency and when there will be a bright side to bad fit. The implication here is that, precisely when the organization may be maximally effective, it must begin the changes required for the next stage. The changes we envision concern the people hired to lead the organization into the future.

In summary, we have argued in this section that the apparent dilemma of simultaneously achieving the bright side of good fit while avoiding its dark side may be resolvable. The resolution involved asking and answering three questions about fit: for whom, on what, and when? The answers to these questions indicate that organizations can simultaneously benefit from the positive consequences of fit by differently addressing the fit issue for top management teams versus others, by differentiating strategic perspectives from deeper values and identity issues, and by considering where in its evolution a particular organization might be.

In the next section we build on these conclusions as we review the steps in the traditional personnel selection process.

CLOSING THE LOOP: PERSONNEL SELECTION AND P–O FIT

In closing the chapter our goal is to outline the typical steps in the personnel selection process and to include some thoughts from a P–O fit perspective on those steps.

Step 1: Recruitment–attraction

It is often forgotten that selection decisions are made from an applicant pool and that, therefore, the quality of the applicant pool sets limits on the quality of those hired. Actually there exists a selection–recruitment–attraction cycle, a kind of infinite feedback loop, the quality of which ultimately contributes to organizational effectiveness. We begin by examining the recruitment–attraction process. The inclusion of the word attraction connotes the idea that the organization's recruitment role is not the only factor determining the applicant pool.

There exists some research on recruitment and P–O fit from both the Realistic Job Preview (RJP; Wanous, 1992) and recruiter interviewing vantage points. Results from RJP research suggest that when applicants are recruited in ways that provide them with a realistic portrait of the job and the company, then the satisfaction and retention of those hired are improved. The evidence suggests that RJPs bring about a fit of applicant expectations to the realities they will encounter if hired. Following on earlier points we have made, RJPs in the future would do well to focus not only on the attributes of the job and the organization (the processes and procedures under which people will work), but the strategy of the organization as well. By strategy we mean whether the organization strives to be a price leader, a service quality leader, a socially responsible corporation, and so forth. Concrete information about the values of the firm should be included in the RJP. RJPs for the TMT might include such job characteristics as the degree of ambiguity in the job, the need to be tough-minded, the degree to which the founder was an achievement-striving person, conflict and turmoil to be experienced as a member of the TMT, and so forth.

The recruitment literature is sparse with regard to P–O fit, but what literature does exist has been summarized by Kristof (1996). She concludes that recruiters consider the organization-specific fit of applicants to firms as they make hiring decisions. In the light of earlier literature we have summarized, this finding suggests the potential for problems in organizations. *If* recruiters were looking only for fit in managers, then they could end up hiring people who promote homogeneity in values, personality, attitudes, beliefs and decision-making styles. This can, as we have noted, be dangerous for organizations in the long run unless managers are *also* seen as attractive because they bring with them divergent perspectives.

There is also a growing literature on what might be called 'natural recruitment', i.e. attraction of persons to organizations in the absence of any formal attempt by organizations to recruit them. The relevance of this growing body of research to P–O fit is summarized in Kristof (1996) and Schneider, Goldstein and Smith (1995). In both cases there is consistent evidence for the conclusion that people are more attracted to organizations with corporate personalities that fit their own personality and to organizations that are perceived to act in ways that fit their personal values. While many of the studies that yield this conclusion were laboratory experiments, enough have been field studies to support the internal and external validity of the conclusions.

These results also should give organizations pause for thought, for they suggest that there is, as Schneider (1987) has hypothesized, a natural inclination to homogeneity in organizations. Organizations must therefore, especially when hiring managers, be very cautious about permitting the fit to get too high in the management talent pool on which the future of the organization will depend, lest the diversity of perspectives required for effectiveness be lacking.

In summary, the literature relevant to P–O fit and recruitment–attraction is consistent and potentially alarming from a long-term organizational effectiveness standpoint—everything points to good fit. We therefore caution practitioners to closely monitor the nature of corporate recruits to ensure that diversity of perspective is present for whom, on what, and when required.

Step 2: Job analysis

The first step in any selection procedure is the job analysis, a process typically initiated to identify the knowledge, skills, abilities and other characteristics (usually abbreviated KSAO) required by a job. Many job analyses do not focus much on the 'O' (other) characteristics because these typically include personality and values which, for 30 years (1960–1990), received scant attention by scholars of personnel selection (cf. Hogan, 1991). Given our focus on P–O fit in this chapter, however, it seems reasonable for the 'O' to be introduced as an important selection variable. Furthermore, with recent changes in judgments about the validity of personality inventories (e.g. Barrick and Mount, 1991; Tett, Jackson and Rothstein, 1991), personality measures have recovered somewhat from a 30-year history of underutilization.

The present chapter emphasizes the need, through an organizational culture analysis, to identify *organizationally relevant* personality and values issues. We emphasize the term organizationally relevant because it is our opinion that generic personality and values constructs, like generic ability constructs, will prove less useful for organizations than more tailored, organization-specific measures of personality and values.

A problem with traditional job analyses is that when a job is studied, the analysis yields the *common* KSAOs required by occupants of that job. We argued earlier, however, that for top management teams it may be dangerous to have all members of the team possessing a common set of attributes. Given our logic, job analysts and selection development researchers will have to determine which jobs require a *common* set of KSAOs and which jobs require a *divergent* set of KSAOs. To our knowledge, such thinking has not been previously presented with regard to job analysis and P–O fit issues.

Thus, our P–O fit model indicates that *across* the jobs in an organization there may be a common set of 'O' characteristics that will promote organizational effectiveness. For example, in a service organization the common values might concern the way people are treated, *all* people, including employee peers, subordinates and superiors as well as customers. Or, in any kind of organization, the presence of 'good soldiers' (Organ, 1988) who are willing to promote organizational well-being through spontaneous (non-specified) acts, might be beneficial. Hiring people with these kinds of attributes could enhance the probability of organizational effectiveness.

To compound the problem further, we have suggested that, over time, organizations may require different configurations of fit for them to be effective; the issue of time must also be taken into account when thinking about job analysis and validation of selection procedures—where in the life cycle is the organization currently? Where is it likely to be in the future? What kinds of KSAOs will be required in that future? Little research on what might be called strategic or future-oriented job analysis exists (see Schneider and Konz, 1989, for an exception; and Sparrow, Chapter 17 in this volume) but our framework suggests such work is important.

We have, obviously, presented a seeming dilemma in our discussion of job analysis within a P–O fit framework. On the one hand, we have identified the need for divergence in KSAOs for TMT and other decision-making positions and, on the other hand, we suggested that some common 'Os' may be necessary across all jobs. Also, we believe that job analyses that focus on the KSAOs for a specific job continue to be important.

In response to this seeming dilemma, it is important to realize that our proposal to conduct organizational culture analyses and derive relevant 'O' attributes is meant to supplement, not supplant, more job-focused analyses. Also, our proposal to seek both divergence and convergence on 'O' attributes should be interpreted as suggesting a need for convergence on *some* attributes but divergence on *other* attributes. Our bottom line regarding job analysis is that, as the basis for the design of selection and training programs, these analyses should determine the *who*, on *what*, and *when*, of fit.

Step 3: Predictor design

The next step in personnel selection involves the design of measurement systems that provide individuals with opportunities to demonstrate the presence of the KSAOs identified in Step 2. Because numerous studies now indicate the validity for general intellectual competencies across all jobs (cf. Gottfredson, 1994) there can develop an inclination to see paper-and-pencil measures of intelligence as a sufficient basis for making all hiring decisions. We demur, however. First, these conclusions apply to measures of cognitive competencies and not to the measures of personality/values that fit the P–O fit model. Secondly, these conclusions are based on evidence collected on the criterion-related validity of predictors against individual performance criteria and not organizational effectiveness.

To conclude from validity generalization studies that measures of general intellectual competence are all that is required to achieve organizational effectiveness is to miss the idea that organizations—their behavior and their effectiveness—are surely a function of more than this. While situations may not moderate the relationship between ability and performance (Schneider, 1978a, 1978b), the evidence is clear that situations and ability combine linearly to enhance the prediction of performance (there is a linear rather than a moderator effect of the situation). This suggests that a consideration of situations, and the fit of persons to those situations, can contribute to prediction, especially when the level of analysis concerns organizational effectiveness.

The assessment of these 'O' attributes is not restricted to paper-and-pencil measures. Just as cognitive competencies may be assessed through situational simulations, so may facets of behavior be reflective of perspectives and values.

For example, decision-making situations can be designed to diagnose predilections of persons for dealing with ambiguity (Moses and Lyness, 1990), orientations to service quality (Schneider and Schechter, 1991), strategies for organizing people into teams (Bass, 1990), and so forth, thus offering opportunities to observe these perspectives and values in action. There is scant literature on the assessment center or other behavior simulation research explicitly tying such simulations to personality, perspectives or values, but we encourage the development and application of such devices because of the consistently modest relationships obtained with standardized personality tests in predicting performance (Barrick and Mount, 1991; Tett, Jackson and Rothstein, 1991). In addition, and especially in selection for management positions, we encourage the development of multidimensional profiles of behavior that the organization will require in its future leaders.

Miner (1993), for example, has shown that different motivations to manage are found in organizations as a function of whether they are start-up, entrepreneurial in nature versus more traditional hierarchical bureaucracies. Unfortunately, the research on leadership, with few exceptions (e.g. Fiedler, 1967), is sparse with regard to P–O fit studies and leadership effectiveness; 'fit' is not even indexed in Bass's (1990) massive review of the literature. Perhaps this general lack of theory and research reflects leadership scholars' inclination to either focus on the personality traits of leaders or the behavior of leaders and to not focus much attention on the integration of person and situational factors in the prediction of that behavior. Some (e.g. Yukl and Van Fleet, 1992) have argued that the failure of trait measurement to yield consistent results across leadership studies is attributable to situational factors; this is a moderator variable (or P × S) explanation, not a fit explanation. Following on the logic of Hambrick and Mason (1984) and Schneider (1987) we suggest increased efforts to explore the issue of fit in understanding managerial behavior and the relationship of that behavior to organizational effectiveness.

Step 4: Criterion development and validation designs

Personnel selection procedures have been dominated by the individual differences model with the implicit hypothesis, as noted earlier, that increasing the number of persons who have specific job-related competencies and other attributes eventually produces organizational effectiveness. On the basis of the concerns raised in the present chapter, organizational effectiveness must also serve as a criterion of effectiveness in personnel selection studies. This will require an additional (not a substitute but an addition) validation design, one that requires another level of analysis and alternative validation models and criteria be used to explore test validity.

The new kind of model required is more akin to evaluation models in training and education (Goldstein, 1992), wherein experimental or quasi-experimental designs are added to the basic individual differences designs. Consider the service quality example used in earlier discussions. Suppose one wanted to design a selection validation study to test the validity of a new interview procedure for hiring persons for the *organization* who fit the strong service quality orientation of the firm. From an organizational effectiveness criterion standpoint, one might collect customer satisfaction data from the customers of the target organization *and the target organization's competitors* over, say, six months prior to implementing the new selection procedure in the target organization. Perhaps one year after the new system is implemented customer satisfaction would be tracked again for six months in both target and competitor organizations and these criterion data would be compared for improvement in the target organization. Having the competitor data for the prior six months, of course, permits judgments to be made regarding the possible effects of the new selection system controlling for effects attributable to environmental or other changes.

This kind of design is unconcerned with validity at the individual level of analysis. The organization is the focus because, in most organizations (especially service organizations), customers deal with the *whole* organization, not specific individuals, and it is this whole organization that should be the focus of the personnel selection effort.

Unbeknown to the reader, we have introduced a new kind of criterion for personnel selection studies as well as a new validation model: the criterion is at the organizational level of analysis (customer satisfaction). In this new validation model, organizational outcomes of all kinds become relevant for the validation of personnel selection strategies—including, but not limited to, such outcomes as market penetration, retention of customers, return on sales, and so forth.

This line of thinking does not imply, however, that studies of individual effectiveness and/or studies of individual satisfaction and adjustment are inappropriate; it does imply that studying *only* individual-level outcomes is inappropriate because organizational effectiveness must become a focus of personnel selection procedures.

In summary, we have noted in this last section of the chapter some consequences of P–O fit thinking for the steps in the personnel selection process. The P–O fit perspective, including ideas presented earlier about the potential unintended negative consequences of good fit for organizational effectiveness, has proven a useful heuristic for identifying some cautions in the traditional personnel selection process. These cautions generally revolve around the concern for a process that has been founded on the assumption that good fit is good; we note that recruitment, job analysis, and examination design can all perpetuate 'right types' to the degree that the organization will be comfortable, content, cohesive—and ineffective. In addition, the benefits of considering organizational-level criteria of effectiveness and validation designs appropriate for organizational-level criteria were noted.

SUMMARY AND CONCLUSIONS

This chapter reveals that the paradigm from which scholarship emerges has long-term consequences for the development of theory and research with regard to a topic. The topic of focus here has been P–O fit, and we have shown how the evolution of P–O fit theory and research from the individual differences, psychological paradigm, and its criteria, may have yielded an incorrect implicit hypothesis that all good things follow from good P–O fit. Thus, the psychological tradition in P–O fit research has emphasized individual, affective outcomes such as adjustment and satisfaction of individuals and ignored organizational effectiveness.

Drawing on work by Hambrick and Mason (1984) and Schneider (1987), some potential negative organizational consequences for high levels of P–O fit were identified and research supporting the validity of such hypothesized negative consequences was presented. Indeed, the tendency for individuals and their employing organizations to move toward homogeneity (good P–O fit) was also documented.

The challenge for the chapter was to integrate the negative consequences for organizational effectiveness with the positive consequences for individuals into a common framework. This was accomplished through the answers to three questions: Good fit for whom? Good fit on what? Good fit when? Possible answers follow: Good fit for employees on the front line (those not involved in decision-oriented teams) but not in top management teams; good fit on dimensions or issues that stand as guiding principles or values of the total organization but not on predilections to view the world in particular ways and/or inclinations to approach strategy and strategy implementation with particular emphases; and, good fit early in the life of the firm to achieve early success but not later in the life of the firm when alternative perspectives are more likely to be required.

Finally, as befits a handbook focused on personnel selection, the chapter concluded with a commentary that applied P–O fit thinking as outlined by us to the traditional steps in the personnel selection process. It became clear that the traditional steps in personnel selection can yield good fit even when that fit may be inappropriate for organizational survival. It also became apparent that existing individual differences validation models may be too narrowly focused on individual outcomes while ignoring organizational effectiveness.

The challenge for organizational scientists is to find ways to balance the bright and dark sides to good fit. This will require models of organizational effectiveness that simultaneously balance issues of individual affect and organizational effectiveness in the light of where in its life history an organization is. It will also require models of personnel selection that focus on organizational as well as job requirements and which conceptualize organizational effectiveness in validation designs. To these ends, the P–O fit framework outlined here provides a convenient vehicle for both conceptualization and practice.

ACKNOWLEDGEMENTS

We wish to thank Dov Eden and Seymour Adler, as well as the editors, for their helpful comments on an earlier version of this chapter.

ENDNOTES

1. Constructivist psychology (e.g. Berger and Luckmann, 1967) also offers a perspective that considers both individual and organizational determinants of criteria. In this field of thought, individuals and organizations mutually 'co-construct' a shared social reality that is organizational life.

2. Whether or not P and E should be gathered from the same source is an interesting conceptual as well as interesting methodological question. In the Murray (1938) and especially in the Lewin (1935) traditions it is the phenomenological environment, the environment as perceived by the individual, that is important. Later scholars, however, have become concerned with the 'out there' environment because, unless there is some agreement on what the environment is, there can be no changes made in it. For example, in the well-known Work Adjustment Project (see Dawis, 1992, for a review), early decisions were made to assess the occupational reinforcer patterns of jobs from persons different from those whose adjustment was being predicted. From the latter group were obtained ratings of the importance of each of the 20 elements of the environment and the measures of satisfaction (the operationalization of adjustment). Our own predilection is to support both kinds of environment operationalizations as a function of the interests of researchers but to not mix the results obtained from these different kinds of studies.

3. The conclusion that there is scant research on the P × E interactional model in personnel selection is particularly true since the advent of the application of meta-analysis (validity generalization) to personnel selection validity studies (cf. Schmidt and Hunter, 1981). Conclusions from validity generalization research appear to indicate that situations do not moderate relationships between predictors and criteria. For many years prior to the conclusions reached by validity generalization studies on this issue, variability in validity coefficients for predictors across situations were attributed to situational differences, an hypothesis of a P × E interaction. Finding such interactions, however, proved elusive. Validity generalization research suggests that variability in validity is attributable not to situational differences but to (primarily) variability in the sample sizes across studies, studies which just happened to be conducted in different situations.

4. Research has also shown, however, that Type A individuals prefer organizational environments characterized by Type A characteristics (e.g. ambition, competitiveness, impatience, high need for achievement, and hostility), and Type B individuals prefer organizational environments not demonstrating these characteristics (Burke and Deszca, 1982).

REFERENCES

Argyris, C. (1957). Some problems in conceptualizing organizational climate: A case study of a bank. *Administrative Science Quarterly*, **2**, 501–520.

Barrick, M.R. and Mount, M.K. (1991). The big five personality dimensions and job performance: A meta-analysis. *Personnel Psychology*, **44**, 1–26.

Bass, B. (1990). *Bass & Stogdill's Handbook of Leadership: Theory, Research, and Managerial Applications*, 3rd edn. New York: Free Press.

Berger, P.L. and Luckmann, T. (1967). *The Social Construction of Reality: A Treatise in the Society of Knowledge*. Garden City, NY: Doubleday.

Bourgeois, L.J., III (1985). Strategic goals, perceived uncertainty and economic performance in volatile environments. *Academy of Management Journal*, **28** (3), 548–573.

Bowen, D.E., Ledford, G.E., Jr and Nathan, B.R. (1991). Hiring for the organization not the job. *Academy of Management Executive*, **5** (4), 35–51.

Bretz, R.D., Jr, Ash, R.A. and Dreher, G.F. (1989). Do people make the place? An examination of the attraction–selection–attrition hypothesis. *Personnel Psychology*, **42**, 561–581.

Burke, R.J. and Deszca, E. (1982). Preferred organizational climates of Type A individuals. *Journal of Vocational Behavior*, **21**, 50–59.

Chatman, J. (1989). Improving interactional organizational research: A model of person–organization fit. *Academy of Management Review*, **14**, 333–349.

Chatman, J. (1991). Matching people and organizations: Selection and socialization in public accounting firms. *Administrative Science Quarterly*, **36**, 459–484.

Dawis, R. (1992). Person–environment fit and job-satisfaction. In C.J. Cranny, P.C. Smith and E.F. Stone (eds.), *Job Satisfaction*, pp. 69–88. New York: Lexington.

Denison, D.R. (1990). *Corporate Culture and Organization Effectiveness*. New York: John Wiley.

Edwards, J.R. (1991). Person–job fit: A conceptual integration, literature review, and methodological critique. *International Review of Industrial/Organizational Psychology*, **6**, 283–357.

Endler, N.S. and Magnusson, D. (eds) (1976). *Interactional Psychology and Personality*. New York: Hemisphere.

Fiedler, F.E. (1967). *A Theory of Leadership Effectiveness*. New York: McGraw-Hill.

Goldstein, I.L. (1992). *Training in Organizations: Needs Assessment, Development and Evaluation*, 3rd edn. Monterey, CA: Brooks/Cole.

Gottfredson, L.S. (1994). The science and politics of group norming. *American Psychologist*, **49**, 955–963.

Grinyer, P. and Norburn, D. (1975). Planning for existing markets: An empirical study. *International Studies in Management and Organization*, **7**, 99–122.

Guzzo, R.A. and Shea, G.P. (1992). Group performance and intergroup relations in organizations. In M.D. Dunnette and L.M. Hough (eds.), *Handbook of Industrial and Organizational Psychology*, 2nd edn, vol. 3, pp. 1–45. Palo Alto, CA: Consulting Psychologists Press.

Hackman, J.R. and Oldham, G.R. (1980). *Word Redesign*. Reading, MA: Addison-Wesley.

Hambrick, D. and Mason, P. (1984). Upper echelons: The organization as a reflection of its top managers. *Academy of Management Review*, **2**, 193–206.

Hambrick, D.C. and Brandon, G.L. (1988). Executive values. In D.C. Hambrick (ed.), *The Executive Effect: Concepts and Methods for Studying Top Managers*, pp. 3–33. Greenwich, CT: JAI Press.

Hogan, R. (1991). Personality and personality measurement. In M.D. Dunnette and L.M. Hough (eds.), *Handbook of Industrial and Organizational Psychology*. Palo Alto, CA: Consulting Psychologists Press.

Holland, J.L. (1985). *Making Vocational Choices: A Theory of Careers*, 2nd edn. Englewood Cliffs, NJ: Prentice-Hall.

Ironson, G.H. (1992). Job stress and health. In C.J. Cranny, P.C. Smith and E.F. Stone (eds.), *Job Satisfaction*, pp. 219–240. New York: Lexington Books.

Judge, T.A. and Ferris, G.R. (1992). The elusive criterion of fit in human resource staffing decisions. *Human Resource Planning*, **15** (4), 47–67.

Karren, R.J. and Graves, L.M. (1994). Assessing person–organization fit in personnel selection: Guidelines for future research. *International Journal of Selection and Assessment*, **2** (3), 146–156.

Kristof, A.L. (1996). Person–organization fit: An integrative review of its conceptualizations, measurement, and implications. *Personnel Psychology*, **49**, 1–49.

Lewin, K. (1935). *A Dynamic Theory of Personality: Selected Papers*. New York: McGraw-Hill.

Magnusson, D. and Endler, N.S. (eds.) (1977). *Personality at the Crossroads: Current Issues in Interactional Psychology*. Hillsdale, NJ: Erlbaum.

Manz, C.C. and Sims, H.P., Jr (1993). *Business Without Bosses: How Self-Managing Teams are Building High-Performing Companies*. New York: John Wiley.

Matteson, M.T. and Ivancevich, J.M. (1982). Type A and B behavior patterns and health symptoms: Examining individual and organizational fit. *Journal of Occupational Medicine*, **24**, 585–589.

Miller, D. (1991). *The Icarus Paradox: How Exceptional Companies Bring About Their Own Downfall*. New York: Harper.

Miner, J.B. (1993). *Role Motivation Theories*. New York: Routledge.

Moses, I.L. and Lyness, K.S. (1990). Leadership behavior in ambiguous environments. In K.E. Clark and M.B. Clark (eds.), *Measures of Leadership*, pp. 327–335. Greensboro, NC: Center for Creative Leadership.

Murray, H. (1938). *Explorations in Personality*. New York: Oxford University Press.

O'Reilly, C.A., III, Chatman, J. and Caldwell, D.F. (1991). People and organizational culture: A profile comparison approach to assessing person–organization fit. *Academy of Management Journal*, **34**, 487–516.

Organ, D.W. (1988). *Organizational Citizenship Behavior: The Good Soldier Syndrome.* Lexington, MA: Lexington Books.

Parkington, J.P. and Schneider, B. (1979). Some correlates of experienced job stress: A boundary role study. *Academy of Management Journal,* **22,** 270–281.

Pervin, L.A. (1984). The stasis and flow of behavior: Toward a theory of goals. In M.M. Page (ed.), *Personality: Current Theory and Research,* pp. 1–53. Lincoln, NE: University of Nebraska Press.

Pervin, L.A. (1992). Transversing the individual–environment landscape: A personal odyssey. In W.B. Walsh, K.H. Craik and R.H. Price (eds.), *Person–Environment Psychology: Models and Perspectives,* pp. 71–87. Hillsdale, NJ: Erlbaum.

Rosenman, R.H. and Friedman, M. (1959). The possible relationship of Type A behavior pattern to coronary heart disease. In *Hormones and Atherosclerosis.* New York: Academic Press.

Schein, E.H. (1992). *Organizational Culture and Leadership,* 2nd edn. San Francisco, CA: Jossey-Bass.

Schmidt, F.L. and Hunter, J.E. (1981). Employment testing: Old theories and new research findings. *American Psychologist,* **36,** 1128–1137.

Schneider, B. (1978a). Person–situation selection: A review of some ability–situation interaction research. *Personnel Psychology,* **31,** 281–298.

Schneider, B. (1978b). Implications of the conference: A personal view. *Personnel Psychology,* **31,** 299–304.

Schneider, B. (1983). Interactional psychology and organizational behavior. In L.L. Cummings and B.M. Staw (eds.), *Research in Organizational Behavior,* vol. 5, pp. 1–31. Greenwich, CT: JAI Press.

Schneider, B. (1987). The people make the place. *Personnel Psychology,* **40,** 437–453.

Schneider, B. and Bowen, D.E. (1995). *Winning the Service Game.* Boston, MA: Harvard Business School Press.

Schneider, B., Goldstein, H.W. and Smith, D.B. (1995). The ASA framework: An update. *Personnel Psychology,* **48,** 747–773.

Schneider, B. and Konz, A.M. (1989). Strategic job analysis. *Human Resource Management,* **28,** 51–63.

Schneider, B., Smith, D.B. and Goldstein, H.W. (1994). The 'dark side' of 'good fit'. Paper presented at the Annual Meeting of the Academy of Management, Dallas, TX.

Schneider, B. and Schechter, D.S. (1991). Development of a personnel selection system for service jobs. In S. Brown, E. Gummesson, B. Edvardsson and B. Gustavsson (eds.), *Service Quality,* pp. 217–236. Lexington, MA: Lexington Books.

Swindle, R.W. and Moos, R.H. (1992). Life domains in stressors, coping, and adjustment. In W.B. Walsh, K.H. Craik and R.H. Price (eds.), *Person–Environment Psychology: Models and Perspectives,* pp. 71–87. Hillsdale, NJ: Erlbaum.

Tett, R.P., Jackson, D.N. and Rothstein, M. (1991). Personality measures as predictors of job performance: A meta-analytic review. *Personnel Psychology,* **44,** 703–742.

Walsh, W.B., Craik, K.H. and Price, R.H. (eds.) (1992). *Person–Environment Psychology: Models and Perspectives.* Hillsdale, NJ: Erlbaum.

Walsh, W.B., Price, R.H. and Craik, K.H. (1992). Person–environment psychology: An introduction. In W.B. Walsh, K.H. Craik and R.H. Price (eds.), *Person–Environment Psychology: Models and Perspectives,* pp. vii–xi. Hillsdale, NJ: Erlbaum.

Wanous, J.P. (1992). *Organizational Entry: Recruitment, Selection, and Socialization of Newcomers,* 2nd edn. Reading, MA: Addison-Wesley.

Yukl, G. and Van Fleet, D.D. (1992). Theory and research on leadership in organizations. In M.D. Dunnette and L.M. Hough (eds.), *Handbook of Industrial and Organizational Psychology,* 2nd edn. vol. 3, pp. 147–198. Palo Alto, CA: Consulting Psychologists Press.

Chapter 20

Selection as Socialization

Neil Anderson

Department of Psychology, Goldsmiths College, University of London, New Cross, London SE14 6NW, UK

Cheri Ostroff

School of Management, Arizona State University West, Phoenix, AZ, USA

INTRODUCTION

In this chapter we argue for the utility of an integrative perspective to research into selection and socialization. Each of these topics has developed largely independently of the other, displaying little overlap or synergy in drawing from advances in the other field. We contend that selection and socialization are facets of essentially the same overarching process—the screening and integration of newcomers into an organization and their learning of specific knowledge relevant for work role performance.

Both selection and socialization have the same underlying goal, namely that of identifying and integrating effective organizational staff members. This requires that employees have the skills and abilities required for job performance (person–job fit) *and* that they adopt the normative attitudes, values, goals and culture of the organization (person–organization fit). Selection procedures have traditionally emphasized *predicting* person–job fit with a more recent focus on predicting person–organization fit; socialization procedures have traditionally emphasized *facilitating* person–organization fit, with some attention devoted to facilitating person–job fit. We argue that selection and socialization are more accurately conceived of as stages in a single, longitudinal process of newcomer integration whereby both person–job fit and person–organization fit are achieved. Socialization begins during selection as the applicant experiences the organization's formal procedures for the first time and attempts to make sense of the organization;

International Handbook of Selection and Assessment, Edited by N. Anderson and P. Herriot.
© 1997 John Wiley & Sons Ltd.

selection is continued during socialization as those appointed learn more about the organization and may then decide themselves to withdraw or may fail to meet training and probation criteria imposed by the organization. In this chapter, as opposed to viewing selection solely as a means of *predicting* work role performance and person–job fit, we explore the ways in which selection techniques act as *facilitators* in the pre-entry socialization process to promote person–organization fit and as *affectors* of the candidate's future attitudes and behaviour on the job.

FIT AND EMPLOYEE INTEGRATION IN SOCIALIZATION AND SELECTION

A well-regarded assumption in organizational psychology is that both individuals and organizations will be more effective when the attributes of the person and organization fit or are congruent (Schneider, 1987). A good fit or match between people and the work environment is believed to result in better work-related attitudes and behaviours than when people do not fit the work context. Two dimensions of fit between people and the work environment can be distinguished: person–job fit and person–organization fit. In person–job fit, the assumption is that employees whose skills and abilities match the skills and abilities required by the job will be better at performing job tasks and duties (Brousseau, 1984). In person–organization fit, the assumption is that individuals whose personalities, values, goals and attributes fit the climate, values, goals and attributes of the organization will be more effective employees, exhibiting higher levels of satisfaction, commitment, performance, and lower levels of turnover, stress, and absenteeism (cf. Chatman, 1991; Pervin, 1989; Schneider, 1983, 1987). Enhancing both person–job fit and person–organization fit simultaneously should result in employees who are fully integrated into the work environment and should produce more positive work-related outcomes than considering either one independently.

The notion of fit has been an underlying premise in both socialization and selection. Socialization has been implicitly aimed at facilitating both person–job fit and person–organization fit. Traditional views of socialization have focused on enhancing new employees' adoption of the values, goals and culture of the organization; in other words, traditional socialization practices have been geared to facilitate person–organization fit. In more recent years, socialization researchers have begun to recognize the importance of the learning process of newcomers, including their learning of the work tasks, duties and role (person–job fit) as well as learning work group norms and values, and organizational attributes (person–organization fit; e.g. Anderson and Ostroff, 1995). In essence, socialization concerns the integration of new employees into an organization through their acquisition of knowledge needed to perform the job function, and their assimilation into the organization's culture and climate to the extent that they fit in with its established work practices and norms.

Selection researchers have also long recognized the importance of fit, but have tended to do so in a more limited vein. Selection techniques have almost exclusively focused on achieving person–job fit by attempting to predict which applicants have the requisite skills and abilities that match those required for effective performance on specific job tasks and duties (Ostroff and Rothausen, 1996). Hence, integration of employees is achieved on the basis of knowledge and skills required for job performance, and largely ignores fit between personal attributes and organizational attributes. In more recent years there has been growing recognition that a focus on predicting person–organization fit during selection can enhance work-related outcomes (e.g. Bowen, Ledford and Nathan, 1991; Schneider, 1987; Chatman, 1991). Furthermore, there is growing recognition that various types of selection practices can provide employees with information about the organization's goals and values (e.g. Gilliland, 1994, 1995; Thornton, 1993), thereby facilitating person–organization fit and beginning the socialization and integration process prior to organizational entry. Although there is on-going debate over the degree of person–organization fit which is desirable (e.g. Ostroff and Rothausen, 1996; Schneider *et al.*, Chapter 19 in this volume) it is clear that a sufficient degree of fit is likely to be beneficial to both the organization and the individual, although it can simultaneously be argued that excessive fit across too many employees may lead to homogeneity, a lack of variety of behavioural responses, and thus to the inhibition of certain outputs such as constructive controversy, creativity, and innovation at work.

Socialization has focused on facilitating integration of employees through fit to jobs and fit to the organization. Selection has focused on the integration of employees by predicting fit to jobs. The two have been falsely separated. In this chapter we argue that employee integration, incorporating both person–job fit and person–organization fit, is a longitudinal process which begins prior to entry during recruitment and selection and continues after organizational entry with socialization.

SELECTION AND SOCIALIZATION PARADIGMS

Table 20.1 presents a summary of both paradigms—selection versus socialization—and illustrates our impression of the status of each as a body of research and practice. We view the selection paradigm as substantially more developed and mature than the socialization paradigm, although this is of course a function of the historical efforts of work psychologists in Europe and North America in both the academic and practitioner wings of the discipline.

The traditional paradigm in selection has regarded prediction of job performance as the prime objective; a sacrosanct property to be sought-out, maximized and enshrined within a selection system, albeit within defined ethical, legal and practical limitations. Consequently, selection and assessment methods are referred to as 'predictors', their role being to measure qualities correlated with successful job performance held to be in finite availability amongst any applicant pool (de Wolff and van den Bosch, 1984; Herriot, 1984, 1992, 1993). Selection methods, if perceived solely as predictors, perform the function of screening-out a majority of applicants to thereby screen-in a minority who are likely to perform

Table 20.1 The dominant ideologies of two disparate areas of research and practice

	Selection and recruitment	Socialization and organization entry
Primary objective	• To predict on-the-job performance through valid and reliable methods of assessment	• To understand and facilitate organization entry and work role transitions
Secondary objectives	• To reduce a large applicant pool to manageable numbers for in-depth assessment • To screen applicants with due regard for equal opportunities and adverse impact • To operate procedures that are perceived as fair and valid by candidates • To generate empirical finding capable of informating our understanding of predictor validity, reliability and fairness	• To understand newcomer learning in task-related and non-task-related domains • To facilitate newcomer cultural assimilation into the organization • To facilitate newcomer work role transitions and thus positive outcomes over time (e.g. job performance, satisfaction, commitment, etc.) • To generate empirical findings into newcomer assimilation and integration
Paridigmatic assumptions over justifiable issues for research	Selection is pre-eminently about accurate but fair prediction, therefore: • Validity and reliability levels *per se* are critical—why techniques are valid or reliable is an intriguing but esoteric aside • Expert knowledge rests with the I/O psychologist to predict person–environment fit—the applicant is merely subject to measurement	Socialization is pre-eminently about assimilation conducive to effective job performance, therefore: • Understanding the socialization process is critical—how newcomers learn, fit-in, and become assimilated into an organization supersedes snap-shot predictions of likely job performance • Expertise development rests with the newcomer—the I/O psychologist can only support and facilitate this process
Predominant research methodology and methods	*Positivist-empirical*, e.g. • Quantitative validity studies correlating predictor/predictors with criterion/criteria • Quantitative studies into adverse impact of predictors • Meta-analyses of the validity and reliability of predictors	*Ethnographical-empirical/positivist-empirical*, e.g. • Case study and anecdotal accounts of newcomers' experiences of socialization • Normative models of the socialization process • Increasingly, longitudinal/repeat measure designs examining changes in self-assessed variables by newcomers (e.g. information seeking tactics, self-esteem, commitment, etc.)
Relative maturity of the research body	*Highly mature* • Construct and concept refinement well developed and extensively debated • Methodological advancement notable—sophisticated and generally accepted techniques available (e.g. meta-analysis, utility analysis) • Predictor validation studies spanning over eight decades for some methods • Research body vast—probably running to several thousand separate studies and publications	*Embryonic/maturing* • Constructs and concepts still under debate • Methodological advancements particularly recently as I/O psychologists have become actively engaged in longitudinal studies • Socialization process and seminal theoretical papers date from about the mid-1970s, and empirical studies have gained momentum from about the mid-1980s • Research body restricted but has developed substantially quite recently
Density of involvement by practising I/O psychologists	Extensive (some would claim saturated) but continuing to expand in the UK and US	Notably lacking apart from piecemeal involvements in orientation training and induction
Actual versus potential examples of practitioner involvement	*Actual* • Day-to-day operation of selection systems • Validation of individual techniques and overall systems • Development and introduction of new methods including structured interviews, ACs, biodata forms, etc. • Advising management on 'best practice' issues *Potential* • New technology and its impact upon assessment practices • The impact of organization change, flexible structures, and teamworking upon selection and assessment	*Actual* • A few examples of I/O psychologist-designed orientation programmes and induction procedures *Potential* • Development and design of integrated socialization procedures with due regard to newcomer learning strategies, individual differences and desired outcomes • Monitoring and measuring the socialization process over time, implementing reactive solutions to socialization 'problems' as they emerge • Follow-up of selection predictions via socialization tactics to enhance early job role performance

better on certain criterion measures of job performance. The predictivist paradigm has dominated North American and, to a lesser extent, European selection psychology (de Wolff and van den Bosch, 1984; Hesketh and Robertson, 1993). Pragmatic concerns of ensuring criterion-related validity have rendered questions over why certain methods are valid in certain circumstances less of a pressing concern than conducting empirical checks to ascertain levels of validity for different assessment methods (Ostroff and Rothausen, 1996).

The traditional paradigm in socialization has been to understand and facilitate the organizational entry process. Early work in the socialization area focused largely on tactics to change new employees' behaviours in organizationally relevant ways through cultural assimilation of the organization's goals and values (e.g. Schein, 1968, Van Maanen and Schein, 1979). To a lesser extent, socialization researchers have begun to focus on understanding how newcomers learn about their job and organizational environment (Anderson and Ostroff, 1995). Most of the theoretical and nearly all of the empirical work in the socialization area has been directed at socialization of employees post-entry, ignoring the important pre-entry socialization process.

The selection and socialization paradigms have developed largely independently. This is unfortunate as there are important points of overlap between the two which could enhance the effective integration and subsequent functioning of employees. On the selection side, the primary goal is to find employees who will subsequently fit the job and perform well on the job. Yet, without exception, the socialization process intercedes between predictors and the point in time at which the performance measure is taken, be it training or some form of job performance ratings. It is therefore surprising that selection researchers have not been more concerned with socialization tactics and their influence upon subsequent performance as a notable intermediary between predictor and job performance measures.

On the socialization side, only a handful of studies have been conducted into pre-entry socialization, unfortunately leaving unanswered many questions over the extent to which socialization can be initiated during selection, the impact of selection methods as socialization tactics, and whether selection methods can feasibly be used to develop accurate expectations about the organization to influence person–organization fit and candidate job behaviour and performance in the longer term. As noted by Chatman (1991):

> Thus in theory, the recruitment and selection process can serve as a substitute for socialization. In practice, however, no matter how thorough the recruitment and selection process may be, there is usually a need for at least residual organizational and individual adjustment (Chatman, 1991, p. 478).

Although selection methods may not obviate the need for on-going, post-entry socialization, they can certainly initiate the socialization process and, in some cases, even reduce the need for more sophisticated induction and orientation procedures in the early stages of organizational entry. We argue in this chapter that the sub-disciplines of selection and socialization have remained disparate for too long in work and organizational psychology, the selection methods commence the socialization process, and consequently, that the socialization impact of selection and assessment procedures warrants much greater attention by researchers and practitioners alike. We make the case for an integration of these two artificially divorced approaches to the staffing process and call for additional research to investigate the ways in which selection commences socialization and, subsequently, the ways in which socialization can further selection.

SOCIALIZATION AS SELECTION

Research into organization socialization has proceeded along a number of paths and has addressed a variety of themes over more recent years. Fortunately, regular reviews of the growing number of studies have been published and are useful in providing an overview of advances in this area over the last 20 years (see, in chronological order, Van Maanen, 1978; Louis, 1980; Fisher, 1986; Feldman, 1989; Wanous and Colella, 1989; and Anderson and Thomas, 1996). Clearly, it is not appropriate here to undertake a detailed review of all published research into organization socialization, but rather it is useful to note that across this literature a number of characteristics arise consistently as being key facets of the socialization process. These can be identified as:

- longitudinality
- information acquisition
- social learning
- personal change and
- complex outcomes.

First, the characteristic of *longitudinality* refers to the fairly obvious notion that socialization occurs over time (e.g. Feldman, 1976a, 1976b; Reichers, 1987; Wanous, 1992). Newcomers become increasingly socialized into the organization as they pass through the selection procedure into early induction training, and eventually becoming accepted by their colleagues and supervisors as fully fledged members of the organization. More contentious is the exact timescale needed to become fully socialized across different types of jobs and organizations given that this can be defined in any number of different ways (Fisher, 1986). As a consequence, little research has focused upon the relative duration of the socialization process for different jobs or across different organizations. These problems of completion and duration noted, we argue that the socialization process commences during, and continues throughout, the selection procedure. Organization socialization researchers have drawn a distinction between *pre-entry* socialization, i.e. socialization that occurs before the individual actually joins the organization, and *post-entry* socialization, i.e. socialization that occurs over the initial months of job incumbency (Feldman, 1976a, 1976b). As discussed below, we posit that the organization's recruitment and selection procedures provide the forum through which pre-entry socialization is enacted.

Secondly, recent socialization research has emphasized the characteristic of *information acquisition* by the newcomer as a central element of socialization (Louis, 1980; Ostroff and Kozlowski, 1992; Morrison, 1993a, 1993b; Smith and Kozlowski, 1994). For even the most mundane of jobs the newcomer will need to obtain previously unknown information on a range of issues before they become proficient in their new job role and organizational setting. Ostroff and Kozlowski (1992) propose a four-category framework of types of information typically sought by newcomers: *task* (information on their specific job demands), *role* (information on wider aspects of their work role including interpersonal networks and communication channels), the *group* (information on the proximal work group, its structure, norms and climate), and the *organization* (information on goals, values, structure, history, etc.). Morrison (1993a) expands this typology to put forward five types of information inherent in socialization: *technical* (information on how to perform the job), *referent* (information on role demands and role clarity), *normative* (information on expected attitudes and behaviours and on group norms), *performance feedback* (information on others' perceptions of their early job performance), and *social feedback* (information on their acceptability to others and the extent to which they fit in with their colleagues). These studies, and others besides, have begun to illustrate the types of information sought by newcomers at different stages in the socialization process. At a more basic level, these typologies imply that newcomers need information to facilitate person–job fit, e.g. task, technical, and performance feedback information; and they need information to facilitate person–organization fit, e.g. group, organizational, normative, and social feedback information. Although many questions still remain over the exact mechanisms newcomers use to integrate multiple sources and types of information (Van Maanen and Schein, 1979; Anderson and Thomas, 1996), they illustrate vividly that information acquisition is an integral part of the socialization process. Again, it is important to highlight the role that pre-entry selection and assessment procedures can play in conveying information across all these categories to potential employees. As the applicant progresses through the selection procedure, he or she will be gaining a plethora of information about the job and organization, some of it accurate and some inaccurate. As developed below, we argue that this job-related and organization information gleaned during the selection process through encounters with various selection tactics begins the socialization process.

The third characteristic of the socialization process is not unrelated to this point, but we separate out *social learning* as a distinct facet omnipresent in newcomer socialization. Several authors have held social learning, sometimes referred to as 'acculturation', to be a key outcome of socialization over and above that of learning task-related information (Louis, 1980; Wanous and Colella, 1989). Whilst Morrison (1993a) includes social learning in her typology of information acquisition, others have argued that acculturation implies more than this; it infers the integration of the newcomer into the organization's culture such that their behaviour, attitudes and norms are modified to a greater or lesser extent. That is, the goal of social learning is to achieve person–organization fit. The extent of this modification process during socialization will be moderated by the system of selection operated by an organization (e.g. Chatman, 1991). The more the selection process is able to screen-out diverse applicants and to select-in an homogeneous minority of candidates similar in educational background, attitudes, values, beliefs, and personalities to those already in the organization, the less the socialization process will need to supplement this process of screening-out diversity (see also, Schneider 1987, and Schneider *et al.*, Chapter 19 in this volume). Conversely, when an organization is unable to pre-screen applicants to any meaningful degree (e.g. national military service, where numbers of vacancies equal or exceed numbers of applicants) or when the pre-screening process focuses exclusively on skills and abilities for person–job fit, the socialization system will be called upon more to modify the behaviour of newcomers toward that desired by the organization (see Wanous, 1992, for a discussion of this issue). Again, then, in terms of social learning, there is a demonstrable inter-relationship between the selection and socialization systems in relation to the desired goal of securing job incumbents who are competent job performers and who behave in organizationally desired ways on the job.

Fourthly, through the information acquisition and social learning processes that occur during socialization, this transition assumes an element of *personal change* on the part of the newcomer (e.g. Arnold, 1994; Nicholson, 1984; Posner and Powell, 1985). Van Maanen and Schein (1979) propose that one dimension along which socialization procedures vary between organizations is the extent to which they either build upon the newcomer's existing experience, skills, attitudes and work-related behaviour, or alternatively deconstruct the individual's self-identity by interventive means to later re-build them in the preferred image of the organization, so-called 'investiture versus divestiture' tactics. Examples of investiture tactics in socialization include the hiring of specifically qualified, mid-career professionals who operate within a closely regulated environment or industry with whom the organization wishes to continue to work in this manner (e.g. banking executives, investment consultants, lawyers, and medical consultants). Examples of divestiture procedures tend to proliferate in job roles either requiring the suppression of individual personality and values (e.g. basic military recruits, fast-food restaurant operatives, and Disney themepark employees: Van Maanen, 1995), or at the entry level in professional careers where socialization tactics sometimes entail an unusually demanding period of apprenticeship immediately following formal qualification (e.g. junior doctors, tenure-track academics). Clearly, socialization procedures that are based upon the principles of divestiture will result in more personal change for the newcomer than those based upon investiture, but the point to note is that *all* procedures are likely to result in some degree of change for the individual. Changes are likely to occur on a whole variety of dimensions and variables, including, for instance, newcomer attitudes toward the job (Chao *et al.*, 1994a, 1994b; McFarlane Shore and Tetrick, 1994), attitudes towards co-workers and supervisors (Anderson and Thomas, 1996), expectations of the work role versus the experienced reality on the job (Herriot, 1989), and at a more observable level, changes in newcomer behaviour in response to particular job scenarios and situations (Van Maanen and Schein, 1979). Furthermore, to the extent that the selection process results in incumbents whose skills and abilities match those needed for the job, a lesser degree of knowledge and skill-related changes will be required during post-entry socialization. Likewise, selection procedures that result in the hiring of employees with values and goals that match the attributes of the organization, a lesser degree of divestiture type socialization procedures will be required post-entry, (Saks, 1995).

The fifth and final characteristic of organizational socialization is that of *complex outcomes* for both the organization and the newcomer. Amongst many positive outcomes for the organization, the following can be highlighted: the addition of an effective job performer to its ranks of employees; the receipt of pro-social behaviours including a willingness to contribute 'above and beyond the routine calls of duty'; work role innovations in improving existing work practices and methods; and commitment of the individual to the organization in terms of willingness to continuously work on behalf of the organization's goals. Positive outcomes for the newcomer include a sense of growth and self-esteem resulting from conquering the challenge of a new work role; job satisfaction, psychological well-being and a sense of personal development; and gaining new work experiences and skills which may be highly marketable in the future. The preceding comments would suggest then that job performance, as strictly defined in many selection validation studies, is only one of a whole host of important work-relevant outcomes. If one takes the view of a single, continuous process of employee integration that begins with selection and socialization at pre-entry and continues post-organizational entry, the importance of considering an integration of selection and socialization for facilitating a wide range of outcomes is revealed.

To summarize: these five characteristics are key features of organization socialization. Quite substantial research has been conducted into some of these characteristics, whereas in others much remains to be done to flesh out our understanding of how effective socialization is achieved following the selection of individuals predicted to be more likely to become successful job performers. At several points we noted briefly the links between selection and socialization, and especially the notion that the foundations for longer-term socialization are laid during the selection procedure. We develop these links below since, as already noted, both processes have the same ultimate goal for any organization: to provide it with competent and committed employees, knowledgeable in their job function and possessing the necessary attitudes and competencies for effective organizational functioning.

SELECTION AS SOCIALIZATION

We have acknowledged that socialization is a longitudinal process, occurring in several stages over time. Numerous authors have postulated stage-based models of the socialization process (e.g. Buchanan, 1974; Feldman, 1976a, 1976b; Porter, Lawler and Hackman, 1975; Schein, 1978; Wanous, 1980). Table 20.2 is reprinted from Wanous, Reichers and Malik (1984) and illustrates these models in summary.

While the models differ slightly in content and the exact progression of newcomers through various socialization stages, general themes across the models

Table 20.2   Stage models of the socialization process

Feldman's (1976a, 1976b) three-stage entry model	Buchanan's (1974) three-stage early career model	Porter, Lawler and Hackman's (1975) three-stage entry modal	Schein's (1978) three-stage socialization model	Wanous's (1980) integrative approach to stages of socialization
Stage 1: Anticipatory socialization—'getting in' • Setting of realistic expectations • Determining match with the newcomer Stage 2: Accommodation—'breaking in' • Initiation into the job • Establishing interpersonal relationships • Roles clarified • Congruence between self and organization • Performance appraisal Stage 3: Role management—'settling in' • The degree of fit between one's life interests outside of work and the demands of the organization • Resolution of conflicts at the work place itself	Stage 1: First year—basic training and initiation • Establish role clarity for newcomer • Establish cohesion with peers • Clarify relationship of peers with rest of organization • Confirmation/disconfirmation of expectations • Loyalty, conflicts with organizational and outside interests Stage 2: Performance—years two, three, and four at work • Commitment to organization according to norms • Reinforcement of self-image by organization • Resolution of conflicts • Feelings of personal importance Stage 3: Organizational dependability—the fifth year and beyond • All succeeding years are in this stage • Diversity due to individual experiences	Stage 1: Pre-arrival • Setting of newcomer expectations • Reward and punishment of behaviours Stage 2: Encounter • Confirmation/disconfirmation of expectations • Reward and punishment of behaviours Stage 3: Change and acquisition • Alteration of newcomer's self-image • Form new relationship • Adopt new values • Acquire new behaviours	Stage 1: Entry search for accurate information • Creation of false expectations by both parties • Inaccurate information is basis for job choice Stage 2: Socialization • Accept organizational reality • Cope with resistance to change • Congruence between organizational climate and person's needs • Organization's evaluation of newcomer's performance • Cope with either too much ambiguity or too much structure Stage 3: Mutual acceptance • Signals of organizational acceptance • Signals of newcomer's acceptance • Commitment to the organization • Commitment to work	Stage 1: Confronting and accepting organizational reality • Confirmation/disconfirmation of expectations • Conflicts between personal values and organizational climates • Discovering rewarded/punished behaviours Stage 2: Achieving role clarity • Initiation to the job's tasks • Definition of interpersonal roles • Coping with resistance to change • Congruence between self and organizational performance appraisals • Coping with structure and ambiguity Stage 3: Locating oneself in the organizational context • Learning behaviours congruent with the organization's desires • Outside and work interests conflicts resolved • Job challenge leads to work commitments • New interpersonal relations, new values and altered self-image Stage 4: Detecting signposts of successful socialization • Company dependability and commitment • High general satisfaction • Feelings of mutual acceptance • Job involvement and intrinsic motivation increases

Source: J.P. Wanous, A.E. Reichers and S.D. Malik (1984). Reprinted with the kind permission of the Academy of Management Association.

emerge. First, prior to organizational entry, potential employees set expectations regarding their role, work group, terms of employment, reward contingencies, and what organizational life is really like. Upon entry, newcomers concentrate on establishing relationships with peers, learning about the tasks necessary for job performance, clarifying their role in the organization, resolving conflicts between pre-entry expectations and organizational reality, and resolving conflicts between personal values and organizational climate and values. These models are useful in that they further illustrate the chronological and processual overlaps between socialization and selection.

Two of the models summarized in Table 20.2 (Feldman, 1976a, 1976b; and Porter, Lawler and Hackman, 1975) specifically incorporate pre-entry stages of socialization during which potential newcomers set expectations. For example, Feldman identifies two process variables which he suggests are indicative of progression through this stage:

> **Realism.** Realism is the extent to which individuals have a full and accurate picture of what life in the organization is really like. It indicates how successfully they have completed the information sharing and information evaluation part of their recruitment.
>
> **Congruence.** This is the extent to which the organization's resources and individual needs and skills are mutually satisfying. It indicates how successful individuals have been in making decisions about employment (Feldman, 1976a, pp. 434–435).

We argue that the pre-entry processes of realism and congruence are likely to occur primarily through the applicant's sense-making of their pre-entry experiences gained throughout their exposure to the selection process. As an example, consider the situation when realistic job previews (RJPs) are included during recruitment or as part of the selection process. Realism is a pivotal concern in the design of any RJP (Wanous, 1992; Wanous and Colella, 1989). By providing candidates with accurate 'warts and all' previews of the job and organization, the assumption is that this permits applicants to self-select-out if they consider that the job and/or organization is not suited to them, thereby avoiding a lack of congruence between the self and organizational context. Congruence, we would argue, is a key personal measure of the degree to which the candidate has been successful in his or her decision-making between job offers.

Similarly, Porter, Lawler and Hackman (1975) propound that pre-entry socialization is facilitated through recruitment and selection. The applicant is argued to be generating a host of expectations regarding the job role, terms and conditions of employment, the work group, organizational human resource management (HRM) procedures, promotion opportunities, and so forth. The degree to which these expectations are subsequently met is held to be a critical determinant of effective socialization, and therefore job performance in the longer term.

Apart from a few notable exceptions, however, there has been little research into pre-entry socialization, almost certainly for the reasons noted earlier of the lack of synergy between selection and socialization in the literature. Despite this paucity of research into pre-entry socialization, the work of Schneider (1987;

Schneider *et al.*, Chapter 19 in this volume) and Herriot (1984, 1989) provides theoretical rationales for considering selection as socialization.

Schneider's well-known *attraction–selection–attrition* (ASA) framework proposes that individuals and organizations will inevitably gravitate toward mutual similarity and fit in their employment relationships over time. Schneider (1987) puts forward the ASA framework as a bi-directional cycle applying to both organizations and individuals as prospective or actual employees. Early on, applicants are attracted to organizations they perceive as work environments into which they would fit in terms of the organization's goals, values, climate and work practices. Similarly, organizations tend to be attracted to individuals who appear to complement rather than compromise their attitudinal and behavioural repertoires, and who would therefore fit in more easily. At the selection stage, Schneider's framework suggests that each party will select the other with these kind of criteria uppermost in mind; the organization selecting candidates who share many personal attributes with those already employed, and likewise the applicant opting for a job offer from the organization whose goals, values, and climate appears to most closely match his or her own personal idiosyncrasies. During the ongoing phase of attrition, Schneider again argues for a two-way process. Individuals who mistakenly join an organization which, it subsequently transpires, is quite different to their own preferred style of working, will leave voluntarily. Organizations 'failing' to screen-out individuals during selection who later turn out not to fit in may be forced to resort to involuntary termination during the early phases of socialization.

The ASA framework is in keeping with our view that socialization is actively commenced during selection procedures. Assessment methods provide the candidate with a veritable plethora of information—information on the culture and climate of the organization (Iles and Robertson, 1989; Chapter 27 in this volume; Rynes, 1993), on its treatment of prospective staff and the procedural and distributive justice of its selection techniques (Arvey and Sackett, 1993; Gilliland, 1993, 1994), and on the expectations held of employees' behaviour at work (Herriot, 1984, 1989; Thornton, 1993). These types of information inform candidates about organizational attributes and may cause them to self-select out of the selection process if they view fit as poor, or accept job offers if they view fit as good. Empirical evidence supports this proposition that job-seekers are affected by congruence between their personalities and personal attributes and organizations' attributes (e.g. Bretz, Ash and Dreher, 1989; Cable and Judge, 1994; Judge and Bretz, 1992). Poorly received or unprofessionally administered methods may cause an organization's top choices to turn down their offers of employment, regardless of the benchmark level of average generalized validity attached to the method (Murphy, 1986; Rynes, 1993). Moreover, selection methods will inform and influence candidate expectations of acceptable behaviour by the organization facilitating subsequent person–organization fit, an issue to which we return later in this chapter.

In this vein, Herriot (1984, 1989) argues that selection procedures comprise a 'series of social episodes' (1989, p. 175) wherein both parties negotiate a viable psychological contract. His theoretical stance differs from Schneider's, however, in that the central measure he suggests is one of *congruence* between the parties' expectations rather than either simply the organization's or the applicant's singular view. Herriot's perspective is thus rather more concerned with the congruence of expectations during selection and the outcome of either party exiting from the process. It also obviously relates to Feldman's (1976a, 1976b) socialization model and the process variables of realism and congruence he identifies as key measures in person–job and person–organization fit. In Herriot's terms, exit on the grounds of accurately construed expectations, for both parties, is a 'valid negative' decision—the organization avoiding the appointment of an unsuitable candidate, and the candidate withdrawing from the possibility of a job role that would have proven to be untenable. Herriot's view also hints at the part that selection methods play in creating expectations of the other for both parties. Such expectations created during selection can act as potent sources of influence upon subsequent workplace behaviour and attitudes.

In summary, the longitudinal process of socialization begins prior to organizational entry when candidates encounter recruitment and selection procedures. Important information about job activities, work roles, and the organizational context, including its goals values and climate, can be gleaned during the selection process. Such information can result in candidates accurately or inaccurately assessing their fit with the organization, thus influencing their job choice decision. Furthermore, information gleaned during selection can result in candidates setting expectations about what the organization will be like facilitating the subsequent social learning process upon organizational entry. To the extent that expectations established during selection are met, a lesser degree of personal change on the part of newcomers will be necessary. Finally, information gained during selection and its impact on the setting of expectations can have a profound influence on the subsequent attitudes and behavioural outcomes of newcomers.

AFFECTIVE REACTIONS, PSYCHOLOGICAL IMPACT AND SOCIALIZATION IMPACT

Existing research into candidate reactions to selection techniques has uncovered a number of interesting findings. Several studies into candidate preference for different methods show distinct patterns of liking for certain techniques (see Rynes, 1993; and Iles and Robertson, Chapter 27 in this volume, for detailed reviews). Candidates understandably prefer methods that appear to be more job-relevant (Robertson *et al.*, 1991; Rynes, 1993), that are non-intrusive (Ryan and Sackett, 1987), that do not violate confidentiality nor invade personal privacy (Rynes and Connerley, 1991), and that generally seem to be fair and objective as an experience for candidates (Rynes and Connerley, 1991). Rynes (1993) argues that such 'affective reactions' are open to wide individual differences between candidates, some being content to accept even highly intrusive and seemingly irrelevant procedures whilst others may react most negatively and even withdraw from the selection process.

In many respects these studies paint a useful picture of candidate reactions in terms solely of their liking for particular methods compared with others.

Candidate liking, conversely, is often perceived by recruiters as being of little import, particularly where labour market conditions and thus the selection ratio favours the organization (de Wolff and van den Bosch, 1984; Herriot, 1989). Provided the affective impact of assessment methods is not so great as to cause the very best candidates to withdraw or to decline an offer of employment, the view of hard-bitten recruiters is likely to remain that it is they who select between a surplus of candidates whose role it is to comply with organizational procedures (Anderson, 1992). But such a view is myopic because it conveniently ignores other evidence which would strongly suggest that selection methods are liked or disliked for definite reasons, one of which is that they can have more permanent psychological impacts upon candidates.

Robertson and his colleagues have proposed the concept of 'psychological impact' to describe such outcomes and have developed and refined a general model portraying the psychological impact of selection procedures (e.g. Robertson and Smith, 1989; Iles and Robertson, 1989; Chapter 27 in this volume; Robertson *et al.*, 1991). Three main outcomes are specified—work commitment, self-esteem, and job and career withdrawal—and the model also incorporates two moderator variables—career stage and personal characteristics. The model has been applied in field studies into the psychological impact of methods, mostly focusing upon any significant differences between successful and unsuccessful candidate groups following final-stage assessment centre procedures (Robertson *et al.*, 1991; Fletcher, 1991). Robertson *et al.* (1991) report correlations between accepted candidates' perceptions of their treatment during selection and their subsequent organizational commitment and intention to quit. This research, then, illustrates the longer-term impact that selection methods can have upon accepted candidates.

In a series of articles, Gilliland (1993, 1994, 1995) has examined candidates' reactions to distributive and procedural justice in selection systems. Distributive justice refers to the fairness of organizationally allocated outcomes, whilst procedural justice concerns the fairness of the procedures, in this case selection, used to allocate such outcomes. Applicants' reactions to selection procedures vary considerably depending on the perceived fairness of the selection method.

A final strand of research into the effects of selection methods upon candidates argues that these techniques have a potent influence upon candidate perceptions of the wider organization, and more crucially, upon job satisfaction, commitment, turnover, and job performance (Thornton, 1993). Drawing· from earlier studies into the effects of interviewer behaviour upon interviewee impressions, Thornton (1993) suggests that applicant perceptions will also inform and influence subsequent job performance and other performance-related variables. The model he proposes has not yet been the subject of empirical validation, but again his argument centres on the perspective of the applicant as influenced by organizational assessment procedures, and there is indeed ample evidence to support the contention that interviewer behaviour exerts a longer-term impact upon candidate perceptions (Rynes and Miller, 1983; Liden and Parsons, 1986).

To summarize: this research indicates convincingly that selection methods have more permanent impacts upon candidates which may be preference-related, psychological, expectational, and performance-related in nature. To the extent that selection procedures impact the subsequent attitudes and behaviours of candidates, socialization and integration into the organization can be affected either positively or negatively. Unfortunately, studies into these strands of research (candidate preference, psychological impact, procedural justice, and influence on candidate attributions to organizational facets) have developed somewhat piecemeal, each theme being addressed largely independently of the others as relatively recent concerns amongst selection researchers. There is a need for integration and synergy across the four themes and, perhaps most notably, for guiding theoretical models and frameworks to summarize the likely types of impact of selection procedures upon candidates. We therefore now turn our attention to developing such an integrative conceptual framework, and to propose the notion of *socialization impact* as a term to describe the array of sorts of influence that selection methods can have upon candidates.

THE SOCIALIZATION IMPACT OF SELECTION METHODS

We propose the concept of 'socialization impact' as a general variable to categorize the socialization capacity of a selection method. A five-domain framework of socialization impact is advanced to categorize the different types of impact that selection methods may have upon candidates, and in conjunction with this framework, we explore assessment methods with respect to their potential for socialization impact. In essence, the argument we present in the remainder of this chapter is based upon four main premises:

1. That socialization impact is measurable in five constituent domains
   - information provision
   - preference impact
   - expectational impact
   - attitudinal impact
   - behavioural impact.
2. That different selection methods possess varying degrees of socialization impact.
3. That selection methods are not just predictors of job performance but can be designed and used via their socialization impact as facilitators in pre-entry socialization.
4. That socialization impact can be 'designed-in' to a selection procedure and should therefore be considered along with validity, reliability and fairness as a major factor in system design.

The concept of socialization impact implies that a particular organizational practice or procedure can have some impact on the integration of employees into the organization. We postulate a five-domain framework as follows:

1. *Information provision*
2. *Preference impact*

3. *Expectational impact*
4. *Attitudinal impact*
5. *Behavioural impact*

The five areas of socialization impact are urged to provide a general typology of the spectrum of ways in which selection methods can influence candidates from the perspective of commencing the process of socialization and assimilation. Each type of socialization impact is described below.

Information provision

Virtually all pre-screening and selection methods convey some sort of information to the candidate, but from the candidate's perspective, some are more informative than others. Even the most rudimentary application form gives a modicum of information on the type of details needed by an organization to reach hiring decisions and may therefore be interpreted as a loose indication of organization culture and HRM policy (Iles and Robertson, Chapter 27 in this volume). Other methods, however, can provide detailed and comprehensive information—RJPs during recruitment and work samples, for instance. In some sense, then, this level of impact is factual rather than affective; it relates simply to the degree and type of information conveyed by selection methods to candidates. Conversely, such information will form the basis upon which candidates develop expectations of the organization, its personnel procedures, the future job role, and so forth (Herriot, 1984; Rynes, 1993; Thornton, 1993). It is therefore important to consider this type of 'impact' initially and to define it as a distinct category of socialization impact in selection.

   First, information provision may be intentional or unintentional on the part of the organization. It is likely that the majority of organizationally sent messages in selection are sent unintentionally. Indeed, few organizations will have intentionally 'designed-in' the range of messages sent throughout the selection process. That is to say, the selection procedure is not designed to explicitly convey any particular type of information to candidates; rather it is designed to assess applicant attributes and predict job performance. Yet, as noted above, selection procedures can and do portray a great deal of information about the organization to applicants. For example, applicants make inferences about the type of job duties involved, the fairness of the organization, its climate and culture and so forth. Likewise, exposure to assessors during an assessment centre can give candidates information on how individuals interact with one another within the organization. It should be noted that while selection procedures *per se* are rarely designed to convey information, some recruitment procedures are designed to do so. For example, RJPs are designed expressly for the purpose of conveying realistic information about the job and/or organization to candidates. Owing to the wide variety of information provided by the selection procedures, we believe it is important that more attention is devoted to defining the types of information provided by various selection procedures and refining existing procedures to convey intended information to applicants.

Secondly, regardless of whether the information provided is intentional or unintentional, the accuracy of the information provided and the accuracy with which candidates perceive the information is critical. Information provided during selection can be an accurate reflection of the job and organization or a misrepresentation of the organization. For example, some information sent by the organization may be intentionally false, i.e. organizational faking good and intentional impression management (e.g. interviewers over-representing the positive aspects of the organization) or unintentionally false. Likewise, candidates can interpret such information either accurately or inaccurately. Thus, accurate interpretation and extrapolation is important in the 'attraction' phase of Schneider's ASA model for the candidate to be able to make valid judgements over their likely fit into the organization.

Inaccurate perception of information, or the naive acceptance of information that has been subject to impression management by recruiters is therefore likely to result in unrealistic expectations and beliefs. As Schein (1988) argues, both parties to the selection process have a vested interest to fake-good and to present themselves in the most favourable light to the other. Considerable research has been conducted into candidate impression management (Giacalone and Rosenfeld, 1991), whereas the topic of impression management by recruiters and organizations has received too little research attention. Adopting these dimensions of accuracy from the organizational and individual perspective gives a simple 2 × 2 factorial (Figure 20.1).

The accuracy of the information sent and the accuracy with which the information is perceived is likely to have important impacts on job choice and subsequent socialization and integration. Quadrant 1 is the most desirable state. Here, realistic

Organizational message

	Accurate	Inaccurate
Accurate	Quadrant 1 Realistic — correctly construed	Quadrant 2 Unrealistic — correctly construed
Inaccurate	Quadrant 4 Realistic — misconstrued	Quadrant 3 Unrealistic — misconstrued

Candidate perception (row label)

Figure 20.1

information about the job and/or organization is sent and is correctly construed by candidates. In this case, candidates can determine if the organizational context is an appropriate fit for them, and if so, should self-select into the organization. Integration and socialization should be facilitated in such a case since expectations about the job and organization are realistic and newcomers may already possess some degree of fit to the organization. When accurate and realistic information is provided by the organization, but misconstrued by candidates, candidates are likely to make poor job choice decisions. For example, candidates may form unrealistic expectations about the job or may choose a job under the assumption that they fit the organization, both of which impede effective socialization. Similarly, when inaccurate information is sent by the organization, 'good' candidates may inappropriately select-out of the process owing to misinformation. Likewise, candidates who do select into the organization may have unrealistic expectations or may not fit the organization owing to misinformation.

Finally, both information about the extent to which the candidate fits the job and the extent to which he or she fits the organization can be conveyed by assessment techniques. Selection techniques that are content valid and focus on assessing job-specific knowledge and skills, such as structured interviews, situational interviews, work samples, assessment centres, and leaderless group discussions, provide information about the types of job tasks and activities a candidate will experience on the job. Such information will allow applicants to gather some information as to their fit with specific jobs. Information about the organizational environment, its goals, values and climate can be derived, to some extent, from nearly all assessment methods. Candidates are likely to make inferences about the organization's goals, value and culture on the basis of the type of selection procedure used and the manner in which they are treated during the selection process (e.g. Judge and Bretz, 1992; Gilliland, 1994, 1995).

Information that applicants obtain from their encounters with selection procedures is likely to impact the socialization process in several ways. First, information may affect candidates' initial preferences, expectations and attitudes about the organization, each of which is explored below. Secondly, information gleaned during pre-entry should influence the types of information needed and sought by newcomers as they begin their post-entry socialization process. Recent empirical evidence strongly supports the notion that assimilation and learning are directly influenced by the amount and types of information obtained from various sources during the socialization process. At a general level, newcomers who obtain a greater degree of relevant information are likely to adjust more quickly, be more satisfied, committed, and less likely to leave than newcomers with less information (e.g. Morrison, 1993a; Ostroff and Kozlowski, 1992). Hence, to the extent that accurate information is obtained about the job and organization during pre-entry, the burdens of obtaining such information post-entry when adjusting to the job are lessened. Furthermore, newcomers who are able to obtain critical information that allows them to understand, make sense of, and adjust to the organizational context become socialized more quickly (Ostroff and Kozlowski, 1992). Thus, to the extent that accurate information about the job context is provided during selection, newcomers will be freer to engage in obtaining information about the organizational context; to the extent that accurate information about the organizational context is provided during selection, newcomers can concentrate on learning about their jobs. These propositions suggest that, depending on the type of information gleaned during selection, newcomer information acquisition behaviour during socialization will differ in its required extent and the types of outstanding information to be sought post-entry.

From the organizational perspective, a set of related arguments can be offered. Different types of selection procedures provide information about the degree to which applicants are predicted to fit the job or fit the organization. A selection strategy that is designed to assess individuals' specific knowledge, skills, and abilities (e.g. work sample tests, ability tests, situational interviews or assessment centres) should increase the probability that selected applicants will have the skills and abilities required for the job. Likewise, a selection strategy that emphasizes person–organization fit (e.g. personality-testing and to some degree biodata, interviews and reference checks) is likely to result in employees who match the company, and want to perform well, but may not be able to do so owing to a lack of job-specific fit (Ostroff and Rothausen, 1996). The implications of the type of information obtained about applicants on the basis of the selection method used (skill-based versus person-based) should influence the types of socialization tactics that are most appropriate. That is to say, with a person–job fit type of selection strategy, socialization tactics should be geared more toward achieving person–organization fit, with a lesser emphasis on person–job fit. A selection strategy that strongly emphasizes person–organization fit should be complemented with a socialization strategy that emphasizes the learning of job-related information.

Preference impact

The second domain in our framework of socialization impact concerns the preference impact of selection methods. We use this term to include candidate liking, positive affective reactions, and relative preference for particular techniques in the selection process (Gilliland, 1993, 1994, 1995; Rynes, 1993). It is clear that candidates prefer some methods over others (for a detailed review see Iles and Robertson, Chapter 27 in this volume). What is more questionable is the longer-term influence of candidate liking for assessment techniques upon their decision-making, their expectations of the employment relationship, and their subsequent behaviour on the job. In all likelihood it is probable that candidate preferences for particular methods will affect these longer-term outcomes to only a limited degree. However, this type of socialization impact is also likely to be a pervasive bias affecting candidates' feelings and expectations of the organization. The use of notably unpopular methods (e.g. drug testing, the polygraph, stress interviews), or the use of generally acceptable techniques in unprofessional or insensitive ways (e.g. contacting referees without prior permission, neglecting to give feedback on psychometric test results) is most likely to establish negative job-related expectations amongst candidates. Such abuse is also liable to be extrapolated to suppose that this is the typical level of procedural and distributive justice accorded to its employees by the organization (Gilliland, 1993, 1994, 1995).

When candidates accept a job after a negative experience with an assessment technique, an overall negative affective reaction to the organization is likely to result. In such a case, socialization is likely to be impacted in several ways. Socialization may occur more slowly as initial negative impressions on the part of the newcomer must be overcome. Learning about the job and organization may be impeded. Furthermore, socialization tactics will need to focus more directly on the organizational context, social learning and acculturation as negative affects may inhibit fit to the organization. In either case, the use of a selection method conveying a negative preference impact is inadvisable, even where the method has been found to have relatively good predictive validity, as the hidden socialization-related costs of retarded integration and longer-term candidate distrust of the organization are likely to outweigh moderate selection-related utility gains.

Expectational impact

As a third dimension of socialization impact we propose that selection methods can generate candidate expectations on a host of issues including, for instance, the psychological contract for employment, expectations of the future job role, organizational climate and culture, HRM practices, and career and promotion opportunities (Herriot, 1984, 1989; Rynes, 1993). Stage models of socialization (e.g. Feldman, 1976a, 1976b; Porter, Lawler and Hackman 1975) elucidate the notion that newcomers set expectations about the job and organization during pre-entry socialization. To the extent that expectations are disconfirmed, the socialization process is impeded and negative outcomes, such as poor performance or turnover, can result. There is an unfortunate paucity of research regarding the role expectations play during the socialization and integration process. Nevertheless, it is clear that expectations are indeed created and that met expectations of newcomers can impact organizationally relevant outcomes such as satisfaction, performance and tenure (Wanous *et al.*, 1992).

Exactly how different selection methods create expectations and the types of expectations created by different selection techniques is open to question. One way in which expectations may be formed during selection is based on Herriot's social process perspective described earlier in this chapter. Herriot's perspective centres around both parties' expectations of their relationship with the other and the way in which selection methods facilitate the agreement of a viable work-related psychological contract. During encounters within the selection process, expectations are generated on both sides which form the basis of the psychological contract. These, in turn, may influence the socialization process. For example, newcomers may acquire information during socialization which confirms or disconfirms their expectations. When expectations inherent in the psychological contract are violated, negative attitudes and behaviours may result (Rousseau, 1989; Robinson and Rousseau, 1994). Similarly, the organization will undoubtedly establish expectations of the newcomer, their subsequent work performance either exceeding, satisfying, or failing to meet these expectations.

Attitudinal impact

A fourth type of impact we propose is that assessment methods can influence candidate attitudes and beliefs. In the socialization literature the modification of newcomer attitudes, beliefs and their wider self-concept has long been asserted as target dimensions for socialization procedures to modify and adapt to suit the needs of the organization (Wanous, 1992). The advantage of using socialization procedures, of course, is that the process is on-going and open-ended, perhaps over several months or even years, and interventions can be designed to reinforce and reward certain changes over time (Van Maanen and Schein, 1979; Louis, 1980). The timescale in selection is notably shorter, usually spanning only days or weeks and, furthermore, the degree of candidate involvement with, and affiliation to, the organization is considerably less. Candidates will typically be invited in for a single assessment or a serial selection procedure, thereby gaining only fleeting glimpses of the organization and its culture rather than a continuous employment experience. Nevertheless, while selection procedures may have minimal impact on attitude change owing to their short time-span, they can have a substantial impact on initial attitude formation by candidates, attitudes that will set their frame of mind for the post-entry socialization process.

The selection process can be argued to comprise of a series of critical incidents from the candidate's perspective, each demanding careful preparation and self-presentation and each likely to provoke not inconsiderable stress at the prospect of having one's competence delved into in detail and one's future career options determined in this manner. Thus, candidates have substantive *psychological investment* in the selection process, sometimes extending to spending days preparing for each assessment method, feeling acute stress over attending the organization for procedures, and generating scenarios of what it would be like to work for the organization and to hold such-and-such a position. Do candidates treat their experience of selection methods as critical incidents for information acquisition and the formation of attitudes and beliefs? One is forced to retort 'what else can they possibly use?!' The likelihood is, then, that selection methods *do* impact upon candidate attitudes, the extent of this impact probably being a function of prior expectations of fair treatment (i.e. 'procedural justice': Gilliland, 1995), the conduct of particular assessment methods by recruiters, and the degree of psychological investment by the candidate in the selection process.

Thus, pre-entry attitudes formed during selection encounters will influence later stages of the socialization process. As noted earlier in this chapter, modifying newcomer attitudes is a key objective of many socialization procedures. The *extent* of this change will vary, as will the *balance* of systemic impact between the selection and socialization systems with increasing degrees of pre-screening via selection proportionately reducing the need for attitude modification via socialization. In their seminal typology of socialization tactics, Van Maanen and Schein (1979) distinguish between socialization procedures that are designed to build upon the newcomer's existing beliefs, knowledge and self-identity as opposed to those that attempt to deconstruct the individual and to fundamentally modify and rebuild their attitudes and beliefs in the preferred image of the organization (so-called 'investiture' and 'divestiture' tactics). Selection methods that form appropriate and organizationally desired attitudes should be favoured, and similarly, the extent to which different types of socialization tactics will be needed should take into account the pre-entry attitudes formed during selection encounters.

Behavioural impact

Lastly, we propose that selection methods have the potential to *affect* as well as *predict* candidate behaviour. First, we argue that selection methods may actually *create* desired behaviours in candidates. That is, exposure to selection methods may encourage appropriate behavioural responses via a pre-entry socialization process. Consider the situation candidates find themselves in having applied to an organization. The likelihood is that they will be expected to undergo a multi-stage selection procedure, each stage successively reducing the numbers of applicants remaining in the procedure. Within what is effectively a competitive tournament procedure, 'acceptable' behaviours are rewarded and reinforced by being shortlisted to the next stage of the process. It is not unreasonable to suppose that candidates skilled in impression management and high on self-monitoring will be able to perceive and display the desired behaviours (Giacalone and Rosenfeld, 1991). Indeed, in a multi-stage selection system it is feasible that shortlisting acts as a behavioural reward, thus reinforcing and replicating certain behaviours deemed to be those desired by the organization. This could lead to escalating self-presentation strategies by applicants keen to impress an organization with their willingness and ability to learn how to behave and fit it. In essence, we argue that socialization begins in earnest during selection as candidates learn which behaviours are appropriate.

In addition, encounters with selection procedures may influence subsequent post-entry behaviours in either a positive or negative way. The expectations and attitudes formed during pre-entry should influence the extent to which newcomers begin to engage in a variety of organizationally relevant behaviours. For example, false expectations formed during selection that the organizational environment is highly competitive should inhibit newcomers from initially engaging in pro-social, helping and altruistic behaviours. Socialization tactics will need to overcome these false expectations, and encourage the behaviours more appropriate for the organizational environment.

In summary, this framework is put forward as a comprehensive typology of socialization impact. We do not infer that selection methods possess a unique or generalizable 'amount' of socialization impact, rather that socialization impact may be situation-specific and moderated by a host of contextual factors. As a rough guide, Table 20.3 presents a summary of the likely degree of impact of methods of pre-screening and candidate assessment.

IMPLICATIONS OF SELECTION AS SOCIALIZATION

Effective integration and socialization of new employees requires fit to both the job and the organizational context. This socialization and integration of

Table 20.3 Five domains of socialization impact of selection and assessment methods

Selection method	Domain 1: Information provision	Domain 2: Preference impact	Domain 3: Expectational impact	Domain 4: Attitudinal impact	Domain 5: Behavioural impact
Pre-screening methods					
• Application form	Low	Low	Low	Low	Low
• Biodata inventory	Low	Medium*	Low	Low	Low
• Recruitment brochure	Medium	High	Medium/high†	Medium	Medium
• Realistic job previews (RJPs)	High	High	High	High	Medium
Assessment methods					
• Unstructured interviews	Low/medium	Medium	Medium	Medium	Low
• PBD interviews	Low	Medium	Low	Low	Low
• Situational interviews	High‡	Medium‡	Medium‡	Medium‡	Low‡
• Cognitive ability tests	Low	Medium*	Low	Low	Low
• Personality tests	Low	Low/medium	Low	Low	Low
• Integrity/honesty tests	Low	Medium*	Medium§	Low	Low
• Drug/alcohol tests	Low	High†	Medium§	Low	Low
• Work samples	High	High	High	High	High
• Leaderless group discussions (LGDs)	Medium	Medium	Medium	Low	Low
• Presentation exercises	Medium	Medium	Medium	Low	Low

* Biodata inventories, cognitive ability tests, integrity/honesty tests, and especially drug/alcohol test are likely to have a *negative* preference impact if unprofessionally administered and/or in circumstances where candidates have other employment opportunities open to them.

† Recruitment brochures are likely to have a higher expectational impact if their contents provide specific details than if they merely provide generalized information.

‡ Situational interviews, being constructed from critical job-relevant incidents, in principle pose candidates with a number of highly relevant and informative scenarios. Whether interviewees commit them to memory or are affected by them longer term is doubtful, but the situational interview may impact unconsciously upon candidate expectations and/or attitudes to the job role.

§ Integrity/honesty tests and drug/alcohol tests are likely to affect candidate expectations of the subsequent treatment by the organization (see also footnote *). Such methods may even *sensitize* candidates to these issues and, perversely, might suggest that the candidate should learn to lie well and/or cover-up their use of controlled substances if they wish to work for this organization!

employees has positive effects for both individuals and organizations. While socialization models indicate that this process can begin prior to organizational entry, little theoretical or empirical work has specified the mechanisms through which the socialization process can commence pre-entry. In this chapter we proposed that socialization begins during selection and that the selection process is an important mechanism that impacts the socialization process. Selection procedures and applicants' encounters with such procedures can influence both the process of socialization and the outcomes of socialization.

Selection procedures can have profound impacts on socialization by providing information, influencing expectations and attitudes, and affecting behaviours. Research is sorely needed to further establish the links between selection procedures and their socialization impact. In particular, studies are needed which elucidate further the particular types of impact (e.g. informational, preferential, expectational, attitudinal and behavioural) and the extent of such impact of different types of selection procedures. Some selection procedures, for example work sample tests, can provide a great deal of realistic job-relevant information but may fail to provide realistic information about the organizational context; hence their socialization impact is limited to job-specific information and expectations. Other procedures may provide little in the way of specific job information (e.g. personality tests, drug tests), but can have profound influences at the organizational level on the expectations and attitudes of candidates.

Given that the areas of socialization and selection have developed independently, most of the socialization impact of selection procedures has proceeded unintentionally. That is, most organizations are unaware, regardless of having conducted predictive validity studies, of the socialization impact of their selection procedures. However, if selection conveys messages, establishes expectations, promotes attitude formation and impacts behaviours, all of which can impact newcomers' subsequent socialization and integration, it is of both theoretical and real practical concern to understand more specifically such impact. And, not only should organizational practitioners *intentionally* build into selection procedures desired types of socialization impact, they should also ensure that the messages conveyed provide realistic information, expectations, and appropriate attitudes.

Of further concern is the creation of complementary selection and socialization procedures and practices. Rarely, if ever, are selection and socialization considered as a continuum. Yet, as we have argued, socialization clearly can begin during pre-entry and selection and post-entry socialization can be strongly impacted by these pre-entry processes. Taking the view that the ultimate goal is to integrate employees through person–job fit *and* person–organization fit, the appropriate combination of selection and socialization can achieve this goal. The impact of selection procedures on both types of fit should first be evaluated, then post-entry socialization practices should be designed to 'fill in the gaps' with more or less emphasis placed on job-specific versus organizationally specific aspects of achieving fit.

Relatedly, in the traditional selection model, criteria focus on the candidate's ability to perform aspects of the job or job duties either directly or indirectly (see Guion, Chapter 13 in this volume). Yet, taking the view that selection and socialization are a single, longitudinal process creating integration of employees into the organization implies that a focus on job-specific behaviours as the sole criteria for evaluation of the utility of a selection procedure is too restrictive. For example, it is likely that some selection procedures may have low criterion-related validity, in the traditional sense, but may have stronger validity for satisfaction, commitment, adjustment, person–organization fit, and other outcomes of socialization and integration (Chatman, 1991; Schneider and Schmitt, 1986; Ostroff and Rothausen, 1996). Indeed, there are even circumstances where we can envisage that an organization may choose to use an assessment technique having lower predictive validity in order to maximize the socialization impact of its selection procedure. Thus, a broader view of criteria should be considered when evaluating the usefulness of any selection procedure owing to impact on socialization and the outcomes of socialization and integration.

CONCLUSION

We have argued in this chapter that selection and socialization are systemic elements of a single overarching process of integration, and therefore that selection methods possess varying degrees of impact upon candidates. We proposed the concept of socialization impact as an integrative framework, which was subdivided into five types of impact—informational, preference, expectational, attitudinal, and behavioural. Selection has traditionally focused on predicting job-specific fit. Yet, full integration into the organization requires more than job-specific fit; fit to the organization is required as well. While post-entry socialization has traditionally been the means through which full integration and person–organization fit is achieved, we argue that selection begins the socialization and integration process. Selection techniques are not only predictors of job-specific fit, but because they possess varying degrees of socialization impact, they facilitate socialization, and hence may impact broader attitudes and behaviours of employees. When socialization and selection systems are designed in such a way to complement each other, full integration and effective functioning of employees can be achieved appropriately and efficiently.

ACKNOWLEDGEMENT

We thank the staff of Personnel Decisions Research Institute, Minneapolis, for participating in an idea generation session which contributed to an earlier draft of this chapter.

REFERENCES

Anderson, N.R. (1992). Eight decades of employment interview research: A retrospective meta-review and prospective commentary. *European Work and Organizational Psychologist*, **2**, 1–32.

Anderson, N.R. and Ostroff, C. (1995). *The Socialization Process: Organizational Tactics, Individual Differences, Learning, and Outcomes.* Symposium conducted at the Tenth Annual Conference of the Society for Industrial and Organizational Psychology, Orlando, USA, May 1995.

Anderson, N.R. and Thomas, H.D.C. (1996). Work group socialisation. In M. West (ed.), *Handbook of Work Groups.* Chichester: John Wiley.

Arnold, J.D. (1994). Opportunity for skill use, job changing, and unemployment as predictors of psychological well-being amongst graduates in early career. *Journal of Occupational and Organizational Psychology*, **67**, 355–370.

Arvey, R.J. and Sackett, P.R. (1993). Fairness in selection: Current developments and perspectives. In N. Schmitt and W. Borman (eds.), *Personnel Selection*, pp. 171–202. San Francisco, CA: Jossey-Bass.

Bowen, D.E., Ledford, G.E. and Nathan, B.R. (1991). Hiring for the organization, not the job. *Academy of Management Executive*, **5**, 35–51.

Bretz, R.D. Jr, Ash, R.A. and Dreher, G.F. (1989). Do people make the place? An examination of the Attraction–Selection–Attrition hypothesis. *Personnel Psychology*, **42**, 561–581.

Brousseau, K.R. (1984). Job–person dynamics and career development. In K.M. Roland and G.R. Ferris (eds.), *Research in Personnel and Human Resources Management*, vol. 2, pp. 125–154. Greenwich, CT: JAI Press.

Buchanan, B. (1974). Building organizational commitment: The socialization of managers in work organizations. *Administrative Science Quarterly*, **19**, 533–546.

Cable, D. and Judge, T.A. (1994). Pay preferences and job search decisions: A person–organization fit perspective. *Personnel Psychology*, **47**, 317–348.

Chao, G.T., Kozlowski, S.W.J., Major, D.A. and Gardner, P. (1994a). The effects of organizational tactics and contextual factors on newcomer socialization and learning outcomes. In

S.W.J. Kozlowski (chair), *Transitions During Organizational Socialization: Newcomer Expectations, Information-seeking, and Learning Outcomes.* Symposium conducted at the 9th Annual Conference of the Society for Industrial and Organizational Psychology, Nashville, TN, April 1994.

Chao, G.T., O'Leary-Kelley, A.M., Wolf, S., Klein, H.J. and Gardner, P.D. (1994b). Organizational socialization: Its content and consequences. *Journal of Applied Psychology*, **79**, 730–743.

Chatman, J.A. (1991). Matching people and organizations: Selection and socialization in public accounting firms. *Administrative Science Quarterly*, **36**, 459–484.

Feldman, D.C. (1976a). A contingency theory of socialization. *Administrative Science Quarterly*, **21**, 433–452.

Feldman, D.C. (1976b). A practical program for employee socialization. *Organization Dynamics*, Autumn, 64–80.

Feldman, D.C. (1989). Socialization, resocialization and training: Reframing the research agenda. In Goldstein (ed.), *Training and Development in Organizations*, pp. 376–416. San Francisco, CA: Jossey-Bass.

Fisher, C.D. (1986). Organizational socialization: An integrative review. In K. Roland and G. Feris (eds.), *Research in Personnel and Human Resources Management*, vol. 4, pp. 101–145. Greenwich, CT: JAI Press.

Fletcher, C. (1991). Candidates' reactions to assessment centres and their outcomes: A longitudinal study. *Journal of Occupational and Organizational Psychology*, **64**, 117–127.

Giacalone, R.A. and Rosenfeld, P. (eds.) (1991). *Applied Impression Management: How Image-Making Affects Managerial Decisions.* London: Sage.

Gilliland, S.W. (1993). The perceived fairness of selection systems: An organizational justice perspective. *Academy of Management Review*, **18**, 694–734.

Gilliland, S.W. (1994). Effects of procedural and distributive justice on reactions to a selection system. *Journal of Applied Psychology*, **79**, 691–701.

Gilliland, S.W. (1995). Fairness from the applicant's perspective: Reactions to employee selection procedures. *International Journal of Selection and Assessment*, **3**, 11–19.

Herriot, P. (1984). *Down from the Ivory Tower: Graduates and their Jobs.* Chichester: John Wiley.

Herriot, P. (1989). Selection as a social process. In M. Smith and I.T. Robertson (eds.), *Advances in Staff Selection.* Chichester: John Wiley.

Herriot, P. (1992). Selection: The two subcultures. *European Work and Organizational Psychologist*, **2**, 129–140.

Herriot, P. (1993). A paradigm bursting at the seams. *Journal of Organization Behavior*, **14**, 371–375.

Hesketh, B. and Robertson, I.T. (1993). Validating personnel selection: A process model for research and practice. *International Journal of Selection and Assessment*, **1**, 3–17.

Iles, P.A. and Robertson, I.T. (1989). The impact of personnel selection procedures on candidates. In P. Herriot (ed.), *Assessment and Selection in Organizations: Methods and Practice for Recruitment and Appraisal*, 1st edn. Chichester: John Wiley.

Judge, T.A. and Bretz, R.D. (1992). Effects of work values on job choice decisions. *Journal of Applied Psychology*, **77**, 261–217.

Liden, R.C. and Parsons, C.K. (1986). A field study of job applicant interview perceptions, alternative opportunities, and demographic characteristics. *Personnel Psychology*, **39**, 109–122.

Louis, M.R. (1980). Surprise and sense making: What newcomers experience in entering unfamiliar organizational settings. *Administrative Science Quarterly*, **25**, 226–251.

McFarlane Shore, L. and Tetrick, L.E. (1994). The psychological contract as an explanatory framework in the employment relationship. In C.L. Cooper and D.M. Rousseau (eds.), *Trends in Organizational Behaviour*, vol. 1, pp. 91–109. Chichester: John Wiley.

Morrison E.W. (1993a). Longitudinal study of the effects of information seeking on newcomer socialization. *Journal of Applied Psychology*, **78**, 173–183.

Morrison, E.W. (1993b). Newcomer information seeking: Exploring types, modes, sources and outcomes. *Academy of Management Journal*, **36**(3), 557–589.

Murphy, K.R. (1986). When your top choice turns you down: Effects of rejected offers on the utility of selection tests. *Psychological Bulletin*, **99**, 133–138.

Nicholson, N. (1984). A theory of work role transitions. *Administrative Science Quarterly*, **29**, 172–191.

Ostroff, C. and Kozlowski, S.W.J. (1992). Organizational socialization a learning process: The role of information acquisition. *Personnel Psychology*, **45**, 849–874.

Ostroff, C. and Rothausen, T.J. (1996). Selection and job matching. In D. Lewin, D. Mitchell and M. Zaidi (eds.), *Handbook of Human Resources*, Greenwich, CT: JAI Press.

Pervin, L.A. (1989). Persons, situations, interactions: The history of a controversy and a discussion of theoretical models. *Academy of Management Review*, **14**, 350–360.

Porter, L.W., Lawler, E.E. and Hackman, J.R. (1975). *Behavior in Organizations*. New York: McGraw-Hill.

Posner, B. and Powell, G.N. (1985). Female and male socialization experiences: An initial investigation. *Journal of Occupational Psychology*, **58**, 81–85.

Reichers, A.E. (1987). An interactionist perspective on newcomer socialization rates. *Academy of Management Review*, **12**(2), 276–278.

Robertson, I.T. and Smith, M. (1989). Personnel selection methods. In M. Smith and I.T. Robertson (eds.), *Advances in Selection and Assessment*, pp. 89–112. Chichester: John Wiley.

Robertson, I.T., Iles, P.A., Gratton, L. and Sharpley, D. (1991). The impact of personnel selection and assessment methods on candidates. *Human Relations*, **44**, 963–982.

Robinson, S.L. and Rousseau, D.M. (1994). Violating the psychological contract: Not the exception but the norm. *Journal of Organizational Behavior*, **15**, 245–259.

Rousseau, D.M. (1989). New hire perceptions of their own and their employer's obligations: A study of psychological contracts. *Journal of Organizational Behavior*, **11**, 389–400.

Ryan, A.M. and Sackett, P.R. (1987). Pre-employment honesty testing: Fakability, reactions of test-takers, and company image. *Journal of Business and Psychology*, **3**, 248–256.

Rynes, S.L. (1993). Who's selecting whom? Effects of selection practices on applicant attitudes and behavior. In N. Schmitt, W. Borman & Associates (eds.), *Personnel Selection in Organizations*, pp. 240–274. San Francisco, CA: Jossey-Bass.

Rynes, S.L. and Miller, H.E. (1983). Recruiter and job influences on candidates for employment. *Journal of Applied Psychology*, **68**, 147–154.

Rynes, S.L. and Connerley, M.L. (1991). Selecting with an eye to attraction: Applicant reactions to alternative selection procedures, Working paper, University of Iowa, Iowa City, USA.

Saks, A.M. (1995). Longitudinal field investigation of the moderating and mediating effects of self-efficacy on the relationship between training and newcomer adjustment. *Journal of Applied Psychology*, **80**, 211–225.

Schein, E.H. (1968). Organizational socialization and the profession of management. *Industrial Management Review*, **9**, 1–16.

Schein, E.H. (1978). Entry into the organizational career. In R.H.J. Hackman, E.E. Lawler III and L.W. Porter, *Perspectives on Behaviour in Organizations*. New York: McGraw Hill.

Schein, E.H. (1988). *Organizational Psychology*, 3rd edn. London: Prentice-Hall.

Schneider, B. (1983). Interactional psychology and organizational behavior. In L.L. Cummings and B.M. Staw (eds.), *Research in Organizational Behavior*, vol. 5. Greenwich, CT: JAI Press.

Schneider, B. (1987). The people make the place. *Personnel Psychology*, **40**, 437–453.

Schneider, B. and Schmitt, N. (1986). *Staffing Organizations*. Glenview, IL: Scott Foresman.

Smith, E.M. and Kozlowski, S.W.J. (1994). Socialization and adaption: Individual and contextual influences on social learning strategies. Paper presented at 9th Annual Conference of the Society for Industrial and Organizational Psychology, Nashville, TN, April 1994.

Thornton, G.C., III (1993). The effects of selection practices on applicants' perceptions of organizational characteristics. In H. Schuler, J.L. Farr and M. Smith (eds.), *Personnel Selection and Assessment: Individual and Organizational Perspectives*. London: Lawrence Erlbaum Associates.

Van Maanen, J. (1978). People processing: Strategies of organizational socialization. *Organizational Dynamics*, **14**, 19–36.

Van Maanen, J. (1995). The smile factory: Work at Disneyland. In B. Staw (ed.), *Psychological Dimensions of Organization Behavior*, 2nd edn, pp. 290–302. Englewood Cliffs, NJ: Prentice-Hall.

Van Maanen, J. and Schein, E. (1979). Toward a theory of organizational socialization. *Research in Organizational Behaviour*, **1**, 209–264.

Wanous, J.P. (1980). *Organizational Entry: Recruitment, Selection and Socialization of Newcomers*, 1st edn. Reading, MA: Addison-Wesley.

Wanous, J.P. (1992). *Organizational Entry: Recruitment, Selection, Orientation and Socialization of Newcomers*, 2nd edn. Reading, MA: Addison-Wesley.

Wanous, J.P. and Colella, A. (1989). Organizational entry research: Current status and future directions. In K. Rowland and G. Ferris (eds.), *Research in Personnel and Human Resources Management*, vol. 7, pp. 59–120. Greenwich, CT: JAI Press.

Wanous, J.P., Poland, T.D., Premack, S.L. and Davis, K.S. (1992). The effects of met expectations on newcomer attitudes and behaviors: A review and meta-analysis. *Journal of Applied Psychology*, **77**, 168–176.

Wanous, J.P., Reichers, A.E. and Malik, S.D. (1984). Organizational socialization and group development: Towards an integrative perspective. *Academy of Management Review*, **9** (4), 670–683.

de Wolff, C.J. and van den Bosch, G. (1984). Personnel selection. In P.J.D. Drenth, H. Thierry, P.J. Willems and C.J. de Wolff (eds.), *Handbook of Work and Organizational Psychology*. Chichester: John Wiley.

Chapter 21

From Job Analysis to Work Profiling: Do Traditional Procedures Still Apply?

Coert F. Visser and Wieby M. M. Altink

Adviesbureau Psychotechniek Utrecht B.V., Arthur van Schendelstraat 612, P.O. Box 1047; 3500 BA Utrecht, The Netherlands

Jen A. Algera

ARBONED hoogovens, P.O. Box 10.000; 1970 CA IJmuiden, The Netherlands

INTRODUCTION

Jobs are seen as interlinked building blocks of work within organizations. They are patches of tasks and responsibilities that, together, are intended to cover the work that needs to be done (Bridges, 1994). From this point of view, any job contributes in its own particular way to the achievement of organizational goals. It is essential for personnel managers and line managers to have adequate knowledge about the structure and dynamics of work and the relationship between work and people. Many decisions they have to make relate in one way or another to the match between people and jobs. That is why many human resources management decisions need to be preceded by a systematic analysis of work, traditionally referred to as 'job analysis'. In this chapter we first describe job analysis from a traditional perspective: What is it and why and how is it used? Then, some well-known job analysis techniques and instruments are reviewed and the use of a multi method approach is recommended. The second part of the chapter focuses on changes in organizations, in work, in human resources management and the consequences those changes have for the practice of analysing work. Contributors in Howard (1995) claim that not since the industrial revolution has the world experienced such a vast transformation in the nature of work as is now in progress. Jobs are no longer the rather static entities they have been in the past. In

International Handbook of Selection and Assessment, Edited by N. Anderson and P. Herriot.
© 1997 John Wiley & Sons Ltd.

fact, we believe that human resources management today requires a fundamentally new way of analysing work.

JOB ANALYSIS FOR SELECTION AND APPRAISAL

Many uses of job analysis have been identified (Levine, 1983). Cascio (1992), for instance, distinguishes 15 different applications within the area of human resources management. Although some methods for job analysis are supposed to be useful for many applications, in practice it turns out that speicifc methods are appropriate for specific areas of human resources management (Algera, 1991). In this chapter we focus on using job analysis in selection and appraisal, areas in which the role of job analysis has become increasingly important.

Ever since World War I, industrial and occupational psychologists have been actively involved in personnel selection. The importance of job analysis in personnel selection was recognized long ago. Freyd (1923) described personnel selection as a process consisting of 10 steps, job analysis being step one. He proposed job analysis as an indispensable basis for personnel selection. Most experts today agree that without an analysis of the job and the job demands, a recruitment and selection procedure cannot be done well. Job analysis has several different applications throughout selection procedures, like:

- a text for a personnel advertisement can be drawn up on the basis of it;
- it provides useful information for letting applicants know about the job content and job context;
- it provides information to be used for self-selection of potential candidates in the recruitment phase;
- a profile of job demands (criteria) can be formulated on the basis of job analysis;
- a set of selection tools (predictors) can be chosen or specifically designed;
- rejected candidates can be informed specifically about the decision in terms of the job profile produced through job analysis; by comparing the profile of the applicant with the profile of the job, a prediction can be made about his or her future performance in the job;
- selection tools, including the interview, can be specifically aimed at gathering information about the job demands.

In other words: job analysis is a binding and crucial element in a selection procedure (Algera and Greuter, 1993).

As in selection, job analysis plays an increasingly important role in designing performance appraisal systems. This is specifically the case in the United States where any performance appraisal instrument should be based on a systematic job analysis procedure in order to satisfy legal challenges. The legal requirements for performance appraisal systems in the United States are basically no different from those for any selection test. Such systems must be based on a job analysis that facilitates decisions with reliability and validity (Latham and Wexley, 1994).

WHAT IS JOB ANALYSIS?

Job analysis is usually defined as the systematic procedure of collecting and analysing information about jobs. By using some kind of structured job analysis method, or a combination of different methods, jobs are broken down into components. Basically job analysis consists of two elements: a job description and a job specification. A *job description* is a written description of the activities that have to be performed. Generally, a job description also contains information about tools and equipment used in the job and about the working conditions. So job descriptions specify the job content and the job context. The *job specification* indicates which specific skills, competences, knowledge, capabilities and other physical and personal attributes one must have to perform the job successfully. An acronym that is used to describe which types of attributes are referred to in job analysis is KSAO: knowledge, skills, abilities and other characteristics.

There are several methods of gathering information about jobs. The most frequently used method of collecting data is the *interview*. Interviews can be held with job incumbents, supervisors, human resources managers and other people who have knowledge about the job. In most cases interviews are held individually, but group interviews can be quite useful too. An example of these are the so-called SME (subject-matter expert) panels. A second way of collecting information is by *observing* someone performing the job. This method is only applicable for jobs with short cycle tasks that are dominated by *physical activities and observable routines*. A third method is using *questionnaires*. Through the years many different types of questionnaires have been developed. There are structured, semi-structured and open-ended questionnaires. A fourth method is using documentation about the job, like existing job descriptions. A final possibility of gathering job information is to perform the job itself as a job analyst.

Throughout the years numerous job analysis methods and approaches have been developed. One way of distinguishing approaches from each other is to look at the way jobs are described. Job analysis methods can be task oriented, behaviour oriented or attribute oriented.

Task-oriented (or work-oriented) methods analyse and describe jobs in terms of results or performed tasks. They yield very specific information. Because of that the descriptions are almost exclusively applicable for the analysed job. The comparability of different task oriented analyses usually is limited. An example of a task-oriented job analysis instrument is CODAP (Comprehensive Occupational Data Analysis Programs; Christal, 1974).

Behaviour-oriented (worker-oriented) methods describe work in terms of more general behaviours necessary to perform the job. This approach gives more opportunities to compare jobs with each other. An example of a predominantly behaviour oriented method is the Position Analysis Questionnaire (PAQ; McCormick, Jeanneret and Mecham, 1972).

Attribute-oriented (or trait-oriented) methods describe jobs in terms of personal characteristics demanded to perform the work successfully. Examples of these attributes are capabilities, personality traits, skills and knowledge. This method seems attractive for personnel selection, because comparisons between the attribute-oriented job profile and the person profile are easily made. A problem, however, is that the translation from job content and context to attributes is a hard one. This translation seems to be the exclusive domain of experts. Examples of attribute oriented job analysis methods are the ARS (Ability Requirements Scales; Fleischmann and Quaintance, 1984), the MJRQ (Minnesota Job Requirements Questionnaire (Desmond and Weiss, 1973) and the TTA (Threshold Traits Analysis (Lopez, Kesselman and Lopez, 1981).

UTILIZATION OF JOB ANALYSIS IN PRACTICE

In the selection literature authors have emphasized repeatedly the necessity of using job analysis in selection and appraisal. In practice, however, job analysis has proved to be much less popular than would be expected. (Ryan and Sackett, 1987). One reason for this is that practitioners often lack knowledge about the topic and about the value of job analysis. A second reason could be a shortage of good and easy-to-use job analysis systems. A third reason, related to the limited interest in practice, is that for a long period there has been little research or innovation (Pearn and Kandola, 1993).

A further factor has been that within the industrial and occupational psychology literature a fundamental doubt has been raised about the value of doing a job analysis in the selection context, by *meta-analyses* (Schmidt and Hunter, 1981). On the basis of results of this type of research it has been concluded that the validity of cognitive capacity tests can be generalized to a wide range of jobs (*validity generalization*). In other words, differences in job content and context would be of little or no significance in predicting future work performance. Although meta-analytical research has been a major breakthrough in research and has yielded a lot of significant knowledge, the above-mentioned conclusion regarding the value of job analysis seems premature. First, there has been methodological criticism against the procedure with which jobs have been grouped together into rather heterogeneous clusters. Secondly, incremental validity can be gained by using situation-specific predictors in addition to cognitive capacity tests. Thirdly, job analysis has more than one purpose and application in the selection and appraisal context. Besides being the basis for designing prediction models, job analysis has an important informative role. Finally, the development of currently popular selection methods such as assessment centres and situational questionnaires makes the use of *molecular* job analysis necessary. The relevance of job analysis for designing appraisal systems seems almost self-evident, especially since an increasing focus on fairness in performance appraisal has emerged in many countries, for example the United States, Canada and the United Kingdom (see Fletcher, Chapter 28 in this volume).

Since the mid-1970s there has been considerable attention in the United States to the topic of fairness in selection and appraisal both in the literature and in practice. The aim is to decrease the probability of adverse (or 'disparate') impact of selection and appraisal decisions on minority groups. A selection procedure can be defined as having adverse impact when proportionately fewer members of one (for instance) ethnic or gender group can meet the criteria. There has been quite a 'litigation explosion' that has put organizations under pressure to ensure that their selection and appraisal procedures are legally defensible. Arvey and Faley (1993) and Greuter and Algera (1989) discuss the topic more specifically. Cascio (1995) discusses the impact of the US 1990 Disabilities Act.

Relevancy for the content of the job to be performed has become a major demand of selection and appraisal systems and procedures. *Job relatedness* of predictors and criteria is something that has to be proven by (human resources) managers. Thompson and Thompson (1982) specified the following considerations if job analysis is used as evidence in legal proceedings:

- A formal job analysis must be performed. It is not enough to rely on informal knowledge about a job that 'everyone' knows that may be based on inaccurate stereotyped notions of the job demands. It must also occur before choosing a selection system, rather than as a retrospective analysis after the event.
- It must be well documented. It is not enough to simply carry around job information in the analyst's head.
- It should be collected from several, up-to-date sources. This will probably entail using different methods of analysis.
- The sample of people interviewed should be sufficient in number to capture the job information. The sample should present the full diversity of job incumbents (e.g. ethnic minorities, females, people with and without formal qualifications) to ensure the validity of the data.
- The job analysts should be properly trained in the different techniques to ensure that they collect objective information and are as free from bias as possible.
- The job analysis should determine the most important and critical aspects of the job and it is upon these that the key attributes and selection and evaluation for the job should be based.

These demands are rather strict. Recently, however, there seems to be a shift in the US provisions in favour of the employer rather than the employee (Latham and Wexley, 1994).

MULTI-METHOD APPROACHES TO JOB ANALYSIS

There is no one best way for doing a job analysis (Ash, 1988; Dunnette, 1976; Levine, Thomas and Sistrunk, 1988). Every method has its own strengths and weaknesses. Algera and Greuter (1993) mention frequently appearing shortcomings such as too little attention of job analysis methods to cognitive processes, like decision-making, assessing, problem-solving, prioritizing, etc. and too little attention to the context of the job. A way of overcoming specific shortcomings of separate methods is to combine different approaches in one procedure. An approach that leads to good results in practice is using interview techniques with more structured job analysis systems. A nice example of using a combination of job analysis methods is presented by Pearn and Kandola (1993). Below we describe a combination of two interview techniques (CIT and Repertory Grid) with a computerized structured job analysis system like PAQ and the Work Profiling System (WPS; Saville and Holdsworth Ltd, 1995a).

Critical Incidents Technique (CIT)

Four decades ago at the American Institute of Research, J. C. Flanagan developed the Critical Incidents Technique (CIT; Flanagan, 1954). The CIT is an interview technique used to investigate actual episodes of on-the-job behaviour. A critical incident is an event that:

- has actually happened
- had an effect that was of crucial importance for being successful in the job
- is not frequently occurring
- is relatively short lasting
- has directly involved the respondent him or herself
- has happened not too long ago.

The procedure is aimed at collecting observed incidents that are very important to job performance in the sense that they make the difference between success and failure, for example dealing with a serious complaint of a customer. The incidents are recorded as notes, stories or anecdotes about how a job-holder handles certain situations and from these a composite picture of job behaviour is built up. The interview itself can be structured as follows:

Introduction
- Explaining goal and approach.
- Explaining the technique.
- Explaining follow up after the interview.

Interview
- Warming up, focusing on the general objectives of the job.
- Thinking up critical incidents:
    Let the interviewee in 15 minutes describe globally several critical incidents. The incidents should be related to job objectives. Incidents with positive outcomes as well as negative outcomes should be included.
- Analysing the critical incidents
    (a) Globally.
    (b) Probing the situation.
    (c) Probing the role and the judgement of the person involved.
    (d) Analysing behaviours and personal attributes involved.

Example of a Critical Incident (Cascio, 1995)

On 14 January Mr Vin, the restaurant's wine steward, was asked about an obscure bottle of wine. Without hesitation, he described the place of vintage and bottling, the meaning of the symbols on the label, and the characteristics of the grapes in the year of the vintage.

The situational character of the CIT makes it very useful for developing assessment centres and appraisal systems, also because assessment and feedback on the level of behaviour can be done. This is probably the most important reason why this method is so popular.

Repertory Grid

The Repertory Grid is a technique developed from the Personal Construct Theory of Kelly (1955). Kelly described a construct as being like 'a basic dimension of appraisal', providing a bipolar basis for classifying information about the environment. In job analysis it is used for identifying the specific skills and characteristics possessed by effective job performers, which differentiate them from less effective. The Repertory Grid is usually applied with managers. They are asked to compare employees in order to identify the skills associated with success.

Position Analysis Questionnaire (PAQ)

The PAQ was developed by Ernest McCormick, one of the most important pioneers in the field of job analysis (McCormick, Jeanneret and Mecham, 1972). It has been one of the best known job analysis questionnaires for many years. The PAQ is a predominantly worker-oriented questionnaire. It contains 194 items (which McCormick calls *job elements*) of which 187 relate to job activities and the rest to other information. The items are divided into six categories that make up the job data section of the PAQ: Information input, Mental processes, Work output, Relationships with other persons, Job context and Other characteristics. Recently, the following computer-processing options have been added to the PAQ: Item analysis, showing the highest percentage scores; Dimension scores, providing scores of the job on 45 underlying clusters of elements; Human attribute scores; and Estimates of aptitude requirements. The validity of the PAQ is based on research that has tested the 'gravitation hypothesis', a supposition stating that people tend to gravitate into jobs they are able to perform successfully.

Work Profiling System (WPS)

A more recently developed job analysis system is the Work Profiling System (Saville and Holdsworth Ltd, 1995a). The WPS is a job analysis system containing three different questionnaires, respectively related to the following job groups: (1) Managerial and professional, (2) Service and administrative, and (3) Manual and technical. These three questionnaires each consist of a *job content* part (establishing the main tasks) and a *job context* part (physical environment, responsibility for resources, remuneration, etc.). The WPS is an integrated computerized job analysis system offering many output options. The WPS Technical Report provides a detailed and comprehensive picture of a job. Alternatively, the WPS can print out a number of simplified, modular reports that are appropriate for different applications. The WPS report options are:

1. Job description: a summary of the key job tasks and responsibilities.
2. Person specification: a summary of the key human attributes that a job requires.
3. Assessment methods: a selection of appropriate tests, personality questionnaire scales and interview questions that could be used to assess candidates for the job.
4. Individual development planner: a tailored development plan for job incumbents.
5. Performance review form: a tailored appraisal document for the job.
6. Person–job match: a facility for matching candidates against the key requirements for a job.

Recent developments in the WPS, incorporated in the 1995 update of the system, are discussed later in the chapter.

TRANSFORMATIONS IN WORK AND ORGANIZATIONS

The content of work and the concept of jobs is changing fast. This is caused by changes in organizations, work design, technological developments and views on managing human resources. To explore the context for applying job analysis in the future, we briefly describe some important changes below.

Changing organizations and work processes

For almost any organization the *complexity* of its environment is increasing. Demands of customers have become increasingly important. As customers, we nowadays require of products and services high quality, low prices and uniqueness. Furthermore, as customers, we constantly want new products and services.

At the beginning of the century, under the influence of the technology and insights of Scientific Management (Taylor, 1911), companies emerged with a high degree of labour division. Tasks were analysed and divided into sharply demarcated sub-tasks. Researchers worked out how each sub-task could be performed as efficiently as possible.

Tasks were divided into sub-tasks that resulted in very simple, short-cycle activities. Work became horizontally divided (a carpenter should hammer, not carry around planks) as well as vertically (thinking and doing, control and operation, supervision and operation). This labour division was carried through to such an extent that it resulted in *management as a profession*: processes became so complex that co-ordinators became necessary. Tasks became so simple that people had to be hired for thinking, deciding, assessing, prioritizing, etc. It also led to *functionally organized organizations*: work units were formed that performed tasks of only one type, for instance the Quality Control Department. Finally, it led to *staff departments*: tasks that required a specific knowledge were pulled out of the primary process of the organization, which resulted in departments like the Personnel Department.

The conditions that made the above processes useful and logical have changed. The current conditions do not allow such a high degree of labour division. Put simply, in the past, organizations had simple tasks and complex processes, which led to inflexible and slow production processes, that were however very efficient and thus very suitable for mass production. Nowadays, customers demand flexibility, speed and continuous product innovation, which demands that production processes be kept very simple but highly flexible. These simple processes lead to complex, broad, integrated tasks. So there is a *reversion of the process of labour division*, leading to complex tasks and simple processes.

The most important catalysts in the development of customer demands and competition between companies have probably been developments in information technology and communication facilities. The first has made new products and services possible, whereas the latter means that customers will instantly have knowledge of new possibilities.

These changes currently are a major focus of managers. Many recipes for improving organizations are related to the process of reversing labour division, like Sociotechniek (De Sitter and De Hartog, 1990), semi-autonomous work groups and Business Process Re-engineering (Hammer and Champy, 1993).

Changes in work

Coinciding with these organizational changes, work itself has changed (Bridges, 1994) in the following ways:

- Technology has changed virtually every workplace in a drastic way and will continue to do so in the years to come. Many workplaces have been *informated* (Van der Spiegel, 1995). More and more people have become used to working with computers, expert systems and computerized performance support systems (Winslow and Bramer, 1994).
- There is an increasing emphasis on working with data, information and knowledge. Drucker (1993) talks about the post-industrial economy as an 'Information Age', Tapscott (1996) talks about the 'Digital Economy'. There has been a significant shift in workplaces from manufacturing and transporting things to manipulating and transforming data and information, a development which management writer Peter Drucker has been emphasizing for a long time. He

used the label *knowledge work* to describe this new way of working. In Drucker's vision, those workers that are not educated enough will become service workers.

- New *communication technologies* change work. Because of new communication facilities, time and distance are no longer effective buffers against change. Tapscott (1996) describes the influences of things like the Internet and group-ware technologies on work, which will probably be enormous.
- There are *change-driven changes*. The changes mentioned above have caused more changes by the way organizations react to them. Organizations seem to be caught in a spiral of ever-increasing competition.
- *Simplification of work processes* is a major change factor.
- Organizations are limiting their activities to those parts of the business where they have special competence and are *outsourcing* the rest to external vendors.
- In order to be able to produce in a flexible manner, work is being packaged more and more in *projects*, carried out by temporary task forces.

New ways of managing human resources

Human resources management (HRM) is a movement or trend in personnel man-agement that has become influential since the early 1980s (Fombrun, Tichy and Devanna, 1984; Beer, 1984). Until that period personnel management in many cases was seen as a necessary evil with no relation whatsoever to organizational strategy. Through the influence of HRM thinking, managing human resources today has become a top priority of both line and top managers in most organiza-tions. There are four key aspects of HRM:

- *Coherence:* there has to be coherence between different personnel management activities.
- *Development orientation:* personnel management should be focused on develop-ing individuals.
- *Strategic:* personnel management should be derived from the organizational strategy and aimed at achieving organizational goals.
- *Line responsibility:* managing human resources should primarily be a respon-sibility of line management.

The extent to which these prescriptions have been realized in practice is, however, very patchy.

Jobshift: Workplaces without jobs?

A job analysis can only be useful when or if a job is reasonably stable and not in a period of rapid evolution. Recently Bridges (1994) observed that jobs have lost that stability for good. He argues that the very conditions (mass production and the large organization) that created jobs 200 years ago are disappearing. He thinks we have lost the need to package work into jobs. Bridges describes several disad-vantages of working with the concept 'job':

- It encourages hiring personnel by cutting work into turfs and by giving managers a level of power commensurate with the number of turf areas for which they are responsible.
- It discourages accountability, because it rewards people not for getting the necessary work done but for doing their jobs.
- It is a rigid solution to an elastic problem, because the work that needs to be done changes constantly.
- Jobs are change inhibitors: conventional jobs inhibit flexibility and speedy response to the threats and opportunities of a rapidly changing market.

Many organizations are concentrating on their most important tasks and outsourcing the rest to temporary and contract workers or to external vendors. Bridges' observation: in a job-based organization, work is not done but passed around.

Furthermore, Bridges proposes that new ways of dealing with employment insecurity have to be found. Employability, vendor-mindedness and resiliency, in his opinion, need to be central focuses.

Next, new ways of packaging work have to be developed. Bridges proposes: self-employment, freelance work, part-time work and working as full-time employees but under fluid and idiosyncratic arrangements. With the latter he refers to flexible job profiles, sets of competencies and working with role instead of job descriptions. Pritchard and Murlis (1992) also refer to roles, rather than to jobs. They define 'role' as an entity within the organization which takes account of the organization's requirement (the 'job') as well as of the characteristics of the person doing the job. They operationalize the role concept as:

- Achievements and outputs required by the organization.
- Skills, knowledge and expertise required in the role.
- The competencies which characterize the role.

Finally, employees' attitudes toward work should be changed with the help of education. People should be educated about the higher outcomes the organization is trying to achieve and show them that their 'piece of work' fits in the larger pattern.

Jobs seem to lose their stability more and more. Alternatives must be found both for the concept of job as we know it and for the systems and procedures built around the concept. In relation to the above described processes Pritchard and Murlis (1992) see as main features of organizational change:

- Delayering of organizations to yield much flatter structures.
- Increasing recognition of project and team work.
- Organizational flexibility.
- Multiple reporting relationships.
- Job flexibility.
- Jobs designed to expand, not constrain.
- People make jobs.

How will all of this influence work? Howard (1995) thinks work in the post-industrial economy will be:

1. Cognitive: the focus will be on cerebral skills rather than manual.
2. Complex: organizations, tasks, and role scripts will be complex and broad.
3. Fluid: jobs will be difficult to tie down, they will continuously change.
4. Uncertain: uncertainty in the organization environment causes uncertainty in jobs.
5. Interconnected: through information technology work and people will be interconnected.
6. Invisible: the abstraction of work form hands-on, manual labour to manipulation of electronic images on a computer screen is making work invisible.

JOB ANALYSIS IN THE FUTURE

Below we try to describe some major challenges for job analysis in order to be able to cope in the environment described above. Job analysis procedures should be able to:

1. *Measure dynamics of the work:* Measuring the kind, the degree and the rate of change in a job.
2. *Identify job families:* In the past, jobs were grouped by the tasks performed. With the rate of the changes in tasks and considering the mobility of personnel, new ways of grouping job have to be found.
3. *Teamwork analysis:* We think it will be necessary for job analysis systems in the future to analyse work on a team level. Team tasks will continue to show far more continuity than tasks at an individual level. Job analysis systems will have to be able to describe team tasks, context and specifications. Also they will have to be able to specify different roles to be performed in order by team members (see West and Allen, Chapter 24 in this volume).
4. *Strategy orientation:* Within job analysis more attention for the organization strategy will have to be built in.
5. *Competence, behaviour and trait orientation:* The trend towards behaviour-oriented (or worker-oriented) systems will be continued. However, the trait-oriented approach will still remain necessary, to predict performance trans-situationally.
6. *More focus on the 'O' in KSAO.* In the future more focus on the Other characteristics will be needed because workers will be more self-managing. They will have more authority in and control over their work (Landy, Shankster-Cawley and Kohler Moran, 1995).
7. *Stronger orientation towards knowledge work:* Job analysis should be focused more to cognitive behaviours in order to be able to describe knowledge work.
8. Integrated HRM systems: The trend of integrating job analysis in computerized HRM systems will probably be an important future development.

Some innovative systems have been designed recently. A good example of a system is the earlier mentioned recently updated version of Work Profiling System (WPS;

Saville and Holdsworth Ltd, 1995a) which already incorporates a lot of the answers to the developments described above. For instance, in the new Windows-based WPS much advanced information technology is applied: the questionnaire can be administered by computer; reports can be generated by computer (supported by an expert system); competencies can be generated by computer. Furthermore, it is a typical HRM supporting system. It can be used as a module in an integrated computer-based HRM system (HURMIS; Saville and Holdsworth Ltd, 1995b). Among the advantages and possibilities of such systems are:

- Incorporating a family of products (such as occupational assessment, job analysis, expert, translating, scanning and statistical systems) within one shell (a series of modules that can be installed separately).
- Interoperating products: the products can work together with one another and share data and functions.
- Common interface: all products work under one operating system and share tools, displays, etc.
- Data-sharing: information on tests, questionnaires, etc. needs to be only in one place in the system (and not duplicated).

Also, the HRM style of thinking is recognizably present in WPS. It is concentrating on outputs like job descriptions and person specifications, performance management, remuneration and reward, competency building and individual development. Finally, it creates a possibility for working organization-oriented. The system contains pre-tailored reports, which can be tailored for organizations in terms of used competency models.

Although the nature of work is changing drastically and continuously, job analysis stays important. In the future new job analysis systems and new versions of older ones will continue to appear. We advise practitioners to pay proper attention to job analysis, specifically to new topics like teamwork, changes in jobs, and new demands.

REFERENCES

Algera, J.A. (1991). Arbeidsanalyse tenbehoere van motivatie en satisfactie. In J.A. Algera (ed.) *Analyse van arbeid vanuit verschillende perspectieven*, 143–177. Amsterdam/Lisse: Swets & Zeitlinger.

Algera, J.A. and Greuter, M.A.M. (1993). Functie-analyse. *Nieuw Handboek A&O-psychologie*, aflevering 11.

Arvey, R.D. and Faley, R.H. (1993). *Fairness in Selecting Employees*, 2nd edn. Reading, MA: Addison-Wesley.

Ash, R.A. (1988). Job analysis in the world of work. In: S. Gael, ed., *The Job Analysis Handbook for Business, Industry and Government*, pp. 3–13. New York: John Wiley.

Beer, M. (ed.) (1984). *Managing Human Assets*. New York: The Free Press.

Bridges, W. (1994). *Jobshift: How to Prosper in a Workplace Without Jobs*. Reading, MA: Addison-Wesley.

Cascio, W.F. (1992). *Managing Human Resources, Productivity, Quality of Worklife, Profits, Third edition*. New York: McGraw Hill.

Cascio, W.F. (1995). *Managing Human Resources, Productivity, Quality of Worklife, Profits, Fourth edition*. New York: McGraw-Hill.

Christal, R.E. (1974). *The United States Air Force Occupational Research Project* (AFHRL-TR73-75). Lackland Air Force Base, Texas: Occupational Research Division.

Desmond, R.E. and Weiss, D.J. (1973). Supervisor estimation or abilities required in jobs. *Journal of Vocational Behavior*, **3**, 181–194.

Drucker, P.F. (1993). *Post-Capitalist Society*. New York: HarperCollins.

Dunnette, M.D. (1976). Aptitudes, abilities, and skills. In M.D. Dunnette (ed.), *Handbook of Industrial and Organizational Psychology*, pp. 473–520. Chicago, Rand McNally.

Flanagan, J.C. (1954). The critical incident technique. *Psychological Bulletin*, **51**, 327–358.

Fleischmann, E.A. and Quaintance, M.K. (1984). *Taxonomies of Human Performance*. New York: Academic Press.

Fombrun, C.J., Tichy, N.M. and Devanna, M.A. (1984). *Strategic Human Resources Management*. New York: John Wiley.

Freyd, M. (1923). Measurement in vocational selection: An outline of a research procedure. *Journal of Personnel Psychology*, **2**, 215–249, 377–385.

Greuter, M.A.M. and Algera, J.A. (1989). Criterion development and job analysis. In P. Herriot (ed.), *Assessment and Selection in Organizations*. New York: John Wiley.

Hammer, M. and Champy, J. (1993). *Reengineering the Corporation*. New York: HarperCollins.

Howard, A. (ed.) (1995). *The Changing Nature of Work*. San Francisco, CA: Jossey-Bass.

Kelly (1955). *The Psychology of Personal Constructs*, 2 vols. New York: Norton.

Landy, F.J., Shankster-Cawley, L. and Kohler Moran, S. (1995). Advancing personnel selection and placement methods. In A. Howard (ed.), *The Changing Nature of Work*. San Francisco, CA: Jossey-Bass.

Latham, G.P. and Wexley, K.N. (1994). *Increasing Productivity Through Performance Appraisal*. Reading, MA: Addison-Wesly.

Levine, E.L. (1983). *Everything You Always Wanted to Know About Job Analysis and More . . . A Job Analysis Primer*. Tampa, FL: Marines Publishing.

Levine, E.L., Thomas, J.N. and Sistrunk, F. (1988). Selecting a job analysis approach. In S. Gael (ed.), *The Job Analysis Handbook for Business, Industry and Government*, pp. 3–13. New York: John Wiley.

Lopez, F.M., Kesselman, G.A. and Lopez, F.E. (1981). An empirical test of a trait-oriented job analysis technique. *Personnel Psychology*, **34**, 479–502.

McCormick, E.J., Jeanneret, P.R. and Mecham, R.C. (1972). A study of job characteristics and job dimensions as based on the Position Analysis Questionnaire (PAQ). *Journal of Applied Psychology*, **56**, 347–368.

Pearn, M. and Kandola, R. (1993). *Job Analysis: A Manager's Guide*, second edition. London: IPM House.

Pritchard, D. and Murlis, H. (1992). *Jobs, Roles and People, the New World of Job Evaluation*. London: Nicholas Brealey.

Ryan, A.M. and Sackett, P.R. (1987). A survey of individual assessment practices by I/O psychologists. *Personnel Psychology*, **40**, 455–487.

Saville & Holdsworth Ltd (1995a). Work Profiling System (WPS, updated version). London: SHL.

Saville & Holdsworth Ltd (1995b). HURMIS, Human Resources Management Information System. London: SHL.

Schmidt, F.L. and Hunter, J.E. (1981). Old theories and new research findings. *American Psychologist*, **36** (10), 1128–1137.

Sitter, L.U. de and Hartog, J.F. den (1990). Simple organizations, complex jobs: The Dutch sociotechnical approach. MERIT, paper presented at the American Academy of Management, San Francisco.

Tapscott, D. (1966). *The Digital Economy, Promise and Peril in the Age of Networked Intelligence*. New York: McGraw-Hill.

Taylor, F.W. (1911). *The Principles of Scientific Management*. New York: Harper.

Thompson, D.E. and Thompson, T.A. (1982). Court standards for job analysis in test validation. *Personnel Psychology*, **35**, 865–874.

Van der Spiegel, J. (1995). New information technologies and changes in work. In A. Howard (ed.), *The Changing Nature of Work*. San Francisco, CA: Jossey-Bass.

Winslow, C.D. and Bramer, W.L. (1994). *Future Work: Putting Knowledge to Work in the Knowledge Economy*. New York: The Free Press.

Chapter 22

Structured Selection Interviews: Why Do They Work? Why Are They Underutilized?

ROBERT L. DIPBOYE

Department of Psychology, Rice University, 6100 Main Street, Houston, TX 77005, USA

INTRODUCTION

The ubiquitous use of the unstructured selection interview in organizations attests to the faith that both employers and applicants have in the casual and unrestrained face-to-face conversation as a technique of selection. Several decades of research have challenged this faith by showing that a more formal and structured approach is needed for interviews to achieve acceptable levels of reliability and validity. This chapter presents evidence that structuring the interview can improve reliability and validity as the result of avoiding and overcoming biases inherent in human judgment. But should selection interviews be evaluated solely on the basis of psychometric standards (Anderson, 1992; Herriot, 1993)? And can interview types that fall short on psychometric standards be justified on the basis of their other contributions to the organization (Dipboye, 1994)? The irony is that so many organizations persist in the use of intuitive approaches to selection despite the empirical evidence. Largely ignored in the research on interviews is the possibility that selection procedures fulfill other functions besides providing a good fit of employees to their jobs. This chapter considers some of the forces that work against structured interviews and calls for a reconciliation between psychometric concerns and the diverse organizational functions served by selection techniques.

International Handbook of Selection and Assessment, Edited by N. Anderson and P. Herriot.
© 1997 John Wiley & Sons Ltd.

META-ANALYSES OF INTERVIEW VALIDITY

A major conclusion emerging from several recent meta-analyses is that structured interviews are more valid and reliable than interviews that are unstructured (Huffcutt and Arthur, 1994; McDaniel *et al.*, 1994; Wiesner and Cronshaw, 1988). For instance, Huffcutt and Arthur (1994) distinguished four levels of interview structure on the basis of the standardization of questioning and response scoring. The observed validities for the four levels were 0.11, 0.20, 0.34, and 0.34 for levels 1 (least structure) through 4 (most structure), respectively. After correcting for criterion unreliability and range restriction, the validities were 0.20, 0.35, 0.56, and 0.57. Similar conclusions are found in previous qualitative reviews, but these meta-analyses have provided more precise estimates as the result of correcting for the statistical artifacts that attenuate validity estimates. Moreover, the corrected validities for highly structured interviews are surprisingly high and comparable with the validities obtained with cognitive ability tests (Searcy *et al.*, 1993; Wiesner and Cronshaw, 1988; McDaniel *et al.*, 1994; Huffcutt and Arthur, 1994).

The evidence is convincing that structured interviews are highly valid, but the studies providing the input to the meta-analyses have left unresolved several important questions. Perhaps the most basic question is: What are the features in structured interviews that can account for their superior psychometric qualities? Several programs of structured interviewing have been proposed. The following five are perhaps the most prominent structured interviewing programs.

Situational interview

Latham *et al.* (1980) base this approach on the hypothesis that intentions are among the best predictors of behavior. In the design of a situational interview, a critical incident job analysis is first conducted to identify the dimensions on which applicants are evaluated. Those incidents that best represent each of the dimensions are turned into questions that take the basic form: What would you do if you were in this situation?

Interviewers do not preview the application or other ancillary data on the applicant prior to the interview. In the actual conduct of the session, interviewers ask each of the questions exactly as they are worded in the guide, with no follow-ups or variations allowed. The applicant is then rated on each of the dimensions using behaviorally anchored rating scales that are anchored with exemplars of good, mediocre, and poor answers. The mean of these ratings forms the final judgment of the applicant.

The highly structured interview

This is an eclectic interviewing approach that combines a mix of biographical, situational, patterned behavior description, and knowledge questions. However, it is the most structured of all the interviewing formats proposed so far. In this approach, Campion, Pursell and Brown (1988) list a set of requirements to guide the development of the procedure: (1) a job analysis is conducted to determine the dimensions used to evaluate applicants and questions are constructed on the basis of this analysis; (2) interviewers ask exactly the same questions with no follow-ups or variations allowed; (3) anchored scales are used to evaluate applicants and to ensure consistency across interviews; (4) note-taking is encouraged to avoid memory decay; (5) interviewers do not preview the paper credentials of the applicants prior to the sessions; (6) panels are used in interviewing and rating the applicants; (7) the final judgment is formed by a simple average of the panel members' ratings; (8) the process is administered in exactly the same way for all applicants with no variations. An underlying philosophy of this approach is adherence to the legal guidelines for non-discrimination as set forth in US laws and regulations.

Patterned behavior description interview

Unlike the situational interview which asks the applicant 'what would you do if . . .?', the patterned behavior description interview (PBDI) asks 'what did you do when . . .?' (Janz, Hellervik and Gilmore, 1986). As in the case of the situational interview, the design of a PBDI begins with a critical incidents job analysis to determine the dimensions on which applicants are evaluated. Questions are developed from these incidents that ask about past behaviors that are related to each dimension. For instance, if the critical incident analysis of sales job revealed that dealing with difficult customers is an important part of the job, then an applicant might be asked: 'Tell us about the most difficult new client contact you made in the last six months.' Interviewers are encouraged to take concise notes and to use follow-up questions to probe the applicant's answers. As soon after the interview as possible, the interviewers use graphic scales to rate the applicants on the dimensions identified in the critical incidents analysis.

The LIMRA structured interviewing guide

The Life Insurance Marketing and Research Association (LIMRA) in the United States has developed a semi-structured interviewing package for the selection of life insurance agents that has been thoroughly researched over the last three decades. Prior to the conduct of the interview, the interviewer is given the opportunity to preview the applicant's scored biodata. A structured guide sets forth questions to ask for each of 11 dimensions that have been identified through job analysis as important in the performance of insurance agents (e.g. communication ability, ability to control situations, interpersonal relations skills, time management and administrative ability). Interviewers are allowed to ask follow-up questions and are expected to take notes on the applicant's answers. At the end of the interview the interviewer rates the applicant on each of the 11 qualifications dimensions and indicates whether the applicant should be considered for employment.

Multimodal interview

Perhaps the least structured of these alternative interviewing formats is the multimodal employment interview (MEI). As described by Schuler and Funke (1989), the MEI is a semi-structured, task-oriented procedure that adapts several different procedures for use in Germany. Highly structured procedures are often in-appropriate in Germany because of legal and cultural mandates that selection techniques be acceptable to applicants and the unions. The first step in the development of the interview is to conduct a critical incidents job analysis to determine the dimensions for evaluating applicants. Situational, PBDI, and self-presentation questions are then constructed to gather information on these dimensions. In the actual conduct of a session, interviewers follow the same pattern: (1) an introductory period of small talk, (2) self-presentation questions to assess expression, self-confidence, and liveliness, (3) questions about vocational interests and choices, (4) a period in which interviewers can ask whatever questions they wish, (5) biographical questions (some of which were structured along the lines of the PBDI), (6) a realistic job preview, and (7) a series of situational questions. Finally, applicants are allowed to ask the interviewer questions.

All these programs are highly job-related and are standardized in that they require coverage of the same topics. They differ, however, in the extent to which they impose constraints on the process. The situational interview and the highly structured interview allow very little discretion on the part of the interviewer and applicant, whereas the remainder impose common standards but allow some freedom in the conduct of the session. Programs of structured interviewing differ in other respects as well, and these are covered later in this chapter when the various strategies for improving interviews are discussed. An important area for future research is to determine the relative impact on validity and reliability of the various strategies that are contained in these interviewing programs.

Three other issues have been neglected that should be addressed in future valida-tion research. First, the criteria used in validating the interview need to be broad-ened to include contextual performances such as volunteering, good citizenship, and prosocial behavior. Although these criteria are almost always ignored, inter-views may be more suited to predicting performance in these contextual dimen-sions than in the core tasks of the job. Secondly, the research needs to take into account differences among individual interviewers. Not only is there evidence of substantial variation among interviewers but some individual interviewers may achieve very high levels of validity (Graves, 1993). A third recommendation is that researchers need to assess the incremental validity of interviewer judgments as well as their simple validity. Questions have been raised about whether interviews can contribute to the prediction of criteria beyond the contributions of less expensive paper-and-pencil measures such as cognitive ability tests (i.e. incremental validity: Campion *et al.*, 1988; Walters, Miller and Ree, 1993). Higher levels of incremental validity seem possible if structured interviews are explicitly designed to assess factors that are non-redundant with cognitive abilities (Roth and Campion, 1992; Campion, Campion and Hudson, 1994).

WHAT CAN GO WRONG IN THE INTERVIEW?

To understand why structured interviews are more valid and reliable than un-structured interviews, it is important to examine what can go wrong in a casual face-to-face session that would threaten the quality of interviewer judgments. The research on the selection interview has shown a variety of problems that seem more likely to occur in unstructured than structured interviewing.

Biased and undifferentiated theories of the ideal applicant

Problems in the typical unstructured interview process often appear to result from the idiosyncratic beliefs that individual interviewers bring to the session (Rowe, 1984). In selecting applicants, interviewers rely on their implicit theories of job requirements that are more vague than the detailed information on the knowledge, skills, and abilities (KSAs) that a formal job analysis would provide. These idiosyncratic and undifferentiated implicit theories (Hakel and Schuh, 1971) or cognitive prototypes (Anderson and Shackleton, 1990) appear to provide a poor basis for evaluating applicants for specific positions. One might expect that experienced interviewers would have more accurate and differentiated conceptions of job requirements than inexperienced interviewers (Graves, 1993), but the few studies directly addressing this issue have failed to show this (Dipboye, 1992).

Biased information-gathering

Possibly reflective of their implicit theories of job requirements, interviewers conduct interview sessions in ways that can bias information-gathering. Ideally, applicant behavior in an interview session is a window to the true attributes of the applicant and is uncontaminated by the way that the interviewer conducts the session. Contrary to this ideal, interviewers appear to form impressions of applicants early in the interview that can then bias the conduct of the session (Dipboye, 1992). The interviewer's opinions of the applicant can be communicated unintentionally (i.e. can 'leak') in the non-verbal and paralinguistic behavior of the interviewer and, in turn, the conduct of the session can influence how well applicants perform in presenting their qualifications (Dougherty, Turban and Callender, 1994). Among the interviewer behaviors that influence the applicant's performance in the interview are the effect displayed in non-verbal and paralinguistic behavior, the degree to which questions are open-ended vs. closed-ended, and the extent to which the interviewer dominates the session. These and other interviewer behaviors appear to influence self-presentation, especially among applicants who are low in self-esteem and perhaps more vulnerable to external influence (Liden, Martin and Parsons, 1993). In some circumstances, self-fulfilling prophecies can occur in which interviewer impressions bias applicant behavior in the direction of confirming these impressions (Dougherty, Turban and Callender, 1994). The outcome of these biases in the conduct of the session is that the information gathered reflects more on interviewer behavior in the session than the applicant's actual knowledge, skills, and abilities (KSAs).

Categorical and biased judgments

Prior to, during, and after gathering information on an applicant, interviewers are involved in judging the fit of the applicant's characteristics to the requirements of the job. Ideally, interviewers focus their attention on the KSAs important to the position and then infer from the information they have gathered the degree to which the applicant possesses each KSA. Moreover, they evaluate each separate KSA on its own merits without being influenced by information on other KSAs or other applicants. Contrary to this ideal, research suggests that the initial reaction of interviewers is to *categorize* the applicant as qualified or unqualified (Rowe, 1984). This initial judgment can occur automatically without much self-insight into the underlying reasons. Suggestive of this automaticity, Judge and Ferris (1992) have observed college recruiters to grasp for an explanation when asked to explain their evaluations of applicants, often attributing their evaluation to some nebulous 'fit' of the applicant to the situation. The specific categories that influence the perception of the applicant and the job can be activated in a serendipitous manner by factors irrelevant to the KSAs of the job, including the mood of the interviewer or the particular mix of candidates. Following the initial categorization is a process of *characterization* in which traits are inferred from the applicant's answers to questions and other behavior. Biases at this stage include the underestimation of the influence of the interviewer's own conduct of the session and the overestimation of the importance of the applicant's traits (Herriot, 1989a).

As information is encountered that contradicts initial categorization, one would expect interviewers to engage in a process of *correction* as they attempt to change their impressions to incorporate new information on an applicant. However, interview research has demonstrated numerous factors that can influence the ratings of applicant qualifications, including halo, negativity, primacy, contrast, similar-to-me effects, and personal liking for the applicant (Dipboye, 1992). These rating biases possibly reflect the continuing influence of initial categorizations. There is also evidence that impressions formed from information available before the interview are substantially related to impressions formed after the interview (Macan and Dipboye, 1990). The verbal and non-verbal style of the applicant's self-presentation can have a powerful influence on ratings of qualifications and can overwhelm objective information on the applicant. Finally, the race, age, disability, gender, and physical attractiveness of applicants can influence interviewer judgments, although the strength, consistency, and generalizability of these effects have been disputed (Stone, Stone and Dipboye, 1992).

Biases in decision-making

In some cases interviewers not only judge the applicant but also make decisions such as to hire, not hire, or gather more information. One would hope that these decisions are based on careful weighing of benefits and costs, but the organizational literature has repeatedly shown that decision-making in organizations can deviate from a rational model. According to Beach's (1990) image theory 'most decisions are made quickly and simply, on the basis of "fittingness", and only in particular circumstances are they made on the basis of anything like the weighing and balancing of gains and losses that is prescribed by classical decision theory ...' (p. xiii). Consistent with this observation, interviewers have been shown to make their decisions well before the end of the interview and sometimes very early in the process (Tullar, Mullins and Caldwell, 1979).

STRATEGIES FOR IMPROVING THE INTERVIEW PROCESS

Structuring the interview should allow more valid and reliable judgments as the consequence of avoiding or eliminating the biases in information-gathering, processing, and decision-making. What follows is a consideration of alternative strategies of structuring the interview and the ways that these strategies might improve the psychometric qualities of interviewer judgments.

Increasing the job-relatedness of the interview

One likely source of advantage for most structured interview procedures is that they are based on formal job analyses and are more content-valid than unstructured procedures. To ensure job-relatedness, a job analysis is conducted to determine the tasks that are critical to job performance of the KSAs needed to perform them. The KSAs are then translated into interview questions and well-defined rating scales. In support of this strategy, enhancing the job-relatedness of an interview has been shown to reduce the effects of irrelevant information and to increase the ability of raters to discriminate between qualified and unqualified applicants (Dipboye, 1992). Additional support comes from the meta-analyses of interview reliability and validity. Interview procedures that are based on formal job analyses have been found to yield higher validities (Wiesner and Cronshaw, 1988) and reliabilities (Conway, Jako and Goodman, 1994) than procedures based on informal or no job analyses. Also, interviews assessing psychological traits (e.g. dependability, leadership) are less valid than interviews assessing job-related factors (McDaniel *et al.*, 1994).

Increasing the job-relatedness of an interview improves validity and reliability, possibly as a result of enhancing information-gathering and processing. One benefit of this strategy is that it provides decision-makers with a common perspective on job requirements and thereby lessens the influence of the interviewers' idiosyncratic conceptions of the position. It also could focus the attention of the interviewer on the verbal content of the applicants' answers to questions while minimizing the effects of physical appearance, non-verbal behavior, gender, and other potentially irrelevant information. Still another benefit is that it could ensure that the interview will directly sample the criterion domain.

Limiting access to ancillary data

In the typical unstructured procedure, interviewers are given access to other data such as test scores and biographical data, and are free to use this information as they wish. The highly structured interview (Campion, Pursell and Brown, 1988) and the situational interview (Latham *et al.*, 1980) do not allow previews of ancillary information. Consistent with this practice, previewing the application has been shown to lower the reliability and accuracy of assessments as the result of increasing the variability with which the interview is conducted (Dipboye, Fontennelle and Garner, 1984). Also, previously meta-analyses have shown higher validities when interviewers do not have access to test scores (McDaniel *et al.*, 1994) and do not preview ancillary data (Searcy *et al.*, 1993).

Regardless of the negative effects that paper credentials might have on interviewer judgments, the chances are slim that these findings will deter interviewers from continuing to review paper credentials prior to the interview. Fortunately, there is evidence that interviewers can glean important information about applicants from previewing applications (Brown and Campion, 1994; Dalessio and Silverhart, 1994). Another important area for future research is to devise procedures for assessing ancillary data that complement rather than detract from the face-to-face interview.

Standardizing the information-gathering process

A key feature of structured interviews is that they standardize the process by which information is gathered by holding interviewers to the same line of questioning. In the case of highly structured (Campion, Pursell and Brown, 1988) and situational (Latham *et al.*, 1980) interviews, exactly the same questions are asked in the same order with no follow-ups or probes. Requiring the same questions of all interviewers should help ensure that information gathered in the session reflects the actual qualifications of the applicant rather than biases in the conduct of the session. However, not all selection researchers agree with this prescription. For example, European I/O psychologists have been critical of imposing a highly standardized process, arguing that it is too mechanical, too inflexible, and artificially inflates validity and reliability by minimizing 'processual variance' between interview interactions (Anderson, 1992; Herriot, 1989b). Moreover, some structured interviewing procedures run the risk of becoming orally administered biodata instruments (Dipboye, 1989; Robertson and Smith, 1989). A possible compromise is represented by the PBDI (Janz, Hellervik and Gilmore, 1986) and the LIMRA structured interview guide (Dalessio and Silverhart, 1994), which hold interviewers to the same general topics but allow them to pursue independent lines of questioning.

Improving the rating process

Structured interviews incorporate a variety of rating procedures that have been shown in previous research to enhance the accuracy and reliability of judgments. Note-taking is encouraged in some structured procedures to reduce errors in recall (Janz, Hellervik and Gilmore, 1986). Additionally, interviewers rate applicants on separate dimensions using well-defined rating scales, such as behaviorally anchored scales. These decomposed ratings are then combined statistically through summing or averaging. In contrast, unstructured interviews typically require holistic ratings of overall qualifications, use poorly defined graphic scales, and rely on intuitive strategies of combining data on the applicant.

Note-taking could be discouraged as well in the interest of facilitating a two-way conversation between applicant and interviewer.

Laboratory research has generally supported the rating procedures that are frequently incorporated in structured interviews. More accurate interview ratings have been observed with behaviorally anchored rating scales (Vance, Kuhnert and Farr, 1978) and note-taking (Macan and Dipboye, 1994). Decomposed rating procedures have been shown to improve the quality of evaluations and to encourage more complex decision strategies (Dipboye, 1992), although the effectiveness of decomposed ratings is dependent upon whether the dimensions encompass the important KSAs (Searcy *et al.*, 1993). Finally, a statistical approach to combining data is almost always superior to an intuitive approach (Meehl, 1986).

Using multiple interviewers

Using more than one interviewer to judge the qualifications of applicants is not considered an essential aspect of structured interviewing, but it is frequently mentioned as an important means of improving validity and reliability. Although it is a possible means of correcting for the idiosyncratic biases of individual interviewers, previous meta-analyses have either concluded that the use of multiple interviewers yields levels of validity that are the *same as* (Wiesner and Cronshaw, 1988; Marchese and Muchinsky, 1993) or *lower than* (Searcy *et al.*, 1993; McDaniel, *et al.*, 1994) the validities found with single interviewers.

Unfortunately, the research that has been the source of data in these meta-analyses provides a limited basis for comparing the effectiveness of single and multiple interviewers. Very few studies have examined the problems that could prevent a group of interviewers from making valid judgments. One exception is a recent study in the United States in which the racial composition of an interview panel was found to influence evaluations (Lin, Dobbins and Farb, 1992). Predominately black panels tended to be biased in favor of black applicants and predominately hispanic panels were biased in favor of hispanic applicants.

Previous research has also failed to distinguish among the various forms of group interviews. Interviewers can conduct the session and evaluate applicants either together as a group (i.e. the classic panel interview) or separately. Likewise, a variety of different methods can be used in reaching a decision. In simple averaging, panel members independently rate the applicant and then average their ratings to form a final judgment (see Campion, Pursell and Brown, 1988). In consensus decision-making the panel members discuss the applicant until they reach an agreement as to the rating that the applicant should receive. In the nominal group technique, the panel would minimize discussion by silently generating ideas about the candidate and then voting on the rating that the applicant should receive. After each round of voting there is a period of discussion that clarifies the opinions of the panel. Among the more confrontational of the techniques are dialectical inquiry and devil's advocacy. In dialectical inquiry one subgroup develops a recommendation and a second subgroup is appointed to present the opposite recommendation. The second subgroup attempts to negate the assumptions of the first subgroup. In the devil's advocacy approach one subgroup presents a recommendation and the second attacks this recommendation without presenting an alternative. In both of these last two approaches the subgroups are expected to come back together and eventually agree on mutually acceptable solutions. A fruitful direction for research is to delve into the relative benefits of these various group procedures on the evaluation of applicant qualifications.

Training the interviewer in interviewing skills

Training usually accompanies the implementation of structured interviewing. Interviewers typically are instructed in how to conduct the session and evaluate applicants to increase the consistency of information-gathering and judgments and thereby enhance reliability and validity. Improving interviewing skills should also release cognitive resources that can be allocated to processing information and rendering judgments. There are only a few studies that have evaluated interviewer training, however, and the few that exist have failed to provide convincing evidence of its efficacy in improving the psychometric qualities of interviewer judgments (Conway, Jako and Goodman, 1994). In the only study that has examined the effects of training on interviewer validity (Dougherty, Ebert and Callender, 1986), an extensive four-day training program was found to increase validity. This study involved only three interviewers, however, and will need to be replicated with larger samples to determine its generalizability. Given that training is the most common strategy for improving interviews, much more research is needed to determine its value in improving the quality of interviewer judgments and to identify the features of successful training programs.

IF STRUCTURED INTERVIEWS ARE SO EFFECTIVE, WHY AREN'T THEY USED MORE FREQUENTLY?

There are several strategies of structuring an interview that can be used to raise the validity and reliability of interviewer judgments, including increasing job-relatedness, providing limited access to ancillary data, and standardizing questions. It should be noted that the recent upsurge of interest in the structured interview possibly reflects a North American concern with compliance to equal employment legislation. Europeans are not faced with the same equal employment constraints and have been much less receptive. Even in North America, however, the unstructured interview remains the most popular approach to selecting employees despite the evidence to support structured approaches. In those situations where structured interviews are implemented, one can question whether they remain structured (Anderson and Shackleton, 1993; Dipboye, 1994; Latham and Saari, 1984).

The preference for unstructured interviews seems to be part of a widespread reliance on intuitive decision procedures (Beach, 1990; Dawes, 1988). For instance, basic research on decision processes has shown a general tendency to go beyond simple decision rules to the detriment of the accuracy of judgments, even when the rules clearly aid accuracy (Arkes, Dawes and Christensen, 1986). It is proposed here that forces are at work in organizations that tend to support unstructured interview procedures and that act against structured procedures. The remainder of this chapter examines some of these forces. Given the scant research that has been conducted on this issue in the context of employment interviews, however, what follows could be considered more a list of hypotheses than a statement of fact.

Sources of resistance to structured interviews

Why would organizations persist in the use of interview procedures that are inferior in their reliability and validity? It could be that structured interview formats are not fully accepted because the evidence presented on their behalf is not persuasive. Research on utility has raised hopes that expressing the benefits of these innovations in terms of financial gain will win decision-makers over to structured procedures. Contrary to this supposition, however, a recent study found that managers were not readily influenced by utility analyses demonstrating the financial benefits of a selection procedure (Latham and Whyte, 1994). A more fundamental issue, according to Johns (1993), is that administrators frame personnel practices such as interview procedures as 'matters of administrative style' rather than in technical terms. It could be further argued that unstructured interviews serve legitimate functions that structured interviews fail to fulfill (Dipboye, 1994). These other functions include recruiting, the personal needs of the decision-maker, providing a good fit to the job content, maintaining and acquiring power, and expressing the values of the organization.

Concerns about recruiting

To provide a good fit to the context, the right type of person must be attracted to join the organization. While structured selection procedures allow an accurate assessment of candidates, those procedures may harm the ability to recruit applicants. There are several reasons why unstructured procedures may provide a better basis for recruiting. Applicants are more favorably disposed to interviewers who are attentive, warm, thoughtful, socially perceptive, and likable in their conduct of the session (Dipboye, 1992), and unstructured interviews are likely to allow the communication of these qualities better than structured interviews. The flexibility of the unstructured procedure enables the interviewer to shift away from assessment and concentrate on recruitment when the applicant is highly qualified. Finally, and perhaps most importantly, unstructured procedures seem to be preferred by applicants, possibly because they allow more control over the situation (Schuler, 1993; Latham and Finnegan, 1993).

The personal needs of the interviewer

For structured interview procedures to be successfully implemented, interviewers must want to use the procedures as they were originally intended (Lewis and

Seibold, 1993). Thus, failures to implement structured procedures could reflect the personal dissatisfaction of interviewers with these procedures. For interviewers who value the role of interviewing and see it as an important part of their position, a highly structured procedure could be seen as deskilling the task and reducing it to a boring, monotonous exercise, while an unstructured interview could offer challenge and autonomy. Individual differences seem likely to moderate these preferences. Interviewers who see interviewing as a burdensome task and who place little importance on the interviewing role may well prefer structured procedures. Self-image is another potential moderator (Meehl, 1986, p. 374). Interviewers who have faith in the validity of their judgments may be the most reluctant to use structured procedures, whereas those who have a more modest view of their perceptiveness could be the most accepting of structured procedures.

Providing a good fit of the applicant to the job context

The emphasis in structured interviewing is on providing a good fit to the KSAs of the job, and yet an increasing number of organizations are moving toward a model of staffing in which persons are selected for *organizational membership* (Bowen, Ledford and Nathan, 1991). In this emerging model, the ideal candidate becomes the person who not only has KSAs that fit a job but who shares the values and goals of the organization, is prosocial, and is a good organizational citizen. This pressure to provide a good fit to the context can pull decision-makers in the direction of intuitive practices and can lead to a degradation of structured procedures. For instance, Bowen, Ledford and Nathan (1991) observe that the attempt to achieve a good person–organization fit has led some organizations to engage in selection practices that seemingly violate the prescriptions of structured interviewing. Not only are the procedures costly, extravagant, and inefficient, but the process is 'full of ambiguity, lacks formal rules, and demands that all employees engage in problem solving to get themselves hired' (p. 35). Judge and Ferris (1993) argue that 'calls for structured interviews as a way to improve the validity of the interview may be misplaced if the true goal, and utility, of the interview lies not in selecting the most technically qualified, but the individual most likely to fit into the organization' (p. 23). (See also Schneider *et al.*, Chapter 19 in this volume.)

Just as an unstructured procedure allows the organization a better basis for assessing fit to the context than structured procedures, unstructured procedures also allow the applicant to make better choices among organizations and jobs. There are at least two reasons for this. In an unstructured procedure the interviewer can provide realistic previews of the job, while the applicant is able to ask questions about whether there is a match to his or her abilities, interests, goals, values, and needs. Additionally, the interviewer and applicant are better able to negotiate a mutually agreeable psychological contract. By contrast, a highly structured interview allows the applicant little opportunity to gather information or influence the conditions of employment. Whether unstructured procedures can actually lead to better applicant decisions remains untested, but the *perception* that they are superior in this respect is an additional reason why they are preferred over structured procedures.

Another advantage of unstructured interviews in providing a good person–organization fit is that they can serve as a preliminary socialization tactic used to change the prospective employees' attitudes to conform to the culture (see also Anderson and Ostroff, Chapter 20 in this volume). As the first significant encounter with the organization, selection procedures can be used to 'unfreeze' potential new hires and shake them loose from previous attitudes, values, and norms, perhaps as a consequence of subjecting the applicant to a stressful interrogation. Interviews in the Tandem Corporation, for example, have been described as 'inquisitions', conveying the message that employment is a privilege reserved for the very few who qualify (Deal and Kennedy, 1982). Southwest Airlines, one of the most successful airlines in the United States, uses teams of current employees to interview applicants. These freewheeling sessions make the hiring process an important initiation into the organizational culture. On the other hand, the exclusive focus on the KSAs of the job of structured procedures seem less likely to allow this early socialization of the new hire.

Maintaining procedural and distributive justice

Unstructured procedures may be preferred because they are seen as fairer by both interviewer and applicant. At first glance this statement may seem counterintuitive considering that structured procedures should ensure consistency in the treatment of the applicants (see also Iles and Robertson, Chapter 27 in this volume). However, an unstructured interview may be *perceived* as fairer by those who must implement it because they allow the decision-maker the flexibility to implement whichever rule seems to fit the situation (e.g. equality, equity, need). Take, for example, an interviewer who believes that minority applicants have been disadvantaged in past hiring decisions. In the interest of fairness, this interviewer might well prefer an unstructured procedure because it allows him/her to bias the session in favor of minority applicants. Likewise, structured procedures are avoided because their inflexibility prevents the interviewer from bending the rules to fit what seems most fair in the situation.

When evaluated in terms of a procedural justice perspective, unstructured interviews appear to be fairer than structured interviews in some respects but unfair in other respects. Consider the 10 procedural rules that Gilliland (1993) has applied in judging the fairness of selection systems: (1) job relatedness, (2) opportunity to perform, (3) reconsideration opportunity, (4) consistency of administration, (5) feedback, (6) justification for the decision, (7) honesty, (8) interpersonal effectiveness, (9) two-way communication, and (10) propriety of questions. Structured interviews should be more consistent, more job-related, and less vulnerable to improper questioning, but unstructured interviews are likely to have more two-way communication, a higher quality of interaction, and more opportunity to perform. Recent research on so-called interactional justice (Tyler and Bies, 1990) suggests that these latter three attributes are especially important and can overshadow other aspects of procedural justice.

Acquiring and maintaining power

A potentially 'dark side' of unstructured interviews is that they offer several advantages to decision-makers seeking power and influence. With unstructured procedures the interviewer can influence the decision by controlling the alternatives and the information on the alternatives, and by stressing those criteria that favor their preferences (Pfeffer, 1981). Unstructured procedures also make it easier to use perhaps the most blatant source of power, i.e. coalition building. For instance, Pfeffer (1981) has described how executives at General Motors Corporation built a power base by promoting unqualified candidates. Obviously, selection procedures that are based on careful analysis of job requirements and that are standardized would make coalition tactics such as these hard to accomplish without revealing the underlying motivation for those using them. The inherent ambiguity of unstructured interviews can prevent close scrutiny and monitoring of the selection process, providing still another reason why they would be preferred over structured interviews. Thus, unstructured interview procedures might allow departments in an organization to avoid monitoring of their selection practices by outside parties, such as the HRM department or governmental agencies. Although potentially harmful to the organization, a blanket condemnation of political activity seems naive. In situations characterized by rapid change and uncertainty, a strict adherence to predetermined rules could be disastrous while political activity may be essential to organizational well-being and survival (Pfeffer, 1981).

The symbolic functions of the interview

The last and most compelling reason why unstructured procedures might dominate the selection process is that they serve the symbolic function of conveying the values that are at the core of the organization's culture. So strong are the cultural functions of many organizational practices that they persist even though there is little evidence that they serve their manifest goals effectively. Similarly, the typical unstructured interview can be akin to a ritual conveying to others the important attributes of the organization and sending the message that great care is being taken to select a qualified applicant. Even though unstructured interview procedures may not allow the interviewer to make reliable and valid assessments, they are a richer vehicle for communicating values than structured interviews.

The idea that interview procedures are devoid of instrumental value but rich in symbolic value is consistent with institutional theory (Meyer and Rowan, 1977). From this perspective, selection procedures acquire symbolic value as the result of demonstrating to participants in the environment of the organization (e.g. potential customers, stockholders, competitors, government agencies) that legitimate techniques are being used in the hiring of employees. Innovative procedures may be avoided out of fear that important constituencies of the organization will see them as bizarre or unusual. Thus, unstructured interviews are embraced, especially in attempting to fill higher level positions, because they are considered normal, universally accepted ways of hiring people. Structured interviews, on the other hand, are deviations from the norm and may be avoided in the interest of pleasing the constituencies of the organization. An example would be the hiring of faculty in universities. One of the reasons that faculty do not subject prospective colleagues to structured interviews is to avoid the negative image that such procedures would convey to the academic community. It should be noted that the absence of structured interviews in faculty selection could reflect other factors that have been discussed (i.e. power, recruiting, etc.) as well as the difficulty of developing and validating structured procedures in 'small settings'. Still, the failure of those in academia who advocate the highly structured approach to practise it themselves is an interesting irony.

Slippage in the implementation of structured interviews

Once structured interviews are introduced, all the above-mentioned forces could prevent them from being fully implemented. Lewis and Seibold (1993) have reviewed evidence of slippages in implementation in the form of low matches between the intended and actual use of innovations (i.e. lack of fidelity) and unevenness in their implementation across situations and time (i.e. lack of consistency). Structured interviews are subject to similar slippages as the result of a dynamic interplay among selection procedures, the social system that these procedures serve, and the personal needs of those implementing the procedures.

A lack of fidelity and inconsistency in the implementation of structured interviews seems more likely in some situations than in others. Ouchi's (1977) model of organizational control offers some potential hypotheses for situations in which structured interviews are more likely to be fully implemented. He proposes that two task dimensions need to be considered when deciding on the type of management control to exert in a situation: (1) the completeness of knowledge of cause–effect relationships, and (2) the degree to which there are crystallized standards of desirability on which participants can evaluate outcomes. Where there is clear knowledge of cause–effect relationships and a consensus as to preferred outcomes, structured selection procedures seem more likely to be embraced and successfully used by the organization. Where there is incomplete knowledge of cause–effect relationships and disagreement over the preferred objectives, it could be hypothesized that unstructured procedures are not only preferred but may be more appropriate. Using highly structured procedures in this situation assumes that there is knowledge about how work is accomplished in the job and what constitutes a good performance, when in fact there is considerable uncertainty about both. By imposing a false sense of certainty, a structured procedure may do more harm than good, especially when the organization is undergoing rapid change and having to compete in a turbulent environment.

CONCLUSIONS

Two major themes were expressed in this chapter that run parallel to the division that exists between human resource management and organizational behavior.

On the one hand, much of the research on the interview has stressed psychometric concerns. The major emphasis has been on assessing individual differences so as to provide a good fit of the person to the position. This research has provided clear support for structuring the interview process to constrain what can be asked and to focus evaluations on the KSAs required in the job. On the other hand, the research and theory in organizational behavior provide insight into the multiple functions that selection procedures serve in addition to providing a fit to the job. While structured interviews clearly achieve higher levels of reliability and validity, unstructured interviews are likely to continue as the dominant mode of selection because they fulfill a variety of functions and provide flexibility to the user.

What are the implications of this dilemma for the practitioner? The evidence is compelling that structuring the interview process can improve the reliability, accuracy, and validity of interviewer judgments. At the least, practitioners should use job analyses as the basis for designing interview procedures and should standardize to some extent the questioning and rating procedures. The unbridled confidence that so many interviewers have in the value of unstructured procedures is clearly unwarranted. At the same time that practitioners can clearly benefit from incorporating structured elements into their interviewing procedures, however, they can go too far in this direction. Not only is there evidence that increasing structure beyond a moderate level may fail to enhance validity (Huffcutt and Arthur, 1994), but over-structuring the process may frustrate other functions served by the selection process. The other functions that I have discussed in this chapter can serve as a checklist for thinking about the implications of interviewing procedures. In structuring the interview, the practitioner needs to carefully consider the impact of the procedures on the needs of those who must do the interviewing, the politics and culture of the organization, recruiting, fairness, and providing a good fit to the job context. In some cases, a highly structured interview procedure may be quite compatible with all of these factors (e.g. the author was informed by a colleague that a highly structured procedure was warmly embraced by the US Federal Bureau of Investigation). In many situations, however, the author suspects that a semi-structured procedure may be a wiser alternative. In any case, pracitioners should attempt to obtain the commitment of those who will implement the interviewing procedure by involving them in its development.

The implication for practice should become clearer as more research is conducted on the dynamics involved in implementing structured interviews and other innovations in human resource management. Research is needed that tracks the use of structured techniques over time and that explores the various factors that can inhibit acceptance of innovative selection practices. Such empirical investigation should allow the identification of the conditions under which structured interviews achieve the best long-term results and ways of integrating the best aspects of structured procedures with the best of aspects of unstructured approaches. In short, it is time to start building bridges to span the gaps that exist in research on the interview between psychometric concerns and the often messy dynamics of the organization.

REFERENCES

Anderson, N.R. (1992). Eight decades of employment interview research: A retrospective meta-review and prospective commentary. *European Work and Organizational Psychologist*, **2** (1), 1–32.

Anderson, N.H. and Shackleton, V.J. (1990). Decision making in the graduate selection interview: A field study. *Journal of Occupational Psychology*, **63**, 63–76.

Arkes, H.R., Dawes, R.M. and Christensen, C. (1986). Factors influencing the use of a decision rule in a probabilistic task. *Organizational Behavior and Human Decision Processes*, **37** (1), 93–110.

Beach, L.R. (1990). *Image theory: Decision making in personal and organizational contexts.* Chichester: John Wiley.

Bowen, D.E., Ledford, G.E., Jr and Nathan, B.R. (1991). Hiring for the organization, not the job. *Academy of Management Executive*, **5** (4), 35–50.

Brown, B.K. and Campion, M.A. (1994). Biodata phenomenology: Recruiters' perceptions and use of biographical in résumé screening. *Journal of Applied Psychology*, **79** (6), 897–908.

Campion, M.A., Campion, J.E. and Hudson, J.P. (1994). Structured interviewing: A note on incremental validity and alternative question types. *Journal of Applied Psychology*, **79** (6), 998–1002.

Campion, M.A., Pursell, E.D. and Brown, B.K. (1988). Structured interviewing: Raising the psychometric properties of the employment interview. *Personnel Psychology*, **41** (1), 25–42.

Conway, J.M., Jako, R.A. and Goodman, D.F. (1994). A meta-analysis of moderators of selection interview reliability. Paper presented at the Ninth Annual Conference of the Society for Industrial and Organizational Psychology, Nashville, TN.

Dalessio, A.T. and Silverhart, T.A. (1994). Combining biodata test and interview information: Predicting decisions and performance criteria. *Personnel Psychology*, **47** (2), 303–315.

Dawes, R.M. (1988). *Rational Choice in an Uncertain World.* San Diego, CA: Harcourt Brace Jovanovich.

Deal, T.E. and Kennedy, A.A. (1982). *Corporate Cultures: The Rites and Rituals of Corporate Life.* Reading, MA: Addison-Wesley.

Dipboye, R.L. (1989). Threats to the incremental validity of interviewer judgments. In R.W. Eder and G.R. Ferris (eds.), *The Employment Interview: Theory, Research, and Practice*, pp. 45–60. Newbury Park, CA: Sage.

Dipboye, R.L. (1992). *Selection Interviews: Process Perspectives.* Cincinnati, OH: South-Western.

Dipboye, R.L. (1994). Structured and unstructured selection interviews: Beyond the job-fit model. In G. Ferris (ed.), *Research in Personnel and Human Resources Management*, vol. 12, pp. 79–123. Greenwich, CT: JAI Press.

Dipboye, R.L., Fontenelle, G.A. and Garner, K. (1984). Effects of previewing the application on interview process and outcomes. *Journal of Applied Psychology*, **69** (1), 118–128.

Dougherty, T.W., Ebert, R.J. and Callender, J.C. (1986). Policy capturing in the employment interview. *Journal of Applied Psychology*, **71** (1), 9–15.

Dougherty, T.W., Turban, D.B. and Callender, J.C. (1994). Confirming first impressions in the employment interview: A field study of interviewer behavior. *Journal of Applied Psychology*, **79** (5), 659–665.

Gilliland, S.W. (1993). The perceived fairness of selection systems: An organizational justice perspective. *Academy of Management Review*, **18** (4), 694–734.

Graves, L.M. (1993). Sources of individual differences in interviewer effectiveness: A model and implications for future research. *Journal of Organizational Behavior*, **14** (4), 349–370.

Hakel, M.D. and Schuh, A.J. (1971). Job applicant attributes judged important across seven diverse occupations. *Personnel Psychology*, **24** (1), 45–52.

Herriot, P. (1989a). Attribution theory and interview decisions. In R.W. Eder and G.R. Ferris (eds.), *The Employment Interview: Theory, Research and Practice*, pp. 97–109. Newbury Park, CA: Sage.

Herriot, P. (1989b). Selection as a social process. In M. Smith and I.T. Robertson (eds.), *Advances in Staff Selection*. Chichester: John Wiley.

Herriot, P. (1993). A paradigm bursting at the seams. *Journal of Organizational Behavior*, **14** (4), 371–375.

Huffcutt, A.I. and Arthur, W., Jr (1994). Hunter and Hunter (1984) revisited: Interview validity for entry-level jobs. *Journal of Applied Psychology*, **79** (2), 184–190.

Janz, T., Hellervik, L. and Gilmore, D.C. (1986). *Behavior Description Interviewing: New, Accurate, Cost-Effective*. Boston, MA: Allyn and Bacon.

Johns, G. (1993). Constraints on the adoption of psychology-based personnel practices: Lessons from organizational innovation. *Personnel Psychology*, **46** (3), 569–592.

Judge, T.A. and Ferris, G.A. (1992). The elusive criterion of fit in human resources staffing decisions. *Human Resource Planning*, **15**, 47–67.

Latham, G.P. and Finnegan, B.J. (1993). Perceived practicality of unstructured, patterned, and situational interviews: In H. Schuler, J.L. Farr and M. Smith (eds.), *Personnel Selection and Assessment: Individual and Organizational Perspectives*, pp. 41–55. Hillsdale, NJ: Lawrence Erlbaum.

Latham, G.P. and Saari, L.M. (1984). Do people do what they say? Further studies on the situational interview. *Journal of Applied Psychology*, **69** (4), 569–574.

Latham, G.P., Saari, L.M., Pursell, E.D. and Campion, M. (1980). The situational interview. *Journal of Applied Psychology*, **65** (4), 422–427.

Latham, G.P. and Whyte, G. (1994). The futility of utility analysis. *Personnel Psychology*, **47** (1), 31–46.

Lewis, L.K. and Seibold, D.R. (1993). Innovation modification during intraorganizational adoption. *Academy of Management Review*, **18** (2), 322–354.

Liden, R.C., Martin, C.L. and Parsons, C.K. (1993). Interviewer and applicant behaviors in employment interviews. *Academy of Management Journal*, **36** (2), 372–386.

Lin, T., Dobbins, G.H. and Farb, J. (1992). A field study of race and age similarity effects on interview ratings in conventional and situational interviews. *Journal of Applied Psychology*, **77** (3), 363–371.

Macan, T.M. and Dipboye, R.L. (1990). The relationship of interviewers' preinterview impressions to selection and recruitment outcomes. *Personnel Psychology*, **43** (4), 745–768.

Macan, T.M. and Dipboye, R.L. (1994). The effects of the application on processing of information from the employment interview. *Journal of Applied Social Psychology*, **24** (14), 1291–1314.

McDaniel, M.A., Whetzel, D.L., Schmidt, F.L. and Maurer, S. (1994). The validity of employment interviews: A comprehensive review and meta-analysis. *Journal of Applied Psychology*, **79** (4), 599–616.

Marchese, M.C. and Muchinsky, P.M. (1993). The validity of the employment interview: A meta-analysis. *International Journal of Selection and Assessment*, **1** (1), 18–26.

Meehl, P.E. (1986). Causes and effects of my disturbing little book. *Journal of Personality Assessment*, **50**, 370–375.

Meyer, J.W. and Rowan, B. (1977). Institutionalized organizations: Formal structure as myth and ceremony. *American Journal of Sociology*, **83** (2), 340–363.

Ouchi, W.G. (1977). The relationship between organizational structure and organizational control. *Administrative Science Quarterly*, **22** (1), 95–113.

Pfeffer, J. (1981). *Power in Organizations*. Marshfield, MA: Pittman.

Robertson, I.T. and Smith, M. (1989). Personnel selection methods. In M. Smith and I.T. Robertson (eds.), *Advances in Selection and Assessment*. Chichester: John Wiley.

Roth, P.L. and Campion, J.E. (1992). An analysis of the predictive power of the panel interview and pre-employment tests. *Journal of Occupational and Organizational Psychology*, **65** (1), 51–60.

Rowe, P.M. (1984). Decision processes in personnel selection. *Canadian Journal of Behavioral Science*, **16** (4), 326–337.

Schuler, H. (1993). Social validity of selection situations: A concept and some empirical results. In H. Schuler, J.L. Farr and M. Smith (eds.), *Personnel Selection and Assessment: Individual and Organizational Perspectives*, pp. 11–26. Hillsdale, NJ: Lawrence Erlbaum.

Schuler, H. and Funke, U. (1989). The interview as a multimodal procedure. In R.W. Eder and G.R. Ferris (eds.), *The Employment Interview: Theory, Research and Practice*, pp. 183–189. Newbury Park, CA: Sage.

Searcy, C.A., Woods, P.N., Gatewood, R. and Lance, C. (1993). The validity of structured interviews: A meta-analytical search for moderators. Presented at the Society of Industrial Organizational Psychology, San Francisco.

Stone, E.F., Stone, D.L. and Dipboye, R.L. (1992). Stigmas in organizations: Race, handicaps, and physical attractiveness. In K. Kelley (ed.), *Issues, Theory, and Research in Industrial and Organizational Psychology*, pp. 385–457. Amsterdam: Elsevier Science.

Tullar, W.L., Mullins, T.W. and Caldwell, S.A. (1979). Effects of interview length and applicant quality on interview decision time. *Journal of Applied Psychology*, **64** (6), 669–674.

Tyler, T.R. and Bies, R.J. (1990). Beyond formal procedures: The interpersonal context of procedural justice. In J.S. Carroll (ed.), *Applied Social Psychology and Organizational Settings*, pp. 77–98. Hillsdale, NJ: Lawrence Erlbaum.

Vance, R.J., Kuhnert, K.W. and Farr, J.L. (1978). Interview judgments: Using external criteria to compose behavioral and graphic ratings. *Organizational Behavior and Human Performance*, **22**, 279–294.

Walters, L.C., Miller, M.R. and Ree, M.J. (1993). Structured interviews for pilot selection: No incremental validity. *The International Journal of Aviation Psychology*, **3**(1), 25–38.

Wiesner, W.H. and Cronshaw, S.R. (1988). The moderating impact of interview format and degree of structure on interview validity. *Journal of Occupational Psychology*, **61** (4), 275–290.

Chapter 23

The Big Five as a Framework for Personality Assessment

GERALD MATTHEWS

Department of Psychology, University of Dundee, Dundee DD1 4HN, UK

INTRODUCTION: THE BIG FIVE AS A STRUCTURAL MODEL FOR PERSONALITY

Origins of the Big Five in lexical and questionnaire studies of personality

The search for a comprehensive system of personality description has been pursued for over 100 years. There is now a growing consensus among personality psychologists in favour of a five-factor model of broad traits: the Big Five. Goldberg (1993) has traced the development of the Big Five from two sources. The first source, pioneered by Galton, and Thurstone, is personality-descriptive terms in natural language. There are around 4500 trait-descriptive terms in the English language, which respondents may use to rate their own or others' personality. Factor analyses of systematically sampled selections of ratings consistently identify five major factors. Table 23.1 lists the 'lexical' Big Five, and some of the marker adjectives for each dimension identified by Goldberg (1992) from extensive psychometric investigations. Matthews and Oddy (1993) have used similar adjectives in developing the TOPAS adjective checklist measure for use in occupational settings, although they also identify some methodological difficulties in identifying the Big Five from lexical data alone.

The second, more recent, source of evidence is the identification of the Big Five in personality questionnaires. One of the most widely used questionnaires of this kind is Costa and McCrae's (1992a) Revised NEO Personality Inventory (NEO-PI-R), which assesses 30 trait facets, which define the five factors as shown in the lower part of Table 23.1. I shall use Costa and McCrae's abbreviations for the scales in the remainder of the chapter: E, N, C, A and O. Other questionnaires

---

International Handbook of Selection and Assessment, Edited by N. Anderson and P. Herriot.
© 1997 John Wiley & Sons Ltd.

Table 23.1 Big Five descriptors: Examples of Goldberg's (1992) marker adjectives, and the facet scales of the NEO-PI-R (Costa and McCrae, 1992a)

	Extraversion	Neuroticism	Conscien-tiousness	Agreeableness	Openness
	E	N	C	A	O
Adjectives	Talkative	Anxious	Organized	Kind	Intellectual
	Assertive	Moody	Systematic	Cooperative	Creative
	Verbal	Envious	Thorough	Sympathetic	Complex
	Energetic	Emotional	Neat	Warm	Imaginative
	Bold	Irritable	Efficient	Helpful	Artistic
vs.					
	Shy	Unemotional	Disorganized	Cold	Unintellectual
	Quiet	Relaxed	Careless	Unkind	Unimaginative
	Reserved	Imperturbable	Inefficient	Distrustful	Simple
	Inhibited	Unexcitable	Impractical	Harsh	Imperceptive
	Withdrawn	Undemanding	Sloppy	Rude	Shallow
Facet scales	Warmth	Anxiety	Competence	Trust	Fantasy
	Gregariousness	Angry hostility	Order	Straightforwardness	Aesthetics
	Assertiveness	Depression	Dutifulness	Altruism	Feelings
	Activity	Self-consciousness	Achievement striving	Compliance	Actions
	Excitement-seeking	Impulsiveness	Self-discipline	Modesty	Ideas
	Positive emotions	Vulnerability	Deliberation	Tender-mindedness	Values

measuring Big Five-like constructs include the Hogan Personality Inventory (Hogan, 1986) and the Professional Personality Questionnaire (Kline and Lapham, 1992). Further evidence for the generality of the Big Five is provided by studies showing that the Big Five may be identified in personality questionnaires developed to assess alternative dimensional models (Costa and McCrae, 1992b).

How basic are the Big Five?

There is little dispute that it is relatively easy to obtain measures of the Big Five from a variety of types of measurement of personality. A conservative reaction might be that the Big Five model provides a convenient, if somewhat arbitrary and artificial, means of characterizing some of the aspects of personality. However, proponents of the Big Five typically wish to advance beyond this conservative position, and claim that the Big Five represent some fundamental underlying psychological reality. Costa and McCrae (1992b) have defended this view in a paper entitled 'Four ways five factors are basic'. Their four criteria for basic dimensions are as follows:

1. The reality of factors
2. The pervasiveness of factors
3. The universality of factors
4. The biological basis of the factors

The reality of factors

The five-factor structure of personality may be obtained from self-ratings, ratings of known others such as peers and spouses, and even from ratings made on complete strangers. Ratings of particular traits made by different observers typically show a substantial level of inter-correlation. Furthermore, the Big Five are highly stable over time and predict important real-world criteria, as discussed below. Costa and McCrae (1992b) reject the social psychological view that personality traits are no more than socially constructed fictions.

The pervasiveness of factors

Concepts related to each of the Big Five appear to be indispensable in psychological theory; each has reappeared in many guises over the years. Empirical support for pervasiveness is demonstrated by the comparability of Big Five dimensions extracted from lexical data and from various questionnaires.

The universality of factors

The Big Five have been identified in many different cultures, although there may also be important differences between cultures (Yang and Bond, 1990). In Western societies, factor structures appear to be similar across men and women, different age groups and white and non-white respondents (Costa and McCrae, 1992a).

The biological basis of the factors

All five factors may be genetically influenced; Zuckerman (1991) suggests that personality traits typically have broad heritabilities in the range 0.4–0.6. Zuckerman (1991) has provided a comprehensive review of psychophysiological correlates of Big Five-like traits (particularly E and N): the evidence is extensive but confusing.

Criticisms of the five-factor model

Although many studies have extracted five-factor solutions from various data sets (Costa and McCrae, 1992b), the pervasiveness of the Big Five is not universally accepted. Eysenck (1992) has argued over many years for a three-factor dimensional model of personality super-factors, comprised of Extraversion (E), Neuroticism (N) and Psychoticism (P). Eysenck does not question the validity of the Big Five E and N factors, which his own work has done so much to establish (Eysenck and Eysenck, 1985). However, he suggests that A and C are primary facets of P, such that high P individuals tend to be disagreeable and lacking in conscience, and that O is a primary facet of Extraversion. Possibly, three- and five-factor models represent equally valid alternative levels of description (Zuckerman *et al.*, 1993).

Conversely, it might be argued that five factors are too few. No one, of course, claims that the Big Five fully accounts for variation in personality, and there is much debate (but no consensus) over descriptions of personality in terms of primary factors, such as Costa and McCrae's (1992a) 30 facet scales. There have been various attempts to develop fundamental systems of six or more dimensions, typically by splitting Big Five factors as summarized in Table 23.2.

Table 23.2   Some modifications and extensions to the Big Five

	E	N	C	A	O
Brand (1994)	Energy	Neuroticism	Conscience	Will (-)	(1) Intelligence (2) Affection
Hough (1992)	(1) Affiliation (2) Potency	Adjustment (-)	(1) Achievement (2) Dependability	Agreeableness	Intelligence
Hogan (1986)	(1) Sociability (2) Ambition	Adjustment (-)	Prudence	Agreeableness	Intelligence
Zuckerman *et al.* (1993)	(1) Sociability (2) Activity	Neuroticism– anxiety	Impulsive unsocialized sensation- seeking (-)	Aggression– hostility (-)	

For example, Brand (1994) argues that self-ratings of intelligence and intellectual interest are on a par with the Five. Intellectual openness, or 'general intelligence', should be distinguished from openness to feelings and to other people ('affection'), so that there are six rather than five basic factors.

Another area of difficulty is the place of traits such as achievement striving and activity within the Big Five. Such characteristics are of particular importance in occupational contexts, for identifying individuals with entrepreneurial, proactive qualities. Achievement orientation is normally seen as part of C, but it may be desirable to distinguish qualities of being dependable, meticulous, and painstaking from achievement-related qualities such as striving for success, and seeking a high degree of involvement in work (Hough, 1992). Matthews and Oddy (1993) found support for this distinction in lexical data. Ambition may also relate to E, which Hogan (1986) splits into sociability and ambition factors, giving a six-factor model. Activity or energy is often seen as a component of E too. Zuckerman *et al.* (1993) claim that the Big Five does not give sufficient importance to activity as a broad trait, and suggest it should be included in an 'Alternative Five'.

A final problem is that different 'Big Five' factor solutions may not, in fact, be psychometrically equivalent. For example, correlations between the Costa and McCrae scales and the Goldberg lexical factors range from 0.69 for E and N to 0.46 for O (Goldberg, 1992). These values are substantial, but (even allowing for unreliability of measures) are insufficiently high to demonstrate exact dimensional equivalence. As discussed in a recent special issue of the *European Journal of Personality* (1994, vol 8, number 4), on *The Fifth of the Big Five*, the nature of the Openness factor appears to present particular problems. However, correlations between questionnaire and lexical factors may under-estimate the true degree of convergence between different Big Fives, because of uncontrolled method variance (see Borkenau and Ostendorf, 1990).

ASSESSMENT OF THE BIG FIVE IN THE OCCUPATIONAL DOMAIN

Costa and McCrae (1992b) argue that the five factors should be identified in any reasonably comprehensive personality measure, including those used in applied

contexts. Results of such studies are critically dependent on f
of statistical methods which has proved controversial, beca
solutions may often be justified for any particular data set
1993). Statistical issues are beyond the scope of this ch
cautioned that it is generally agreed that factor analysis cannu.
resolve personality structure (Costa and McCrae, 1992b). In additiu.
tions are influenced by the sampling of items or scales in the questionna.
tigated; recovery of the Big Five is less likely if some of the Five are n.
extensively sampled than others.

Next, I briefly review evidence on recovery of the Big Five from two questionnaires based on comprehensive structural models for selection and assessment,
the 16PF and the OPQ. The role of the primary factor scales provided by these
instruments is also discussed. Costa and McCrae (1992a, 1992b) discuss various
other questionnaires used in occupational settings within which Big Five factors
have been identified, including the Myers–Briggs Type Indicator, the Revised
California Personality Inventory, the Edwards Personal Preference Schedule and
Holland's measure of vocational interests.

16PF and 16PF5

Cattell's (1973) structural model of personality has for many years distinguished
between primary and secondary factors, with the secondary factors extracted
from the inter-correlations of the 16 primary scales assessed by the 16PF. Cattell
(1973) describes eight second-order factors (which include the ability dimension
of Intelligence), but not all of these secondaries appear to be robust. Krug and
Johns (1986) ran a large-scale study which obtained six factors, resembling the Big
Five plus intelligence. Noller, Law and Comrey (1987) extracted seven factors
from a joint factor analysis of the 16PF and personality scales developed by
Eysenck and Comrey, of which the first five resembled the Big Five. Other studies
of the 16PF have obtained fewer second-order factors (Eysenck, 1992). Matthews
(1989) used criteria validated against simulation data to determine the optimal
number of factors to extract, which suggested that three secondary factors resembling Eysenck's dimensions should be extracted.

The 16PF has recently been extensively revised, and relaunched as the 16PF5
(Russell and Karol, 1994). Revision has been extensive: 51% of the items are new or
significantly changed. It now has a five-factor secondary structure (see Table 23.3),
comprising the five personality factors identified by Krug and Johns (1986), though
no overt reference to the Big Five structure is made. The new secondaries do not
fully correspond to those of the previous version of the 16PF. Russell and Karol
(1994) provide correlations between the 16PF secondary factors and the NEO-PI-R
facet scales. There appear to be fairly good correspondences between Extraversion
and E, Anxiety and N, and Self-Control and C. Tough-mindedness is more weakly
related to O (inversely). The remaining factor, Independence, is associated with
both high E and low A; there is no close correspondence between A and any of the
16PF5 secondaries. Hence, there are some similarities but no direct equivalence
between the Costa and McCrae Big Five and the secondaries of the 16PF5.

Table 23.3 Five secondary factors in the 16PF5 (Russell and Karol, 1994): factor pattern loadings > 0.4 are listed

Secondary factor	Big Five equivalent	Primary factor	Loading
Extraversion	E	Q2 (Self-reliance)	−0.81
		A (Warmth)	0.74
		F (Liveliness)	0.70
		N (Privateness)	−0.67
		H (Social boldness)	0.44
Anxiety	N	Q4 (Tension)	0.86
		O (Apprehension)	0.76
		C (Emotional stability)	−0.70
		L (Vigilance)	0.57
Self-control	C	Q3 (Perfectionism)	0.82
		G (Rule-consciousness)	0.78
		M (Abstractedness)	−0.58
Independence	E, A-	E (Dominance)	0.87
		Q1 (Openness to change)	0.49
		H (Social boldness)	0.43
Tough-mindedness	O-	I (Sensitivity)	−0.75
		Q1 (Openness to change)	0.68

Occupational Personality Questionnaire (OPQ)

The OPQ (Saville *et al.*, 1984) was developed to assess the personality constructs of most relevance to occupational psychologists. It is based on an a priori hierarchical model of personality, comprising four levels of description: the Concept Mode (30 scales), Factorial Model (14 scales), Octagon Model (eight scales), and Pentagon Model (five scales). Four of the five Pentagon Model dimensions resemble the Big Five dimensions E, O, C and N, but there is no equivalent to A. The fifth Pentagon Model dimension, Vigour, does not correspond closely to any Big Five dimension. In two studies, Matthews *et al.* (1990) and Matthews and Stanton (1994) factor-analysed the OPQ Concept Model scales, using validated criteria to determine the correct number of factors to extract. The two studies were remarkably consistent in demonstrating a clear Big Five factor structure. However, the five factors obtained showed only an approximate correspondence with the Pentagon Model factors, implying that Saville *et al.*'s five-factor structure was difficult to obtain empirically. The Factorial and Octagon Models were poorly supported by the data. Ferguson, Payne and Anderson (1994) report an OPQ study using a 'confirmatory' factor-analytic procedure, in which a specified factor solution is tested for fit to the empirical data. They showed that a five-factor solution resembling the Big Five provided the best fit of the various factor models tested, and confirmed that the Pentagon Model fitted the data poorly.

Assessment of primary factors

Both the 16PF and the OPQ are marketed on the basis that the more fine-grained primary factor level provides useful information over and above that available from measures of higher-order factors. In fact, the primary scales of the 16PF became notorious for poor internal consistency. In addition, a variety of studies (e.g. Matthews, 1989) showed that its primary factor structure did not appear to correspond to that described by Cattell (1973). These problems appear to have been addressed in the 16PF5; Russell and Karol (1994) report a mean internal consistency (coefficient alpha) of 0.74 for the 16 revised primary scales. Primary factor structure also seems to be improved, though past experience with the 16PF suggests there is a pressing need for independent confirmation of the factor structure.

It is claimed that the 30 Concept Model scales of the OPQ are based on a theoretical model and item analyses, rather than on factor analysis (Saville *et al.*, 1984). Matthews *et al.* (1990) showed that most of the scales did measure reliable variance additional to the variance associated with the Big Five. An item factor analysis conducted by Matthews and Stanton (1994) showed that some of the Concept Model scales were, in fact, poorly discriminated, and a system of around 20 primaries was to be preferred.

In summary, there is little doubt that the primary scales of questionnaires such as the 16PF5 and OPQ measure variation unexplained by the Big Five. The importance in applied contexts of this extra variance is unclear. Some unique primary factor variance may relate to narrow but important qualities; other variance may be too specific and trivial in nature to be worth measuring. Given the lack of correspondence between different primary factor systems, psychometric evidence is unhelpful in resolving the issue. Of more importance is whether primary factors provide incremental criterion validity, a question that is returned to in a later section.

CRITERION VALIDITY OF THE BIG FIVE

The Big Five and job performance

It is well known that personality measures are often relatively poor predictors of occupational criteria. Three key meta-analytic reviews of the validity of the Big Five and related constructs (Barrick and Mount, 1991; Tett, Jackson and Rothstein, 1991; Hough, 1992) reinforce this point. For example, Barrick and Mount (1991) report a mean N-weighted correlation between personality and occupational criteria of only 0.03. Table 23.4 reproduces data from the Barrick and Mount meta-analysis which shows that all five factors are weak predictors of job performance. However, as Eysenck and Eysenck (1980) have argued, in an important commentary on the validity of personality measures, such averaged coefficients have little meaning. Correlation magnitudes are lowered by various statistical artifacts, such as unreliability of measures and restriction of range. Averaging also lumps together both well-conducted and poorly-conducted studies, which will also attenuate the averaged correlation. Furthermore, personality theory suggests any given trait will only predict certain external criteria, so the averaging process includes correlations which would be expected to be zero.

Both meta-analyses took some of these points into account. Table 23.4 includes correlations corrected for factors such as unreliability of measures of personality

Table 23.4   Selected data from two meta-analyses of correlations between the Big Five and job proficiency

	Study		E	N	C	A	O
Job proficiency (uncorrected *r*)	BM	*r*	0.06	−0.04	0.13	0.04	−0.02
		(N)*	(12 396)	(11 635)	(12 893)	(11 526)	(9454)
	TJR	*r*	0.10	−0.15	0.12	0.22	0.18
	(Confirmatory studies)†	(N)	(2302)	(900)	(450)	(280)	(1304)
Job proficiency (corrected *r*)	BM	*r*	0.10	−0.07	0.23	0.06	−0.03
		(N)	(12 396)	(11 635)	(12 893)	(11 526)	(9454)
	TJR	*r*	0.16	−0.22	0.18	0.33	0.27
	(Confirmatory studies	(N)	(2302)	(900)	(450)	(280)	(1304)

Note. BM: Barrick and Mount (1991); TJR: Tett, Jackson and Rothstein (1991).
  * Number of subjects contributing data.
  † Studies testing confirmation of an hypothesis specified a priori.

and performance, which are larger than the raw correlations. Tett, Jackson and Rothstein (1991) also distinguished confirmatory studies, in which researchers had a theoretical rationale for relating personality to performance, from exploratory analyses in which there was no a priori rationale. Table 23.4 shows that correlation magnitudes are higher in confirmatory studies, particularly when correlations are corrected for artifact. Correlations are still fairly modest, but it is now generally realized that even correlations of 0.2 or 0.3 are useful in guiding selection. The procedures used by Tett, Jackson and Rothstein (1991) for correcting correlation magnitudes have been criticized by Ones *et al.* (1994). In response, Tett *et al.* (1994) showed that an improved correction procedure tended to lower correlations slightly, but the main conclusions of their earlier paper were unaffected. For example, the corrected mean correlations for exploratory and confirmatory studies dropped from 0.12 to 0.03, and from 0.29 to 0.24, respectively. Unfortunately, Tett *et al.* (1994) did not re-analyse data discriminating the correlates of the Big Five, but the corrected correlation estimates given in Tables 23.4 and 23.5 may be a little inflated.

Moderating factors

Tett, Jackson and Rothstein (1991) identify a number of moderating factors that influence the magnitude of correlations. Some of these may be essentially methodological, such as the larger effect sizes reported in published articles, compared with dissertations. Others relate to contextual factors. Barrick and Mount (1993) hypothesized that personality may be more important in jobs providing a high degree of autonomy. In a study of managers, they showed that high C, high E and low A were more strongly related to supervisor ratings of job performance when job autonomy was high than when autonomy was low.

   Contextual factors may, in part, relate to variation in the specific activities and tasks required for specific jobs. Experimental studies show that associations

Table 23.5 Relationship between the Big Five, training proficiency and personnel data (Barrick and Mount, 1991)

Criterion		E	N	C	A	O
Training proficiency	*r*	0.15	−0.04	0.13	0.06	0.14
(Uncorrected *r*)	(*N*)*	(3101)	(3283)	(3585)	(3685)	(2700)
Personnel data	*r*	0.06	−0.06	0.11	0.08	0.01
(Uncorrected *r*)	(*N*)	(6477)	(5644)	(6175)	(4474)	(3785)
Training proficiency	*r*	0.26	−0.07	0.23	0.10	0.25
(Corrected *r*)	(*N*)	(3101)	(3283)	(3585)	(3685)	(2700)
Personnel data	*r*	0.11	−0.09	0.20	0.14	0.01
(Corrected *r*)	(*N*)	(6477)	(5644)	(6175)	(4474)	(3785)

* Number of subjects contributing data.

between personality and performance are often highly sensitive to variation in the information-processing demands of the task (Deary and Matthews, 1993). Studies of E show that relationships between this variable and performance may be positive, negative or zero, depending on task demands and contextual factors. Broadly, extraverts perform better when the task makes high demands on attention and short-term memory, and requires speeded response, whereas introverts are superior at vigilance and reflective problem-solving (Matthews and Dorn, 1995). The low magnitudes of the E–performance correlations shown in Table 23.4 may result from neglect of task factors. There is good evidence that extraverts are indeed better at tasks requiring rapid information-processing such as military flying (Eysenck and Eysenck, 1985) and semi-automated mail sorting (Matthews, Jones and Chamberlain, 1992). We would also expect extraverts to perform better on jobs requiring sociability and assertiveness. Consistent with this prediction, Barrick and Mount (1991) report higher (though still small) correlations between E and occupational criteria in sales and managerial jobs, compared with other occupational groups.

As expected, N (Neuroticism) is negatively correlated with performance, but the relationship is of modest magnitude, even in confirmatory studies (Tett, Jackson and Rothstein, 1991). Again, experimental studies suggest moderating factors which should be investigated in future research. In general, neurotic individuals cope ineffectively with stress, and perform badly on cognitively-demanding tasks (Matthews and Dorn, 1995). Cortina *et al.* (1992) report a study of the Big Five in police recruits. Low neuroticism was one of the most consistent predictors of various indices of superior performance during training, a finding which Cortina *et al.* relate to the high stress of police work.

Evidence is lacking on the role of task factors in moderating effects of the other three dimensions. C appears to be a fairly general influence on performance across a variety of occupations, which is relatively insensitive to moderator effects (Barrick and Mount, 1991). Effects of C on performance may be mediated by motivational factors such as goal-setting and goal commitment (Barrick, Mount and Strauss, 1993). Possibly, the high C individual is able to choose performance-enhancing strategies across a variety of specific tasks. Moderators of A are likely to relate to social rather than task factors. Although Tett, Jackson and Rothstein (1991) found evidence for beneficial effects of A in confirmatory studies, Barrick and Mount (1993) showed that agreeable managers receive poorer supervisory ratings, particularly when the job has high autonomy. High A may be incompatible with ruthless, competitive qualities which contribute to success in some business occupations. Hough's (1992) review suggests that high A relates to superior teamwork, but reduced creativity; there may be a tradeoff between accommodating the needs of others and independence of thought. O would be expected to be more beneficial when the work environment offers greater change and variety, but there is little relevant evidence.

The Big Five and other occupational criteria

The Big Five appear to predict criteria other than job performance. Table 23.5 reproduces Barrick and Mount's (1991) correlations between personality, training proficiency and 'personnel data' (e.g. salary level, tenure and status change). Again, high C appears to be generally beneficial; its positive association with training is consistent with data indicating that C predicts educational success (Hough, 1992). In these data, E and O relate more strongly to training proficiency than to job proficiency. Barrick and Mount (1991) point out that most of the training programs concerned were demanding and required interaction with others; factors which may moderate effects of E, as discussed above. In other contexts, such as education, there is no simple linear association between E and learning (Eysenck and Eysenck, 1985). The effect of O is consistent with the interest in new experiences reported by the high scorer on the dimension.

C is of special interest as a predictor of deviant and antisocial behaviour in occupational settings. Hough (1992) reviews data on the Achievement and Dependability components of C, summarized in Table 23.6. Both aspects of C relate to measures of law-abiding and commendable behaviour. Table 23.6 also suggests that Achievement is the stronger predictor of all criteria except law-abiding behaviour; note that correction of correlations would tend to increase magnitudes of differences between them. Ones, Viswesvaran and Schmidt (1993) report a meta-analysis of correlates of integrity tests, which attempt to measure honesty, responsible behaviour and reliability at work. Integrity measures included both 'overt' tests, which directly assess attitudes to dishonesty, and broader personality tests (see also Murphy and Luther, Chapter 18 in this volume). Table 23.7 summarizes some of their findings; both types of test predict performance and counterproductive behaviours, but overt tests have greater validity for the latter criterion. As Ones, Viswesvaran and Schmidt (1993) state, integrity tests may primarily measure C.

Finally, the Big Five may be useful in profiling the personality characteristics associated with various occupations (Kline and Lapham, 1992). Figure 23.1 shows standard scores on the TOPAS lexical scales developed by Matthews and Oddy (1993), for five business occupations. As suggested by Brand (1994), Openness is split into intellectual and emotional components. Notable features of the data include the high extraversion of salespersons, and the disagreeableness and lack

Table 23.6 Relationships between Achievement and Dependability components of Conscientiousness and occupational criteria (Hough, 1992)

Criterion		Achievement	Dependability
Job proficiency	*r*	0.15	0.08
(Uncorrected *r*)	(*N*)*	(2800)	(46 100)
Training success	*r*	0.21	0.11
(Uncorrected *r*)	(*N*)	(1200)	(4700)
Educational success	*r*	0.29	0.12
(Uncorrected *r*)	(*N*)	(12 600)	(18 700)
Commendable behaviour	*r*	0.33	0.23
(Uncorrected *r*)	(*N*)	(4100)	(87 600)
Law abiding behavior	*r*	0.42	0.58
(Uncorrected *r*)	(*N*)	(25 900)	(36 200)

Note. Commendable behaviour: Derived from employee records of commendations, disciplinary actions, reprimands, demotions, involuntary discharge, ratings of effort, hard work.
Law-abiding behaviour: Derived from records of theft, delinquent offences, criminal offences, imprisonment.
* Number of subjects contributing data.

Table 23.7 Relationships between integrity tests and occupational criteria (Ones, Viswesvaran and Schmidt, 1993)

Criterion		Test type	
		Personality based	Overt
Job performance (all criteria)	*r*	0.22	0.20
(Uncorrected *r*)	(*N*)*	(37 683)	(31 089)
Job performance (supervisor ratings)	*r*	0.22	0.18
(Uncorrected *r*)	(*N*)	(27 081)	(12 932)
Counterproductive behaviours	*r*	0.22	0.39
(Uncorrected *r*)	(*N*)	(158 065)	(349 623)
Job performance (all criteria)	*r*	0.35	0.33
(Corrected *r*)	(*N*)	(37 683)	(31 089)
Job performance (supervisor ratings)	*r*	0.37	0.30
(Corrected *r*)	(*N*)	(27 081)	(12 932)
Counterproductive behaviours	*r*	0.32	0.55
(Corrected *r*)	(*N*)	(158 065)	(349 623)

Note. Counterproductive behaviours: Various disruptive behaviours including actual and admitted theft, illegal activities, absenteeism, tardiness and violence.
* Number of subjects contributing data.

of emotional openness of senior management (Chief Executive Officers and executives). Matthews and Oddy (1993) suggest that the low C of CEOs is a consequence of having already achieved career goals.

Incremental validity of primary factors

There is some evidence that predictive validity may be improved by using primary factors in place of the Big Five (see Schmit and Ryan, 1993). Many relatively

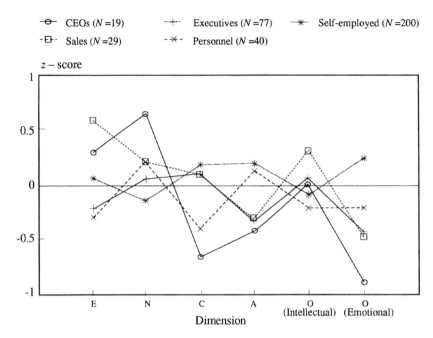

Figure 23.1   Personality profiles for five business occupations using the TOPAS measure of Brand's (1994) modified Big Five. Data re-analysed from Matthews and Oddy (1993), using standard Big Five labels for scales

narrow traits have proved useful in occupational psychology (see Furnham, 1992, for a comprehensive review). Hough (1992) concludes that the Big Five are too broad and heterogeneous for predicting occupational criteria successfully. In addition to dividing C into distinct Achievement and Dependability constructs, as previously discussed, she suggests that E should be split into Potency and Affiliation, and extra dimensions of Rugged Individualism and Locus of Control should be considered essential constructs (giving nine fundamental dimensions in total). More generally, there is little direct evidence from studies systematically comparing primary factors with standard measures of the Big Five such as the NEO-PI-R, and more research is clearly needed.

RESPONSE BIAS IN ASSESSMENT OF THE BIG FIVE

The problem of social desirability

As with any other personality questionnaire, Big Five scales are potentially vulnerable to response biases such as acquiescence, inter-item variability of response and social desirability. Although such factors may reduce construct validity somewhat, it appears that, in general, variation in response style is not, in general, a major threat to validity in either questionnaire (Costa and McCrae, 1992a) or lexical data (Matthews and Oddy, 1996). The 16PF5 offers perhaps the most comprehensive measurement of response styles, providing indices of impression management (social desirability), infrequency (for detection of unusual or random responding) and acquiescence (Russell and Karol, 1995).

A special problem in occupational contexts is that job applicants may well be motivated to 'fake good'. In principle, such tendencies should be detectable from social desirability scales, such as the Eysenck Lie scale. However, social desirability scores appear to measure two distinct constructs: impression management, which includes outright lying, and self-deception, naively believing oneself to lack common faults and so forth (Paulhus, 1986). Hence, a high social desirability score may actually reflect a substantive (and possibly advantageous) personality trait, rather than faking good.

There have been several empirical attempts to assess the impact of impression management in occupational studies of the Big Five. Tett, Jackson and Rothstein (1991) point out that if faking good lowers criterion validity, the effect should be larger in job recruits or applicants than in job incumbents, who should be less motivated to dissimulate. However, their meta-analysis showed that validity was not reduced in job applicants. Hough *et al.* (1990) used a mixture of experimental and correlational methods to investigate response biases in military personnel, in a study of Big Five-like measures. Although explicit instructions to 'fake good' or 'fake bad' altered scale scores, motivation to fake had little effect on either mean scores or on criterion-related content validities in samples given standard instructions. In addition, social desirability score had only a small moderating effect on correlations between scale scores and various occupational criteria. However, validity was reduced in subjects identified as responding randomly.

Use of ipsative measures to control response bias

A potential method for reducing response bias, in cases where it is believed to be a problem, is to use forced-choice or ipsative measures. Such measures are known to be subject to artifact, in that any one scale score is linearly dependent on the others, and it may not even be possible to rank order individuals using ipsative measures (e.g. Cornwell and Dunlap, 1994). In defence of ipsative measures, Saville and Willson (1991) have reported OPQ data which suggest that equivalent ipsative and normative scales are highly correlated, and have similar validity in predicting external criteria. They conclude that both normative and ipsative measures have disadvantages, but both types of scale may have practical uses.

However, Saville and Willson's (1991) analyses were based on the 30-scale OPQ, for which the predicted average intercorrelation between scales is −0.03. With only five scales, as provided by a Big Five measure, the average intercorrelation will be −0.25, implying that the problems of ipsativity will be more acute. Matthews and Oddy (submitted) conducted a study using normative and ipsative versions of the 6-factor TOPAS scales previously described. They showed that normative–ipsative scale correlations were of moderate magnitude only (0.49–0.64), but correlation magnitudes were increased by controlling for normative response bias and ipsative scale artifact. Structural equation modelling of the data suggested that both normative and ipsative scales provided acceptable, though biased, estimates of the underlying 'true' scores. Hence, although ipsative scales must be used with considerable caution, they may be useful in contexts where there is strong response bias on normative measures. However, ipsative scales are entirely unsuitable for investigating personality structure, through factor analysis for example (Cornwell and Dunlap, 1994).

PROFESSIONAL ISSUES: THE DEMYSTIFICATION OF PERSONALITY
ASSESSMENT?

Professional issues in selection and assessment are largely beyond the scope of this chapter, but it should be noted that the potential for abuse of personality question-naires is leading to concern in a number of countries, including the United Kingdom (see Smith and Sutherland, 1993; special issue of *The Psychologist* on *Testing in the Workplace*, vol. 7, January 1994). The British Psychological Society (BPS), for example, has launched a 'Level B' certificate for personality assessment in occupational settings. Certification requires both knowledge of test theory and professional skills such as providing appropriate feedback to clients and candidates, typically acquired from training courses run by test suppliers or by occupational psychology consultants. The BPS has also published an independent review of commercially published instruments as part of its efforts to promote expertise in personality assessment (Bartram *et al.*, 1995). In the United Kingdom, such efforts have been stimulated by increasing use of personality measures in selection (e.g. Williams, 1994), with the consequent increase in the scope for misuse of personality assessment. The extent to which other countries will introduce similar schemes is unclear.

Although there are good reasons for relatively stringent controls on the availability of personality questionnaires, there are also some hazards. In particular, there is a danger that detailed knowledge of tests may become restricted to a relatively small number of occupational psychologists, whose livelihood requires that they go to the trouble and expense of certification. Restrictions on availability may stifle independent academic research, which is already in short supply (Fletcher, 1994). It is also not unreasonable to suggest that psychologists working in selection and assessment have a commercial interest in presenting personality assessment as a complex and difficult process, requiring somewhat esoteric professional skills. A business client is more likely to be impressed by a 20-scale personality profile than a three-scale one, even if the three scales account for most of the reliable variance in the 20 scales.

The five-factor model may provide a check on these dangers. First, the academic researcher who does not have to provide professional advice to testees requires a more limited range of professional skills for access to measures. Table 23.8 reproduces in full Costa and McCrae's (1992a) statement for professional requirements for the NEO-PI-R to illustrate this point. It is important for theory development that questionnaires are available to the spectrum of research psychologists, as well as to individuals with expertise in occupational psychology. The five-factor model also puts forward a case for the relative simplicity of personality structure, in terms of constructs which should be accessible to anyone

Table 23.8 Professional requirements for using the NEO-PI-R (Costa and McCrae, 1992a, p. 4)

'The NEO-PI-R and NEO-FFI are essentially self-administered instruments. Thus the administration and scoring of these instruments can be performed by individuals who do not have formal training in clinical psychology, personality, or related fields. The administration and scoring procedures detailed in this manual should be carefully studied by the examiner.

In keeping with the *Standards for Educational and Psychological Testing* (American Educational Research Association, American Psychological Association, & National Council on Measurement in Education, 1985), *interpretation* of the NEO-PI-R and NEO-FFI requires professional training in psychological testing and measurement (e.g., reliability and validity, use of norms, etc.), in addition to familiarity with the materials and procedures presented in this manual. The utility of the NEO-PI-R and NEO-FFI is clearly related to the professional's background and knowledge.'

with a reasonable knowledge of psychology (see Costa and McCrae, 1992b). At the least, the parsimony and predictive validity of the Big Five puts the onus on occupational test companies to demonstrate incremental predictive validity for additional personality scales. It is in the long-term interests of the personality assessment industry to support independent research on validity, even though independent studies may be potentially embarrassing to individual companies. In addition, the increasing availability of Big Five measures in the public domain (e.g. Goldberg, 1993) may result in test companies marketing products on the basis of questionnaire-specific validity data and comprehensive norms, rather than on the company's unique insights into personality structure.

CONCLUSIONS AND PRACTICAL RECOMMENDATIONS

The Big Five is firmly established as a useful and widely-accepted general framework for the description of broad personality traits. All five factors appear to have predictive validity in occupational contexts. Some psychometric issues remain to be resolved, particularly the relationship to the Big Five of intelligence, achievement striving and activity traits. It is possible that some additions to the current Five will eventually become necessary (see Brand, 1994; Hough, 1992). The relative importance of primary factors also remains uncertain. The most serious difficulty in using the Big Five is the lack of a detailed theoretical basis for the five factors. Each may be linked to pre-existing psychological constructs in general terms (Costa and McCrae, 1992a), but there is currently no detailed account of the biological and cognitive processes underpinning each dimension (Eysenck, 1992; McAdams, 1992). Improved articulation of theory is necessary for predicting the moderator effects discussed in the section 'Moderating factors', and so is of practical relevance.

Implications for practice

- Assessment of the Big Five is strongly recommended for a general description of personality. Such descriptive information is useful in a variety of practical contexts. The empirical evidence reviewed supports use of Big Five measures to select those individuals who are likely to perform well at a particular job, who will enjoy doing that job, and who will benefit from training. Big Five scales are potentially valuable also in assessment of integrity and prosocial behaviour.

- The various Big Five measures available will provide similar, but not identical, information on personality. Choice of personality measure should be guided primarily by evidence on its validity in the occupational context of interest. It is criterion validity that allows personality data to improve decision-making, and hence to be cost-effective. There is little point in administering a personality measure if it is unlikely to predict practically important criteria. Hence, the practitioner requires expertise in evaluating scientific evidence. Companies try hard to give materials a professional appearance, but the visual attractiveness of a questionnaire and associated products provides no information on its predictive validity.

- Other criteria are important too, especially fairness. Scientifically, the central aim of personality testing is to discriminate—between individuals who are more or less suitable for a particular job, for example. However, discrimination in the scientific sense should not be associated with discrimination in the legal sense, i.e. unfairly favouring one group over another. In fact, gender differences and cross-cultural differences in the Big Five are typically fairly small in magnitude. Nevertheless, the test user must be able to defend assessment procedures used, which may require empirical evidence that procedures are non-discriminatory, or use of separate norms for different groups. A further aspect of fairness is 'face validity', the degree to which questionnaire items appear to the respondent to relate to the constructs measured. Face validity is scientifically irrelevant, but it is desirable to avoid irritating respondents with questions that appear meaningless.

- Social desirability does not, in general, threaten the validity of Big Five measures taken in selection and assessment contexts. However, there may be some circumstances in which it is desirable to monitor response biases, or to use ipsative measures.

- Use of measures of primary dimensions of personality may add to predictive validity, but there is no consensus among personality psychologists regarding the assessment of primaries. As with Big Five measures, assessment of primary dimensions should be guided by an a priori rationale, which takes into account the occupational context.

- Even in methodologically sound studies, the validities of Big Five measures are typically moderate in magnitude. It will normally be essential to supplement Big Five measures with other types of assessment; reliance on personality measure alone is unwise.

REFERENCES

Barrick, M.R. and Mount, M.K. (1991). The Big Five personality dimensions and job performance: A meta-analysis. *Personnel Psychology*, **44**, 1–26.
Barrick, M.R. and Mount, M.K. (1993). Autonomy as a moderator of the relationships between the Big Five personality dimensions and job performance. *Journal of Applied Psychology*, **78**, 111–118.

Barrick, M.R., Mount, M.K. and Strauss, J.P. (1993). Conscientiousness and performance of sales representatives: Test of the mediating effects of goal setting. *Journal of Applied Psychology*, **78**, 715–722.

Bartram, D., Anderson, N., Kellet, D., Lindley, P. and Robertson, I. (eds.) (1995). *Review of Personality Assessment Instruments (Level B)*. Leicester: British Psychological Society.

Borkenau, P. and Ostendorf, F. (1990). Comparing exploratory and confirmatory factor analysis: A study on the 5-factor model of personality. *Personality and Individual Differences*, **11**, 515–524.

Brand, C. (1994). Open to experience—closed to intelligence: Why the 'Big Five' are really the 'Comprehensive Six'. *European Journal of Personality*, **8**, 299–310.

Cattell, R.B. (1973). *Personality and Mood by Questionnaire*. New York: Jossey-Bass.

Cornwell, J.M. and Dunlap, W.P. (1994). On the questionable soundness of factoring ipsative data: A response to Saville and Willson (1991). *Journal of Occupational and Organizational Psychology*, **67**, 89–100.

Cortina, J.M., Doherty, M.L., Schmitt, N., Kaufman, G. and Smith, R.G. (1992). The 'Big Five' personality factors in the IPI and MMPI: Predictors of police performance. *Personnel Psychology*, **45**, 119–140.

Costa, P.T., Jr and McCrae, R.R. (1992a). *Revised NEO Personality Inventory (NEO PI-R) and NEO Five-Factor Inventory (NEO-FFI) Professional Manual*. Odessa, FL: Psychological Assessment Resources, Inc.

Costa, P.T., Jr and McCrae, R.R. (1992b). Four ways five factors are basic. *Personality and Individual Differences*, **13**, 653–665.

Deary, I.J. and Matthews, G. (1993). Personality traits are alive and well. *The Psychologist*, **6**, 299–311.

Eysenck, H.J. (1992). Four ways five factors are *not* basic. *Personality and Individual Differences*, **13**, 667–673.

Eysenck, H.J. and Eysenck, S.B.G. (1985). *Personality and Individual Differences: A Natural Science Approach*. New York: Plenum.

Eysenck, M.W. and Eysenck, H.J. (1990). Mischel and the concept of personality. *British Journal of Psychology*, **71**, 191–204.

Ferguson, E., Payne, T. and Anderson, N. (1994). Occupational personality assessment: Theory, structure and psychometrics of the OPQ FMX5-Student. *Personality and Individual Differences*, **17**, 217–225.

Fletcher, C. (1994). Validity, test use and professional responsibility. *The Psychologist*, **7**, 30–31.

Furnham, A. (1992). *Personality at Work: The Role of Individual Differences in the Workplace*. London: Routledge.

Goldberg, L.R. (1992). The development of markers for the Big-Five factor structure. *Psychological Assessment*, **4**, 26–42.

Goldberg, L.R. (1993). The structure of phenotypic personality traits. *American Psychologist*, **48**, 26–34.

Hogan, R. (1986). *Hogan Personality Inventory Manual*. Minneapolis: National Computer Systems.

Hough, L.M. (1992). The 'Big Five' personality variables—construct confusion: Description versus prediction. *Human Performance*, **5**, 139–155.

Hough, L.M., Eaton, N.K., Dunnette, M.D., Kamp, J.D. and McCloy, R.A. (1990). Criterion-related validities of personality constructs and the effect of response distortion on those validities [Monograph]. *Journal of Applied Psychology*, **75**, 581–595.

Kline, P. and Lapham, S.L. (1992). The PPQ: A study of its ability to discriminate occupational groups and the validity of its scales. *Personality and Individual Differences*, **13**, 225–228.

Krug, S.E. and Johns, E.F. (1986). A large-scale cross-validation of second-order personality structure defined by the 16PF. *Psychological Reports*, **59**, 683–693.

Matthews, G. (1989). The factor structure of the 16PF: Twelve primary and three secondary factors. *Personality and Individual Differences*, **10**, 931–940.

Matthews, G. and Dorn, L. (1995). Cognitive and attentional processes in personality and intelligence. In D.H. Saklofske and M. Zeidner (eds.), *International Handbook of Personality and Intelligence*, pp. 367–396. New York: Plenum.

Matthews, G., Jones, D.M. and Chamberlain, A.G. (1992). Predictors of individual differences in mail coding skills, and their variation with ability level. *Journal of Applied Psychology*, **77**, 406–418.

Matthews, G. and Oddy, K. (1993). Recovery of major personality dimensions from trait adjective data. *Personality and Individual Differences*, **15**, 419–431.

Matthews, G. and Oddy, K. (1996). Ipsative and normative scales in adjectival measurement of personality: Problems of bias and discrepancy, submitted.

Matthews, G. and Stanton, N. (1994). Item and scale factor analyses of the Occupational Personality Questionnaire. *Personality and Individual Differences*, **16**, 733–743.

Matthews, G., Stanton, N., Graham, N.C. and Brimelow, C. (1990). A factor analysis of the scales of the Occupational Personality Questionnaire. *Personality and Individual Differences*, **11**, 591–596.

McAdams, D.P. (1992). The five-factor model in personality: A critical appraisal. *Journal of Personality*, **60**, 329–361.

Noller, P., Law, H. and Comrey, A.L. (1987). Cattell, Comrey, and Eysenck personality factors compared: More evidence for the five robust factors? *Journal of Applied Psychology*, **53**, 775–782.

Ones, D.S., Viswesvaran, C. and Schmidt, F.L. (1993). Comprehensive meta-analysis of integrity test validities: Findings and implications for personnel selection and theories of job performance [Monograph]. *Journal of Applied Psychology*, **78**, 679–703.

Ones, D.S., Mount, M.K., Barrick, M.R. and Hunter, J.E. (1994). Personality and job performance: A critique of the Tett, Jackson and Rothstein (1991) meta-analysis. *Personnel Psychology*, **47**, 147–156.

Paulhus, D.L. (1986). Self-deception and impression management in test responses. In A. Angleitner and J.S. Wiggins (eds.), *Personality Assessment Via Questionnaire*, pp. 143–165. New York: Springer.

Russell, M.T. and Karol, D.L. (1994). *The UK Edition of the 16PF5: Administrator's Manual.* Windsor, Berkshire: NFER-Nelson.

Saville, P., Holdsworth, R., Nyfield, G., Cramp, L. and Mabey, W. (1984). *Occupational Personality Questionnaires Manual.* Esher, Surrey: Saville & Holdsworth, Ltd.

Saville, P. and Willson, E. (1991). The reliability and validity of normative and ipsative approaches in the measurement of personality. *Journal of Occupational Psychology*, **64**, 219–238.

Schmit, M.J., and Ryan, A.M. (1993). The Big Five in personnel selection: Factor structure in applicant and nonapplicant populations. *Journal of Applied Psychology*, **78**, 966–974.

Smith, M. and Sutherland, V. (eds.) (1993). *International Review of Professional Issues in Selection and Assessment*, vol. 1. Chichester: John Wiley.

Tett, R.P., Jackson, D.N. and Rothstein, M. (1991). Personality measures as predictors of job performance: A meta-analytic review. *Personnel Psychology*, **44**, 703–742.

Tett, R.P., Jackson, D.N., Rothstein, M. and Reddon, J.R. (1994). Meta-analysis of personality–job performance relations: A reply to Ones, Mount, Barrick, and Hunter (1994). *Personnel Psychology*, **74**, 157–172.

Williams, R.S. (1994). Occupational testing: Contemporary British practice. *The Psychologist*, **7**, 11–13.

Yang, K. and Bond, M.H. (1990). Exploring implicit personality theories with indigenous or imported constructs: The Chinese case. *Journal of Personality and Social Psychology*, **58**, 1087–1095.

Zuckerman, M. (1991). *Psychobiology of Personality.* New York: Cambridge University Press.

Zuckerman, M., Kuhlman, D.M., Joireman, J., Teta, P. and Kraft, M. (1993). A comparison of three structural models for personality: The Big Three, the Big Five, and the Alternative Five. *Journal of Personality and Social Psychology*, **65**, 757–768.

Chapter 24

Selecting for Teamwork

MICHAEL A. WEST

Institute of Work Psychology, University of Sheffield, Sheffield, UK

NATALIE J. ALLEN

Centre for Administration and Information Studies, University of Western Ontario, Ontario, Canada

INTRODUCTION

The use of teams in organizational settings is increasing in the Western indus-trialized world (Sundstrom, DeMeuse and Futrell, 1990) partly because managers see teams as a medium for empowering individuals, but also because research evidence suggests that setting group goals increases productivity (Weldon and Weingart, 1993), promotes innovation (Pillinger and West, 1995) and improves company financial performance (Guzzo, 1996). The immediate practical reason for working in groups, however, is the need to combine efforts, knowledge and skills, since many complicated tasks cannot be accomplished effectively by one person. As organizations have grown in size and become more complex in their structure, the need for people to work together in coordinated ways to achieve objectives which contribute to the overall aims of the organization has also become clear. By coordi-nating the activities of groups with clearly defined and organizationally relevant objectives, it is easier to translate organizational strategy into practical action.

However, despite the popularity of work groups, or teams, in organizational settings, very little research attention has been given to the issue of how best to select people for team-based work. Indeed, in contrast to research on the relation-ship between selection devices and individual job performance, the ground for developing research in this area has barely begun to be prepared.

To be sure, determining the appropriate selection devices to use in predicting individual job performance is a complex process. As in many areas of work and

International Handbook of Selection and Assessment, Edited by N. Anderson and P. Herriot.
© 1997 John Wiley & Sons Ltd.

organizational research, however, even further complexities arise when one considers the issues at the group level. In the case of selecting personnel for work in groups, for example, there are many more possible criterion measures against which predictors of performance could be validated since both individual behaviour/performance and group behaviour/performance could reasonably be examined. A further complication is that some situations involve several personnel who are being selected to form newly created teams while, in others, a single individual is being selected to fill a spot in an already existing team. Despite these complications, and the limitations in the selection literature, the psychological literature on groups is extensive and contains much of relevance to the staffing of teams. In this chapter we outline the limited research that specifically focuses on selecting for teams and draw together relevant information from other areas of research within the groups literature. In doing so, we address two distinct, but related questions:

1. How can we select individuals who will be good at working within a group or team setting?
2. What do we know about the composition of groups that may be relevant to the issue of staffing teams?

But first it is important to address some prior questions that have considerable bearing upon the general issues addressed in this chapter. What is a work group or team? Why work in groups? What structural characteristics optimize team functioning?

DEFINING AND STRUCTURING WORK TEAMS

Throughout the chapter, work group, group, and team are used interchangeably to refer to a set of employees who are characterized by the following:

1. Team members have shared objectives in relation to their work.
2. Team members interact with each other in order to achieve those shared objectives.
3. Team members have more or less well-defined roles, some of which are differentiated from one another (for example, in a health care team, there are nurses, receptionists and doctors).
4. Teams have an organizational identity—that is, they have a defined organizational function and see themselves as a group within the larger organization (e.g. the R&D Department for a medium sized manufacturing company).
5. Teams are not so large that they would be better defined as an organization. In practice this means that few are likely to exceed 20 members.

Before selecting personnel for a particular team, attention should be given to the design or structure of the work that team members will do and the roles they will occupy. Research examining how to maximize team effectiveness (see reviews in Guzzo and Shea, 1992; West, 1996; but also see Pritchard *et al.*, 1988) suggests seven important principles:

1. Individual roles within the teams should be indispensable and therefore valued. Prior to selection it is important to determine each team member's role and identify team and individual objectives in order that team members can see and demonstrate the value of their work to team success.
2. Individual roles should be meaningful and intrinsically rewarding. If individuals are to be selected who are committed and creative, then their team tasks must be rewarding, engaging and challenging.
3. Individual contributions to the team should be identifiable and subject to evaluation. Those selected to work in teams, not only have to feel that their work is important, but also that their performance will be visible to other team members.
4. The team should have an intrinsically motivating and interesting set of tasks to perform. Selecting motivated people to work in teams requires that team tasks are intrinsically engaging and challenging.
5. Perhaps of greatest importance, there should be clear team goals with clear team performance feedback.
6. The team should have a just sufficient number of members to successfully complete its task, but should not be so big that participation becomes difficult (Hackman, 1990; West, 1994).
7. The organization should provide adequate (though not necessarily abundant) resources to enable the team to achieve its targets or objectives (Payne, 1990). Resources include: having the right number and skill mix of people; adequate financial resources to enable effective functioning; necessary secretarial or administrative support; adequate accommodation; adequate technical assistance and support.

The above principles help to define the 'ideal group'. But what do we know that will assist in achieving this ideal from the perspective of staffing? In what follows we turn our attention to research relevant to our two central questions, those involving the selection of team players and the composition of teams.

SELECTING 'TEAM PLAYERS'

Typically, individuals are recruited and selected to work as part of a group because they appear to have the particular set of technical skills and experience deemed necessary for particular aspects of the job. This is, of course, entirely reasonable. Also reasonable, however, would be an examination of the degree to which candidates have the personal characteristics necessary to work effectively as part of a team. Indeed, since it is unlikely that people are equally well-suited, or interested in group-based work, characteristics of this sort may well play an important role in the recruiting and selection of group members. Though promising, research of relevance to this general issue is very much in its early stages, and, not surprisingly, consensus does not exist about the most effective way to assess team-relevant characteristics—or even what they may be. It is encouraging to note, however, that organizations wishing to incorporate individual differences in 'team playing' into their selection strategy have some viable options to explore.

Teamwork and person characteristics

One approach involves the possibility that some people are simply better suited psychologically to team-based activity than others. Research to date is suggestive, though limited and hardly conclusive, that this is the case. In an early study, for example, Davis (1969) asked people to state their preference for working individually or in groups; task groups made up of those who prefer group work performed better on tasks requiring interaction and coordination. More recently, Earley (1994) reported that people characterized by a 'collectivist' orientation performed better when given group-focused training, while 'individualists' performed better under self-focused training.

Another approach focuses on skills. Cannon-Bowers *et al.* (1995), for example, distinguish between team-specific and team-generic competencies. Team-specific competencies are those that are contextually determined—that is, they depend on the other members of the particular team (e.g. knowledge of team characteristics, team cohesion). For this reason, team-generic competencies may be more useful in the selection context. They include individually held communication skills, leadership skills, and attitudes toward teamwork and are hypothesized to influence team performance directly and regardless of the characteristics of other team members. Cannon-Bowers *et al.* further distinguish between team-generic competencies that are also generic with respect to task (e.g. conflict-resolution skills) and those that are task-specific. It is argued that team-generic/task-specific competencies are crucial for individuals who work in teams with particularly fluid membership (e.g. emergency crews, high turnover teams, aircraft crews). It would be important, for example, for all cockpit crew members and members of surgical teams to be working under similar operational and attitudinal assumptions—regardless of whether they had worked together before (Gregorich, Helmreich and Wilhelm, 1990).

To date, this approach has been used to inform training, rather than the selection, of team members (Cannon-Bowers *et al.*, 1995). Given that training research has demonstrated the value of the general competencies framework, however, it seems reasonable to suggest the assessment of generic team skills could be implemented into a system aimed at selecting 'team players'.

Indeed, explicit attempts to do something of this nature have been made. Stevens and Campion (1994a, 1994b), for example, argue that, because knowledge, skills, and abilities (KSAs) are better predictors of individual job performance than are personality attributes, that this is also likely to be the case for teamwork. On the basis of the literature on team functioning, they identified two broad skill areas (interpersonal KSAs and self-management KSAs), consisting of a total of 14 specific KSA requirements for effective teamwork. From this taxonomy, Stevens and Campion (1994b) developed a 35-item multiple choice test in which respondents are presented with challenges they may face in the workplace and asked to identify the strategy they would most likely follow. Available validity evidence appears promising. Using both supervisor and peer ratings of individual job performance, Stevens and Campion report substantial criterion-related validities, some in excess of 0.50. In addition, they report that this measure outperformed predictions made using traditional employment tests.

Finally, a rather novel approach to assessing teamwork abilities has been taken recently by Davey (1995) who developed a video format measure. Viewers are shown 25 scenarios in which actors portray team-relevant dilemmas, each with two possible behavioural solutions, and are asked to choose which solution they believe is most appropriate. In addition to its face validity, initial work with the measure suggests that it converges with several personality measures that would seem theoretically linked with teamwork. Relations between the measure and actual performance in teams have not yet been examined.

To conclude this section, although preliminary evidence suggests that people whose preferences, personal styles, and/or KSAs seem more 'team-worthy' perform better, as individuals in teams, than do less team-worthy individuals, several important issues deserve further attention. It is not clear, for example, how well the criteria used in the existing research capture the 'team player' construct; thus, we look forward to criterion development work in this area. Related to this is the point, raised earlier, that validation research should be conducted at both the individual and group levels of analysis. It may well be that parallel results will be obtained when considered at the group level of analysis; to our knowledge, however, such studies have not been conducted. Nor do we know the impact of introducing a strong team player into any of the various 'combinations' that existing teams could represent (e.g. a group of all weak team players; a group with some weak, some strong). Too many 'team players' might also, for example, produce a climate of conformity, subjecting their decision-making processes to the dangers of 'group think' (Janis, 1982).

We turn now to an examination of research on the membership composition of teams.

TEAM COMPOSITION

Team composition—used here to refer to the 'mix' of members making up a team—has been examined in two somewhat distinct lines of research. Though neither have been applied explicitly to the problem of structuring teams, both have relevance for it.

One line of research examines the very general question of whether heterogeneity is advantageous or disadvantageous to groups and their members. It is 'better' to belong to a group whose members are quite different from each other— for example, in terms of abilities, personality, or demographic characteristics? Or are groups, and/or their individual members, disadvantaged by such diversity? The theoretical perspectives that have guided much of the research in this area include the attraction–selection–attrition model (Schneider, 1987), similarity-attraction theory (Byrne, 1971), and self-categorization theory (Turner, 1987). A basic premise of all three is that we are attracted to those who are similar to us and, thus, contrive to organize, and evaluate, our social worlds accordingly.

In the second line of research it is assumed that heterogeneity is valuable but that, in order to work effectively, groups need to be made up of the 'right mix' of members. At issue in this line of research, then, are questions about which combination of roles, styles, or skills fit together particularly well and which types of people are needed within groups.

Team heterogeneity: Do differences matter?

Although group members can differ from each other in a wide variety of ways, research in this area has tended to focus on heterogeneity in terms of skills, ability, and both general, and organizational, demographic variables. Dependent variables have included those at both the group level (e.g. team performance, turnover rates, cohesion) and the individual level (e.g. satisfaction, turnover). Although much of the early research on group heterogeneity examined experimental laboratory-based groups, focus on 'real-world' groups has typified more recent research in this area.

Heterogeneity and performance

At the group level of analysis, several studies suggest facilitative effects of heterogeneity. This pattern is most likely when the attributes in question are skills or educational specialization and the dependent variable is team performance. Wiersema and Bantel (1992), for example, reported that strategic management initiatives were more likely to be made by groups that were heterogeneous with respect to educational specialization, while Bantel (1993) reported that banks whose teams were heterogeneous with respect to education and functional background developed clearer corporate strategies (see also Bantel and Jackson, 1989; O'Reilly, Caldwell and Barnett, 1989). Several experimental studies, particularly those involving complex tasks or requiring innovation, have shown similar effects (McGrath, 1984). Presumably, skill heterogeneity means that each group member is more likely to have non-redundant expertise to contribute to the team activities.

Although some debate has surrounded the question of whether it is advantageous to have groups that are homogeneous or heterogeneous with respect to cognitive ability, most research results support the view that level of ability, not heterogeneity of ability, is the critical factor. At least for tasks that are truly interdependent, high ability homogeneous groups outperform, for example, low ability homogeneous groups. This was demonstrated in Tziner and Edens' (1985) study of military groups in which they found that the contribution of one team member of high ability to the performance of the team was greatest when all other crew members were high in ability.

In one of the very few longitudinal studies in this area, Watson, Kumar and Michaelsen (1993) reported that groups that were heterogeneous with respect to culture initially performed, on a series of business case exercises, more poorly than culturally homogeneous groups. As group members gained experience with each other over time, however, performance differences between culturally homogeneous and heterogeneous groups largely disappeared.

Heterogeneity and affective reactions

A somewhat different, though not entirely consistent, pattern emerges when heterogeneity with respect to other attribute/outcome combinations is examined. Specifically, when significant relations between 'demographic heterogeneity' (e.g. tenure, age, gender) and affective outcomes (e.g. turnover, work attitudes) are reported, they are more likely to be negative than positive. This is the case at the group level of analysis, and particularly so, at the individual level of analysis.

At the group level, for example, research has shown that turnover rates are higher in groups that are heterogeneous with respect to age (Jackson *et al.*, 1991; Wagner, Pfeffer and O'Reilly, 1984; Wiersema and Bird, 1993), team (or department) tenure (McCain, O'Reilly and Pfeffer, 1983; Wiersema and Bird, 1993), prestige of the university attended (Wiersema and Bird, 1993) and non-industry work experience (Jackson *et al.*, 1991).

At the individual level, Tsui, Egan and O'Reilly (1992) reported that being dissimilar from one's cohort with respect to education and organizational tenure was associated with stronger commitment to, and greater intention to stay with, the organization. Positive effects of individual dissimilarity, such as these, however, are extremely rare. Typically, where significant relations between individual dissimilarity and affective outcomes are observed, they are negative. For example, both gender and race dissimilarity were associated with lower affective commitment to the organization and more absenteeism (Tsui, Egan and O'Reilly, 1992) and dissimilarity with respect to tenure was associated with lower affective attachment to the team (Allen *et al.*, 1996). Finally, turnover has been shown to be more likely for individuals who are dissimilar from team members on educational level, college major, and non-industry work experience (Jackson *et al.*, 1991) and on team tenure and university attended (Wiersema and Bird, 1993). It is important to make clear that, in all these cases, 'being dissimilar' refers not to absolute levels of a particular variable—these are controlled for in this research—but rather the degree to which the target individual is different from other members of the team on the attribute in question.

Teams as jigsaw puzzles: Achieving the 'right mix'

A second line of research relevant to team composition views teams somewhat like jigsaw puzzles, in which the different shaped 'pieces' (people) must 'fit together' or complement each other. Thus, this work has focused on the effects of skill homogeneity and heterogeneity with respect to personality or personal style, on group level variables (e.g. group effectiveness, group cohesion).

Skill mix

As indicated above, research evidence indicates that group performance is positively linked to the task-related ability of group members (Hill, 1982). Taking this theme further, a currently popular notion, particularly within teams in health service settings (NHSME, 1992), is that of skill mix. Skill mix is defined as

> . . . the balance between trained and untrained, qualified and unqualified, and su-pervisory and operative staff within a service area as well as between different staff groups . . . Optimum skill mix is achieved when the desired standard of service is provided, at the minimum cost, which is consistent with the efficient deployment of trained, qualified and supervisory personnel and the maximisation of contributions from all staff members. It will ensure the best possible use of scarce professional skills to maximise the service to clients.

A skill mix review involves discovering what activities need to be carried out within the team; who is currently doing them; the skill level of people doing them; the minimum level of skill required to do them; and the potential for combining tasks in new ways to create in some cases new roles and staff groupings. This orientation to selecting for teams therefore focuses on the identification of particular technical skills required by the team that are not already supplied, or are supplied at higher cost, by others in the team. Finally, in thinking about this issue, it is important to note that the skill mix required by some teams may well fluctuate over time as they undergo changes in focus, technology, or positioning within the organization.

Personality and personal styles

Given that team members must frequently interact with each other, the extent of their personal compatibility would seem to play an important part in team effectiveness. What personality types work best together? What mix of personalities is needed for a team to be effective? In what ways must group members be compatible in order to work together effectively?

Although a number of models of personality in teams have been proposed in the psychological literature, little research has examined relationships between personality compatibility and team performance. An exception is the work of Schutz (1955, 1958, 1967). Schutz's theory of fundamental interpersonal relations orientations (FIRO) seeks to explain how the personal attributes of members affect group performance. Schutz sees three basic human needs expressed in group interaction: needs for inclusion, control and affection. Groups composed of people with compatible needs will be more effective, according to Schutz's theory, than groups composed of those with incompatible needs. Compatible groups have a balance of initiators and receivers of control, inclusion and affection. In an incompatible group, for example, some members may want more affection than others are able to provide. Schutz has developed a psychometric measure (the FIRO-B) which enables the application of his ideas in the selection process (Schutz, 1958). Although some research has shown that compatibility on the dimensions of control and affection predicted time to task completion in groups of managers working in a laboratory setting, there is a good deal of evidence showing no relationships between compatibility and group performance (for example, Hill, 1982; Moos and Spiesman, 1962; Shaw and Nickols, 1964). Indeed, Hill (1982) found that incompatibility on FIRO-B was associated with higher productivity in teams of systems analysts!

Another popular approach to team personality issues is Belbin's Team Roles Model (Belbin, 1981, 1993). Belbin suggests that there are nine team personality types and that a balance of these team personality types is required within teams. These include: the co-ordinator—a person-oriented leader; the shaper—a task-focused leader; the plant—the creative person within the group; a resource investigator—who explores opportunities and develops contacts; an implementer—who works for the team in a practical and realistic way; a monitor evaluator—who prudently judges quality of decisions; a team worker—who makes helpful interventions to avert potential friction and maintain team spirit; a completer finisher—who aims to complete and to do so thoroughly; and the specialist—who provides knowledge and technical skills within the team. Belbin argues that a balance of all nine team roles is required for a team to perform effectively. Individuals usually incorporate several of these team role types in their personality profiles and so, within teams of only three or four individuals, there may nevertheless be primary and secondary team role types which cover the nine areas of team role functioning. However, there is little evidence to support these predictions and the instruments developed to measure the team role types (Belbin, 1981, 1993) do not appear to have good psychometric properties (Furnham, Steele and Pendleton, 1993). Scales have low internal consistencies and very high intercorrelations. In light of this, the widespread use of the Belbin model in organizational settings is curious.

A similar approach to identifying team roles and selecting for teams is described in the Team Management System developed by Margerison and McCann (1984) which describes nine team roles very similar to the Belbin categories, including reporter–adviser, creator–innovator, explorer–promoter, assessor–developer, thruster–organizer, concluder–producer, controller–inspector, upholder–maintainer, and linker. Again, the empirical evidence supporting this model is limited, with little well-controlled research assessing the predictions of the model.

IMPLICATIONS FOR RESEARCH AND PRACTICE

In this chapter we have taken a broad look at issues involving team selection and composition. The existing research in these areas can serve as a guide, we feel, for both researchers and practitioners. Though it is certainly premature to make definitive statements about how best to select for, and structure, work teams, much of practical use has been learned. In addition, the existing research highlights some directions in which future research could profitably head.

What are the implications of this research? Particularly promising, we feel, is work on the development of selection instruments assessing individual suitability for teamwork (e.g. Stevens and Campion, 1994b). At the practical level, this research reminds us that there is indeed individual variation in 'teamworthiness' and that, though some might prefer to believe otherwise, teamwork simply may not be for everyone (especially in the absence of team-relevant training).

Clearly, however, there is not yet consensus as to whether individual suitability for teams is best thought of in terms of personality, knowledge, skills, or abilities. Moreover, much validation work is needed. To date, predictors of team KSAs have been validated only at the individual level (Stevens and Campion, 1994b). While individual performance criteria are important—and critical in order to defend the use of such predictors in selection—team-level performance criteria must also be incorporated into further validation studies. Though this will add considerable complexity to validation efforts, failing to do so is to ignore the fact that, ultimately, the products or services provided by team members are the result of their collective efforts.

Related to this is the need for something akin to job analysis done at the team level. As described above, the notion that particular combinations of personal styles or personalities are needed to produce particularly successful teams has received very little support. At this point it is not entirely clear why this is the case, leaving us somewhat reluctant to abandon the general idea completely. It may well be that this is a reasonable idea, but that our hunches to date about 'what goes with what' are badly informed—perhaps because we have spent too little time examining and describing how effective and ineffective teams differ. To return to the jigsaw puzzle analogy used earlier, in order to know which pieces of the puzzle to choose and where to place them, one needs to know what the puzzle ought to look like. Team-level job (or task) analyses, augmented with good descriptive studies of team behaviour (e.g. Ancona, 1990; Gersick and Hackman, 1990), could provide this sort of information.

Turning to the other stream of team composition research, it is clear that differences between team members do have implications. Groups do seem to be advantaged, for example, by heterogeneity with respect to expertise or skills. Increasingly, organizations will want to examine heterogeneity of expertise to find not only a skill mix that will work, but one that will do so in the most cost-effective manner. We suggest that such efforts should go beyond traditional performance variables and consider skill/expertise mixes that will enhance such things as group and individual innovation (West, 1994), boundary-spanning (Ancona, 1990), and the ability of the group to modify its habits when needed (Gersick and Hackman, 1990).

The picture that emerges from research on sources of heterogeneity other than expertise/skills is much less clear. Group variability, on some attributes, is related to some group outcomes. Individual dissimilarity, on some attributes, is related to some individual outcomes. Many, though certainly not all, of the studies suggest that attribute variability can be problematic both for groups and for their individual members. Thus, despite its popular appeal, the idea that advantages will inevitably accrue to heterogeneous groups, and their members, is not well supported by the data. Obviously, however, it makes neither ethical nor practical sense to suggest that team staffing proceed with a view to maintain/increase the attribute of homogeneity of the team. Neither, however, would we recommend that organizations simply overlook the challenges presented by team heterogeneity. Instead, it is clear that both practitioners and researchers need to learn much more about this issue.

As a first step, we recommend that researchers focus attention on the processes that link team composition variables and outcome variables of interest. If we are to explain the complex pattern of observed links, and draw any practical implications from them, we may well need to go beyond the general notion underlying much of this research—that of similarity attraction—and become more precise in our theorizing. At the very least, we need to articulate clearly why 'being different' on a particular attribute would be expected to make an individual feel or behave in a particular way and how, in the longer term, this is related to team-level performance. Unfortunately, research with a focus on process and contextual variables is extremely rare (Zenger and Lawrence, 1989; Wiersema and Bird, 1993). We look forward to more such studies.

In addition, we recommend that team leaders be selected, in part, for their ability to deal with the team composition effects—that is, their ability to enhance the positive effects of heterogeneity and reduce its negative effects. At its core, this may require the ability to mobilize team members under a common banner. Strategies may include: the articulation by the leader of clear team-based goals, the use of socialization tactics that focus on what team members have in common rather than how they differ, and the development of mentoring relationships that capitalize on mentor/mentoree similarity (Anderson and Thomas, 1996). Team leaders will need to be able to do all this while, at the same time, maintaining the differentiation among roles that provide team members with a sense of their unique contribution to the team. Above all, they need to facilitate the exploration and integration of diverse and often conflicting viewpoints, in ways that enable teams to derive synergistic benefits from their diversity. These benefits could include enhanced creativity, innovation and effectiveness, along with skill-sharing and development.

Finally, as with other team/group issues, those interested in staffing cannot ignore the growing consensus amongst researchers that the effectiveness of teams is strongly dependent upon supports supplied by the organizational context within which the team is located (Guzzo and Shea, 1992; Hackman, 1990). By organizational supports we are referring to technical and training assistance available to the group, information systems enabling the group to set goals and plan performance, resources available to the group (staff, equipment, money), constraints in the work technology, and the structure of the reward systems within the organization. If team members are encouraged to work interdependently, for example, yet are rewarded only in terms of individual performance, what message is the organization sending about the value of teamwork (cf. Wageman, 1995)? Other elements of the organizational context include the structure of, and climate within, the organization. If the organizational structure is hierarchical and the climate authoritarian, for example, then the effectiveness of teamwork may be limited, since team members will be unlikely to have the autonomy and control needed to maximize the benefits accruing from team performance. In short, the organization must provide a context that reinforces the notion that team work is valuable and valued. Taken together, the research and practitioner literatures suggest that organizational support for teams may be the exception rather than the rule. From a staffing perspective, this is of considerable concern. Indeed, we would argue that, in the long run, any payoffs associated with selecting the best person for the team will be severely limited if organizational supports for teamwork are not in place.

REFERENCES

Allen, N.J., West, M.A., Nolan, J.M. and Anderson, N.R. (1996). Attribute dissimilarity and attachment to the team among senior managers. Unpublished manuscript.

Ancona, D.G. (1990). Outward bound: Strategies for team survival in an organization. *Academy of Management Journal*, **33**, 334–365.

Anderson, N.R. and Thomas, H.D.C. (1996). Work group socialization. In M.A. West (ed.), *The Handbook of Work Group Psychology*, pp. 423–450. Chichester: John Wiley.

Bantel, K.A. (1993). Strategic clarity in banking: Role of top management team demography. *Psychological Reports*, **73**, 1187–1201.

Bantel, K.A. and Jackson, S.E. (1989). Top management and innovations in banking: Does the composition of the top team make a difference? *Strategic Management Journal*, **10**, 107–124.

Belbin, R.M. (1981). *Management Teams: Why They Succeed or Fail*. London: Heinemann.

Belbin, R.M. (1993). *Team Roles at Work: A Strategy for Human Resource Management*. Oxford: Butterworth, Heinemann.

Byrne, D.E. (1971). *The Attraction Paradigm*. New York: Academic Press.

Cannon-Bowers, J.A., Tannenbaum, S.I., Salas, E. and Volpe, C.E. (1995). Defining competencies and establishing team training requirements. In R. Guzzo and E. Salas (eds.), *Team Effectiveness and Decision-Making in Organizations*, pp. 333–380. San Francisco, CA: Jossey-Bass.

Davey, L.M. (1995). *Kelly Service Industrial Applicant Screening Video: Test Manual*. Waterloo, Ont.: University of Waterloo.

Davis, J.H. (1969). Individual-group problem solving, subject preference, and problem type. *Journal of Personality and Social Psychology*, **13**, 362–374.

Earley, P.C. (1994). Self or group? Cultural effects of training on self-efficacy and performance. *Administrative Science Quarterly*, **39**, 89–117.

Furnham, A., Steele, H. and Pendleton, D. (1993). A psychometric assessment of the Belbin Team-Role Self-perception Inventory. *Journal of Occupational and Organizational Psychology*, **66**, 245–257.

Gersick, C.J. and Hackman, J.R. (1990). Habitual routines in task-performing groups. *Organizational Behavior and Human Decision Processes*, **47**, 65–97.

Gregorich, S.E., Helmreich, R.L. and Wilhelm, J.A. (1990). The structure of cockpit management attitudes. *Journal of Applied Psychology*, **75**, 682–690.

Guzzo, R.A. (1996). Fundamental considerations about work groups. In M.A. West (ed.), *The Handbook of Work Group Psychology*, pp. 3–23. Chichester: John Wiley.

Guzzo, R.A. and Shea, G.P. (1992). Group performance and inter group relations in organisations. In M.D. Dunnette and L.M. Hough (eds.), *Handbook of Industrial and Organizational Psychology*, vol. 3, pp. 269–313. Palo Alto, CA: Consulting Psychologists Press.

Hackman, J.R. (ed.) (1990). *Groups That Work (And Those That Don't): Creating Conditions for Effective Teamwork*. San Francisco, CA: Jossey-Bass.

Hill, M. (1982). Group versus individual performance. Are $N + 1$ heads better than one? *Psychological Bulletin*, **91**, 517–531.

Jackson, S.E., Brett, J.F., Sessa, V.I., Cooper, D.M., Julin, J.A. and Peyronnin, K. (1991). Some differences make a difference: Individual dissimilarity and group heterogeneity as correlates of recruitment, promotions, and turnover. *Journal of Applied Psychology*, **76**, 675–689.

Janis, I.L. (1982). *Groupthink: A Study of Foreign Policy Decisions and Fiascos*, 2nd edn. Boston, MA: Houghton Mifflin.

Margerison, C.J. and McCann, D.J. (1984). *How to Lead a Winning Team*. Manchester: MCB University Press.

McCain, B.E., O'Reilly, C. and Pfeffer, J. (1983). The effects of departmental demography on turnover: The case of a university. *Academy of Management Journal*, **26**, 626–641.

McGrath, J.E. (1984). *Groups: Interaction and Performance*. Englewood Cliffs, NJ: Prentice-Hall.

Moos, R.H. and Spiesman, J.C. (1962). Group compatibility and productivity. *Journal of Abnormal and Social Psychology*, **65**, 190–196.

NHSME (1992). *The Nursing Skill Mix in District Nursing*. London: HMSO.

O'Reilly, C.A., Caldwell, D.F. and Barnett, W.P. (1989). Work group demography, social integration, and turnover. *Administrative Science Quarterly*, **34**, 21–37.

Payne, R.L. (1990). The effectiveness of research teams: A review. In M.A. West and J.L. Farr (eds.), *Innovation and Creativity at Work: Psychological and Organizational Strategies*, pp. 101–122. Chichester: John Wiley.

Pillinger, T. and West, M.A. (1995). *Innovation in UK Manufacturing*. University of Sheffield: Institute of Work Psychology.

Pritchard, R.D., Jones, S.D., Roth, P.L., Stuebing, K.K. and Ekeberg, S.E. (1988). Effects of group feedback goal settings, and incentives on organizational productivity. *Journal of Applied Psychology*, **73**, 337–358.

Schneider, B. (1987). The people make the place. *Personnel Psychology*, **40**, 437–453.

Schutz, W.C. (1955). What makes groups productive? *Human Relations*, **8**, 429–465.

Schutz, W.C. (1958). FIRO: A Three Dimensional Theory of Interpersonal Behavior. New York: Holt Rinehart.

Schutz, W.C. (1967). *JOY: Expanding Human Awareness*. New York: Grove Press.

Shaw, M.E. and Nickols, S.A. (1964). *Group Effectiveness as a Function of Group Member Compatibility and Co-operation Requirements of the Task*. Technical Report No. 4, ONR Contract NR 170–226, Nonr – 580 [II]. Gainesville: University. Cited in Shaw, M.E. (1981). *Group Dynamics*, 3rd edn. New York: McGraw-Hill.

Stevens, M.J. and Campion, M.A. (1994a). The knowledge, skill, and ability requirements for teamwork: Implications for human resource management. *Journal of Management*, **20**, 503–530.

Stevens, M.J. and Campion, M.A. (1994b). Staffing teams: Development and validation of the Teamwork–KSA test. Paper presented at the annual meeting of the Society of Industrial and Organizational Psychology, Nashville, TN.

Sundstrom, E., DeMeuse, K.P. and Futrell, D. (1990). Work-teams: Applications and effectiveness. *American Psychologist*, **45**, 120–133.

Tsui, A.S., Egan, T.D. and O'Reilly, C.A. (1992). Being different: Relational demography and organizational attachment. *Administrative Science Quarterly*, **37**, 549–579.

Turner, J.C. (1987). *Rediscovering the Social Group: A Self-Categorization Theory*. Oxford: Blackwell.

Tziner, A. and Eden, D. (1985). Effects of crew composition on crew performance: Does the whole equal the sum of its parts? *Journal of Applied Psychology*, **70**, 85–93.

Wageman, R. (1995). Interdependence and group effectiveness. *Administrative Science Quarterly*, **40**, 145–180.

Wagner, W.G., Pfeffer, J. and O'Reilly, C.A. (1984). Organizational demography and turnover in top-management groups. *Administrative Science Quarterly*, **29**, 74–92.

Watson, W.E., Kumar, K. and Michaelsen, L.K. (1993). Cultural diversity's impact on interaction process and performance: Comparing homogeneous and diverse task groups. *Academy of Management Journal*, **36**, 590–602.

Weldon, E. and Weingart, L.R., (1993). Groups goals and group performance. *British Journal of Social Psychology*, **32**, 307–334.

West, M.A. (1994). *Effective Teamwork*. Leicester: BPS Books.

West, M.A. (ed.) (1966). *The Handbook of Work Group Psychology*. Chichester: John Wiley.

Wiersema, M.F. and Bantel, K.A. (1992). Top management team demography and corporate strategic change. *Academy of Management Journal*, **35**, 91–121.

Wiersema, M.F. and Bird, A. (1993). Organizational demography in Japanese firms: Group heterogeneity, individual dissimilarity, and top management team turnover. *Academy of Management Journal*, **36**, 996–1025.

Zenger, T.R. and Lawrence, B.S. (1989). Organizational demography: The differential effects of age and tenure distributions on technical communication. *Academy of Management Journal*, **32**, 353–376.

Chapter 25

Selection for Potential: The Case of Graduate Recruitment

Tony Keenan

*Department of Business Organisation, Heriot-Watt University,
Edinburgh, UK*

Even a cursory glance at how selection is carried out in practice strongly suggests that, in many selection situations, evaluation of previous relevant work experience is a critical element in the process. Indeed, relevant work experience is often explicitly stated as a requirement in job advertisements, and common sense suggests that the decision to invite for interview will be influenced by the perceived fit between job requirements and previous experience. Furthermore, although we know surprisingly little about the topics discussed in interviews (Keenan, 1989; Graves, 1993), it seems likely that discussion of previous relevant work experience would be a significant part of many selection interviews.

However, there are many circumstances where organizations find it necessary to recruit from applicant pools where candidates have little or no relevant work experience. In this case, where selection is being made for potential rather than current capability, how can recruiters make effective decisions in the absence of a substantial track record?

To analyse this issue in depth, the case of graduate recruitment has been selected as the subject of the present chapter, although many of the issues raised will be relevant to recruitment for other entry-level situations such as, for example, school leavers. There were a number of reasons for focusing on graduates. For example, in the United Kingdom and elsewhere they represent a large, and significant, sector of the employment market. They are also becoming an increasing proportion of the labour market with 30% of young people in the United Kingdom now in higher education, compared with 15% 10 years ago.

International Handbook of Selection and Assessment, Edited by N. Anderson and P. Herriot.

Furthermore, recruiters of graduates see these individuals as having potentially critical roles in their organizations both in the medium term and in the longer term.

There are several features of graduate recruitment which make the process particularly difficult for the recruiter. As already mentioned, most graduates lack significant work experience This is especially true in the United Kingdom where most students go straight from school to university. Also, because applicants typically come from a wide range of degree disciplines, and because they have studied at institutions with varying standards and systems of operation, recruiters are likely to have difficulty evaluating the experience they have had outside of the work environment. Frequently, they are not being selected for specific work roles initially, but rather with the intention of placement at a later date, perhaps even years ahead, say at the end of a lengthy training period. This in turn raises the tricky question of how to identify generic competencies that will be applicable across a variety of work roles. Even more problematic in terms of the job analysis process is the dilemma faced by many recruiters as to whether they should be aiming to select for short-term to medium-term performance or for long-term potential. Finally, graduates come from a population that has already been heavily pre-selected by the universities in terms of prior educational attainment and therefore, to some extent at least, cognitive ability. Thus recruiters have to select from a highly intelligent and relatively homogeneous group in terms of cognitive abilities, and the consequences of this for effective selection are unknown.

Further complications are created by the nature of the annual graduate recruitment cycle, at least as it operates in the United Kingdom. First, there is the sheer volume of applications many organizations are confronted with, which can run into hundreds or even thousands for a very small number of vacancies. Apart from the administrative headaches this creates, it also often leads to heavy pre-screening based on application forms. Most graduates make multiple applications to several organizations over the course of the annual recruitment cycle.[1] Given the fact that most graduates are likely to be naive and inexperienced in their approach to the job application process at the beginning of the cycle and if, given their high learning capacity, their impression management skills improve over the cycle, there is a danger that a given applicant's perceived suitability may be almost as much a function of where the person is on this learning curve as of his or her job-related abilities. As if all these problems were not enough, the whole process has to be completed within narrow predetermined windows of time dictated by university semesters, final examination schedules, and so on.

All these difficulties lead one to wonder about the overall effectiveness of the graduate recruitment process. One way to approach this question would be to evaluate each of its component parts separately and to examine how the effectiveness of each might be increased. This is the approach taken here and separate sections below will discuss graduate recruitment in relation to job analysis; application forms and biodata; interviews; and assessment centres.

GRADUATE RECRUITMENT IN PRACTICE

Job analysis

The need for systematic job analysis to identify selection criteria has long been recognized among researchers, although the extent to which this is a view that is also held by practising graduate recruiters is unknown. However, some years ago Keenan (1976), in a study of graduate recruitment interviewers from 79 organizations, found that the personal qualities sought in graduates were more a function of personal preferences than systematic selection criteria laid down by their organizations. However, in the intervening years since that study was carried out, greater prominence has been given to the whole issue of the specification of criteria in relation to selection, notably with the increasing popularity of various competency frameworks (Sparrow, 1997). It is not clear, however, how far this trend has influenced actual graduate recruitment practice. There is little systematic evidence on this issue, although a recent study by Knights and Raffo (1990) suggests that relatively little change has occurred in reality. Following a survey of 20 major graduate recruitment companies, they drew rather similar conclusions to Keenan (1976) reporting that 'the graduate specification . . . is often no more than a reflection of the particular prejudices and expectations of personnel managers'. Although this sample is too small to enable definite conclusions to be drawn, it is worth noting that the companies involved recruit a significant proportion of the total output of UK graduates.

As already mentioned, many organizations do not seek to place graduates in specific work roles at the outset, so that the most appropriate criteria for them would seem to be a set of generic abilities that would be applicable across a variety of managerial work roles. Paradoxically, there are also circumstances where organizations seeking to place applicants in specific work roles immediately also concentrate on generic abilities. This occurs in organizations where the number of job functions to be filled is large but the numbers to be recruited into each are small. Under these circumstances, many organizations feel they simply do not have the time or resources to carry out a whole series of separate job analyses for each work role. How can this situation be resolved in practice?

The first question that needs to be addressed here is: Is it possible to produce a generic list of abilities that would be applicable to a range of jobs? There is impressionistic evidence, gathered by the present author in a series of job analyses for several major organizations recruiting graduates, which suggests that it may be possible to identify generic abilities of this type. The method used in these analyses seeks to identify the behavioural requirements for high performance and is a variation on that described in Campbell *et al.* (1973). As defined here, behavioural requirements have much in common with the notion of behavioural competencies discussed by Sparrow (Chapter 17 in this volume). Briefly, behavioural statements are generated in brainstorming sessions with managers who are familiar with graduates' jobs in the organization. These are then grouped into dimensions. Separate groups of managers then rate statements for importance and evaluate the accuracy of behavioural allocations to dimensions. The next stage is to refine the list on the basis of a number of factors, such as importance, clarity, overlap, and so on. Experience using this method in over 30 organizations for a very diverse set of jobs can be summarized as follows. There is considerable commonality across both job functions and organizations in the initial list of behavioural statements and dimensions generated. At a rough guess most lists have about 70% of statements that closely resemble each other. The number of dimensions generated varies between four and eight, with certain core dimensions (e.g. planning and organizing, interpersonal skills) almost always present. This commonality could be interpreted as the generic component of graduate selection criteria.

This method is also applicable where organizations need to go beyond generic criteria and wish to specify criteria for particular roles. This can be done by examining importance ratings, several of which differ markedly across functions and organizations. To take an illustrative example, the statement 'able to persuade others effectively' was rated as 'highly important' by 16% of managers when the job in question was a research scientist. The same item was given a 'highly important' rating by 70% of managers when the job in question was that of production engineer. An example where importance varies at the level of the organization is 'ability to adapt to change'. All organizations value this to some extent, but it is more critical for some companies than others.

The method for developing criteria described above is based on the premise that selectors are primarily attempting to match abilities to job performance requirements. However, in practice, many selectors may be looking for person–organization fit as much as person–job fit, i.e. does the person share the values and 'modal personality' of the organization? While few would seriously question the logic of seeking to maximize person-job fit, the wisdom of focusing excessively on person–organization fit is much more questionable in many circumstances. For example, person–organization fit could actually be counterproductive if innovation is a key organizational requirement.

Assuming that the organization has carried out a systematic specification of the behavioural requirements for effective job performance, the next logical step in the recruitment process is to consider where to look for evidence of these abilities. This is the question of choice of selection devices. Commonly used selection tools would include application forms, cognitive tests, interviews and assessment centres. Even when optimal selection tools have been identified, it is also essential to use them appropriately in a graduate recruitment context if selection is to be effective. To address these issues, it is necessary to consider each of the selection tools commonly used for graduate recruitment in turn.

Application forms

A conventional application form is capable of influencing selection decisions in at least three ways. First, if paper pre-screening is operating, it leads to the direct elimination of candidates. Secondly, for those shortlisted, it may influence prior perceptions of their suitability before interviews take place. Thirdly, it may function as a guide for the interviewer suggesting areas to explore and develop in the interview. As far as the United Kingdom is concerned, it is clear that virtually all organizations currently pre-screen, often quite heavily, thus reducing their applicant pool considerably (Keenan, 1995). To take the second point, there is now considerable evidence that pre-interview impressions gained from application forms can significantly affect final selection outcomes (Macan and Dipboye, 1990), although the extent to which this is due to pre-interview initial perceptions or to an influence on question content in the interview is unclear. In any event, the information in application forms appears to have an important influence on selection outcomes in graduate recruitment. All of this would lead one to expect that the majority of organizations would take considerable care in the design and use of application forms for graduate recruitment.

A recent survey of graduate recruitment practices of 536 organizations in the United Kingdom (Keenan, 1995) found that this was frequently not the case, even though virtually all of the organizations in question were using the application form for pre-selection and many were rejecting a high proportion of candidates at this stage. Consider first the question of application form design. Very few organizations in the survey appeared to design their form around selection criteria, and over half did not even have their own application form but relied instead on off-the-shelf products. Even when an in-house form was used, in only half of cases had it been designed specifically for graduates.

All of this leads to the interesting question of the content of the typical graduate application form. In other words: What type of information is actually requested from graduates? In an earlier investigation Keenan (1983) classified the content of 100 randomly selected graduate application forms into free response and closed formats. Academic qualifications, work experience and spare-time interests were typically in closed format (i.e. applicants provide a statement of facts without opportunity to comment). The most common free response questions related to: reasons for wanting to join the organization; reasons for selecting a particular work area; career ambitions; and self-assessment of strengths and weaknesses. Given the fact that in many of these forms most of the available space was given over to the free response sections, how applicants actually respond to this type of question is an important issue. In a follow-up, previously unpublished, study a group of graduates who had just completed real job application forms were asked to indicate in which sections of the form they had made up answers purely to please the recruiter (as opposed to answering honestly). The results are shown in Table 25.1, from which it can be seen that the areas most favoured for 'impression management' were also those identified in the Keenan (1983) study as the most popular with employers in terms of free-format questions. In the light of this finding a further investigation was undertaken as part of the Keenan (1995) survey. In this case recruiters themselves were asked to identify sections of the form where *they* thought graduates would make up answers. These data are also shown in Table 25.1, and it can be seen that the recruiters' views correspond quite closely to the reality as described by the students. Thus, we have the interesting situation where the most popular free-format questions on graduate application forms are those that encourage graduates to fake answers, even though the majority of recruiters apparently know this to be the case! Perhaps this is not as paradoxical as it seems since the respondents in the Keenan (1995) survey were mainly the users of application forms in organizations, rather than those who had been responsible for designing them.

Table 25.1   Comparisons between recruiters' opinions about how graduates complete application forms and self-reports of graduates themselves

	Recruiter sample	Graduate Sample
	In which sections of the application form are students more likely to make up answers simply to please the recruiter?	In which sections of the application form did you make up an answer simply to please the recruiter?
	(% saying Quite/Very Likely)	(% saying 'Quite' or 'Very' True)
Subjects taken at university	4	5
Demographic details, i.e. age/sex/address	1	3
Hobbies and interests	56	40
Attitudes, skills, personal qualities	67	45
Career ambitions	69	57
Reason for choice of type of work	66	49
Reasons for choice of company	81	73

All of this leads one to wonder how graduate application forms are actually used in practice. The importance of the pre-screening task, and the fact that many forms seem to be less than ideal from a design point of view, both suggest the need to train screeners carefully in their use. Training in how to interpret applicants' responses would seem to be particularly critical, because of the apparent problem of faking discussed above. However, Keenan (1995) found that, although half of the sample of recruiters claimed to have received some training in this area, its quality seemed questionable in many cases. Thus for one-third of respondents it consisted of no more than observing an 'experienced' screener at work. Also, only one in three of those trained was given guidance in how to interpret answers. Finally, it also turned out that those organizations that were screening most heavily were actually less likely to provide any training for their screeners.

While the above discussion implies that the processes graduate recruiters use to make pre-screening decisions are often less than systematic, there is actually little published research that directly addresses this question. Wingrove, Glendinning and Herriot (1984) found that, in addition to qualifications and achievements, applicants' form-filling behaviour and aspects of their background predicted pre-screening decisions made by graduate recruiters. Knights and Raffo (1990) found that, although superficially managers claimed to operate in a systematic way in this respect, the practical reality was very different, with individuals effectively adopting their own rule-of-thumb procedures to reach decisions. By way of illustration, they cite two screeners from the same organization one of whom focused mainly on reasons for joining the organization, while the other concentrated on academic qualifications. The Knights and Raffo study was based on interviews with recruiters. The present author, in a previously unpublished study in a single organization, took a different approach to investigate these decision-making processes. Eight screeners, working with guidelines supplied by the organization, were asked to make 'accept for interview' or 'reject' judgements on the same 100 application forms. They were also asked to rate the information provided in each subsection of the form for favourability using Likert-type scales. The results revealed virtually no agreement among screeners in accept–reject recommendations. A more detailed ideographic analysis was carried out by treating each screener as the unit of analysis and using favourability ratings for each subsection to predict decisions using multiple regression procedures. It turned out that, on the whole, individuals were reasonably consistent in the type of information they used to arrive at decisions, although some were more so than others. However, the information utilized differed from one screener to another. In one case perception of favourability of academic record at school predicted decisions with little unique variance being added by other sources of information. For another screener extra-curricular interests was the main predictor, while for a third the crucial information was that pertaining to reasons for wanting to join the organization.

These studies suggest that, at least in some circumstances, application form screening is far from being the systematic process it ought to be. The detrimental effects of such a situation of essentially random pre-selection for the later stages of selection cannot be over-emphasized. Because the final selection stages are often highly costly in terms of time and money, companies typically expect to recruit a relatively high proportion of those invited for final assessment. But a randomly screened sample is unlikely to contain a high proportion of high quality applicants. This explains the not infrequently experienced paradox where an organization can have an extremely large number of initial applications and yet still end up with a shortfall at the end of the day. What is not known is how widespread the practices described above are. That is a question that should be addressed in future research.

Biodata

Clearly one of the major problems of pre-screening using traditional application forms is the subjective nature of the judgements made. Given this, and the associated problems outlined above, an alternative approach which could be adopted would be to use biodata. While it is time consuming to set up, once developed, biodata provides a method that is both economical in time and objective in terms of the method used to evaluate the information. Also in favour of its use is the fact that the evidence indicates that biodata can be one of the more valid predictors for a number of different jobs (Hunter and Hunter, 1984). As far as graduate recruitment is concerned, two key questions need to be asked about biodata. First, is it practicable to adopt this approach given the time that has to be invested in development work? Secondly, can we reasonably assume that it will still be a valid procedure in the particular case of graduate recruitment?

The answer to the first question will of course depend on the circumstances of individual organizations, not just in terms of the resources available, but also in terms of the numbers being recruited annually. As far as the latter question is concerned, it is worth noting that in the Keenan (1995) survey, around 40% of organizations were expecting to recruit less than 10 graduates each year. It is questionable whether many of these organizations could be readily convinced that investment in biodata would be justified. Of course, if it proves possible to develop biographical items that are sufficiently robust to generalize across situations, as has been suggested recently (Rothstein *et al.*, 1990), then a biodata approach may be a viable one even when the numbers being recruited are small.

The question of validity of biodata for graduate populations is more difficult to answer given the dearth of published empirical studies on this particular applicant population. However, one important consideration here is the type of biodata item that can be used with graduates. There are many different types of biodata item, and indeed there is no agreed definition of what actually constitutes biodata (Mael, 1991). One useful distinction is between 'hard' items which consist of factual information that is actually verifiable, and 'soft' non-verifiable items dealing with attitudes, opinions, and so on. The question is: Would biodata for graduate populations be likely to use predominantly verifiable or non-verifiable items? Given the relative homogeneity of graduates with regard to at least some verifiable items (e.g. age, length of previous employment, educational qualifications) one suspects there might be a tendency to opt more for attitudinal types of item. This could create difficulties as far as validity is concerned, given the increased possibility of faking these items compared with items where the accuracy of the responses can be checked, at least in theory. The evidence is scant on how far individuals can and do fake such items, although recently Becker and Colquitt (1992) were able to show that individuals did fake some biodata items in a real selection situation and that these were the less verifiable ones. In a study of impression management in completing biodata items, Stokes, Hogan and Snell (1993) reported that job incumbents responded differently to items than did actual job applicants. The latter exhibited greater responding in the direction of high social desirability with differences between the two groups being less for verifiable items. Furthermore, items that were valid in one sample had no validity in the other. This last point highlights the dangers of developing scoring keys for biodata on existing employees and assuming that they can be safely used to pre-select actual job applicants without carrying out further confirmatory validation. In fact, the present author in one such, as yet unpublished, confirmatory validation study on graduate biodata where the scoring keys had been developed on existing employees, found that the biodata score had no predictive validity when used on applicant populations.

In summary, while there is evidence that biodata can be a valid predictor of performance for many jobs, caution should be exercised in applying it in a graduate recruitment context, especially if homogeneity with regard to verifiable items leads to a heavy reliance on non-verifiable ones. At the very least, careful validation checks on applicant samples would seem to be indicated in these circumstances.

The interview

In graduate recruitment the majority of organizations use interviews both for pre-screening and in the final stages of the selection process.

Until relatively recently, the research evidence indicated that interviews lacked validity (Wagner, 1949; Mayfield, 1964; Ulrich and Trumbo, 1965). Indeed, studies of the way in which graduate recruitment interviews are typically conducted suggest that, in all probability, they are likely to fit this general pattern. Thus, Keenan (1977) found that personal liking for the candidate was strongly associated with evaluation of suitability. More recently, Graves and Powell (1988), and Anderson and Shackleton (1990), also found that both personal liking as well as perceived similarity were associated with suitability ratings in graduate recruitment interviews. A few studies have investigated the content of graduate recruitment interviews and these also provide circumstantial evidence of lack of validity. Keenan and Wedderburn (1980) found that interviewers did not cover the topics they believed were important and did not cover topics consistently across interviews. Also, they gave greater emphasis to topics related to their own organizations than to candidates' past achievements. Taylor and Sniezek (1984) reported broadly similar results for an American sample of college graduates. Knights and Raffo (1990) found that interviewers often used an 'amalgam of idiosyncratic and personal approaches' when interviewing. According to these authors one reason for this was the feeling that graduates were too well rehearsed and prepared for the interview to allow the use of what they referred to as 'standard techniques' (p. 33).

In recent years the pessimistic conclusions on interview validity drawn by the early reviewers have been increasingly questioned. Evidence from meta-analysis suggests that the interview can be valid provided it is highly structured (Weisner and Cronshaw, 1988; Wright, Lichtenfels and Pursell, 1989; McDaniel *et al.*, 1994; Huffcutt and Arthur, 1994). While there is no universally agreed definition of what constitutes a structured interview, it would appear to have four main distinguishing features. These are: prior systematic job analysis to identify essential behavioural requirements for effective job performance; all questions asked are job related; scoring guides and rating scales are provided for interviewers; and ratings of specific abilities are combined to arrive at an overall rating. Of these four requirements, the second is probably the most problematic with regard to graduate selection.

Two well-known models of the structured interview are the situational interview (Latham and Saari, 1984) and the patterned behaviour description interview (PBDI) (Janz, 1982). The description of what constitutes job-related questions in these two models illustrates the difficulty. In the situational interview, applicants are invited to describe how they think they *would* deal with a pre-determined set of job-related hypothetical situations. All applicants are asked the same questions and it is assumed that their actual behaviour would correspond to their intended behaviour as described to the interviewer. The patterned behaviour description interview (PBDI), on the other hand, requires candidates to describe their *past* job behaviour in detail. In this case the questions vary to some extent from one candidate to another, reflecting each person's unique past experiences. The basic assumption here is that past behaviour predicts future behaviour. Taking the situational interview first, the questions are typically derived from critical incident analysis of the particular job for which candidates are being considered. Were this approach to be applied to graduate recruitment a problem would arise in so far as, in many cases, the organization does not actually know at the selection stage which particular job the graduate will ultimately be doing. Perhaps more fundamental are the difficulties arising from many graduates' limited job experience. If, because of lack of relevant work experience, a person has no awareness of the key parameters and contextual factors surrounding critical events as applied to a particular job role, how can he or she tackle the questions in a sensible and informed way? After all, we are talking about individuals who may have never had experience of anything even remotely related to the job role that is under discussion. It is easy to see how the graduate's position here is quite different from that of the typical experienced applicant, who can bring his knowledge to bear to analyse the situation and debate possible courses of action. Turning to the PBDI approach, this requires candidates to discuss experiences and achievements from previous job roles that have analogous elements to the job for which the person is being recruited. But most graduates may not have had these kind of experiences since they have not had similar job roles to those for which they are applying. To summarize, it seems that, if graduate recruitment interviews are to adopt the successful structured interview model, then a key issue to be addressed is how to generate appropriate job-related questions in the absence of experience in similar work roles to the jobs for which they are being recruited.

Assessment centres

Assessment centres are relatively popular with graduate recruiters in the United Kingdom. In the Keenan (1995) study, just under half of respondents reported that their organizations used them. Keenan found that the interview was almost always an integral part of the assessment centre, and use of cognitive (91%) and personality tests (80%) was also high. Popular simulations included group discussions, in-trays, and presentations. However, there was no discernible relationship between the apparent validity of a particular test or exercise and its popularity with recruiters. For example, cognitive tests and personality tests were almost equally popular, despite the fact that the evidence for validity is much stronger for the former than for the latter (Hunter and Hunter, 1984). Another notable feature of these assessment centres was the extent to which the interview was dominant in the final decision. When asked to rank components of the assessment centre for importance in determining the final decision, four out of five respondents in the survey placed the interview top of the list. This is particularly worrying in view of the evidence cited above that graduate interviews can often be of poor quality.

Why was the interview apparently so dominant in its influence on decision-making in these assessment centres? There was certainly circumstantial evidence that decision-making was often more a matter of intuitive judgement than of following systematic decision-making rules. But why should intuition favour interview data rather than data from any of the other tests and exercises? On the one hand, it could be simply that the face-to-face nature of the interview encounter inevitably creates a strong impression which then feeds through to decision-making. Recruiters may just have a lot of faith in the interview. However, it is possible to look at the problem from the opposite perspective. Perhaps the particular simulations were not producing as much valid information in the graduate recruitment context as is typical in other selection situations. There is some, admittedly circumstantial, evidence to support this from an unpublished validation study of a graduate assessment centre carried out by the author in a large engineering company. This particular assessment centre included a variety of psychometric tests and simulations and a structured interview. Only the interview score significantly predicted subsequent job performance.

Another way to look at this issue is to examine the precise nature of the exercises used in assessment centres for graduate recruitment. Unfortunately, there are no systematic data available on this and all that can be offered is the author's, admittedly anecdotal, experience of working with a number of organizations who have installed such systems. The majority of exercises seem to follow the established model of designing simulations around elements of managerial jobs, either tailor-made for a particular organization, or perhaps more often bought as off-the-shelf products. This is presumably based on the premiss that participants have sufficient relevant experience to interpret and act upon the situation they are presented with in a realistic way. Yet again, this is precisely what graduates lack. For example, how can someone who has never even been inside a factory be expected to deal sensibly with a production manager's in-tray? How can someone who has no real concept of the marketing function or how it fits into an organization realistically take on the assigned role of the marketing manager in a group discussion? As far as the latter is concerned, someone who has taken a degree in business studies may be able to do this if the role of the marketing function had been explained to him or her in lectures. But, if this is so, many would see this as an example of one candidate having an unfair advantage over another, rather than anything else. The potentially de-motivating effect of this type of exercise, where candidates are assigned roles with which they have no familiarity, is well illustrated by the remarks of one history graduate who, on the basis of his lack of contribution to a group exercise, had (unknown to him) just been rated as lacking in the interpersonal skills needed for team working. His comments to the author were: 'They asked me to play the role of finance director. I know nothing about finance or what finance directors do. Since I make it a rule in life not to shoot my mouth off about things I know nothing about, I did not say anything in the discussion.'

Once again we have come up against the situation where approaches that work well when candidates have significant relevant work experience may be falling down when applied to new graduates. Clearly some way has to be found to fill the vacuum this creates in order to make graduate recruitment more effective. It is to this issue that we now turn.

AN ALTERNATIVE APPROACH TO GRADUATE RECRUITMENT

It has been argued above that graduates' lack of experience in work roles similar to those for which they are applying effectively means that tried and tested approaches to the various elements of the selection process are unlikely to work very well with this population. This would appear to be the single most difficult aspect of graduate selection. The underlying assumption behind the focus on previous experience in all selection situations is the simple but well-founded notion that past behaviour and achievements predict future behaviour and achievements. The logic behind assessment centre simulations is, in principle, not very different, i.e. behaviour in the here-and-now will be predictive of future actions. Of course the formula works best where past and future situations share common elements, and this is where the root of the present problem, and indeed the answer, lies. The solution is not, as some recruiters seem to believe, to abandon the basic principle in favour of a focus on more intuitive and impressionistic methods. Rather, the approach advocated here is to continue applying the basic principle but to look for significant experiences which can substitute for relevant work role experience. This involves analysing the major experiences that graduates have had, at university and elsewhere, to identify activities that share common elements with critical tasks to be carried out in employment. To the author's knowledge this is seldom done in the systematic and comprehensive manner that is necessary to ensure successful recruitment.

This approach has been used by the author on a number of occasions. The process can be described as follows. The first stage is to identify major areas of experience which are shared by most graduates during their university careers. For example, in the academic sphere, many have to complete a major project or dissertation. All will be subjected to formal assessment and examinations and many will have to spend significant time in small group, seminar-type, situations. These constitute the main elements of academic experience which have been the focus of this approach. These broad areas of experience are then subjected to more detailed analysis, the object of which is to establish the key behavioural requirements needed in order to be able to complete the tasks involved in each area successfully. In some respects this procedure is analogous to the job analysis process, but for the 'job' of student.

The next stage can only be carried out once the key behavioural requirements for effective performance in the jobs for which candidates are being recruited have been established through job analysis. Once this has been done, the two sets of information are cross-referenced and commonalities identified. As a result of this process the recruiter knows precisely where in the typical graduate's experience to look for each of the abilities he or she is interested in. By way of illustration, experience of using the technique indicates that there is a pool of around 20 or so behavioural requirements needed to produce a high quality undergraduate project which are also relevant to successful performance in a range of graduate-level jobs. These include: setting and meeting deadlines; dealing effectively with setbacks; learning from mistakes; and so on. A similar number of relevant behaviours can be identified in the academic performance area. Once again, behavioural requirements defined in this way are similar in many respects to the notion of behavioural competencies (see Herriot and Anderson, Chapter 1 in this volume).

The next stage in the process is to link this information to the various selection instruments as illustrated below.

The application form

Using this approach, the application form can be designed in such a way as to be criteria based, as can the judgements based on the information it contains. For example, suppose that one of the criteria for effective job performance is 'continues to put in effort even on disliked tasks'. This is a behavioural requirement for success in certain examinations. (How many students like all of the courses they are required to take?) By designing the form in such a way that applicants give details of relative performance in liked and less-liked courses, information can be obtained on this issue. To take another example, if 'ability to overcome setbacks' is a job performance requirement, candidates could be asked to provide information about their project in which they are explicitly required to describe something that went wrong and how they overcame the problem. One assumption underlying this approach is that applicants will be less likely to fake responses to questions that refer to specific past events compared with the more generalized motivational questions illustrated in Table 25.1. However, this assumption still awaits empirical test. In any case, the kind of information described above can also be used for questioning in the interview to explore issues further and verify its authenticity.

When this approach to application form design is taken, it has been the author's experience that many previously popular questions are excluded from the form (e.g. reasons for joining the company) because they are seen by recruiters as irrelevant. The approach taken here is unlike biodata, since recruiters still have to make a subjective decision about candidates. Nevertheless, it is possible to encourage a systematic approach to decision-making on the part of recruiters, both by giving them guidelines on which criteria are being evaluated in each section, and through the use of benchmark training in the form of providing examples of answers of varying quality for each section of the form.

The interview

It is possible with this approach to devise a structured interview which meets all four of the requirements for a structured interview outlined above. In particular, job-related questions can be constructed without relying solely on the typical graduate's limited work experiences. A structured interview designed according to this method typically covers the following areas of the graduate's experience: academic performance; project work; work experience; and extra-curricular activities. Critical behaviours and achievements to be explored in each area are identified as described above, and a comprehensive list of questions is provided for investigating each of them. Intensive training in using the technique is necessary, not just in the usual interviewing skills, but also in giving recruiters an in-depth understanding of how the university system operates, of the demands placed on students, and of how students behave in response to these. All of this is necessary, not just to enable interviewers to obtain high quality relevant information, but also to enable them to interpret that information and make appropriate evaluations against their selection criteria.

To date the author has carried out only one, as yet unpublished, predictive validity study of interviews conducted using this technique. In the investigation, interview scores of 90 technical graduates were correlated with job performance between one and four years later. The criterion used was supervisors' ratings. Interviewers provided ratings on six behavioural dimensions plus an overall rating. The predictive validity of the latter, corrected for criterion unreliability but not range restriction, was $r = 0.38$. Validity coefficients varied significantly across the dimensions, and combining the three 'best' dimensions to provide a summated score produced a validity coefficient of $r = 0.48$.

Assessment centres

Since many of the behavioural requirements for effective job performance have counterparts in graduates' university environment, it follows that simulation exercises can be built around university, rather than organizational, scenarios. These should not only be more realistic given their experience of this environment, but graduates should have a better understanding of the context of the situations and the parameters involved than is likely to be the case with organizationally based exercises. This, in turn, should allow a greater range of relevant behaviours to be observed than would otherwise be the case. The author has developed just such a set of simulations and they are in use in a number of organizations. Over 200 graduates were involved in the development of these exercises. As part of the development work their views on the approach being adopted were requested. Reactions were almost universally favourable. However, the development of these exercises is a recent innovation and no data are yet available on whether this approach produces a more valid outcome than the more conventional approach of using exercises built around organizational scenarios.

THE FUTURE OF GRADUATE RECRUITMENT

This chapter has discussed some of the problematic areas in graduate recruitment as it is currently being carried out and has offered an alternative approach as a way of improving its effectiveness. However, the world of both work and education is changing rapidly and as a result more radical approaches than those outlined above may have to be contemplated in the future.

In the United Kingdom, if not elsewhere, there has been a very marked increase in the number of students attending university over the last few years and this is now beginning to have an impact on the graduate labour market. Thus, increasingly, organizations will be faced with even larger numbers of applicants than before, at a time when there is no reason to expect a corresponding increase in job vacancies. This means that there will be pressure to pre-select out even more applicants at an early stage than at present. Not only will companies have to use state-of-the art methods for this, but it may be that entirely new methods of pre-screening will need to be developed. Also, organizations will have to take the issue of self-selection as a way of reducing applications much more seriously than they have done in the past. At present, within the United Kingdom at least, it is common to find organizations complaining about the need to reduce numbers of applications while simultaneously designing their recruitment literature to appeal to all graduates, irrespective of their suitability for the jobs in question. In future, recruitment brochures may need to focus much more on pre-selection by providing information that would allow a significant number of potential applicants to decide that they are not suited for, or interested in, the jobs in question. There are a number of ways of doing this, not all of which need be expensive. Two examples are realistic work diaries showing everyday job experiences and job knowledge questionnaires (with answers attached).

Of course, it is not just the recruitment literature that can be used to reduce applications through rational self-selection. In the author's experience, criterion-related application forms of the type described above almost always result in a significant reduction in the number of applicants. In one, admittedly unusual, case the reduction was so marked that the organization was able to take applicants directly to an assessment centre after paper pre-screening without the need for preliminary interviews. In this particular case, self-selection seemed to have worked well, since the quality of the candidates at the assessment centre was judged to be so high that all applicants were judged to be acceptable for the jobs in question.

The increasing internationalization, and indeed globalization, of the market place also has implications for recruitment practices. For example, additional abilities may be needed in the more internationally oriented managers of the future leading to a modification and elaboration of selection criteria for graduates. However, evidence from a study of how organizations were adapting their practices to one particular aspect of this phenomenon—the development of the free market in Europe in 1992—indicated that, while there was plenty of awareness of the issue, in reality precious little was being done to modify graduate recruitment practices in the light of these changes (Keenan, 1992). For example, very few of the organizations studied were making a significant effort to recruit graduates from other countries and hardly any of them had modified their selection criteria to embrace abilities needed to function effectively at an international level.

Organizations are also changing markedly in their structures and this may also have significant implications for future graduate recruitment. For example, trends towards downsizing, de-layering, and so on may mean that traditional hierarchical career structures may be becoming a thing of the past. If, in response to this, individual career satisfaction in future has to come from a series of horizontal moves to different jobs rather than vertical progression, then this has implications for selection criteria. For example, flexibility, learning ability, positive reactions to change, and the ability to manage change may become more critical qualities than the match between a specific set of abilities to a particular job role. In this new work environment, organizations may seek to recruit fewer people, but these few may be more critical to the effective functioning of the organization. This makes it even more vital for the selection process to be as valid as possible. This in turn may stimulate organizations to develop more elaborate selection procedures than in the past. An example might be two-stage selection (Hanisch and Hulin, 1994). This is a sequential selection process where the first stage involves traditional selection procedures such as interviews and ability tests. Employees are then hired on a trial basis and subsequent training performance becomes an integral part of selection as the second stage in the process. In a simulation study, Hanisch and Hulin (1994) were able to show that the incremental validity of training performance was both statistically and practically significant in the prediction of overall task performance.

A number of the alternative approaches to graduate recruitment discussed in this chapter could turn out to be more costly and time consuming for organizations than what is being done currently. However, in the final analysis the amount of time and energy an organization should put into its graduate selection should really be dictated not by short-term cost considerations but by the extent to which it wants and needs top grade performance from its future managers.

ENDNOTE

1. In the United Kingdom, the cycle typically begins in the October–December period when graduates make multiple applications. Following screening, initial interviews take place from January to March. These are followed by final selection interviews and often assessment centres in the April–June period.

REFERENCES

Anderson, N. and Shackleton, V. (1990). Decision making in the graduate selection interview: A field study. *Journal of Occupational Psychology*, **63**, 63–76.

Becker, T.E. and Colquitt, A.L. (1992). Potential versus actual faking of a biodata form: An analysis along several dimensions of item type. *Personnel Psychology*, **45**, 389–406.

Campbell, J.P., Dunnette, M., Arvey, R.D. and Hellervik, L.V. (1973). The development and evaluation of behaviourally based rating scales. *Journal of Applied Psychology*, **57**, 15–22.

Graves, L.M. (1993). Sources of individual differences in interviewer effectiveness: A model and implications for future research. *Journal of Organizational Behavior*, **14**, 349–370.

Graves, L.M. and Powell, S.N. (1988). An investigation of sex discrimination in recruiters' evaluation of actual applicants. *Journal of Applied Psychology*, **73**, 20–29.

Hanisch, K.A. and Hulin, C.L. (1994). Two-stage sequential selection procedures using ability and training performance: Incremental validity of behavioural consistency measures. *Personnel Psychology*, **47**, 767–785.

Huffcutt, A.I. and Arthur, W. (1994). Hunter and Hunter re-visited: Interview validity for entry-level jobs. *Journal of Applied Psychology*, **79**, 184–190.

Hunter, J.E. and Hunter, R.F. (1984). Validity and utility of alternative predictors of job performance. *Psychological Bulletin*, **96**, 72–98.

Janz, T. (1982). Initial comparisons of patterned behavior description interviews versus unstructured interviews. *Journal of Applied Psychology*, **67**, 577–580.

Keenan, A. (1976). Interviewers' evaluations of applicant characteristics: Differences between personnel and non-personnel managers. *Journal of Occupational Psychology*, **49**, 223–230.

Keenan, A. (1977). Some relationships between interviewers' personal feelings about candidates and their general evaluation of them. *Journal of Occupational Psychology*, **50**, 275–283.

Keenan, A. (1983). Where application forms mislead. *Personnel Management*, February, 39–43.

Keenan, A. (1989). Selection interviewing. In C.L. Cooper and I. Robertson (eds.). *International Review of Industrial and Organizational Psychology*. New York: John Wiley.

Keenan, A. (1992). Graduate recruitment and the Single European market. *European Management Journal*, **10**, 485–493.

Keenan, A. (1995). Graduate recruitment in Britain: a survey of selection methods used by organizations. *Journal of Organizational Behavior*, **16**, 303–317.

Keenan, A. and Wedderburn, A.A.I. (1980). Putting the boot on the other foot: Candidates' descriptions of interviewers. *Journal of Occupational Psychology*, **53**, 81–89.

Knights, D. and Raffo, C. (1990). Milk round professionalism in personnel recruitment: Myth or reality? *Personnel Review*, **19**, 28–37.

Latham, G.P. and Saari, L.M. (1984). Do people do what they say? Further studies of the situational interview. *Journal of Applied Psychology*, **69**, 569–573.

Macan, T.H. and Dipboye, R.L. (1990). The relationship of interviewers' pre-interview impressions to selection and recruitment outcomes. *Personnel Psychology*, **43**, 745–768.

Mael, F.E. (1991). A conceptual rationale for the domain and attributes of biodata items. *Personnel Psychology*, **44**, 763–792.

Mayfield, E.C. (1964). The selection interview: A re-evaluation of published research. *Personnel Psychology*, **17**, 239–260.

McDaniel, M.A., Whetzel, D.R., Schmidt, F.L. and Maurer, S.D. (1994). The validity of employment interviews: A comprehensive review and meta-analysis. *Journal of Applied Psychology*, **79**, 599–616.

Rothstein, H.R., Schmidt, F.L., Erwin, R.W., Owens, W.A. and Sparks, C.P. (1990). Biographical data in employment selection: Can validators be generalizable? *Journal of Applied Psychology*, **75**, 175–184.

Sparrow, P.R. (1997). Organizational competencies: Creating a strategic behavioural framework for selection and assessment. In N. Anderson and P. Herriot (eds.), *Handbook of Selection and Appraisal*. New York: John Wiley.

Stokes, G.S., Hogan, J.B. and Snell, A.F. (1993). Comparability of incumbent and applicant samples for the development of biodata keys: The influence of social desirability. *Personnel Psychology*, **46**, 739–762.

Taylor, M.S. and Sniezek, J.A. (1984). The college recruitment interview: Topical content and applicant reactions. *Journal of Occupational Psychology*, **57**, 157–168.

Ulrich, L. and Trumbo, D. (1965). The selection interview since 1949. *Psychological Bulletin*, **63**, 100–116.

Wagner, R. (1949). The employment interview: A critical summary. *Personnel Psychology*, **2**, 17–46.

Weisner, W.H. and Cronshaw, S.F. (1988). A meta-analytic investigation of the impact of interview format and degree of structure on the validity of the employment interview. *Journal of Occupational Psychology*, **61**, 275–290.

Wingrove, J., Glendinning, R. and Herriot, P. (1984). Graduate pre-selection: A research note. *Journal of Occupational Psychology*, **57**, 169–172.

Wright, P.M. Lichtenfels, P.A. and Pursell, E.D. (1989). The structured interview: Additional studies and a meta-analysis. *Journal of Occupational Psychology*, **62**, 191–199.

Section 4

Individual Assessment for a Changing Context

Assessment practices take an expansive variety of forms and perform a variety of functions in organizational settings apart from that of recruitment and selection. In fact, as most practitioners and researchers will undoubtedly appreciate, the context and purpose of assessment exerts a powerful influence upon its day-to-day practice. In selection, for instance, the timescale is short, recruiter and candidate availability is limited, cost considerations may be more pressing because expenditure is explicit and often charged to specific budgets, and the candidate is still an 'outsider' to the organization. These and other factors largely determine the practice of assessment for selection by an organization that will often be attempting to cope with large numbers of applicants, high selection ratios and, most recently, acute pressures to cut identifiable costs in the recruitment process.

In other contexts, though, assessment practices will be influenced by a different range of factors. Once assessment is of individuals who are already members of an organization, such evaluation of the 'insider' takes on a quite different guise: its main function being to facilitate performance improvements, rather than to determine whether to accept or reject for employment. Furthermore, whatever the outcome of the assessment process, the individual is likely to remain in the organization, because even in the case of selecting for redundancy, a number of survivors will remain in employment. The impact of assessment procedures upon individuals is therefore of paramount concern. It is this context of the assessment of individuals for different HR purposes which is the common theme binding all of the chapters in Section 4 of the Handbook.

In Chapter 26, Irwin Goldstein develops this theme with some aplomb. His chapter sets out to construct practical relationships between two HR systems: selection and training. Confronting squarely the lack of previous integration between these two systems, the author commences the seemingly mammoth task of building bridges between the two. Initially Goldstein draws parallels between construct, criterion-related, and content approaches to selection and training, arguing that the two systems share more in common than their past treatment by researchers and practitioners would suggest. His chapter extends these links to consider commonalities between evaluation, validation and job analysis for selection and training procedures.

Paul Iles and Ivan Robertson contribute the second chapter (Chapter 27) of the six comprising Section 4. As the only chapter in the Handbook that was commissioned as an update to their chapter originally published in Herriot's (1989) volume, this contribution examines recent developments in research into the psychological impact of assessment procedures on individuals. Evidently, this area of research has burgeoned quite substantially over this period, and, one would hope, has done so in recognition of the importance of evaluating assessment procedures from the candidate's perspective. Although this chapter focuses upon the psychological impact of selection procedures, one is struck by the probable generalizability of these findings to other assessment contexts. In keeping with this point, at the commencement of their chapter the authors explore alternative approaches to selection and assessment, arguing that the traditional psychometric paradigm has tended to overlook social psychological approaches to assessment processes. Iles and Robertson proceed then to review research into applicant rights in selection, including legislative provisions to counter the invasion of personal privacy. They subsequently examine findings over the impact of different selection methods upon candidates, proposing a testable model of these relationships.

In Chapter 28 Clive Fletcher once again emphasizes the importance of the context of assessment, in this case concentrating upon challenges to, and widespread developments in, performance appraisal. In common with several other chapters, he highlights early on in his contribution the effects that the internationally felt changes in organization structures and work design are having upon appraisal and assessment practice. The view that assessment, for whatever purpose, can exist as a neutral technology standing in isolation above this context is again challenged by the author. Fletcher examines disparate issues in performance appraisal, including the choice of appraiser, performance-related pay (PRP) and motivation, appraising for performance management, and the appraisal of development potential. His juxtaposition of the purposes, contents and objectives of appraisal in the 1990s and beyond with those prevalent in the 1980s is particularly noteworthy and highlights just how this context has been transformed over the last decade.

Jeroen Seegers authors Chapter 29. His theme, assessing for developmental needs, picks up neatly from where Fletcher finishes off. His lucidly presented argument will appeal especially to practitioners since he explores, from a pragmatic, consultancy perspective, the organizational realities of assessing an individual's developmental needs. He links such developmental activities to strategic personnel planning and presents a general model of this process. Finally, Seegers describes the processes of criterion-based training and mentoring as essential elements of transforming developmental needs into plans and activities for the individual at work.

Jennifer Kidd, who offers up the following contribution, Chapter 30, adopts a somewhat different view. In focusing upon the proactive role that individual employees can themselves play in the development process she expounds the belief that individuals will need increasingly to take owernship of, and respon-sibility for, their own career planning activities. She reviews evidence in support of her position from various sources: self-designing organizations, self-assessment, and career theory, for instance. The author concludes by evaluating the utility of different methods of assessing career development.

The final chapter of Section 4, and indeed of the Handbook as a whole, reminds us of one less optimistic aspect of the context within which personnel and selec-tion psychologists have to operate today. Paul Jackson (Chapter 31) examines in detail an important—some may claim inevitable—growth area in assessment re-search and practice, namely selection for redundancy. Wisely avoiding any of the numerous euphemisms for such negative scenarios which seem to have entered into managerial vocabulary over recent years (e.g. 'outplacement', 'rightsizing', even 'external career development counselling'), Jackson presents a balanced and comprehensive review of the economic forces toward downsizing, the changing patterns of employment across many industrialized countries, and the effects of job loss both upon those laid off and upon the survivors who remain in the organ-ization. He concludes by raising important professional issues for selection researchers and practitioners alike of how best to deal with selecting for redun-dancy. Such issues are unlikely to just fade away; indeed, this final context for assessment is likely to remain as a particularly challenging one, professionally, ethically, and pragmatically, for selection psychologists at least into the foresee-able future.

NEIL ANDERSON
August 1996

REFERENCE

Herriot, P. (ed.) (1989). *Assessment and Selection in Organizations: Methods and Practice for Recruitment and Appraisal.* Chichester: John Wiley.

Chapter 26

Interrelationships between the Foundations for Selection and Training Systems

College of Behavioral and Social Sciences, University of Maryland, 2141 Tydings Hall, College Park, Maryland 20742-7225, USA

There are many issues involved in the interrelationships between selection and training systems. Some concern the choice of the appropriate job analysis and evaluation design and whether the same approaches are useful for both selection and training. Other questions concern the *use* of selection and training systems. For example, is it appropriate to use an entry test for the presence of particular knowledge, skills and abilities, or should training be provided with no assumption that the individual already has those skills in his or her repertoire? Further issues involve the degree to which the same interventions can serve both selection and training purposes. In many instances, the same principles serve as foundations for both selection and training systems. Thus, researchers and practitioners working in these areas can benefit from understanding these interrelationships.

VALIDATION AND SELECTION SYSTEMS

The usefulness of any intervention, be it a selection or a training system, starts with the question of validity. This is made particularly clear in the description of validity concerning test usage provided in the *Standards for Education and Psychological Tests*, hereafter referred to as the *Standards*:

> Validity is the most important consideration in test evaluation. The concept refers to the appropriateness, meaningfulness, and usefulness of the specific inferences from

International Handbook of Selection and Assessment, Edited by N. Anderson and P. Herriot.
© 1997 John Wiley & Sons Ltd.

test scores. Test validation is the process of accumulating evidence to support such inferences. (AERA, APA and NCME, 1985, p. 9)

Although the evidence may be collected in a variety of ways, an essential point is that validity refers to the degree to which the evidence supports the inferences made from the scores. In the case of selection, inferences refer to whether scores on a selection instrument allow inferences to be made about probable job behavior. The *Principles for the Validation and Use of Personnel Selection Procedures* (SIOP, 1987), hereafter referred as the *Principles*, make it clear that validity is a unitary concept and that there are a variety of strategies which can be used to collect evidence concerning inferences about scores. Further, the *Principles* describe three major strategies: construct, criterion-related, and content. In the remainder of this section, a brief summary of these strategies is presented, with a particular focus on selection systems. Following this material, these strategies regarding validation systems are related to training systems and comparisons are made. The closing section of the paper discusses other similarities and differences between selection and training systems, such as the types of job analyses employed.

Construct strategies

Constructs refer to a trait or characteristic (e.g. spatial visualization, introversion, verbal reasoning) underlying behavior. More specifically, Binning and Barrett (1989) state that 'a construct is merely a hypothesis about which behaviors will reliably co-vary' (p. 479). Thus, to be useful for selection systems, there must be evidence that the construct is important for job performance (SIOP, 1987). This requires a thorough understanding of the job based upon a complete job analysis that shows the logical relationship between the construct and the job demands. Second, evidence is required that shows the testing instrument itself is a measure of that construct and not of other constructs. Thus, the development of evidence for establishing a construct requires the collection of information, often involving criterion and content strategies, until the patterns of relationships establish evidence concerning the construct.

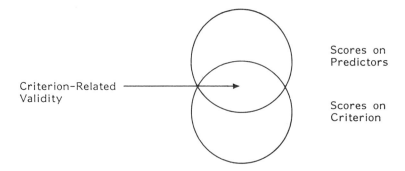

Figure 26.1   Diagram illustrating criterion-related validity

Criterion-related strategies

Figure 26.1 presents a diagram which illustrates conceptually that criterion-related strategies are based upon a useful relationship between the selection device(s) (predictor) and job performance (criteria).

When the scores on the predictor are related to (overlap) the scores on the criterion in a statistically meaningful way, evidence is collected about the validity of the test and it is possible to make inferences from scores on the test about job behavior. Of course, both the test and the criterion measure are expected to meet a series of measurement standards such as satisfactory reliability. In addition, the criterion measure is also expected to be content-relevant in that it reflects critical job components. In that sense, a criterion that only meets measurement standards is not good enough. This was exceptionally well stated by Wherry (1957) who made the following statement about emphasis on measurement without a corresponding concern about the content validity of the criterion measure: 'We don't know what we are doing, but we are doing it very carefully, and hope you are pleased with our unintelligent diligence' (pp. 1–2).

Figure 26.2 presents the conceptual relationship, illustrating the content validity of a criterion measure.

When the criterion measure overlaps the important components of the job identified in the job analysis, it is considered relevant or content-valid. Of course, there are often multiple criteria involved in job success and thus it is possible to think of these relationships as a series of intersecting circles. If there are major aspects of performance identified in the job analysis which are not measured in the criterion, it is deficient. If there are components measured in the criterion which are not identified as important job success components in the job analysis, the measure is contaminated.

One interesting aspect of this analysis is that even in a criterion-related validity strategy, content validity strategies should be employed to establish the relevance of the criterion measure. However, few investigators are concerned with whether the test itself is content-valid when a criterion-related validity procedure is utilized. Rather, there is a bottom-line view that the demonstration of a statistical relationship between the test and a content-valid criterion measure provides evidence concerning validity. Unfortunately, there is often not enough attention given to formally establishing the content validity of the criterion measure.

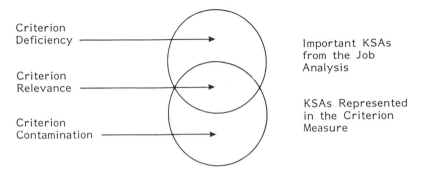

Figure 26.2   Diagram illustrating the content validity of a criterion measure

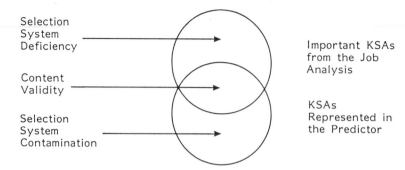

Figure 26.3   Diagram illustrating the content validity of a predictor

Content strategies

In determining the content validity of a test or predictor, the emphasis is on inferences concerning the degree to which the critical knowledge, skills and abilities from the job are represented in the selection techniques (Goldstein, Zedeck and Schneider, 1993). This relationship is demonstrated in Figure 26.3.

In summary, if it can be shown that the test measures the critical aspects of the job performance domain, inferences about job performance based on the test are justified. Here the concern is on the content of the test itself. As described by Schmitt and Landy (1993), if the test and performance domain are interchangeable, inferences about the scores based on a content validity strategy can be made. Goldstein, Zedeck and Schneider (1993) describe the type of detailed job analysis necessary for establishing a foundation for content validity. They also describe the detailed procedures involving the collection of judgments from subject matter experts as a way of providing evidence for the establishment of content-related evidence.

It is clear that one major difference in content and criterion-oriented strategies is that in content approaches, statistical evidence is not collected showing that the scores on the test actually predict job performance. This is made obvious from a comparison of Figures 26.1 and 26.3. As shown in Figure 26.3, the evidence concerns the degree of congruence or overlap in knowledge, skills and abilities (KSAs) between the critical job components and the test components. Indeed, the conceptual foundation for content validity is much more similar to Figure 26.2, which is the content validity model for the establishment of criterion measures. There is an assumption that if it is possible to demonstrate great congruence between the KSAs required for the job and the KSAs present in the testing instrument, then it would be possible to make inferences about the scores as one would in a criterion-related validity study. Such assumptions are clearly based on the degree of fit between the specific KSAs critical for job performance and the specific KSAs being assessed in the testing instrument. Thus, if as shown in Figure 26.3 there are KSAs in the test which are not required for job performance, then the test is contaminated and inferences concerning the scores is more problematical.

Contamination can occur because the wrong KSAs are tested or because the testing method introduces required KSAs which may not be critical for job performance. For example, a job analysis for the position of a lieutenant in a fire department in the United States might indicate that, when arriving at a fire scene, he or she gives short orders indicating where the firefighters should place themselves and what equipment to take into a fire. If, in the testing situation, the testee is required to respond to a fire scene by writing an essay concerning what he or she would do, there is the question as to whether that is content-valid; the question would arise as to whether writing an essay requires KSAs that the job analysis indicates might not be job-relevant for the position of a supervisory firefighter. If the candidate is required to write the essay in perfect English, and the exam is scored for spelling and the quality of the written essay, then there are more serious issues about content validity. If we added the fact that in the fire department under study, the lieutenant does not perform any writing of essays or reports, then there is the further question of whether the examination format requires KSAs that are not required by the job.

One strategy to resolve this problem could be to give examinees a tape recorder and instruct them to respond to the fire scene situations by speaking the directions and orders he or she would have given. However, the point is that in establishing content validity, the job analysis needs to be very detailed and carefully performed. For interested readers, Arvey and his colleagues (Arvey *et al.*, 1992) describe an example of a construct validity approach to the development of a physical ability test for police officers which does not utilize a content approach. In their approach, they are able to demonstrate the establishment of a nomological net and the construct validity of strength and endurance constructs for police officers.

As will be discussed below, these foundations for the establishment of content validity are particularly pertinent to the design of training systems. Another aspect of this situation also shown in Figure 26.3 is that, if there are key aspects of the job that the test is expected to assess but it does not, then the selection system is deficient. For example, a job analysis might show that there are a number of important components to the job ranging from ability to communicate effectively with other individuals to the ability to be able to read. Often, when testing large numbers of individuals, it is difficult to test the ability to communicate effectively because this might require an assessment exercise. On the other hand, it is quite possible to test the ability to read with large numbers of individuals by employing paper and pencil methodology. If large important components of the job are not tested then questions occur about the degree to which the selection system is deficient. The question of how much of the job a selection system needs to measure in order to be considered acceptable is not easily determined and, of course, the same issue exists regardless of whether a criterion strategy or content strategy is employed.

Since content validity involves inferences about congruence between test and job components and does not have a direct test of the relationship between the scores on the test and the scores reflecting job performance, it is possible to ask why content validity strategies are used. One reason is that there is an increasing number of situations where content validity is the only strategy for developing information to support inferences about validity. Many times, this occurs because the sample size is not large enough for a criterion-related validity study, such as the situation that occurs in testing small samples of persons for promotion purposes. In other instances, reliable criterion information cannot be obtained for a variety of reasons, such as the adversarial conditions that often occur as a result of fair employment practice lawsuits or union actions which forbid the collection of job performance information. Most interestingly, the emphasis on the use of content validity strategies as a method for validity has resulted in furthering our understanding of the interrelationships between testing and training situations. As will be described below, these particular concepts are especially relevant for the development of training programs.

VALIDATION AND TRAINING SYSTEMS

In this section we first discuss the traditional model used to evaluate training programs, and then we relate those systems to the validation models employed in the examination of selection systems.

Criterion measurement

Establishing the validity of a training program requires evidence to support inferences that the training intervention produces changes in individuals, resulting in improved performance on the job. There are two important components in evaluating training programs:

- There is the need to develop criteria that systematically assess the trainees in order to determine how learning in the training program changes their performance on relevant dimensions.
- The choice of relevant dimensions must come from the job analysis and reflect those aspects of job performance that are the focus of the training program.

The relationships are very similar to those shown in Figure 26.2 for the content validity of a measure used to validate a test measure. When there are components in the criterion that are not relevant to the job, it is considered contaminated. If critical job components are not represented in the criterion measures, then they are deficient. If they were deficient, there is great difficulty in assessing whether a trainee has learned these critical components because there is no measurement of that aspect of performance. Thus, even if the training program were successful, it is not possible to demonstrate this without content-valid criterion measures. All of the same principles concerning criterion measures for selection systems are equally applicable here.

One additional aspect concerning criterion systems devoted to the evaluation of training systems is that there typically needs to be a number of different measures at different points in time to assess the program. Thus, measures might be developed to assess the reactions of the trainees to the program, others might be developed to assess learning in training, others for determination of how performance transferred on to the job and yet still others to establish the utility or value of the program to the organization (Goldstein, 1993; Boudreau, Sturman and Judge, 1994). While the use of multiple criteria is more common in evaluating training, multiple measurements can be just as useful in providing information about selection systems. Thus, researchers might be interested in predicting early indicators of performance and also to later measures of success.

Evaluation design

A second aspect of training evaluation is that most investigators consider training programs to be interventions that are expected to produce change. The measurement of change necessarily requires using evaluation designs that require measurement of performance at different points in time, such as before and after training, in order to establish that change has occurred. Of course, that is why training evaluation must be concerned with multiple criteria that are used at varying points in time. In addition, training evaluation employs various procedures such as control groups to establish whether the change is due to the training intervention or to some other factors. Thus, in order to determine whether evidence exists to make inferences concerning the validity of the training program, various sorts of designs are used to document both that change occurred and that it occurred as a result of the intervention. In recent years, considerable thought (e.g. Cook, Campbell and Peracchio, 1990) has been given to developing innovative evaluation designs that are useful in interpreting the effects of interventions in organizational settings.

Above, it was indicated that the establishment of criterion measures to assess training programs involves many of the same principles as those used in both establishing the content validity of tests and the content validity of criterion measures used in criterion-related validity studies. In addition to these similarities, another useful possibility is to treat selection programs as interventions and to collect before-and-after data. There is no reason why one cannot ask about the capabilities of the workforce as measured by a pre-test before a selection or promotion system is designed. Then, it is possible to ask at a later time, using a post-test, whether significant changes occurred that were meaningful to the organization. It is even possible to consider the use of a control group, such as another unit of the organization that has not employed the intervention. Then, it would be possible to ask whether changes in the workforce are a result of the use of the test or of other variables such as changing demographics or court-imposed procedures in the selection of the workforce.

Unfortunately, these type of analyses have not been used very frequently. Rather, attention is focused on whether a particular test predicts successful behaviour. It is clear that it is important to have that information, but from an organizational perspective it is just as important to know whether the intervention has had an impact. If a test is expected to select individuals who perform better, it is appropriate to ask whether there is a difference in workforce productivity after a period of time. If that is not the case, then it is important to ask what other variables are affecting these results. The use of evaluation designs that permit tracing the effects of interventions can be very useful in these instances.

The point is that many of the procedures involved in assessing training strategies are just as relevant for selection systems, and vice versa. Being aware of these different models and their application would actually increase the amount of relevant information for decision-makers.

FURTHER RELATIONSHIPS BETWEEN SELECTION AND TRAINING SYSTEMS

This section will focus on the similarities and differences between selection and training systems on two dimensions: validation strategies and job analysis strategies.

Validation strategies

As noted above, establishing the validity of selection systems involves evidence concerning inferences from test scores and their relationship to job performance. In the validation of training systems, evidence is being collected to support inferences concerning whether an intervention produced changes on criterion measures that also have a relationship to job performance. Owing to the emphasis in training evaluation on change and whether the intervention produced the change, the validation strategies applied to selection systems are somewhat different, but in most instances they are very applicable to training systems. Those issues will be examined next.

Construct validity

Construct validity as used in selection terms is just as relevant to training systems but it is applied in a different way. The question is not whether a test instrument measures a construct; rather, it is whether an intervention (training) can improve performance underlying the construct such that it changes on-the-job performance. Since improving performance on a construct necessarily demands that performance is measured, it is clear that instruments must be developed which measure the construct reliably. Those measurement issues are the same for testing and training systems. The extra dimension is that for a training program to be shown to be valid, an instructional system needs to be designed to change behavior on dimensions related to that construct. For example, if the job analysis shows that behaviors related to decision-making are critical, it is not only necessary to measure that behavior, but also to design instructional programs to change it in a way consistent with the goals and objectives of the organization.

Criterion-related validity

As noted above, all of the methodology related to establishing relevant criterion measures used in criterion-related validity strategies are appropriate for the design of measures to assess training interventions.

In addition, there is the interesting question of whether it is possible to assess the impact of the training program by examining the relationship between scores in training and scores on the job in the same way as examining the relationship between test performance and job performance. Certainly, it is useful to know that persons who perform better on training performance criteria also perform better on the job. If both measures are examining the same constructs or dimensions, you would expect such co-variation. However, this is an instance where the criterion-related validity methodology does not permit an assessment of the intervention (the training program). It is possible to have a training program where relatively little learning occurs and yet the scores on the training criterion predict scores on the job. It simply says that persons who perform better (or worse) on one measure (training criterion) also perform better (or worse) on the job.

One way to understand this phenomenon is to consider a situation where pre-test scores (before training) are correlated with on-the-job scores. For example, Kraut (1975) found that peer ratings obtained from managers attending a month-long training course predicted several criteria including future promotion and performance-appraisal ratings of job performance. Bartlett and Goldstein (1974) found that a road test, which was part of a bus driver-trainer program, predicted accidents on the job for those same trainees. However, this relationship might occur regardless of whether the training program is effective. In other words, Kraut, and Bartlett and Goldstein, might have designed very effective tests which predict future job performance. Those tests might predict regardless of whether the training program is effective, and certainly the fact that they predict does not provide information about the effectiveness of the training program.

Determining that the training program accomplished its objectives requires showing a significant improvement in group performance after training which can be traced to be a result of the intervention. That determination requires before-and-after measurements showing differences that can be inferred to have occurred because of the training intervention. The typical methodology employed in criterion-related validity strategies usually does not provide that information.

Content validity

The other validation strategy, known as content validity, is particularly relevant to the design and assessment of training programs. If the reader examines Figure 26.3 and substitutes the words 'training program' for 'selection program', all of the other components would be just as pertinent to training design as to selection design. Goldstein, Zedeck and Schneider (1993) point out that, while the content strategy for test validation is also concerned with better understanding of constructs, it does so by an emphasis on attending to observables; i.e. to focus on the overlap or similarity between the knowledge, skills and abilities (KSAs) necessary to perform on the test and the same KSAs required for the performance domain.

This focus on the issues involved in making inferences concerning the content validity of a testing instrument are identical to the issues concerned with the development of a content-valid training program. For both testing and training, the focus is on the degree to which the critical job KSAs are represented in the selection or training device. While the emphasis in this approach is on the KSAs, it is not my intention to ignore the tasks that are performed on the job. Tasks describe what a worker actually does on the job; the closer the test or training program approximates the tasks, the greater the physical fidelity of the test or training program. However, when a test or assessment device is being designed, it is not usually the case that the actual physical fidelity that constitutes the job tasks is being replicated. Rather, a test is a simulation of the physical components of the job such that the KSAs required to perform those tasks are called forward. When these KSAs are called forward, the test has psychological fidelity. Similarly, when a training program is designed, the focus is on choosing tasks that permit the learning of the required KSAs. In this instance, the training program has psychological fidelity. Often, these are not the exact same tasks that occur on the job. Sometimes, this is done because it is too dangerous or not feasible to have the exact duplicate of the job. In other cases, it is because it is not possible to teach the KSAs with the exact job tasks because it would be overwhelming. Thus, teaching a beginning person to fly by using a real airplane is dangerous, too expensive, not feasible, and overwhelming for the learner. On the other hand, the design of part simulators that have psychological fidelity in the sense that they permit the learning of the KSAs can provide an effective training environment.

Thus, the establishment of the content validity of the training program is a critical first step in ensuring that the appropriate KSAs are being taught. It is important to note that this does not mean that it is certain that learning has occurred in the training program. It is possible to have the appropriate content while the techniques used are not appropriate for the trainees, and as a result learning may not occur. The assessment of learning again refers to before-and-after measurement. On the other hand, if the training program is not content-valid and the correct KSAs are not being taught, it would be hard to argue that before-and-after measurement is a worthy endeavor.

Job analysis issues

When a job analysis is used in designing a training system, this is usually called a 'needs assessment strategy'. The term 'needs assessment' reflects the point that the approach to job analysis in the development and evaluation of training systems requires a much broader systems-oriented analysis than that usually employed in the development of selection systems. In training design, needs assessment has various components.

Organizational analysis

Organizational analysis refers to an examination of system-wide components of the organization that may affect a training program. For example, organizational analysis attempts to determine what the organizational goals are and whether the training program fits the organizational plan. We would probably all agree that it may not be sensible to design training programs for a technology that will not be employed for a long period of time. Also, organizational analysis recognizes that in order for training to work, what is learned in the training program will need to be transferred into the work situation. To ensure that this will occur, information needs to be collected to help determine the constraints and facilitators to effective transfer.

Rouiller and Goldstein (1993) examined a situation where managers were all trained at a central facility and then were randomly assigned to one of a hundred different fast-food franchises. As expected, they found that manager trainees who had learned more in training performed better on the job. However, they also found that trainees who were assigned to sub-organizations that were more supportive of what had been learned in training performed better than trainees who were assigned to sub-organizations where the climate was less supportive. This effect was independent of performance in training. This meant that regardless of how well trainees had performed in training, their actual job performance was also affected by the climate of the organization to which they were assigned. Some examples of the determinants of the transfer climate which was independently measured at each of the 100 sub-organizations, included whether trainees were supported by managers and peers for using the behaviors taught in training, and whether managers and peers already used the same learned behaviors.

In addition, organizational analysis can identify the external and legal constraints that may affect the implementation of a training program.

While there are many different components to organizational analysis, the main point is that information is collected to ensure that the training system fits the organization. Interestingly, this is another example where both training and selection systems can benefit from examining each others' practices.

It is clear that the concern about organization fit, constraints, facilitators, and so forth is just as important for the design of selection systems as it is for the design of training systems. For example, designing selection systems without knowing what future changes are being planned for the organization does not make much sense. Nor is it worthwhile to design selection systems without formally understanding the legal requirements facing the organization. It is the case that persons involved in selection systems are usually aware that there is a need for exploring such issues. The present difference is that in training this is a formal part of the job analysis system, and methodologies (e.g. Goldstein, 1993) have been developed to ensure that the information is collected. This should result in fewer mistakes and oversights. Selection systems can benefit from the development of similar approaches.

Recently, Sparrow (1994) introduced such an overall approach for human resource management (HRM) based upon the concept of organizational competencies. He notes that in the 1990s, HRM will be dominated by the need to redesign organizations to tie all of the aspects of human resources together. Thus, for example, it will make no sense to select on the basis of one set of competencies while the organization moves in a different direction requiring other sets of competencies. Sparrow notes that it is not unusual for pay systems to tell you to behave one way, while career systems assess other sets of competencies, while the organizational culture espouses something else, none of which is translated into recruitment strategies. Certainly, organizations which recently have wanted to move towards a service orientation have found this difficult to achieve because individuals have been hired based upon other skills. Sparrow correctly points out that his approach requires a broad-based type of job analysis approach that examines many facets, including individual and organizational competencies. Interestingly, this concept again makes the approach to selection and training systems even more similar.

Tasks and KSAs

Another aspect of needs assessment and job analysis is the collection of information concerning tasks and KSAs. There are many different types of systems available for collecting such information (Harvey, 1991). It is possible to ask whether these systems are equally useful for selection and training systems.

Sometimes when a criterion-oriented validity approach is being used to evaluate a selection system, the job analysis system used is not very detailed in terms of the tasks or the KSAs required for the job. This can create problems if the approach does not permit the kind of criterion development which would make it more likely for tests to be validated. However, the bottom line is still that, if the test predicts the criterion measure, most investigators would argue that evidence for validity is being established. If content-validity procedures are being used for the validation of tests or training interventions (Goldstein, Zedeck and Schneider, 1993), the need is for detailed job analyses. As described above, the key aspect for the content validation of selection systems is to show that the specific KSAs required on the job are represented in the test or predictor.

Interestingly, the exact same thing is true for the design of content-valid training programs. Indeed, since effective training is dependent upon learning specific KSAs, that information is absolutely required in order to design programs as well as to evaluate them. Thus, the content-validation strategy for analyzing selection systems and the design and validation of training systems could both benefit from the same type of specific oriented job analyses.

CONCLUSIONS

It is hoped that the above discussion will help to develop the idea that many of the approaches to selection and training have common features. No doubt, there are many other ways to benefit from these considerations. Often, the organization needs to decide whether it wishes to select persons with particular capabilities or whether training needs to be provided. Of course, usually both selection and training are required to ensure the most capable workforce; but the level of training, and the capability level at which training needs to begin, is determined by the types of individuals selected.

Sometimes the differences between selection and training systems are hard to distinguish. For example, assessment centers use a standardized set of simulated activities, and are often used as a way of testing *and* selecting managers. It is also the case that these simulated activities can be designed to provide information to the candidates about which skills need to be developed in order for them to qualify as future managers. Also, it is possible to design these exercises so that candidates have the opportunity to practise (or be trained) in performing assessment-center simulations requiring these various skills and abilities. This kind of assessment, training and feedback may provide useful information which can be used to plan career development.

REFERENCES

American Educational Research Association (AERA), American Psychological Association (APA) and National Council on Measurement in Education (NCME) (1985). *Standards for Educational and Psychological Tests.* Washington, DC: American Psychological Association.

Arvey, R.D., Landon, T.E., Nutting, S.M. and Maxwell, S.E. (1992). Development of physical ability tests for police officers: a construct validity approach. *Journal of Applied Psychology,* **77**, 996–1009.

Bartlett, C.J. and Goldstein, I.L. (1974). *A Validity Analysis of Employment Tests for Bus Drivers.* Training and Educational Research Programs Technical Report. College Park, MD: University of Maryland.

Binning, J.F. and Barrett, G.V. (1989). Validity of personnel decisions; a conceptual analysis of the inferential and evidential bases. *Journal of Applied Psychology,* **74**, 478–494.

Boudreau, J.W., Sturman, M.C. and Judge, T.A. (1994). Utility analysis: what are the black boxes, and do they affect decisions? In N. Anderson and P. Herriot (eds) *Assessment and Selection in Organizations: First Update.* Chichester: John Wiley.

Cook, T.D., Campbell, D.T. and Peracchio, L. (1990). Quasi-experimentation. In M.D. Dunnette and L.M. Hough (eds) *Handbook of Industrial and Organizational Psychology.* Palo Alto, CA: Consulting Psychologists Press.

Goldstein, I.L. (1993). *Training in Organizations.* Belmont, CA: Brooks–Cole.

Goldstein, I.L., Zedeck, S. and Schneider, B. (1993). An exploration job analysis–content validity process. In N. Schmitt and W.C. Borman (eds) *Personnel Selection in Organizations.* San Francisco: Jossey-Bass.

Harvey, R.J. (1991). Job analysis. In M.D. Dunnette and L.M. Hough (eds) *Handbook of Industrial and Organizational Psychology.* Palo Alto, CA: Consulting Psychologists Press.

Kraut, A.I. (1975). Prediction of managerial success by peer and training-staff ratings. *Journal of Applied Psychology,* **60**, 14–19.

Rouiller, J.Z. and Goldstein, I.L. (1993). The relationship between organizational transfer climate and positive transfer of training. *Human Resource Development Quarterly,* **4**, 377–390.

Schmitt, N. and Landy, F.J. (1993). The concept of validity. In N. Schmitt and W.C. Borman (eds) *Personnel Selection in Organizations.* San Francisco: Jossey-Bass.

Society for Industrial and Organizational Psychology (SIOP) Inc. (1987). *Principles for the Validation and Use of Personnel Selection Procedures,* 3rd edn. College Park, MD: SIOP.

Sparrow, P.R. (1994). Organizational competencies: creating a strategic behavioural framework for selection and assessment. In N. Anderson and P. Herriot (eds) *Assessment and Selection in Organizations: Methods and Practices for Recruitment and Appraisal.* Chichester: John Wiley.

Wherry, R.J. (1957). The past and future of criterion evaluation. *Personnel Psychology,* **10**, 1–5.

Chapter 27

The Impact of Personnel Selection Procedures on Candidates

PAUL A. ILES

Liverpool Business School, Liverpool John Moores University, 98 Mount Pleasant, Liverpool L3 5UZ, UK

IVAN T. ROBERTSON

Manchester School of Management, UMIST, PO Box 88, Manchester M60 1QD, UK

Systematic, effective and efficient staff selection has always been regarded as a major contributor to effective organizational functioning. Recent developments in job design and organizational structuring (flexible working, cellular working, self-directed teams, Total Quality Management, delayering and decentralization, *inter alia*) have placed even greater importance on the identification and selection of employees with appropriate skills, knowledge and attitudes (Kanter, 1989; Drucker, 1988).

A growing current interest in managerial competencies, for example, is just one illustration of a concern to identify and select individuals with the qualities to manage contemporary organizational structures (Sparrow, 1994). Considerable academic interest has been shown in selection and assessment practices within work and organizational psychology. In its dominant psychometric form, this discipline has approached the study of organizational selection systems and processes from the assumption that the objectives of the analysis are the improvement of the *effectiveness* and *efficiency* of the selection process, and that the process of analysis involves the objective and systematic discovery and analysis of objective data.

An alternative approach of growing importance (e.g. Hollway, 1991; Knights, 1992; Townley, 1989) considers the process of enquiry into organizational practices, including selection and assessment practices, from another direction. Drawing on the work of Foucault and others, this addresses the *technologies of*

International Handbook of Selection and Assessment, Edited by N. Anderson and P. Herriot.
© 1997 John Wiley & Sons Ltd.

government within organizations, and their impact on employees' subjectivity and identity, specifically with reference to the *power–knowledge relationship*. As Hollway (1991) remarks, this approach assumes that the psychology of work, '. . . like other applied social sciences, is a body of knowledge which has been produced rather than discovered' (Hollway, 1991, p. 1). Psychological knowledges, as other knowledges, are seen as part of the 'ensemble formed by the institutions, procedures, analyses and reflections, calculations and tactics that allow the exercise of this very specific albeit complex form of power' (Foucault, 1980, p. 20). In practice this approach means that conventional psychometric approaches to organizational selection are seen as supporting the 'expert' scientific practices through which power relations and dynamics are translated and operationalized.

Within this approach the main focus of interest is the ways in which, within organizations, 'human technologies' such as assessment and selection carry certain assumptions about the subjectivities of those who work within them, and which attempt to develop or discourage certain qualities and behaviours in line with certain bodies of 'expert' knowledge. In this perspective the process of selection and the knowledge which supports this process is seen as central to these wider processes of regulation and control in the light of current organizational efforts to identify and select individuals with the qualities demanded by ongoing changes in organizational and work forms. This approach seeks not to enhance performance but to unscramble relationships between power and expert knowledge within the context of current conceptualizations of necessary occupational and managerial competencies (Iles and Salaman, 1994; Iles, 1995).

This is not the place to enter into further consideration of either the psychometric or the post-modern approaches. The psychometric approach in particular has been discussed extensively, and there is extensive evidence on which methods are good predictors of performance. However, it is worth noting that these approaches have their origins in very different academic traditions. The psychometric tradition has been very firmly driven by a primarily American model drawn from the psychology of individual differences, albeit a model very influenced by earlier British work in this area.

This model is represented in a variety of forms in most textbooks of HRM personnel management and organizational psychology as 'good professional practice', if not fully represented in actual organizational practice. Its paradigm status in work psychology and personnel management owes much to its application to mass vocational selection in the USA in both world wars. Its principal focus is the 'job', conceived of as a set of discrete tasks. In this model, performance criteria are selected and individual 'attributes' of various kinds are chosen as predictors of job performance. The attributes selected are then measured through a variety of procedures, and the assessment process validated primarily in terms of criteria-related predictive validity. This model appears to value individualism (individual attributes are taken to predict individual performance), managerialism (the major criteria of performance are the achievement of organizational goals as defined by top management) and utility (cost-benefit analysis of the monetary benefits conferred on organizations in using different selection procedures). Recent developments in utility theory in assessing the benefits of investing in good selection practice are often attempted so as to give psychologists an equal say in the 'language of business' to other business professionals (Herriot, 1992, 1993; Smith and George, 1992; Boudreau, Sturman and Judge, 1995).

Clearly this model has a number of considerable strengths. Individual differences in performance *do* contribute significantly to differences in organizational performance, a contention underlying much of the growth in HRM in recent years. However, many other factors also affect organizational performance, and it does seem as if people do change as a result of job experiences. The kinds of attributes assessed by psychologists—for example, locus of control, self-directedness, intellectual flexibility—do seem to be affected by such work experiences as occupational success, racial discrimination, and the kinds of jobs one performs (e.g. Kohn and Schooler, 1982).

As organizations change, decentralize, restructure, get flatter, and devolve accountability, the conception of the 'job' as a stable collection of discrete tasks has come under pressure (e.g. Atkinson, 1984). Multiskilling, flexible specialization, and self-directed work teams have made this notion rather outdated, and these and other changes such as downsizing and the growth of 'portfolio careers' have changed our concepts of career success and career development. Knowledge and skill-based reward systems have also undermined the use of job evaluation and the role of the 'job' as the basis for reward systems (e.g. Armstrong, 1993; Luthans and Fox, 1989). In addition, in Western Europe in particular, assessment has come to play a more strategic role in facilitating individual development and cultural and organizational change, rather than in selection alone (Iles, 1992; Mabey and Iles, 1993; Sparrow, 1994).

A more long-standing challenge to the psychometric paradigm of assessment has come from political and legal challenges to the fairness and validity of assessment and selection procedures. In the USA, in particular, such challenges have come over groups with 'visible differences' such as race, age and gender. Similar concerns, especially with regard to gender but less markedly with regard to age and race, have been manifest in recent years in Europe. Assessment instruments have increasingly been seen as exhibiting unfair and illegal discriminatory features, and the criterion of 'bias' or 'adverse impact' has become an increasingly important 'evaluative standard' against which to judge selection procedures. In part this situation led to a drop in the use of psychometric tests in the 1970s in the USA; in part it stimulated research into 'validity generalization' to show that tests *were* valid across situations. It has also stimulated research into creating selection procedures which were as valid, if not more valid, than psychometric tests but which generated less 'adverse impact', such as work samples, assessment centres and structured, criteria-related interviews.

This overview shows that the agenda for the psychometric model has not in fact been set by neutral, scientific interests but by political, social and legal pressures (Anderson, 1992). As Hesketh and Robertson (1993) argue:

> the selection literature has been atheoretical, with a primary focus on identifying approaches and techniques that have practical utility. Comparatively little emphasis has been placed on the development of conceptual frameworks for selection or on trying to understand why some procedures work and others not. (p. 3)

Their call is for developing a *process* model of selection that places it in a broader theoretical perspective of human abilities, personality, motivation and skill acquisition. The more radical post-modern tradition would see the broader theoretical context in terms of power, regulation, identity and subjectivity. We share its concerns for more exploration of the impact of selection and assessment processes on individuals and their role in influencing identity, but here take a more interactionist, social process view of assessment and selection, one much more influenced by a *European* social and political agenda and one much more rooted in social rather than in differential psychology. The concerns here are less with measurement, prediction and job performance than with relationships, attributions, attitudes, interaction, negotiation, identities and self-perceptions—distinctly social psychological concerns (e.g. Herriot, 1992, 1993).

We contend that people can and do change in the course of their careers in organizations, an assumption underlying much of the British work on career and work-role transitions and providing much of the impetus to European training and development work which often makes extensive use of action learning and work-based learning in contrast to the dominant North American emphasis on lectures, case-studies, simulations and role-plays. We also contend that subjective self-perceptions are critical determinants of work motivation and performance, and that these are influenced by assessment and selection processes. Since individual assessment is playing a growing role in informing and guiding individual and organizational development efforts, it is important to identify those features which characterize assessment procedures with high motivational and developmental value.

Some American research has examined assessment processes from a social psychological perspective. Much of this has examined the role of 'non-relevant' variables like appearance, attractiveness, gender, dress, race, ethnicity, disability, age and non-verbal behaviour on interview ratings. In the individualistic tradition of American social psychology, much of this has employed rather artificial experimental scenarios where student raters typically rate 'interviewees' after very brief exposure to paper transcripts, résumés, photographs, or videotaped or audiotaped interview extracts. Such scenarios are likely to exaggerate the intensity of the effects observed (e.g. Powell, 1993). European research has been perhaps more likely to employ field studies of real-life raters rating real-life candidates. Examples include our own work on the effects of gender, appearance and attractiveness on ratings in a UK bank asessment centre (e.g. Iles, 1990) and Salaman and Thompson's (1978) work on Army selection procedures. This study demonstrated the existence of a set of social class-linked values, assumptions and understandings among selecting officers as part of a shared 'officer culture'. These values, such as the importance of 'cool', affected selection outcomes, but were masked by the deployment of, and reference to, formal procedures.

The responses of applicants to selection procedures are therefore important in two ways. First, they are an element in the relationship between the individual and the organization. Second, they imply that people change, even during the period of the selection procedure itself. In this chapter we will explore the impact of selection and assessment processes on candidates from three perspectives. First we shall review candidates' *reactions* to a variety of selection procedures. Then we shall discuss a recent American perspective on the impacts of selection and assessment which employs the social–psychological concepts of procedural and distributive justice, first employed in the legal and judicial field. Finally we shall review some recent European work in this area employing the social–psychological concepts of attitude, self-perception, identity and transition. Both frameworks contend that not only do candidates display different attitudes towards assessment and selection procedures, but that these affect a range of important work, organizational and career-related attitudes and behaviours. Indeed, we are in agreement with Messick (1989) that focusing too narrowly on one value base when evaluating the use of an assessment procedure—which is what the psychometric tradition has done—is to narrow the focus of enquiry and to reduce our awareness of possible adverse side-effects. Indeed, we feel that this area is of sufficient importance that validity considerations need to be broadened to include what we have called 'impact validity' (e.g. Robertson and Smith, 1988); that is, the extent to which a measuring instrument has an effect on a subject's psychological characteristics.

APPLICANT RIGHTS: VULNERABILITY AND PRIVACY

In much of Continental Europe, reservations about the 'American model' of personnel selection, with its concern for predictive validity, were initially expressed in concerns over the applicant's vulnerable position *vis-à-vis* the organization (de Wolff and van den Bosch, 1984; Herriot, 1992). Candidates were seen as unable to engage the organization on equal terms, with their labour market position rendering them more vulnerable. In addition the organization might claim for itself the right to ask the candidate to divulge various kinds of personal information, but retain the right to refuse to disclose to the candidate information it considered 'confidential'. In particular, the applicant was increasingly seen as having rights and interests including a right to 'privacy'. Though the applicant was seen as needing to provide some information about himself or herself in any job application, he or she was also seen as having rights over its possible misuse (de Wolff and van den Bosch, 1984).

Not much empirical research has addressed the issue of applicant perceptions of invasion of privacy in personnel selection situations. Some American research suggests that applicants' perceived control over how any personal information disclosed is treated is of prime importance. Individuals perceiving that they had some control over the uses to which the information could be put appear to experience less of a sense of having their privacy invaded (Fusilier and Hoyer, 1980). The instrumental value of the selection outcome also seems important. People experiencing a positive outcome decision appear to feel less of an invasion of privacy than those experiencing a negative outcome, such as rejection. This may have practical implications in relation to the growing use of polygraphs and drug testing, especially in the USA. We will explore this area in more detail. In addition, some studies have shown that the *type* of disclosure has some impact. Disclosure outside the organization such as to another employer seems to be perceived more negatively in this respect. The type of information disclosed seems also to have some impact, with information perceived as 'job-relevant', such as productivity data, being less sensitive than information perceived as less job-relevant, such as personality data (Fusilier and Hoyer, 1980).

This area has legal as well as psychological implications for organizations and individuals, especially with the growing computerization of personnel information storage. For example, the UK Data Protection Act of 1984 covers the use of computers for applicant screening, regulating the storage of personal information held on computerized information systems. Certain rights are conferred on the applicant, such as the right to demand a copy of the details held on file and knowledge of the assessment criteria used.

Trying to protect one's rights to privacy by omitting to include requested information on an application form, such as details of previous convictions, may not be a very viable strategy. Stone and Stone (1987) found that this resulted in applicants being viewed as less suitable for jobs than those reporting no convictions, and non-response seemed treated as an attempt to conceal.

It might be argued that individuals have a right to see any test scores or assessment ratings and to have feedback on their performance. Some controversy exists about when this feedback should be given, by whom, and in what form. Providing full and detailed feedback on a separate occasion, but relatively close in time to the original assessment, might seem a useful strategy, especially if development plans are to be used and acted on. There is a risk that individuals who have obtained an unfavourable assessment might be further damaged by such a full disclosure, with their self-esteem further affected and their work motivation and commitment further lowered. This has been confirmed in empirical work on the impact of negative feedback following assessment centres (Fletcher, 1991). In some circumstances relatively full oral feedback might be better, with some emphasis on strengths and concentration on only one or two specific areas for development (Fletcher, 1986).

The point is that applicants do not respond passively to selection procedures, but actively interpret their experiences, both seeking out practice, coaching and courses in interviewee strategies and withdrawing their application if the experience is perceived too negatively. Given the rise, especially in the United States, of such invasive and privacy-threatening techniques as drug, integrity and honesty testing (Rynes, 1992), understanding the way selection procedures impact on candidates is becoming a question of growing practical and scientific interest (e.g. Ryan and Sackett, 1987). In the next section, we examine the research evidence on the reactions of candidates to a variety of recruitment, selection and assessment processes and procedures.

ASSESSMENT EXPERIENCES AND OUTCOMES: EFFECTS ON CANDIDATES

There has been some research into client perceptions of the assessment and selection process, and client reactions towards selection procedures. Most studies seem to have been of the initial recruitment process, of interview procedures, and of candidates' reactions to assessment centre procedures.

The recruitment process

With regard to organizational recruitment practices, most interest has been on the influence of various recruitment practices on applicants' decisions to pursue job applications. Herriot and Rothwell (1981) found that career information issued by organizations had some effect on UK engineering student's intentions to apply for particular jobs. However, Quaglieri (1982) found that US business studies graduates in trainee management and accountancy jobs felt that informal sources of job information and referral, such as word of mouth recruitment, provided more specific and accurate job information than formal organizational sources such as job advertisements. Breaugh and Mann (1984) found that US social service workers, recruited through referrals from existing employees, had more realistic job expectations and showed longer tenure with the organization than those recruited through direct applications or newspaper advertisements. However, given the reality of personal and social networks, referals are unlikely to open recruitment opportunities to presently under-represented minorities (Iles and Auluck, 1991).

This link between realistic expectations and job tenure is also stressed in the realistic job preview literature. Offering potential candidates a 'realistic preview' of the job in question, rather than the over-inflated view of prospects and conditions often offered in glossy recruitment brochures, appears to lower applicant expectations of the rewards a job has to offer to a more 'realistic' level and offers potential candidates more opportunity *not* to pursue their application if the position is not perceived as meeting their needs. Those candidates who do pursue their application, if selected, appear to show greater commitment to the organization, greater job satisfaction, better performance and longer tenure (Premack and Wanous, 1985).

One might question, however, how 'realistic' a job preview can be if conducted by means of films or videos, discussions with organizational personnel and recent recruits, and members of the company. One of the advantages of using work sample tests or assessment-centre type exercises is that they provide the candidate with an accurate picture of the job, allowing him or her to make a decision as to whether to continue with an application. Non-managerial staff wishing to be considered for a managerial position may, for example, decide that such a career is not for them after sampling various aspects of a management job in a managerial assessment centre. Examples of what the job involves based on realistic job samples may provide much more 'realistic previews' than the oral, visual or written descriptions commonly encountered in 'realistic job previews' and have similar or greater effects on commitment, satisfaction and turnover. For example, Cascio and Phillips (1979) found that introducing work sample tests for US city government employment seemed to reduce significantly the annual turnover rate for new staff compared with those engaged through interviews or paper-and-pencil tests.

Interviews

There has been increasing recognition of the social processes involved in personnel selection interviews, and increasing interest in the nature of the decisions taken by candidates as well as by assessors (Herriot, 1988). Herriot (1987) presents a review of such processes. It seems as if candidates form favourable impressions of interviewers who show interest and empathy, demonstrate good listening and counselling skills, and display interpersonal sensitivity. These favourable impressions are likely to lead to a greater willingness to accept any job offer made, especially if the interviewers are perceived as typical or representative of the organization in general. Candidates also appear to expect interviewers to ask technical questions in their area of competence, and to present useful information on the job and the organization. In general, studies on interviews have shown that characteristics of interviewers do have some impact on applicants' perceptions of organizational attractiveness. Some of the work in this area has been done in laboratory settings but there is also work in field settings. In their field study, Harris and Fink (1987) found that candidates' perceptions of such characteristics of the interviewer as personableness, competence and informativeness affect their perceptions of job attributes and their regard for both the company and job. The likelihood that they would take up a job offer was also affected. It is likely that the ways interviews are actually conducted (e.g. in offensive, discriminatory or superficial ways) will negatively affect applicant reactions. Marchese and Muchinsky (1993) showed both that the interview has moderate predictive validity and that interview structure moderated its validity. Superior predictive validity was associated with structured interviews.

Some research has also looked at structured interviews. Robertson *et al.* (1991) compared independent groups of candidates who had been assessed by situational interviews or assessment centres. The candidates revealed more positive views about the adequacy of the assessment centres than the interviews. Firm conclusions about candidates' preferences for assessment centres could not be drawn from this study, since the groups were independent and had not both been assessed by the same methods. Further research by Janz and Mooney (1993) on interviewer and interviewee reactions to traditional and patterned behaviour description interviews showed that interviewers were in general more positive about the patterned interviews, seeing them as more complete and thorough, fairer, and better at preparing candidates for understanding what was required of the job. However, the superiority of the more structured interview was less clear-cut for interviewees. They did see them as more complete and thorough and as giving them a clearer understanding of position requirements. Of course, those selected via thorough and perhaps stressful interviews may not so much be put off as attracted to the organization, liking its apparent high standards and selectivity.

Rynes and Connerley (1991; quoted in Rynes, 1992) also found mixed reactions to patterned behaviour description interviews. Some candidates liked them for their in-depth approach; others had encountered them so often they thought them both boring and fakeable. Students with little work experience also thought themselves disadvantaged in relation to applicants with 'real-life' experiences.

A recent study of interviewers' behaviour and interview characteristics by Turban and Dougherty (1992) has confirmed the importance of interviewer behaviours for candidates' perceptions of both expectancy (the likelihood that they would be invited for a second interview and offered a job) and value (their regard for the company and the attractiveness of the job). For student interviewees rating campus interviewers, the *interest* of the interviewer and his or her informativeness seemed to be the major influence on candidate attraction. Recruiter similarity to candidates, as manifested by alumni status and gender similarity, seemed less influential. Recruiters' reports of interview focus (recruitment versus selection) and interview structure were related to applicant perceptions of recruiter behaviour. Interview focus was related to perceptions of attractiveness; if the interviewer was seen as selection-oriented, candidates saw it as more structured, less selling-oriented, and more intimidating. However, when recruiters spent more time discussing a job and company, presumably to market the firm, applicants were less attracted—perhaps because they felt there was something wrong with the job! Interestingly, interview structure was not related to either expectations or value perceptions.

Work samples

Candidates appear to have particularly positive reactions to the use of work samples for selection purposes, perceiving them as fair and valid and as presenting them with opportunities to demonstrate their potential in ways that paper-and-pencil tests or interviews do not. Robertson and Kandola (1982) review studies of the reactions of candidates to work samples and to analogous 'trainability tests' or 'miniaturized training tests'. Studies in the United States have shown that black, Hispanic and white applicants all showed equally positive attitudes towards their use, and that their introduction results in a significant decline in the number of complaints received from applicants about selection procedures (Schmidt *et al.*, 1977; Cascio and Phillips, 1979). It seems clear from various studies (see Rynes, 1992) that work samples and other methods with a strong link to job content such as simulations are generally favoured by applicants.

Assessment centres

The high face validity and positive endorsement of work-sample tests by applicants also extends to the use of assessment centres, probably because they often include managerial work samples such as in-basket exercises or group discussions. Early work with IBM managers in various countries reported that, in general, assessment centres were positively regarded by clients as a fair and valid way of measuring managerial potential (Kraut, 1972). Canadian research has also shown that the use of assessment centres is generally positively received, with candidates reporting that they had received a realistic view of their strengths and weaknesses and that participation in an assessment centre had had a positive effect on morale (Bourgeois *et al.*, 1975). A survey (Nirtaut, 1977) of the use of assessment centres by US organizations also showed that companies uniformly reported positive reactions from clients. The major adverse effects reported were some discouragement of low performers due to perceived harmful career impacts and some problems caused by high performers perceiving a mismatch between their expectations for promotion and the limited opportunities for such promotion often present in their company.

Dodd (1977) has reviewed many such studies and concludes that assessment centres are in general favourably regarded by candidates and generally perceived as measuring important job-related qualities accurately and fairly. Data collected using a standard questionnaire recommended by him have continued to confirm this generally positive picture, such as the UK study by Dulewicz, Fletcher and Wood (1983). This study found that, in particular, analogous exercises such as in-basket, business decisions simulation, and business plan presentations were favourably regarded, presumably because of their high face validity and perceived job relevance. However, there seem to be differences in how people react to assessment procedures, depending on how well they have performed. A small-scale US study, while reporting similarly favourable endorsements generally, found that assessment-centre high-scorers had more positive views of the assessment process than low-scorers (Teel and DuBois, 1983). Low-scorers tended to rate the centres as less accurate and less fair, and to report fewer perceived career benefits. They also tended to see their assessment-centre behaviour as less like their 'real-life' behaviour.

Robertson *et al.* (1991) studied two assessment centres using a cross-sectional, post-only research design. In one case they found that pass and fail groups differed in their beliefs about the adequacy of the centre (with the fail group expressing less positive views). In the other, pass and fail groups did not differ. In fact, the results from this study suggest that, although fail groups might sometimes express less positive views, candidates show no greater thought of leaving job and career. They found no differences in post-assessment self-esteem or psychological well-being. Participants in general reported quite favourable impressions of assessment centres. Even the lowest scoring fail group in their study had a mean of over 3.5 on a 5-point Likert scale (Robertson *et al.*, 1991). Clearer differences emerged between pass and fail groups when candidates' views of the impact of the assessment on their careers were examined. As expected, pass groups perceived greater positive career impact. Robertson *et al.* (1991) also explored differences between pass and fail groups on organization commitment, job and career withdrawal cognitions, psychological health and self-esteem. For the situational interviews and one of the assessment centres they found differences, with the fail group showing lower organizational commitment.

Fletcher (1991) conducted a longitudinal examination of the impact of assessment centres on candidates. He used a single group pre-post design, with pre-measures taken immediately before the assessment centre. Post measures were taken immediately after the centre and six months later. His results showed a drop in self-esteem and lower scores on some aspects of need for achievement for unsuccessful candidates. Iles, Robertson and Rout (1989) also conducted a longitudinal study involving two development centres (i.e. assessment centre procedures used to collect information for use in development rather than selection processes). In this study the results for one of the centres indicated some change in career planning and career withdrawal cognitions. Measures were taken immediately before and immediately after participation.

Other methods: Biodata, peer appraisal, drug and integrity testing and polygraphs

In contrast to these positive reactions to the use of both work-sample tests and assessment-centre procedures, some studies have reported less positive reactions to the use of some other selection procedures. For example, Robertson *et al.* (1991) reported negative views held by internal candidates about the use of *biodata* to select managerial applicants in their study of selection procedures in a major UK organization. Candidates rejected by this procedure tended to express doubts about its accuracy, validity and usefulness. However, situational interviews seemed reasonably well regarded, though not as well regarded in terms of accuracy, fairness or validity as most of the assessment centres used in the same management development programme.

Peer assessments, often used in military selection contexts and as part of an assessment centre process (e.g. Tziner and Dolan, 1982; Schmitt and Hill, 1977; Fletcher and Dulewicz, 1984), also seem less acceptable to candidates than work-sample tests or assessment centres. Cederblom and Lounsbury (1980), in a study of peer evaluation schemes in a US university, found them often perceived to suffer from friendship bias and to have a discouraging effect on staff morale. A higher degree of user acceptance of peer appraisal in an industrial setting, especially its use for developmental purposes, has been reported by McEvoy and Buller (1987).

Drug testing, integrity testing, polygraphs and *genetic screening* represent emerging methods of personnel selection which seem to be increasingly used in North America, if not yet in Europe. All appear to be very 'intrusive' methods, likely to generate negative reactions from candidates. *Integrity* or 'honesty testing', attempting to assess the likelihood that individuals will engage in counter-productive behaviour such as theft, has not been extensively researched. However, merely administering such tests may sensitize potential employees to the organization's concern for honesty and so perhaps deter the behaviour they are designed to predict. Woolley and Hakstian (1993) found that four published integrity scales were correlated significantly with self-reports of counter-productive behaviour and that individual scales from mainstream personality inventories assessing 'conscientiousness' were as highly correlated as integrity test scales. Personality traits held to be conceptually distinct from integrity were also related to counter-productivity. The item content of such tests is likely to be seen in many cases as invasive and potentially offensive, with job applicants becoming angry and indignant and perhaps initiating legal or other challenges. Canadian surveys by Thacker and Cattaneo (1987, 1993) showed honesty testing to be used by only a very small proportion of organizations.

Drug testing of samples of urine for illegal substances raises a whole host of questions concerning its legality, its accuracy and the establishment of dosage levels which impair performance. A survey of mainly US public sector agencies in 1992 showed that 63% used drug screening (IPMA, 1992). Around 20% of Canadian transportation companies had drug testing processes in place in one survey (MacDonald and Dooley, 1991). Canadian human rights legislation appears to suggest that drug testing may be acceptable in high-risk jobs, but should be administered only after a conditional offer of employment has been made (Rowe, Williams and Day, 1994).

Polygraphs, measuring physiological reactions such as heart rate and perspiration, may also be used to select people for a job, and though in the US its use for pre-employment screening among private sector employers is banned, its use in the Federal government in the national security and law enforcement areas appears to be growing. Integrity tests have often been correlated against polygraph criteria. A 1992 survey of the selection practices of US public agencies showed that 37% used polygraph examinations (IPMA, 1992).

Genetic screening appears to be becoming increasingly used to identify 'hyper susceptible' individuals so as to minimize their exposure to toxic effects in the work environment.

Rynes (1992) notes that many of these methods are potentially invasive, lack obvious job-relatedness, and have generated considerable public controversy. Such procedures may be generally accepted in the abstract since drugs and dishonesty may be accepted as serious problems and so many employers may be using them that objections may seem pointless. However, there appear to be wide individual differences in reactions, suggesting promising areas for future research.

Overall attitudes towards selection systems

A Flemish study of 769 employees, primarily young graduates, found that in general applicants were reasonably positive towards the selection procedures they encountered. Interviews and behavioural simulations were however the most positively regarded. Applicants had less favourable attitudes towards intelligence tests and towards personality inventories (de Witte, van Laere and Verraecke, 1992). Intelligence tests were found to be perceived as irritating, but less so if used with other techniques. Personality questionnaires were seen as efficient only when used alongside intelligence tests but as superfluous if used with other techniques. Procedures containing both interviews and behavioural simulations were experienced as most efficient and as providing significant information on the job; the presence of an interview was necessary for applicants to evaluate the whole procedure positively. de Witte *et al.* (1992) argue that this positive attitude towards interviews and simulations can be understood with reference to perceptions of applicant control and face validity, and hypothesize that three ethical principles are present in the interview and in simulations but absent in tests and inventories. These are:

- the right of the applicant to receive information on the job and the selection procedure

- the applicant's right to privacy
- the applicant's right to be treated as an active negotiator.

These principles are similar to those put forward by Iles and Mabey (1993) and Mabey and Iles (1991) on the basis of a study of the reactions of 120 British managers on an MBA course to a variety of selection, assessment and career development techniques. This study found that procedures such as biodata and psychometric tests of personality and cognitive ability (especially if used without feedback) were in general seen as less fair, accurate, or helpful for personal, career and organizational development than procedures such as assessment and development centres and interviews. The authors argued that managers appear to react more positively to procedures which are prospective rather than retrospective, that is looking forward rather than backward; procedures which are overt rather than opaque, that is appearing face-valid and job-relevant; procedures which are anchored rather than abstract, that is including line managers; and procedures which are collaborative rather than controlling, that is enabling the participant to have some influence over the process. In this case, 'anchored' refers to the procedures being rooted in organizational realities—e.g. by using criteria manifestly relevant to the organization's strategic direction, by using activities and examples drawn from organizational life, and employing the language of the organization and by using line managers with organizational power and influence over career progress as interviewers, assessors and feedback providers.

In general, it seems as if applicants prefer some assessment and selection procedures to others, seeing work-sample tests and analogous devices as more valid and more appropriate than paper-and-pencil tests, biodata, or peer assessment. These techniques, based on a 'sample' approach rather than a 'sign' approach (Wernimont and Campbell, 1968) with predictors as close to criterion behaviour as possible, seem to be regarded more favourably and are perceived to be more job-relevant, especially when administered in formats that avoid paper-and-pencil testing. Rynes and Connerley (1991; cited in Rynes, 1992) reported negative reactions to psychological assessment and to handwriting analysis, in part because applicants were sceptical about the need to acquire such information and in part because of scepticism about the employer's ability to evaluate it accurately.

The evidence also suggests that applicants want to be treated sensitively and sympathetically in the selection procedure, and not to have their privacy invaded unduly. They also seem to want to be presented with realistic job information. Not only will this result in candidates being more favourably disposed to the selection procedure used and more accepting of it, it will also probably generate more realistic expectations of the job and organization. The candidate seems also more likely to accept a job offer and to be more committed to the organization. This may be reflected in longer tenure and perhaps better work performance, though further research is needed here.

Having reviewed the evidence here concerning candidates' reactions to selection procedures and their effects on subsequent work-related attitudes and behaviours, we now move on to attempts to construct a conceptual framework that will help us understand the impact process more fully.

PSYCHOLOGICAL IMPACT: A CONCEPTUAL BASIS

The impacts of selection processes and selection outcomes or decisions on candidates have only recently begun to be considered as an important area needing further study. Selection procedures have tended to be regarded as neutral measuring instruments, assessing various candidate attributes or characteristics with greater or lesser validity but with their impact on these characteristics, or any other candidate characteristics, either not considered at all, or treated as intrusions or 'biases' disturbing otherwise clean psychometric evaluations. The increasing emphasis on selection as a social process (Herriot, 1988, 1992, 1993), and the increasing evidence that candidates have definite attitudes towards selection procedures and that these affect the decisions they make, indicate the importance of further research in this area. One perspective primarily adopted in the United States, is organizational justice theory.

Organizational justice theory

One framework becoming increasingly popular in the USA is organizational justice theory, already applied to performance appraisal and pay rises (Folger and Konovsky, 1989). In this conception, the primary justice distinction made is between procedural and distributive justice, conceptualized in this context as the distinction between the fairness of the selection procedure and the fairness of the selection decision. Perceptions of procedural and distributive justice are likely to influence such outcomes as job satisfaction, organizational commitment, and job performance. For example, the perceived procedural fairness of a drug testing programme has been shown to influence organizational commitment, job satisfaction, intentions to quit and job performance (Konovsky and Cropanzano, 1991), whilst fairness perceptions have also been shown to influence organizational citizenship behaviour (Moorman, 1991) and employee theft (Greenberg, 1990).

'Organizational citizenship' here refers to employees exhibiting 'out of role' behaviours; that is, going above and beyond their job descriptions and acting in a generally helpful, conscientious way. Citizenship includes becoming involved in the governance of the organization and taking steps to improve aspects of a job, even when such innovation is not required or explicitly related to the formal reward system of the organization. Specific examples of such behaviour would include altruism (e.g. helping others who have been absent or have heavy workloads), courtesy (e.g. informing and consulting with others), sportsmanship (e.g. not complaining unduly), and conscientiousness (e.g. punctuality).

The importance of procedural justice has also been shown by McFarlin and Sweeney (1992). Though distributive justice was there the more important predictor of pay satisfaction and job satisfaction, procedural justice was the more important predictor of organizational commitment and the subordinate's evaluation of the supervisor. In addition, both justice dimensions interacted: resentment seems most likely when the outcome is poor. When people perceive the procedure to be fair, resentment may be minimal even when distributive justice is low, since it would be difficult for employees to envisage alternative fairer procedures that could have led to the outcome. Employees' resentment is not only a function of low distributive justice, but also of the opportunity to blame their misfortune on the actions of others, rather than on their own behaviour. The combination of unfair procedures and low distributive justice produced the lowest ratings, whereas fair procedures produced high commitment and positive supervision evaluations regardless of the level of distributive justice. This is likely to be of particular relevance to the selection situation. Robertson *et al.* (1991) found, for example, that candidates 'failing' an assessment centre were less likely to see the procedure as unfair. With biodata procedures or situational interviews 'failed' candidates who see the assessment procedure as unfair seem particularly likely to show distrust of the organization and its representatives.

If this is the case, then investigations of the determinants of the perceived fairness of selection procedures as one dimension of procedural justice along the lines of Greenberg's (1986) examination of performance appraisal would be welcome. It is likely that the perceived fairness of a procedure is associated with perceived job-relatedness, opportunities to perform, fakeability and consistency of administration. It may also be linked to the kind of performance feedback offered, the information given on the selection process, the degree of honesty exhibited by the organization in its treatment of the candidate, and the interpersonal, communication and counselling skills and lack of bias shown by the recruiter/assessor (e.g. Gilliland, 1993; Arvey and Sackett, 1992; Fletcher, 1995).

These principles in the selection and assessment area resemble the general procedural rules defined by Leventhal (1980) as characterizing fair procedures: consistency, bias suppression, accuracy, correctability, representativeness and ethicality. Procedural justice has been seen as consisting of two categories by Greenberg (1996): fair formal procedures increasing employee voice in decision-making and decreasing bias or errors, and interactional justice, the fairness of treatment employees receive in enacting formal procedures or in explaining such procedures. Selection and assessment methods that display both kinds of procedural justice are more likely to be seen as fair by individuals and more likely to generate feelings of commitment to the organization.

However, Rynes and Connerley (1991; cited in Rynes, 1992), using open-ended interviews, did not find 'fairness' mentioned particularly frequently by candidates when asked to react to selection procedures. They found the perceived likelihood of accurate evaluations, the perceived employer need to acquire the information, and the perceived ability to do well in the procedure (distributive justice?) to be the characteristics mentioned most often. As Rynes (1992, p. 248) puts it:

> Applicants evaluate selection devices more on the basis of perceived legitimacy than on personal self interest . . . a more serious concern seems to be whether justice theory, by itself, adequately captures the entire set of factors that influence applicant impressions.

The above discussion indicates that features of the selection procedure, such as perceived fairness, seem to influence applicant reactions and behaviour. The organizational justice model also points out that features of the selection decision, especially concerns relating to distributive justice, will also be influential. Though not taking an explicit organizational justice perspective, recent British research has also explored the impacts of both selection procedures and selection decisions from a social psychological perspective.

A European perspective on assessment impacts

Experiences with selection outcomes or decisions appear to have major impacts on candidate and organization health and performance (e.g. Fletcher, 1991). In essence, when selection and assessment methods are utilized, there are three broad classes of outcome: accept, reject, or feedback on strengths and weaknesses. Sometimes feedback may be combined with accept or reject decisions, as is the case of internal assessment centres used to identify candidates for a management development programme. In any true 'selection' situation, at least some of the candidates will be rejected. Some recent speculation has concentrated on possible negative consequences of such decisions, such as immediate stress and later re-duced work commitment and lowered job involvement. Reduced career commit-ment and lower organizational commitment have been shown to lead to thoughts of leaving one's job, organization or career field and to greater absenteeism, reduced work performance, and greater turnover (Griffin and Bateman, 1986). It is possible that negative selection decisions might also lead to damaging psycho-logical consequences for the individual, such as lowered self-esteem, ill-health, and lowered psychological well-being, analogous to the effects of such transitions as unemployment or downward mobility (Warr, 1987).

The research conducted so far, and reviewed above, has not provided un-equivocal findings concerning the impact of assessment experiences on candi-dates. Some evidence of differences in candidates' reactions to methods and preferences for methods has been accumulated but there is too little for general-izations to be drawn. The research focusing on the psychological impact of assessment experiences has not produced consistent findings. Robertson _et al._ (1991), for example, found no evidence for an effect on self-esteem whereas Fletcher (1991) did. The studies conducted so far have all had methodological shortcomings (cross-sectional design, lack of control group, etc.) and there is a clear need for methodologically sound field research, building on the suggestive findings and measurement tools used in these initial studies. Although there is a possibility of negative impacts from assessment experiences, it is also possible that even rejected candidates could benefit if feedback is handled well. Some candidates receiving a negative decision may develop a more realistic and accu-rate self-image and a more realistic view of their strengths and weaknesses, with a clearer view of attainable career goals (inside or outside of their present organization). This possibility may be increased if clear feedback is provided, realistic developmental plans are drawn up with input from the participant as well as the organization and immediate line managers, and action taken on such plans. It may also help if the organization makes available realistic career planning and career counselling, training opportunities, and alternative job openings and lateral transfers as well as upward promotions (Hall and Goodale, 1986).

Assessment-centre exercises or work-sample tests, with their opportunities for self-assessment, have been shown to have an impact on candidates' self-perceived abilities and to allow candidates to develop a more accurate picture of their strengths and weaknesses (Schmitt, Ford and Stults, 1986), even in the absence of feedback on performance. Assessments may have an impact on later career behaviour and job attitudes. Individuals' motivation to experiment with managerial skills and seek further work experiences and job-and-career-related information seems to be influenced by assessment-centre evaluations (Noe and Steffy, 1987). Lower expectations as a result of negative assessment-centre evaluations here resulted in lower levels of exploratory behaviour, lower job involvement, and less searching for information on managerial jobs and career paths. Again there is a clear need for research designed to explore the extent to which the impact of assessment experiences may be moderated by feedback, design features, outcome decisions and other aspects of the assessment process. Little research has focused on these issues in an assessment context but research into the psychological impact of unemployment (Warr, 1987) has demonstrated that the impact of unemployment on psychological well-being, self-esteem and mental health is moderated by factors such as age and previous levels of employment commitment.

A preliminary model of the impact process

There is relatively little in the way of theoretical ideas which seek to conceptualize the impact process, as previously noted. Robertson and Smith (1989) introduced the concept of impact validity as 'the extent to which a measuring instrument has an effect on a subject's psychological characteristics'. This concept focuses attention on the previously neglected issue of the impact of psychological assessment on an individual and indicates the need for a model of the impact process. Robertson and Smith proposed a tentative model of the impact process in which features of the assessment process and the decision help to determine the psychological impact on candidates. Dreher and Sackett (1983) have also put forward a model to explain candidates' responses to rejection during a selection procedure. The essence of their model involves an initial cognitive appraisal of the selection decision followed by possible affective consequences. Robertson *et al.* (1991) built on the ideas of Dreher and Sackett (1983) and Robertson and Smith (1989) to propose a more general model covering the impact of assessment processes. Their model incorporates three sets of variables: *independent* variables (assessment decision and the procedures used); *mediating* variables (cognitive reactions) and *outcome* variables (affective reactions, psychological states and job and work attitudes). In their empirical work Robertson *et al.* (1991) investigated the extent to which cognitive reactions (beliefs about the adequacy of the assessment and the perceived career impact of the assessment) mediated the impact of a selection decision. In general their results offered support for the mediating role of cognitive reactions. In other words, the impact of the assessment decision on candidates is dependent on their beliefs about the adequacy of the assessment process and their view of the impact of the assessment on their careers. It should be stressed that although the results obtained by Robertson *et al.* (1991) fit this explanation, they note that their research design was not strong enough to rule out alternative explanations of the results. The role of cognitive reactions as mediators would also fit with ideas on the role of attribution in the impact process put forward by Silvester and Brown (1993) who suggest that the extent to which candidates attribute the causes of the outcome to themselves (internal attribution) or external factors such as the assessment process will moderate the impact on factors such as self-esteem.

Though further research needs to be undertaken before the factors which influence candidates' reactions to selection processes and selection outcomes can be fully identified, it seems likely that these will include the social and organizational context in which the decision is taken, the method used, and the personal characteristics of the candidate. Figure 27.1 provides an indication of possible key variables and how they are related.

For example, characteristics of the method, such as its perceived intrusiveness, its face-validity, its perceived job-relevance, and the opportunities it provides for feedback and self-assessment, would seem likely to influence candidates' affective and cognitive reactions to the selection process. This seems especially the case if the method is perceived as providing a valid and accurate indication of the true strengths or deficiencies of the candidate, or is perceived as being biased, inaccurate or invalid, implying no accurate information about the individual. The actual nature of the selection and assessment decision such as accept, reject, accept with feedback, reject with feedback, etc. and the kinds of feedback provided (such as how timely and specific it is, what kinds of

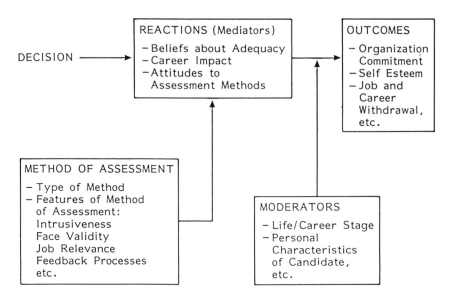

Figure 27.1   Key variables involved in the impact process

training needs are identified, what kinds of career development are recommended and what kinds of developmental action plans are devised and acted upon) also seem likely to be influential in determining applicant reactions. A variety of candidate personal characteristics, such as life and career stage, current level of job and career involvement, strength of self-efficacy with regard to job and career, degree to which an internal locus of control is present, current career plans, current level of self-esteem, and previous knowledge of and experience with the selection procedure, also seem likely to moderate candidate reactions. The degree of organizational or extra-organizational social support candidates receive may influence their reactions. Effects on candidates may be expressed in terms of work commitment variables and thoughts about leaving both job and career field. In addition, reactions in terms of psychological well-being (such as lower or higher mental health) may occur, as well as a variety of behaviours related to career planning and exploration, job search, training and development and job/career movements. Such a model implies that research in this area will need to be longitudinal, in contrast to cross-sectional, as applicant reactions are likely to change over time (Fletcher, 1991; Iles, Mabey and Robertson, 1990). Table 27.1 gives an overview of the research available so far of relevance to Figure 27.1.

Table 27.1 Studies of relevance to the components of the model in Figure 27.1

Relevant studies	Interpretation of results
Iles and Mabey (1993) de Witte, van Laere and Verraecke (1992) Mabey and Iles (1991) Rynes and Connerly (1991) Robertson *et al.* (1991) Dulewicz, Fletcher and Wood (1983) Dodd (1977)	Candidates prefer methods that are seen to be job-relevant, forward-looking and giving them some control; e.g. assessment centres and job-related interviews are preferred to psychological tests or handwriting analysis
Robertson *et al.* (1991) Teel and Dubois (1983)	Candidates who perform well react more favourably than those who do badly
Robertson *et al.* (1991) Fletcher (1991) Noe and Steffy (1987)	Candidates who are not successful, in terms of job outcomes, may experience loss of self-esteem and organization commitment; they may also lose motivation to seek further experiences
Robertson *et al.* (1991)	Candidates' views of the adequacy of the assessment process and the impact that it has on their careers may mediate the impact of the assessment on job and work attitudes
Schmitt, Ford and Stults (1986)	Job-relevant assessment procedures may have an impact on candidates' later behaviour even in the absence of feedback

CONCLUSIONS

This chapter has focused on an area of personnel selection research which, in parts, is seriously under-researched, yet is potentially of great significance both to individuals and organizations. Traditional research within the personnel selection domain has focused on establishing which are the best methods for choosing candidates for jobs. If selection is to be useful for individuals and organizations, this traditional line of enquiry is of continuing importance. Nevertheless, as the material contained in this chapter serves to emphasize, the need to identify selection methods that are valid and predict future job performance accurately is not sufficient. Care needs to be taken about the effect that selection technology has on individual candidates. With the exception of work on bias/adverse impact, a coherent research programme into these effects is only just beginning.

Some selection techniques, while providing useful predictions of future job performance, may have adverse side-effects. Methods that are demonstrably related to the job seem to be better received by candidates, particularly when they are forward-looking and provide candidates with some control over the assessment process (see Table 27.1). This provides further support (see Tett, Jackson and Rothstein, 1991) for the importance of job analysis being used to help design selection and assessment procedures.

The research reviewed in this chapter suggests that for organizations to use selection methods that have good criterion-related validity may be a necessary but not sufficient condition for effective personnel selection. It also seems important to use methods that candidates feel positive about since this is more likely to ensure their committed participation in the selection process and may minimize any damaging side-effects.

It is clear, nevertheless, that even with the use of valid methods that are well-thought of by candidates, there is still room for unsuccessful candidates to react badly. With this in mind, it seems important (particularly for schemes using internal candidates) that organizations strive to develop procedures which also minimize negative impacts on unsuccessful candidates. When less transparent methods (such as psychological tests) are used it may be helpful if organizations ensure that both assessors and candidates are given clear information about the rationale for using the method and its role in organizational decision-making.

REFERENCES

Anderson, N.R. (1992). Eight decades of employment interview research: a retrospective meta-review and prospective commentary. *European Work and Organizational Psychologist*, **2** (1), 1–32.

Armstrong, M. (1993). *Managing Reward Systems*. Buckingham: Open University Press.

Arvey, R.D. and Sackett, P.R. (1992). Fairness in selection: current developments and perspectives. In N. Schmitt and W. Borman (eds) *Personnel Selection*. San Francisco, CA: Jossey-Bass.

Atkinson, J. (1984). Manpower strategies for flexible organizations. *Personnel Management*, August, 28–31.

Boudreau, J.W., Sturman, M.C. and Judge, T.A. (1995). Utility analysis: what are the black boxes, and do they affect decisions? In N. Anderson and P. Herriot (eds) *Assessment and Selection in Organizations: First Update*. Chichester: John Wiley.

Bourgeois, R.P., Leim, M.A., Slivinski, L.W. and Grant, K.W. (1975). Evaluation of an assessment centre in terms of acceptability. *Canadian Personnel and Industrial Relations Journal*, **22** (3), 17–20.

Breaugh, H.A. and Mann, R.B. (1984). Recruiting source effects: a test of two alternative explanations. *Journal of Occupational Psychology*, **57**, 261–267.

Cascio, W.F. and Phillips, N.F. (1979). Performance testing: a rose among thorns? *Personnel Psychology*, **32**, 751–766.

Cederblom, D. and Lounsbury, J.W. (1980). An investigation of user acceptance of peer evaluation. *Personnel Psychology*, **33**, 567–569.

Dodd, W.E. (1977). Attitudes towards assessment center programs. In J.L. Moses and W.C. Byham (eds) *Applying the Assessment Center Method*. New York: Pergamon.

Dreher, G. and Sackett, P. (1983). *Perspectives on Employee Staffing and Selection: Readings and Commentary*. Homewood, IL: Irwin.

Drucker, P. (1988). The coming of the new organization. *Harvard Busines Review*, Jan/Feb, 45–53.

Dulewicz, V., Fletcher, C. and Wood, P. (1983). A study of the internal validity of an assessment centre and of participants' background characteristics and attitudes: a comparison of British and American findings. *Journal of Assessment Center Technology*, **6**, 15–24.

Fletcher, C. (1986). Should the test score be kept a secret? *Personnel Management*, April, 44–46.

Fletcher, C. (1991). Candidates' reactions to assessment centres and their outcomes: a longitudinal study. *Journal of Occupational Psychology*, **64**, 117–127.

Fletcher, C. (1995). Performance appraisal in context: organizational changes and their impact on practice. In N. Anderson and P. Herriot (eds) *Assessment and Selection in Organizations: First Update*. Chichester: John Wiley.

Fletcher, C. and Dulewicz, V. (1984). An empirical study of a UK based assessment centre. *Journal of Management Studies*, **211**, 83–87.

Folger, R. and Konovsky, M.A. (1989). Effects of procedural and distributive justice on reactions to pay raise decisions. *Academy of Management Journal*, **32**, 115–130.

Foucault, M. (1980). *Power/knowledge: selected interviews and other writings by Michel Foucault 1972–77* (C. Gordon, ed.). Brighton: Harvester.

Fusilier, M.R. and Hoyer, W.D. (1980). Variables affecting perceptions of invasion of privacy in a personnel selection situation. *Journal of Applied Psychology*, **65**, 623–626.

Gilliland, S.W. (1993). The perceived fairness of selection systems: an organizational justice perspective. *Academy of Management Review*, **18** (4), 694–724.

Greenberg, J. (1986). Determinants of perceived fairness of performance evaluations. *Journal of Applied Psychology*, **71**, 340–342.

Greenberg, J. (1990). Employee theft as a reaction to underpayment inequity: the hidden cost of pay cuts. *Journal of Applied Psychology*, **75**, 561–568.

Griffin, R.W. and Bateman, T.S. (1986). Job satisfaction and organizational commitment. In C.L. Cooper and I.T. Robertson (eds), *International Review of Industrial and Organizational Psychology*. Chichester: John Wiley.

Hall, D.T. and Goodale, J. (1986). *Human Resource Management: Strategy Design and Implementation*. Glenview, IL: Scott Foresman.

Harris, M.M. and Fink, R.S. (1987). A field study of applicant reactions to employment opportunities: does the recruiter make a difference? *Personnel Psychology*, **40**, 765–784.

Herriot, P. (1987). The selection interview. In P.B. Warr (ed.) *Psychology at Work*, 3rd edn. Harmondsworth: Penguin.

Herriot, P. (1988). Selection as a social process. In J.M. Smith and I.T. Robertson (eds) *Advances in Selection and Assessment*. Chichester: John Wiley.

Herriot, P. (1992). Selection: the two subcultures. *European Work and Organizational Psychologist*, **2**, 129–140.

Herriot, P. (1993). A paradigm bursting at the seams. *Journal of Organizational Behavior*, **14** (4), 371–376.

Herriot, P. and Rothwell, C. (1981). Organisational choice and decision theory: effects of employers' literature and selection interview. *Journal of Occupational Psychology*, **54**, 17–31.

Hesketh, B. and Robertson, I.T. (1993). Validating personnel selection: a process model for research and practice. *International Journal of Selection and Assessment*, **1** (1), 3–17.

Hollway, W. (1991). *Work Psychology and Organizational Behaviour*. London: Sage.

Iles, P.A. (1990). Using assessment and development centres to facilitate equal opportunity. *Equal Opportunities International*, **8** (5), 1–26.

Iles, P.A. (1992). Centres of Excellence? Assessment and development centres, managerial competencies and HR strategies. *British Journal of Management*, **3** (2), 79–90.

Iles, P.A. (1995). *Managing Assessment Processes*. Buckingham: Open University Press.

Iles, P.A. and Auluck, R.K. (1991). The experience of black workers. In M. Davidson and J. Earnshaw (eds) *Vulnerable Workers*. Chichester: John Wiley.

Iles, P.A. and Mabey, C. (1993). Managerial career development techniques: effectiveness, acceptability and availability. *British Journal of Management*, **4**, 103–118.

Iles, P.A., Mabey, C. and Robertson, I.T. (1990). HRM practices and employee commitment: possibilities, pitfalls and paradoxes. *British Journal of Management*, **1**, 147–157.

Iles, P.A., Robertson, I.T. and Rout, U. (1989). Assessment-based development centres. *Journal of Managerial Psychology*, **4** (3), 11–16.

Iles, P.A. and Salaman, G. (1994). Recruitment and Selection. In J. Storey (ed.) *HRM: A Critical Perspective*. London: Routledge.

International Personnel Management Association (1992). *PP1 1992 Survey Results*. Alexandra, VA: IPMA.

Janz, T. and Mooney, G. (1993). Interviewer and candidate reactions to patterned behaviour description interviews. *International Journal of Selection and Assessment*, **3**, 165–169.

Kanter, R.M. (1989). The new managerial work. *Harvard Business Review*, Nov/Dec, 85–92.

Knights, D. (1992). Changing spaces: the disruptive impact of a new epistemological location for the study of management. *Academy of Management Review*, **17**, 514–536.

Kohn, M.L. and Schooler, G. (1982). Job conditions and personality: a longitudinal examination of their reciprocal effects. *American Journal of Sociology*, **87**, 1257–1286.

Konovsky, M.A. and Cropanzano, R. (1991). The perceived fairness of employee drug testing as a predictor of employee attitude and job performance. *Journal of Applied Psychology*, **76**, 698–707.

Kraut, A. (1972). A hard look at assessment centers and their future. *Personnel Journal*, May, 317–362.

Leventhal, G.S. (1980). What should be done with equity theory? New approaches to the study of fairness in social relations. In K.J. Gergen, M.S. Greenberg and R.H. Willis (eds) *Social Exchange: Advances in Theory and Research*, pp. 27–55. New York: Plenum.

Luthans, F. and Fox, M.L. (1989). Update on skill-based pay, *Personnel Management*, **66** (3), 26–32.

Mabey, C. and Iles, P.A. (1991). HRM from the other side of the fence. *Personnel Management*, Feb, 50–53.

Mabey, C. and Iles, P.A. (1993). The strategic integration of assessment and development practices: succession planning and new manager development. *Human Resource Management Journal*, **3** (4), 16–34.

MacDonald, S. and Dooley, S. (1991). The nature and extent of EAPs and drug screening programs in Canadian transportation companies. *Employee Assistance Quarterly*, **6** (4), 23–40.

Marchese, M.C. and Muchinsky, P.M. (1993). The validity of the employment interview: a meta-analysis. *International Journal of Selection and Assessment*, **1** (1), 18–26.

McEvoy, G.M. and Buller, P.F. (1987). User acceptance of peer appraisals in an industrial setting. *Personnel Psychology*, **40**, 785–797.

McFarlin, D.B. and Sweeney, P.D. (1992). Distributive and procedural justice as predictors of satisfaction with personal and organisational outcomes. *Academy of Management Journal*, **35** (3), 626–637.

Messick, S. (1989). Validity. In R. Linn (ed.) *Educational Measurement*, 3rd edn. New York: Macmillan.

Moorman, R.M. (1991). The relationship between organizational justice and organizational citizenship behaviours: do fairness perceptions influence employee citizenship? *Journal of Applied Psychology*, **76**, 845–855.

Nirtaut, D.J. (1977). Assessment centers: an examination of participant reaction and adverse effects. *Journal of Assessment Center Technology*, **1**, 18–23.

Noe, R.A. and Steffy, B.D. (1987). The influence of individual characteristics and assessment center evaluation on career exploration behaviour and job involvement. *Journal of Vocational Behavior*, **30**, 187–203.

Powell, G.N. (1993). *Women and Men in Management*, 2nd edn. Newbury Park, CA: Sage.

Premack , S.Z. and Wanous, J.P. (1985). A meta-analysis of realistic job preview experiments. *Journal of Applied Psychology*, **70**, 706–719.

Quaglieri, P.L. (1982). A note on variations in recruiting information obtained through different sources. *Journal of Occupational Psychology*, **55**, 53–55.

Robertson, I.T. and Kandola, R.S. (1982). Work sample tests: validity, adverse impact and applicant reaction. *Journal of Occupational Psychology*, **55**, 171–182.

Robertson, I.T., Iles, P.A., Gratton, L. and Sharpley, D.S. (1991). The impact of personnel selection and assessment methods on candidates. *Human Relations*, **44**, 963–982.

Robertson, I.T. and Smith, J.M. (1989). Personnel selection methods. In J.M. Smith and I.T. Robertson (eds) *Advances in Selection and Assessment*. Chichester: John Wiley.

Rowe, P.M., Williams, M.C. and Day, A.L. (1994). Selection procedures in North America. *International Journal of Selection and Assessment*, **2**, 74–79.

Ryan, A.M. and Sackett, P.R. (1987). Pre-employment honesty testing: fakeability, reactions of test takers and company image. *Journal of Business and Psychology*, **1**, 248–256.

Rynes, S.L. (1992). Who's selecting whom? Effects of selection practices on applicant attitudes and behaviours. In N. Schmitt and W. Borman (eds) *Personnel Selection*. San Francisco: Jossey-Bass.

Salaman, G. and Thompson, K. (1978). Class culture and the persistence of an elite: the case of army officer selection. *Sociological Review*, **26** (2), 283–304.

Schmidt, F.L., Greenthal, A.C., Hunter, J.E., Berner, J.G. and Seaton, F.W. (1977). Job samples *vs* paper and pencil trades and technical tests: adverse impact and examinees' attitudes. *Personnel Psychology*, **30**, 187–197.

Schmitt, N., Ford, J.K. and Stults, D. (1986). Changes in self-perceived ability as a function of performance in an assessment center. *Journal of Occupational Psychology*, **59**, 327–336.

Schmitt, N. and Hill, T.E. (1977). Sex and race composition of assessment center groups as a determinant of peer and assessor ratings. *Journal of Applied Psychology*, **62** (3), 261–264.

Silvester, J. and Brown, A. (1993). Graduate recruitment: testing the impact. *Selection and Development Review*, **9**, 1–3.

Smith, M. and George, D. (1992). Selection methods. In C.L. Cooper and I.T. Robertson (eds) *International Review of Industrial and Organizational Psychology*, vol. 7. Chichester: John Wiley.

Sparrow, P.R. (1994). Organizational competencies: creating a strategic behavioural framework for selection and assessment. In N. Anderson and P. Herriot (eds) *Assessment and Selection in Organizations: First Update*. Chichester: John Wiley.

Stone, D.L. and Stone, E.F. (1987). Effects of missing application-blank information on personnel selection decisions. Do privacy protection strategies bias the outcome? *Journal of Applied Psychology*, **72**, 452–456.

Teel, K.S. and DuBois, H. (1983). Participants' reactions to assessment centers. *Personnel Administrator*, March, 85–91.

Tett, R.P., Jackson, D.N. and Rothstein, M. (1991). Personality measures as predictors of job performance: a meta-analytic review. *Personnel Psychology*, **44**, 703–742.

Thacker, J.W. and Cattaneo, R.J. (1987). The Canadian personnel function: status and practices. *Proceedings of the Administrative Sciences Association of Canada Supplement: Personnel and Human Resources*, 55–66. Toronto, Canada.

Thacker, J.W. and Cattaneo, R.J. (1993). *A Survey of Personnel Practices in Canadian Organizations: A Summary Report to Respondents*. Working Paper series no. W93–04. Windsor, Ontario: University of Windsor.

Townley, B. (1989). Selection and appraisal: reconstituting 'social relations'. In J. Storey (ed.) *New Perspectives on Human Resource Management*, pp. 92–108. London: Routledge,

Turban and Dougherty (1992).

Tziner, R.A. and Dolan, S. (1982). Validity of an assessment centre for identifying future female officers in the military. *Journal of Applied Psychology*, **67**, 728–763.

Warr, P.B. (1987). Workers without a job. In P.B. Warr (ed.) *Psychology at Work*, 3rd edn. Harmondsworth: Penguin.

Wernimont, P.F. and Campbell, J.P. (1968). Signs, samples and criteria. *Journal of Applied Psychology*, **52**, 372–376.

de Witte, K., van Laere, B. and Verraecke, P. (1992). Assessment techniques: towards a new perspective? Paper submitted to workshop on psycho-social aspects of employment, Sofia, Bulgaria, September.

de Wolff, C.J. and van den Bosch, G. (1984). Personnel selection. In P.J.D. Drenth, H. Thierry, P.J. Willems and C.J. de Wolff (eds) *Handbook of Work and Organizational Psychology*, vol. 1. Chichester: John Wiley.

Woolley, R.M. and Hakstian, A.R. (1993). A comparative study of integrity tests: the criterion-related validity of personality-based and overt measures of integrity. *International Journal of Selection and Assessment*, **1** (1), 27–40.

Chapter 28

Performance Appraisal in Context: Organizational Changes and their Impact on Practice

CLIVE FLETCHER

Department of Psychology, Goldsmiths College, University of London, New Cross, London SE14 6NW, UK

Over the last decade, many—perhaps most—organizations have undergone quite radical restructuring. They have become more organic and less mechanistic, with fewer levels and more flexible modes of operating. Managers now typically have to build and manage teams that cross organizational boundaries and which may exist only for the duration of the immediate task. They also have to deal with more information and take on a wider range of responsibilities (Cockerill, 1989). The kinds of staff they manage are changing too; an increasing proportion of them are knowledge workers, and they span an ever-widening range of cultural and ethnic backgrounds—many companies are grappling with the problems of managing such diversity.

Some of these changes have come about as a result of wider social and political shifts, some as a result of new concepts in management (such as Total Quality, and Performance Management), but probably the main driving force has been economic pressures. Taken together, they form the backdrop against which performance appraisal has had to operate and evolve. The magnitude of the differences between now and ten years ago is such that appraisal schemes operating then could not possibly be appropriate or effective in any but a handful of present day organizations.

However, this does not mean that performance appraisal is no longer relevant; in fact, it has become more rather than less important. There are two main reasons for arguing this. One is that the application of appraisal has been extended to new

International Handbook of Selection and Assessment, Edited by N. Anderson and P. Herriot.
© 1997 John Wiley & Sons Ltd.

work settings; for example, in the UK it has been introduced in schools, universities and the British National Health Service. The other is that it is seen as a central element in the concept of Performance Management, with its more strategic and holistic approach to organizational and individual performance; this places performance appraisal in a central role in a more integrated and dynamic set of HR systems (Bevan and Thompson, 1992).

What the impact of the changes does mean, though, is that the nature and aims of performance appraisal are now very different. In this chapter, five key aspects of appraisal will be considered in detail to see how the contemporary situation and thinking have had an impact on them.

WHO APPRAISES?

With fewer management layers and more direct reports to each manager, with increased use of matrix or project management, and with greater geographical spread of staff, the old principle of the immediate boss carrying out the appraisal becomes unworkable in many instances. A manager may have too many appraisees to deal with, or see them too infrequently to know how they are doing. An appraisee may work for several different bosses throughout the year. Who, then, should be the appraiser?

There have been a variety of responses to this problem. The practice of having several bosses contribute to the appraisal process has become common in matrix management organizations. Typically, this involves one line manager—or sometimes a functional head—consulting the appraisee's other bosses over the period in question and trying to feed back a representative view based on their replies. Increased use of self-appraisal is another alternative; who else sees as much of his or her performance as the appraisee? This helps, but is not without problems; it will only be useful where the expectations generated by the introduction of self-appraisal have been carefully managed and where the appraisers have been trained to use it. At least one study has shown how self-appraisal can lead to appraisees feeling that they have less influence over the appraisal and expressing more disagreement where these conditions are not met (Robertson *et al.*, 1993).

Whilst a combination of self- and superior appraisal is still the most common one, the involvement of peers and even of subordinates as appraisers is gaining popularity. The involvement of peers in the appraisal process is not something that has as yet become widespread. It has an appeal in academic and teaching institutions, where there is often a dislike of formal hierarchical management structures. In British universities, it is commonly an important input to promotion decisions, external assessors being asked to comment on the candidate's work and its impact on the field. But as an element in the assessment of performance on a shorter time scale, it has seldom been employed. In theory, it should have a lot to offer, as peers may be in a position to give a unique insight into an individual's team contribution—no small concern when there is pressure for people to achieve what might sometimes lead them to put their own concerns ahead of the team effort. In fact, peer rating in general is not all that accurate or unbiased, judging from the research evidence (Kane and Lawler, 1978). This does not mean that it cannot be developed and that effective ways of utilizing it as part of the appraisal process cannot be found. The biggest stumbling block is likely to be the administrative one—the time it takes to collect peer ratings would add substantially to the workload involved in appraisal. There is also the danger, mentioned by Williams (1989) that peer involvement in appraisal could cause friction and disrupt team harmony.

Upward appraisal, the appraisal of bosses by their subordinates, whilst also not very common as yet, is clearly a practice that is gaining ground. This takes two forms. In one, an element of upward appraisal is integrated into subordinate appraisal. For example, one major oil company included an item on the appraisal preparation form that asked the appraisee to identify occasions in the last year on which the appraiser could have provided them with more support. The alternative approach, however, is more common. This involves having an external agency send questionnaires to a manager's subordinates, seeking their views on various aspects of their boss's performance; the results are then collated into a report which is discussed in a feedback session between the manager and a consultant or someone designated for the role within the organization. Redman and Snape (1992) suggest that upward appraisal has the advantages both of facilitating the empowerment of employees and of making appraisal decisions more defensible against legal challenge (because they are based on a wider assessment input). There are inevitably some difficulties with it, though—e.g. the frequently voiced concern that either the managers being so appraised will feel their position to be undermined and react badly, or that their subordinates will not be frank enough to make any meaningful comments anyway, or both. The conditions for upward appraisal to work would seem to include:

- anonymity for the subordinate respondents
- a manager having enough subordinates to facilitate that anonymity and also to ensure a reasonable sample on which to base feedback
- the focus of upward appraisal has to be on those aspects of managerial performance that subordinates are most able to comment on (i.e., various aspects of staff management)
- a sufficient degree of trust has to be built up to gain the manager's support for the exercise

Upward appraisal is likely to become more frequently used in the next few years, but it is really an occasional, additional developmental activity rather than an integral and regular part of the ongoing appraisal process. Therefore, to return to the question posed at the start of this section, namely—who should appraise? The answer is no longer clear-cut; it depends on the structure of the organization, the quality of relationships (especially levels of trust) between the people in it, and how it conceives of appraisal—as a narrow, bottom-down process for communicating organizational needs and allocating rewards, or as a broader development tool.

THE QUALITY PERSPECTIVE AND ACCURACY IN APPRAISAL

Perhaps it is not surprising that, with all these pressures and shifts in thinking that have taken place, some people might question whether there is any place at all for appraisal in the modern organization. No one has put this more strongly than the 'guru' of Total Quality, W. Edward Deming, who has identified performance appraisal as one of the seven deadly diseases of current management practice (Deming, 1986). The crux of his argument is that appraisal does harm because it leads to the erroneous perception that variations in performance are caused by individual employees, as opposed to the real situation of such variations being caused by the systems created and controlled by managers. This leads to a focus on the wrong responses to quality shortcomings and to low morale amongst those appraised. Deming believes: (a) that individuals do not differ significantly in terms of their performance, with such variation as there is being attributable to random observations and sampling error; (b) variations in performance are due mainly to factors outside the individual's control; (c) managers cannot effectively differentiate between individuals and systems as the cause in performance variation. Deming's ideas have had widespread impact, and not just in relation to quality issues. Carson, Cardy and Dobbins (1991) report that Ford in the USA have been experimenting with reducing the appraisal categories from nine to three; they have taken on Deming's point that most people perform within the limitations of the system, and have decided that only 5–11% of staff should be rated higher or lower than the middle category.

Is Deming right? In most respects, he surely is. The strenuous efforts that have been made to avoid having to come to this conclusion are demonstrated by the extensive literature on attempts to improve the quality of assessment through different rating scale formats (Landy and Farr, 1980; Gomez-Mejia, 1988) and through varying approaches to training raters (Smith, 1986). Overall, though, the results of these have been inconsistent and somewhat disappointing. The inability of appraisers to assess accurately has been frequently observed (Bernadin and Cardy, 1982; Fletcher and Williams, 1992a). Much of what Deming says reflects the kind of attributional error described by psychologists as affecting appraisal ratings (e.g. Mitchell and Wood, 1980; Nieva and Gutek, 1980). Perhaps the only point of disagreement is his suggestion that there are no substantial differences between individuals in their performance. This flies in the face of a great deal of research on human performance across a wide range of settings. However, this contention on his part possibly does not matter much anyway from an appraisal viewpoint; if appraisers are not good at assessing performance differences and attributing them correctly, and if external factors are more important in determining performance than are individual capabilities, then there is little point in having performance appraisal based primarily on assessment.

Deming's thesis is in line with the argument (Fletcher, 1993) that the traditional, assessment-oriented approach to appraisal, with its emphasis on comparing people and linking assessment with rewards, fails to deliver on almost every count. It might well be regarded as a deadly disease, but it does *not* mean that other approaches to appraisal are equally lethal. This leads neatly on to the concept of appraisal as a process for motivating and developing people.

APPRAISAL, PAY AND MOTIVATION

Many, perhaps most, appraisal schemes pay at least lip service to the aim of motivating those appraised. For some of them, it is one of their main purposes. Yet they seldom make explicit just how this motivation is to be achieved; their documentation rarely addresses the nature of work motivation and how it relates to the appraisal process. It seems to be simply assumed that if feedback on performance is given by way of conveying an assessment in the appraisal, and if this is linked to rewards, then appraisal will be a motivating experience. Nor, come to that, does one find motivation being dealt with as part of appraisal training courses.

Simply giving feedback on performance is by no means automatically motivating, as was demonstrated many years ago by Meyer, Kay and French (1965). Indeed, it may sometimes have the opposite effect. Pearce and Porter (1986) studied the impact of a new appraisal scheme and found that those appraisees who were marked as average (by definition, most of them) were unhappy with their assessment and that they suffered a significant and stable drop in organizational commitment as a result. Given the doubts about the accuracy of appraisers' ratings, this is perhaps not surprising. But the use of appraisal as a motivational mechanism has actually increased recently, in the sense that performance-related pay (PRP) has been more widely adopted (Bevan and Thompson, 1992) and has usually been related to the appraisal process with varying degrees of directness.

Survey findings repeatedly show support for the principle of PRP amongst employees across a wide range of jobs and organizations. There is a strong and widely shared belief in the idea that those who perform well should gain greater benefits, and that allocating rewards this way is the fairest principle to follow. The basis of the support for PRP is, however, rather questionable. It is illustrated by the work of Meyer (1980) in which he asked all staff in a major company how they felt they were performing compared to their peers. He found that *on average*, people thought they were performing better than 75% of their peers! And the more senior the staff level in the company, the greater this proportion became. The implication of this is that people may think PRP is fine chiefly because they are going to benefit from it. No doubt this is behind the example given by Wright (1991) of a financial services company where 75% of the staff were in favour of PRP, but more than 70% of them were rated as superior on their appraisals.

To some extent, then, the popularity of the idea of PRP may be based in part on widespread, overly-positive self-appraisal, and an erroneous anticipation of the direct benefits it will bring to the individual. Consequently, there is a substantial problem of dealing with peoples' expectations when PRP is introduced—the majority are going to find they are getting less than they expected, and in some cases, a lot less. Because if money is to be attached to appraisal assessments, organizations cannot afford to go on permitting very positively skewed distributions of ratings, as it would have a serious impact on their financial viability. They have to make sure that the assessments follow a more normal distribution. Not surprisingly, in view of this, PRP seems to have just as much power to de-motivate as to motivate. Recent research by Thompson (1993) suggests that it may even fail to motivate those staff rated as high performers. Nor does it seem to be associated with high levels of organizational performance (Bevan and Thompson, 1991).

It would be foolish to suggest that financial reward is completely unimportant. But the simple-minded way in which appraisal-linked pay is trotted out as the answer to motivating people at work contradicts most of the evidence. Certainly, financial reward can be a motivator for some people, some of the time. However, its effect is likely to vary hugely. There are wide individual differences in what motivates people, and even within one person, the power of money as a motivator is likely to change radically depending on what life and career stage the individual is at. As long ago as the 1960s, research (Nealy, 1964) demonstrated that employees of different ages had very different reward preferences, and that the application of one incentive system to all employees in a particular job group did not make sense in motivational terms.

Can appraisal have a motivating function, then? Fortunately, there is more to reward than just PRP. There is a potentially vast array of non-financial rewards, and these do not usually generate the kind of problems associated with PRP. Perhaps this is because they are more individual and do not invite direct comparison, and because they often do not lead to permanent differentials. They are not valued the less for this, though. Many of them have the distinct advantage of being closer to intrinsic motivation than to extrinsic motivation. In other words, giving greater recognition, more responsibility, higher exposure to senior management and the like are all rewards that tap into the individual's pride in their work and achievement. Simply seeking to motivate with money sends a message that the reason for performing at a high level is down to personal financial reward. The question then arises—what happens to motivation and performance if (for various reasons, like economic recession) the money is not there any more?

The other important aspects of appraisal as a reward mechanism stem from its capacity to serve as a vehicle for personal development (which will be dealt with later in this chapter) and its objective-setting component. The evidence—reviewed by Locke, Shaw, Saari and Latham (1981) and Latham and Lee (1986)—repeatedly shows how goal setting is effective in raising performance levels. Many appraisal systems have goal setting and review as one of their chief components although, as will be noted below, not always as part of a single appraisal session.

APPRAISAL AS PART OF PERFORMANCE MANAGEMENT

The past ten years have seen the emergence of performance management as an approach not only to HR policies but to running the business as a whole. For many organizations, it is clear that the term performance management is synonymous with performance appraisal, or with performance-related pay (PRP). But a performance management system (PMS) is much more than either or both of these. There is no one, universally accepted definition; indeed, it is perhaps better to think of it more as a philosophy than as a clearly-defined process or set of policies. The notion of performance management that is most prevalent is one that is associated with an approach to creating a shared vision of the purpose and aims of the organization, helping each individual employee to understand and recognize their part in contributing to them, and in so doing to manage and enhance the performance of both individuals and the organization (Fletcher and Williams, 1992b).

The main building blocks of such a PMS are:

1. The development of the organization's mission statement and objectives.
2. Associated with this, the development of a business plan (business being interpreted here in the broadest sense of the word).
3. Enhancing communciations within the organization, so that employees are not only aware of the objectives and the business plan, but can contribute to their formulation.
4. Clarifying individual responsibilities and accountabilities (which means, amongst other things, having job descriptions, clear role definitions, and so on, and being willing to be held accountable).
5. Defining and measuring individual performance (with the emphasis on individuals being measured against their own objectives rather than being compared with one another).
6. Implementing appropriate reward strategies.
7. Developing staff to further improve performance, and their career progression, in the future.

Performance appraisal has a central role to play in PMS. The vehicle by which organizational goals and objectives are translated into individual objectives is usually the appraisal. It also remains the chief means by which development of the individual is discussed and acted on. The difference is that within the context of PMS, appraisal is now much more closely linked with the broader business context. There are, however, a number of issues that arise or which gain greater prominence when appraisal operates within the framework of PMS. These are as follows.

Individual vs team achievement. One of the potential problems of creating a performance culture—which is what many organizations are seeking to do through adopting PMS—is that there is a risk of encouraging individual achievement at the expense of team effort and cohesion. This risk can be overstated, but it is important that when objectives are set in the appraisal process, they reflect the priorities of the unit and not solely the narrower focus of the individual. This suggests that there has to be a clear understanding of what the team goals look like, and that it would be helpful for some sort of group review and discussion to take place to facilitate this, before individual appraisals are carried out.

Line-driven appraisal. The emphasis on line management driving PMS has implications for how appraisal operates. In terms of the purpose of appraisal, it emphasizes the point made by Dulewicz and Fletcher (1989) on the necessity of finding a formula for appraisal that meets the needs of the participants as well as the requirements of the organization. It is essential that line management have a major input to determining the nature of the appraisal system. Part of the rationale for this is that line input will be sensitive to local needs and requirements, and will develop appraisal to suit those better than any centrally imposed scheme is likely to—which is of considerable importance in modern, devolved-authority structures.

Appraisal as part of a feedback loop. Another aspect of PMS that impacts on the role of appraisal is the operation of a feedback loop. If PMS is to work effectively, it cannot be an exclusively top-down process. There has to be some mechanism whereby the strategic goals of the organization and their implications at lower levels can be influenced and modified by the line. Without it, the chances of gaining commitment to the aims of the organization are reduced. To some extent, this is covered by the emphasis on team discussion and framing of team targets mentioned earlier. This necessitates an interim stage in the process, before individual targets are set in appraisal, and can act as an opportunity to feed back to senior management reactions to strategic objectives. The appraisal itself thus has some capacity to act as a feedback mechanism too; appraisees should be in a position to agree realistic and important targets rather than simply accepting those imposed on them.

Excessive bottom-line emphasis. The main thrust of PMS in many organizations is about bottom-line or service-delivery issues. This is understandable, but it can be taken too far, leading to an excessive emphasis on ends rather than means. The concern becomes one of achieving short-term results at the expense of the longer term aims—not least of which may be the development of the individual. Where it is part of PMS, appraisal may become so focused on the individual's targets and their achievement that the developmental aspect is neglected. Where this happens, the appraisal process will fail to generate as much commitment from those appraised and will suffer in effectiveness. Worse still, there is evidence that excessive bottom line emphasis in PMS can induce high stress levels that detract from employee psychological well-being (Fletcher and Williams, 1992b).

To some extent, the twin aims of achieving improved performance and developing individuals can go hand in hand. However, it may be the case that in the context of PMS, holding development reviews separate from—but not unrelated to—the objective setting and review process makes good sense. This kind of separation of appraisal functions into different occasions and sessions has long been advocated (Meyer, Kay and French, 1965; Randell, Packard and Slater, 1984), though more often driven by the need to take pay discussion out of the appraisal arena. With the emerging popularity of PMS, the merit of such an approach is increasingly evident.

APPRAISAL AND THE ASSESSMENT AND DEVELOPMENT OF POTENTIAL

Traditionally, appraisal has been conceived of as having both a short-term performance focus and a long-term perspective in contributing to the assessment and development of potential. The economic pressures of the early 1980s seem to have caused something of a rethink on this aspect of appraisal. A survey by Long (1986) showed how the proportion of organizations listing the assessment of promotability and potential as one of their main purposes of appraisal had fallen appreciably, from 87% to 71%. Career planning was also less often seen as an important aspect of appraisal. The causes of this shift in emphasis are probably the uncertain economic outlook of the time, which made it harder to project ahead and to envisage growth with much confidence, and the fact that many organizations had shed labour in the previous five years and consequently had fewer promotion opportunities on offer. However, with the changes in organizations that have taken place in the last few years—not least the continued slim-lining and delayering—and the recession of the early 90s, these problems have scarcely improved. In some ways, they have got worse. There are fewer promotion opportunities as such, and given the rate of organizational change, when and where they occur is less predictable. The pattern of career progression is consequently less stable for many people, and less likely to be continued within the same organization than was the case hitherto.

These circumstances, far from suggesting that promotability and potential should be taken off the appraisal agenda, indicate that the career progression of the individual needs to be addressed with much greater care. If there are fewer promotions to be had, then it is even more essential that the process of deciding who will get them is seen to be fair and effective. If career development opportunities increasingly lie outside the organization, then the latter cannot rely quite so much on loyalty and company commitment of individual employees as a motivating force. Moreover, the nature of career development, either inside or outside organizations, is changing. With flatter hierarchies and fewer senior positions, for many people development is going to involve sideways moves or job enlargement rather than straight promotion.

There are two main ways in which appraisal systems have adapted to this new scenario. The first is the growth of competency-based appraisal (see also Sparrow, Chapter 17 in this volume). The notion of 'competency' has been defined in a myriad of ways, which understandably leads to some confusion. Boyatzis (1982), whose work in the USA led to much of the interest in this area, defines competence as 'an underlying characteristic of a person', which could be 'a motive, trait, skill, aspect of one's self-image or social role, or a body of knowledge which he or she uses'. This is a very broad definition, and others adopt more succinct descriptions of what constitutes a competence, such as 'an observable skill or ability to complete a managerial task successfully' or 'behavioural dimensions that affect job performance' (Jacobs, 1989; Woodruffe, 1990; Sparrow, Chapter 17 in this volume). Once it has been established what the key competencies are—often through the use of repertory grid methodology—they can be built into the appraisal system.

This does not mean that they become part of what is essentially an *assessment* process, with people being rated and compared on their levels of competence. Competencies cannot be equated with ratings of single job-related abilities—they are much broader and more complex than that. An individual may have mastered some aspects of a competence but not others. Competency-based appraisal does allow some scope for comparing people, but its real strength is in analysing the progress of the individual and in directing attention to those areas where skills can be improved (Fletcher, 1993). It is developmentally-oriented, and as such is likely to be motivating for the person appraised. The emphasis is on both parties in the appraisal process working together to chart the levels of competence attained by the appraisee and deciding on the appropriate training and experience needed to make further progress. Because it is behaviourally based, it is likely to be more objective and less likely to generate disagreement or conflict; however, competency-based appraisal is still fairly new and has yet to be subject to thorough research.

The other way in which appraisal has changed to meet the new career development situation is in terms of the methods used to augment its capacity to identify promotability and potential. The conventional appraisal process is not generally seen as a very effective means of assessing long-term potential, though it does have a more worthwhile contribution to make to immediate promotion decisions. The problems of using performance appraisal in this context are numerous, but two of the main ones are:

1. Where judgements about long-term potential for senior management levels are needed, line managers are not necessarily the best people to comment, as they may not have reached that level themselves and hence not possess first-hand experience of what is required.
2. The limited breadth of perspective of individual managers can mean that they are unaware of the performance standards required for promotion and of the extent of the range of opportunities available—which may give rise to the creation of false (unduly high or low) expectations in the appraisee.

These problems are accentuated in appraisal schemes that are highly-devolved and line-owned—i.e. precisely the conditions which are on the increase. This suggests that in such circumstances it is especially unwise to let the assessment of potential rest solely on the appraisal process. Because of the limitations of appraisal in this context, there has been a strong contemporary trend towards using psychometric tests or assessment/development centres as the main assessment method. The huge growth in the use of psychometric tests over the last ten years or so, in large organizations in the UK and elsewhere in Europe (Shackleton and Newell, 1991) has included an increase in their use to assess promotability and potential. There are a variety of ways in which tests are applied for these purposes:

1. They may be given to external candidates as part of a selection procedure, not only to assess suitability for the job vacancy but also to get some idea of the individual's potential beyond that.

2. Internal candidates for a promotion vacancy may be given a battery of tests to assess their suitability for the promotion in question.
3. Individuals may go through a testing session as part of a career assessment process that is not related to a specific promotion or job vacancy, but which has the assessment of potential as one of its aims.
4. Tests are often included as an element of an assessment centre process. Assessment Centres (ACs), rather like psychometric tests, have only become popular in the UK and Europe in the last ten years or so. ACs are currently used by 47% of UK organizations employing 1000 or more staff (Mabey, 1992).

There is still a place for the annual appraisal in assessing promotability, but where the appraisal is of the traditional kind it is a limited one; this is not one of the functions it serves well. The way so many organizations have taken to using psychometric tests and assessment centres in recent years suggests that this point has been widely recognized. As a trend, it looks set to continue and strengthen for some time yet. One of the advantages of this kind of strategy is that it allows appraisal of performance to be very much line-led, but puts the assessment of potential into a wider perspective that cannot usually be provided by line management alone. It also offers a superior level of objectivity and predictive power in assessment. If handled sensibly, tests and ACs can still leave line managers with a substantial role in implementing career development plans and decisions for their staff.

CONCLUSIONS AND IMPLICATIONS

This chapter has reviewed a wide range of changes in organizations and their associated trends in appraisal practice. What do such changes mean for the future of performance appraisal? One thing seems to be clear, and that is the steady decline of the traditional, monolithic appraisal system. This approach has typically involved a universally applied, personnel-driven, standard procedure, often with a heavy emphasis on the appraisal documentation and on using the process primarily for assessment purposes. In its place there are evolving a number of separate but linked processes, applied in different ways according to the needs of local circumstances and staff levels. Table 28.1 illustrates the emerging picture and how it contrasts with the earlier approach.

Essentially, appraisal seems to be breaking down into the two parts mentioned above when the relation of appraisal to PMS was discussed:

1. A performance planning session that involves reviewing achievement of objectives over the period in question and setting objectives for the period ahead. If PRP comes into the picture, this is often what it is related to.
2. A development review, probably based on competencies or skill dimensions, that looks at the training and development needs of the individual.

As noted earlier, this view of how appraisal should operate is not new; in various and sometimes rather different forms, it has been around since Meyer and his

Table 28.1   The contrasting pictures of appraisal, 1984–1994

1984		1994
Personnel Department	ORIGINS	Senior Management and HR Department jointly
Single event	NATURE	Multiple events: • Objective Setting and Review (OSR) • Personal Development Review (PDR) • Use of other methods to assess promotability/potential
Annual	FREQUENCY	Objective setting annually Objective Review quarterly PDR annually Potential assessed as needed
Immediate boss	APPRAISER	One or more bosses Some input from subordinates
Middle/junior management, mainly private sector	APPRAISED	Senior management down to clerical/secretarial; some coverage of operatives. Both public and private sector
Immediate job	FOCUS	Immediate job, team targets, organizational objectives and mission

Ratings of job abilities
 	
Objective setting and review
 	
Overall performance assessment
 	
Assessment of potential (on closed, separate form)
	CONTENT	OSR—objective setting/review
		    —assessment of performance for pay purposes
		PDR—competency review or other form of development need identification
		    —development planning

Possible use of overall assessment in pay decisions
 	
Use of appraisal data in promotion procedure
	LINKS WITH OTHER HR OR BUSINESS PROCESSES	OSR—links with business plan
		    —links with pay decisions
		
		PDR—links with Career Panels
		    —links with Career Workshops
		    —links with Development Centres
		    —links with organizational perceptions of future skill/competency needs

colleagues (Meyer, Kay and French, 1965) called for split roles in performance appraisal as a result of their work in the American company GEC in the 1960s. But it is far more relevant now than at any previous time. A third function or aspect of appraisal, the assessment of potential, is increasingly often supplemented by the use of more objective assessment methods such as psychometric tests or assessment centres.

The various elements in this new concept of appraisal may go by a variety of names, and perhaps the term performance appraisal has in some way outlived its usefulness—though it will probably refuse to go away. The main point is that these elements are more likely now and in the future to be properly integrated into the human resource policies of the organization as a whole. The research evidence is beginning to show that such policies do make an impact on employee attitudes and commitment (Ogilvie, 1987; Caldwell, Chatman and O'Reilly, 1990; Kinicki, Carson and Bohlander, 1992), which in turn can impact on organizational performance (Ostroff, 1992). Future research in this area might usefully mirror this broader perspective, spending less time and effort on seeking to achieve what usually turn out to be very modest improvements in the psychometric properties of various rating methods and instead focusing on the motivational and developmental consequences of appraisal, and how these can be enhanced within the wider context of continually changing, modern organizational structures and policies.

In parallel with this shift in research orientation, I/O psychologists and other practitioners working in this field should perhaps focus their own training and applications on gaining a broader organizational perspective, with greater emphasis on a holistic picture combining HR and business objectives. It is no longer enough to look at performance appraisal, selection, motivation, career development and related topics separately and individually, in an isolated and exclusively HR context; they have to be viewed as dynamic, interacting systems serving the needs both of individuals and of their employing institutions. This implies that, in future, I/O psychologists will increasingly be called upon to operate at a more macro level, and will thus need to have the requisite skills and knowledge to do so.

REFERENCES

Bernardin, H. J. and Cardy, R. L. (1982). Appraisal accuracy: The ability and motivation to remember the past. *Public Personnel Management,* **11**, 352–357.

Bevan, S. and Thompson, M. (1991). Performance Management at the crossroads. *Personnel Management,* November, 36–39.

Bevan, S. and Thompson, M. (1992). *Performance Management in the UK: An Analysis of the Issues.* London: Institute of Personnel Management.

Boyatzis, R. (1982). *The Competent Manager.* New York: Wiley.

Caldwell, D. F., Chatman, J. A. and O'Reilly, C. A. (1990). Building organizational commitment: A multifirm study. *Journal of Occupational Psychology,* **63**, 245–261.

Carson, K. P., Cardy, R. L. and Dobbins, G. H. (1991). Performance appraisal as effective management or as deadly management disease: Two initial empirical investigations. *Group & Organization Studies,* **16**, 143–159.

Cockerill, T. (1989). The kind of competence for rapid change. *Personnel Management,* September, 52–56.

Deming, W. E. (1986). *Out of the Crisis.* Cambridge, MA: MIT Institute for Advanced Engineering Study.

Dulewicz, S. V. and Fletcher, C. (1989). The context and dynamics of performance appraisal. In P. Herriot (ed.), *Assessment and Selection in Organizations.* London: John Wiley.

Fletcher, C. (1993). *Appraisal: Routes to Improved Performance.* London: Institute of Personnel Management.

Fletcher, C. and Williams, R. (1992a). *Performance Appraisal and Career Development,* 2nd edition. London: Stanley Thornes.

Fletcher, C. and Williams, R. (1992b). *Performance Management in the UK: An analysis of the Issues*. London: Institute of Personnel Management.

Gomez-Mejia, L. R. (1988). Evaluating employee performance. Does the appraisal instrument make a difference? *Journal of Organizational Behaviour Management*, **9**, 155–172.

Jacobs, R. (1989). Getting the measure of managerial competence. *Personnel Management*, October, 32–37.

Kane, J. S. and Lawler, E. E. (1978). Methods of peer assessment. *Psychological Bulletin*, **85**, 555–586.

Kinicki, A. J., Carson, K. P. and Bohlander, G. W. (1992). Relationship between an organization's actual human resource efforts and employee attitudes. *Group and Organization Management*, **17**, 135–152.

Landy, F. J. and Farr, J. L. (1980). Performance rating. *Psychological Bulletin*, **87**, 72–107.

Latham, G. P. and Lee, T. W. (1986). Goal setting. In E. Locke (ed.), *Generalising from Laboratory to Field Settings*. Boston, MA: Lexington Books.

Locke, E. A., Shaw, K. N., Saari, L. M. and Latham, G. P. (1981). Goal setting and task performance: 1969–1980. *Psychological Bulletin*, **90**, 125–152.

Long, P. (1986). *Performance Appraisal Revisited*. London: Institute of Personnel Management.

Mabey, W. (1992). The growth of test use. *Selection and Development Review*, **8** (3), 6–8.

Meyer, H. H. (1980). Self appraisal of job performance. *Personnel Psychology*, **33**, 291–295.

Meyer, H. H., Kay, E. and French, J. R. P. (1965). Split roles in performance appraisal. *Harvard Business Review*, **43**, 123–129.

Mitchell, T. R. and Wood, R. W. (1980). Supervisors' responses to subordinate poor performance: A test of the Attributional model. *Organizational Behavior and Human Performance*, **25**, 123–128.

Nealy, S. M. (1964). Determining worker preferences among employee benefit programs. *Journal of Applied Psychology*, **48**, 7–12.

Nieva, V. F. and Gutek, B. A. (1980). Sex effects on evaluation. *Academy of Management Review*, **5**, 267–276.

Ogilvie, J. R. (1987). The role of human resource management practices in predicting organisational commitment. *Group and Organizational Studies*, **11**, 335–359.

Ostroff, C. (1992). The relationship between satisfaction, attitudes and performance: An organizational level analysis. *Journal of Applied Psychology*, **77**, 963–974.

Pearce, J. L. and Porter, L. W. (1986). Employee responses to formal appraisal feedback. *Journal of Applied Psychology*, **71**, 211–218.

Randell, G. A., Packard, P. M. A. and Slater, A. J. (1984). *Staff Appraisal: A First Step to Effectiveness*, 3rd edition. London: Institute of Personnel Management.

Redman, T. and Snape, E. (1992). Upward and onward: Can staff appraise their managers? *Personnel Review*, **21**, 32–46.

Robertson, L., Torkel, S., Korsgaard, A., Klein, D., Diddams, M. and Cayer, M. (1993). Self appraisal and perceptions of the appraisal discussion: A field experiment. *Journal of Organizational Behavior*, **14**, 129–142.

Shackleton, V. J. and Newall, S. (1991). Management selection: A comparative survey of methods used in top British and French companies. *Journal of Occupational Psychology*, **64**, 23–36.

Smith, D. E. (1986). Training programs for performance appraisal. *Academy of Management Review*, **11**, 22–40.

Thompson, M. (1993). *Pay and Performance 2: The Employees' Perspective*. Sussex: Institute of Manpower Studies.

Williams, R. (1989). Alternative raters and methods. In P. Herriot (ed.), *Assessment and Selection in Organizations*. London: John Wiley.

Woodruffe, C. (1990). *Assessment Centres: Identifying and Developing Competence*. London: Institute of Personnel Management.

Wright, V. (1991). Performance-related pay. In F. Neale (ed.), *The Handbook of Performance Management*. London: Institute of Personnel Management.

Chapter 29

Assessing Developmental Needs

Jeroen J. J. L. Seegers

Assessment and Development Consult, Zypendaalseweg 47, 6814 CC Arnhem, The Netherlands

'Our focus is on people' and 'good management is scarce': two frequently heard statements which indicate the crucial importance of the human element in the production process. In practice, however, many companies seem to regard the process of developing their own management as a sort of exotic stepchild. While the topic of management development has been in vogue for some time now, it has only in recent years become the focus of serious attention. Organizations expend a good deal of energy every year on the selection of graduates for top management positions. These so-called management trainees are selected for management positions which they will occupy 6–10 years later. Since, in terms of management behaviour, many graduates are poorly prepared for their managerial tasks, the actual selection process takes place in the form of interim appraisals. When self-assessment and mentoring are integrated into the selection and appraisal process, both selection and appraisal gain strength. But this, of course, implies the mobilization of successful practising managers and executives (Bartz and Calabrese, 1991).

An examination of job descriptions reveals that line managers who are supposed to be responsible for the quality of their personnel never actually seem to be held accountable for this. In daily practice, apparently, the quality of a manager's personnel is of secondary importance. What counts are results, no matter whether they are achieved because of, or despite, the quality of the personnel. This attitude leads to 'depletion' of human capital: short-term profits may be booked, but nothing constructive is done on the assets side of the personnel balance sheet. Metaphorically speaking, it is as if a farmer were to harvest crops continually without ever adding any fertilizer to his land; the result, of course, would be exhaustion. One may select and appraise ever so carefully, but when the results of

International Handbook of Selection and Assessment, Edited by N. Anderson and P. Herriot.
© 1997 John Wiley & Sons Ltd.

the selection and appraisal process do not provide input for continual development, the efforts put into selection will not, in the end, yield all the fruits they
could have (Boudreau, 1983; Wright and Werther, 1991).

Many managers find that they are actually penalized for good personnel policy.
Skilfully trained and guided people are soon recommended for promotion and
disappear into other jobs. This is fine for the employees, of course, but the managers have to pay the price. They lose their best employees and have no option
but to begin all over again. Moreover, the former boss is seldom rewarded with a
salary increase for supplying 'high potential'. No wonder if such managers think
twice in the future before singing the praises of their 'star pupils' so openly. And
yet a good personnel policy is of increasing strategic significance for any organization. For an organization or company to survive, the creation of an internal
labour market is of crucial importance.

In other words, it is necessary to pursue a strategic personnel policy focused on
placing the right people in the right positions. In this chapter, the characteristics of
effective strategic personnel policy will be discussed. The role of 'management
development' in such policy will then be examined and it will be argued that
management training should no longer be approached as a *system* but as an on-
going *process*. The last section of this chapter will be devoted to the technique of
criterion-based training.

STRATEGIC PERSONNEL POLICY

> A strategy is a pattern in a stream of decisions. A strategy integrates significant plans
> (objectives, policies, programmes) and decisions (agreements, commitments) into a
> coherent whole and provides a sense of direction for the entire organization. The
> strategy thereby indicates how the great variety of resources available to the organ-
> ization (people, money, raw materials, machines, technologies, developmental ca-
> pacity, etc.) are to be deployed in order to compete with products and services in a
> number of different markets. (Groot, 1992)

It should be obvious from this very lucid description that strategic personnel
policy forms part of the total organizational strategy. Strategic personnel policy
means acquiring insight today into the organizational picture of tomorrow. Strategic personnel policy also means having a clear perception of the organization's
own internal labour market. This implies that the assessment process does not
stop with initial selection. Strategic personnel policy means continual selection
and appraisal of employees against the background of ever more radically changing jobs. Only then will selection lead to success.

In 1988, a study by Nicholson and West confirmed the increasing importance of
creating an internal labour market. Organizations are going through drastic
changes, becoming flatter and more mobile and demanding a high degree of
adaptability from management. The same study revealed that more than half of
the managers on active duty changed jobs within a period of three years. Experience has taught that these new jobs and positions were not easy to predict.
Careers are no longer pursued in the familiar manner, one rung after the other on

the same ladder. Making a career now means finding one's way in a maze of possibilities. With the prevalence of mergers, takeovers, privatizations, radical reorganizations and the like, any career strategy which presupposes a stable organization is hopelessly out of date. And unfortunately for the policy-makers, this is becoming more and more the case (Herriot, 1989). Moreover, continuing cutbacks in education budgets make it increasingly necessary to offer postgraduate education or supplementary training within the organization.

In the external labour market, the increasing availability of female staff is a significant factor. The simple fact that women bring children into the world gives them a different position in the *internal* labour market. As the care of small children is still left largely to women to arrange (which implies, among other things, the necessity to work part-time for certain periods), they are not always in an equal position with their male colleagues. Organizations cannot afford to ignore this fact, quite apart from discussions about equal opportunities and non-discrimination.

Strategic management of the internal labour market demands a good plan and a good personnel prognosis. A mere printout of personnel data is not enough. Moreover, the performance of many personnel information systems is woefully inadequate. Owing to their frequently static character, the data tend to be out of date just when you need them, usually because the organization has changed as well. There is thus little sense in trying to formulate a strategic personnel prognosis for the whole organization, especially when the organization is confronting a high rate of employee turnover.

Owing to all kinds of new developments, success is defined differently nowadays. No longer is it merely a question of being successful in a given job; what counts more is the ability to switch jobs rapidly. A shorter 'switching time' increases profitability. Many existing management development systems are inadequate and very inefficient. An average management development course of six years (three blocks of two years each) often yields no more than three really productive years. The first half-year is devoted to the breaking-in process, after which a year of productivity follows. Then another half-year is spent on preparing for the next step, with a good deal of energy being invested in the succession procedure. The process is repeated in the second job and again in the third block. The result is a wave-like movement in which performance is continually being interrupted by periods of breaking-in and winding-up.

When people are better prepared for the next step, there is less loss of productivity. This is only possible when the steps are coherently linked, which brings us back to the need for a good prognosis. Such a prognosis, however, goes a good deal further than *ad hoc* prediction. A good personnel audit can be a godsend here, but such audits demand thorough preparation and a highly project-based approach (see also Fombrun, 1984).

In brief, an audit proceeds something like this: A project team begins by drafting an organizational profile which includes the organization's basic strategy, mission and objectives. The current state of affairs is outlined in terms of both the internal situation (strengths/weaknesses) and external developments. Trends and possible new activities are analysed. This should result in a strategic personnel plan indicating the requirements to be met by future personnel. This needs analysis will lead to budget adjustments, since it is to be expected that extra money will have to be invested in assessment and development.

Central elements in the auditing process are a strengths/weaknesses analysis of the present workforce and an analysis of the discrepancies between presently available personnel and the workforce which should be available in the future (Figure 29.1). An evaluation based only on performance in the current job is not sufficient, since future jobs will frequently involve entirely new elements. Assessment centres can be of considerable help here. After all, the assessment-centre method enables line management to evaluate personnel strengths and weaknesses, which can subsequently be worked out in greater detail by the personnel department. Formulating the internal and external mobility policy, however, is again a line management responsibility.

A personnel audit forms the basis for a well-balanced management selection policy, for a better distribution of tasks between line management and the personnel department, for a more adequate use of personnel information systems, and for the proper utilization of various personnel instruments. It does not make sense for an organization to launch a particular business strategy if it is unlikely to be able to develop competencies to implement it (see also Schuler, 1992).

THE SELECTION OF FUTURE MANAGERS

A properly functioning management selection policy belongs within the framework of a strategic personnel policy—or to formulate it more accurately, within a strategic human resource management policy. Human resource management goes much further than management development and comprises, based on the Harvard approach, all management decisions and activities which influence the nature of the relationship between the organization and its employees—the human 'resource' (Beer *et al.*, 1984; Miles, 1974; Schein, 1978; Vloeberghs, 1989). Although organizations are becoming increasingly aware of the importance of human resource management, many organizations still give it even less chance to live up to its promise than management development. Factors such as market turbulence and demographic changes are compelling organizations to take strategic action (Nicholson and West, 1988). In simple terms, proper management development should result in an adequately functioning management which not only takes internal and external developments into account but anticipates them as well (Gratton, 1989).

Nowadays, too many people still see management development as a system (Fisscher, 1988). Consider, for example, the so-called *formalistic management development system*. This is an exceptionally methodical plan which lets recent graduates know exactly what to expect in terms of both jobs and training programmes during their first six years. It amounts to a cram course for a line or staff career. The basic premise of such a system is that it is possible to predict the type of situations people are going to encounter and the capacities that are going to be required of them six to eight years in advance. Experience, however, indicates

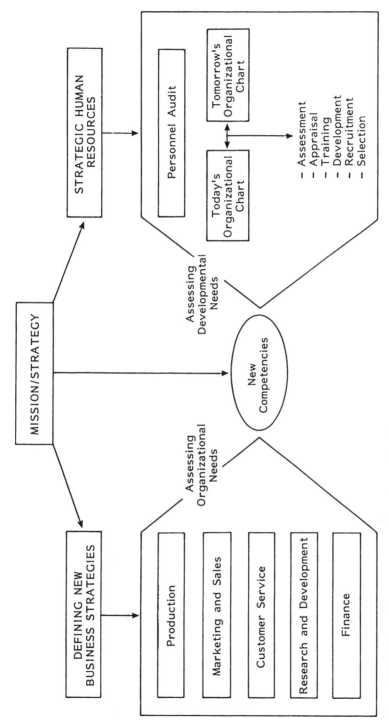

Figure 29.1 Towards a competency-based organization

that such predictions are becoming increasingly difficult to make in today's turbulent environment.

The *breeding ground model* is a system based on a somewhat different approach. Recent graduates are hired as 'supernumeraries' and follow a management trainee programme. During the first two years they have no specific posts but occupy themselves with projects and assignments. The idea behind this programme is that the trainees will discover their strong and weak points on the job. The Achilles' heel of this model is found in the supervision given by a sort of mentor in the organization. This mentor—often from sheer necessity—will generally be a personnel officer or senior executive. It can be questioned whether either of these persons is the right choice: the personnel officer usually lacks adequate line experience; and the senior executive, being too far removed from the trainee's learning situation as a model, is more likely to have a frustrating than an encouraging effect.

Finally, there is the so-called *ad hoc model*, which actually means no model at all. By means of careful prognoses, the organization tries in a fairly short time to assess what management qualities are needed and appoints *ad hoc* officers to certain positions. This takes place very systematically and consciously, however, making use of external expertise.

The striking thing about these 'models' is that they are based on the needs and patterns of the organization and not on the individual's pattern of growth and needs. It still remains to be seen whether people with *real* talent will have the patience to wait six to eight years before being allowed to show what they can do. Moreover, since the initial jobs are not likely to be very challenging, such people may begin to get restless after one year, let alone two. Companies are often in the market for 'dynamic, young, enterprising future managers'. This type of person is characterized by the following behavioural profile: energetic, enterprising and with plenty of drive. An enterprising person is someone who both creates and utilizes opportunities; a person who shows initiative and dares to take risks; a self-starter, a leader, an achiever. This sounds superb, of course, but it can also be seen in another light, as a 'healthy dose' of recklessness, opportunism, nonconformity, independence, insensitivity, dominance and ambition. And it goes without saying that someone who displays a somewhat too healthy dose of such qualities at the beginning of his or her career will, almost by definition, be penalized for it. Any young, ambitious manager, dominant and self-starting, blessed with plenty of nerve and initiative, who dares to wander from the beaten path (and it is fairly likely that he or she will do so) will immediately be reined in with comments such as 'be patient', 'don't move too fast', 'wait until you have a bit more seniority'. Justifiably or not, the effect is that really talented people feel that they are being 'penalized' and are likely to leave the organization, while slightly less talented people are systematically 'cured' of such behaviour within four to six years.

A child who is punished whenever he or she does something wrong will think twice before making another false move. Deviant behaviour results in penalties. Both the formalistic and the breeding ground systems tend to induce deviant behaviour. This is less true for the *ad hoc* system, in which people are hired on the basis of actual needs; but the danger here is that a good culture match may be lacking: an organization may well attract talented people, but they don't play the game the way the organization has always played it. They are unfamiliar with the organization's playing style and are used to playing other games in other organizations.

This definitely seems to argue for a dynamic model of management development. This model is not limited strictly to management positions but covers the whole field of personnel development. Management development can best be considered as a *continuous process of competence assessment and development geared to the future requirements of the organization and its personnel.* This definition is based on a number of premises:

- The organization has (or can form) a good picture of what will be demanded from individual employees by the *future* organization.
- These demands can be translated into measurable *capabilities*.
- These capabilities can be *developed*.
- The organization has sufficient *developmental capacity*.

The last two points in particular are rather troublesome. For one thing, development is not always possible. In such cases, some sort of selection procedure will have to be employed. Secondly, not all organizations, by any means, have sufficient developmental capacity. The 'management' aspect of management development often receives more attention than the 'development' side. It is well known that people do not change their behaviour 'just like that' (Howard and Bray, 1988): people need to be motivated to change their behaviour, and the new behaviour must subsequently be 'reinforced'. (Why should I change my behaviour when my boss doesn't value my efforts positively?) Worse yet, people who try, cautiously and somewhat uncertainly, to put what they have learned in a course into practice are frequently chided with remarks such as 'Just back from the course I see!' or 'Please try to act like a normal human being again!'. This is simply deadly for the new behaviour.

Management progression is a continuous process of assessment and development. The word 'assessment' has purposely been used here rather than 'evaluation'. Evaluation is a retrospective process (and of course we are all wise in retrospect). Assessment is a process of evaluation in advance: what are the organization's future requirements and are employees capable of meeting them? The use of the word 'process' does not imply that no control is possible. To borrow an analogy from measuring and control engineering, 'control mechanisms' can be developed to make the process manageable. All control systems are characterized by feedback: information on events and their effects.

It is possible to speak of management development at a micro-level and a macro-level. At the micro-level, it is concerned with the 'control' of the individual at the operational level. It will be obvious that the line manager functions as 'controller' here; the training process is in his or her hands. This is a recurring process, put into operation each time at a slightly higher level. For the controlling managers are themselves the subjects of developmental processes controlled by their own managers.

At the macro-level, another form of control takes place. Based on the organization's strategic policy and the results of a personnel audit, a strategic personnel plan is formulated. On the basis of this plan, top management directs its human resources. Teamwork between top management and human resource specialists in the organization is of decisive importance here. Only then can top management and middle management effectively translate the strategic policy plan into operational plans for the organization. These objectives are focused on the development of both individuals and teams. Each manager is responsible not only for his or her own development but also for that of his or her team. These developmental goals are also taken into consideration in the evaluation process and are valued and rewarded. Line managers must realize that they are responsible for managing human resources; they and they alone are responsible for both the quantity and the quality of their personnel.

CRITERION-BASED TRAINING

The assessment-centre method—or rather, assessment-centre technology—can be employed successfully for the development of personnel. This is true, above all, when it is not a question of attitude training but of conveying certain skills and teaching specific job-relevant behaviour. Anyone who has ever tried to write, or even read, a set of instructions for repairing a punctured cycle tyre will appreciate the advantages of a learning model based on the principle of behavioural modelling.

Criterion-based training is based on the theory of behaviour modelling (Bandura, 1971; Zemke, 1978; Robinson, 1982). It is a 'back-to-basics' approach composed of the following elements: example, imitation and practice, reinforcement and reward. Because it is so closely linked with day-to-day activities, the manager plays a central role. A true 'people manager' must in the first place be a competent coach and instructor.

The technique of criterion-based training consists of the following five phases:

1. *Formulate behavioural goals.* The first phase in criterion-based training involves the formulation of behavioural goals. The desired objective is described in terms of behaviour. These behavioural goals must be based on what the trainee needs to learn; there should also be some indication of the extent to which the 'new' behaviour is or can be effective. The point is to make the trainee aware of the positive effects which the new behaviour can have. In this first step, then, it is important to discuss the behavioural goals with the trainee in advance.

   In order to formulate behavioural goals properly, an analysis of the job and job requirements is necessary. This involves an analysis of the desired capacities or capabilities, expressed in terms of behaviour. This last element is essential for day-to-day practice is always the starting point.

   A subsequent section of the job analysis involves the selection of 'good' and 'bad' behaviour. If properly performed, evaluations based on the integrated approach will provide sufficient information for this purpose. Compare the behaviour displayed by 'good' and 'poor' performers and determine what sort of behaviour is desirable. Identify effective and ineffective behaviour and eliminate the ineffective: ineffective behaviour should not be included in the behavioural goals. Analyse the critical situations in which effective behaviour must be displayed and organize the forms of behaviour which are to be learned in a structured, orderly fashion. Develop model behaviour for this purpose. Use can be made of the same critical situations utilized in the assessment centre. Critical behaviours should be developed for each situation that has been identified. Once these critical behaviours have been determined, the behaviours should be tested. The best way to do this is through a behavioural demonstration. If, for instance, you are looking for future middle managers, you would select at least six competent middle managers who will test the different behaviours in different situations to determine whether these behaviours are effective or should be re-examined. A fundamental concept of behaviour modelling is 'If you can't describe it in behavioural terms, don't try to teach it' (Robinson, 1982).

2. *Demonstrate model behaviour.* The second phase in criterion-based training involves the demonstration of model behaviour, which in fact is the behaviour the trainee needs to learn. If the 'model' is not perceived as credible and positive, the trainee will not be inclined to adopt the behaviour. The role of the manager as coach is obvious here. The model behaviour is to be displayed in a simulated practical situation. Here also, the assessment-centre method offers a solution.

3. *Practise new behaviour.* In the third phase, the new behaviour is practised in a practical simulation. It is important to bear in mind that this is no informal role-playing session. The participant must acquire both the skill and the self-confidence that goes with it, which implies intensive supervision. Conveying the skill without self-confidence is not sufficient. A person may have learned how to give presentations, for example, but still not dare to actually do so. In such a case, the exercise has not in fact led to effective job behaviour.

4. *Give direct feedback.* The fourth phase of criterion-based training involves the giving of feedback. There is no good basis for changing behaviour without feedback. It is important that feedback be provided directly, in a positive and encouraging manner, focused on specific forms of behaviour and presenting possible behavioural alternatives.

5. *Reinforce behaviour in practice.* In the fifth and crucial phase, the newly learned behaviour is reinforced in daily practice. The key role of the line manager as mentor and coach is evident here, which is why it is necessary to train managers in reinforcing newly learned behaviour. In this phase, it becomes manifest that experience in itself is not enough to lead to changes in behaviour. People only learn from mistakes when the consequences of their mistakes are tangible. Many management development programmes fail to lead to effective changes in behaviour because behavioural changes play no role in the evaluation and remuneration system.

Table 29.1 Behavioural Modelling: Basis for Management Development (Reproduced from *Developing Managers through Behaviour Modeling* by J.C. Robinson. Copyright © 1982 by J.C. Robinson. Published by Pfeiffer & Company, San Diego, CA. Used with permission of the publisher)

Learning principles	Behaviour modelling precepts	Programme development considerations	Classroom procedures
MODELLING	*Behavioural objectives* If you can't describe it in behavioural terms, don't try to teach it	Define behavioural objectives that • are based on needs • specify *effective* behaviour	1. Introduce need for skill 2. Present critical steps 3. Show modelling display
	Model If you can't demonstrate how to do it, don't teach it	Develop modelling displays that • are positive • are credible	
BEHAVIOURAL REHEARSAL	*Skill practice* If you can't practise the skill, you can't develop it	Develop skill-practice exercises that • provide each learner extended opportunities to perform the behaviours • provide success experiences	4. Review critical steps 5. Provide skill practices for learners
REINFORCEMENT	*Immediate feedback* Without feedback there's no accurate basis for changing some behaviours and strengthening others	Develop instructor competencies for managing feedback process that • reinforce effective behaviours • provide alternative behaviours	6. Manage process of group feedback on the learners' performances after each skill practice
	On-the-job reinforcement Without reinforcement on-the-job, the new skills will be extinguished	Arrange for separate management-reinforcement workshop for learners' immediate superiors	

The behaviour modelling approach has close links with the assessment-centre method: they are on the same wavelength. The assessment-centre method enables assessors to establish precisely which behavioural aspects require development. By indicating the effectiveness of behaviour in assessment reports, they thus lay the foundation for the first step in the behaviour modelling concept. The central role of the line manager was made clear in the previous paragraph. Teaching line managers to function as trainers or mentors will also enable them to handle the following steps, using assessment simulations as training aids.

Many assessment or selection procedures are exclusively focused on selection and not on providing a thorough, in-depth diagnosis. A selection procedure such as a test, for example, can indicate that a given person is weak in leadership. A diagnostic assessment centre, in contrast, may show that while a person displays mediocre leadership qualities in an open group discussion, he or she scores far above average when it comes to leading a two-person talk. Another example: a selection procedure merely indicates that someone is weak in judgment. In a diagnostic assessment centre, however, it would be noted that this person has good judgment when dealing with facts and figures but is weak when it comes to evaluating less concrete matters such as human relations. The conclusion is that the assessment-centre method makes it possible to discern more contrasts and nuances in respect of a given behavioural criterion, which is of essential import-ance for training and development purposes.

MODELLING: MENTORS AT WORK

Once developmental needs have been assessed, a course could give the solution. However, a course is generally an expensive solution. Besides, most young trainees have just finished a long period of education and are not looking forward to having more courses again. Mostly they are very eager to learn from other experiences. A day spent chatting with an experienced colleague and observing him or her on the job might produce almost the same result. And the employee's individual learning style is also relevant here, of course. Does he or she learn best by reading a book on 'how to chair a meeting' or by actually doing it and discuss-ing the experience? It is important to select a developmental activity which is in line with the individual learning style. Although an external course is often the first thing people think of when the question of 'development' comes up, such courses generally cover more topics than the employee actually has need of. Following a course or a training programme is but one option out of a number of possible developmental activities, such as:

- talking to colleagues who possess the relevant knowledge and skills
- reading books, articles, etc.
- on-the-job training
- job or task rotation
- self-study
- computerized education
- sitting in on activities which need to be mastered (chairing a meeting, for example)
- learning by example
- therapy, particularly in cases of attitude and personality problems.

Another, even more important, issue has been raised by Lawler (1993) in con-nection with competency-based organizations: 'The basic problem is that the development and management of individuals is a second order effect of the management system which has as its major focus filling jobs with individuals, who can perform them. 'The central issue is how to best manage individuals so that they develop and maintain the correct competencies. The challenge in a competency-based organization is to focus on what individuals need to be able to do in order to make the work processes operate effectively. In practice, there are two possible diagnoses:

- The manager determines that an employee does not perform adequately. This may be due to a developmental need (the employee does not know how to do the job properly), but it can also be caused by other factors. In the analysis phase, it is important to define the cause clearly. People are so often sent off to courses that are of no real use to them.
- The employee is performing adequately. The manager talks to the employee about his or her overall performance and attempts to detect whether any developmental needs are present. When the employee indicates insufficient mastery of certain activities (although this may not be directly apparent in his or her performance and achievements) or needs to develop certain skills which are not directly related to the present job, boss and employee can sit down together and focus their attention on possible developmental activities. In other words, even if the employee is performing well at a given time, it is still the manager's task to see whether enough attention is being given to further development.

Once it has been established that an employee is not functioning and performing properly, it is the manager's job to get to the bottom of the problem. Does the employee really 'fit' in the present job? Sending an employee who generally dislikes the present job off to a course is no solution at all. Reshuffling tasks or giving him or her another job (if possible) will be much more helpful. Another possible developmental activity is to hold consultation sessions: talks in which employees can express their feelings about their work and managers can suggest ways of approaching certain tasks which might help them feel more comfortable in their jobs.

The manager gives the employee the opportunity, as it were, to think about his or her own behaviour and its effects on others, hoping that by doing so it will be possible to determine whether the cause of the performance problem lies in the employee's unfamiliarity or ineptitude with the desired behaviour. Research by de Graaff (1992) has shown that 'lack of mastery of the required behaviour' is the cause of only 5% of performance problems; sending an employee to a course may thus be an adequate solution in a maximum of only 5% of all cases. Most performance problems originate in the situation. Employees perform poorly because something in the situation hinders them from carrying out their assignments effectively. They may have the right behavioural skills, like their work and know what is expected of them, but something in the situation prevents them from achieving their goals.

When the cause of the performance problem lies in the employee's personality or behaviour, developmental activities can provide a solution. When the problem originates in the situation or in the employee's perception of the situation, there is no question of a developmental need. Instead, managers should help such employees to either change their attitudes or change the situation so that they can do their jobs properly.

In the analysis phase, the precise origin of the performance problem is identified. Is it lack of knowledge? If so, which knowledge? Is it lack of (behavioural) skills? If so, which skills exactly? Does the employee's attitude (personality) hinder his or her performance? If so, what is this attitude and how does it have to change? Once the precise developmental need has been identified (knowledge, behaviour, attitude), developmental activities can be planned. The selection criteria for developmental activities are the efficiency of the course and the trainee's learning style.

Together, the manager and the employee determine the most effective and efficient developmental activities. They draw up a training or development plan and schedule progress review meetings. In effect, a 'contract' is concluded between manager and employee. The manager is committed to support the employee during the developmental phase and in applying what has been learned in practice. The employee is committed to making a real effort and working actively on his or her own development.

In their roles as mentors and coaches, managers are particularly responsible for guiding their employees in integrating and applying the newly acquired knowledge and skills in practice. Many developmental activities have no visible results owing to lack of support for new behaviour on the job. 'We can see you are just back from a course, but do act normally again!' is a (notorious) catchphrase familiar to anyone who has ever tried to put what has been learned on a training course into practice. It is the manager's responsibility to help employees utilize their newly learned skills and he or she will have to create space, time and opportunity for this.

When a manager assumes the role of coach, this implies that he or she will have to give more attention to accommodating and guiding employees who have followed courses. The success or failure of a developmental activity is determined by the 'aftercare' provided on the job. When, after a thorough analysis of developmental needs, manager and employee have established the correct developmental activities, it is no more than logical that the employee, once back on the job, should be given the chance to apply what has been learned. The fact that this still happens so rarely reveals something about the prevailing view of courses and other developmental activities: not so much as 'developmental activities' in themselves (after all, it may not be known what the precise developmental need is!), but rather as rewards for services rendered.

When it appears in practice that the performance problem has not been entirely solved following completion of the developmental activities, the manager will have to look into the precise origins of the problem again. In effect, the whole analytical process will have to be repeated. What follows are some suggestions to support the manager in his or her mentor role.

Train managers in mentoring. This type of training demands a specific approach. The goal is to make managers aware that training and coaching their employees on the job will require spending quite a lot of time on supervision, which in many companies is still too often seen as a job for the personnel department or professional trainers. It is, however, an explicit line responsibility and the ability to supervise employee development should be considered as an important management characteristic. Anyone in a management position should also be evaluated in terms of this skill.

Senior management involvement. Set up what is known as a 'sponsor' system. Sponsors are senior managers whose position in the organization enables them to approve projects. In addition, they supervise the managers involved as mentors and coaches in the coaching process. They must be able to take whatever action is required to guarantee the continuation of the development process. Coaches and sponsors meet regularly to discuss trainee progress (Wright and Werther, 1991).

Development handbook. Put together a handbook for training and developmental activities. The handbook should indicate possible activities for each criterion and provide managers with the means to develop their employees. Each organization which utilizes the assessment-centre method for training and development objectives should in fact compose its own handbook geared to its own prevailing behavioural criteria. Ideally, the handbook will offer more than one developmental activity for each behavioural criterion. An example of this, concerning the use of the handbook at Cadbury Schweppes, is given by Glaze (1989).

Use of project teams and special assignments. Place a manager in a team which must make recommendations for the solution of a problem or the execution of another assignment. This is an outstanding developmental technique. Such an assignment makes it possible to observe the participant(s) while leading or collaborating with their colleagues in the project team. It can also, certainly when the group is composed of participants from different disciplines, make an important contribution towards the acquisition of insight and understanding into the operation of the organization as a whole. Particularly for management trainees who have been selected to fill leadership positions at a later date, directing a project team is an excellent manner of training managerial capacities. Normally, a trainee at the beginning of his or her career will not soon be given the opportunity to demonstrate these managerial capacities, even though he or she will have definitely been selected at least partially on this basis.

Special assignments provide the manager with opportunities for in-depth training and development. Usually of relatively short duration, special assignments involve the trainee with a given problem or area of special attention within the organization (ideally one outside his or her own professional field). The trainee will generally report to another line manager rather than to his or her immediate boss. Such special assignments may help the trainee acquire more in-depth or comprehensive knowledge or may be specifically focused on developing capacities for analytical thought, decision-making processes, etc.

Use of critical incident training. Utilize job analysis to sub-divide a job into given work situations that are critical for success. Such incidents may include: analysis reports, planning sessions, meetings, discussions, purchasing and sales talks, progress checks, etc. Training in dealing with these critical incidents is given under the supervision of a coach, who provides immediate feedback on strong and weak points, etc.

Use of the case method. For this purpose, use can be made both of cases which have actually occurred in the company and examples included in management handbooks (e.g. Klabbers, 1988). Company cases (preferably recent) can be subjected to strengths/weaknesses analyses. Examples are: the start of a new or a renovated production line; problems with the introduction of new equipment or systems; launching a new product; etc. All available memos and reports in connection with such incidents are collected and studied and interviews are held with the managers involved. The findings are compiled in the form of a final report and/or presentation.

Each learning situation provides opportunities for training in new behavioural criteria: judgment, problem analysis, written communication. If a presentation with group discussion results, criteria such as persuasiveness and leadership come into play. Depending on the job characteristics, learning situations are selected which actually occur as critical incidents on the job.

Use of assessment-centre exercises. As has already been mentioned, assessment-centre exercises (especially the 'in-tray') are excellent for training in specific behavioural criteria or clusters of criteria. The exercises have been verified in practice and are designed to evoke the desired behaviour. An extra advantage is that line managers get additional opportunities to practise their skills in the assessment-centre observation technique (Seegers, 1989).

CONCLUSIONS

The selection of management trainees has more in common with compiling a weather report than an investment plan. The return on investment depends to a great degree on the instruments employed, as well as coaching on the job. Selection can be greatly enhanced by making use of assessment centres, role play, 'in-tray' exercises, games and criterion-based training. These techniques, however, must always be supported by a good mentoring programme, utilizing successful practising managers and executives.

A number of studies have described in detail the advantages and disadvantages of mentoring and criterion-based training, particularly with respect to the role of line management in employee development (Mager and Pipe, 1970; Robinson, 1982; Piskurich, 1991). The most significant disadvantage is the time that line managers must be prepared to invest in the development of their employees. As a result of their numerous 'hit-and-run' chores, managers often make no time for this or fail to give it adequate priority. But criterion-based training also has many advantages:

- *It is goal-oriented training.* Development is focused exclusively on the behavioural criteria that are relevant for the job. Training is only given in behaviour which is clearly important for successful job performance.
- *There is efficient use of time.* The advantage of the modular character of the training sessions is that the amount of time spent by each trainee is kept to a minimum. Trainees follow only the modules that are of importance for these (based on their strengths/weaknesses analyses).
- *There is practical versatility.* The training is focused not merely on providing insight but also on imparting new behaviour. After all, it is the task of an assessment centre to generate insight. When no use has been made of an assessment centre, trainers can employ criterion-based interviews and simulations to prepare a strengths/weaknesses analysis. In other words, intake for training sessions can also be carried out by means of the assessment-centre method.
- *It is directly applicable in practice.* The training sessions have a very practical character. Whenever possible, trainees present their own cases and practise the 'new' behaviour. The relevance of the training for their own jobs is thus abundantly clear.
- *There is motivated development.* The trainees know which behavioural criteria are important for their own jobs. If use has been made of the assessment-centre method, they also know which criteria they still need to work on. They thus come to the training session or module with very explicit developmental demands. In other words, trainees realize the immediate significance of the training and are very motivated to participate in it.

The idea of being able to identify the key competencies an organization needs for competitive advantage and designing systems that will develop these competencies raises a variety of effectiveness issues regarding selection and development.

Traditional selection activities focus on finding individuals who fit particular job openings. In the competency-based organization, selection is best thought of as finding individuals who fit the learning environment that is provided by the organization (Lawler, 1993).

Instead we should rather look for individuals for organizational membership. This means that the selection process needs to focus on identifying people who can learn and follow the various career tracks that are available in the organization.

Assessment of developmental needs, as well as the development process itself, by existing members of the workforce (i.e. the managers) may be a helpful way of deciding whether an individual will fit the culture of an organization and whether he or she has specific work-relevant competencies. Mentors at work can help.

REFERENCES

Bandura, A. (1971). *Psychological Modeling.* New York: Lieber-Atherton.
Bartz, D.E. and Calabrese, R.L. (1991). Enhancing graduate business school programmes. *Journal of Management Development,* **10** (1), 26–32.

Beer, M., Spector, B., Laurence, P.R., Mills, D.Q. and Walton, R.E. (1984). *Managing Human Assets.* New York: Macmillan.

Boudreau, J.W. (1983). Economic considerations in estimating the utility of human resource productivity improvement programmes. *Personnel Psychology*, **36**, 551–576.

Fisscher, O.A.M. *et al.* (1988). *Management Development.* Brentford: Kluwer.

Fombrun, C.J. (1984). *Strategic Human Resource Management.* Chichester: John Wiley.

Glaze, A.C. (1989). A competency-based approach to human resource development. Paper presented at the 2nd European Congress on the Assessment Centre Method, London.

de Graaff, M.J.C. (1992). Coaching; een kunst en een kunde. In *Handboek voor Managers.* Holland: Van de Wolk.

Gratton, L. (1989). Work of the manager. In P. Herriot (ed.) *Assessment and Selection in Organizations.* Chichester: John Wiley.

Groot (1992). *Strategie in de Bedrijfsprautijk*, p. 13. Dordrecht: Kluwer.

Herriot, P. (1989). The future of managerial work and implications for assessment centres. Paper presented at the 2nd European Congress on the Assessment Centre Method, London.

Howard, A. and Bray, D.W. (1988). *Managerial Lives in Transition.* New York: Guilford Press.

Klabbers, J.H.F. (ed.) (1988). *Simulation-Gaming: On the Improvement of Competence in Dealing with Complexity, Uncertainty and Value Conflicts.* Oxford: Pergamon Press.

Lawler, E.E. (1993). *From Job-based to Competency-based Organizations.* CEO Publication G93-8 (228), University of Southern California.

Mager, R.F. and Pipe, P. (1970). *Analyzing Performance Problems.* Belmont: Fearon.

Miles, R.E. (1974). Human relations or human resources? In D.A. Kolb, I.M. Rubin and J.M. McIntyre (eds) *Organizational Psychology.* Englewood Cliffs, NJ: Prentice-Hall.

Nicholson, N. and West, M.A. (1988). *Managerial Job Change.* London: Oxford University Press.

Piskurich, G. (1991). Training: the line starts here. *Training and Development*, **12**.

Robinson, J.C. (1982). *Developing Managers Through Behavior Modeling.* Texas: Learning Concepts.

Schein, E.H. (1978). *Career Dynamics: Matching Individual and Organizational Needs.* Reading, MA: Addison-Wesley.

Schuler, R.S. (1992). Strategic human resources management: linking the people with the strategic needs of the business. *Organizational Dynamics*, **21** (1), 18–32.

Seegers, J.J.J.L. (1989). Assessment centres for identifying long-term potential and for self-development. In P. Herriot (ed.) *Assessment and Selection in Organizations.* Chichester: John Wiley.

Vloeberghs, D. (1989). *Human Resource Management: Visie, Strategieën en Toepassingen.* Leuven: Acco.

Wright, R.G. and Werther, W.B. (1991). Mentors at work. *Journal of Management Development*, **19** (3), 25–32.

Zemke, R. (1978). Behavior modeling: using the monkey see, monkey do principle in training. *Training*, **15** (6), 21–26.

Chapter 30

Assessment for Self-Managed Career Development

Jennifer M. Kidd

Department of Organizational Psychology, Birkbeck College, University of London, Malet Street, London WC1E 7HX, UK

Organizationally based models of careers portray career development as movements through corporate structures. However, changes in the business context have meant that this view of careers as progression within one organization is becoming less and less appropriate. Pressures to adapt to changing and more competitive environments are leading organizations to downsize and to remove the rungs of career ladders, with the result that employees are experiencing much more uncertainty about their future. Lateral moves are becoming more common and individuals are increasingly required to accept temporary employment contracts.

Weick and Berlinger (1989) argue that the organizations that can best deal with continuous environmental change are those that have the capacity to 'self-design'. They cope with change by evolving as the environment evolves and, accordingly, they need employees who can be adaptable and capable of dealing with uncertainty. As Hall (1991) suggests, employees in these more organic organizations need career competencies at the level of meta-skills: the skills of acquiring new skills of career management.

In self-designing organizations, the usual markers of the objective career, such as advancement and stable career paths, are rare. Subjective careers take the place of objective structures as the framework for career development. When viewed from the individual's subjective perspective, careers reflect self-perceptions of needs, abilities, interests, beliefs about work and changing aspirations. Perhaps most importantly, the subjective career emphasizes self-direction and personal responsibility for choices made.

International Handbook of Selection and Assessment, Edited by N. Anderson and P. Herriot.
© 1997 John Wiley & Sons Ltd.

These changes within organizations and their career systems appear to characterize a number of European countries, as well as the United States and Canada. Japanese firms also report flatter hierarchies, more promotions from within, less precise job descriptions and control systems based on self-discipline (Kagono *et al.*, 1989), and the policy of life-time employment in one organization in Japan is now less common.

A range of policy initiatives in Europe address the need to encourage self-awareness and flexibility in career development. In Sweden, for example, the selection process for managers frequently incorporates an offer of a career consultation with a psychologist (Ekvall, 1980). Furthermore, in several countries assessment is increasingly based on records of personal achievement, which broaden the range of attributes assessed and emphasize the process of assessment as well as its outcomes (European Commission, 1985). In the UK, a proposal by the Confederation of British Industry (CBI) has introduced the notion of 'careership', which puts the individual at the heart of continued learning and training through adult life (CBI, 1989). Accordingly, steps have been taken to implement one system of records of achievement and action planning. This would begin at school, but would be carried with individuals throughout their working lives to provide a life-long basis for reflection and development. Other examples in the UK are the 'Investors in People' initiative, and the emerging National Vocational Qualification (NVQ) system, which both emphasize the importance of individuals taking responsibility for their own development.

Partly in response to these developments, some large organizations are beginning to recognize the importance of giving employees opportunities to engage in career planning activities. The term 'personal development planning' is increasingly being used to describe the process by which there is a greater sharing of responsibility between the organization and its employees for their personal and career development. Personal development planning typically involves a range of activities. In British Petroleum, for example, employees work through self-assessment materials and a computer-aided careers guidance system, and attend career workshops. Progress is slow in this area, however. In a British survey of 120 managers on MBA programmes, although 77% of respondents' organizations provided formal career reviews with superiors, only 14% offered career planning workshops (Iles and Mabey, 1993).

Career development activities are often described as being of two types: those which focus on the organization's needs; and those which centre on the employee's concerns. Examples of the former include fast-track programmes, developmental assessment centres, and provision of information about career ladders and paths. A key (though not exclusive) aim in these activities is assessment, by the organization, of potential, particularly abilities and competencies. Activities which focus on employees' concerns include career planning workshops, self-study materials and individual career counselling. Here, the emphasis tends to be more on self-assessment of interests, skills and values and the development of action plans.

Over the last two decades, a number of writers in the United States have conducted reviews of practice in this area. Russell (1991), for example, has examined the types of intervention used by US companies, and Leibowitz, Farren and Kaye (1986) have proposed practical guidelines for the introduction of career development programmes into organizations. In Britain, however, there have been few attempts to share and integrate knowledge, although Jackson (1990) has provided a useful analysis of possible ways forward.

Given the increasing importance of the subjective career as the building block of development in organizations, the main focus of this chapter is on self-assessment tools which facilitate individual career planning. It is suggested that different perspectives on the concept of career imply different domains for self-assessment. Viewing careers as sequences of positions, for example, emphasizes the need for awareness of interests and skills and how job opportunities might match these attributes. Alternatively, taking a developmental perspective on careers points to the desirability of helping individuals become aware of their life or career stage. Five distinct perspectives on career are outlined below, and some of the relevant conceptual frameworks and tools are identified. Some of the implications of using these tools for organizations are then noted. (Space precludes a comprehensive review of the range of instruments and techniques available; for this the reader is referred to Walsh and Betz (1990) and Bartram, Lindley and Foster (1990) for descriptions of psychometric instruments, and to Hopson and Scally (1989) and Bowles (1991) for self-help materials.) The discussion of different views of careers is followed by a summary of some of the features of the organizational context about which individuals need information. The chapter concludes with an overview of how career planning interventions have been evaluated, and the benefits to individuals and organizations which appear to ensue.

Before moving on to examine tools and techniques, it is helpful to outline some of the practical advantages of using self-assessment devices in place of (or in addition to) instruments which require skilled administration and interpretation. The most important of these are that: individuals can work independently, and at their own pace; expensive test administration and scoring facilities are unnecessary; and, arguably, self-assessment encourages individual ownership of the results. Furthermore, there is evidence to suggest that the typical employee is able to assess interests and personality traits with some accuracy (Zytowski and Borgen, 1983) (though self-estimates of ability tend to be less accurate—Lowman and Williams, 1987). In areas where psychometric devices are unavailable, or where their use is not possible for other reasons, self-assessment is likely, therefore, to be an effective way of developing self-awareness. Furthermore, since much of the value of assessment is that it enables individuals to acquire *cognitive structures* to organize their ideas about self and situation (Holland, Magoon and Spokane, 1981), simply providing models or frameworks on aspects of career development may well be as effective as more formalized methods, as the popularity of self-help materials suggests. Accordingly, the following review will identify first the relevant conceptual frameworks and models in each domain which might be employed simply as tools for reflection. Subsequently to this, and where they exist, selected self-assessment tools and psychometric instruments will be described.

CAREER PATTERNS

Models of individual (as opposed to institutional) careers are of two types: those that describe the *objective* individual career, which may be observed and defined publicly, and those focusing on the *subjective* individual career, which can only be understood in terms of the individual's specific experiences (Watts, 1981). For the reasons expressed in the introduction to this chapter, the main concern here is with subjective individual careers. However, it is appropriate first to examine a model of careers which draws upon properties of both the individual and the external context.

Driver (1982; 1988) has proposed a typology of career patterns which attempts this kind of integration. Four 'career concepts' are described which underlie an individual's thinking about careers, but which also incorporate structural features of occupations and organizations. An integration of situational characteristics and individual psychology is achieved by linking particular career patterns with motives and cognitive styles, as described in Table 30.1.

The little research that has been carried out into this view of career patterns seems to confirm that all four patterns exist in a range of occupations, and that career motives are related to career concepts (Driver and Coombs, 1983), though a broader range of motives seems to be linked to each.

Fewer promotion opportunities in organizations suggest the need for employees to understand the potential for and benefits of lateral movements. Yet in the United States, at least, it would appear that employees increasingly have linear orientations to their careers and spiral patterns are becoming less rather than more frequent (Driver, 1988).

A Career Concept Questionnaire (Driver and Brousseau, 1981) is available for individuals to assess career patterns (though it should be noted that this measures the 'ideal' career concept, rather than allowing individuals to reflect on their

Table 30.1 Driver's career concepts and their relationship to motivation and cognitive styles (adapted from Driver, 1988)

Career concept	Motivation	Cognitive style
STEADY STATE Initial career choice leads to lifetime commitment to an occupation	Security	Decisive
LINEAR Initial career choice leads to upward movement	Achievement	Hierarchic
SPIRAL Career evolves through a series of occupations, where each choice (related or unrelated to the last) builds on the past and develops new skills	Growth	Integrative
TRANSITORY Individual changes employment frequently without any periods of stability	Independence	Flexible

pattern of job moves so far). The value of Driver's model lies more in the conceptual framework it offers for self-assessment.

CAREER STAGES

An early stage theory (Super, 1957) viewed careers as consisting of five stages:

- *Growth* (0–14 years). The self concept develops through identification with members of the immediate family and other key figures. With increasing social participation and reality testing, interests and capacities become more important.
- *Exploration* (15–24 years). The self concept increases in clarity through the processes of experimentation and reality testing. The young person tests out ideas of self in the environment through exploration of roles and occupations at school, leisure activities and part-time work, and later in a first job.
- *Establishment* (25–44 years). The individual makes efforts to establish a permanent place in an occupational field. Early in this period, there may be some further experimentation, and this may result in one or two job changes before a 'life work' is found, or before it becomes clear that the career will consist of a succession of unrelated jobs.
- *Maintenance* (45–64 years). The individual is concerned to hold on to the place that has been established in the world of work. Usually little new ground is broken, but the career continues along existing lines.
- *Decline* (65+ years). Mental and physical powers decline, and the pace of work slackens and finally ceases.

Although Super's model has stimulated a large amount of research into the exploration stage of development, particularly on the role of self concepts in the entry into work, much less attention has been given to issues within the establishment and maintenance stages. One reason for this is that the processes set out as being characteristic of the later stages are discussed in a very general descriptive way. Super's more recent work, however, explores these later stages in a little more detail (Super *et al.*, 1988). It also incorporates a revised view of the relationship between age and stage. Individuals are acknowledged to 'recycle' through career stages—those experiencing mid-career change, for example, would be expected to demonstrate some of the concerns of early working life. The model incorporates four stages and, within each of these, three substages (or career concerns):

- *Exploration*: crystallization, specification, implementation
- *Establishment*: stabilizing, consolidating, advancing
- *Maintenance:* holding, updating, innovating
- *Disengagement:* deceleration, retirement planning, retirement living.

A more interactive model of career stages has been proposed by Arthur and Kram (1989). They describe a framework of individual and organizational needs where each successive need at either the individual or organizational level of analysis has a reciprocal counterpart at another level. Individuals are viewed as progressing through three career stages, each characterized by a particular need. In their early career, the dominant individual need is to *explore*; in mid-career it is to *advance*; and in late career the need is to *protect* self and others. In turn, organizations are seen as proceeding through stages where needs for *exuberance*, *directedness* and *stewardship* successively predominate.

Exuberance is mostly concerned with the organization adapting to the external environment through entrepreneurial activity, innovation and creativity. Directedness involves achieving organizational objectives, producing results and developing a reputation. During the third stage of organizational evolution, stewardship, the main concern is with maintaining the organization internally. This analysis results in a matrix of combinations of individual needs which suggests particular patterns of individual–organizational fit and misfit. Maximum fit is achieved when the individual's stage matches that of the organization (i.e. exploring–exuberance, protecting–stewardship). Where stages are out of line, pressures towards change are experienced by both parties.

A self-assessment exercise to identify life stage is described by Hopson and Scally (1989). Scores are provided on seven stages: pulling up roots (ages 16–20); provisional adulthood (20–28); age 30 transition (28–32); rooting (32–39); mid-life transition (39–45); restabilizing and flowering (45–55); and mellowing (55–65+).

Super's more recent stage model is operationalized in the Adult Career Concerns Inventory (Super *et al.*, 1988). Items require self-reports, on a five-point scale, of concern with particular career tasks characteristic of the four stages (e.g. 'consolidating my career position'; 'planning well for retirement'). This instrument should be used with caution, however, as although internal consistency reliabilities of the various scales are adequate, no test–retest reliability data are reported in the manual and there is little evidence for its validity.

Stage models can be criticized in relation to a number of features. They fail to reflect adequately the increasingly common patterns of lateral movements within organizations, career plateauing, changes of employer and changes of occupation. Moreover, they are normative: they merely describe the average or typical experience. The danger is that descriptions of development become prescriptions, as in the case where individuals expecting career advancement experience frustration when plateaued, and where employers discriminate against older workers because they are assumed to be uninterested in development opportunities. Nevertheless, awareness of career stage can be helpful in understanding feelings of being out of step with organizational career systems (Lawrence, 1984). It may also contribute to anticipatory socialization, helping individuals look ahead to the issues and transitions they may have to face in the future, and enhancing the capacity for behaving in an autonomous way.

CAREER POSITIONS

This view of careers emphasizes sequences of jobs within and between organizations. It is informed by trait–factor theories of occupational choice (e.g. Betz,

Fitzgerald and Hill, 1989), which are based on the assumption of relatively static dispositional differences. Their theoretical bases are in differential psychology, particularly analyses of individual differences in interests and abilities, and in Parsons' (1909) 'matching' approach to occupational choice and careers guidance; and accordingly they emphasize the need to assess individual differences and understand the ways in which correspondence between individuals and environments leads to job satisfaction and successful performance at work.

One of the most widely researched trait–factor theories is that of Holland (1973) who proposed that people seek occupational environments that are congruent with their occupational interests (or preferences for particular work activities). The theory states that:

- People fall into six interest types: Realistic; Investigative; Artistic; Social; Enterprising and Conventional.
- Occupational and organizational environments can be classified in the same terms.
- Occupational choice is the result of attempts to achieve congruence between interests and environment.
- Congruence results in job satisfaction and stability.

Research into Holland's theory supports the view that individuals generally make occupational choices that are congruent with their interests (Spokane, 1985). However, a recent meta-analysis has cast doubt on the assertion that those in 'congruent' occupations are more satisfied than others who are in less congruent work roles (Tranberg, Slane and Ekeberg, 1993). This finding may reflect the increasing diversity necessary in organizations as innovation becomes more important for survival and competitive advantage.

One of the problems with much of the research into the validity of Holland's theory is that the studies generally employ cross-sectional rather than longitudinal designs. Current congruence between interests and environment may be due to socialization within the organization, or to *post hoc* rationalization to minimize dissonance. Furthermore, little is known about what happens to 'incongruent' people over time. We need to know more about how socialization practices affect incongruence and how organizations might respond to incongruence to maximize commitment and performance.

Examples of instruments for the assessment of occupational interests are the Strong–Campbell Interests Inventory (Hansen and Campbell, 1985) and the Vocational Preference Inventory (Holland, 1985a). Over the years, an impressive amount of evidence for their reliability and validity has accumulated. From the individual's point of view, however, it is debatable how useful it is to assess interests in isolation. There is evidence to suggest that abilities and needs are also important in determining satisfaction and performance (Dawis and Lofquist, 1984). With this in mind, self-reports on skills have been included in self-assessment devices: for example, the Self-Directed Search (Holland, 1985b) and the Campbell Interest and Skill Survey (Campbell, 1992). The latter provides scores on seven orientation (or interests) scales, 29 'basic' interest and skill scales (sub-scales of the orientation scales) and 58 occupational scales.

Standardized tests of performance (as opposed to self-reports) for the assessment of abilities and skills include the Differential Aptitude Tests (Bennett, Seashore and Wesman, 1981), the General Aptitude Test Battery (US Government Printing Office, 1970) and the Morrisby Differential Test Battery (Morrisby, 1989). Reviews of these are readily available (e.g. Bartram, Lindley and Foster, 1990). Less well known, however, are methods to help individuals identify 'transferable skills' from previous experiences in work and other settings such as leisure activities. Self-assessment checklists or structured interviews are used to provide the framework for identifying skills which may not be formally accredited but which may be applied to paid employment (e.g. Kidd, 1988).

CAREER CONSTRUCTIONS

An examination of recent writing on careers reveals a shift towards more dynamic, interactionist explanations of career development: towards the portrayal of individuals as active organizers and interpreters of events (Kidd and Killeen, 1992). One example is the interactionist model proposed by Vondracek, Lerner and Schulenberg (1986), who take an ecological view of development. Individuals are treated as being involved in the continuous process of selecting and shaping their contexts. Another is the literature on employees' attributions of the criteria for career progression (e.g. Beehr and Taber, 1993). As Nicholson and West (1989) have neatly put it, careers can be seen as either 'autobiographical fictions' constructed by individuals to emphasize what may be an exaggerated sense of self-direction, or, on the other hand, as 'opportunities' which self-directed individuals mould to fit their own routes. Either way, subjective constructions of careers are paramount.

An interesting feature of this view of careers is the possibility of its incorporating and extending opportunity structure theories of career development (e.g. Roberts, 1968). Career decisions, initially constrained by the range of occupations available, are justified retrospectively. Furthermore, subsequent opportunities are opened up by reconstructions and reassessments of aims and goals.

Following Betz (1992), we can distinguish two approaches to assessment in this area: the measurement of cognitive *processes* (notably problem-solving and information-processing) and the assessment of cognitive *products* (for example, locus of control and the appropriateness of beliefs about careers).

Little progress has yet been made in relation to cognitive processes, though Rounds and Tracey (1990) have made a start in their application of information-processing principles to career development. With regard to cognitive products, an instrument to assess locus of control in organizational environments has been developed by Spector (1988). This scale measures the extent to which outcomes at work (e.g. salary increases, career advancement) are believed to be controlled by one's own activities (internality) or by external factors (externality). The measure appears to have adequate internal consistency and validity.

With respect to career beliefs, common 'myths' or irrational beliefs about career development are the subject of a framework developed by Krumboltz, derived from social learning theory, and operationalized in his Career Beliefs Inventory (Krumboltz, 1991). These are organized into five groups: 'current career beliefs'; 'what seems necessary for my happiness'; 'factors that influence my decisions'; 'changes I am willing to make'; and 'effort I am willing to make'. Reviewers have been critical of this instrument, however, since the available evidence suggests poor reliability and validity (e.g. Killeen *et al.*, 1994).

The notion of career-self efficacy also has potential here, though models which incorporate career-related concerns are not well-developed. Hackett, Betz and Doty (1985), however, have summarized the competencies or areas of efficacy that appear to be important to success for professional women.

It might be argued, as Savickas (1992) has done, that emphasizing subjective constructions of careers requires a phenomenological approach to assessment, which identifies the meanings given to events, and overall 'life themes'. Savickas provides a comprehensive overview of these approaches, which are derived from narrative psychology. His methods include autobiographies, structured interviews and card sorts.

CAREER PURPOSES

The portrayal of careers as constructions emphasizes making sense of the past. Equally important are the individual's conceptions of the future. Notions of purposeful activity as a central feature of careers have surfaced a number of times in contemporary writing. In relation to early career development, for example, Law (1981) discusses how young people negotiate possible future selves with significant others. Furthermore, Kidd (1984) showed how, in their attempts to implement *ideal* rather than *actual* self concepts in their choice of occupation, young people seemed to be thinking about work in terms of future possibilities, rather than just current realities.

In the organizational context, Ballantine (1993) offers a model of career development which incorporates considerations of individual and organizational purposes. He argues that a consideration of individual purpose involves taking account of the individual's sense of direction, which is for the most part independent of the organization. Ballantine further suggests that there are benefits in making individual purpose explicit, through negotiating the psychological contract. If purpose remains tacit, this amounts to allowing organizational ownership of the employee, restricting the individual's sense of direction.

Career assessment frameworks which incorporate these ideas of purpose are of two types. First, there are those that take account of the various motivations which propel people towards particular occupations and organizations. Secondly, there are those that portray work in the context of other life roles and thus point up areas of balance and imbalance.

Frameworks of the first type include models of work values and needs (e.g. Pryor, 1983; Dawis and Lofquist, 1984) which cover the range of intrinsic and extrinsic satisfactions sought from work. Published inventories include the Work Aspect Preference Scale (Pryor, 1983) and the Minnesota Importance Questionnaire (MIQ) (Rounds *et al.*, 1981).

The MIQ covers 20 work-related needs, each of which is described by a representative statement. These are grouped into six clusters: achievement; comfort; status; altruism; safety; and autonomy. Internal consistency reliability coefficients for the clusters are good, and sound evidence for convergent and discriminant validity is offered by MacNab and Fitzsimmons (1987) in a study measuring the relationship among needs and values assessed by four different instruments. As a further aid to interpretation, occupations are described in terms of Occupational Reinforcer Patterns, according to which needs they are more or less likely to satisfy.

Of more relevance to adults is Schein's concept of career anchors (Schein, 1992). An individual's career anchor consists of perceptions of abilities, needs, motives and values. Anchors evolve through experiences at work and are influenced by relevant feedback from these experiences. Once a career anchor has developed it becomes a stabilizing force and constrains future development.

Schein's career anchor categories were derived from longitudinal studies of managers, teachers and members of various other occupations. They are as follows:

- *Security/stability*: concern to stabilize the career; preference for stable predictable work
- *Autonomy/independence*: concern with freedom from organizational rules and restrictions
- *Technical or functional competence*: concern for work which permits the use of particular skills
- *General managerial competence*: concern to integrate the efforts of others and tie together different functions of an organization
- *Entrepreneurial creativity*: concern to create something new, by own efforts; may involve risk
- *Service/dedication to a cause*: concern to achieve something of value; unlikely to take a job with an organization that was hostile to own values
- *Pure challenge*: concern to solve seemingly insurmountable problems and surmount difficulties
- *Life-style integration*: concern to make all major sectors of life work together in an integrated whole.

Schein suggests that these anchors be assessed using structured interviews, but a self-diagnostic questionnaire is also available (Jansen and Chandler, 1989).

A second framework in this area allows for the assessment of involvement in and commitment to other individual life roles. Super's Life–Career Rainbow (Super, 1980) portrays various roles within the 'life-space' of the individual. The bands of the rainbow represent the different roles a person may assume during the course of his or her life. During adulthood many people experience seven or eight roles, as when a person is employed in an occupation, studying part-time, being a spouse, being a parent, maintaining a home, supporting ageing parents and pursuing leisure interests. The rainbow also depicts the impact of both internal and external forces upon life-roles. The use of this or similar tools for examining roles (for example, the Salience Inventory—Super and Nevill, 1986) can be a powerful means of helping individuals appreciate work–family linkages and conflicts. (It is important, however, that individuals are able to use the 'rainbow' concept in ways that make sense to them, rather than being constrained by any normative assumptions.)

IMPLICATIONS FOR ORGANIZATIONS

This chapter has identified a broad range of tools which may be used in individual career planning. An attempt has been made to evaluate the frameworks, and information on the reliability and validity of instruments has been presented where it is available. However, potential users will need to consider other strengths and limitations of the various tools. The following are particularly relevant:

- *Ease of use.* Are special skills needed to administer and interpret the instrument? How much time is needed for administration, analysis and feedback? Does the instrument depend on rare professional skills and knowledge for its use? Simple frameworks and self-administered and self-scored checklists may be preferable to standardized psychometric tests in some circumstances.
- *Face validity.* Is the instrument likely to have credibility with users? This will depend on the context within which it is used and employees' needs. Some tools may be considered to be over-elaborate ways of assessing career-related attributes.
- *Consistency with the organizational culture.* Are the aims of the instrument in line with the underlying beliefs and values of the organization and its human resource systems? Offering employees career planning activities which highlight their development needs will have implications for organizational practices.

Some of the implications of this last point are considered in Table 30.2, which suggests some of the things organizations may need to do to ensure that employees are better able to translate self-knowledge into action. It also lists the instruments identified earlier and summarizes the various outcomes of assessment in relation to each perspective on careers.

ASSESSMENT OF CONTEXT

Whichever view of careers is taken, individuals also need to be aware of the organizational context in which careers are enacted. The kind of information individuals need about organizations is in some respects similar to that needed about occupations. Whilst occupational information is in the public domain, however, and therefore readily available, information about organizations is less accessible. Some of the features of organizations that individuals need information about are as follows:

Table 30.2   Outcomes of different types of assessment and some implications for organizations

Instruments	Outcomes of assessment	Implications for organizations
CAREER PATTERNS Career Concept Questionnaire (Driver and Brousseau, 1981)	Understanding of career movements Consideration of nonlinear as well as linear development opportunities	Provide more information on nonlinear as well as linear paths
CAREER STAGES Adult Life Stage Questionnaire (Hopson and Scally, 1989) Adult Career Concerns Inventory (Super *et al.*, 1988)	Understanding of current experience in relation to social norms Anticipatory socialization	Address career concerns of employees according to career stage
CAREER POSITIONS Strong–Campbell Interests Inventory (Hansen and Campbell, 1985) Vocational Preference Inventory (Holland, 1985a) Self-Directed Search (Holland, 1985b) Campbell Interest and Skill Inventory (Campbell, 1992) Differential Aptitude Tests (Bennett *et al.*, 1981) General Aptitude Test Battery (US Govt Printing Office, 1970) Morrisby Differential Test Battery (Morrisby, 1989)	Understanding of interests and abilities Cognitive structures to assess these in future	Provide comprehensive job information
CAREER CONSTRUCTIONS Work Locus of Control Scale (Spector, 1988) Career Beliefs Inventory (Krumboltz, 1991)	Understanding of extent of self-determination in career development Increased autonomy	Promote self-development culture
CAREER PURPOSES Work Aspect Preference Scale (Pryor, 1983) Minnesota Importance Questionnaire (Rounds *et al.*, 1981) Career Orientation Inventory (Jansen and Chandler, 1989) Life–Career Rainbow (Super, 1980) Salience Inventory (Super and Nevill, 1986)	Understanding of long-term career aims and changing balances between life roles	Provide opportunities to negotiate and renegotiate psychological contract

Structure and processes
- The pattern of the organizational structure
- How decisions are made
- Predominant leadership styles

Career systems
- How people are promoted
- Career paths
- Possibilities for lateral movement
- Internal or external labour market
- Training and development opportunities
- Support for career transitions

Strategy
- Organizational strategic type
- Business plans
- Predictions of future skill requirements

As Herriot (1989) has pointed out, the selection interview is (or could be) the primary means of gathering information about a prospective employer. For employees already in the organization, there is a need to provide such information within career development programmes, for as Iles and Mabey (1993) observe, it appears that employees react more positively to activities that are 'anchored' within organizational realities.

EVALUATION

Although extensive research has been carried out into the effectiveness of career interventions with young people at school and students in higher education (Kidd and Killeen, 1992), little has been done to evaluate career planning activities in organizations. Possible criteria of effectiveness are of four types: individual reactions; learning outcomes; behavioural outcomes; and effects on organizations.

Reaction measures simply assess participants' satisfaction with the intervention. Learning outcomes may be related to self or situation. Self-related learning outcomes include greater self-awareness and self-determination, improved decision-making and goal-setting skills, and knowledge of how to implement goals and cope with transitions. Learning about situations includes greater knowledge about occupational and organizational opportunities. Examples of behavioural outcomes are participation in developmental activities, career actions taken (e.g. promotions; cross-functional moves), and less directly, improved performance and commitment, and better communication between employees and their managers. Effects at the organizational level which might be examined are better management of promotions and transfers, improved succession planning, and reduced turnover and absenteeism.

Before discussing what is known about the effectiveness of interventions, it may be instructive to say a little about the instruments that are available to assess learning and attitudinal outcomes. Over the last few decades a considerable amount of effort has been devoted to the development of tools to assess individuals' readiness to cope with the tasks of early career development, particularly initial choice of occupation. The best known of these measures of 'career maturity' are Crites' Career Maturity Inventory (Crites, 1978) and Super's Career Development Inventory (Super *et al.*, 1984). A number of reviewers, however, have expressed concern with the value-laden nature of these measures, as well as with their psychometric adequacy (e.g. Kidd, 1981; Savickas, 1990).

Career assessments with adults need to attend to broader aspects of coping with career tasks, rather than just decision-making. These include early 'sense making' (Louis, 1981), responses to new work roles, and preparation for the next transition (Nicholson, 1984). Crites' Career Mastery Inventory (Crites, 1990) purports to assess individuals' degree of coping with some of these tasks. Part 1 consists of six scales which measure the mastery of the following career tasks:

- *Organizational adaptability*: processes involved in socialization and 'learning the ropes'
- *Position performance*: learning the duties and responsibilities of the job
- *Work habits and attitudes*: being dependable and having a positive attitude to work
- *Coworker relationships*: getting on with others and dealing with interpersonal conflicts
- *Advancement*: moving up the organizational hierarchy
- *Career choice and plans*: planning for the future

Part 2 of the Career Mastery Inventory assesses work adjustment mechanisms along three dimensions: integrative; adjustive; and nonadjustive. Psychometric data are lacking on this measure, though an earlier version (the Career Development and Adjustment Inventory) was characterized by low internal consistency values. A more serious drawback with the instrument is its assumption of the desirability of a 'custodial' response to the work role, rather than innovative behaviours (Van Maanan and Schein, 1979). Furthermore, the scales appear to be as much concerned (if not more so) with job performance as with career issues.

An instrument developed by London (1993) may have more potential in this area. It assesses three components of 'career motivation', namely, 'career resilience', 'career insight' and 'career identity'. Of particular relevance here is the seven-item resilience scale, which measures the ability to adapt to changing circumstances, and the five-item insight scale, which assesses realism and clarity of career goals. Internal consistency reliabilities exceed 0.80 (though this may be expected, given that some items address virtually identical construct areas). Sample items for the career resilience scale are: 'welcome job and organizational changes'; and 'willing to take risks'. Examples of items within the career insight scale are 'recognize what you can and cannot do well'; and 'have realistic career goals'.

Somewhat surprisingly, an examination of the literature on the evaluation of career development interventions in organizations revealed only two studies

Table 30.3 Benefits of career development interventions

Criteria	Authors
REACTIONS	
Ratings of helpfulness of career workbook some years later (80% rated it helpful)	Kotter *et al.* (1978)
Ratings of effectiveness of career planning programme (85% rated it 'very', 'moderately' or 'partially' effective)	Walker and Gutteridge (1979)
Ratings of helpfulness of career development programmes (44% of managers in Fortune 500 companies found them very helpful)	Keller and Piotrowski (1987)
Ratings of usefulness of range of career development activities (e.g. 77% found self-assessment materials helpful; 100% found developmental assessment centres helpful)	Iles and Mabey (1993)
LEARNING OUTCOMES	
Perceptions of being in control of career actions	Hanson (1982)
Self-esteem, growth motivation, decision-making (among others)	Kingdon and Bimline (1987)
Clarity of career objectives, familiarity with career options	Nusbaum (1986)
Career resilience, insight and identity	London and Bray (1984)
Career resilience and insight	Noe *et al.* (1990)
BEHAVIOURAL OUTCOMES	
Achievement of career goals, job performance	Stump (1987)
Communication with managers	Moses and Saltrese (1989)
Organizational commitment	Minor (1986)
ORGANIZATIONAL EFFECTS	
Participants' ratings on increased organizational effectiveness (e.g. 50% for career planning workshops; 75% for self-assessment materials)	Iles and Mabey (1993)

which used instruments, such as those described above, especially designed to measure coping with career-related tasks.

Some of the positive benefits of career development interventions in organizations are listed in Table 30.3. The interventions used cover a wide range of the possible activities described earlier.

The studies listed in Table 30.3 are indicative of the (limited) range of positive findings in this area. To draw any firm conclusions from these would be dangerous, for two reasons. First, there is the common problem of the possibility of negative or inconclusive findings being unpublished. Secondly, few studies have employed rigorous methodologies, using pre-post designs, control groups, random allocation to groups and long-term follow-up of subjects.

As the table shows, there is little evidence relating to organizational effects. For this, we must wait for more evaluation research. In the meantime, it is possible to suggest some further ways in which organizations might benefit from offering career development programmes to their employees.

Improved information about human resources

There is evidence that individuals taking part in career planning activities become more articulate in describing their interests, goals and development needs to management (Moses and Saltrese, 1989). Moreover, developing new descriptive skills for thinking and talking about careers is likely to enable employees to look beyond current job titles and identify the competencies they can bring to future work tasks.

Improved organizational commitment among employees

Research has confirmed the notion that individuals at different career stages have different career concerns. For example, those in the establishment stage are more interested in achievement and recognition than those in maintenance (Veiga, 1983), and managers who have reached maintenance have a greater need to act as mentors (Evans and Gilbert, 1984). Recognizing and supporting these concerns results in greater organizational commitment and less turnover (Eisenberger, Fasolo and Davis-La Mastro, 1990; Veiga, 1983). Research also suggests that those who have a clear view of their future careers are likely to show more commitment to their organizations (Arnold and Mackenzie-Davey, 1993).

Increased readiness of employees to engage in nonlinear career patterns

As we saw earlier, it has been argued that a 'spiral' view of career appears to be the most suitable career pattern in organizations that adapt well to changing environments (Weick and Berlinger, 1989). Providing opportunities for self-assessment and action planning is likely to lead employees to recognize the value of lateral and functional moves where vertical mobility is not possible. Furthermore, offering opportunities for individuals to assess long-term aims and preferred balances between work and other activities could lead to changes in perceptions of work centrality. Arrangements such as job sharing and periods of parental leave may then be seen as more desirable, thus facilitating the introduction of more flexible working arrangements.

There is some evidence that employees perceive career development interventions as more useful when they are clearly integrated with other human resource systems within organizations (Iles and Mabey, 1993). But there may be a price to pay for greater integration. Career planning programmes which are set up as self-contained activities for employees to use for their own private purposes offer a relatively safe environment for self-exploration (particularly, perhaps, where they are run by external consultants, who are more likely to be seen as offering confidentiality). On the other hand, programmes which are more closely linked to development opportunities within the organization may be seen to be connected to the organization's power structure and its performance management functions.

Where this is the case, participants will be less likely to be prepared to engage in self-disclosure, and gains in self-knowledge will be more limited.

This issue of individual and organizational 'ownership' arises in relation to the 'products' of the assessments (for example, skills profiles; action plans) as well as to the assessment processes. Career progression within an organization may require sharing some of the results of assessments with managers, and knowledge that this will happen may affect the kinds of activities employees are willing to engage in voluntarily. There are no easy answers to these matters. What is essential, however, is that individuals and their managers are clear about the purposes of the assessment process and the use to be made of its products.

CONCLUSIONS

This chapter has discussed some of the ways in which employees can be helped with their career planning. It would seem that the potential benefits to organizations may be far-reaching. As yet, however, there is little hard evidence to suggest that this is so. Most of the small number of studies carried out so far have evaluated the effects of career development interventions on managers in large organizations, and more research is needed to identify the kinds of interventions that might be suitable for other groups of workers in a wider range of organizations.

Further development in this area requires more communication between those attempting to implement programmes in their organizations. At the moment there are very few opportunities to share experiences and views on practice. Furthermore, it is clear from the UK experience of the introduction of records of achievement and action planning in schools and higher education that much benefit would be gained by a cross-fertilization of ideas between those responsible for implementing and evaluating these initiatives in education and in work organizations. It is becoming clear that the same sorts of issues need to be addressed in both sectors—for example, the appropriate criteria for evaluating effectiveness and clarity over matters of ownership. Moreover, greater sharing of theoretical perspectives and practical issues is likely to help us progress towards a much-needed integration between vocational psychology, careers guidance and organizational psychology.

REFERENCES

Arnold, J. and Mackenzie-Davey, K. (1993). Predictors of organizational commitment and intention to leave amongst graduates in early career. Paper presented at BPS Occupational Psychology Conference, January.

Arthur, M.B. and Kram, K.E. (1989). Reciprocity at work: the separate, yet inseparable possibilities for individual and organizational development. In M.B. Arthur, D.T. Hall and B.S. Lawrence (eds) *Handbook of Career Theory*. Cambridge: University Press.

Ballantine, M. (1993). A new framework for the design of career interventions in organisations. *British Journal of Guidance and Counselling*, **21**, 233–245.

Bartram, D., Lindley, P.A. and Foster, J. (1990). *Review of Psychometric Tests for Assessment in Vocational Training*. Newland Park Associates Ltd., University of Hull.

Beehr, T.A. and Taber, T.D. (1993). Perceived intraorganizational mobility: reliable versus exceptional performance as means to getting ahead. *Journal of Organizational Behavior*, **14**, 579–594.

Bennett, G.K., Seashore, H.G. and Wesman, A.G. (1981). *Differential Aptitude Tests*. New York: Psychological Corporation.

Betz, N.E. (1992). Career assessment: a review of critical issues. In S.D. Brown and R.W. Lent (eds) *Handbook of Counseling Psychology*, 2nd edn. Chichester: Wiley.

Betz, N.E., Fitzgerald, L.F. and Hill, R.E. (1989). Trait-factor theories: traditional cornerstone of career theory. In M.B. Arthur, D.T. Hall and B.S. Lawrence (eds) *Handbook of Career Theory*. Cambridge: University Press.

Bowles, R.N. (1991). *What Color is your Parachute?* Berkeley, CA: Ten Speed Press.

Campbell, D. (1992). *The Campbell Interest and Skill Survey*. Minneapolis: National Computer Systems.

Confederation of British Industry (1989). *Towards a Skills Revolution*. London: CBI.

Crites, J. (1978). *Career Maturity Inventory*. Monterey, CA: McGraw-Hill.

Crites, J. (1990). *Career Mastery Inventory*. Boulder, CO: Crites Career Consultants Inc.

Dawis, R.V. and Lofquist, L.H. (1984). *A Psychological Theory of Work Adjustment*. Minneapolis: University of Minnesota Press.

Driver, M. (1982). Career concepts: a new approach to career research. In R. Katz (ed.) *Career Issues in Human Resource Management*. Englewood Cliffs, NJ: Prentice-Hall.

Driver, M. (1988). Careers: a review of personal and organizational research. In C.L. Cooper and I. Robertson (eds) *International Review of Industrial and Organizational Psychology*. Chichester: John Wiley.

Driver, M. and Brousseau, K. (1981). *The Career Concept Questionnaire*. Los Angeles, CA: Decision Dynamics Corporation.

Driver, M. and Coombs, M. (1983). Fit between career concepts, corporate culture, and engineering productivity and morale. Paper presented at the IEEE Careers Conference, New York.

Eisenberger, R., Fasolo, P. and Davis-La Mastro, V. (1990). Perceived organizational support and employee diligence, commitment and innovation. *Journal of Applied Psychology*, **75**, 51–59.

Ekvall, G. (1980). Industrial psychology in Sweden. In X. Zamek-Gliszezynska (ed.) *Work Psychology in Europe*. Warsaw: Polish Scientific Publishers.

European Commission (1985). *Transition of Young People from Education to Adult and Working Life*. Brussels: EC.

Evans, M. and Gilbert, E. (1984). Plateaued managers: their need gratifications and their effort–performance expectations. *Journal of Management Studies*, **21** (1), 99–108.

Hackett, G., Betz, N.E. and Doty, M.D. (1985). The development of a taxonomy of career competencies for professional women. *Sex Roles*, **12**, 393–409.

Hall, D.T. (1991). Twenty questions: research needed to advance the field of careers. In R.F. Morrison and J. Adams (eds) *Contemporary Career Development Issues*. Hillsdale, NJ: Erlbaum.

Hansen, J.C. and Campbell, D.P. (1985). *Manual for the SVIB SCII*, 4th edn. Palo Alto, CA: Consulting Psychologists Press.

Hanson, M.E. (1982). Career development: maximising options. *Personnel Administrator*, **23**, 58–61.

Herriot, P. (1989). The selection interview. In P. Herriot (ed.) *Assessment and Selection in Organizations*. Chichester: John Wiley.

Holland, J.L. (1973). *Making Vocational Choices: a Theory of Careers*. Englewood Cliffs, NJ: Prentice-Hall.

Holland, J.L. (1985a). *Manual for the VPI*. Odessa, FL: Psychological Assessment Resources.

Holland, J.L. (1985b). *The Self-Directed Search: Professional Manual*. Odessa, FL: Psychological Assessment Resources.

Holland, J.L. Magoon, T.M. and Spokane, A.R. (1981). Counseling psychology: career interventions, research, and theory. In *Annual Reviews in Psychology*. Hillsdale, NJ: Erlbaum.

Hopson, B. and Scally, M. (1989). *Build Your Own Rainbow: a Workbook for Career and Life Management*. Leeds: Lifeskills Associates.

Iles, P. and Mabey, C. (1993). Managerial career development programmes: effectiveness, availability and acceptability. *British Journal of Management*, 4, 103–118.

Jackson, C. (1990). *Careers Counselling in Organizations: the Way Forward*. IMS report no. 198, Institute of Manpower Studies, University of Sussex.

Jansen, E. and Chandler, G. (1989). *Career Orientation Inventory*. University of Utah.

Kagono, T., Nonaka, I., Sakakibara, K. and Okumura, A. (1985). *Strategic vs. Evolutionary Management: a US-Japan Comparison of Strategy and Organisation*. Amsterdam: North Holland.

Keller, J. and Piotrowski, C. (1987). Career development programs in Fortune 500 firms. *Psychological Reports*, 61, 920–922.

Kidd, J.M. (1981). The assessment of career development. In A.G. Watts, D.E. Super and J.M. Kidd (eds) *Career Development in Britain*. Cambridge: CRAC/Hobsons Press.

Kidd, J.M. (1984). The relationship of self and occupational concepts to the occupational preferences of adolescents. *Journal of Vocational Behavior*, 24, 48–65.

Kidd, J.M. (1988). *Assessment in Action*. Leicester: NIACE.

Kidd, J.M. and Killeen, J. (1992). Are the effects of careers guidance worth having? Changes in practice and outcomes. *Journal of Occupational and Organizational Psychology*, 65, 219–234.

Killeen, J., Kidd, J.M., Hawthorn, R., Sampson, J. and White, M. (1994). *A Review of Measures of the Learning Outcomes of Guidance*. Cambridge: NICEC.

Kingdon, M.A. and Bimline, C.A. (1987). Evaluating the effectiveness of career development training for women. *Career Development Quarterly*, 35, 220–227.

Kotter, J.P. Faux, V.A. and McArthur, C.C. (1978). *Self Assessment and Career Development*. Englewood Cliffs, NJ: Prentice-Hall.

Krumboltz, J. (1991). *Career Beliefs Inventory*. Palo Alto, CA: Consulting Psychologists Press.

Law, B. (1981). Community interaction: a 'mid-range' focus for theories of career development in young adults. *British Journal of Guidance and Counselling*, 9, 142–158.

Lawrence, B.S. (1984). Age grading: the implicit organizational timetable. *Journal of Occupational Behavior*, 5, 23–35.

Leibowitz, Z.B., Farren, C. and Kaye, B.L. (1986). *Designing Career Development Systems*. San Francisco, CA: Jossey-Bass.

London, M. (1993). Relationships between career motivation, empowerment and support for career development. *Journal of Occupational and Organizational Psychology*, 66, 55–69.

London, M. and Bray, D.W. (1984). Measuring and developing young managers' career motivation. *Journal of Management Development*, 3, 3–25.

Louis, M.R. (1981). Surprise and sense making: what newcomers experience and how they cope in entering unfamiliar organizational settings. In D.A. Kolb, I.M. Rubin and J.M. McIntyre (eds) *Organizational Psychology: Readings in Human Behavior in Organizations*. Englewood Cliffs, NJ: Prentice-Hall.

Lowman, R.L. and Williams, R.E. (1987). Validity of self-ratings of abilities and competencies. *Journal of Vocational Behavior*, 31, 1–13.

MacNab, D. and Fitzsimmons, G.W. (1987). A multitrait–multimethod study of work-related needs, values and preferences. *Journal of Vocational Behavior*, 30, 1–15.

Minor, F.J. (1986). Computer applications in career development planning. In D.T. Hall and associates (eds) *Career Development in Organizations*. San Francisco, CA: Jossey-Bass.

Morrisby, J.R. (1989). *Morrisby Differential Test Battery*. Hemel Hempstead: Educational and Industrial Test Services Ltd.

Moses, B. and Saltrese, K. (1989). Implementing a career planning program. *International Journal of Career Management*, 1, 19–24.

Nicholson, N. (1984). A theory of work role transitions. *Administrative Science Quarterly*, 29, 172–191.

Nicholson, N. and West, M. (1989). Transitions, work histories, and careers. In M.B. Arthur, D.T. Hall and B.S. Lawrence (eds) *Handbook of Career Theory*. Cambridge: University Press.

Noe, R.A., Noe, A.W. and Bachhuber, J.A. (1990). Correlates of career motivation. *Journal of Vocational Behavior*, 37, 340–356.

Nusbaum, H.J. (1986). The career development program at DuPont's Pioneering Research Laboratory. *Personnel*, 63, 68–75.

Parsons, F. (1909). *Choosing a Vocation.* Boston: Houghton–Mifflin.

Pryor, R.G.L. (1983). *The Work Aspect Preference Scale.* Hawthorn, Victoria: Australian Council for Educational Research.

Roberts, K. (1968). The entry into employment: an approach towards a general theory. *Sociological Review,* **16,** 165–184.

Rounds, J.B., Henley, G.A., Dawis, R.V. Lofquist, L.H. and Weiss, D.J. (1981). *Manual for the Minnesota Importance Questionnaire.* University of Minnesota, Minneapolis: Vocational Psychology Research.

Rounds, J.B. and Tracey, T.J. (1990). From trait-and-factor to person–environment fit counseling: theory and process. In W.B. Walsh and S.H. Osipow (eds) *Career Counseling: Contemporary Topics in Vocational Psychology.* Hillsdale, NJ: Erlbaum.

Russell, J.E.A. (1991). Career development interventions in organizations. *Journal of Vocational Behavior,* **38,** 237–287.

Savickas, M.L. (1990). Career choice process scales. In C.E. Watkins and V.L. Campbell (eds) *Testing in Counseling Practice.* Hillsdale, NJ: Erlbaum.

Savickas, M.L. (1992). New directions in career assessment. In D.H. Montross and C.J. Shinkman (eds) *Career Development: Theory and Practice.* Springfield, IL: Charles C. Thomas.

Schein, E.H. (1992). Career anchors and job/role planning: the links between career planning and career development. In D.H. Montross and C.J. Shinkman (eds) *Career Development: Theory and Practice.* Springfield IL: Charles C. Thomas.

Spector, P.E. (1988). Development of the Work Locus of Control Scale. *Journal of Occupational Psychology,* **61,** 335–340.

Spokane, A.R. (1985). A review of research on person–environment congruence in Holland's theory of careers. *Journal of Vocational Behavior,* **31,** 37–44.

Stump, R.W. (1987). Evaluating career development: fact and fantasy. *Training and Development Journal,* **41,** 38–40.

Super, D.E. (1957). *The Psychology of Careers.* New York: Harper & Row.

Super, D.E. (1980). A life-span, life-space approach to career development. *Journal of Vocational Behavior,* **16,** 282–298.

Super, D.E., Thompson, A.S., Lindeman, R.H., Jordaan, J.P. and Myers, R.A. (1984). *Career Development Inventory.* Palo Alto, CA: Consulting Psychologists Press.

Super, D.E., Thompson, A.S., Lindeman, R.H., Myers, R.A. and Jordaan, J.P. (1988). *Adult Career Concerns Inventory.* Palo Alto, CA: Consulting Psychologists Press.

Super, D.E. and Nevill, D.D. (1986). *The Salience Inventory.* Palo Alto, CA: Consulting Psychologists Press.

Tranberg, M., Slane, S. and Ekeberg, S.E. (1993). The relationship between interest congruence and satisfaction: a meta-analysis. *Journal of Vocational Behavior,* **42,** 253–264.

US Government Printing Office (1970). *General Aptitude Test Battery.* Washington, DC: US Government Printing Office.

Van Maanen, J. and Schein, E.H. (1979). Toward a theory of organizational socialization. In B.M. Staw (ed.) *Research in Organizational Behavior,* vol. 1. Greenwich, CT: JAI.

Veiga, J.F. (1983). Mobility influences during managerial career stages. *Academy of Management Journal,* **26,** 65–85.

Vondracek, F.W., Lerner, R.M. and Schulenberg, J.E. (1986). *Career Development: a Life-Span Perspective.* Hillsdale, NJ: Erlbaum.

Walker, J.W. and Gutteridge, T.G. (1979). *Career Planning Practices: an AMA Survey Report.* New York: AMACOM.

Walsh, W.B. and Betz, N.E. (1990). *Tests and Assessment,* 2nd edn. Englewood Cliffs, NJ: Prentice-Hall.

Watts, A.G. (1981). Career patterns. In A.G. Watts, D.E. Super and J.M. Kidd (eds) *Career Development in Britain.* Cambridge: CRAC/Hobsons.

Weick, K.E. and Berlinger, L.R. (1989). Career improvisation in self-designing organizations. In M.B. Arthur, D.T. Hall and B.S. Lawrence (eds) *Handbook of Career Theory.* Cambridge: University Press.

Zytowski, D.G. and Borgen, F. (1983). Assessment. In W.B. Walsh and S.H. Osipow (eds) *Handbook of Vocational Psychology. II: Applications.* Hillsdale, NJ: Erlbaum.

Chapter 31

Downsizing and Deselection

PAUL R. JACKSON

Institute of Work Psychology, University of Sheffield, Sheffield, UK

INTRODUCTION

Unemployment is high in almost all Western industrial economies, and recent estimates are of over 17 million people unemployed within the European Union. In a recent survey of 400 employers, Mirvis (1993) found that 80% had downsized between 1986 and 1991, reducing the workforce by 12.4% on average. Since 1980, 3.4 million jobs have been lost from the Fortune 500 companies often described in ever more creative ways. For IBM, 'rightsizing' translates into 35 000 redundancies; for Boeing, 'adjusting to the market downturn' meant 28 000 redundancies; for Kodak, 'real progress in reducing our cost base' meant 12 000 redundancies; and for GE, 'streamlining facilities' equals 10 000 redundancies (adapted from *Time Magazine*, 1994).

Furthermore, growth in Western economies has not been successful in creating jobs at the same rate, and the structure of labour markets has changed fundamentally in recent years. Research effort has not kept up with these changes: we know a great deal about traditional full-time permanent jobs and about full-time unemployment, but much less about other kinds of employment relationship. Most of the efforts of academic researchers have been understandably directed towards understanding the effects of unemployment on those who want to be in paid work; though there is also some research looking at the effects of redundancies and layoffs within a company on those who remain afterwards.

The aims of this chapter are threefold: first, to describe the structure of the labour market, and in particular the changes associated with increased flexibility; secondly, to examine the research literature on the impact of downsizing and redundancy on those who lose their jobs; and finally, to consider the impact of downsizing on layoff survivors. The chapter closes with a discussion of the

International Handbook of Selection and Assessment, Edited by N. Anderson and P. Herriot.
© 1997 John Wiley & Sons Ltd.

dilemmas facing organizations that seek to utilize non-traditional forms of employment contract.

THE FLEXIBLE LABOUR MARKET

The term 'flexibility' is one of the buzz words of 1990s debates about the structure of the labour market, and the current UK government's commitment to flexibility is now enshrined in the overall aim of the Employment Department: 'to support economic growth by promoting a competitive, efficient and flexible labour market'. For this aim to have substance, it is obviously important to define what the term means, and here difficulties arise. Watson (1994) has listed a number of components which are usually taken to denote flexibility, and they are listed in Table 31.1. Flexibility includes the extent to which pay levels are responsive to market conditions, the extent of barriers to freedom of movement of employees, demarcation lines between jobs, and flexibility in the pattern and organization of work. It is the last form of flexibility that is the focus of this chapter, and it includes numerical flexibility and working time flexibility.

An influential model in research on the flexible firm is that developed by Atkinson at the Institute of Manpower Studies in the United Kingdom (Atkinson, 1984) which contains a distinction between a *core* workforce of full-time permanent employees, whose commitment was encouraged by high investment in their skill, and a *peripheral* workforce of part-time, temporary and self-employed people (see Figure 31.1). The model involves a departure from traditional demarcations between blue-collar and white-collar jobs, in favour of distinctions based on skills that are specific to the organization and those which are not. Organization-specific jobs are represented in the *core*, and consist of permanent full-time employees who are flexible in terms of the function they perform. For them, job security is won at the cost of accepting functional flexibility, both in the short term (by diffuse role boundaries) and in the long term (accepting the continual need for

Table 31.1   Forms of labour market flexibility (based on Watson, 1994)

Wage/earnings flexibility: the responsiveness of pay levels to market conditions, including performance-related pay, bonuses linked to company performance.

Labour mobility: the movement of workers between jobs, between companies, and between geographical areas.

Functional flexibility: the reduction of demarcations between different jobs.

Flexibility in the pattern and organization of work:
- *flexibility in the place of work*—homeworking and teleworking,
- *numerical flexibility*—adjustment of the number of workers or hours worked in response to production requirements, by the use of part-time, temporary or self-employed workers,
- *working time flexibility*—changes in the number and timing of hours worked from day to day or week to week, by the use of overtime or short-time working, annualized hours contracts, or flexitime.

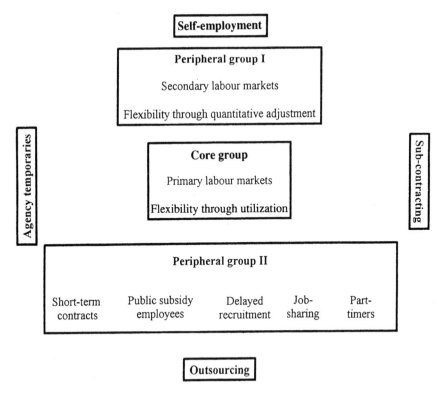

Figure 31.1   The Atkinson model of the flexible firm

career change and retraining). The *first peripheral group* is also full-time employees, but enjoy lower levels of job security and have less access to career opportunities. Occupations in the first peripheral group are not organization-specific, and may include clerical, supervisory, assembly and testing work. External labour markets are used to meet requirements, and flexibility is afforded by adjusting the numbers of workers employed. Finally, the *second peripheral group* includes workers on non-standard contracts: trainees, part-timers, and temporary employees.

Handy (1989) uses the analogy of the shamrock to present a similar picture of the emerging organization. The first leaf of the shamrock represents the *core* workers whom Handy sees as made up of qualified professionals, technicians and managers, essential to the organization, highly committed and highly paid. The organization cannot do without them, and rewards them well. The second leaf is *contractors*, specialized people and firms, who are often outside the organization itself and perform tasks that are not crucial to the organization. Thus, many manufacturing firms do not actually make anything, rather they assemble components made by someone else. The Japanese practice of just-in-time delivery is probably the most sophisticated example of how organizations can export uncertainty to others, while at the same time binding sub-contractors to themselves. The use of sub-contractors in this way allows smaller organizations to specialize in a service or product, and supply it to perhaps a range of customers. The third leaf of the shamrock is the *flexible workforce* of part-time and temporary workers, who provide a buffer to the core workforce in order to allow organizations to manage fluctuations in demand for their products and services.

While recent surveys have shown that few firms are deliberately adopting the strategy of the flexible firm model, there is abundant evidence that they are using some of its elements and labour markets in the United Kingdom (and in the rest of the Western economies too) are changing rapidly. The 1993 UK Labour Force Survey (Watson, 1994; Naylor, 1994) showed that 38% of all in employment—over 9.6 million people—were in the flexible workforce, defined as part-time, temporary, self-employed and those on government training schemes. This figure represents an increase of 1.25 million people since 1986; and most of that increase has been amongst men. The proportion of women workers who are part of the flexible work force has remained around 50% since the early 1980s; while the proportion for men has increased from 18% in 1981 to 27% in 1993. The most common form of non-standard employment is part-time working, representing almost a quarter of the UK labour force. Thurman and Trah (1990) show that this trend towards reliance on part-time workers is growing in most other industrialized nations. O'Reilly (1993) reports high levels of use of part-time working in Britain, Denmark and the Netherlands; while France, Germany and Belgium have relatively low rates. In all six of the countries she studied the rate of part-time work has increased in the last 20 years, with the biggest increases for the Netherlands (from 9.5% in 1975 to 29.4% in 1987), Britain (from 17.1% in 1975 to 27.3% in 1992), France (from 6.4% in 1975 to 11.9% in 1991) and Belgium (from 4.9% in 1975 to 9.9% in 1987). Less common in the United Kingdom are other forms of non-standard employment: almost one in five people are employed in shiftwork of some kind, and 12% are either self-employed or working flexitime. The other forms of working time flexibility are much less common.

In what sectors of the labour market are these flexible jobs? Table 31.2 summarizes findings from the 1993 Labour Force Survey (and reported by Naylor, 1994 and Watson, 1994) showing that there are large variations in the distribution of different forms of flexibility. For example, part-time working, flexitime, and term-time working are particularly prevalent in the service sector; compressed working week and shiftwork are more common in manufacturing; while annualized hours are equally likely in the service and manufacturing sectors.

Davis (1995, pp. 124–125) has documented trends within Western economies towards what he calls *virtual staff*—employees who come together temporarily to work on projects. Under this heading he includes members of the flexible workforce, temporary and contract workers who work in lieu of full-time workers, as well as full-time employees of other organizations who cooperate on joint projects. The use of virtual staff allows organizations to reduce their fixed costs, while maintaining access to more than its own resources.

Organizational downsizing can have a range of consequences: for the efficiency and profitability of the organization itself, for individuals who leave the organization, and for those who remain within the organization, layoff survivors. While

Table 31.2   Patterns of UK working time flexibility by occupational group and industry (based on Watson, 1994; Naylor, 1994)

	Percent	Occupational group	Industry sector
Temporary employment	5	na	na
Self-employed	12	na	na
Govt. training schemes	1	na	na
Part-time working	24	Sales; other services	Services; retail and catering
Flexitime	12	White-collar staff in large offices	Banking; financial and business services; public administration
Annualized hours	9	Teachers; plant and machine operatives	Services; manufacturing
Term-time working	5	Teachers; personal, protective occupations	Public sector; retail, hotels and catering
Job-sharing	1	Clerical and secretarial occupations	Public administration, education, health
Compressed working week	3	Craft and related occupations	Manufacturing
Shiftwork	18	Personal and protective occupations; plant and machine operatives	Manufacturing; transport and communication

Notes: na = information not reported; the categories for part-time, temporary and self-employed overlap (for example, some temporary employees work part time).

there is some study of the organizational impact of downsizing (Freeman and Cameron, 1993), the primary focus of this chapter is on individual impacts, on those who leave and those who stay.

CONSEQUENCES OF DOWNSIZING FOR THOSE WHO LOSE THEIR JOBS

Most research on the effects of unemployment has concentrated on layoffs and job loss, predominantly among male blue-collar workers (e.g. Warr, Jackson and Banks, 1988). The phenomenon of large-scale clerical and professional unemployment is relatively recent, and there is less research evidence to go on. Nevertheless, the pattern that emerges from reviews of the literature gives a quite consistent picture, at least for the effects of job loss, though the pattern for the impact of unemployment among those who are entering the labour market for the first time is more mixed.

Effects of job loss

The psychological consequences of job loss have been well documented for a wide range of different groups. In both cross-sectional comparisons between employed and unemployed people and in panel studies of changes in employment status it has been noted that unemployment brings with it marked deterioration in many aspects of psychological health and sometimes physical health too (Jackson, 1994; Smith, 1987). Specific measures of anxiety and depression, measures of generalized mental health such as the General Health Questionnaire (Goldberg, 1972), life satisfaction, and self-esteem all show deteriorations with job loss. The dominant pattern of responses has been subsumed under the heading *resigned adaptation* (Warr and Jackson, 1987), reflected in the adoption of a passive lifestyle, a reduced aspiration level and a resigned acceptance of unemployment. There is evidence that proactive responses to unemployment are possible (Fryer and Payne, 1984; Walsh and Jackson, 1995), particularly for those who are able to pursue valued personal goals; but such *constructive adaptation* is rare given the dominant societal construction of the unemployment role.

Having described the overall psychological effects of unemployment, it is important to recognize that there is great diversity, both in the effects of unemployment and in vulnerability to those effects. Indeed, identification of risk factors has been a primary goal of research since 1980; and the most important are demographic and psychosocial factors, including individual value systems and personal and social resources (Warr, Jackson and Banks, 1988).

From this research, a primary risk factor for severe psychological consequences of unemployment is the level of centrality of the employment role to the individual, measured in terms of employment commitment (e.g. Jackson *et al.*, 1983). For those in paid work, strong commitment to the employment role is associated with poorer well-being. Studies of transitions between employment and unemployment show that the effects on well-being are amplified among individuals with high employment commitment. There are two important aspects of the salience of paid employment. First, and most obviously, paid employment is, in our society, the primary means whereby an individual is able to support dependants financially. It is not surprising therefore that psychological health is worse for individuals under greatest financial pressure (e.g. Kessler, Turner and House, 1987; Price, 1992; Rowley and Feather 1987). In a sample of 953 adult unemployed men, Warr and Jackson (1984) found a curvilinear relationship between age and psychological health: worst off were men of middle age, who were also those most likely to be married with dependent children. The second aspect of the salience of the employment role is in terms of individual self-concepts. For many people, the job that they do defines in part their identity—who they are—such that the loss of a job carries a threat to that identity. The erosion of the sense of self that unemployment can bring is shown vividly by one respondent in the Warr and Jackson panel study of unemployed men. At the first interview he described himself as an 'unemployed electrician'; at the second interview nine months later, he said 'I'm unemployed, and I used to be an electrician; by the third interview, ten months after the previous one, he described himself simply as 'unemployed'.

Initial entry into the labour market

In general, the negative consequences of job loss have also been observed among school leavers and graduates on initial entry into the labour market. Banks and Jackson (1982) found poorer psychological health among unemployed young adults while there were no differences in their psychological health when measured while still at school. These findings are consistent with a deterioration in psychological health on becoming unemployed. Studies of Australian school leavers (Tiggeman and Winefield, 1984) have also found employment status differences after leaving school, but the authors have interpreted them differently. They argued that unemployment at this age does not exert positive damage on well-being; rather the experience of unemployment retards aspects of personal development which would otherwise accompany entry into the adult world of work. Whichever detailed explanation is preferable, both are consistent with the general conclusion that unemployment keeps young people in the same state of dependency as when they were in full-time education; while employment marks a status shift into adult independence.

While the evidence for an impact of unemployment on school leavers is clear, findings are less clearcut for graduates who fail to find paid work. Borgen, Hatch and Amundson (1990) found evidence for an initial 'vacation period' when respondents felt positive and optimistic followed by a downward trend characterized by fluctuating emotions and decreased self-confidence. However, Schaufeli and Van Yperen (1992) found no evidence in a Dutch graduate sample for such a downward trend, and speculated that this result might reflect the typically high self-esteem of their sample, the favourable benefit system in place at the time of the study, and the cultural acceptability of unemployment.

In general, then, we may conclude that paid work gives individuals access to many 'markers' of adulthood as well as making it possible to live independently, and unemployment severely threatens that transition except for those with favourable personal and social resources.

THE IMPACT OF DOWNSIZING ON LAYOFF SURVIVORS

While there is an enormous amount of research on the effects of unemployment on those who lose a job (and to some extent on the families of those who lose a job), there is much less known about the consequences for survivors who remain within organizations after layoff programmes and for those who live their employed lives with the threat of job insecurity, the fear of job loss. Personnel professionals are becoming increasingly aware of a pattern of reactions in layoff survivors which is systematic enough to merit a media label—*survivor syndrome*. The features of survivor syndrome include decreased motivation, morale and loyalty to the organization, and increased stress and scepticism.

Evidence comes from a recent survey on the financial services industry conducted by Working Transitions and the Human Resource Research Centre at Cranfield in the United Kingdom (Doherty and Horsted, 1995). They interviewed

170 personnel and HR specialists from 131 financial services organizations, and found an imbalance between the high level of support to those made redundant and the relative lack of support to those that remained. The focus of support for survivors was on training for new work roles as a result of the restructuring that was associated with redundancies. The pressure for downsizing was cost, and most companies that had recently made redundancies expected to make more in future years. What most companies missed out on was succession planning and career management; all the more important given the fire-fighting focus on the immediate task requirements coupled with the threat of future job losses. The study found, disturbingly but understandably, that loyalty to the organization decreased: employees felt that the organization had made its own future more secure, but that their own career security had decreased. Instead, employees showed an increase in loyalty to colleagues; and many companies recognized a shift in the psychological contract, the ties between the individual and the organization, away from employment and towards employability. Similar patterns emerge from US research, summarized by Church (1995).

One of the key findings, both from academic research and from case studies of organizations' experiences, is that employees are affected much more by *how* restructuring is done than by *what* is done (see also Iles and Robertson, Chapter 27 in this volume). The two key elements are perceived fairness (both *procedural* and *distributive* justice) and communication, and have been addressed in an important and extensive programme of research by Brockner and colleagues. In a number of papers (Brockner *et al.*, 1987, 1992, 1993) they have reported the results of a study based on a sample drawn from employees of a chain of 773 small, company-owned retail stores throughout the United States. Many stores in the chain had been closed in the 12-month period prior to the study, and questionnaires were distributed to employees of 300 of the remaining stores. Each store employed between 2 and 11 people, and replies were obtained from 597 people, almost all of them female.

The dependent variables that they examined were:

- *organizational commitment*—individuals' identification with and pride in the company
- *work effort*—change in expenditure of effort in the job since before layoff announcements.

The main predictor variables were:

- *perceived job quality*—the extent to which the job is seen as intrinsically interesting or enjoyable, relative to before layoffs
- *perceived distributive fairness*—the extent to which the organization offered concrete benefits to layoff victims (generous severance pay, help in finding work inside and outside the company, continuation of health insurance)
- *perceived procedural fairness*—the extent to which the procedures for implementing layoffs were seen as fair or unfair
- *perceived co-worker reactions*—the favourability of the reactions of co-workers

- *job insecurity*—beliefs that further layoffs were likely in the foreseeable future (perceived threat) and that management would meet the respondent's need if he/she were laid off (perceived control)
- *prior attachment to layoff victims*—the closeness of professional relationships with layoff victims.

The main findings of the research were as follows. *Organizational commitment* went down for those who had strongest links with people laid off, and markedly so where the company was perceived as acting unfairly towards layoff victims (distributive justice). Interestingly, perception of distributive justice was not a significant predictor of organizational commitment overall, but only in the presence of strong attachments to those laid off. A decrease in commitment was also associated with reports of a reduction in job quality, low procedural fairness, and a perception that other co-workers had reacted negatively. Greater *work effort* resulted for those who felt that the quality of their jobs had improved. A U-shaped relationship was found relating work effort to the two components of job insecurity: for both very high and very low insecurity, work effort was less than at moderate levels of insecurity. Low job insecurity plausibly leads to complacency and low work effort; while high job insecurity produces low work effort by a different mechanism— helplessness arising from a high perceived risk to their jobs accompanied by a belief that the organization will offer little help to anyone laid off.

The behaviour of organizations when staff are made redundant is clearly of vital importance therefore, and Cameron (in Church, 1995) comments that two-thirds of the organizations he has been associated with did it poorly. These companies were worse off at the end of downsizing than they were when they started the process. Those employees who remain after redundancies have been carried out do not easily forget what the company did, and are more likely to leave when they get the opportunity. Furthermore, as Crofts (1991) points out: 'it is poor public relations to have former employees out in the marketplace complaining about how shabbily they have been treated' (pp. 24–25).

The case of the closure of the Duracell factory in Crawley, England (described in Pickard, 1993) illustrates vividly how the findings of academic research can be taken out of the laboratory and applied in the real world. The company spent eight months planning the closure of the plant with the transfer of battery component production to Belgium. They set up a taskforce of directors, senior managers, public relations advisers, outplacement consultants and pension experts, all of whom were pledged to secrecy during the planning phase. When the closure programme was announced and 150 were made redundant straight away, information was available about severance entitlements and the services of the outplacement consultancy was offered to all. Moreover, the taskforce had contacted 5000 companies confidentially and were able to offer 100 unadvertised vacancies immediately. A major concern was to maintain production capability with the remaining staff right up to the final shutdown, and in this the company succeeded. 'The strategy met its objectives: a smooth rundown, production back to normal in two days and even an increase in productivity during the rundown period' (Pickard, 1993, p. 20).

The 1990s may well be the decade of the outplacement industry, and many employers have a jaundiced view of outplacement. However, there are examples of employers acting humanely and effectively, meeting many of the requirements of procedural justice highlighted in the academic research. Marks and Spencer (summarized in Crofts, 1991) removed several hundred management-level jobs from its head office early in 1991 and set up its own career counselling outplacement consultancy, Compass, in order to help those made redundant. By the end of the year half of those who approached Compass had been placed, and they planned to keep this consultancy in existence until the numbers not placed were so small as to make the operation unviable.

THE FLEXIBLE WORKFORCE AND INDIVIDUAL CAREERS

Restructuring, downsizing, outsourcing and re-engineering have taken their toll on employees and changed fundamentally the relationship between the individual and the organization. So far in this chapter we have looked at the effects of the transition to unemployment, and what downsizing can do to those who remain. Now we turn to an analysis of the impact of the growing flexible workforce, and in particular what it means for the psychological contract between employer and employee. Rousseau and Wade-Benzoni (1995) define the psychological contract as 'the individual's understanding of the employment relationship's terms' (p. 294); and it is clear that the terms of this contract have changed and are changing still. Job insecurity is much greater now; there is greater pressure to perform (in terms of intensity of work and in working hours) especially for those in the organization's core; and there is reduced benefit provision.

Hall and Mirvis (1995, p. 326) sum up the new contract in terms of a message found posted on the bulletin board of a company experiencing widespread layoffs:

- We can't promise you how long we'll be in business.
- We can't promise you that we won't be bought by another company.
- We can't promise that there'll be room for promotion.
- We can't promise that your job will exist until you reach retirement age.
- We can't promise that the money will be available for your pension.
- We can't expect your undying loyalty and we aren't sure we want it.

This anecdote points clearly to changes in what an organization is either willing or able to offer employees, and what it can expect in return. To understand the impact of the flexible workforce, we need to consider both of these aspects.

What is it that people are looking for in a job? While it is obvious that people value the monetary rewards of paid employment, there are many aspects of work and employment that are rewarding in other ways. It is helpful to be able to define what these non-monetary rewards are, and then to consider the extent to which they can be achieved outside the traditional contract of full-time permanent paid employment. Jahoda (1982) and Warr (1987) have summarized these rewards in related, but different, ways. Jahoda argues that social roles carry with them the ability to meet five latent functions:

- time structure
- social contact
- goals and purposes outside the person
- personal status and
- enforced activity.

Warr includes these within a broader framework of nine 'vitamins' which are important factors underlying positive mental health:

- *Opportunity for control* over activities and events within a person's life. Within job settings there are large differences in the degree to which workers are given autonomy over the scheduling of work activities, over work methods and over work objectives (Jackson *et al.*, 1993).
- *Opportunity for skill use,* although many jobs are very routine and impose heavy constraints on the use that people can make of their skills.
- *Externally generated goals* are important in that they encourage activity and achievement. Indeed, people will tend to establish goals for themselves in the absence of external pressure to do so.
- *Variety* in activity rather than repetitiveness is associated with positive mental health.
- *Environmental clarity* relates to feedback about the consequences of actions, to predictability in the environment, and to the clarity of social norms and expectations.
- *Availability of money* is obviously important to psychological well-being in that poverty does not allow individuals and families the resources to meet their requirements.
- *Physical security* is clearly important in relation to physical threat, personal territory and the right to privacy.
- *Opportunity for interpersonal contact* provides access to friendship relationships with other people, provides sources of help (whether emotional or instrumental), provides for social comparisons, and allows individuals access to achieve goals using collective effort beyond what could be achieved by the person alone. An important aspect of relationships at work is a leadership style that reflects treating staff with personal respect, rather than adopting a style that bullies employees.
- *Valued social position* arises from membership of social institutions. Role memberships are important sources of identity for most people, and allow them to derive esteem from the fact that they belong to, for example, a prestigious organization.

What opportunities does the flexible workforce offer people relative to these nine vitamins? Since there is so little research on other than the traditional full-time permanent employee, answers must be somewhat speculative, but let us

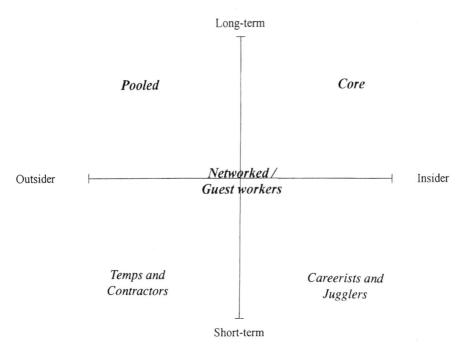

Figure 31.2   Employment relations attachment map (from Rosseau and Wade-Benzoni, 1995)

consider the possibilities by using Rousseau and Wade-Banzoni's (1995) framework of two basic dimensions of employment relations: short- or long-term time frames and embeddedness (internal or external to the organization). Figure 31.2 shows what they call an attachment map, which distinguishes five types of employment relationship.

Core employees are long-term insiders around whom the organization is built, and the mutual attachment of individual and organization is clear. These are the ones who are left after downsizing and outsourcing, and it may well be that the research on organizational commitment (e.g. Shore and Wayne, 1993) gives a good account of their position. Delayered management structures and flexible work roles offer potential opportunities for autonomy, skill use and a degree of security. On the debit side, delayering and the short shelf-life of job specifications are likely to obscure clarity in terms of role expectations and future career routes.

Secondly, *careerists and jugglers* are short-term insiders, whose attachments are to personal goals other than promotion or advancement within an organization. Careerists use temporary organizational membership as a path to advancement within an industry or profession, while jugglers are people for whom employment is not a central life interest. From the organization's perspective, short-term insiders need to bring expertise with them, or learn it very quickly, and need to fit in sufficiently to meet company goals. Investment in developing the expertise of such people is a low priority: they 'do not reflect the organization's distinctive present and future competencies as core workers do' (Rousseau and Wade-Benzoni, 1995, p. 309). Instead, short-term insidership offers temporary access to the 'vitamin' opportunities of organizational membership, while maintaining the integrity of personal goals beyond the organization.

Pooled workers are long-term outsiders who work irregularly for the organization over a period of time, and often may be former long-term employees whose circumstances have changed. Hospitals and schools have long used pooled staff to cope with variations in demand, and many manufacturing organizations are beginning to introduce similar arrangements often as a way of reducing staffing costs. Comparisons in the form of the psychological contract between core staff and pooled staff show both similarities and differences. Because both categories are long term, the organization has a continuing need for their expertise, and therefore has an incentive to offer conditions that merit attachment. These may include challenging work assignments which allow autonomy, skill utilization, variety, interpersonal contact, and valued social position during the period of employment. However, the key difference is that those conditions do not include a full-time or indeed a predictable employment contract. For some people this may be a benefit, allowing them to pursue personal goals which are larger than organizational membership; others may see the contractual arrangement as a cost that needs to be paid.

Temps and contractors are short-term outsiders from whom the organization requires neither continued nor regular commitment, and typically offers little in return beyond a wage for work done. Access to the 'vitamins' is likely to be low for this group. Furthermore, Rousseau and Wade-Benzoni suggest that extensive reliance on temporary staff brings problems for organizations in that it creates two classes of employees: secure workers with high-paid employment and temps with sporadic and low-paid jobs.

Finally, Figure 31.2 shows a category of employee relationships that are 'floating' and may cut across the other four categories. These are *networked or guest workers* whose work is performed beyond the boundaries of the organization, and access to vitamins will depend on the precise nature of the working arrangement. A particular problem for networked workers may be that geographical remoteness denies access to both formal and informal communication channels, and therefore influences the extent of opportunity for interpersonal contact and perhaps too occupation of a valued social position.

THE ASSESSMENT IMPLICATIONS OF DOWNSIZING AND THE FLEXIBLE WORKFORCE

The final section of the chapter considers some of the assessment implications of downsizing and restructuring. The context for this discussion is the commonly reported conclusion that downsizing exercises often fail to achieve their intended purpose, and may even leave the organization worse off than before! To a large extent this can be put down to a short-term emphasis on headcount reduction aimed at cutting costs rather than the exercise of a strategic process of analysing individuals' contribution to the future needs of the organization (Sanchez, 1994).

Failure to follow a coherent strategy can lead companies into the kind of nightmare position described by Sparrow (Chapter 17 of this volume). A division of a large pharmaceutical organization reduced its workforce from 2500 to 1200, with a fall in management posts from 160 to 60. Afterwards, they found that only 16% of the surviving managers scored above halfway on several key dimensions of leadership: 'the new "delayered" organization with its "empowered" managers simply would not be "competent" enough'. The two key elements which can be identified in a strategic approach to restructuring are a focus on work that needs to be done to meet business needs rather than on existing job boundaries and role definitions, and a future orientation looking to the long term rather than a present orientation concerned purely with the next quarter's profit figures.

Conventional job analysis (Altink, Visser and Castelijn, Chapter 14 in this volume; Harvey, 1992) is concerned with defining the work activities and worker requirements of a specific job. To a large extent this emphasis on a well-defined job grew out of Scientific Management principles of a rigid division of labour and the creation of jobs where workers are paid to *do*, while managers are paid to *think* about what workers do. It is now clear that this is damaging to the competitiveness of modern organizations; job boundaries are becoming blurred and change frequently, organizations are becoming flatter, and the responsibilities of employees are broadening. As a result, many commentators have questioned the continued usefulness of conventional job analysis. Instead, Sanchez (1994) proposes that we concentrate on the processes involved in the flow of work, rather than on archaic job boundaries. He suggests that such 'work analysis' can use many of the formal tools familiar to occupational psychologists and HR professionals while at the same time giving a shift in aim 'from defining and documenting clear-cut job boundaries to facilitating the design of enlarged and multi-functional classifications' (p. 58).

The environment within which most organizations operate is so uncertain and turbulent that today's jobs are obsolete tomorrow and what is needed to perform jobs today is not necessarily needed tomorrow. A strategic approach to downsizing should therefore be future-oriented, concerned with the competencies required for tomorrow, rather than present-oriented. Sparrow and Bognanno (1993) have applied what they call a life-cycle perspective to this issue of the shelf-life of organizational competencies:

> Rather than create generic lists of competencies associated with 'coping with change' or 'making change happen', organizations will need to develop an even more sophisticated picture of competencies that allows them to analyse how the relevance of any competency to the organization as a whole (or to a career stream, or individual job) waxes and wanes. (p. 55)

They distinguish between four categories of competencies: those that are emerging, maturing, transitional, and core (see their Figure 3). *Emerging* competencies are those that may not be relevant now, but will be relevant in the future given the organization's strategic path. By contrast, *maturing* competencies are those that have been important to the past success of the organization (and to jobs within it), but will become less relevant in the future, either because of strategic change or because of technological obsolescence. *Transitional* competencies are those that are important neither for current performance nor for the proposed strategic plan, but are vital to the smooth management of change from 'here' to 'there'. Sparrow and Bognanno suggest that many organizations' 'competencies for change' are really transitional competencies, which may not be required in the longer term. Under this heading they include capacity to live with uncertainty, to manage stress and to cope with pressure. Finally, *core* competencies are those whose importance is enduring, at the heart of effective performance regardless of the vagaries of organizational change fashion.

Following the life-cycle perspective, it is clear that organizations will want to keep the people who possess the core competencies which they have identified for business effectiveness, as well as those who currently possess (or can learn through training or personal development) the emerging competencies necessary following restructuring. Identification of people with the appropriate transitional competencies is likely to be important too, given the level of turbulence in many organizations. The new kinds of work require flexibility and adaptability, and team-working is increasingly common at all levels within organizations (West and Allen, Chapter 24 in this volume). Moreover, the fit between the person and the organization's culture and values is increasingly seen as vital. It is not surprising therefore that assessment practice has broadened to include not just ability and reasoning but also personality, motivation and styles of working.

There is strong evidence for cognitive ability tests as valid predictors of job performance across a wide range of jobs (Hunter and Hunter, 1984), and recent reviews have also suggested that some personality characteristics are associated with job performance across a range of jobs (Barrick and Mount, 1991; Tett, Jackson and Rothstein, 1991). It is not surprising therefore that both ability tests and personality inventories have been used as aids in making decisions about who should be laid off during restructuring. However, there is considerable controversy surrounding the use of personality inventories in redundancy settings. Most notably, in the United Kingdom Southwark Council and Anglian Water are facing industrial tribunals over their use of such methods in making employees redundant. There are many practical and conceptual difficulties involved in deciding that an individual is not capable of meeting the organization's new requirements based on a personality profile (Karren and Graves, 1994). Self-report measures such as personality inventories are obviously vulnerable to distortion; and it will not help much to argue that honesty is in the individual's best interests, especially in the context of threatened restructuring and downsizing which create an environment not conducive to openness and honesty. Furthermore, a 30-minute self-report measure used as a basis for redundancy after many years of service understandably evokes highly negative reactions, especially since leavers have nothing to lose in bringing an Equal Opportunities case to a court or tribunal. Finally, the link between specific elements of a profile (or configuration of elements) and organizations' culture or strategic goals is likely either to be weak or unknown. The best advice to an organization wanting to ···· personality inventories as a psychometric basis for individual de-selection decisions is almost certainly—don't.

The kinds of jobs that there will be in the world of the flexible labour market are radically different from what many of us have known in our working lives. We will need to learn to live with broader, boundary-less jobs within (and sometimes outside) organizations which constantly change in size and structure. Lawler (1994) suggests that we should discard traditional thinking in terms of systems organized around jobs in favour of a competency-based approach: 'the task is to select individuals for organizational membership, not for a particular job' (p. 9). Like most prescriptions that are easy to say, putting this one into practice is possibly the biggest challenge facing organizations today.

REFERENCES

Atkinson, J. (1984). Manpower strategies for flexible organizations. *Personnel Management*, August, 28–31.

Banks, M.H. and Jackson, P.R. (1982). Unemployment and risk of minor psychiatric disorder in young people: Cross sectional and longitudinal evidence. *Psychological Medicine*, 12, 789–798.

Barrick, M.R. and Mount, M.K. (1991). The big five personality dimensions and job performance: A meta-analysis. *Personnel Psychology*, 44, 1–26.

Borgen, W., Hatch, W. and Amundson, N. (1990). The experience of unemployment for university graduates: An exploratory study. *Journal of Employment Counselling*, 27, 104–112.

Brockner, J., Grover, S., Reed, T.F. and DeWitt, R. L. (1992). Layoffs, job insecurity, and survivors' work effort: Evidence of an inverted-U relationship. *Academy of Management Journal*, 35, 413–425.

Brockner, J., Wiesenfeld, B.M., Reed, T., Grover, S. and Martin, C. (1993). Interactive effect of job content and context on the reactions of layoff survivors. *Journal of Personality and Social Psychology*, 64, 187–197.

Brockner, J., Grover, S., Reed, T.F., DeWitt, R.L. and O'Malley, M. (1987). Survivors' reactions to layoffs: We get by with a little help for our friends. *Administrative Science Quarterly*, 32, 526–541.

Church, A.H. (1995). From both sides now organizational downsizing: What is the role of the practitioner? *The Industrial/Organizational Psychologist*, July.

Crofts, P. (1991). Outplacement: A way of never having to say you're sorry? *Personnel Management*, May, 46–50.

Davis, D.D. (1995). Form, function and strategy in boundaryless organizations. In A. Howard (ed.), *The Changing Nature of Work*, pp. 112–138. San Francisco, CA: Jossey Bass.

Doherty, N. and Horsted, J. (1995). Helping survivors to stay on board. *People Management*, 12, 26–31.

Freeman, S.J. and Cameron, K.S. (1993). Organizational downsizing: A convergence and reorientation framework. *Organizational Science*, 4, 10–29.

Fryer, D. and Payne, R.L. (1984). Proactive behaviour in unemployment: Findings and implications. *Leisure Studies*, 3, 273–295.

Goldberg, D.P. (1972). *The Detection of Psychiatric Illness by Questionnaire*. Oxford: Oxford University Press.

Hall, D.T. and Mirvis, P.H. (1995). Careers as lifelong learning. In A. Howard (ed.), *The Changing Nature of Work*, pp. 323–361. San Francisco, CA: Jossey Bass.

Handy, C. (1989). *The Age of Unreason*. London: Business Books.

Harvey, R.J. (1992). Job analysis. In M.D. Dunnette and L.M. Hough (eds.), *Handbook of Industrial and Organizational Psychology*, 2nd edn. Palo Alto, CA: Consulting Psychologists Press.

Hunter, J.E. and Hunter, R.F. (1984). Validity and utility of alternative predictors of job performance. *Psychological Bulletin*, 96, 72–98.

Jackson, P.R. (1994). Influences on commitment to employment and commitment to work. In A. Bryson and S. McKay (eds.), *Is It Worth Working?*, pp. 110–121. London: Policy Studies Institute.

Jackson, P.R., Stafford, E.M., Banks, M.H. and Warr, P.B. (1983). Unemployment and psychological distress in young people: The moderating role of work involvement. *Journal of Applied Psychology*, **68**, 525–535.

Jackson, P.R., Wall, T.D., Martin, R. and Davids, K. (1993). New measures of job control, cognitive demand and production responsibility. *Journal of Applied Psychology*, **78**, 753–762.

Jahoda, M. (1982). *Employment and Unemployment*. Cambridge: Cambridge University Press.

Karren, R.J. and Graves, L.M. (1994). Assessing person–organization fit in personnel selection: Guidelines for future research. *International Journal of Selection and Assessment*, **2**, 146–156.

Kessler, R.C., Turner, J.B. and House, J.S. (1987). Intervening processes in the relationship between unemployment and health. *Psychological Medicine*, **17**, 949–961.

Lawler, E.E. (1994). From job-based to competency-based organizations. *Journal of Organizational Behavior*, **15**, 3–15.

Mirvis, P.H. (ed.) (1993). *Building a Competitive Workforce: Investing in Human Capital for Corporate Success*. New York: John Wiley.

Naylor, K. (1994). Part-time working in Great Britain—an historical analysis. *Employment Gazette*, December, 473–484.

O'Reilly, J. (1993). Part-time work and employment regulation: A comparison of Britain and France in the context of Europe. Paper presented to the Employment Service/PSI Conference on 'Unemployment in Focus', Rotherham, UK, November 1993.

Pickard, J. (1993). Outplacement and the run-up to redundancy. *Personnel Management*, April, 18–20.

Price, R.H. (1992). Psychosocial impact of job loss on individuals and families. *Current Directions in Psychological Science*, **1**, 9–11.

Rousseau, D.M. and Wade-Benzoni, K.A. (1995). Changing individual–organization attachments. In A. Howard (ed.), *The Changing Nature of Work*, pp. 290–322. San Francisco, CA: Jossey-Bass.

Rowley, K.M. and Feather, N.T. (1987). The impact of unemployment in relation to age and length of unemployment. *Journal of Occupational Psychology*, **60**, 323–332.

Sanchez, J.I. (1994). From documentation to innovation: Reshaping job analysis to meet emerging business needs. *Human Resource Management Review*, **4**, 51–74.

Schaufeli, W.B. and Van Yperen, N.W. (1992). Unemployment and psychological distress among graduates: A longitudinal study. *Journal of Occupational and Organizational Psychology*, **65**, 291–305.

Shore, L.M. and Wayne, S.J. (1993). Commitment and employee behavior: A comparison of affective commitment and continuance commitment with perceived organizational support. *Journal of Applied Psychology*, **78**, 774–780.

Smith, R. (1987). *Unemployment and Health*. Oxford: Oxford University Press.

Sparrow, P.R. and Bognanno, M. (1993). Competency requirement forecasting: Issues for international selection and assessment. *International Journal of Selection and Assessment*, **1**, 50–58.

Tett, R.P., Jackson, D.N. and Rothstein, M. (1991). Personality measures as predictors of job performance: A meta-analytic review. *Personnel Psychology*, **44**, 699–742.

Thurman, J.E. and Trah, G. (1990). Part-time work in international perspective. *International Labour Review*, **129**, 23–40.

Tiggeman, M. and Winefield, A.H. (1984). The effects of unemployment on the mood, self-esteem, locus of control, and depressive affect of school leavers. *Journal of Occupational Psychology*, **57**, 33–42.

Time Magazine (1994). Bumstead, you're downsized! *Time Magazine*, April, p. 22.

Walsh, S. and Jackson, P.R. (1995). Partner support and gender: Contexts for coping with job loss. *Journal of Occupational and Organizational Psychology*, **68**, 253–268.

Warr, P.B. (1987). *Work, Unemployment and Mental Health*. Oxford: Oxford University Press.

Warr, P.B. and Jackson, P.R. (1984). Men without jobs: Some correlates of age and length of unemployment. *Journal of Occupational Psychology, 57,* 77–85.

Warr, P.B. and Jackson, P.R. (1987). Adapting to the unemployment role: A longitudinal investigation. *Social Science and Medicine, 25,* 1219–1224.

Warr, P.B., Jackson, P.R. and Banks, M.H. (1988). Unemployment and mental health: Some British studies. *Journal of Social Issues, 44,* 47–68.

Watson, G. (1994). The flexible workforce and patterns of working hours in the UK. *Employment Gazette,* July, 239–247.

Index

Abbey National, 238
Ability requirements, 72
Ability Requirements Scales (ARS), 444
Ability test, 185
Abstraction, 140–1
Academic conformity, 15–16
Academic models, 35
Acculturation, 151
Accumulated experience curve, 223–5
Achievement versus ascription, 19
Acquisitions, 6
Adaptability, 24, 279
Adaptation issues, China 76–7
Adaptive testing, 136
Adaptiveness, 290
Ad hoc model, 586–7
Advocates, training, 183
Affective reactions, 425–7
Affectively neutral versus affectivity,
    19
Aggregation problem, 339
Alcohol tests, 371, 381
Alpha change, 253, 263
Anglo-Saxon cultures, 19
Applicants
    attitudes towards selection systems,
        554–5
    rights, 30, 547–8
Application forms, 88–9
    graduate recruitment, 510–13, 519
Appraisal results, 72
Aptitude tests, 170–1
Armed Services *see* Military staff
Armed Services Vocational Aptitude
    Battery (ASVAB), 165–7, 170, 174, 176,
    177, 211
ARS (Ability Requirements Scales), 444
ASA framework, 402
Assessment, 35

changes in techniques and procedures,
    132–42
classification of procedures, 132–3
computer-assisted, 136
cost-effectiveness of, 142
emergent themes, 21–30
more efficient and faster, 135–8
of dynamic criteria, 138–9
of general characteristics, 133–5
of learning potential, 139–40
situational, 141–2
Assessment centres, 90, 91, 93, 262, 297
    China, 69–70
    competencies, 358
    diagnostic, 591
    exercises, 595
    graduate recruitment, 516–17, 520–2
    impact of, 551–3
    meta-analysis of validity, 328–9
    military staff, 168
    predictive power, 358
    technology, 588
Assessment dimensions, construct validity
    of, 360
Assessment practices, changing context,
    525–7
Assessment processes, 389–92
    European perspective, 558–9
    impact process model, 559–61
    in organizational turnaround, 262
    outcomes and effects on candidates, 548–55
    psychological impact of, 543–66
    psychometric paradigm of, 545
Attitudinal impact of socialization impact,
    433–4
Attraction-selection-attrition (ASA)
    framework, 399, 424
Authentic performance assessment, 271
Automation, 129

Balance of power between employer and job applicants, 235–6

Bankruptcies, 6

Bar
Mark I selection process, 185–91
Mark II selection process, 191–6
results from 1996 selection process, 196–8
training for, 183–5

Bar Council, 184, 185

Bar Vocational Course, 183, 185

Barristers, 183

Behaviour in work organizations, 393

Behaviour modelling in criterion-based training, 588–91

Behaviour reinforcement in practice, 589

Behavioural competencies, 345, 346, 360
application, 349–53
HRM content benefits, 351
HRM process benefits, 351
management change programmes, 352
performance management, 352
post hoc labelling process, 348–9

Behavioural cues to deception, 382–4

Behavioural goals, formulation, 588

Behavioural impact of socialization impact, 434

Behavioural indicators, content validity of, 360

Behavioural measures, 274–5

Behaviourally Anchored Rating Scales (BARS), 272

Beta change, 253, 263

Bi-directional decision-making, 30

Big Five
and job performance, 481–2
and occupational criteria, 484–5
assessment in occupational domain, 478–81
criterion validity, 481–6
in personality assessment, 475–92
practical recommendations, 489–90
relationship with training proficiency and personnel data, 483
response bias in assessment, 486–8

Bimodal prediction, 22–3

Biodata, 88–9, 172
graduate recruitment, 513–15
impact of, 553–4

Biographical data, 374–5

BITNET, 103

Boston Consulting Group model, 224

BP, 239

Breeding ground model, 586

British Army recruit battery (BARB), 174, 175, 177

Bulletin boards, 104

Business changes, 35
psychological responses to, 215–18

Business goals, strategies facilitating attainment of, 221

Business level strategies and HRM implications, 228

Business maturity, 223–5

Business process re-engineering, 6, 108, 121

Business strategy, 220–2

Business unit size, 231

Cadbury Schweppes, 594

California Personality Inventory, 375

Campbell Interest and Skill Survey, 605

Campus wide information systems (CWIS), 104

Canadian automated pilot selection system (CAPSS), 171

Candidates
conceptual basis, psychological impact on, 556–61
impact of personnel selection procedures, 543–66

Career anchor categories, 608

Career beliefs, 607

Career constructions, 606–7

Career development
assessment of context, 609–11
effectiveness of interventions, 611–15
employee's concerns, 600
evaluation, 611–15
implications for organizations, 609
organization's needs, 600
self-managed, 599–618

Career Development Inventory, 612

Career identity, 612

Career insight, 612

Career management, 10

Career Mastery Inventory, 612

Career motivation, components, 612

Career patterns, 237
nonlinear, 614
objective, 602–3
subjective, 602
typology, 602

Career planning
programmes, 614
self-assessment tools in, 601

Career positions, 604–6

Career purposes, 607–9

Career resilience, 612

Career stages, 603–4
  models, 603–4
  self-assessment exercise, 604
  theory, 603
Case method in development, 595
Cash Cow businesses, 224, 225
CD-ROM, 105, 107
Change
  drivers of, 3–5
  increasing pace of, 5
  organizational responses to, 5–7
  selecting for, 1–34
  strategic responses to, 5
  see also Organizational change; Selection
    for change; Strategic change
Change-driven changes, 450
Chief Executive Officers (CEOs), 240, 260–1
China, 63–79
  adaptation issues, 76–7
  ancient views on personnel
    characteristics, 63–4
  assessment centre, 69–70
  basic characteristics, 64
  cadre leadership assessment and
    selection, 69
  capability characteristics, 64
  comprehensive leadership appraisal,
    67–8
  context and practice of selection and
    appraisal, 65–8
  Cultural Revolution, 68
  independent criteria, 75
  information utilization in personnel
    selection, 72–4
  institutional single-pattern approach in
    selection, 67
  integrated approach to selection,
    appraisal and decisions, 77–8
  job analysis, 70–1
  joint ventures, 74
  labour market development, 65–6
  methodological concerns about quality
    of assessment instruments, 74
  moral characteristics, 64
  needs for selection and appraisal, 65–6
  personnel assessment and appraisal,
    68–71
  personnel selection and appraisal
    systems, 64–5
  personnel selection and decision-making,
    71–4
  psychometric knowledge, 75–6
  public bidding in selection of
    management teams, 71–2
  rating bias, 76–7
  rating skills, 75–6
  situational simulation, 69–70
  social desirability effects, 75
  state-owned companies, 74
  structure of personnel systems, 66–7
  task analysis, 70–1
  testing and assessment, 65
  traditions in selection and assessment,
    63–8
Chinese performance-maintenance (CPM)
  study, 68–9
Civil Rights, 53
COBRA Project, 105, 108
Co-construction of mutual realities, 30
CODAP, 443
Cognitive ability tests, 633
Cognitive competencies, 239
Cognitive processes, measurement, 606
Cognitive products, assessment, 606
Cognitive styles, 602
Cohesiveness, 400
Collectivism, 48
Commitment
  hypothesis, 261
  personnel, 253
  see also Organizational commitment
Communication systems, 127
Communication technologies, 450
Communication tool, criterion
  development as, 297–300
Communication with colleagues, 110
Communicative skills, 290
Community teleservice centre, 106
Compensation systems, 113
Competencies, 443
  assessment centres, 358
  categories, 632–3
  challenges to, 357
  changing context, 353
  current usage, 344–5
  elements, 348
  future-oriented, 358–61
  measurements, 91
  methodological and research
    development needs, 365–6
  nature of, 343–5, 358–61
  new resourcing equations, 353
  required to identify organizational
    comptencies, 365
  requirement forecasting techniques, 364
  selection perspectives, 356
  strategic, 361–2
  technical, 83
  vocational, 345
  see also Organizational competencies

Competency-based organizations, 585, 591–2
Competency-profile changes, 251–2
Competition, 5
Competitive advantage, 289, 360
Competitive parity, 289
Competitive strategy, 226–7
Competitiveness, cost, 6
Complimentary interaction, 27
Compressed design cycles, 23
Compressed validation cycles, 23–4
CompuServe, 102, 105, 109
Computer adaptive testing, 174
Computer-assisted assessment, 136
Computer-assisted screening test (CAST), 174
Computer-based HRM system, 453
Computer-based situational exercises, 138–9
Computer-based testing (CBT), 173, 174, 176
Computer use, 108
Computerized testing, 135–8
Condition-action sequences, 204
Confederation of British Industry, 226
Congruence in socialization, 423
Conscientiousness, 25, 375
Construct strategies, 530
Construct theory, 279–80
Construct validity, 536
    of assessment dimensions, 360
Constructive adaptation, 624
Constructivist psychology, 410
Content strategies, 532–4
Content validity, 537–8
    of behavioural indicators, 360
Contextual criteria, 278
Contextual performance, 26
Contingency theory, 100
Continuous competence assessment and development, 587
Contractors, 621, 631
Contradictory interactions, 27
Control Question Techniques, 379, 380
Control systems, 127
Cooperativeness, 290
Coping hypothesis, 261
Core employees, 630
Core workers, 621
Corporate strategy, 219–45
Corruption, 369
Cost competitiveness, 6
Cost cutting, 5
Cost-effectiveness of assessment, 142
Cost reduction strategy, 228

Council of Legal Education (CLE), 184
Co-worker evaluations, 47
Creativity, 7, 25
Criteria definition, 312–13
Criteria-in-use, impact of change, 237
Criterion-based training, 588–91
    behaviour modelling in, 588–91
    phases, 588–9
Criterion constructs, 277
    choosing for practicality, 281
    choosing for understanding, 280–1
    defining, 279
    normative measures vs. standards, 282
    refining, 279–83
    typical vs. maximum performance, 283
Criterion development, 287–301
    and environmental change, 288–90
    and organizational change, 288–90
    and organizational performance, 294–7
    and P–O fit, 407–8
    as communication tool, 297–300
    changing role of the professional, 300–1
    for growth, 298–9
    for management development purposes, 299–300
    organizational considerations, 292–4
    organizational rebuilding, 297–8
    problems, 290–2
    procedures, 290–2
    psychometric considerations, 292–4
    reasons for, 288
    requirements, 293
Criterion dimensionality, 280
    over time, 282
Criterion measures, 267–86
    critical commentary, 275–6
    frequently used, 268–76
    training systems, 534–5
    see also Specific measures
Criterion performance, standard level, 282
Criterion problem, 276–9
    psychometric solutions, 276
    understanding, 276–7
Criterion-related strategies, 531
Criterion-related validity, 536–7
Criterion samples, 348
Critical Incidents Technique (CIT), 297, 446–7
Critical Thinking Appraisal (CTA), 186
Criticality of employees, factors affecting, 229
Criticality of human resource, 227–9
Criticality of people, impact of change, 234
Cross-cultural applicability of meta-analysis, 27–9

Cross-cultural training, expatriate
     employees, 155–6
Cultural assumptions, 10–12
  artefacts, 12
  fundamental, 11
  general beliefs, 11
  regarding self, 46
  specific values, 11
Cultural diversity, 19, 35–8, 86–8, 233
Cultural effects on HR practices, 48
Culturally tied features, 42
Culture change, organizational, 238
Curriculum vitae, 88–9

Databases, 104–5, 109
Deception
  assessment, 371
    costs and benefits, 384–6
  behavioural cues to, 382–4
  in job applicants and/or incumbents, 369
Deception tests, 378–84
Decision-making
  China, 71
  selection, 25
Decision support systems, 355
Decision-making, bi-directional 30
Declarative knowledge, 277
Delayering, 5, 7
DELPHI, 102
Dependability, concept, 371
Deregulation, 3, 253
Deselection, 619–36
Design cycles, 3
  compressed, 23
Development costs, 231
Development courses, 591
Development handbook, 594
Developmental model of mutual
     accommodation, 30
Developmental needs assessment, 581–97
Devolution, 5
Dial-up networks, 98, 99
Differential aptitude tests, 170, 606
Differentialization/generalization
     hypothesis, 252
Diplomatic service personnel, 149
Directional competencies, 239
Discussion list, 102, 103
Dishonesty
  control methods, 385–6
  future prediction, 371
  in job applicants and/or incumbents, 369
  in the workplace, 369
Distributive justice, 30, 556

Dog businesses, 224
Downsizing, 5–8, 97, 619–36
  assessment implications, 631–4
  job losses through, 623–5
  layoff survivors, 625–8
  organizational commitment in, 627
  work effort in, 627
Drug tests, 90, 371, 381
  impact of, 553–4
  validity, 382
Drug usage, 90
Dynamic testing, 136–7

East Midlands Electricity, 238
Education, 48–52
  and work, 50
  implications, 52
  links with industry and social contracts
     of employment, 50–1
  work-relatedness of, 49
  workforce assessment, 49
Edwards Personal Preference Schedule, 479
Electronic customer, 108
Electronic homework, 105
Electronic libraries, 104, 109
Electronic mail (e-mail), 102, 110
Electronic malls, 108
Electronic media, 13
Electronic trading, 98, 101, 107–8
Elite groups, 49
Embezzlement, 369
Employee integration in socialization and
     selection, 414–15
Employee job property rights and
     entitlement, 53
Employee movement representation of
     multiple criteria, 312
Employee retention, 261
Employment relationship, 7
Environmental change
  coping with, 252–3
  effect on criteria, 288–90
  implications of, 233–8
Environmental drivers, 2, 5, 10
Environmental features, 43
Environmental forces, on human resources,
     41
Environmental variables, 83
ERASMUS programme, 82
Ethnic differences
  military staff, 164–5
  within-country, 53
European Union (EU), 233
Exchange perspective, 84–6

Executives, recruitment of, 261
Expatriates, 147–60
  categories of attributes of success, 153
  competence retention, 149
  cross-cultural training, 155–6
  cultural context, 150–1
  failure rate, 83
  implications for research and practice,
    156–8
  in global expansion, 82–3
  language skills, 154
  mutually satisfactory relational contract,
    149
  nature and context of assignments, 150–2
  needs of, 149
  problematic issue of, 250
  retention failure, 147–8, 154
  selection criteria, 28, 152–4
Expectational impact of socialization
  impact, 432

Fairness, impact of change, 236
Family situation, 83
Feedback
  in criterion-based training, 589
  in PMS, 574
  personnel, 262
Financial control versus organic growth
  strategies, 226
FIRO-B, 500–1
Flexibility, 24
  labour market, 620–3
  personnel, 253
Flexible firm, 620
Flexible work roles, 8
Flexible workforce, 622
  and individual careers, 628–33
  implications of downsizing, 631–4
Floating workers, 631
Fordism, 289
Foreign employees, role of, 83–4
Formalistic management development
  system, 584
40–70% rule, 232
Fraud, 369
Frequently-asked questions (FAQs), 102,
  110, 111
Functional strategy, 220–2
Fundamental interpersonal relations
  orientations (FIRO), 500

Gamma change, 253, 263
GATES project, 177–8

Gender differences
  military staff, 163–4
  teleworking, 119–20
General Aptitude Test Battery (GATB), 170,
  192, 606
General Health Questionnaire, 624
General intelligence, 25
  measures of, 201
General trainability index (GTI), 175
Genetic compatibility, 90
Genetic screening, impact of, 553–4
Genetic testing, 90
GEnie, 102
Global assignment selection process, 157
Global economy, 5, 39–61, 147
  see also Expatriates
Global expansion, expatriates in, 82–3
Globalization, 248–51
  graduate recruitment, 521
Goal-oriented training, 596
Government influence, 253
Graduate recruitment, 507–27
  alternative approach, 518–20
  annual cycle, 508
  application forms, 510–13, 519
  assessment centres, 516–17, 520–2
  biodata, 513–15
  future, 520
  globalization, 521
  internationalization, 521
  interviews, 515–16, 519–20
  pre-screening, 512–13
Graphic rating scales, 272–4
Graphology, 89–90, 376–8
  validity analysis, 377–8
Group work *see* Team; Teamwork
Guilty Knowledge Technique, 379, 380

Handwriting analysis *see* Graphology
Hierarchical management vs. horizontal
  management, 131
Hiring and firing, 53
Hogan Personality Inventory (HPI), 373,
  476
Hogan Reliability Index, 373
Holland's measure of vocational interests,
  479
Home-based telework, 105
Homeworking, 8, 97
Honesty
  assessment, 370, 376
    potential costs and benefits, 384–6
  concept, 371
  in the workplace, 369

see also Integrity
Horizontal management vs. hierarchical
    management, 131
HR practices, 40
    and law, 52–4
    cultural effects on, 48
    future research, 56–7
    global, 41
    innovations, 55
    institution-based, 56
    local nature of, 40–1, 54
    options for rejecting, adopting, adapting
        or creating, 55
    relevance and legitimacy, 42–3
HR practitioners, 13, 29
HR research, global agenda, 54
HR strategy, 40
HR technologies, 42
    adaptation, 43
    adoption, 43
    awareness of locational factors, 43
    outcomes from exposing foreign
        students to, 42
    rejection, 42
HR tools, 42
Human resource *see* HR
Human resource management (HRM), 7,
    15, 220, 539
    computer-based, 453
    criticality of, 227–9
    environmental forces on, 41
    key aspects, 450
    local, 39–61
    specialists, 91–2
    supporting system, 453

Illegal activity, 369
Incentives, 53
Individual applicant, 35
Individual-organizational continuum, 394
Individualism, 48
    versus collectivism, 19
Industrial espionage, 369
Industrial Revolution, 97–8
Informatics, 129
Information about human resources, 614
Information acquisition, in socialization,
    419
Information collection
    and processing systems, 127
    KSAs, 540
    tasks, 540
Information provision in socialization
    impact, 428–31

Information technology (IT), 3, 5, 35–8, 99,
    100, 109
    applications, 126–8
    as means of production, 125
    current developments, 126–8
    impact on personnel selection and
        assessment, 125
    interface management, 130–1, 131
    output standardization, 131–2
    symptoms caused by, 121
    upgrading of function content, 129–30
Information utilization in personnel
    selection, 72–4
Innovation, 6, 7, 9, 56, 290
    potential, 25
    strategy, 228
Inns of Court, 183
Inns of Court School of Law (ICSL), 184
Institutional linkages, 50
Integrated approach to selection, appraisal
    and decisions, China, 77–8
Integrated broadband communication, 120
Integrated services digital network (ISDN),
    120
Integrity
    assessment, 371–8
        potential costs and benefits, 384–6
    concept, 371
    see also Honesty
Integrity/dependability measures, 370
Integrity interview, 383
Integrity tests, 90, 371–4
    clear-purpose or veiled-purpose, 372
    examples, 373
    impact of, 553–4
    paper-and-pencil, 371
    validity, 372–4
Intellectual skills, 290
Intelligence, 237
Intelligence tests, 91, 209
    see also IQ
Interactive levels of analysis, 26–7
Internal versus external locus of control,
    19
International assessment and selection,
    81–95
International assignments, 82
International differences in selection
    methods, 86–8
International employees, 82
    see also Expatriates
International generalizability, 28
International managers, 233
International organizations, 81
International recruitment, 92–3

national selection methods,
explanations for differences in, 91
ernational senior managers, 82
ernational strategy, 82
Internationalization, 233, 248–51
  ethnocentric phase, 249
  geocentric phase, 249
  graduate recruitment, 521
  implications, 249–50
  political issues in, 250
  polycentric phase, 249
Interviewers
  biases in decision-making, 460–1
  multiple, 463–4
  training, 464
Interviews, 50, 89, 172, 443
  biased and undifferentiated theories of
    ideal applicant, 459
  biased information-gathering, 459
  categorical and biased judgements,
    459–60
  graduate recruitment, 515–16, 519–20
  impact of, 550–1
  job-relatedness of, 461
  potential problems, 458–61
  situational, 456, 461–2
  structured *see* Structured selection
    interviews
  unstructured, 458–61
    acquiring and maintaining power, 468
    comparison with structured
      interviews, 464–9
    maintaining procedural and
      distributive justice, 467
    symbolic functions of interview, 468–9
  validity meta-analysis, 456
  see also Structured selection interviews
Ipsative measures to control response bias,
  487–8
IQ, 201–2, 205, 210–11
ISDN (Integrated Services Digital
  Network), 111

Job analysis, 12, 261, 270, 441–54, 456, 632
  and P–O fit, 405–6
  applications, 442
  attribute-oriented (or trait-oriented)
    methods, 443
  behaviour-oriented (worker-oriented)
    methods, 443
  China, 70–1
  definition, 443
  for selection and appraisal, 442
  future, 452–3

graduate recruitment, 509–17
in legal proceedings, 445
molecular, 444
multi-method approaches, 445–8
requirements, 452–3
task-oriented (or work-oriented)
  methods, 443
training systems, 538–40
utilization in practice, 444–5
Job applicants, balance of power,
  235–6
Job characteristics, teleworking, 114
Job concept, changes in, 450–1
Job content domain, 270
Job content universe, 270
Job descriptions, 12, 443
Job design, 231
Job enlargement vs. enrichment, 110
Job loss
  negative consequences, 625
  psychological consequences, 624
  through downsizing, 623–5
Job performance, 633
  and Big Five, 481–2
  theory, 277–8
  variation in, 230
Job preview, 261
Job profiles, 451
Job-related criteria, 261
  see also Criteria measures
Job-relatedness, 445, 461
Job requirements, 72
  and operational criteria, 239
Job security, 620
Job specification, 443
Job stability, 451
Job success, 201–13
Jobs, decline of, 7–8
Joint ventures, inernational, 74

Knowledge
  growth of, 3
  priority, 290
Knowledge-driven companies, 128–9,
  139–40
Knowledge, skills, abilities and other
  characteristics (KSAOs), 24–5, 405, 443,
  459, 460, 461, 463, 466, 467, 532–3,
  537–8
  and P–O fit, 405–6
  information collection, 540
  predictor design, 406–7
Knowledge society, 51
Knowledge work(ers), 50, 450

Labor markets, local, 40
Labor pool, 40
  accessing and effectively developing, 57
Labour division process, reversion of, 449
Labour market
  flexibility of, 620–3
  initial entry, 625
  international, 81
  power, 9
  segmentation, 9–10
Language differences, 233
Language skills, expatriate employees, 154
Laptop computers, 98
Law and HR practices, 52–4
Leadership
  appraisal, China, 67–8
  cadre assessment and selection, 69
  charismatic, 256
  CPM study, 68–9
  personal characteristics, 256–9
  requirements in organizational
    turnaround, 255–9
  strategic change, 239–40
  transformational, 255–6
Learning abilities measurement program
  (LAMP), 171, 176
Learning potential, assessment of, 139–40
Learning styles, 591
Legal proceedings, job analysis in, 445
Legal profession, 183–99
Lie Control Technique, 379
Lie detector *see* Polygraph examinations
Life-Career Rainbow, 608
Life-cycle perspective, 633
Life-long learning, 129
LIMRA structured interview guide, 457,
  462
Local area networks (LANs), 109
Long-term outsiders, 631
Lotus Development Corporation, 100

Management
  competencies, 343, 346, 356
  fads, 6
  progression, 587
  work processes, 110–11
Management change programmes,
  behavioural competencies, 352
Management Charter Initiative (MCI), 345
Management development
  macro-level, 587–8
  micro-level, 587
Management selection policy, 584–8
Management teams, China, 71–2

Managers
  as mentors, 591–5
  international, 82, 233
  selecting for transnational companies,
    83–4
Manpower delivery system, 222
Manpower demand system, 222
Market growth rate, 224
Market share, 224
Mass assessment, 77
Mathematical knowledge, 50
Mentors, managers as, 591–5
Mergers, 6, 251
Meta-analysis, 12, 323–42, 444
  application, 324
  assessment centre validities, 328–9
  Big Five and job performance, 481–2
  combining validities from diverse
    sources, 338–9
  contributions and challenges of,
    335–40
  cross-cultural applicability of, 27–9
  improving the quality of research, 337
  improving the use of research, 336
  in advance of science and practice,
    339–40
  integrity test validities, 373
  interview validity, 456
  methods, 324–6
  quality of data base, 337–8
  selection perspectives, 356
Micro-analytical issues, 27
Midland Bank, 343
Military staff, 161–81
  academic qualifications and personal
    record, 168
  adjustment to educational trends, 165
  appraisal process, 169–70
  assessment and appraisal systems, 166
  assessment and appraisal tools, 170–3
  assessment centres, 168
  assessment scales, 172–3
  changes in selection and appraisal
    policies, 163–6
  conditions of service, 165–6
  ethnic differences, 164–5
  future developments, 178
  gender differences, 163–4
  matching abilities with tasks and
    training, 176
  matching ability measures to
    performance assessments, 176–7
  matching people with jobs, 177–8
  matching tests with abilities, 175
  new developments, 173–8

Military staff (*cont.*)
    pressures for change, 161–3
    principal approaches to selection, 167
    recruitment and selection operations,
        166–7
    sequential process, 169
MIME protocols, 102
Minnesota Importance Questionnaire
    (MIQ), 608
Minnesota Multiphasic Personality
    Inventory (MMPI), 375–6
MJRQ (Minnesota Job Requirements
    Questionnaire), 444
Mobile work, 106
Mobility of workforce, 233
Model behaviour, demonstration, 589
Monitoring of work processes, 110–11
Moral character, 90
Morrisby Differential Test Battery, 606
Motivation, 278
    career concepts, 602
    competencies, 239
    in development, 596
Multi-attribute utility (MAU) analysis, 310,
    312–13
Multi-cultural framework, 18–20
Multi-dimensional criteria, 310–14
Multi-faceted model of personnel
    assessment, 77
Multi-modal employment interview (MEI),
    457–8
Multi-nationals, 82, 233
Multi-stage selection and decisions, 78
Multiple criteria
    and multiple predictors, 314
    employee movement representation of,
        312
Multiple levels of analysis, 26–7
Multiple predictors and multiple criteria,
    314
Multivariate criteria, representation by
    single-criterion validity, 310–11
Multivariate validity over time, 307–9
Mutual accommodation, developmental
    model of, 30
Mutual attraction, 30
Myers–Briggs Type Indicator, 479

National cultures, 20–1
National Vocational Qualifications (NVQs),
    345, 600
NatWest, 239
NEO–PI–R, 479, 486, 488, 489
Nepotism, 48

Networking, 97–124, 631
Neutral interactions, 27
New behaviour, practising, 589
Newly created jobs (NCJs), 8–9
Nissan, 239
Non-procedural control, 77–8
Non-procedural information, 73, 74

Obsolescence, 5
Occupational environments, trait-factor
    theories of, 604–5
Occupational Personality Questionnaire
    (OPQ), 479–81, 487
Occupational profiles, teleworkers, 115
Occupational Reinforcer Patterns, 608
On-line networks, 99
On-line services, 99
On-line shoppers, 98
Open electronic networking, 101, 102
Operational criteria, 235
    and job requirements, 239
Organic growth strategies, 226
Organization fit, 9
Organization socialization *see* Socialization
Organizational analysis, training systems,
    538–40
Organizational appraisal, 77
Organizational attributes, 393
Organizational change, 448–9
    effect on criteria, 288–90
    enabling, 360
    main features, 451–2
    reacting to and capitalizing on, 359
Organizational citizenship behaviour, 556
Organizational commitment, 614
    in downsizing, 627
Organizational competencies, 343–68, 539
    concepts of, 346
    identification, 365
    implications for psychologists, 364–6
    life-cycle perspective, 362–4
Organizational effectiveness, 396
Organizational justice theory, 556–8
Organizational performance
    and criterion development, 294–7
    maximizing, 316–17
Organizational rebuilding, criterion
    development, 297–8
Organizational requirements
    criterion development, 292–4
    integration with HRM and selection,
        240–2
Organizational research, 40
Organizational response to change, 5–7

Organizational strategy
  nature of, 220–2
  perspectives, 220–2
Organizational survival, 5
Organizational theory and global HR
    research agenda, 54–8
Organizational turnaround, 247–65
  facilitation using assessment procedures,
    262
  general qualifications, 262
  general types of major changes, 253–5
  impact on assessment and selection,
    255–62
  leadership requirements in, 255–9
  procedures of selection and assessment,
    259–62
  trends, 248–53
  types of changes, 248–55
Out-group members, 47, 48
Outsourcing, 8, 450
Overall assessment ratings (OARs),
    358

Panacea predictors, 25
Part-time workers, 622
  employment contracts, 6
Patterned behaviour description interview
    (PBDI), 457, 462, 515–16, 550
PDI Employment Inventory, 373
Peer appraisal, impact of, 553–4
Peer rating, 262
Performance appraisal, 567–80
  accuracy in, 570–1
  and assessment and development of
      potential, 575–7
  appraiser, 568–9
  as performance management, 572–4
  in PMS, 573–4
  pay and motivation, 571–2
  quality perspective, 570–1
  self- and superior appraisal, 568
  upward appraisal, 569
Performance components, 278
Performance constructs, 277–8
Performance criteria, 112
  challenges of, 357
  for future-oriented competencies, 359
Performance effectiveness measures,
    268–74
Performance-maintenance (PM) scale, 68–9
Performance management, 6, 572
  behavioural competencies, 352
  performance appraisal as, 572–4
  system (PMS), 573–4

Performance measures, 233
Performance models, 291
Performance proficiency determinants,
    277–8
Performance ratings, 12, 272–4
  cognitive processes of raters, 274
Performance records, 269
Performance-related pay (PRP), 6, 571–2
Performance tests, 269–71, 606, 633
Peripheral workforce, 620–1
Person–environment (P–E) fit, 260
  research, 394–6
Person–environment psychology (PEP),
    394–6
Person–job fit, 29, 68, 73, 74, 413, 414
Person–organization (P–O) fit, 26–7, 312,
    394, 413, 414, 424
  and criterion development, 407–8
  and job analysis, 405–6
  and KSAOs, 405–6
  and personnel selection, 403–8
  and recruitment-attraction, 403–5
  and validation designs, 407–8
  contemporary theory and research,
    396–400
  good fit for whom?, 401, 409
  good fit on what?, 401–2, 409
  good fit when?, 403, 409
  historical introduction, 394–6
  social learning in, 419
  striking the balance, 400–3
Person–team (P–T) fit, 26–7
Person–work role fit, 26–7
Personal change in socialization, 420
Personal computers, 23
Personal qualifications versus social
    acceptability, 47
Personal Question Manager (PQM), 137
Personal support systems, 127
Personality assessment, 24–5
  Big Five, 475–92
  demystification, 488–9
  from handwriting, 89–90
Personality issues, organizationally
    relevant, 405
Personality tests, 173, 375
Personality traits, 83
Personnel appraisal procedures, 262
Personnel archives, 72
Personnel feedback, 262
Personnel management environment, 72
Personnel policy, strategic, 582–4
Personnel psychology *see* Psychology of
    personnel and selection
Personnel selection, 389–92

Personnel selection (*cont.*)
   emergent themes, 21–30
   strategic, 241
Personnel specialists, 91–2
Personologists, 393
Political issues, in internationalization, 250
Polygraph examinations, 378–80
   impact of, 553–4
   techniques, 379
   validity, 380
Pooled workers, 631
Portfolio assessment, 271
Portfolio planning, 223–5
Position Analysis Questionnaire (PAQ),
   443, 447
Positive Control Technique, 379
Potential assessment and development,
   575–7
Power–knowledge relationship, 544
Practical versatility, 596
Predictivist paradigm, 13
Preference impact domain of socialization
   impact, 431–2
Pre-screening, 371, 376
   graduate recruitment, 512–13
Princples for the Validation and Use of
   Personnel Selection Procedures, 530
Privacy of applicant, 547–8
Private education, 49
Private teleworking companies, 106
Privatization, 253
Probabilistic models, 139
Procedural control, 77–8
Procedural justice, 30, 556
Procedural knowledge, 278
Product cycle, 5
   and HRM, 225
Product life cycle, 223–5
Productivity, 5, 6, 108
Professional Personality Questionnaire, 476
Programmer Aptitude Test (PAT), 303, 307,
   308
Project teams, 594
Psychological characteristics, 72
Psychological contract, 7
Psychological impact, 425–7
   of assessment processes, 543–66
   of selection procedures, 30
   on candidates, conceptual basis, 556–61
Psychological responses to business
   change, 215–18
Psychological tests, 90
Psychology of personnel and selection,
   1–34
   changing nature of, 4

   dominant paradigm, 10–21, 12
   predominant paradigm, 14
   role of, 91–2
   status, 12
   see also Personnel psychology
Psychometric knowledge, China, 75–6
Psychometric methods, 276
Psychometric paradigm of assessment
   process, 545
Psychometric processes, 543–7
Psychometric requirements, criterion
   development, 292–4
Psychometric tests, 232
Psychometric view of selection and
   recruitment, 84
Psychopathology assessment, 375–6
Pupillage, 183–4

Quality enhancement strategy, 228
Question-mark businesses, 224, 225

Radical feminist perspectives, 30
Rank Xerox, 240
Rating bias, China, 76–7
Rating scales, 272–4
Rating skills, China, 75–6
Rational Estimate methodology, 231, 232
Real time conversations, 103
Realism in socialization, 423
Realistic Job Preview (RJP), 239, 404,
   423
Re-assessment, 25–6
Recruitment
   executives, 261
   for transnational companies, 83
   impact of, 549
   international, 92–3
   psychometric view of, 84
   requirements, 35
Recruitment–attraction and P–O fit, 403–5
Redundancies, 5
References, 89
Reid Report, 373
Relational abilities, 83
Relevant Control Technique, 379
Remote access to organizational
   information, 109
Repertory Grid, 447
Research and development (R&D), 3
Research questions, 13–14
Resource dependence, 55
Restructuring, 5–8
Résumé fraud, 369

Revised California Personality Inventory, 479
Revised NEO Personality Inventory (NEO–PI–R), 475
Rightsizing, 619
Risks, 7
Role of values, 209–10
Rorschach Inkblot Test, 375

Salience Inventory, 609
Satellite work centres, 105
Satisfaction, 400
Scholastic Aptitude Test (SAT), 168
Schooling, 48–52
Scientific knowledge, 50
Security, 7
Segmented labour market, 9–10
Selection
  and socialization, 413–40
  and training interrelationships, 530–41
  for change, 1–34
    issues, 22–6
  paradigms, 415–18
  procedures, 12
  psychometric view of, 84
  theory and practice, 2
Selection criteria, 73, 232–4
  impact of change, 234, 236
  in strategic change, 238–9
Selection decision-making, 25
Self, cultural assumptions regarding, 46
Self-assessment, 140–1
Self-assessment tools in career planning, 601
Self-characterizing individualist cultures, 47
Self-designing organizations, 599
Self-Directed Search, 605
Self-management, 290
Self-managing teams, 401
Self-report methods, 374
75% rule, 327–8
Shared-facility centre, 106
Shell Canada, 360
Short-term insiders, 630
Simulation *see* Work simulations
Single European Market, 81
Situational assessment, 141–2
Situational interviews, 456
  limiting access to ancillary data, 461–2
Situational specificity
  assessment difficulties, 330–5
  implications, 330
  lack of situational model, 333–5

of test validities, 335
outcomes, 329
role of sample size, 333
vs. validity generalization, 327–9
16PF, 479
16PF5, 479
Sixteen Personality Factor Questionnaire, 116
Small to medium sized companies, 8
SME (subject-matter expert) panels, 443
Social contracts, 43–5, 50
  compliance with, 56
  enhanced understanding of role of, 57
  legal implications, 54
Social desirability, 486–7
  China, 75
Social events, 51, 233
Social learning in socialization, 419
Social norms, 49
Social stratification, 49
Socialization
  and selection, 413–40
  attitudinal impact of, 433–4
  behavioural impact of, 434
  complex outcomes in, 421
  expectational impact of, 432
  impact of, 425–7
    concept, 427–34
    five-domain framework, 427–8, 435
    information provision in, 428–31
  information acquisition in, 419
  key facets, 418–21
  longitudinality, 418–19
  paradigms, 415–18
  personal change in, 420
  preference impact domain, 431–2
  social learning in, 419
  stage-based models, 421–3
Societal culture, 45–8
Societal trends in internationalization, 251–2
Societal wealth, 49
Solicitors, 183
Special assignments, 594
Specific versus diffuse, 19
Sponsor system, 594
Standards for Education and Psychological Tests, 530
Stanton Survey, 373
Star businesses, 224
Strategic analysis, 221
Strategic change
  environmental implications, 233–8
  leadership, 239–40
  role of selection in promoting and enabling, 238–42

Strategic change (*cont.*)
  selection criteria in, 238–9
Strategic choice
  and criticality of people, 227–9
  impact on selection criteria, 232–4
  impact on selection utility, 229–32
  implications for HRM and selection, 222–33
Strategic competencies, 361–2
Strategic design issues, 231
Strategic personnel policy, 582–4
Strategic personnel selection, 241
Strategic responses to change, 5
Strong–Campbell Interests Inventory, 605
Structured selection interviews, 455–73, 515, 519, 550, 608
  approach, 456–8
  comparison with unstructured interviews, 464–9
  improving rating process, 462–3
  interviewer needs, 465–6
  limiting access to ancillary data, 461–2
  procedural requirements, 456–7
  providing a good fit of applicant to job context, 466–7
  reasons for infrequent use, 464–9
  recruiting concerns, 465
  slippage in implementation, 469
  sources of resistance to, 465
  standardizing information-gathering process, 462
  strategies, 461–4
  training of interviewers, 464
  use of multiple interviewers, 463
Subject-matter expert (SME) panels, 443
Superior Equivalents technique, 232
Survivor syndrome, 625–8

Tacit knowledge, 201–13
  acquisition, 203–4
  categories, 204
  concept, 202–3
  form, 204–5
  local, 204
  measuring, 205–10
    scoring, 208–9
  questionnaires, 211
  self, 204
  studies, 210–12
  test limitations, 212
  tests, 206–8
  theoretical basis for understanding and assessing, 203
Takeovers, 251

Task analysis, 448–9
  China, 70–1
Task-oriented selection procedure, 47
Tasks, information collection, 540
Taylorism, 7
Team composition, 497–501
Team definition and structuring, 494–5
Team heterogeneity
  and affective reactions, 499
  and performance, 498–9
Team level fit, 27
Team selection
  achieving the 'right mix', 499
  implications for research and practice, 501–4
  personality and personal styles, 500–1
  skill mix, 499–500
Teamwork, 7, 9, 26, 290
  and person characteristics, 496–7
  selection, 493–506
  selection criteria, 495–7
Technical competence, 83
Technology transfer, 42
TeleCentres, 105
Telecommunications, 108
Telecommuterland, 98, 99, 102
  work-related facets inside, 114
Telecommuting, 100, 101–3
  implications for selection and appraisal, 112–19
Telecustomers, 108, 110
Telehealth, case study, 119–20
Telematic systems, 97
Telemedicine, case study, 120
Teletrading, 101, 106–8
Teleworkers, 104, 108, 110, 111
  addiction to on-line services, 117
  occupational profiles, 115
Teleworking, 8, 98, 101, 105–6, 130
  appraisal, 117–19
  areas of concern for employee and employer, 119
  barriers, 111–12
  basic issues concerning selection, 117–19
  criticism, 121
  gender differences, 119–20
  implications for selection and appraisal, 112–19
  introduction, 121
  job characteristics, 114
  organizational barriers, 111–12
  psychological barriers, 112
  workplace circumstances, 114
Temporal validity variations, 309
Temporary staff, 622, 631

employment contracts, 6
Termination, 53
Theft, 369, 374
    control methods, 385–6
Time, efficient use, 596
Top management teams (TMTs), 399, 401,
    402, 403, 404
TOPAS adjective checklist measure, 475,
    487
Toshiba, 238
Total quality management (TQM), 128, 355
Trade barriers, 3
Trainability, 279
Training costs, 231
Training programs
    evaluation, 534
    evaluation design, 535–6
Training systems
    and selection interrelationships, 530–41
    and validation, 534–6
    criterion measurement, 534–5
    job analysis, 538–40
    organizational analysis, 538–40
Trait-factor theories of occupational
    environments, 604–5
Transformational criteria, 235, 239
Transnational companies, 81
    recruitment for, 83
    selecting managers for, 83–4
Triarchic theory, 203
Truth Control Technique, 379
Truthfulness, concept, 371
TTA (Threshold Traits Analysis), 444
Type A/type B personality, 260, 399, 410

Uncertainty, 231
Unemployment, 619, 623
    impact on school leavers, 625
Unimodal prediction, 22
Universalism versus particularity, 19
USENET, 102, 103
Utility analysis, 12, 17, 303–22
    and organizational performance, 316–17
    costs of implementing, 317–18
    definition, 304
    evolution, 304
    example application, 305–7
    factors affecting costs of implementing
        selection systems, 306
    factors affecting the value of quality
        change in job performance per
        person year, 306
    future research, 318–20
    impact of change, 236

multi-attribute, 312–13
    practitioner–researcher collaboration,
        318–20
    quantity of person–years afected, 306
    SD_y, 307, 310–14
    $\bar{Z}_x$, 314–17
Utility formula, Schmidt *et al.*, 230

Validation
    and selection systems, 530–4
    and training systems, 534–6
    compressed cycles, 23–4
Validation designs and P–O fit, 407–8
Validation strategies, 536–8
Validation techniques, 8
Validity, impact of change, 236
Validity coefficient, 307, 324, 325,
    338
Validity generalization (VG) analysis, 12,
    27–9, 323–42, 444
    and consistency of validities, 326–30
    applications, 326
    basic rationale, 325–6
    combining validities from diverse
        sources, 338–9
    contributions and challenges of, 335–40
    implications, 330
    improving the quality of research, 337
    improving the use of research, 336
    in advance of science and practice,
        339–40
    outcomes, 329
    power to detect variability in validities,
        331–2
    selection perspectives, 356
    variability in levels of test validity,
        331
    vs. situational specificity, 327–9
Value-free tests, 209–10
Values
    organizationally relevant issues, 405
    role of, 209–10
Videoconference, 103
Virtual firms, 107
    implications for selection and appraisal,
        112–19
Virtual staff, 622
Visionary criteria, 235, 236
Vocational competencies, 345
Vocational Preference Inventory, 605
Voice e-mail programs, 102
Voice stress analysis, 380–1
    reliability and validity evidence, 380–1
Vulnerability of applicant, 547–8

Watson-Glaser test, 186, 187, 191–3
Wilful disruption, 25
Work Adjustment Project, 410
Work Aspect Preference Scale, 608
Work design, 290
Work effort in downsizing, 627
Work groups *see* Teamwork selection
Work packaging, 451
Work processes
  management of, 110–11
  monitoring of, 110–11
  simplification, 450
  transformations, 448–50
Work Profiling System (WPS), 447–8, 452–3
Work-relatedness of education, 49

Work roles, 7–8
  changing nature of, 5–10
  shorter-term stability, 23
Work samples, 270
  impact of, 551
  tests, 171
Work simulations, 171, 232, 270
Worker rights, 53
Workforce, mobility of, 233
Workplace circumstances, teleworking, 114
World Bank, 250
World Wide Web, 104, 107

Zero hour contracts, 6